DATE DUE			
Nov 4 78			
Feb21 80			
Mar 10 80			
Apr 25'80			
Feb9 '81			

DEVELOPMENT

DEVELOPMENT

N. J. BERRILL
Swarthmore, Pennsylvania

GERALD KARP
Department of Microbiology
and Cell Science
University of Florida

McGraw-Hill Book Company
New York St. Louis San Francisco Auckland Düsseldorf Johannesburg
Kuala Lumpur London Mexico Montreal New Delhi Panama Paris São Paulo
Singapore Sydney Tokyo Toronto

DEVELOPMENT

2 3 4 5 6 7 8 9 0 V H V H 7 9 8 7 6

This book was set in Primer by Progressive Typographers. The editors were William J. Willey and Richard S. Laufer; the designer was Merrill Haber; the production supervisor was Thomas J. LoPinto. New drawings were done by J & R Services, Inc.
Von Hoffmann Press, Inc., was printer and binder.

Cover photograph
Dark-field autoradiograph of a section of a sea urchin gastrula that had been incubated for ten minutes in ^{3}H-amino acids prior to fixation. [*G. Karp.*]

Library of Congress Cataloging in Publication Data

Berrill, Norman John, date
  Development.

  Includes bibliographical references.
  1. Developmental biology. 2. Embryology.
I. Karp, Gerald, joint author. II. Title.
QL955.B37   591.3   75-26740
ISBN 0-07-005021-X

Contents

Part V   RECONSTITUTIVE, SELF-ORGANIZING
           SYSTEMS

Part VI   APPENDIX

Preface

Developmental biology has become an immense field whose confines are difficult to delineate. The focus has been and remains on the embryo; on the gradual emergence of form and structure from what appears to be a very modest beginning. The essence of embryonic development is change—transition from one stage to another. Embryos are a fleeting state, a continuum along the axis of time.

The transformation of an organism or its component cells from one state to another can also be identified in a variety of biological processes not specifically related to embryonic development. Of prime interest among these processes are regeneration, aging, and malignancy, each of which is characterized by a shift, either gradually or suddenly, in cellular activities, and each has fallen into the province of the developmental biologist.

The study of developmental biology transcends the levels of organization of living systems from the molecular to the organismal. At each level different types of questions have been asked and different types of observations made. As a result, developmental biology is a multilevel discipline composed of descriptive, experimental, and biochemical components which must, to some extent, be integrated.

Development has several emphases: Uppermost, this book attempts to provide an analysis of development, i.e., an insight into underlying mechanisms responsible for that which can be observed to the extent that such an insight is presently available. The traditional approach in embryology is the experimental approach, and a large part of this book concerns itself with what has been and what can be learned by mechanical, chemical, or genetic disruption of normal developmental processes.

The analysis of mechanisms of development is inevitably an analysis at the cellular and molecular levels, and it is with molecules and cells that several of the chapters are primarily concerned. Two comprehensive introductory chapters on molecular assembly and the eukaryotic cell (Chapters 2 and 3) have been included, from which students can review the most important concepts that have been formulated at this level. In addition an appendix is included (Chapter 25) in which explanations are given of the means by which information presented in the text was obtained.

Inquiries and concepts are stressed throughout the book, rather than accomplishments and answers, the treatment reflecting the fact that at all levels the inquiry is open-ended. Names and dates are included to some extent, both in the text and in lists of readings at the end of the chapters, partly to emphasize the continuity of investigation and conceptual thinking throughout the history of the subject, and more importantly to serve as leads into current literature.

We are grateful to the following persons for their helpful comments upon reading the manuscript: Robert Atherton, Ira Fritz, Mary Gilbert, Duane Heath, Norman Hecht, Charles Lambert, David Lindsay, Hironobu Ozaki, Michael Solursh, David Stocum, and Fred Wilt, with special thanks to Timothy Fitzharris.

N.J. Berrill
Gerald Karp

DEVELOPMENT

CHAPTER 1

Introduction to Development

What is development? No one has completely defined it, any more than the organism itself has been fully defined. In all cases a cell or a group of cells becomes separate from the organism as a whole, either physically or physiologically, and progressively becomes a new complete organism or a new part thereof. A fern spore settles and develops into a fern gametophyte. An insect egg may become a caterpillar which transforms into a pupa and emerges as a butterfly. The stump of a salamander leg regenerates a new limb. A microscopic cell, the human egg, proliferates and develops into a giant creature able to contemplate its own nature and origin.

All cells arise from preexisting cells. There is no other way for a cell to be produced, unless scientists eventually succeed in synthesizing cells from simple elements or molecules in the laboratory. At this late stage in the history of the planet, however, a single cell may be a bacterial or a protistan organism which through division gives rise to successive new generations. Or it may be a constituent cell of a multicellular organism—animal or plant—and by multiplication contribute to the growth of the whole. In such a system it may become a relatively very large cell indeed, an egg, and by a series of divisions give rise to an integrated cell assembly, a multicellular organism of the next generation.

Both in the prolonged evolution of organisms and in the development of all kinds of individual organisms at the present time we see matter in action in its most complex form, as processes of self-assembly, directed assembly, functional activity, disassembly, reconstitution, and replication. The main problem in studying such phenomena is to perceive what is actually going on behind the facade of the changing visible form. The philosopher A. N. Whitehead has said that process itself is the reality. Development has also been said to be an expression of the irreversible flow of biological events along the axis of time. Although abstract, these are undoubtedly valid concepts that emphasize the dynamic and sequential character of reality and development. For development is a clearly ordered process whereby structural and functional organization of the system, whether of a single cell or of a multicellular organism, becomes progressively expressed. Apart from energy supply and utilization, the fundamental phenomena appear to be the production of differentiated structural substances and the organization of such materials into patterns distinctive of cell, tissue, or organism. The end point is highly structured matter in action. The aim of developmental biology is to discover what processes are involved in producing this culmination, how they are related, and how they are controlled.

UNITY OF DEVELOPMENT

Following activation, an animal egg undergoes successive cleavages to become a multicellular organism consisting of a multitude of small more or less differentiated cells cohering and functioning together as a whole. Such an organism must be viable, i.e., capable of self-maintenance, by the time the various processes released during activation have run their course. The fertilized egg has an obvious unity to begin with, as a single cell with but one zygote nucleus and with a single unbroken surface layer of plasma membrane and cortical material. The division of the egg into cells does not alter the fact that the developing organism remains an integral protoplasmic system. This needs to be kept in mind, in spite of the elusive nature of the integration, particularly since analytical studies tend to break the whole developmental process into separate components that appear to be independent.

An egg, any egg, at the moment of activation is awesome in its potential. It is essentially always a single cell, however large. Small eggs may develop into prodigious organisms, particularly in mammals, although only with major nutritive assistance from the maternal organism. Large eggs, enormously rich in yolk, may develop independently and directly into near replicas of the adult, as in birds, reptiles, sharks, and some others. Very small eggs, entirely self-contained and unassisted, develop into adult-type creatures only when the adult itself is of minute dimensions, as in rotifers where the egg divides into about a thousand cells and that number suffices to make a rotifer; otherwise such development is indirect, the small egg becoming only what is possible with the material it is endowed with, and attaining adult size and character by devious and diverse means at later times. Yet whatever the course of development or the final destiny, all eggs undergo various progressive changes simultaneously in a strictly coordinated manner.

Development and evolution may both be regarded as a process of attaining successively higher levels of organization of matter by means of self-assembly and directed assembly. During evolution, matter progressively evolved from prebiotic assemblies to procaryotic cells to eucaryotic cells to multicellular organisms, collectively constituting ecosystems of increasing magnitude and complexity, successive generations being linked in time by replication. In development, as in evolution, the organism passes from one level of organization to a higher level with the emergence of new properties at each such translation. But whereas evolution has occupied several billion years of planetary time, development expresses a comparable phenomenon in hours, days, or weeks.

The Cell and Development

The concept now widely accepted is that there is organizational structure in cells and that this structure has a profound influence on the chemical activities that occur within a cell. A cell is truly structure in action, in the same indivisible sense that the human organism has been defined as a "minding body," rather than an association of mind and body. All development depends on it.

As the developing organism proceeds from level to level in the organizational scale, something new emerges at each step. This is the principle underlying the phenomenon of epigenesis. A simple example is that when an egg cell or a spore undergoes successive divisions, the property of cohesiveness becomes apparent, together with all the complexities of the multicellular situation. The nature and origination of intercellular cohesion on the one hand and the consequences of such cohesion and its variability thus become vitally important to an understanding of the developmental process. At a later stage in the development of most animals some tissue shifts to a location internal to the remainder, so that environmental conditions become different for the two components and in addition there is opportunity for interactions between the two. Each new circumstance leads to new possibilities, and development is primarily the orderly and ordered sequence of transformations.

The Organism as a Whole

Historically there have been two prevailing points of view in biology: *reductionism* and *holism*. The first assumes that complete knowledge of the constituent parts of the whole—the whole could be cell, organ, organism, species, population, etc.—can explain the entire character of that whole. The second holds that the properties of the whole emerge as a result of the organization of the parts, the whole being neither comprehensible nor predictable from knowledge of the individual parts.

Molecular biology is the most reductionist branch of biology. There is great and justifiable hope that many of the more intractable problems of development will be solved through it. But alone it cannot solve all the problems. The nature of the whole must be kept in view at the same time. This is very obvious in the study of the brain, and is no less important in the study of development.

The organism as a whole, though clearly recognizable, is practically indefinable. An organism is more than an object; it is a happening. A frog, for instance, is all that takes place during its life span. It begins with a cell that becomes an egg, which is fertilized and then progressively transforms to become a tadpole larva equipped with adhesive suckers and external gills, only to change into one with internal gills and no suckers. Growth continues, but at some point, depending on the species, metamorphosis intervenes and what was a tadpole becomes a froglet different in almost every character. The froglet grows to adult size, attains sexual maturity, undergoes tissue aging, and ends its life span. All this is "frog." The potential lies in the cell that becomes an egg, either in the genes alone or together with cytoplasmic properties not yet identified.

So it is with human development. The cell that becomes the human organism is one of many thousands dormant in the ovary from before birth. Of these only about 200 in each ovary ripen during the years between puberty and menopause and but a few become fertilized and develop. A human egg that does develop is therefore from 15 to 50 years old when it starts. During development and growth, it forms transient structures that are integral parts of the organism. The fetal membranes, or amnion, which enclose the fetus, and the placenta and cord, which sustain the fetus in the womb, are cast off or cut at birth. Yet they are as much a part of the developing organism as the embryonic heart or brain is, just as milk teeth are at a later time. In all cases an organism changes with time, sometimes dramatically as in insect metamorphosis, sometimes with little outward sign, but always with incessant loss and replacement of vital cells and substance.

In animals the eggs and sperm are the exclusive means of reproduction in most groups, although in many cases the egg is able to develop without being fertilized by a sperm. The egg is always a relatively large cell specialized to a greater or lesser degree to undergo development. In a few groups new individuals can form without the intervention of an egg, i.e., by asexual reproduction. In animals asexual reproduction consists of the development of tissue fragments usually containing many small somatic cells, in certain cases remarkably few. In plants asexual reproduction is widespread, both by small groups of tissue cells and by asexual spores.

PERSPECTIVES

Foundations

During most of the nineteenth century descriptive embryology dominated the field. Vertebrate embryology became an extension of comparative anatomy and remains so to some degree, as is evident from such excellent illustrative texts as those by Patten and Carlson and by Arey, and from the recent "Atlas of Embryology" by Wischnitzer. Toward the end of the century the emphasis turned from the "what" to the "how" questions, and experimental embryology became the common practice; vertebrate and invertebrate eggs and embryos, together with regenerative phenomena, were all grist to the mill.

From 1885 to 1914 the foundations of present developmental biology were laid. These consisted of:

1 Experiments involving the separation and subsequent development of the first cells (blastomeres) resulting from the earliest divisions of fertilized eggs, particularly those of sea urchins and frogs, by chemical and by mechanical means, primarily by Wilhelm Roux, Hans Driesch, and Theodor Boveri.

2 Cell lineage studies, notably by E. B. Wilson and E. G. Conklin, wherein the descendants of various early blastomeres were painstakingly traced far enough through the course of development to demonstrate their ultimate fate, i.e., their individual contributions to the embryo and larva.

3 Cytological studies establishing the cellular and chromosomal basis of inheritance, many of them under the leadership of Wilson in the United States, but based broadly on the work of many on both sides of the Atlantic.

4 Rediscovery of Mendel's long-forgotten laws of heredity.

5 Culture of tissue (nerve) cells outside the organism, by Ross Harrison.

6 Grafting experiments on amphibian embryos, by Hans Spemann and W. H. Lewis.

7 Extensive studies of regeneration in both vertebrates and invertebrates, particularly by Hans Driesch, T. H. Morgan, and C. M. Child.

The first four of these areas of study were synthesized by Wilson in his book "The Cell in Development and Heredity." First published in 1896 and revised in 1925, it is a classical, monumental, and seemingly immortal work.

It has long been recognized that development and genetics are integral features of the same system. Yet the intellectual and experimental approaches to the two subsciences have been very different. Experimental embryologists saw eggs and embryos as the most suitable tools for their research. They liked them for their amenability to operational procedures and because they need not be reared from one generation to the next. Geneticists, on the other hand, chose the fruitfly *Drosophila* for their research, mainly because of its brief life span and the ease with which sequential generations can be raised. Progress continued on these lines in the following ways:

1 In the development by Spemann and his students, notably Mangold and Holtfreter, of surgical techniques with massive operational results, and in their discovery of the existence of an "organizer" of the vertebrate embryo. (They were finally frustrated in their drive to identify it chemically.) Their work is lucidly summarized in Spemann's "Embryonic Development and Induction."

2 In further experimental (manipulative) analysis of developing sea urchin embryos by Swedish workers, especially Hörstadius.

3 In studies of regeneration processes in both vertebrates and invertebrates.

4 In biochemical embryology, summarized by Needham in 1942.

Eventually developmental genetics emerged as a result of applying the techniques of experimental embryology to the relatively small eggs and embryos of *Drosophila*. This led the way to the unification of the disciplines that constitute contemporary developmental biology.

Since the midcentury biochemical embryology has proceeded on many fronts, but the light remains focused on the molecular events associated with the storage and utilization of information within the cells and the embryo. When the structure of DNA and its manner of duplication became known, particularly its action in controlling enzyme production in bacteria, both geneticists and embryologists recognized the challenge to discover the mechanism by which genes regulate cell differentiation. In other words, how does a developing multicellular organism organize its numerous cells so that they express their genes selectively and thereby become different from one another? This dominant and insistent question pervades present developmental biology.

Advances in biochemical or molecular biology have gone hand in hand with exploitation of the electron microscope, which has portrayed the cell's anatomy as an amazingly complex, fine structure of membranes and granules within the cell and its organelles, differing from cell to cell yet fundamentally the same in all. We are supplied, however, with static pictures of frozen moments in the ongoing life of the individual cell. This life is evident in the studies (by Loewenstein and others) of electrochemical transport and communication between adjacent and adjoining cells, particularly in relation to junctional structures that can be seen in electron micrographs. Studies of living cells, living developing systems, and living organisms are essential accompaniments to the inevitably disruptive procedures of chemical analysis and electron microscopy. Otherwise the essence of the vital phenomenon is lost. At the cell level, the insight afforded by the new knowledge of molecular and cellular phenomena is great indeed. At the level of the developing multicellular system, the problems recognized and formulated by the nineteenth-century pioneers remain the outstanding problems of today. Inasmuch as developmental biology, to date, is a harmless, fascinating, and profoundly enjoyable activity, long may the challenge remain.

Application

Knowledge and understanding of developmental processes are important to human welfare:

1 Many kinds of abnormalities can arise during human development, and comprehension is the first step toward alleviation. These may be caused by genetic defects, drugs, viruses, hormones, or any disturbance of normal circumstances. The kind of abnormality produced depends less on the nature of the effective agent than on the stage of development on which it acts. In human development, whatever processes are most active at a particular time will be the ones most affected.

2 Malignant tumors are in a real sense abnormal forms of tissue development, and the nature and control of malignancy relate to the normal processes of growth and differentiation.

3 The nature of aging is elusive and any understanding, and therefore control, of the process depends on analytical insight into cell, tissue, and organismal growth throughout the life span. The aging process is itself one aspect of development, and in humans and other mammals it can be said to begin within the womb.

4 The control of reproduction and development—at least in livestock and potentially in humans—involves the use of hormones, low-temperature sperm storage, and storage and transfers of early embryos; in effect, seed stocks are maintained and genetic improvement can be made without dependence on the quality of the foster mothers. These techniques are readily applicable to humans and further human evolution may well depend upon their exploitation, even though the social implications are alarming.

Developmental biology consequently holds out both a promise and a threat to the human race. The more that is understood concerning the manifold and integrated processes of development, the more likely we are to ensure the quality of development and growth, not only in the womb but also throughout life. An understanding of development leads to an understanding of aging, and much alleviation of the afflictions of age might follow. Sooner or later it will be understood what it is that enables the human egg and the eggs of certain other creatures to endure in a developing, growing, and maintaining state for nearly a century, in contrast to the short-lived existence of most others. This understanding would be essential if a true extension of the human life span were to be attained, as distinct from merely warding off some of the more deleterious changes that now characterize our aging period.

The threat lies in the prospect of success itself. The more we can do technologically, the more certain it is we will undertake to do it. The technological control of development has already begun in the procedures of: in vitro fertilization of mammalian eggs (including human) and their reintroduction into a suitable host mother; freezing, thawing, and transferring mammalian embryos, with the opportunity to vary the conditions experimentally before implantation into a foster mother; nuclear transplantation, which permits numbers of genetically identical nuclei from one embryo to be introduced into a variety of different enucleated egg recipients, with the goal of producing genetically identical individuals. Each of these techniques has great benefits for animal husbandry, and the temptation exists to meddle where meddling should not be possible.

Other lines of research that have stemmed from the recent success in microbial and viral molecular genetics have provided us with the concept of genetic engineering, i.e., the ability to alter the nature of an individual genome. On the positive side of this issue is the prospect of "gene therapy," in which it is envisioned that persons with genetic defects can be "cured" by modification of their genetic makeup, at least with respect to the cells responsible for the defect's consequences. The general approach to such techniques involves the insertion of the proper gene, from whatever source, into the defective cells.

The techniques needed for gene therapy require the ability to assemble genes from more than one organism. The prospect for such an assemblage has received a boost from the recent discovery of DNA restriction endonucleases. These enzymes chop DNA molecules into smaller pieces with ends that are complementary in nucleotide sequence and thus are "sticky" and can be rejoined. With the aid of these enzymes, DNA fragments from any number of sources can be assembled, and preliminary experiments have involved joining frog or fruit fly genes with those of bacteria. The prospects for the study of gene function in higher animals by the insertion of their genes into microorganisms are enormous, but so are the risks in the wrong recombinant.

The great progress of molecular biology has come mainly from work on the common human colon bacillus, while many virus-induced cancer studies are based on the monkey virus SV40; experiments uniting the two are already conceived and only caution serves as a brake. An experimentally assembled organism that such a fusion would produce might well add insight into the processes of self-assembly that underlie developmental phenomena, but at the same time the prospect of adding viral cancer genes to the human organism is ominous.

The risks inherent in genetic engineering have long been discussed among scientists and nonscientists alike, but a recently proposed moratorium by a number of members of the National Academy of Sciences is a unique attempt by molecular biologists to designate guidelines for the direction potentially dangerous research should take. In a conference report in *Science* it was proposed that research involving the fusion of viral or potentially dangerous bacterial DNA to other bacterial DNA be deferred until proper consideration by the scientific community can determine the risks involved. Innocent inquiry can have devastating aftermaths. The nuclear physicists of the thirties were ivory tower scientists of the purest sort, with no thought of what was to come.

Essence

Why, then, study development at all? The benefits to humanity are there but are not overwhelming. Progress in medicine clearly depends to a great extent on progress in cell biology and to a lesser extent in developmental biology. Public funding of any activity, scientific or other, is generally forthcoming only insofar as public officials can see beneficial application, actual or potential. Yet developmental biology and most other branches of biology exist because a few individuals during the late nineteenth and early twentieth centuries had time and opportunity to be caught up in the esthetic fascination and intellectual challenge of developmental phenomena as such, usually without research funds or assistants.

Few persons who have watched—through a microscope—a fertilized sea urchin egg become an elaborately sculptured, free-swimming larva within two or three days, or who have seen a small ascidian egg become an active tadpole between dawn and dusk, are likely to forget it. The process of self-creation of organisms is an unceasing attraction and a perpetual mental challenge, and those who could devote time and attention to a materially rather unrewarding activity were fortunate. Molecular and cell biology have now progressed to such a high technological level that expensive equipment and technical assistance are necessary. At the developmental level, for the most part, this phase of sophistication has not arrived, and the scope for individual imagination and investigation remains as broad as ever. Humans are by nature wondering, problem-solving creatures with esthetic sense, fascinated by stars, by the presence of life on earth, by the nature of matter, and by the mysterious mind-brain that they feel themselves to be. The phenomenon of development—the process of becoming, at all levels and in all forms of life—is an equally essential part of the whole. A developmental biologist, like all biologists, like all human beings, grows from a single, microscopic cell to become a giant, multicellular complex now self-consciously exploring the process of becoming, together with that of all else. The procedure is both objective and subjective and brings its own reward.

PRIMITIVE SYSTEMS

Most of this book is concerned with the differentiation of cells and the development of animal eggs into embryos, tissues, and organs, and with various associated topics. Chapters 23 and 24 relate to regenerative and asexual development as seen in animals. It is therefore appropriate here to emphasize that single somatic or nonsexual cells of plants are capable of developing into complex, multicellular forms without benefit of the internal reserves that eggs possess. This is seen most clearly in the development of spores, which are specialized for reproduction only in having a protective coat that ruptures under conditions compatible with development. For example, single spores liberated from fern fronds develop in water into *gametophytes*, small multicellular plants that produce eggs and sperm. Such chlorophyll-containing cells are able to grow and multiply as a multicellular unit by virtue of photosynthesis and do not depend on previously built-up reserve.

Cell Division and Morphogenesis

The fern spore cell, moreover, has but one set of chromosomes; it is haploid. Nevertheless it follows a progressive course, demonstrating that the developmental potential may be present in all cells not overly specialized for other functions. Fern spores develop readily in water that contains a mixture of inorganic salts and is exposed to light. The first cell division gives rise to one *rhizoidal* and one *protonema* cell (Fig. 1.1). The protonema cell then begins a phase of successive cell divisions in one direction, resulting in the so-called filamentous protonema. This growth pattern is *primary one-dimensional growth*. After a definite time lapse, the direction of cell division of the protonema apical cell is converted from longitudinal to transverse. The subsequent division of these cells takes place in all directions but in the same plane, forming a platelike, monocellular layer. This growth pattern is *two-dimensional*. The platelike organism resulting from two-dimensional growth develops first into a heart-shaped *prothallium* and then into a mature prothallium that contains antheridia and archegonia, or male and female sex-cell tissue. As a rule the primary one-dimensional growth proceeds to a seven-cell stage. This takes about 25 days, while about 100 days are required for the completion of the mature prothallium, the gametophyte. Fertilized egg cells develop in a different

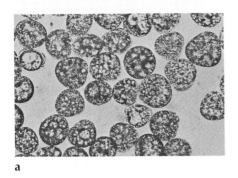
a

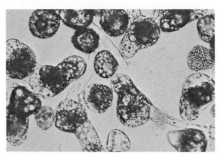
c

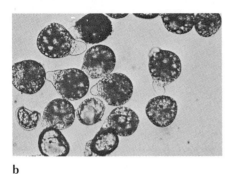
b

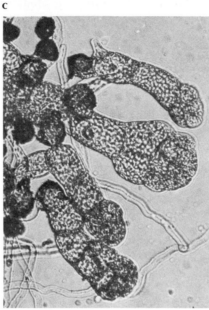
d

Figure 1.1 Development of spore cell of fern *Pteridium*. *a* Dry spores. *b, c* Protonemas in filamentous or one-dimensional stage, after 60 and 84 hours of development. [*Courtesy of A. E. De-Maggio.*] *d* Protonemas in transition to two-dimensional prothallus. [*Courtesy of L. B. Livingstone.*]

manner, in different circumstances, to become the large, spore-producing fern that is more familiar and with which we are not concerned here.

The comparatively simple process just described is a good example of a developmental system suitable for analysis; one point of interest is the nature and cause of the switch from one-dimensional to two-dimensional growth. It can be induced prematurely, for instance, by transferring spores growing in red light to a white light environment, the switch being critically dependent on exposure to the blue light component. It is also known that a sharp increase in protein concentration occurs whenever the two-dimensional growth takes place, associated with a change in the nucleotide composition of the dividing cells. Accordingly a developmental control system exists that combines an environmental agent with gene activation in the cells.

Self-Assembly and Differentiation

Spore cells are found in another developmental system now under intensive investigation, that of the cellular slime molds, of which the species *Dictyostelium discoideum* has received the most attention. Slime molds lie near the taxonomic base of the eukaryotic ladder, classified among the Protozoa by many biologists. Their life cycle has provided developmental biologists with events that resemble many of the more complex processes in the development of higher animals. The life cycle, in brief, is as follows: As spores germinate, each liberates a small amoeba which divides repeatedly. The population of amoebae continue to divide as long as an adequate supply of bacteria (the colon bacillus, *Escherichia coli,* is routinely employed in laboratory cultures) permits them to feed and grow. When the bacterial food supply is exhausted and the population of amoebae sufficiently dense, they begin to stream together to form cell masses, or aggregates. These assume a sluglike form and move about for a while but eventually become upright. The anterior cells of the slug give rise to stalk cells, the posterior cells give rise to spore cells which form an ovoid mass at the tip of the stalk, the whole being known as a *sporocarp.*

An organism with such a life cycle obviously lends itself to the study of many aspects of cell and developmental biology. Primarily three phases predominate:

1   The phase of *aggregation,* whereby a local population of free amoebae congregate at a center and become an integrated mass (Fig. 1.2*a*)

2   The phase of the slug, or pseudoplasmodium, with the degree of *differentiation* that its cells exhibit (Fig. 1.2*b*)

3   The phase of morphogenesis, whereby a slug transforms into a mature fruiting body, the sporocarp, a process known as *culmination* (Fig. 1.2*c*)

Each phase presents problems of its own, though all relate to the attainment of the multicellular state and its subsequent self-assembly into an organized and differentiated reproductive structure.

The aggregation phase represents a profound change in the life-style of the organism, reflecting the transformation of a population of single cells to a single, multicellular structure. Why does it happen? What is the mechanism? What is the consequence? Evolution has selected adaptations that ensure survival and reproduction. In many animals environmental hardship triggers a stage in the life cycle that is resistant to a deleterious environment and contains the potential for the establishment of the next generation, should times improve. In the cellular slime molds the spore provides that capability and factors in the environment trigger a series of rapid developmental activities to ensure the production of the necessary spore cells.

Why should cells living as isolates suddenly aggregate? The aggregation phenomenon has been shown to result from concentration gradients produced by the secretion of certain cells of the nucleotide, cyclic adenosine monophosphate (cyclic AMP). Dispersed cells within a certain distance of a source of cyclic AMP move in the direction of increasing concentration, a condition termed *chemotaxis.* Centers of aggregation may contain more than 100,000 cells or as few as a dozen. The concepts of chemotaxis and chemical gradients as controlling agents in development have prevailed in various forms since the early days of developmental biology.

The attainment of the multicellular state provides the opportunity for specialization so that different cells can accomplish different tasks. In a higher organism, one cell, the fertilized egg, gives rise to a multitude of cell types; in the slime-mold pseudoplasmodium, only two types are clearly recognizable: the prespore cells, which will eventually form the spores at the top of the fruiting body, and the prestalk cells, which will eventually form a slender stalk bearing the mature spores at the apex (Fig. 1.3). What determines which cells will become each type? What characteristics do each of these cells acquire and how

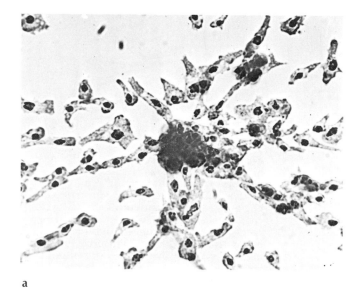

a

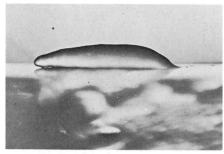

b

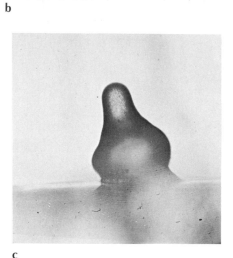

c

Figure 1.2 Self-assembly of cells of slime mold. *a* Stage in aggregation of amoebae at a center showing alignment and head-tail contacts of amoebae in migration. [*Courtesy of J. T. Bonner.*] *b* Side view of slug (pseudoplasmodium) near close of migrating period, showing tip lifting from substratum and a trail of mucus behind. [*Courtesy of David Francis.*] *c* Early culmination phase and beginning of stalk formation in *Dictyostelium discoideum.* [*Courtesy of K. B. Raper.*] *d* Mature sporocarp. [*Courtesy of W. F. Loomis.*]

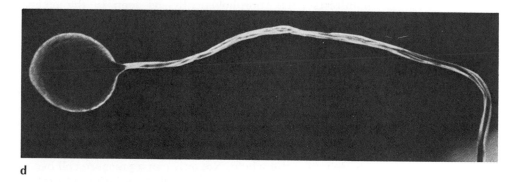

d

does this differentiation come about? How stable are the changes? That is, can the process of differentiation be reversed? This set of questions is just as valid for the differentiation of the cells of a human embryo as it is for those of a slime mold. We cannot provide all the answers in either instance, but it is hoped that the analysis of basic processes in simpler organisms can provide knowledge applicable to all forms of development.

The fate of a given cell depends primarily upon its relative position among the other cells of the aggregate. Those at the leading end of the migratory slug

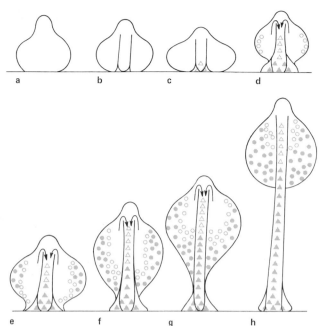

Figure 1.3 Sequential stages in the model for culmination. *a* Stage 17 aggregate. *b* Cellulose tube forming. *c* Stalk cells forming at base. *d* Stalk forming in tube, amoebae entering top of tube, and spores beginning to differentiate at periphery. *e–g* Process continues, spore formation spreading nearer center of rising cell mass, region of undifferentiated amoebae being depleted both by the encroachment of developing spores and by loss of the cells entering the tube to become stalk. *h* Process has limited itself; all the amoebae except those in the tip have either started to become spores or have entered the tube. Closed symbols = fully differentiated cells; open symbols = cells in process of differentiation. [*After P. Farnsworth,* 25th Sympos. Soc. Exp. Biol., *1971, p. 263.*]

become prestalk cells, while the remainder become prespore cells. The differentiation process between these two cell types can be followed biochemically and morphologically. The two cell types in the slug stain differently with certain dyes and have different specific gravities. As the process continues, the parts are characterized by different proteins and different carbohydrates. Presumably, the differentiation into spore cells and stalk cells represents the activation of different genes to provide each cell type with the specific templates needed to carry out its own differentiation. The underlying biochemical differentiation manifests itself morphologically, as seen in the electron microscope, as a changing cytological condition, a process termed *cytodifferentiation*. The prespore cells, e.g., have a type of membrane-bound vacuole that is not found in the prestalk cells.

Even though the cells of the slug have become differentiated in anticipation of their respective positions within the mature fruiting body, their fate is not yet sealed irreversibly. The prespore region of the slug can be isolated from the prestalk region and each can form a complete fruiting body; under these conditions each cell can shift its path of differentiation to produce the missing type. We can conclude from this experiment that differentiation, in this instance at least, is reversible to a relatively late stage and that each part of the slug has an awareness of the whole. Not only can a prespore cell become a prestalk cell and vice versa, but each can halt its differentiation and revert to the single-celled, ameboid stage. For this to happen, a part of the slug is removed, reduced to single cells by mechanical disruption, and provided with a food source, whose absence may have triggered the initial aggregation. If there is no food source, the isolated cells reaggregate and return to the formation of fruiting body. The cells of the slime mold are remarkably plastic in their differentiation.

Of primary interest to developmental biologists is the nature of the agents that cause cell differentiation. In the slime mold the position of the slug cells relative to one another is of utmost importance in the determination of their fate. The relationship of a part to the whole is a causal factor in many developmental events, but the means by which this information is passed to the cells is poorly understood.

One of the consequences of the multicellular state, in a pseudoplasmodium or any other cell mass, is the cell communication that results from cell contact. The outer edge of all cells forms a complex structure capable of transmitting and receiving a wide variety of stimulatory signals. Cells kept in isolation, and therefore free of cell contacts, cannot undergo differentiation into prespore and prestalk cells. An early event in the differentiation of the slime-mold amoebae is a molecular change in the plasma membrane; the intramembrane particles become larger. Whether or not a change at the cell surface is the first step in differentiation in this or any other system remains uncertain, but many examples show that information received at the cell periphery has a profound effect upon the internal activities of the cell.

The latter stages in the life cycle of *Dictyostelium* involve the construction of the fruiting body and provide an example of *morphogenesis,* the development of form and structure. The analysis of morphogenesis includes the study of changes in cell shape, the interaction between cells and extracellular materials such as cellulose and acid mucopolysaccharides, and the assembly of the parts of this complex structure.

The genetic control of morphogenesis is a complex subject, studied in various ways. Biochemical analysis has provided evidence for the role of specific messenger RNAs and proteins in these events, and genetic mutants have been isolated in which morphogenesis proceeds toward a greatly deranged fruiting body.

Events in the life cycle of the cellular slime mold have been included in this introductory chapter to provide an overview of some basic questions of concern to developmental biologists, regardless of the particular organism under study. The processes of differentiation and morphogenesis provide the focus for research in developmental biology and are discussed throughout this book.

READINGS

BERG, P. *et al.*, 1975. Asilomar Conference on Recombinant DNA Molecules, *Science,* **188**:991–994.

BONNER, J. T., 1967. "The Cellular Slime Molds," 2d ed., Princeton University Press.

CHARGAFF, E., 1971. Preface to a Grammar of Biology, *Science,* **172**:637–642.

CHILD, C. M., 1941. "Problems and Patterns of Development," Chicago University Press.

CONKLIN, E. G., 1905. Mosaic Development in Ascidian Eggs, *J. Exp. Zool.,* **2**:145–223.

JOHNSON, L. G., and E. P. VOLPE, 1973. "Patterns and Experiments in Developmental Biology," Wm. C. Brown.

LASH, J., and J. R. WHITTAKER, 1974. "Concepts of Development," Sinauer.

NEEDHAM, J., 1942. "Biochemistry and Morphogenesis," Macmillan.

NEWELL, P. C., J. FRANKE, and M. SUSSMAN, 1972. Regulation of four functionally related enzymes during shifts in the developmental program of *Dictyostelium discoideum, J. Mol. Biol.,* **63**:373–382.

RAGHAVAN, V., 1974. Control of Differentiation in the Fern Gametophyte, *Amer. Sci.,* **62**:465–475.

RAPER, K. B., and D. I. FENNELL, 1952. Stalk Formation in *Dictyostelium, Torrey Bot. Club Bull.,* **70**:25–51.

SPEMANN, H., 1938, "Embryonic Development and Induction," Yale University Press (reissued 1968).

WILLIER, B. H., and J. M. OPPENHEIMER, 1974. "Foundations of Experimental Embryology," Prentice-Hall. Contains classical articles by Roux, Driesch, Wilson, Boveri, Harrison, Child, Spemann and Mangold, Holtfreter, Loewenstein, *et al.*[1]

WILT, F. H., and N. K. WESSELLS, 1967. "Methods in Developmental Biology," Crowell.

[1] For reference throughout this text, the articles in this chronological anthology are listed here. **Contents:** 1888 Contributions to the Developmental Mechanics of the Embryo. On the Artificial Production of Half-Embryos by Destruction of One of the First Two Blastomeres, and the Later Development (Postgeneration) of the Missing Half of the Body (W. Roux). 1892 The Potency of the First Two Cleavage Cells in Echinoderm Development. Experimental Production of Partial and Double Formations (Hans Driesch). 1898 Cell-lineage and Ancestral Reminiscence (Edmund B. Wilson). 1902 On Multipolar Mitosis as a Means of Analysis of the Cell Nucleus (Theodor Boveri). 1907 The Living Developing Nerve Fiber (Ross G. Harrison). 1908 Observations on Oxidative Processes in the Sea Urchin Egg (Otto Warburg). 1913 The Mechanism of Fertilization (Frank R. Lillie). 1914 Susceptibility Gradients in Animals (C. M. Child). 1916 The Theory of the Free-Martin (Frank R. Lillie). 1924 Induction of Embryonic Primordia by Implantation of Organizers from a Different Species (Hans Spemann and Hilde Mangold). 1939 Tissue Affinity, A Means of Embryonic Morphogenesis (Johannes Holtfreter),. 1954 *In Vitro* Experiments on the Effects of Mouse Sarcomas 108 and 37 on the Spinal and Sympathetic Ganglia of the Chick Embryo (Rita Levi-Montalcini, Hertha Meyer and Viktor Hamburger). 1969 Ionic Communication between Early Embryonic Cells (Shizuo Ito and Werner R. Loewenstein). 1973 Positional Information in Chick Limb Morphogenesis (D. Summerbell, J. H. Lewis and L. Wolpert).

PART I

CELL ASSEMBLY AND REPRODUCTION

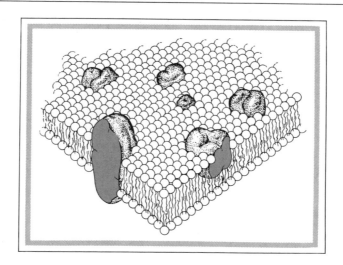

CHAPTER 2

Molecular Biology and Assembly

The Concept of the Gene
The Structure of DNA
DNA Replication
Transcription
Translation
Protein Structure
Selective Gene Activation

The operon concept
Control in eukaryotes

Levels of Control
Self-assembly

Construction and reconstruction of collagen, a structural protein
The ribosome
Virus assembly

Research in many areas of developmental biology is beginning to produce answers to basic questions, questions that until recently could not even be formulated for complex developing systems. The current research leans heavily on the findings and technology of those who have examined the mysteries of metabolic function in the simpler viral and bacterial systems. Many of these studies represent some of the finest endeavors in the history of science. Their elegant yet simple design has allowed questions to be answered on organisms too small to be seen with the light microscope. Their methods and tools have been adopted by biologists working at higher levels of organization, and knowledge of processes in higher animals is rapidly accumulating.

Although many molecular processes found in microorganisms are found in any animal cell, many are not. The bacterial cell is a simple unit by mammalian standards, one that has evolved a direct responsiveness to the foreign environment around it. The cells of higher animals are, instead, responsive to the needs of a supercellular structure, and the levels of regulation are vastly more complex. This is reflected in the complexity of the genome, in the architecture of the cytoplasm and cell surface, in the many intercellular activities. To appreciate current research efforts in developmental biology, one must become familiar with the basic techniques and the core of knowledge of cellular and molecular biology. That is the goal of this chapter.

The most important questions at the molecular level concern the storage and utilization of genetic information. It is clear to all of us that the basic characteristics of any organism are transmitted from generation to generation in the genetic information. In some unexplained way the geometry of a spider's web and the score of a bird's song must be *coded* for, the incredibly complex regulative processes that maintain the homeostatic activities of the cell must also be a part of this genetic code. In many ways we have only scratched the surface in our attempts to understand how this vast genetic inheritance is utilized in the activities of the organism.

17

The credit for the concept of a "unit of inheritance" belongs to the Austrian monk Gregor Mendel, who in 1866 published the results of his studies on the breeding of different races of pea plants. Starting with pure stocks that had recognizably different characteristics, he artificially cross-pollinated the plants and carefully recorded the characteristics of the offspring over several generations. From these data he reached several conclusions that now form the foundation of the science of genetics. He concluded that a pair of discrete "factors" governed each characteristic and that they segregated upon formation of the gametes. We know this pair of factors as the maternally and paternally derived alleles on homologous chromosomes that first come together at fertilization.

Segregation occurs within the reproductive organs in meiosis, when each gamete receives only one of the pair of factors. The *law of segregation* encloses the concept that the units of inheritance come together at fertilization, remain together during the life of the organism, separate at meiosis, and remain unchanged throughout this whole process. How was Mendel able to derive such a law? In one of his experiments he crossed a stock of peas with green seeds with one of yellow seeds. All the offspring (F_1) had yellow seeds. A first conclusion might be that the factor for green color had been lost. When, however, two of these offspring (F_1 generation) were crossed, 25 percent of the next generation (F_2) had green seeds and bred true among themselves. The green factor had not been lost, but was rather in a masked condition and could still emerge intact to direct the characteristics of the next generation.

Mendel's findings, published in an obscure periodical, were rediscovered by 1900, a time when several investigators were beginning to open doors in the science of genetics. During the first half of the twentieth century, genetic studies by many biologists, notably T. H. Morgan, of a number of organisms (especially the fruitfly) were being carried out. They provide much of our present knowledge of genetic inheritance. The geneticists of this period discovered that new genes could appear by mutations of existing genes and that crossing-over and recombination could redistribute maternal and paternal characteristics. They realized that genes occur in a linear sequence, and they described many complex linkage groups, i.e., groups of genes that segregate together. Another branch of genetics, *cytogenetics,* was making great strides in explaining the physical basis of the gene theory. The chromosome was singled out as the carrier of the linear array of genes and the physical basis of the linkage groups. The duplication and separation of the chromosomes and their crossing-over activities were observed and described.

One type of cell of particular interest was discovered and greatly exploited for its usefulness to cytogenetics. This special cell, found in several tissues of the larval fruit fly, contains giant chromosomes which, except for their unusual size, reflect the state of the genome in every cell of the fly. These chromosomes result from duplication of genetic material and failure of the duplicates to separate. This process continues until there are over 1,000 identical units together in perfect genetic register. The giant chromosomes have a banded appearance in the light microscope (Fig. 2.1), and individual bands have been correlated with specific genes. Thus, the cytogeneticist could examine the chromosomes of an individual fly and have before him a visual array of the genes of that fly. Visible alterations in these chromosomes have led to explanations of genetic changes. Missing genes (deletions) were observed, as were a variety of ways in which the chromosomal pieces could be broken and reorganized. Much of our knowledge of chromosomal malformation is based on this work

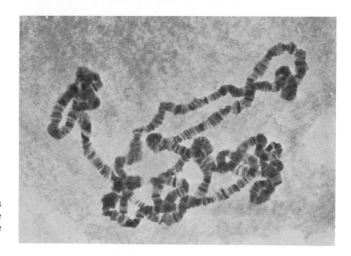

Figure 2.1 Chromosomes isolated from the nucleus of a salivary gland cell of a larval *Drosophila*. Note the irregular banding throughout the length of the chromosome, further illustrated in Fig. 22.7.

In the past quarter-century much of the genetic theory has been explained at the molecular level. The single, most basic question in molecular genetics has been the nature of the genetic material. This is the point of departure of this still-young science. During the first of this century considerable information became available on the composition of macromolecules. Proteins were the logical candidate for the role of genetic carrier, because of the number and variety of the building blocks of which they are made. There are approximately 20 different amino acids in a protein, but only 4 different nucleotides in a nucleic acid molecule. Presumably this greater complexity could better satisfy the requirements of the job.

We know now, of course, that protein is not the genetic carrier. The first report to point directly to deoxyribonucleic acid (DNA) was a report by Avery, MacLeod, and McCarthy in 1944 on transformation in *Pneumococcus*. Two strains of *Pneumococcus* had been isolated: one had a smooth appearance and was able to produce pneumonia in a suitable host; the other had a rough appearance as the result of a defect in its capsule and was nonvirulent. When a cell-free extract of smooth bacteria was added to the medium in which the rough strain was growing, a few of the latter became smooth and virulent. They had been *transformed*. From the time of transformation, the progeny of that cell maintained their smooth appearance, i.e., the transformation was a stable, genetic change. Avery and his coworkers purified the contents of cells after their disruption in detergent and found that only the purified DNA was capable of causing the transformation.

To further corroborate this finding they treated the cell extract with various enzymes that digest specific macromolecules. Treatment of the homogenate with ribonuclease or protease had no effect, indicating that transformation occurred in the absence of RNA or protein; these could not be the genetic material. Enzymes that destroyed DNA, however, eliminated the ability of the homogenate to transform. This suggested that for transformation to occur, DNA fragments entered the recipient cell intact and substituted in the bacterial chromosome for the original DNA that was eliminated; a new genetic microorganism was produced. Subsequent experiments confirmed this finding and the search for the chemical identity of the gene was over.

The elucidation of the physical nature of the gene was yet to come. To appreciate the analysis of DNA structure by Watson and Crick, one must understand the facts available at that time.

19

DNA was known to be a very long, fibrous molecule with a backbone composed of alternate sugar and phosphate groups joined by 3'5'-phosphodiester linkages. To each sugar was attached one of four possible nitrogenous bases. The bases were of two types; the pyrimidines cytosine (C) and thymine (T) and the purines adenine (A) and guanine (G). It was known that the amount of purine equaled the amount of pyrimidine and specifically that adenine content was equal to thymine content and guanine to cytosine. However, the percentage of adenine plus thymine or guanine plus cytosine could vary from source to source. With this information in mind, Watson and Crick in 1953 proposed, from the analysis of x-ray diffraction studies, that DNA had the following structure (Fig. 2.2). DNA was made of two chains coiled around a common axis, with the sugar-phosphate backbone on the outside and the bases pointing in toward the axis. The bases were hydrogen-bonded to each other across the axis and only two possible bonds could exist, adenine to thymine and cytosine to guanine. Both chains formed right-handed helices, but they ran in opposite directions. In addition, they provided the physical dimensions: the nucleotides were 3.4 Å (angstroms) apart and there were 10 pairs of bases per complete turn of the double helix. The distance of the phosphate atoms to the axis was 10 Å.

With this model Watson and Crick speculated on the relationship between DNA structure and several basic genetic functions. They proposed that the information of DNA was coded for by the linear sequence of the bases. They theorized that a mutation could be accounted for by a chance mistake in the formation of the sequence during duplication. Finally they suggested that in duplication each chain would act as a template for the formation of the companion chain. By this mechanism the requirement for self-duplication of the genetic material was met.

One of the most important points demonstrated in the model was *complementarity*. For example, adenine is complementary to thymine, AGC is complementary to TCG, and one entire chain is complementary to the other. If the base sequence of one chain were to become known, then the base sequence of the complementary chain would automatically be available. The concept of complementarity of nucleic acids—in DNA chains or in RNA chains—is of overriding importance in nearly all the activities and mechanisms in which this class of macromolecules is involved. Not only was the elucidation of the DNA structure significant in its own right, but it provided the stimulus for investigation of all the activities in which the genetic material must take part. Once the model for its structure was accepted, any theory of the genetic code, of DNA synthesis, or of information transfer had to be explained on the basis of that structure.

During the next decade the specific nature of the triplet code for amino acids was worked out, the essential events in the process of protein synthesis were uncovered, and the mechanism by which each strand of DNA acts as a template for replication of the complementary strand was described. The process of replication (DNA synthesis) and probably that of transcription (RNA synthesis) require that the DNA double helix be opened up. Each hydrogen bond linking the two strands is weak and is easily broken to allow localized strand separation. On the other hand the tremendous number of H bonds arranged in a linear series provides a very stable double-helical structure. In the bacterium *Escherichia coli,* the chromosome consists of one circular piece of DNA, 1,100μm(microns) in length, while in contrast the DNA of one human X chromosome contains nearly 5 cm double helix, though it is not known if the DNA of each chromosome is one unbroken molecule or many molecules.

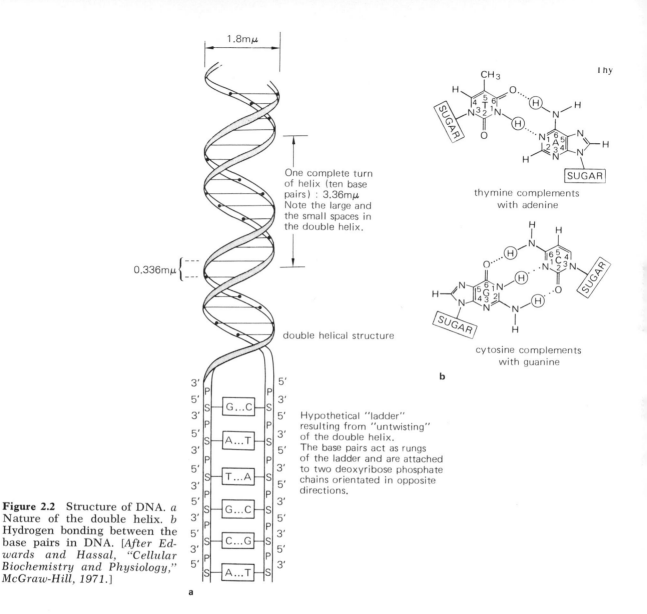

1.8mμ

One complete turn
of helix (ten base
pairs) : 3.36mμ
Note the large and
the small spaces in
the double helix.

0.336mμ

double helical structure

thy

thymine complements
with adenine

cytosine complements
with guanine

b

3' 5'
P   P
5'S G...C SP3'
3'P A...T PS5'
5'S   SP3'
3'P T...A PS5'
5'S   SP3'
3'P G...C PS5'
5'S   SP3'
3'P C...G PS5'
5'S A...T SP3'

Hypothetical "ladder"
resulting from "untwisting"
of the double helix.
The base pairs act as rungs
of the ladder and are attached
to two deoxyribose phosphate
chains orientated in opposite
directions.

Figure 2.2 Structure of DNA. *a*
Nature of the double helix. *b*
Hydrogen bonding between the
base pairs in DNA. [*After Ed-
wards and Hassal, "Cellular
Biochemistry and Physiology,"*
McGraw-Hill, 1971.]

a

Current research centers on the complexity of the eukaryotic genome. This
phase of DNA study began in 1966 with the report by Britten and Kohne that in
the genome of higher organisms some genes are present as many copies (repeated DNA), while other genes are apparently present in only one copy per
haploid set of chromosomes (unique DNA). From the time it was established
that DNA is the genetic material, the question has been asked, "why so much
DNA?" Although some cancer-producing viruses contain DNA for fewer than
10 genes, one *E. coli* bacterium has a single, circular chromosome with enough
DNA for approximately 5,000 genes and the genome of humans has approximately 2,000 times as much DNA as an *E. coli*. If we were to assume that the
only function of DNA is to code for the amino acid sequence of different proteins,
we would expect to find within our body nearly 10 million different proteins. Be-

21

cause, as we will see later in this chapter, many proteins are composed of more than one chain of amino acids, we could divide this number by 2 or 3 and we are still left with an unimaginable number of proteins. From what we know about the relationship of amino acid sequence to the structure and function of proteins, it seems unlikely that so many different-shaped proteins could have any meaningful function. Evidence obtained over the past several years confirms the suggestion that most of the DNA does not code for proteins. We can repeat the question of why so much DNA, but we cannot yet provide the answer. Some relevant studies will be described below, and an optimist would probably state that the answer to this question is not far off.

The techniques used by Britten and Kohne in their studies are relatively complex, but they must be understood before the significance of their findings can be appreciated. (The student will have to understand these techniques also to follow the series of investigations of gene activity that will be described in later chapters.) To begin the analysis, a solution of DNA is prepared and the large DNA molecules are broken into fragments of approximately 400 nucleotides in length. DNA is generally fragmented by means of ultrasonic disruption or high hydrostatic pressure. The next step is to cause the dissociation of the double-stranded complex of the DNA fragments. This is accomplished by heating the solution of DNA fragments to approximately 100°C in the appropriate salt solution, causing the disruption of the H bonds and the separation of the two strands.

Each strand releases a strand of complementary base sequence. Two of these types of fragments are considered here: first, a fragment with the same sequence of several hundred nucleotides that is present in many places on several different chromosomes; second, a fragment with a nucleotide sequence that is found in only one place on one of each set of chromosomes. Clearly, the solution of single-stranded DNA will have many more fragments with the first sequence than the second. In solution these DNA fragments are continually colliding with one another, and inevitably those with a complementary base sequence will come into contact. At 100°C, H bonds cannot form between the colliding complementary strands, but if the temperature of the solution is dropped to about 60°C, stable, double-stranded fragments (reannealed DNA) can result from successful collisions. The sequences most common within the DNA and present at greatest concentration will have the greatest number of successful collisions and will reanneal most rapidly. Therefore, the longer a solution of single-stranded fragments is allowed to remain at 60°C in the appropriate solvent (e.g., 0.12 M phosphate), the greater will be the percentage of the DNA present in a double-stranded, reannealed form. Sequences present at very low concentration will reanneal only after very long periods.

This relationship is shown by the (reannealing) curves of Fig. 2.3 (see Chapter 25). A reannealing curve for mammalian DNA has several components. First there is a fraction representing about 10 percent of the total DNA. It reanneals so rapidly its progress can be followed only in dilute solutions where the concentrations of the reactants are very low. This is called *satellite DNA;* it consists of great numbers of very short nucleotide sequences and has been localized primarily in the centromeres of the chromosomes. Another fraction of 20 percent of the total DNA sequences in the mouse reanneals over a part of the curve that indicates they are present in numerous copies in the genome. This is the *repeated fraction;* its function remains unknown with the exception of the messenger RNAs for the histones and the genes for ribosomal RNA, which constitute a small percentage of the repeated DNA. The bulk of this DNA may have important regulatory functions.

The remaining fraction, 70 percent in the mouse, appears to be present in only one copy, or at best a very few copies, per haploid genome. This is the

Figure 2.3 Reannealing curves of heat-denatured (single-stranded) DNA. DNA is fragmented, converted to single strands, allowed to incubate at a suitable temperature (e.g., 60°C) in a suitable medium (e.g., 0.12 M phosphate buffer) for various times, and the percentage of DNA that has reannealed is determined. The term C_0t is a measure of the concentration-time variable. Either the greater the concentration or the longer the time, the greater will be the number of successful collisions between complementary strands, and the greater will be the percentage of the DNA that has reannealed. A solution containing a high concentration of DNA incubated for a short time will have the same C_0t as one of low concentration incubated for a correspondingly longer time; both will have the same percentage reannealed. In this figure there are two curves: the dotted line represents the reannealing of bacterial DNA and the solid line represents mammalian DNA. The mammalian-reannealing curve starts with a significant percentage already double-stranded, reflecting the reannealing of satellite DNA at very low C_0t. The first part of the mammalian curve represents the reannealing of the repeated DNA sequences. The last part of the curve (from 50 to 100 percent reannealed) represents the nonrepeated sequences. The reannealing curve for the bacterial DNA has a simpler shape. Bacterial DNA has essentially no repeated DNA sequences and therefore reanneals with the same kinetics as nonrepeated mammalian DNA. The reason the bacterial curve is to the left of the nonrepeated mammalian DNA is that the sequences are at a much higher concentration. The bacterial genome is small and, therefore, a comparable amount of bacterial DNA will have a greater number of genomes and thus a greater number of each sequence. [*After Britten and Kohne, 1968.*]

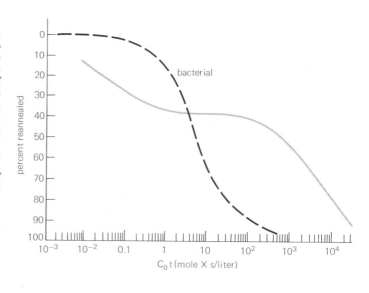

unique (nonrepeated) fraction; it has recently been shown to include the DNA that codes for the hemoglobin mRNA, the silk protein mRNA, and very likely all other mRNAs with the exception of the histones, for which several hundred copies are found. In the sea urchin embryo it appears that histones are transcribed from repeated DNA sequences that are highly clustered. Calculations indicate that one gene per haploid set of DNA can turn out sufficient numbers of mRNA in the time allowed to account for the synthesis of protein, even when one protein greatly dominates the cell's synthetic activity.

The evidence from the analysis of different-sized DNA fragments from both the sea urchin and *Xenopus,* an amphibian, suggests that approximately 50 percent of the genome contains closely interspersed repeated and unique sequences. The repeated sequences average 300 nucleotides in length while the unique are about 800 nucleotides. A significant fraction (about 20 percent in the sea urchin) is made of essentially uninterrupted unique DNA sequences. In the sea urchin about 6 percent apparently contains relatively long regions of repeated DNA. The remaining DNA is made of repeated sequences interspersed with unique sequences of considerable length (4,000 nucleotides). Indications are, therefore, that the organization of the genome of higher organisms is very complex and its significance is yet to be understood.

23

DNA REPLICATION

The term *replication* describes the process of the doubling of DNA or DNA synthesis. The details will not concern us here, but a few of the most important points will be considered. Replication is semiconservative; i.e., each of the strands of the parent molecule remains intact and becomes one of the strands of each of the two daughter molecules. Each strand serves as a template during the copy process for the polymerization of the complementary strand. The separation of strands, the unwinding, and the polymerization are accomplished by an enzyme, DNA polymerase, in association with other proteins. The copy process is precise though a rare mistake is made and an incorrect nucleotide is incorporated in the strand, producing a mutation—i.e., a change in nucleotide sequence. This is a major cause of mutation; another cause is a modification of a nucleotide base that was already incorporated into the DNA backbone.

DNA synthesis is not a continual process in the life of a cell; it is restricted to a period between mitoses and is sandwiched between two periods when DNA is not synthesized, G_1 and G_2. In other words, in a dividing population of cells, there is a period following mitosis when DNA synthesis has not yet begun. This period is G_1 (Gap$_1$). In the following period, the S phase, DNA synthesis begins and continues until the chromosomal DNA is doubled. Studies indicate that DNA synthesis is a carefully controlled event; certain chromosomes are predictably replicated in early S phase and others are predictably replicated in late S phase. Within each chromosome, more that one point of replication is found at a given time. After DNA synthesis is completed, the cell enters G_2 (Gap$_2$) preparatory to its next mitosis.

TRANSCRIPTION

The repository of the nuclear DNA is the chromosome, and with one exception no evidence has been obtained that it is ever found in any other nuclear structure. The exception is the DNA that codes for ribosomal RNA found in the nucleolus; in certain cases this DNA lacks continuity with that of the chromosomes.

The chromosomes are the seats of information storage, and as such can have virtually no direct effect on the cell's activities. To the present time, only one way has been uncovered in which DNA can manifest itself in cell function. This is indirectly via the synthesis of complementary RNA molecules, which is the process of *transcription*. RNA, in general, differs structurally from DNA in three ways: (1) The sugar is ribose rather than deoxyribose. (2) Thymine is not found in RNA but is replaced by uracil, which differs by lacking a methyl group. (3) As a result of the first two points, RNA is generally a single-stranded molecule, though base pairing is still possible and many RNAs have double-stranded regions.

As research continues, the number of types of RNAs discovered continues to grow. The three RNAs first identified are the best studied: messenger RNA, transfer RNA, and ribosomal RNA. As will be discussed in detail below, it is the messenger RNA (mRNA) that contains within its linear sequence of nucleotides the information for the specific sequence of amino acids of one polypeptide chain. The transfer RNAs (tRNAs) are the intermediates in the manufacture of proteins and are responsible for bringing the proper amino acid, as specified by the bases of the mRNA, into the growing polypeptide chain. The ribosomal RNA (rRNA) is found as part of the ribosome. Ribosomal RNA is initially transcribed as one long RNA molecule, which is then broken into several fragments by a complex process within the nucleolus. Two large fragments are retained as ribosomal RNAs and each becomes a part of one of the two subunits of each ribosome. An additional small rRNA (5S RNA) is also present in the large subunit. The role of the rRNAs in ribosome function is unclear; they are distinctly involved in the association of certain proteins that make up the subunits, and they may function in holding the two subunits to each other. The interactions of these RNAs in protein synthesis will be reviewed below.

Transcription is accomplished by the activity of an enzyme, RNA polymerase, of which the cell has more than one type. This enzyme illustrates the working of a typical enzyme and also describes the events of transcription itself. The function of this enzyme is to produce a molecule of RNA with a complementary base sequence to one strand, the sense strand, of the DNA. In a bacterial cell the polymerase consists of a core enzyme, made of five polypeptide chains, and another protein, the sigma factor. In addition, at least one other protein, the rho factor, is needed for transcription. An enzyme made of more than one polypeptide chain is said to have a subunit structure. Some enzymes with a subunit structure are made of more than one identical subunit, while others are composed of different polypeptide chains that are coded for by different genes. The polypeptide chain is defined as a continuous sequence of amino acids joined by peptide bonds. One polypeptide chain is coded for by only one mRNA, though, at least in bacteria, the reverse may not hold true; i.e., one mRNA can code for more than one polypeptide chain, as will be seen later in this chapter. One polypeptide chain is generally used as the defining criterion for one gene. In other words, if a stretch of DNA produces two polypeptide chains, it is said to be composed of two genes even though it may be transcribed into one long mRNA.

The function of the polymerase is complex. The enzyme must recognize where it should bind on the DNA molecule and where transcription should begin. In prokaryotes it is clear that the chromosome is an unbroken molecule of DNA without protein or other material within the DNA chain. There appears to be a special region of the DNA, the promotor region, with which the sigma factor of the polymerase first makes contact. Presumably the specificity of the sigma factor for a specific nucleotide sequence of the promotor region prevents the tight binding of the enzyme to the incorrect DNA strand or internally to a gene. The enzyme, once bound, must be able to move along the DNA toward the gene itself. Movement proceeds from the 3' end to the 5' end of the DNA template. The promotor region itself in the best-studied case is not transcribed, but the enzyme must recognize some sequence in the DNA as the point to begin transcription.

Transcription results in the formation of a growing (nascent) chain of polymerized ribonucleoside phosphates. The enzyme must have the ability to recognize the specific nucleotide in the template strand of DNA and to select the appropriate complementary nucleoside triphosphate from the nuclear sap. The enzyme must then catalyze the reaction, whereby the nucleoside triphosphate is polymerized to the growing chain as the nucleoside monophosphate with the release of pyrophosphate. During the process, the growing chain must therefore also be held by the enzyme. After each nucleotide is added, the enzyme must move to the next position. This process continues a short distance until a codon, TAC (thymine-adenine-cytosine), of the DNA is reached; this is called the *initiation codon*. It is this codon (AUG in mRNA) that will begin the process of amino acid incorporation at the ribosome. Transcription proceeds and the nascent chain grows. Finally, the enzyme reaches a point where a codon signals the end of chain elongation. The termination codon can have

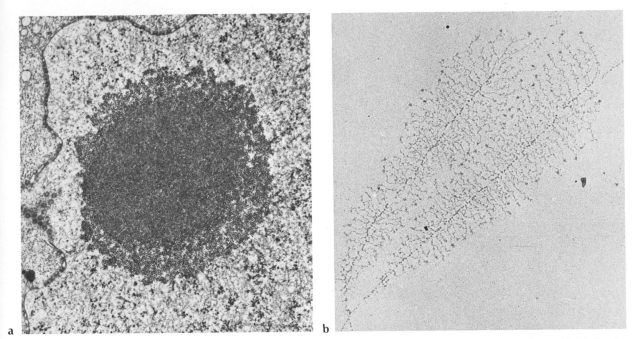

Figure 2.4 Photograph of nucleolus and of ribosomal cistrons transcribing rRNA (in the newt *Triturus viridescens*). Transcription in various stages of completion is evident in the lateral extensions from the central thread of DNA. *a* Thin section of extrachromosomal nucleolus, showing compact fibrous core surrounded by a granular cortex. *b* Portion of a single nucleolar gene showing RNA polymerase molecules located on the DNA axis at the base of each matrix fibril. [*Courtesy of O. L. Miller Jr. and Barbara R. Beatty, Biology Division, Oak Ridge National Laboratory.*]

three different triplet sequences. Termination appears to require an additional protein, the rho factor.

The details of transcription are presented because they illustrate the dynamic processes that occur at the molecular level. These proteins are inanimate objects, capable of performing these complex acts in unison with one another as a result of their geometric shapes and the reactivities of the component amino acids. It must be presumed that each act produces the necessary change in the substrate and the enzyme itself, whereby the next act must inevitably follow. Polymerization follows nucleotide selection, and movement must then occur before the process can be repeated. Enzymes are catalysts; they are constructed in such a way as to facilitate a specific chemical reaction without being themselves altered in the process. Conformational changes in enzymes are well documented and involve subtle alterations in the relative positions of the polypeptide chains. Transcription has been visualized in the electron microscope (Fig. 2.4) by Miller and his coworkers.

TRANSLATION

In a bacterial cell the synthesis of a mRNA strand is followed by the translation of that strand into protein. In the cells of higher organisms there are, clearly, intermediate steps in this process. In studies of mammalian cells growing in tissue culture, it appears that the mRNA molecule (i.e., the stretch of nucleotides that codes for a given sequence of amino acids) is only a small fragment at one end of a much larger molecule (over 10,000 nucleotides at the time of termination). The remainder of this huge RNA molecule is split from the mRNA piece before its release from the nucleus to the cytoplasm; therefore, these large molecules are never found outside the confines of the nucleus itself. Before its relation to mRNA was discovered, the term *heterogeneous nuclear RNA* (HnRNA) was assigned to this fraction. It becomes labeled rapidly by radioactive RNA precursors, is never seen to leave the nucleus, and is degraded with a half-life of about 7 to 30 minutes. The function of this piece, and therefore of most of the RNA synthesized, is unknown. Another aspect of the processing of newly synthesized RNA has recently emerged. After the transcription process is completed, leaving the mRNA as a tail at the 3′ end of the large precursor molecule, a chain of adenosine monophosphate (AMP) molecules is added one at a time to the 3′ end of the mRNA tip. These poly-A fragments are in the order of 200 nucleotides long and may be required for the release of many of the newly synthesized RNAs to the cytoplasm.

The process of polypeptide formation directed by the mRNA template is *translation*. When the mRNA strand moves into the cytoplasm, the ribosomes become attached to it. The mRNA molecule consists of a nucleotide chain that is a complement of one of the DNA strands. The information is coded in the linear sequence of these nucleotides, specifically in the form of a continual sequence of triplets of nucleotide bases (*codons*). Because there are 4 possible nucleotides, there are 64 possible codons but only approximately 20 amino acids. Three of the possible codons specify termination, and the remaining 61 triplets, including the initiation codon, specify amino acids. Obviously there are amino acids with several different codons; i.e., the code is *degenerate*.

There is no obvious steric relationship between a triplet sequence of nucleotides in RNA and any given amino acid; an intermediate must bridge this gap. The intermediate function is performed by the tRNA. One end of the molecule has a triplet sequence (*anticodon*) complementary to a specific triplet in the mRNA. One end becomes charged with a specific amino acid for which that mRNA triplet must code. Each tRNA molecule ends in the sequence cytosine-cytosine-adenine, to which the amino acid is attached. If the amino acid attachment site is identical (CCA) in all tRNAs, the problem of specificity must reside elsewhere on the molecule. It is the function of the amino acid activating enzyme to properly charge the specific tRNA (Fig. 2.5).

Amino acid activation is in two steps. Each amino acid activating enzyme is capable of reacting with ATP and one specific amino acid. This complex then can recognize, presumably by its shape, only one of the possible tRNAs to which the amino acid is transferred; the proper amino acid is linked up opposite the proper anticodon. In one sense it is therefore the amino acid activating enzymes where the specificity of the process and the link between nucleotide sequence and amino acid sequence reside.

Because there are 61 codons that specify an amino acid, one would expect 61 different tRNAs. In *E. coli* this correlation does not exist. There are tRNAs whose anticodon can recognize more than one codon in the mRNA. For example, the amino acid serine has six codons: UCU, UCC, UCA, UCG, AGU, and AGC. Of the three bases that make up the anticodon of the tRNA, the 5′ base can pair with more than one base at the 3′ position of the mRNA triplet. When U is the third anticodon base, it can pair with A or G in the mRNA. If I (inosine) is the 5′ anticodon base, it can pair with U, C, or A in the mRNA. With these rules in mind, the above six codons could be handled by three different tRNAs having the following anticodons: 1 and 2, AGI; 3 and 4, AGU; 5 and 6, UCI. On the other hand, there appear to be different tRNAs having the same anticodon.

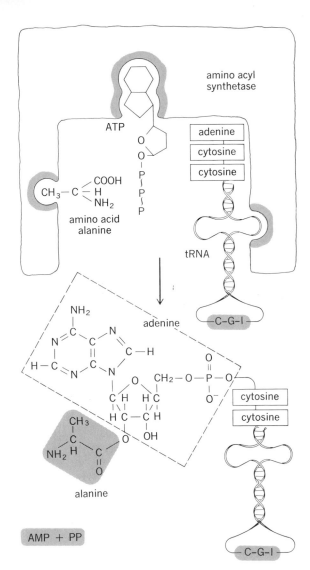

Figure 2.5 Diagrammatic representation of reaction between the amino acid activating enzyme for alanine, ATP, and the specific amino acid (ala). The specificity for the particular amino acid and the specific tRNA is carried by the enzyme. [*From Vander, Sherman, and Luciano, "Human Physiology," 2d ed., McGraw-Hill, 1974.*]

The functional significance of this finding is not known. The events of translation are illustrated in Fig. 2.6, and only the highlights will be considered here.

The components required for protein synthesis include (1) the mRNA strand that bears the information for amino acid sequence within its nucleotide code, (2) the ribosome that is intimately involved in the entire process, (3) the tRNAs that bring in the specific amino acids, (4) a growing number of proteins with a variety of roles, and (5) guanosine triphosphate (GTP), whose exact role is still unclear.

Translation proceeds from the 5′ to the 3′ end of the RNA, producing a polypeptide chain that grows from its amino to its carboxyl end. Each ribosome attaches to the mRNA at a point before the initiation codon, which in higher cells appears to be one of the methionine triplets, AUG. When the ribosome reaches this codon, the tRNA bearing the methionine at its CCA terminus binds to the ribosome; in association with initiation factors, translation begins. After the initiation step, polypeptide chain elongation proceeds.

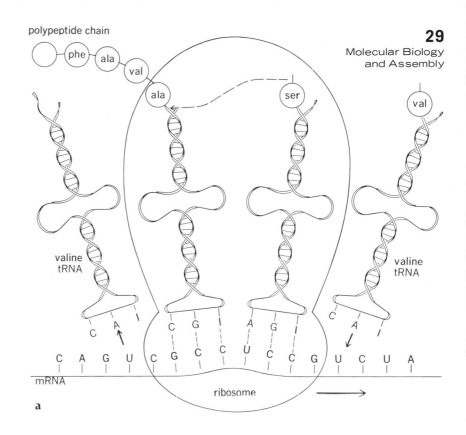

a

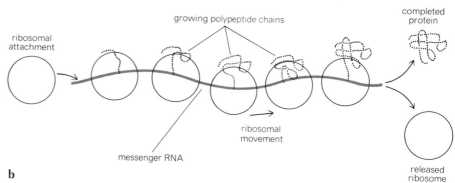

b

Figure 2.6 *a* Diagrammatic representation of the elongation process of protein synthesis. [*From Vander, Sherman, and Luciano, "Human Physiology," 2d ed. McGraw-Hill, 1974.*] *b* Movement of ribosomes into and out of a polysome, showing formation and release of polypeptide chain. [*From "Molecular Organization and Biological Function," edited by John M. Allen: Fig. 3 (p. 25) by Alexander Rich, Harper & Row, 1967.*]

Elongation is a complex event. Each ribosome contains two binding sites for tRNAs, the A site and the P site. At first the P site is occupied by the tRNA bearing the first amino acid, methionine, and the A site is open. The second step is the binding of the next tRNA, as specified by the next mRNA codon, to the A site. Peptide bond formation is effected by the passing of the methionine over to the amino acid at the A site, forming a tRNA with an attached dipeptide. The old methionine-tRNA is displaced from the ribosome, the tRNA with its dipeptide moves to the vacant P site, and a new tRNA attaches to the newly vacated A site. During this process the ribosome has moved on one codon. The movements are called *translocation*. The tRNAs are moved with respect to the

A and P sites of the ribosome to which they are attached, and the mRNA is moved with respect to the small subunit to which it is attached. GTP and several other factors are required for chain elongation. The last step in the process is chain termination, which results when the ribosome reaches one of the three termination codons, UAA, UGA, or UAG. When this happens, it appears that no new tRNA binds to the A site. Instead, a release factor is involved in freeing the ribosome and polypeptide chain from the mRNA. Once the completed polypeptide chain is formed, the methionine can be removed if the protein does not contain this amino acid at its amino end. In the above discussion we have followed the progress of a single ribosome from its point of attachment to its release at the end of the gene.

Protein synthesis is generally carried out by numerous ribosomes attached to the same mRNA at the same time, just as RNA synthesis is accomplished by numerous polymerase molecules operating simultaneously at different sites along the template. The complex of the mRNA and more than one ribosome is called a *polyribosome* or *polysome;* it represents the functional unit for protein synthesis (Fig. 2.7). Typically, the number of attached ribosomes reflects the length of the mRNA chain, though other factors can modify this relationship.

Even the simplest protein is known to be a many-folded, twisted molecule. The question that must be considered is how such a complex, coiled macromolecule can arise.

PROTEIN STRUCTURE

The evidence suggests that the sequence of amino acids, called the *primary structure of the protein,* is responsible for its three-dimensional appearance as well. This theory states that one of the vast number of possible arrangements of the polypeptide chains produces a structure with the most thermodynamically stable organization. Not only does the primary structure have to be specified to form a protein with the required properties, but it has to allow the proper shape to be generated as well.

The overall shape of a protein molecule is a result of the interaction of amino acids that may be located at some distance from one another in their linear arrangement but are brought very close to one another when the molecule becomes folded. This is clearly illustrated in the diagram of the enzyme ribonuclease (Fig. 2.8).

The most important interactions between amino acids in a protein are hydrophobic association, hydrogen bonds, electrostatic interactions, and covalent bonds. The most important generating forces in the folding of most proteins arise in the hydrophobic association. Certain of the approximately 20 amino acids have structures with little regard for the solvent water. These amino acids do not become hydrated; they tend to associate in the center of the protein and water is generally excluded from that region. The hydrophobic core is then surrounded by those parts of the molecule that contain the hydrophilic amino acids, with which water readily associates. After this general type of folding brings the hydrophobic parts together, the other noncovalent bonds—hydrogen and electrostatic—further determine how the parts will interact. Generally the covalent bonds, i.e., those between two cysteine residues that form a disulfide bridge, are a means of fixing the structure rather than causing its formation in the first place.

Much of the evidence for the relationship between primary structure and protein shape has come from studies of proteins that have been fully dena-

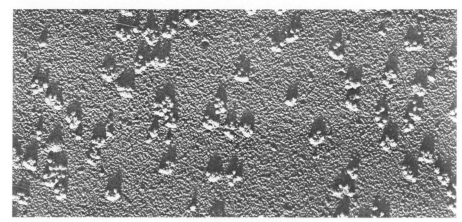

Figure 2.7 Electron micrograph of reticulate polysomes. [*Courtesy of A. Rich.*]

Figure 2.8 *a* The enzyme ribonuclease, consisting of 124 amino acids of 19 different types. The three-dimensional profile of the enzyme is brought about by formation of the four disulfide bonds between cysteine residues. Ribonuclease was utilized by Anfinsen in his early studies of the relationship between the amino acid sequence and the shape of the protein. *b* Native protein molecule in natural configuration, converted to an extended polypeptide chain, spontaneously reconverts to the original folded condition by means of its disulfide bonds. Separated regions of the extended chain are thus brought together to form a specifically structured active center. [*After Anfinsen, 1968.*]

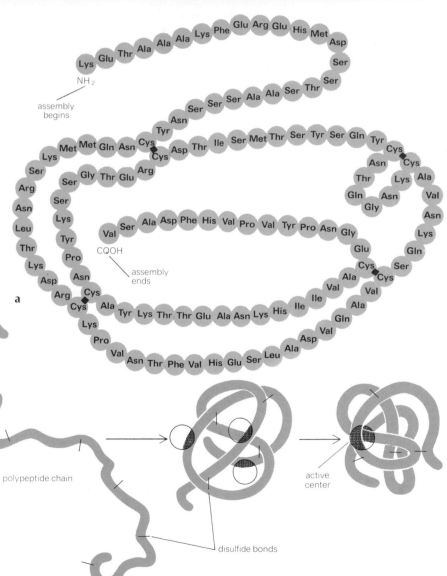

tured—i.e., treated so that all the disulfide and noncovalent bonds are broken—and then have been allowed to re-form. Figure 2.8 illustrates the process for ribonuclease, the protein for which this concept was originally proposed. If a solution of purified ribonuclease molecules is denatured and exposed to conditions that promote re-formation, active enzyme molecules are soon re-formed and they are indistinguishable in structure from those at the beginning of the experiment.

The importance of the shape of a polypeptide chain goes beyond its own activity to its interaction with its neighbors. As mentioned above, many proteins are composed of more than one polypeptide chain. As in the determination of a folded structure, the association of polypeptide chains is also a spontaneously occurring process. The same types of procedures that denature the coiling of a single chain dissociate proteins made of more than one chain; these include high salt concentrations, changes in pH, detergents, presence of urea. Such agents interfere with noncovalent associations, which are responsible for holding subunits together. In certain cases several different types of proteins come together, and again there is evidence that these interactions can occur simultaneously as a direct result of the structure of each individual protein in the complex. These interactions clearly illustrate the potential for complex organization with a minimum of outside input. In a direct way, the primary sequence of amino acids is responsible for the far-reaching consequences of protein organization and, therefore, of protein function. This type of spontaneous development of structure will be considered again in the formation of even more complex products by self-assembly.

Whereas, the nucleic acids are assigned the roles of information storage and transfer, the proteins mediate the many cellular activities. It is the protein that can assume the innumerable geometric and electrostatic configurations needed, though one cannot dismiss other macromolecules in some of these functions. Proteins can be categorized on the basis of shape, charge, amino acid composition, function, etc., and they serve in several capacities. Some are enzymes constructed to catalyze metabolic reactions. Others have structural roles, e.g., ribosomal proteins, membrane proteins, microtubule proteins, collagen, keratin, and the proteins of silk. Many have a regulatory function; these include genetic repressors, corepressors (discussed below), and hormones. There are proteins with specialized functions not easily categorized. Some bind molecules, e.g., hemoglobin and hormone receptors; others tranport molecules through the blood or through a membrane. Antibodies are proteins. There are proteins with elastic properties, contractile properties, and antiviral properties; and undoubtedly there are many unknown proteins with unknown properties.

SELECTIVE GENE ACTIVATION

One of the key words in developmental biology is *differentiation,* the process whereby cells of the body acquire different properties that enable them to carry out their specific functions. To a large extent differentiation is reflected in the production of specialized proteins. As stated earlier, if the DNA content of a variety of cells is examined, it is found that all cells contain approximately the same amount of chromosomal DNA, about twice that in the sperm of that species. Evidence from many sources indicates that—with a few exceptions—each cell of the organism contains a complete set of genes and that differentiation cannot be explained as the selective loss of genes with no function in the progeny of that cell. If all the DNA is present, we must invoke selective utilization to explain the differentiated state. Molecular hybridization techniques clearly indicate that cells contain RNAs with base sequences specific for that type of tissue and not shared with other cell types. For example, liver cells contain RNAs that are not found in other cells tested. This type of evidence suggests that cells become different because specific genes operate in those cells as a result of *selective gene activation,* rather than the selective translation of specific mRNAs from a common RNA pool or the selective use of specific proteins from a common protein pool.

If selective gene activation is the key to differentiation, we have pushed the problem back one level and we must search for the regulatory molecules that cause only certain genes to be transcribed. This search has been fruitful in microorganisms and viruses but has only broken ground in higher cells. Many instances have been described where a specific treatment in higher organisms results in genetic activation, but the exact nature of the molecule that interacts with the DNA to produce the activation is unknown. One intensively studied example is the effect of the hormone ecdysone on the gene activity pattern of giant *Drosophila* chromosomes. This is described in Chapter 22.

The Operon Concept

In this section the best-studied case of genetic activation is described: the activation by lactose of RNA synthesis for a series of enzymes needed for lactose utilization by *E. coli.* A brief account of this process will be presented as a review for the student. Additional readings for an in-depth analysis can be found at the end of the chapter. The genetic activation of the enzymes for lactose metabolism in *E. coli* is the basis of the operon theory proposed in 1961 by Jacob and Monod. Every aspect of this theory has been substantiated and it has been extended to several other genetic units in viral and bacterial systems. The complexity of the eukaryotic genome, however, seems likely to require intricate control mechanisms beyond those in the lowly bacterial cell. It is undoubtedly this area of molecular biology that will receive some of the greatest attention in the coming years.

Every bacterial cell lives in direct contact with its environment, a constantly changing chemical milieu. At certain times a given type of molecule may become available for use, while at other times that compound is absent. It is of obvious selective advantage for these cells to utilize their available resources in the most efficient way, and mechanisms have evolved that allow them to respond to specific environmental changes. There are two classes of response. If a substance that the cell can utilize becomes available, such as an energy source, the hydrolytic enzymes for the breakdown of this molecule will be needed. The cell will have to crank up the machinery for the synthesis of these so-called inducible enzymes. On the other hand, if a substance such as an amino acid becomes available, for which the cell is normally expending energy and material, the enzymes utilized for the synthesis of this amino acid are no longer needed; their synthesis is repressed. An *operon* (Fig. 2.9) is a functional genetic unit whose genes are coordinately controlled.

The elements of an operon are the structural genes, i.e. DNA that codes for the specific enzymes required, and the operator gene (o gene), at which the synthesis of the mRNAs of the structural genes is controlled. Outside the physical region of the operon is the regulator gene (i gene), from which an mRNA is transcribed. This mRNA is subsequently translated into a protein that will physically interact with the DNA of the operator gene to control the synthesis of RNA from the adjacent structural genes.

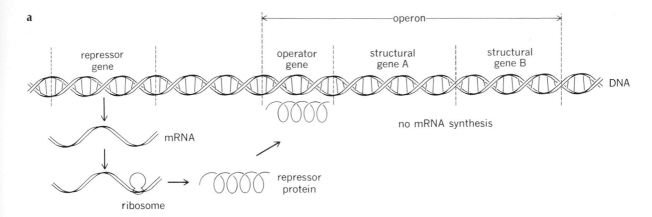

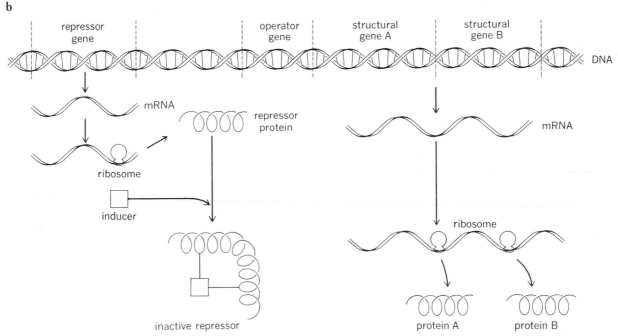

Figure 2.9 Diagrammatic representation of the functioning of the operon in the noninduced (*a*) and induced (*b*) state. *a* The repressor protein, translated from the gene product of the i gene (referred to as repressor gene in this diagram), is bound to the operator gene, thereby blocking transcription of the structural genes. *b* The inducer is present and binds to the repressor protein, converting it into "inactive repressor," which can no longer attach to the operator gene. As a result, the structural genes are transcribed. [*From Vander, Sherman, and Luciano, "Human Physiology," 2d ed., McGraw-Hill, 1974.*]

The lac operon contains a collection of three adjacent inducible enzymes involved in the uptake and breakdown of the disaccharide lactose. In the absence of lactose, these enzymes are not needed and there is less than one mRNA for them per cell. This shutdown results from the attachment of the repressor protein of the i gene at the o gene, thereby inhibiting the movement of RNA polymerase to the structural genes. If lactose is added to the culture, after a lag of a few minutes the enzymes are found within the cell. This activation is explained by the specific interaction of the inducer lactose with the repressor protein, thereby making the complex (lactose-repressor) unable to bind with the

34

operator gene. The inactivation of the repressor results in the synthesis of the mRNAs for the three structural genes that produce β-galactosidase, galactoside permease, and galactoside acetylase. The mRNAs for the polypeptide chains of these three enzymes are synthesized as one long, polycistronic messenger that is translated as three discrete polypeptide chains, each with its own termination codon. In this way all the enzymes that will be needed together can be synthesized together, though they can still be controlled separately by another mechanism. For example, it has been found that more β-galactosidase chains are synthesized than chains of either of the other two proteins. In the induced state there are 35 to 50 mRNAs (of the approximate 1,000 total) per cell and over a thousand times more enzyme than in the absence of inducer. The complex between the inducer and the repressor is a reversible one, just as the complex between the repressor and the DNA can be dissociated. In this way, if the lactose supply becomes exhausted, the repressors will once again interact with the operator and block mRNA transcription of the structural genes.

The operons of repressible enzymes work in a somewhat reversed fashion. One that has been studied most is the histidine operon, which consists of the tandem array of 10 structural genes that code for the enzymes making up the pathway for histidine biosynthesis. Under normal conditions the enzymes are needed, the product of the i gene is unable to attach to the operator gene, and the long, polycistronic mRNA that codes for all these enzymes is produced and translated. If histidine becomes available, the enzymes are not needed. The histidine molecule complexes with the i gene protein, called a *corepressor* in repressible systems, and this complex is now capable of attachment to the operator gene, which then shuts down mRNA synthesis in this operon.

Control in Eukaryotes

The search for the mechanisms that control information transfer from DNA to the synthesis of specific proteins has led in several directions. Various steps along this complicated pathway appear to be under different types of regulation. One possible factor that might be varied is the number of DNA templates available to be transcribed. Differentiation results in cells with specialized functions. Each type of differentiated cell might have extra copies of the genes used for the specific activities of that cell. This process is *selective gene amplification*, selective because only those genes needed in that cell would be amplified in number. Evidence suggests this is not a general method whereby a cell can increase its output of specific protein molecules. In the best-studied case, the affected genes are templates not for mRNA synthesis but for rRNA production. During the development of most oocytes, cell volume enlarges greatly with a corresponding increase in nuclear volume and in the number or size of the nucleoli. If one extracts the DNA from a population of amphibian oocytes, approximately 50 percent of it consists of the genes for ribosomal RNA. The selective amplification is needed to fill a cell of great volume with sufficient ribosomes in the alloted time. Selective gene amplification is also shown in the "DNA puffs" of certain insect chromosomes. The giant chromosomes of the midge *Chironomus*, however, contain bands with a similar amount of DNA, which can be in a varying state of compactness (Fig. 2.10).

If selective gene amplification were a general method to increase protein synthesis, one could predict that cells specialized to synthesize large amounts of one protein, or a few specific proteins, would be prime candidates for this mechanism. The reticulocyte, however, specialized for the synthesis of large amounts of hemoglobin, contains very few copies of this gene. Similarly,

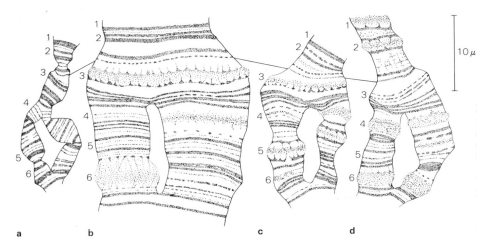

Figure 2.10 A short section of one of the chromosomes of the midge *Chironomus,* from a cell of (*a*) intestine, (*b*) salivary gland, (*c*) excretory tubule, (*d*) rectum. Six prominent bands (numbered) can be recognized in each chromosome. [*After Beermann, 1958.*]

although the silk gland cells of *Bombyx* produce great quantities of the silk protein, fibroin, evidence is against the amplification of this gene. In the liver, cells with DNA in excess of the diploid value have been studied, and the evidence suggests duplication of the entire genome rather than selective gene amplification of a few "liver" genes. It appears, therefore, that selective gene amplification does not generally accompany the formation of the differentiated state.

As has been previously noted, selective gene transcription is widespread in differentiated cells of higher organisms, just as it has been demonstrated to be important in prokaryotic cells. The mechanisms responsible for selective gene activation and repression in higher cells remain uncertain; the search for operons in higher organisms has not been conclusive, and alternate control mechanisms are believed to function. Several models have been presented, the most extensive one by Britten and Davidson in 1969. The Britten-Davidson model is theoretical and complex (to be expected in a model that attempts to explain genetic regulation in higher organisms), and a detailed presentation is beyond the scope of this book. In the model, the redundant DNA sequences are assigned regulatory roles in a hierarchy of genetic function. Certain sequences act as sensors to external stimuli. Others produce secondary signals that could act at receptor sites in the DNA to turn batteries of genes on or off for the production of messengers as required by the activities of each cell at a given time. Though the model remains speculative and is intended more as a framework on which research and discussion can be focused, than as a definitive statement of genetic regulation, evidence has been gained that supports certain of its precepts. This is presented in a recent reexamination by its authors (Davidson and Britten, 1973).

The eukaryotic chromosome is a complex structure containing DNA, RNA, and several types of proteins including the enzymes and factors for transcription. Procedures have been developed whereby this complex of macromolecules can be isolated, fragmented, and its template activity to support RNA synthesis examined in the test tube. Isolated chromosomal material (*chromatin*) is capable of directing the synthesis of RNA, which upon examination appears to be the same species of RNA that was made by the cell before disruption. Reticulocyte chromatin produces hemoglobin mRNA, while liver chromatin does not. The isolation procedure does not seem to turn off previously active genes or to turn on previously inactive ones. If, however, the chromosomal proteins are removed from the chromatin and its template activity is then tested, a much greater variety of RNA molecules are now synthesized, as if the inhibitors had been removed from their association with the inactive genes.

A requirement for any repressor mechanism that works selectively at the DNA level is a high degree of specificity. In other words, if such a mechanism is to operate effectively, it must be able to specifically block unneeded DNA sequences and to unlock those that must become activated. Even in *E. coli,* where the total number of genes cannot exceed 5,000, the lac repressor is a protein made of 4 identical polypeptide chains with a total molecular weight of 160,000. The operator site to which it binds must be at least a dozen bases in length to provide the specificity necessary for this repressor to bind there and not at other places that may accidentally have the same base sequence. In higher organisms, whose genomes are more complex, the problem of specificity becomes even greater.

Whatever the mechanisms for transcription in eukaryotes turn out to be, they will certainly be complex; literally thousands of genes have to be activated and repressed for differentiation to occur.

LEVELS OF CONTROL

After the RNA has been produced, numerous steps precede translation. The large piece of heterogeneous nuclear RNA must be separated from the mRNA, the poly A must be added, proteins must become associated with the naked nucleic acid, and exit to the cytoplasm must occur. Possibilities exist for regulation at any of these and perhaps at many unknown steps. Once the RNA is in the cytoplasm, the decision for translation must be made. Factors operating at this last level in the pathway involve *translational control.* Many claims have been made for such controls, but the question remains controversial.

Translational level control is important during development because the embryo begins its life with a large store of RNAs made during oogenesis for translation after fertilization. The utilization of this "preformed" RNA has been studied in many different embryos. Since it is present in the unfertilized egg but is not translated until after fertilization, translational control mechanisms are presumably involved. The best evidence for translational control during early development is the translation of messages in the sea urchin embryo; this is discussed at length in Chapter 9.

Once a given mRNA has been translated, we must consider the question of how many times it should perform this function. Some mechanism has to be available for a cell to rid itself of RNAs that are no longer needed. Differentiation encompasses the loss of previous function as well as the gain of new properties. It is clear that the cell can distinguish, to some extent at least, between different RNA molecules. Some mRNAs have a long half-life—once produced, they remain intact for days—while others have a much shorter one, possibly as little as 1 hour. The hemoglobin mRNA is an example of a very stable message. After the mRNAs for a protein are destroyed, no further synthesis of that protein can occur in the absence of new transcription of that mRNA. The previously synthesized proteins, however, can remain for a period even if their presence is no longer of value to that cell. Many investigations of a variety of enzymes clearly reveal the way in which previously formed proteins can be inhibited. In an elegant paper, Monod, Changeux, and Jacob predicted in 1963 the mechanism whereby the activity of an enzyme could be modified by its interaction with a small metabolite at a site other than the catalytic site. This is termed the *allosteric* site.

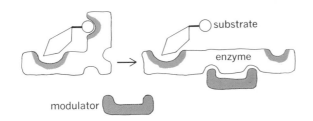

Figure 2.11 Allosteric inhibition. Inhibitor, typically the end product of the reaction, combines with the allosteric site, changing the conformation of the catalytic site, which inhibits enzyme activity. [*From Vander, Sherman, and Luciano, "Human Physiology,"* 2d ed., McGraw-Hill, 1974.]

This method of activity control illustrates the sensitive relation between the shape of a protein molecule and its properties (Fig. 2.11). Interaction of the allosteric site with the allosteric inhibitor produces a general change in the conformation of the catalytic site and the subsequent alteration of activity. No direct contact at the catalytic site is required and the allosteric inhibitor bears no structural resemblance to the substrate. Another term for allosteric inhibition is *end-product inhibition,* which reflects its place in the overall metabolic scheme. Metabolic pathways leading to the formation of biological molecules consist of a series of enzymes where the product of one reaction is the substrate of the next. If, for example, the end product of this series is an amino acid and that amino acid becomes available, it is a waste of resources to continue to manufacture the compound within the cell. Under these conditions the first enzyme of this synthetic pathway is typically under end-product control; this amino acid can bind to an allosteric site of this enzyme and thereby shut down the entire sequence of metabolic reactions.

The foregoing is a brief summary of some of the molecular activities of the cell has been given. These processes do not occur simply in a homogeneous solution but are integrally connected with the structures of the cell itself. The basic nature of the eukaryotic cell is briefly described in Chapter 3.

SELF-ASSEMBLY

In the preceding discussion of protein structure, the concept was presented that protein interaction can be determined simply by the shape of the individual proteins and by the conditions in which they are placed. For example, polypeptide chains can spontaneously organize themselves into enzymes made of these subunits, and in certain cases, several enzymes can spontaneously associate into multienzyme complexes. The term used to describe the spontaneous ordering of components into a more complex structure is *self-assembly.* How far can this mechanism be carried to explain biological organization? In the following sections we will examine this question by presenting several examples of molecular morphogenesis.

Construction and Reconstruction of Collagen, a Structural Protein

Many biological macromolecules exist as very long, thin structures. DNA is one example; a number of fibrous proteins are other examples. These fibrous proteins are polymers of a highly ordered assembly of a single component, the monomer. Collagen is a fibrous protein of high tensile strength characteristic of connective tissues throughout the animal kingdom. It is exploited for many purposes by different organisms and in various ways and places in the same organism. It is generally found outside the cell, secreted in the extracellular matrix, from which it can be extracted and studied outside the living system.

Information derived from x-ray diffraction, electron microscopy, chemical analysis, and other means has shown how collagen fibrils are built up from individual molecular units (monomers) called *tropocollagen*. The tropocollagen molecule has a complex structure made up of three polypeptide chains joined by hydrogen bonds. Each polypeptide chain has about 1,000 amino acids, and the three twist around each other in a characteristic way to form a tropocollagen molecule about 2900 Å long and only 50 Å wide. The tropocollagen monomers are joined to form long fibrils that appear striped in the electron microscope, with a characteristic band spacing of 640 Å.

The question is how a monomer 2900 Å in length is polymerized to form a structure with a banding pattern of 640 Å. The evidence suggests that in the living state, the so-called native state, the monomers are polymerized not with their ends aligned in register but with overlapping of one-fourth their length. This is shown in the middle section of Fig. 2.12, where the tropocollagen monomers are secreted outside the cell and are then aligned to form the native pattern. Notice that each tropocollagen molecule is asymmetrical (one end is different from the other); in the native fibril the molecules are lined up in the same direction and are staggered.

Figure 2.12 Reconstitution of collagen. Collagen fibrils reconstitute spontaneously when an acid solution of native collagen molecules is neutralized. The fibrous long-spacing form of collagen is produced by adding glycoprotein to an acid solution of native collagen. The segment long-spacing form of collagen is produced by adding ATP to an acid solution of collagen. The central block suggests a possible way in which collagen fibrils are formed extracellularly, in vivo, from secreted tropocollagen. [*After Gross, 1956.*]

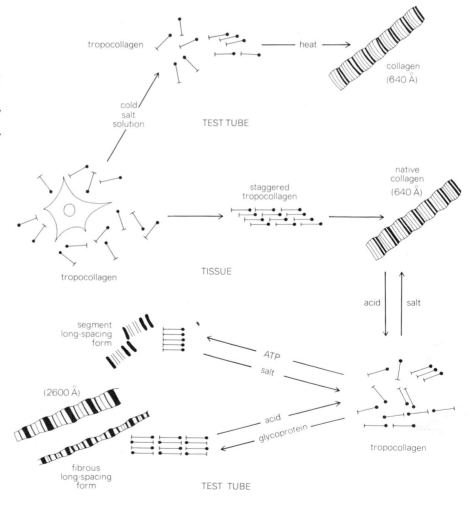

The discovery that collagen fibrils can be disassembled in acid and then reassembled was made in 1892 but was not followed up until 70 years later. The ease with which collagen can be disassembled in a weak acid medium offers opportunities to investigate experimentally the agents that operate in the process of reassembly, or polymerization. The top of Fig. 2.12 shows that when the acidic solution is neutralized, the tropocollagen monomers polymerize to form a structure identical in its finest detail with the native collagen. Because the only ingredients in the solution were the tropocollagen molecules and a certain concentration of inorganic ions, the native structure of collagen is capable of forming by self-assembly; no extraneous factors are needed. All required information is in the structure of the monomer.

If the conditions for reconstruction are altered, however, other possible types of polymerization can be seen; these are illustrated in the lowest section of the figure. If a highly negative charged molecule, such as a glycoprotein, is added to the acid solution of the collagen, a polymer forms whose main bands are 2600 Å rather than 640 Å. This is *fibrous long-spacing* (FLS) *collagen*, in which the monomers do not overlap and face in opposite directions. A similar but nonfibrous material is formed by adding ATP to the acid solution of monomers; this is called *segment long-spacing* (SLS) *collagen*. In this case the polymerization also occurs without overlap but with the monomers facing the same direction. The difference in the orientation of neighboring monomers produces the differences in minor bands that are seen between SLS and FLS polymers. Since the monomers are asymmetrical, the banding pattern will be asymmetrical when they are aligned in the same way, as in the FLS form, and symmetrical when the neighbors run in opposite directions, as in the SLS form.

Any one of these three structurally different forms of collagen can be disassembled and reassembled into either of the other forms, which differ only in the way the tropocollagen is aligned. The in vitro polymerization of collagen illustrates the importance of the composition of the medium (pH, ionic composition, temperature) in the assembly process. Protein-protein interaction (protein-nucleic acid and nucleic acid-nucleic acid as well) clearly depends on the electronic configuration of the molecule, which is very sensitive to changes in its environment. If the conditions are right, the collagen monomers associate in the proper way to form the native structure, which has advantages of strength from both overlap and molecular orientation. Another point to be learned from this example is the ease with which an investigator can be misled when working under test tube conditions. This should be kept in mind throughout the book when interpretations of in vitro experiments are applied to in vivo events of great complexity and little-known nature.

The Ribosome

The ribosome has been extensively studied as a complex molecular structure capable of self-assembly, mainly by Nomura. We will restrict the following discussion to one of the subunits, the smaller 30S subunit, of *E. coli*. This tiny cell organelle consists of one rRNA molecule, of approximately 1.2 million molecular weight, and probably 21 different proteins, present in one copy per subunit. The exact number remains unclear since it is not certain that every one is an integral part of the ribosome. The 30S subunit can be isolated and its components separated and purified. In other words, it is possible to prepare solutions containing a pure population of each of the 21 proteins and the RNA. The spontaneous nature of the ribosome assembly is demonstrated by the complete reconstitution of the 30S subunit from purified rRNA and the separate proteins. These reconstituted particles have the same biological activity as a preparation of 30S subunits isolated directly from the cell. Whether the reconstituted particle is identical with the original structure is not certain. One of the proteins does not seem to be incorporated into the re-formed structure, but the potential for the self-assembly of this complex structure is evident.

By the sequential addition of the various proteins, a partial scheme for the steps that occur during in vitro assembly has been made. Of the 21 proteins, only 5 to 7 appear to bind initially to the RNA; the remaining proteins are capable of binding only to a protein-RNA complex. Considerable work has focused on the position of each of the proteins and RNA within the ribosome and on their roles in ribosome activity. These studies employ several methods, but techniques that accurately focus on one protein alter the properties of another.

In one approach, mutant bacteria that contain an altered protein are selected, and the effect on ribosomal function is studied. Another approach involves chemical modifications of one specific, purified ribosomal protein, its incorporation into a reconstituted ribosome, and the analysis of any malfunction. A similar technique is to reconstitute subunits in the absence of one of the ribosomal proteins and to determine the effect. The results of these studies suggest that some ribosomal proteins are required exclusively for the assembly process, some for the maintenance of the proper conformation of the subunit, and others for specific functional activities of the ribosome. Some proteins may have more than one role. For example, the omission of the ribosomal protein S11 increases the translational errors when the reconstituted subunits are tested. The exact mechanism for this is unknown, but it suggests that this protein has a functional role. Many omissions produce ribosomes devoid of activity, but the interdependence of structure and function makes it difficult to assign specific roles to these proteins.

The 16S rRNA is required for both the assembly and the function of the subunit. Chemical modification of only a few nucleotide bases is sufficient to destroy all activity. In some cases these RNA-modified, inactive subunits are indistinguishable from normal ones by all criteria based strictly on structure.

Studies are now progressing toward the complete sequence of all the ribosomal proteins and rRNAs and their relative places within the ribosome. The 50S subunit has also been reconstituted from its components. There is evidence that the assembly of the 50S subunit is somehow dependent upon the 30S. Mutants in which 30S subunit assembly is altered inhibit the assembly of the 50S particle, although the reverse is not true. The next few years should provide more information on assembly and structure of the ribosome.

Virus Assembly

It is a big step from the construction of the molecular complexes described above to the organization of a whole cell. Even in a small procaryote cell such as *E. coli*, the energy requirements, as shown by the ATP turnover rate, are impressive. At least 2 million ATP molecules are broken down per second to achieve the biosynthesis of all the cell components. Fortunately, virus particles offer opportunity for analysis at a more comprehensible, subcellular level. These "organisms" cannot directly metabolize, grow, or undergo division; yet their nucleic acid contains all the information required for the attachment to a cell, the penetration of the genetic material into that cell, and the control of that cell's activities for its own purposes. It is strikingly clear how a handful of viral genes is capable of entirely rerouting the activities of an infected cell. In most cases the typical activities of that cell are shut down and the production of new virus particles consumes its energy and resources. Even though small virus particles may be 8,000 times smaller than the smallest true microorganism, they may still be regarded as suborganisms of considerable complexity. Whether simple or complex, they all have a central core of nucleic acid enclosed by a protein envelope.

In this section we will briefly analyze the morphogenesis of two viruses. One of these is the relatively simple tobacco mosaic virus (TMV). Its particle is made of approximately 2,000 indentical protein subunits, organized in a helix around one long RNA molecule of 6,300 nucleotides containing the genetic information. If the components are gently dissociated and then brought together under the proper conditions, they reassemble to form complete and infectious rod-shaped virus particles. The entire particle, therefore, can be formed by self-assembly. The manner in which these viruses are assembled from the two components has recently been uncovered and demonstrates the complex interactions and conformational changes that macromolecules can undergo.

The unit of protein is the 4S subunit, but the unit of assembly is a specific complex of 34 subunits. This complex (Fig. 2.13) is a disc made of 2 layers of subunits, 17 per layer, arranged in a circle. If a preparation of these discs is combined with the RNA, complete virus particles are formed in several minutes. If, however, one starts with a preparation of individual 4S subunits, the process takes several hours; the conversion from single subunit to disc is slow. The initiation step in assembly is shown in Fig. 2.13a, where the end of the RNA molecule is wound inside the first disc. The 5' end of the RNA appears to contain a specific nucleotide sequence that combines with one disc to begin the assembly process. If the 5' end of the RNA is digested away by a special ribonuclease which begins only at that end, the ability for assembly is abolished. A similar digestion from the 3' end has no effect on the process.

The assembly results from the ordered accumulation of discs, but how can such discs form the helical structure of the virus? A pile of discs would merely form a cylinder, while a helix is a continuing spiral that requires none of the discs to have a closed shape. The answer to this puzzle is in a comparison of Figs. 2.13a and 2.13b, and reemphasizes the complex conformational changes that protein molecules can make. This transition to a helical unit occurs because of a shift in the way the subunits are organized within the disc; a dislocation produces what is essentially a part of a spiral containing a free end to join with the next disc. This structure is reminiscent of a "lock washer" found in

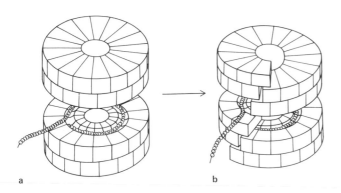

a   b

Figure 2.13 Stages in the assembly of a tobacco mosaic virus. *a* Each disc has two layers and is composed of 34 subunits, each having a sedimentation coefficient of 4S. The RNA is seen coiled in the center of the hollow disc. Initiation reflects a special nucleotide sequence for first disc attachment. *b* The dislocated form ("lock-washer" form) that occurs in response to RNA binding. [*After Klug, 1972.*]

any hardware store. The most thermodynamically stable structure is the disc, and it appears that the dislocation occurs only after the disc has combined with the RNA, which somehow facilitates the change. The requirement for RNA in this transition ensures that particles will never form without the genetic material. The addition of discs and their dislocation into the lock-washer form somehow ensures that the free end of the RNA will protrude for combination with the next disc. Once the discs have consumed the entire RNA molecule, the assembly process automatically comes to an end and the particle is complete.

The analysis of TMV assembly presented above is the most recent explanation in a long series of studies, many of which came to erroneous conclusions based on the variety of ways these subunits can aggregate under varying conditions of ionic strength, pH, and temperature. Here, as in tropocollagen polymerization, the environmental conditions are of critical importance in dictating the manner of association, and the last word on TMV assembly has not been spoken.

TMV is a relatively simple virus whose protein coat is made of one protein and whose genetic material contains only a few genes. Many viruses, including those that attack bacterial cells, the bacteriophages, are much more complex. An electron micrograph of one of these is shown in Fig. 2.14 and a diagram in Fig. 2.15. Several distinct parts can be seen. The double-stranded DNA of the

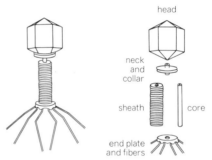

Figure 2.15 The parts and structure of the T bacteriophage. [*From "Cellular Differentiation" by J. Richard Whittaker. ©1968 Dickinson Publishing Company, Inc., Belmont, California.*]

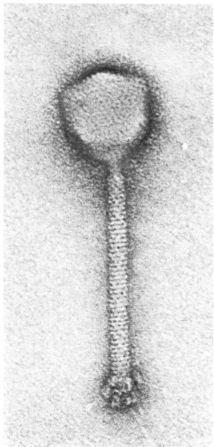

Figure 2.14 Virus particle (*Bacillus subtilis* bacteriophage) showing shell, sheath-enclosing core, and plate with anchoring fibrils. [*Courtesy of A. K. Kleinschmidt.*]

phage is contained within the polyhedral head. A short neck connects the head with a tail consisting of a springlike contractile sheath, or tube, which surrounds a central core and is attached to an end plate. Six slender fibers and six short spikes protrude from the end plate. Altogether the virus is a highly organized structure, not unlike a landing module for the moon.

Before discussing the assembly process, a brief review of the events of the infection will be presented. First, the virus becomes anchored to the bacterial wall by its tail fibers so that the tail and head are perpendicular to the surface, as if guyed by the tail fibers. Within a few minutes after attachment, the sheath shortens to less than half its original length and the core is forced through the wall of the bacterium, allowing the DNA molecules coiled in the head to pass

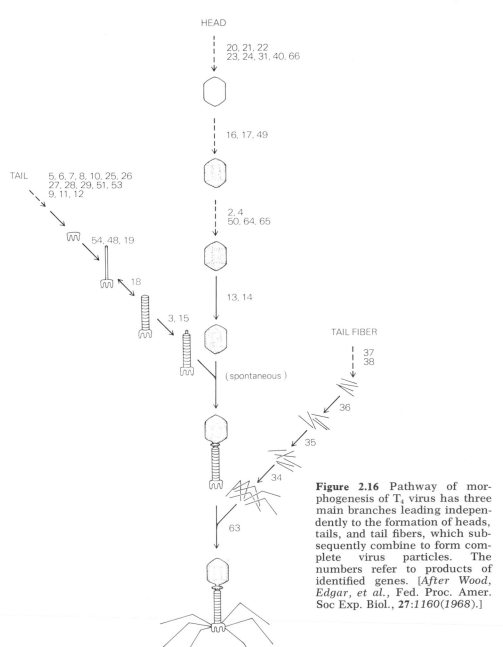

Figure 2.16 Pathway of morphogenesis of T_4 virus has three main branches leading independently to the formation of heads, tails, and tail fibers, which subsequently combine to form complete virus particles. The numbers refer to products of identified genes. [*After Wood, Edgar, et al.,* Fed. Proc. Amer. Soc Exp. Biol., **27**:*1160(1968)*.]

into the bacterium. Once inside, a series of intricate biochemical steps result in the appearance of the first complete virus particle about 13 minutes after infection. The process continues for another 12 minutes until about 200 such particles have been completed and the raw materials of the bacterial cell have been exhausted. A viral enzyme, a lysozyme, then appears and attacks the cell wall, liberating the new viral particles. The known details of this process could easily take up the remainder of this book and would provide a fascinating account of new sigma factors, carefully controlled gene activation, altered host enzymes and ribosomes, and complex assembly steps. Instead we will try to keep to the original question concerning the assembly process.

Studies of T_4 construction indicate there are three independent assembly lines. Each produces one finished part of the virus—the head, the tail, and the tail fibers—and these subsequently combine to form the finished virus particle. This is illustrated in Fig. 2.16. Each of the three assembly lines consists of steps in which specific genes are known to be involved.

How are these genes assigned? Mutant viruses are prepared that are unable to carry out specific steps in the assembly process. The location of the mutation on the chromosome can be determined by standard genetic mapping procedures. The T_4 genetic map is shown in Fig. 2.17. As an example, genes 37 and 38 are involved in the first stages in the formation of the tail fibers. If a mutation occurs in gene 37, no tail fibers will be formed and the infected bacteria will contain particles made by the other assembly lines—heads and tails—but tail fibers will be missing. If a mutation is in gene 13, heads will not form and

Figure 2.17 Genetic map of the T_4 virus showing relative positions of more than 75 genes that had been identified by 1966 on the basis of mutations. Diagrams show viral components of cells infected by mutants defective in the particular gene. The labels and symbols indicate defective phenotypes as follows: *DNA neg.,* no DNA synthesis; *DNA arrest,* DNA synthesis arrested after a short time; *DNA delay,* DNA synthesis commences after some delay; *mat. def.,* maturation defective (DNA synthesis is normal, but late functions are not expressed). A hexagon indicates that free heads are produced; an inverted T, that free tails are produced; *tail fiber,* that fiberless particles are produced. Gene 9 mutants produce inactive particles with contracted sheaths; gene 11 and 12 mutants produce fragile particles which dissociate to free heads and free tails. [*After Edgar and Wood,* Proc. Nat. Acad. Sci., **55**:498 (1966).]

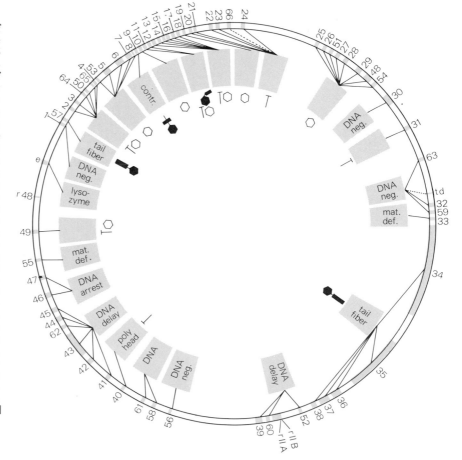

the cell will contain only tails and tail fibers. If these two types of cells are broken in the test tube and their contents are mixed, the heads and tails from one cell can pick up tail fibers from the other, and vice versa, and infective particles are formed. These two mutants "complement" each other. However, if cells containing gene 37 mutants are mixed with cells containing gene 38 mutants, no mature virus particles are formed. These two genes are said to be in the same "complementation group." In this case genes 37 and 38 are known to be separate genes, yet the extracts appear to be deficient in the same component; at least the complementation cannot occur in the test tube. By this process, 13 complementation groups were originally discovered, each containing one or more genes. Two mutants in the same group cannot be mixed to form infective particles. By this procedure it was established that at least 12 assembly steps exist that can occur in mixtures of extracts.

If we return to the original question of whether or not the morphogenesis of this virus can be accounted for simply by self-assembly, the answer appears to be that it cannot. The analysis of this question is complex and requires several approaches; the details will not be given. Of the 150 to 200 genes in T_4 it is likely that 50 to 100 genes are required to direct viral morphogenesis. However, fewer than 40 different species of protein have been identified as part of the virus particle. This does not mean that all the other genes required for morphogenesis do not code for structural proteins—they may be present in nondetectable quantities per virus—but it does seem clear that there are genes whose product is not contained within the virus but instead have some morphogenetic role. In other words, the assembly is not entirely coded for by the structure of the components, but requires the outside intervention of morphogenetic gene products. Mutations in some of these genes may be responsible for many bizarre results that include giant virus particles, polysheaths composed of many sheaths stuck together, etc. Some of these morphogenetic gene products could act as catalysts in the formation or breakage of covalent bonds required to put certain elements together. Others might act as templates or measuring devices to ensure proper assembly of the interacting components.

To illustrate morphogenetic genes we can briefly examine the assembly of tail fibers. Six of the seven genes now known to be required for this branch of assembly are shown in Fig. 2.16. Of these seven gene products, only four have been accounted for as structural elements. Of the remaining three, gene product 63 appears to catalyze the attachment of the tail fiber to the fiberless baseplate, and this event can be studied in vitro. Other examples of morphogenetic genes have come from studies of head assembly. For example, mutants in gene 31 cause the head proteins to aggregate randomly and adhere to the bacterial envelope. There is evidence that this gene product interacts with a component coded for by the bacterial genome that is also required to promote polymerization of head proteins to form a head intermediate. In this case several bacterial mutants have been isolated in which genetically normal virus cannot proliferate as a result of the deficiency in this host protein needed for virus assembly.

Though many of the steps in T_4 construction are by self-assembly, some are not; this suggests that structures of the order of complexity of this virus begin to rely on outside agents to put themselves together. Throughout this book we will discuss biological architecture, for this is the essence of differentiation. In the study of suborganisms such as T_4, it is believed principles will be uncovered that we can apply to the construction of more complex cellular elements. Considering the current effort and past success in the analysis of many viral systems, we should soon possess the blueprints for many of their constructions. Whether or not this information will be useful as models in the analysis of embryonic development remains to be seen.

READINGS

ALLEN, J. M.(ed.), 1967. "Molecular Organization and Biological Function," Harper & Row.

ANFINSEN, C. B., 1973. Principles that Govern the Folding of Protein Chains, *Science*, **181**:223–230.

AVERY, O. T., C. M. MacLEOD, and M. McCARTY, 1944. Studies on Chemical Nature of the Substance Inducing Transformation of Pneumococcal Types, *J. Exp. Med.*, **79**:137–157.

BRITTEN, R. J., and E. H. DAVIDSON, 1969. Gene Regulation for Higher Cells: a Theory, *Science*, **165**:349–357.

———, and D. E. Kohne, 1968. Repeated Sequences in DNA, *Science*, **161**:529–540.

DARNELL, J. E., W. R. JELINEK, and G. R. MOLLOY, 1973. Biogenesis of mRNA: Genetic Regulation in Mammalian Cells, *Science*, **181**:1215–1221.

DAVIDSON, E. H., and R. J. BRITTEN, 1973. Organization, Transcription, and Regulation in the Animal Genome, *Quart. Rev. Biol.*, **48**:565–613.

DICKSON, R. C., J. ABELSON, W. M. BARNES, W. S. REGNIKOFF, 1975. Genetic Regulation: The Lac Control Region, *Science*, **187**:27–35.

DUPRAW, E. J., 1968. "Cell and Molecular Biology," Academic.

GROSS, J., 1956. The Behavior of Collagen Units as a Model in Morphogenesis, *J. Biophys. Biochem. Cytol.*, suppl. **2**:261–274.

JACOB, F., and J. MONOD, 1961. On the Regulation of Gene Activity, *Cold Spring Harbor Symp., Quant. Biol.*, **26**:193–211.

KLUG, A., 1972. Assembly of Tobacco Mosaic Virus, *Fed. Proc. Amer. Soc. Exp. Biol.*, **31**:30–42.

KOLATA, G. B., 1973. Repeated DNA: Molecular Genetics of Higher Organisms, *Science*, **182**:1009–1011.

KORNBERG, R. D., and J. O. THOMAS, 1974. Chromatin Structure, *Science*, **184**:865–871.

LEIININGER, A. L., 1970. "Biochemistry; The Molecular Basis of Cell Structure and Function," Worth.

MENDEL, G., The Birth of Genetics, suppl. to *Genetics*, **35**:(5), part 2, reprinted in 1950.

MILLER, O. L., and B. A. HAMKALO, 1972. Visualization of RNA Synthesis on Chromosomes, *Int. Rev. Cytol.*, **33**:1–25.

MITCHISON, J. M., 1971. "The Biology of the Cell Cycle," Cambridge University press.

MONOD, J., J. P. CHANGEUX, and F. JACOB, 1963. Allosteric Proteins and Cellular Control Systems, *J. Mol. Biol.*, **6**:306–329.

NOMURA, M., 1973. Assembly of Bacterial Ribosomes, *Science*, **179**:864–873.

STEIN, G. S., T. C. SPELSBERG, and L. J. KLEINSMITH, 1974. Nonhistone Chromosomal Proteins and Gene Regulation, *Science*, **183**:817–824.

WATSON, J. D., 1970. "Molecular Biology of the Gene," 2d ed., Benjamin.

———, and F. H. C. CRICK, 1953. The Structure of DNA, *Cold Spring Harbor Symp., Quant. Biol.*, **18**:123–131.

———, ———, 1953. Genetical Implications of the Structure of Deoxyribonucleic Acid, *Nature*, **171**:964–967.

WHITE, A., P. HANDLER, and E. L. SMITH, 1973. "Principles of Biochemistry," 5th ed., McGraw-Hill.

WOOD, W. B., 1973. Genetic Control of Bacteriophage T$_4$ Morphogenesis, 31st Symposium, The Society of Developmental Biology, pp.29–46, Academic.

———, and R. S. EDGAR, 1967. Building a Bacterial Virus, *Sci. Amer.*, July.

CHAPTER 3

The Eukaryote Cell

The cell is the structural and functional unit of living tissue and is a complete entity with a well-defined perimeter and predictable internal organization. One cell can contain all the subcellular organelles. It is the smallest unit that can maintain itself in a living state. In isolation, cells can divide, metabolize, grow, and take part in every basic activity required for the maintenance of life.

CELL AND ENVIRONMENT

The previous chapter was concerned primarily with information storage and utilization. This chapter is a brief survey of the fundamental components of cell structure and function, with a particular emphasis upon those aspects that relate to developmental phenomena. Coordination, more than any other property, characterizes intracellular activity.

A multitude of events occur simultaneously within every cell. If a cell is to maintain itself in a living condition, all these individual activities must be coordinated and controlled, each maintained within the bounds that propagate life rather than lead to its destruction. To maintain the complex homeostatic conditions within the cell, there must be continual exchange of information and material from one part to another in a complex, interwoven network of activity. Ultimately, this drama is under genetic control; the script is locked into the inherited code. The constituents, however, have their own parts to play and are capable of maintaining the action as a consequence of their own structure and of the cues they receive from their surroundings.

PLASMA MEMBRANE

The cell is bounded by the plasma membrane, a structure of extreme thinness (approximately 75 Å) and delicacy. It is of the utmost importance, for it maintains a highly specialized environment within. In this capacity the plasma membrane is a barrier, but a highly selective one. Many substances are kept out, numerous substances are allowed in. Among the substances that enter the cell, some do so simply by diffusion in response to a concentration difference across the membrane. Others are actively carried through the membrane in order to be maintained at a higher concentration on the inner side. Still other materials, including the fluid they are suspended in, are brought inside as a result of the formation of pinocytotic vesicles at the surface, which are then brought inward. In contrast, fusion of vesicles with the membrane are capable of extruding materials from the intracellular space to the outside world. One important consequence of the selective permeability of the plasma membrane and its high electrical resistance is its capacity to separate charged ions and therefore establish a potential difference. This voltage is critical for the so-called excitable cells, the neurons and muscle cells, but it is also of great importance in the ability of all cells to respond to their environment.

In its role of screening the substances that are allowed entrance to the cell's interior, the plasma membrane can determine what types of regulatory influences can be exerted on the cell from the outside. In a more direct sense, several regulatory molecules that have dramatic effects on the activities of the entire cell appear to have their primary site of action at the cell surface. One of these regulatory molecules is the hormone insulin, whose presence has profound effects on cell metabolism and yet its site of interaction with the cell appears to be at the membrane itself. Similarly, there is evidence that the nerve growth factor, a protein that produces dramatic changes in the differentiation of developing neurons, does not penetrate the membrane but instead binds to it in order to initiate its effect.

Membranes serve as supportive structures as well as walls upon which a variety of proteins can be hung. In actuality these proteins are integral parts of the membrane itself, probably serving both a structural and a functional role. Presumably the proteins found in the plasma membrane would be specific in the dealings of the cell membrane with its environment. The membranes of the mitochondria include a sequence of enzymes involved in oxidative metabolism.

Membranes also serve to compartmentalize the cell. They are very thin, continuous sheets, never have free edges, and accordingly separate the cell interior into cytoplasmic compartments. In this capacity, membranes ramify throughout the cytoplasm in an apparently continuous, interconnected system (Fig. 3.1). Taken together, membranes are active participants in virtually all cellular processes and may include a large percentage of the cell's total enzymatic machinery. The observations that membranes are interconnected and

Figure 3.1 Electron micrograph of part of a cell, showing endoplasmic reticulum with ribosomes and secretory granules. [*Courtesy of K. Porter.*]

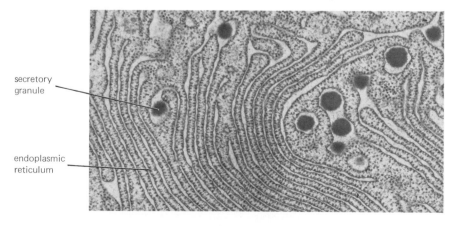

secretory granule

endoplasmic reticulum

capable of giving rise to one another led to the concept of a "unit membrane," i.e., all membranes are essentially alike. This concept remains valid if provision is made for the various cellular membranes to be specialized within a broader framework of similar, overall membrane structure.

MOLECULAR STRUCTURE OF MEMBRANE

From the early development of techniques for the isolation of purified membranes, the basic composition of lipids (including cholesterol) and protein has been well established. These macromolecules are of a heterogeneous nature with several distinct types of phospholipids and a large number of protein species. The structure generally accepted until the past few years is shown in Fig. 3.2. In this model, originally proposed by Davson and Danielli, the phospholipids are organized into a layer two molecules deep, a bimolecular leaflet. Phospholipids have two recognizable ends with widely differing properties; they are molecules with a split personality. At one end is the phosphate group together with a variety of other small charged molecules, while at the other end are long fatty acid chains. The end with the phosphate is soluble in water as are the small charged molecules; it is the hydrophilic end. In contrast, the end with the long organic chain is hydrophobic and insoluble in water. These features are reflected in the model shown in Fig. 3.2a. The lipid molecules are organized in such a way that their hydrophobic ends are pointed inward and their hydrophilic ends lie to the inside and outside of the cell. Associated with the hydrophilic ends on both sides of the lipid bilayer is a layer of proteins. The familiar triple-layered structure seen in the electron microscope (Fig. 3.2b) has always been taken as strong evidence of two layers of protein with a lipid layer between. The difference in thickness of the inner and outer layers has been interpreted as evidence of the asymmetry of the membrane, i.e., one protein edge is different from the other.

With the advent of new techniques for membrane study, a new model has become more generally accepted. This is the fluid mosaic model of Lenard, Singer, and Nicolson. The fluid nature of the membrane is indicated by employing the technique of cell fusion, whereby cells of two different species are joined together to produce one cell with a common cytoplasm and a continuous plasma membrane—in the present case, human and mouse cells. Certain proteins of the cell membrane are readily identifiable as being derived from a human cell rather than of mouse origin. The locations of human and mouse surface proteins were mapped at various times after fusion, and it was found that they did not remain in their original positions. Shortly after fusion the two types of proteins were still present in either one or the other half of the united membrane, but in 40 minutes they were essentially intermixed. These results suggest that the proteins of the membrane are free to move—to actually diffuse—within the membrane itself. In other words, the components of the membrane are not in a static state, but rather are capable of movement in lateral directions within the plane of the membrane. The results also suggest that the

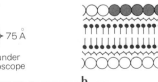

appearance under
electron microscope

a   b

Figure 3.2 *a* Typical appearance of the plasma membrane as seen in the electron microscope, i.e., two electron dense layers with a light layer between. *b* Davson-Danielli model of the membrane. In this model the lipid bilayer is sandwiched between two layers of protein (represented by spheres in this diagram). [*From "Molecular Organization and Biological Function," edited by J. M. Allen: Fig. 14 (p. 129), Harper & Row, 1967.*]

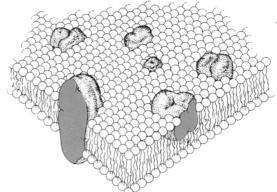

Figure 3.3 The fluid mosaic model of the cell membrane. The phospholipid bilayer is represented as a fluid lipid matrix in which the proteins float on either one side or the other or project through to both sides. [*After Singer and Nicolson, Copyright © 1972 by the American Association for the Advancement of Science.*]

lipid phase of the membrane is in a fluid state, through which the proteins are suspended and capable of migration. The length of time it takes the human and mouse proteins to approach an equilibrium state is a measure of the rate of diffusion of the molecules, which is in turn a measure of the fluidity (or viscosity) of the membrane. Calculations indicate that the viscosity of the lipid solvent phase is approximately 1,000 times that of water.

The fluid mosaic model is shown in Fig. 3.3. The "mosaic" nature of the membrane is provided by the proteins, which are floating as a noncontinuous particle phase within the surrounding lipid. The lipid bilayer, demonstrated by a variety of physical methods, is retained. The asymmetry of the membrane is also retained in this model by assuming that the proteins are free to move laterally but not through the membrane from one side to the other. The reason for this restriction of their freedom relates to the structure of the individual protein molecules, each believed to have a hydrophobic and a hydrophilic region. Just as the arrangement of hydrophobic versus hydrophilic amino acids can determine the shape of the resulting protein, it can also determine the types of interactions the molecule can have with other kinds of materials. If a protein contains a recognizable hydrophobic surface, this part will remain embedded within the lipid solvent. Those regions of the surface that are hydrophilic will project out of the membrane as shown in Fig. 3.3. As a result of the lipid insolubility of the hydrophilic end, it is assumed that the molecule cannot even tumble in the membrane, but must remain as shown. In some cases it is believed that a single protein molecule extends completely through the membrane, having hydrophilic groups at both ends and a hydrophobic region in between dissolved in the lipid. The development of freeze-etch electron microscopy (see Chapter 25) has been of great importance in membrane structural analysis. In this method, membranes are split within the bimolecular lipid leaflet along the interior hydrophobic face, which makes it particularly suited for the analysis of the location of the membrane proteins.

Earlier studies of the turnover of membrane components, i.e., the continual synthesis and destruction of the constituents, indicated the dynamic nature of the membrane in a metabolic sense. The fluid mosaic model illustrates the dynamic nature of the membrane in a structural sense. The model allows for the specialization of membranes that are involved in different activities. Presumably the nature of the proteins that provide the mosaic character of the membrane will vary from cell to cell, depending upon the needs. Similarly, the nature of the various intracellular membranes is readily accommodated to this model; however, the evidence that it can be directly applied to them is hard to obtain because of the difficulty in applying the necessary techniques to membranes deep within the cytoplasm of the cell.

CELL COAT

Though the plasma membrane is at the outer edge of the cytoplasm, there is usually extracellular material on the outer surface of the membrane itself. It is difficult to determine how much of this material is in direct continuity with the membrane and how much is a completely independent cell coat. These extracellular materials include proteins and protein-carbohydrate complexes (glycoproteins and mucopolysaccharides). In many cases this layer is visible in the electron microscope (particularly after it has been stained with a compound such as ruthenium red) as a fuzzy layer of varying thickness and composition. This outer surface layer is of vital importance in determining the manner in which cells will interact with one another as well as other properties such as migratory activity and malignancy. Certain of the macromolecules at the cell surface act as recognition sites for cell-to-cell identification. The nature and distribution of these sites are believed to vary from one type of cell to the next and to facilitate the proper interactions. There are, clearly, differences in the cell surface from one individual to another and these form the basis for the graft-rejection mechanisms described in Chapter 18.

Substances have been isolated from a variety of organisms that will bind to specific carbohydrates projecting from the outer edge of the membrane. These agents, called *lectins,* such as concanavalin A (Con A), have more than one binding site per molecule and can serve to cross-link membrane receptors together. If the receptors are on the same surface, the result is a clustering of the reactive sites together. The ability of reactive sites to become clustered is a reflection of the ease with which they can move toward one another in the membrane, i.e., its fluidity, determined primarily by the nature of the phospholipids and the temperature. Another factor in surface mobility is the degree to which membrane components are anchored to intracellular or extracellular structures. The binding of lectins can be followed by combining them with fluorescent chemicals, or with particles visible in the electron microscope, or by making them radioactive.

CELL JUNCTIONS

One of the primary consequences of the multicellular state is that cells have evolved mechanisms of intercellular interaction. The types of contacts that two cells can form with one another are of great importance to the cooperative activity they might show, and it is the surface that must mediate these contacts. Intercellular connections between cells at the tip of a developing limb are seen in Fig. 3.4. A variety of specialized structures have been described with the electron microscope, though the function in each case has not been resolved. In a recent review, Gilula has placed the major types of cell junctions into five categories; one of them is the *synaptic junction,* which we will not consider further. The *desmosome* (Fig. 3.5a) is a contact junction with considerable space between adjoining plasma membranes (about 150 Å) and extensive modifications in the adjacent cytoplasm; it is believed to be involved with cell-

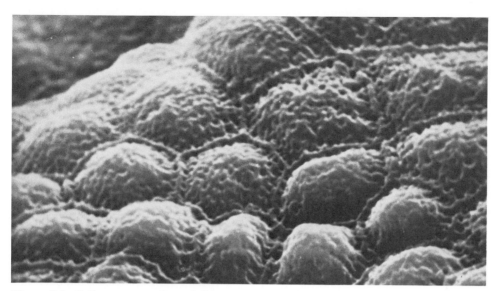

Figure 3.4 Cells at apex of amphibian limb bud (scanning electromicrograph, × 25,000) showing structured surface and intercellular junctional attachment. [*Courtesy of David Tarin.*]

Figure 3.5 *a* Fine structure of a desmosome in newt epidermis, exhibiting five distinct bands of differing stain contrast. The intercellular gap of the desmosome is occupied by moderately dense material which displays a discontinuous midplane density. The cell membranes appear as single dense lines. Subjacent desmosomal plaques are represented as dense lines, separated from the cell membranes by thin lucent bands. Tonofilaments approach plaque from cytoplasm and loop back away at varying distances from the membrane. (× 100,000) [*Courtesy of D. E. Kelly.*] *b* Diagram of flattening cells of the epidermis. Microfilaments in the apical regions of the cell have been replaced by discrete bundles of thicker 100 Å filaments which appear to course the cell from desmosome to desmosome. [*After B. Burnside, Amer. Zool.* **13**:997, 1973.]

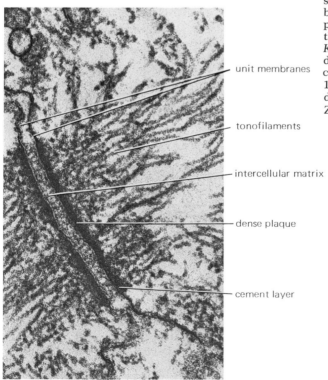

unit membranes

tonofilaments

intercellular matrix

dense plaque

cement layer

a

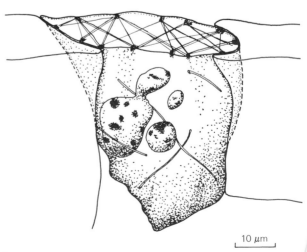

10 μm

b

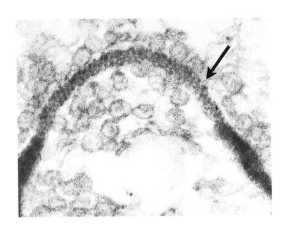

Figure 3.6 Electron micrograph of section through a gap junction. Very dense staining is seen in the extracellular space at the edge of the junction, and a repeating pattern is discernible within the junction (arrow). [*Courtesy of B. W. Payton.*]

to-cell attachment and anchoring, together with associated filaments (Fig. 3.5*b*). The *tight junction* brings the two membranes together in their closest contact and is proposed as a means to prevent materials from passing between cells. Tight junctions are found to completely encircle cells and to seal off the extracellular space on the two sides of the junction. The *septate junction* also encircles the cells it contacts. Septate junctions have a varying cleft between (40 to 150 Å) and are characterized by parallel bars that span the gap. It has been proposed that, along with the gap junction described next, the septate junction allows the flow of small molecular weight materials from one cell to the next. Cells in which a direct communication exists between the cytoplasm of the adjacent cells are said to be "coupled." The *gap junction* (Fig. 3.6) has received the most attention as the means of cell coupling. In this type there is a narrow cleft (20 to 40 Å) between the membranes and evidence of channels between.

There are two principal means to demonstrate the direct exchange of materials from one cell to another without their passing through the extracellular space between. In one technique, materials of different molecular weight are injected into one cell and are seen to diffuse rapidly and directly into the adjoining cell. A variety of tracer studies of this sort indicate that many substances, particularly of small molecular weight, readily pass in some channel across cell membranes. In some cases, particularly embryonic ones, molecules as large as several-hundred molecular weight (such as fluorescein) cannot make the journey; in other tissues considerably larger molecules (possibly up to 10,000 molecular weight) can pass between. In the other method of analysis, electrodes are placed within two cells in a line of cells and the passage of ionic current (a measure of the ability of ions to move between cells) is determined (Fig. 3.7). Cells between which a flow of current can be measured are said to be electrically coupled. Both tracer flow and electric coupling go hand in hand, and both are believed to be mediated by gap junctions. If substances are to be able to diffuse freely from one cell to another without appearing in the extracellular space, some form of pipeline must exist that directly connects the two cytoplasms. A model for the construction of a gap junction is shown in Fig. 3.8. Tiny channels are believed to exist in a latticework within the patches where the membranes of two cells come together. The numerous interconnecting tubes are evident. The dimensions of the interconnecting channels seen in the electron microscope, together with a consideration of the molecular weights of materials that can pass between the cells, suggest that the diameter of these channels are in the order of 10 Å.

Figure 3.7 Measurement of intercellular electrical communication. Light-microscope views of living, unstained material showing microelectrodes inserted: *a* salivary gland epithelial cells of *Chironomus.* larva; *b* cells of Malpighian tubule of prepupal stage of *Chironomus*. (Calibration = 50μm) [*Courtesy of W. R. Loewenstein.*]

Figure 3.8 Model of gap junction shows possible distribution of intercellular channels (*A*) and extracellular channels (*B*) within the junctional membrane complex. [*Courtesy of B. W. Payton.*]

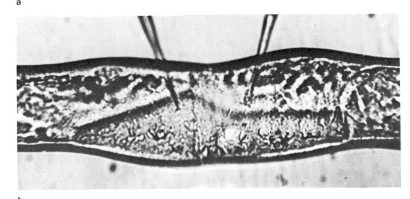

a

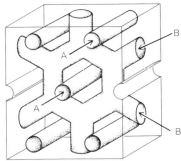

b

One of the most remarkable features of these membrane complexes is the rapidity with which they can be disassembled and re-formed. Treatment of coupled cells with trypsin or removal of divalent ions or micromanipulation readily causes the coupling to be lost. Cells can become coupled in minutes simply by putting their surfaces in contact with one another. Even cells of different tissues or of different species can be coupled one to another and gap junctions will form between them. These results reaffirm the dynamic nature of the cell membrane and the spontaneity with which it can form itself or such derived structures. Presumably the same types of rules discussed in the section on self-assembly apply here as well; the major difference is the presence of a variety of lipid molecules in membranes, in addition to the ever-present protein. The reason for selecting the gap junction for special consideration among the numerous types of intercellular contacts is the potential it provides for intercellular communication. That a large number of cells can be put into intimate cytoplasmic contact with one another provides what is, in essence, one giant compartment. The possibility for embryonic cells to influence one another by this means is apparent. On the other hand, the process of diverse differentiation among a group of cells might be expected to be accompanied by a lack of such communication between cells whose development was continuing along different lines.

CYTOPLASMIC MEMBRANES

Coursing through the cytoplasm of most cells is an extensive series of interconnected cytoplasmic membranes. This membrane is found around spherical vesicles, lining long channels, organized into stacks of flattened discs, and in various other configurations. To a varying degree these membranous components can be categorized into several distinct types of organelles. The endoplasmic reticulum, the Golgi complex, and the lysosomes will be considered. Figure 3.1 shows a cell with an extensive endoplasmic reticulum (ER). In this cell the ER is rough as a result of rows of ribosomes attached to the membranes. Presumably these ribosomes are organized into membrane-bound polyribosomes and are actively engaged in protein synthesis. Newly synthesized proteins come off the polyribosomes and can be carried through the enclosed channels of the ER to a variety of different destinations.

In some cases the rough ER leads into a system of tubular membranes devoid of ribosomes, termed the *smooth endoplasmic reticulum*. Smooth ER is present to varying degrees in different cells and is particularly predominant in epithelial cells, steroid-producing cells, and striated-muscle cells. Cells responsible for the production of large quantities of protein—such as cells producing digestive enzymes in the pancreas—have a greatly expanded rough ER network; others such as muscle and nephron cells, have very little rough ER. Rough ER is primarily involved in protein synthesis and transport, while smooth ER probably serves a variety of specialized functions in the cells in which it is best developed. Smooth ER has been implicated in the synthesis of nonprotein products, in glycogen metabolism, and as a channel for transport through the cell. As in the plasma membrane, specific enzymes have been found to be associated with, and are probably a part of, the membranes of the endoplasmic reticulum.

GOLGI COMPLEX

Another distinct membranous structure is the Golgi complex, formed by a collection of flattened membranous cisternae and vesicles (Figs. 3.9 and 3.10). As with the ER, different types of cells have a varying degree of development of the Golgi. As with the ER, a variety of functions have been ascribed to this organelle; we will mention only a few. Golgi membranes are particularly well developed in secretory cells that pour their contents to the outside. In these cells, such as those of the pancreas, the newly synthesized products are collected within the membranes of the Golgi complex; there they appear to undergo a concentration process, producing vesicles with sufficient protein content to appear dense in the electron microscope after appropriate staining. In the pancreas the last stage in this process is the zymogen granule, which fuses to the plasma membrane, thereby releasing its products to the outside as a preliminary step in its passage to the digestive tract.

The entire process from protein synthesis to expulsion from the cell can be followed by administering radioactively labeled amino acids and waiting various times before fixation of the tissue. As the time after injection is increased, the label moves farther from its site of synthesis in the rough ER, into the Golgi complex, then into the zymogen granules, and in about two hours label is seen to be expelled to the outside of the cells. Other functions of the Golgi complex include the attachment of carbohydrate molecules to newly synthesized proteins to produce glycoproteins and mucopolysaccharides. Certain of

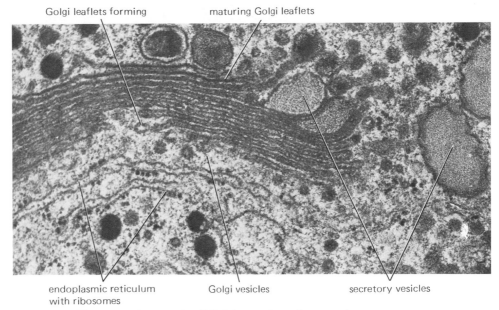

Golgi leaflets forming   maturing Golgi leaflets

endoplasmic reticulum   Golgi vesicles   secretory vesicles
with ribosomes

Figure 3.9 Electron micrograph of Golgi complex of a growing cell. [*Courtesy of O. Kiermayer.*]

Figure 3.10 The Golgi complex, showing origination from rough endoplasmic reticulum, fusion of Golgi vesicles to form stacks of smooth endoplasmic reticulum, and conveyance of product-containing secretory vesicles to the cell exterior, liberating either secretory granules or extracellular coat.

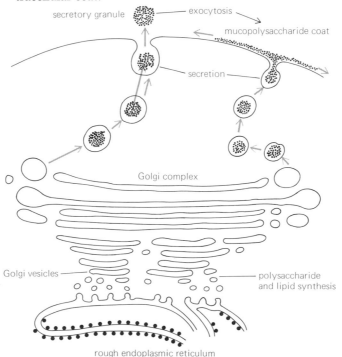

secretory granule — exocytosis

mucopolysaccharide coat

secretion

Golgi complex

Golgi vesicles   polysaccharide and lipid synthesis

rough endoplasmic reticulum
(protein synthesis)

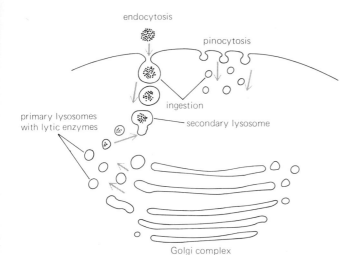

endocytosis

pinocytosis

ingestion

primary lysosomes
with lytic enzymes

secondary lysosome

Golgi complex

Figure 3.11 The GERL (Golgi-endoplasmic reticulum-lysosome) system is shown with primary lysosomes originating from Golgi complex and fusing with endocytic vesicles from cell surface (left) to form secondary lysosomes.

these carbohydrate-bearing proteins become sulfated, and the attachment of inorganic sulfate is accomplished within the confines of the Golgi complex. In many cells, such as mucous-secreting epithelia, these products are also transported to the outside via these membrane-bound vesicles. In at least two cases—the formation of the coelenterate nematocyst and of the acrosome at the tip of most sperm—the Golgi complex undergoes a complex transformation to form the two structures.

The other membranous organelle to be briefly considered is the lysosome. Lysosomes are membrane-bound vesicles formed in a manner similar to that of the zymogen granules described above. The Golgi complex, in its capacity of membrane-former, buds off these vesicles, which become filled with proteins produced by the endoplasmic reticulum (Fig. 3.10). In this case the proteins are a collection of hydrolytic enzymes whose optimal activity occurs at acid pH. Included in the collection of enzymes are proteases, lipases, nucleases, and enzymes to break down polysaccharides and phosphate esters. It is this last capability of lysosomes—i.e., their acid phosphatase activity—that is typically used as the criterion for a vesicle's being considered a lysosome. As would be expected from its contents, lysosomes are involved in intracellular digestion.

In most cases lysosomes function by fusion with vesicles containing material to be digested. One of the properties of the cell membrane is its ability to surround particles or fluid on the outside of the cell and to enclose them within a vacuole that is pinched off inside the cell (Fig. 3.11). These vacuoles (termed *pinocytotic vacuoles* if the contents are more fluidlike and *phagocytotic vacuoles* if the contents are particulate) undergo fusion with the lysosomal vesicle, and their contents are digested by the hydrolytic enzymes. Lysosomes are particularly prominent in cells such as certain leukocytes and macrophages that have roles in intracellular digestion of material. In other cases the hydrolytic enzymes, generally ascribed to lysosomes, are responsible for the death of the cell in which they are contained. In this capacity these organelles provide the capability for self-destruction, termed *autophagy*. This can result either from certain disease states characterized by tissue self-destruction or in the normal course of events of certain tissues, such as resorption of tail tissue in frog tadpole metamorphosis.

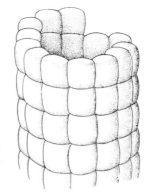

Figure 3.12 Model of a microtubule showing arrangement of the subunits, each a dimer of tubulin. [*After Tilney, 1968.*]

MICROTUBULES AND MICROFILAMENTS

One of the most useful shapes in the constructions around us is the hollow cylinder. We use it in pipe lines to carry fluids or gases from one place to another and as a supporting column to hold up the roofs over our heads. In the construction of living organisms, we find it has evolved to meet similar needs. For example, tubular elements carry fluids of all types within the body in ducts and vessels of a variety of diameters. In the form of the long bones of the body, the tubular column functions to support our body weight. Since the ability of a column to act in a supportive role is proportional to its cross-sectional area, a tubular column provides equivalent support as if it were solid, yet requires a more simple construction and less mass. This same structure is found within cells as microtubules, structures that make up a variety of organelles of widely different appearance and function.

A model of the microtubule is shown in Fig. 3.12. These structures are composed of globular subunits with dimensions of 40 by 50 Å, packed together in a predictable way. Microtubules generally have 12 or 13 subunits composing the circumference, though it is not certain whether they are in a helical arrangement or in rows stacked one on top of the other. The analysis of the chemistry of the microtubule has had a long and confusing history. It appears that the subunit is a dimer with a molecular weight of 110,000 to 120,000, composed of two monomers. If protein is extracted from microtubules and fractionated by electrophoresis, two distinct proteins—alpha and beta *tubulin*—can be separated, having molecular weights of nearly equal number. Since the subunit is a dimer, it might be expected that one of each type of protein makes up the dimer (a heterodimer), though this remains uncertain. It is possible that there are two types of subunits, both homodimers (composed of two identical proteins). For a period there was speculation that tubulin was identical with the protein actin, though this has been clearly shown not to be the case. A similarity, reflecting a possible evolutionary relationship, does exist between these proteins. One of the least understood, and most important, aspects of microtubule study is the mechanism by which they are assembled. Centrioles have long been implicated as a center of microtubule formation, but there are examples where microtubules are present while centrioles are lacking. Present studies are focusing on the nature of microtubule-organizing centers.

Microtubules are found in a variety of circumstances. They are universally present in cilia and flagella (Fig. 3.13), where they provide the force necessary for movement. This derives from a sliding of tubules across one another in a

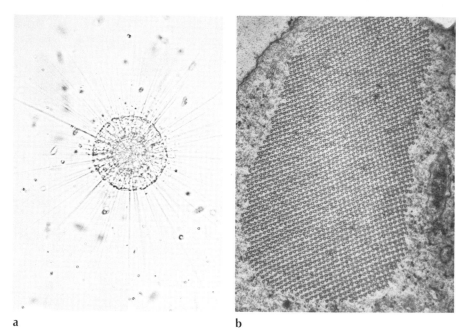

a

b

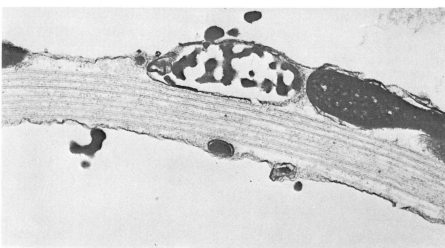

c

Figure 3.13 *a* The helizoan *Echinosphaerium.* Slender axopodial processes radiate from the cell body. Within each axopodium is a birefringent core, or axoneme. [*Courtesy of L. G. Tilney.*] *b* Microtubule array of an axopodium. Reassembly of axoneme structure after dispersion. [*Courtesy T. P. Fitzharris.*] *c* Longitudinal section shows a reforming axopodium after 10 minutes of recovery following dispersion of subunits by ultrasonic treatment. [*Courtesy of L. G. Tilney.*]

manner analogous to sliding muscle filaments. They are universally found in the spindle apparatus as the elements of all the spindle fibers as well as of the centriole. It is believed that in this role the microtubules provide the force by which the chromosomes are pulled apart. The mechanism whereby chromosome movement is accomplished is not known, though there are several theories. In one theory a sliding mechanism between two sets of spindle fibers is invoked, while in another theory the force is believed to result from the disassembly of the tubule at the polar end of the fiber.

Microtubules are widely present in cells, where they appear to function in a transport and support capacity. They have been implicated in the movement of various granules within cells and, in an entirely different capacity, microtubules are believed to be of primary importance in the maintenance of cell shape. The natural shape of a free body with liquid properties is spherical, as seen in the suspended drop of water in oil or in a soap bubble. When free bodies are clustered together—again as seen most readily in a mass of soap bubbles—the exposed surfaces remain curved, but adjoining surfaces become more or less flat. Surface tension and mutually adhesive forces are responsible for these configurations. When other shapes appear, as in most cells, then other agencies must exist that either produce or maintain the distortions. Microtubules seem to be the most likely agent. They are commonly seen to be lined up parallel with and close to cell walls and in general to conform to whatever particular shape a cell may exhibit. A well-suited example of this is in the heliozoan protozoan *Echinosphaerium* (Fig. 3.13). This organism has numerous long axopodia (5 to 10 μm in diameter and up to 400 μm long) whose shape is determined by microtubules arranged parallel with the axopod (Fig. 3.13c). A cross section through an axopod (Fig. 3.14a), particularly near its base, reveals a remarkable structure, the *axoneme;* it consists of numerous microtubules arranged in two interlocking coils or spirals, the number of constituent tubules decreasing as sections are cut progressively toward the axopodial tip. Single tubules appear to traverse the entire length of the axopod.

Microtubules are an example of an organelle in a polymerized condition. In many of its structures, particularly those of spindle fiber and neuronal support, the microtubule is in a fragile state and is readily depolymerized. One theory proposes that a dynamic equilibrium exists between the polymer and the monomers that make up the precursor pool. By control of this equilibrium the cell would control the assembly and disassembly of its microtubules. This relatively fragile condition is easily verified by the disruption of the microtubule by a variety of treatments—including hydrostatic pressure, cold temperature, vinblastine, and a molecule (colchicine) that binds specifically to the dimer subunit. The microtubules of cilia and flagella are more stable structures, probably not in equilibrium with the subunits and not sensitive to disruption by these treatments.

Figure 3.14 *a* Cross section of axopodia shows double spiral arrangement of microtubules. [*From Tilney, 1968, after MacDonald and Kitching.*] *b* Transverse section of a cilium, showing typical 9 + 2 organization of microtubules with arms and secondary fibers. [*After Gibbons, 1967.*] *c* Centriole, showing 9 triplet tubules and no central (axial) tubules.

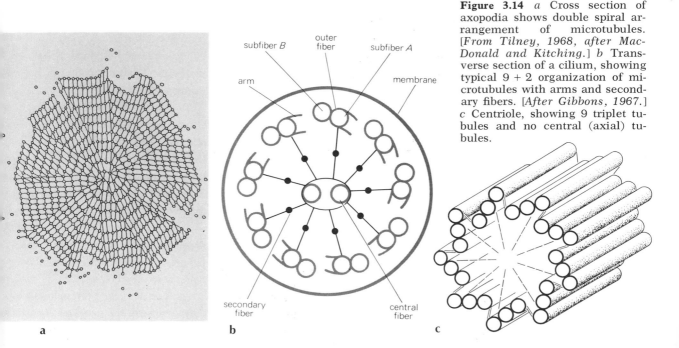

subfiber *B*

outer fiber

subfiber *A*

arm

membrane

secondary fiber

central fiber

a

b

c

Evidence is accumulating that contractile properties of nonmuscle cells are correlated with the presence of microfilaments. These elongated, wirelike structures are approximately 30 to 70 Å in diameter, solid in structure, and very likely identical with the actin filaments found in muscle cells. The mechanism by which microfilaments produce their shortening is unknown; one likely possibility is that the filaments slide relative to one another as in muscle contraction. Microfilaments generally appear in an oriented manner close beneath the cell membrane, running parallel to the membrane. They are capable of a rapid appearance before a contractile event and a rapid disappearance upon its conclusion. These filaments have been implicated in a variety of morphogenetic events that involve a change in cell shape—including cleavage, gastrulation, neurulation, and the formation of certain organs. These will be discussed individually as the topics appear during the book.

Processes requiring microfilaments are disrupted by the addition of cytochalasin B, though its mechanism of action is not understood. We can conclude that both microtubules and microfilaments are responsible for cell shape. The former are correlated with the maintenance of a particular shape as a result of the supportive role of the microtubule. The latter are correlated with more rapid changes in shape, and a contractile property is believed responsible. Table 1 lists the processes believed to require microfilaments. In a few cases there is evidence of a preliminary cell shape change dependent upon microtubules, followed by a second cell shape change involving a constriction of a cell, and this step depends upon microfilaments.

TABLE 1   Processes Sensitive to Cytochalasin B

1	Cytokinesis
2	Single-cell movement
3	Nerve outgrowth
4	Tubular gland formation
5	Cytoplasmic streaming
6	Tail resorption in ascidian metamorphosis
7	Invagination during gastrulation
8	Smooth muscle contraction
9	Cardiac muscle contraction
10	Cortical contraction in eggs

CENTRIOLES AND BASAL BODIES

Apart from any capacity the microtubule components of the various structures may have for self-assembly, disassembly, and reassembly, the basal bodies and centrioles serve as nucleation centers for microtubules production. The fine structures of basal bodies and centrioles are so much alike that these bodies can be regarded as a single type of organelle serving two possible functions in the cell. All may be called centrioles.

A typical centriole is a cylinder about 200 nm (nanometers)[1] wide and about twice as long. Nine evenly spaced fibrils run the length of the centriole; each fibril appears in cross section as a band of three microtubules (Fig. 3.14c), designated the A, B, and C subfibrils, each about 20 nm in diameter. Each band of three microtubules is inclined at an angle to the surface of the centriole. At one end, identified as the proximal or old end, the central part is usually occupied by a characteristic pinwheel structure that consists of a central cylindrical hub and nine delicate spokes extending toward the peripheral fibers.

Characteristically, therefore, centrioles have nine sets of triplet tubules but no central tubules, whereas ciliary and flagellar axonemes have nine sets of double tubules plus central tubules. It is significant that when outer doublets of the ciliary or flagellar axoneme are isolated, depolymerized, and allowed to redevelop *in vitro* without the basal body, only single microtubules are formed.

The primary questions about centrioles—whether mitotic and/or axonemic—concern their role in the assembly process of the associated physically active structure and the process by which they are replicated. During mitotic cell division, the centriole at each pole of the mitotic spindle duplicates, so that each daughter cell has a pair of centrioles. The "daughter" centriole always arises close to the old centriole, with its long axis at right angles to that of the old (see pair of centrioles in midpiece of sperm in Fig. 4.9). Through nearly a century since they were discovered in 1887—independently by Boveri and Van Beneden—centrioles have been considered to be self-replicating bodies, although there are cases where all evidence points to *de novo* formation. This paradoxical situation still defies rational interpretation.

NUCLEUS

The nuclear compartment of the cell retains a unique composition, yet is in continual communication with the cytoplasm in which it is immersed. The organelles of the cytoplasm—mitochondria, endoplasmic reticulum, Golgi complex, lysosomes, and numerous vesicles and inclusion bodies—are not found within the confines of the nuclear membrane. Compared with the diverse functions of the cytoplasm in the many different types of cells that have been studied, the *known* functions of the nucleus are primarily restricted to the storage and replication of genetic information, its selective transcription, and the assembly of ribosomes. Four prominent components make up the typical nucleus: the chromosomes, the nucleolus, the fluid matrix (nucleoplasm or nuclear sap), and the surrounding membrane. We will briefly consider the nature and function of each of these components, though the assumption is made that the student is familiar, to some degree, with these basic cellular parts.

The DNA is contained within the chromosomes, in close association with a great variety of proteins. Chromosomal proteins are generally categorized on the basis of their amino acid composition and thus their solubility. The histones are small proteins, of limited variety and great similarity in amino acid sequence among eukaryotic cells. Histones are rich in basic amino acids (lysine and arginine) and are therefore most soluble in acidic extraction media as a result of their positively charged character. Another group of chromosomal proteins are relatively acidic, i.e., are negatively charged at physiological pH and therefore more readily extracted by basic solutions. A third class of chromosomal proteins, the residual proteins, are least soluble and tend to remain behind after many extraction procedures. Included among the chromosomal proteins are enzymatic, structural, and regulatory molecules; but the manner in which these

---

[1] A nanometer is one-millionth of a millimeter.

various protein fractions are organized into chromatin structure remains the subject of controversy and intensive investigation.

Analysis of chromatin with the electron microscope has been most informative from studies of unsectioned mitotic chromosomes prepared as whole mounts by special techniques. The fibrous nature of the mitotic chromosome is clearly shown in electron micrographs. In the nonmitotic state these chromatin threads are diffusely spread throughout the nucleus with possible attachments to the inside of the nuclear membrane. In at least two other cases, the giant polytene chromosomes of some insect cells and the lampbrush chromosomes of the reproductive cells, an entirely different organization of the components is found. In addition to DNA and protein, RNA is also present in the chromosomes, though its nature and function have not been resolved.

Along with the chromosomes, most nuclei contain either one or two dense structures, the nucleoli (Fig. 3.15), composed of RNA and protein. Ultrastructural analysis indicates that nucleoli are composed of granular and fibrillar regions; biochemical analysis indicates the presence of DNA, which is usually spun out from one or more of the chromosomes to become associated with the nucleoli. Within the nucleolar DNA is the template for ribosomal RNA, and within the nucleolus the synthesis of rRNA occurs. Ribosomal RNA is produced as one large molecule and is then split up into a number of fragments, the rRNA for each ribosomal subunit and other fragments that are discarded. Assembly of each subunit occurs in the nucleolus by the combination of one of the rRNAs with a specific group of ribosomal proteins and an extra RNA molecule (5S RNA of nonnucleolar origin) in the case of the large subunit. The synthesis of the ribosomal proteins occurs on cytoplasmic polyribosomes with the migration of the proteins through the nuclear membrane to the nucleolus for assembly into the subunits. Other than its role in ribosome formation, no other functions of the nucleolus have been clearly established.

The nuclear sap, or nucleoplasm, is the fluid medium in which the chromosomes and nucleoli are found and through which regulatory molecules, synthetic products, substrates, enzymes, etc., must pass on their way to and from

Figure 3.15 *a* Portion of a nucleolus of a molluscan oocyte showing both fibrous and granular regions. *b* Electron microscopic autoradiograph of a cell of a rabbit embryo after incubation of the embryo in ³H-uridine. Nucleoli are seen within the nucleus and are found to contain numerous silver grains reflecting their role in ribosomal RNA synthesis.

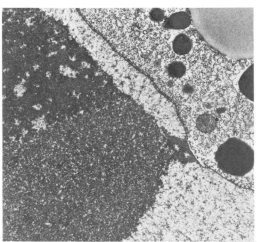

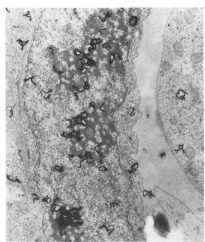

a   b

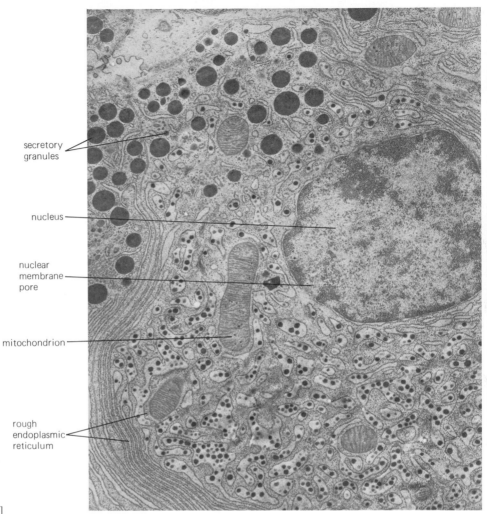

secretory
granules

nucleus

nuclear
membrane
pore

mitochondrion

rough
endoplasmic
reticulum

Figure 3.16 Part of a bat pancreas secretory cell, showing nucleus, nuclear pores, mitochondria, endoplasmic reticulum, and secretory (zymogen) granules. [*Courtesy of K. Porter.*]

the cytoplasm. Analysis of the nucleoplasm reveals a wide variety of proteins, including enzymes capable of anaerobic energy metabolism (glycolysis), and an ionic composition that can be quite different from the cytoplasm that surrounds it.

Surrounding the nucleus is the nuclear membrane, or envelope, consisting of two distinct concentric membranes separated by a space of about 100 to 300 Å. Scattered at frequent intervals along the nuclear membrane are "pores," which give the appearance that the nucleus is open at these sites to the cytoplasm (Fig. 3.16). More careful analysis using ultrastructural and physiological means indicates that these pores are complex structures and that they do not provide an open channel of communication between the cytoplasm and the nucleus. The pore is defined at its edges by the fusion of the two elements of the nuclear membrane; however, within the pore there is additional visible material (annular material), which appears to fill in much of the pore space. The number of pores present per unit surface of nuclear membrane is highly variable and can undergo change during a physiological or developmental process. For example, there is a reduction in nuclear pore density that accompanies the development of the spermatozoa.

The most important question for our purpose concerning the nuclear membrane is the constraint, if any, it places on communication between the two major cellular compartments. Evidence relating to this question has led to some controversy. A variety of techniques have been applied to determine just how porous the nuclear envelope might be. Observations of isolated nuclei that are osmotically active, i.e., capable of swelling when placed in hypotonic media, would suggest that the nuclear membrane can act as a semipermeable membrane to restrict the free diffusion of small ions. Electrophysiological studies of the large nuclei of *Drosophila* larval salivary gland cells indicate that a potential difference is maintained across the nuclear envelope in these cells, which therefore must restrict the movement of small ions across itself. However, in other cases, such as the nuclear membrane of frog oocytes, no such potential is found; this suggests there may be species differences to consider with respect to nuclear membrane permeability.

In another series of experiments, particles of varying diameter were injected into the cytoplasm of cells (amoebae and oocytes); the ability of the various-sized particles to penetrate into the nuclear space was determined in the electron microscope. In these studies it was found that smaller particles could penetrate the membrane and that penetration was restricted to the center of the pores (Fig. 3.17). Particles of about 125 Å or greater remained in the cytoplasm, however, suggesting that this is the upper limit for penetration even though the diameter of the pore itself is considerably greater. That particles of 100 Å can enter the nucleus through the pores does not prove the pores in the envelope are wide open gates in these cells. Mechanisms might exist for capture and penetration of certain materials, maintaining the exclusion of others. Whatever the mechanism, some facility must exist for passage of materials—including particles at least the size of the ribosomal subunits—through the membrane.

MITOCHONDRION

One of the most characteristic structures of the cell is the mitochondrion, present in all cells except the bacteria. Each mitochondrion is typically about 1 μm long and one-third as wide. The number of mitochondria per cell can vary greatly; a renal tubule cell contains about 300, a rat liver cell about 1,000, and an amphibian oocyte 100 times that number. The usual picture of the mitochondrion in section in the electron microscope (Fig. 3.18a) illustrates the main features of mitochondrial structure. The organelle is bounded by an outer, encircling membrane of typical trilaminar appearance. Within the outer membrane and separated from it by a space is an inner membrane, which is thrown into numerous folds that penetrate deeply into the mitochondrion and often connect with the inner membrane of the other side. Within the mitochondrion, bounded by the inner membrane and its foldings, is the fluid phase, or matrix, of the organelle. The electron microscope has provided a detailed examination of the structure of the mitochondrion, leading to the accepted model shown in Fig. 3.18b.

Observations of the mitochondria in living cells with cinematographic techniques have shown a dynamic picture of mitochondrial activity not obtainable in electron micrographs. In these movies the mitochondria are seen in constant motion undergoing branching, fusion, and division with great rapidity, revealing the type of spontaneous behavior characteristic of the plasma membrane previously described. It has been known for a long time that the seat of

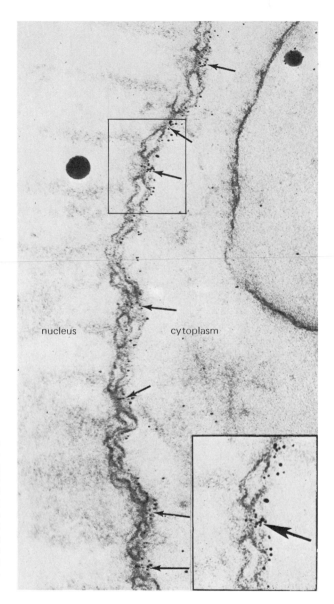

nucleus   cytoplasm

Figure 3.17 Electron micrograph of the nuclear-cytoplasmic border of an amoeba after injection with coated gold particles. These particles are seen to penetrate through the nuclear envelope via the center of the pores. Insert shows a portion of the figure at higher magnification. Arrows correspond to nuclear pores. (*Courtesy of C. Feldherr.*)

oxidative energy metabolism is housed in the mitochondrion, and recent biochemical analysis has localized many of the activities. Anaerobic oxidative metabolism (glycolysis) occurs outside the mitochondria; the products penetrate into the mitochondrial space, where further oxidative metabolism occurs. The intermembranous matrix contains the soluble enzymes of the Krebs cycle, during which electrons are removed from several of the intermediates and passed to a series of proteins and cofactors that constitute the electron transport chain. The location of the components of the electron transport system is confined to the inner membrane, presumably organized in an assembly whereby electrons can be transferred from one component to the next on the path. A single mitochondrion from a liver cell has approximately 17,000 such respiratory assemblies, or about 650 per μm^2.

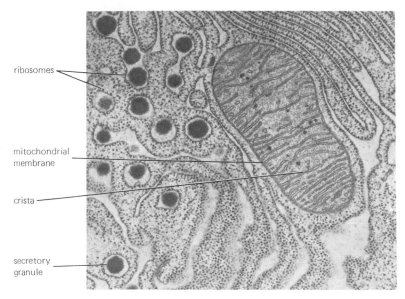

ribosomes

mitochondrial membrane

crista

secretory granule

a

Figure 3.18 *a* Electronmicrograph of mitochondrion, together with secretory granules and rough endoplasmic reticulum. [*Courtesy of K. Porter.*] *b* Model of a mitochondrion showing outer membrane, inner membrane extending inward as folds, or cristae, and possible arrangement of circular DNA within the mitochondrion. The DNA molecules may be attached to portions of the membrane. [*After Nass, copyright ©1969 by the American Association for the Advancement of Science.*]

b

Another basic aspect of mitochondrial function has emerged in recent years: an entirely distinct information storage and utilization system operates in parallel with that of the nucleus. As in the nucleus, the code is in DNA, the utilization in RNA. Mitochondrial DNA occurs in small circles approximately 5 μm in circumference, sufficient to code for approximately 5,000 amino acids (about 20 proteins of 30,000 molecular weight). RNA synthesis takes place in the mitochondria, on mitochondrial DNA templates; protein synthesis follows, using special mitochondrial ribosomes, smaller than cytoplasmic ribosomes and containing ribosomal RNA coded for by the organelle's own genetic material. The nature of the proteins coded for by the mitochondrial DNA has not been fully established, though isolated mitochondria incorporate labeled amino acids into the proteins of the inner membrane, but neither the outer membrane nor soluble compartments. An interesting sidelight to mitochondrial study has been the proposal and speculation that they arose evolutionarily as a distinct prokaryotic organism, which evolved a symbiotic relationship with eukaryotic cells. This proposal is discussed at length by Raff and Mahler (1972).

MITOSIS AND THE CELL CYCLE

The ability of a cell to divide into two cells is at the very foundation of the development of multicellular animals that arise from one cell, the fertilized egg. The division of a cell requires the contents to be parceled out, and the cellular events of mitosis ensure that each cell receives its share. The division of the genetic material is a precise event; each cell receives an entire set of intact, homologous chromosomes. The remaining contents appear to be divided in a less precise, but in most cases an approximately equivalent, manner. The divisional process itself is a relatively short period, preceded and followed by much longer periods of time. Division occurs in two steps: nuclear division (mitosis) followed by cytoplasmic division (cytokinesis).

All cells have their individual period of existence, the cell cycle. They begin in the division of a parental cell; they cease at the end of a period of maturation and special functioning, or else lose their individuality in becoming a pair of daughter cells. Single-celled organisms, the protists, maintain various degrees of differentiated structure throughout the process of division, and only partial reconstruction of new individuals is evident. In multicellular organisms, cells fall roughly into three categories:

1   Cells that retain full capacity for division and exhibit little or no special differentiation, serving principally as limiting membranes and/or as reserves for tissue replacement.

2   Cells that exhibit considerable general differentiation—such as liver cells, the gastrodermal cells of hydras, and the photosynthetic cells of plants—but are still able to undergo division.

3   Cells that when mature have lost their capacity to divide, notably cells with extreme structural or chemical specialization.

If we consider a population of rapidly dividing cells, there are periods of mitosis alternating with periods of interphase in a continual cyclical process. This alternation of periods within the life of a population of cells is the cell cycle. The interphase period is generally divided into three parts, G_1, S, and G_2 (Fig. 3.19). During G_1, which follows immediately upon the completion of mitosis, preparatory synthetic steps begin that will ensure the following mitosis, if such is to occur. In cells that have reached a stage in their differentiation where no further divisions will follow, the cell will remain in the G_1 state. During G_1, proteins are synthesized that are required for the synthesis of DNA during the ensuing S phase. DNA synthesis is restricted to the S phase, which is generally of a predictable length (several hours in mammalian cells in culture) and is followed by G_2. Throughout the interphase period, RNA synthesis and protein synthesis continue; some of these RNAs and proteins are required for the cell to undergo the following mitosis.

As mitosis begins, many dramatic changes in the cell's activities occur (Fig. 3.20). The precision of cell division relates primarily to the division of the chromosomal material that has previously undergone duplication and must be prepared for separation into two cells. In the interphase state the chromosomes are diffuse, interwoven, and each is spread throughout the nucleus.

During *prophase*, the first stage in the continual sequence of mitotic events, the diffuse threads of the chromosome must become packed into the

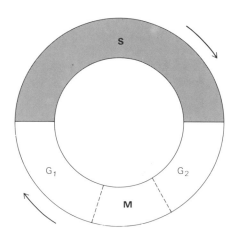

Figure 3.19 The cell cycle, or mitotic cycle, showing relative duration of phases in a growing cell. S, synthesis of DNA; G_1, phase prior to DNA synthesis; G_2, phase following DNA synthesis; M, the period occupied by mitosis (prophase through telophase).

compact structure of the metaphase chromosome. For example, the X chromosome in humans is estimated to contain nearly 5 cm of DNA double helix, which must become packed into a mitotic chromosome of less than 10 μm in length. The nature of the mechanism by which the chromatin threads become coiled and folded is unknown; presumably, certain of the proteins associated with the DNA are of great importance for this process. Other events characteristic of prophase include the breakdown and disappearance of the nucleolus and the separation of two pairs of centrioles located just outside the nuclear membrane; this is followed by the migration of one of the pairs around the nucleus to the opposite end of the cell. Stretching between the centrioles, microtubules of the early spindle fibers can frequently be seen.

The junction between the prophase and the *metaphase* stages is character-

Figure 3.20 Diagrammatic representation of the stages of mitosis (see text) during early cleavage in *Drosophila*. [*After Huettner*, 1933.]

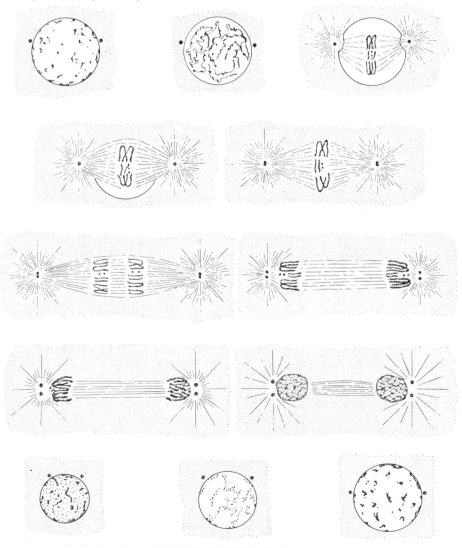

ized by the breakdown of the nuclear membrane, which is followed by the penetration of the growing spindle fibers into the center of the cell, the attachment of some of these fibers to the centromeres (kinetochores) of the chromosomes, and the alignment of the chromosomes at the cell's equator to form the metaphase plate. Spindle fibers are of two types, those that extend from pole to pole and those that extend from pole to chromosome. One theory suggests that chromosome movement at *anaphase* results from the sliding of the chromosome-attached fibers along the continuous pole-to-pole variety. The initiation of anaphase is marked by the synchronous separation of the duplicated chromosomes (chromatids) from each other. Some mechanism within the chromosomes appears to cause the fused centromeres to split apart, because spindle fibers are not needed for the event. Once split, the two chromatids are pulled apart—the centromeres leading the way—by the action of the attached spindle fibers. During *telophase*, nuclear membrane and nucleolus re-form, and the chromosomes disperse to assume their typical interphase condition. The mechanisms underlying the events of cytokinesis are discussed in Chapter 6.

CLONING AND SYNCHRONIZATION

Cell cultures, particularly of mammalian cells, are studied as synchronized populations, i.e., populations with all cells in the same phase of the cell cycle. This situation is brought about by exposure to thymidine, followed by blockading of the cell population with colcemid, which arrests all cells in metaphase. The culture is then grown in fresh medium and all cells continue their regular cycle, but starting at the same point.

A further degree of standardization of cell populations is attained by cloning, which eliminates the possible condition that a cell culture originating from a number of tissue cells consists of cells of subtly diverse kinds. Cloning consists of isolating a single cell from a culture and establishing a new culture which consists only of the descendants of that cell. The genetic and other constitutional characteristics are therefore, at least initially, the same for all the cells of that particular clone. Cloning and synchronization procedures are accordingly generally employed in the study of cell populations, whether of tissue cells of multicellular organisms or of protistan organisms. Various pathways, however, are open to cells following division. These are presented graphically in Fig. 3.21. They consist of continuing cycles of cell division maintaining a particular cell line, or of cycles leading to cell differentiation and eventual death, or to differentiated cells (gametes) that relate to sexual reproduction and development.

CELL DIFFERENTIATION AND
THE CELL CORTEX

If a single fundamental process does exist which leads to cell differentiation, it is the genic control of synthesis of innumerable diverse structural and enzymatic proteins. All else follows from their subsequent interactions, except for possible genic control of the timing of synthesis initiations. The questions, however, remain: To what extent, if any, is essential biological information encoded and transmitted by materials and mechanisms other than the nucleic acid templates? To what extent does organized cell structure itself influence the course of differentiation?

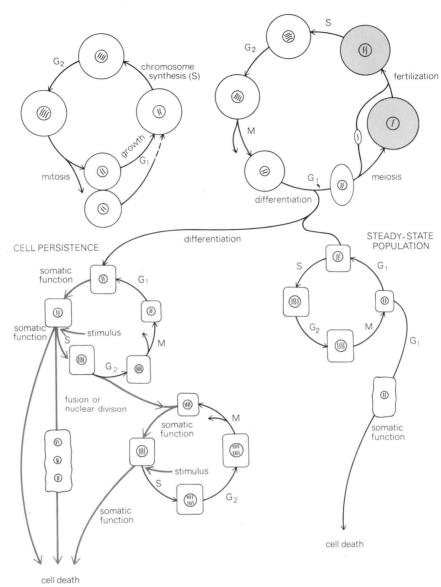

Figure 3.21 Types of cell cycles. [*After Stern and Nanney.*]

Ciliate protozoans have long been studied with such thought as this in mind. They are highly appropriate organisms for several reasons: they are unicellular and readily multiply in laboratory cultures, they are usually comparatively large (some are even very large indeed), and they exhibit cortical structural patterns that are highly differentiated. The ciliate cortex, which may be as deep as 2 μm, contains rows of cilia, each cilium with its own basal body, or *kinetosome;* the rows of cilia typically orient with regard to body shape and locomotory axis, and locally form specific assemblies, particularly feeding organelles. Individual rows of kinetosomes are known as *kineties* (Fig. 3.22).

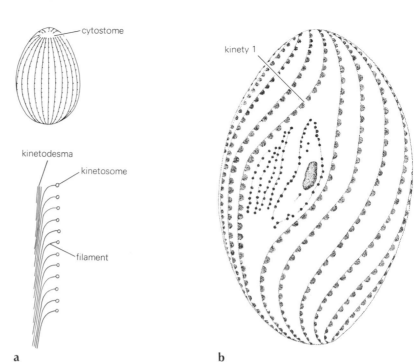

Figure 3.22 Kineties. *a* Kinety consisting of a row of kinetosomes, or basal bodies, with filaments constituting a kinetodesma. *b* Formation of successive rows of new kineties from kinety 1 to give rise to a "field," or oral primordium, associated with an expanding area of the cortex as a whole (typical of the ventral side of many ciliates).

Ciliates are also characteristically equipped with two kinds of nuclei per individual: the micronucleus, which appears to be inactive most of the time but is necessary for mitotic division, and the macronucleus, which is essential to the general functioning of the cell-organism and for processes such as growth and regeneration.

Very small fragments of the whole organism are capable of reconstitution, at least in relatively large ciliates such as *Stentor* (Fig. 3.23). The importance of the cortex in this connection is shown by certain experiments. When all or virtually all of the endoplasm of a stentor is withdrawn through a small incision in the surface, leaving only the cortex and the nucleus, endoplasm is promptly restored and normal growth and reproduction follow. On the other hand, if all the cortex is stripped off, leaving only endoplasm and nucleus, the cell becomes spherical, survives for a while, but finally dies. However, if a piece of cortex is left on the endoplasm, it gradually spreads around it, reconstituting the visible markers of its gradients in the form of gradation in stripe width, and eventually regenerates and reproduces normally. Inasmuch as the kinetosomes are apparently self-replicating bodies and form precise, complex patterns in the cortex, namely, characteristic infraciliatures, the question arises whether such cortical patterns perpetuate themselves more or less independently of nuclear genes.

Apart from this question of the self-propagation of cortical structures and patterns, the very extensive work on *Stentor* by Tartar and by deTerra indicates that (1) changes in the structural organization of the cell surface initiate the process of cell division; (2) during cell division, the cell surface undergoes a series of changes that may control some events of organelle replication; and (3) these regulatory changes do not seem to be caused by release of diffusible substances into the endoplasm. There is, accordingly, evidence that the cell surface controls the time of cell division and also plays a part in determining the replication of the macronucleus and the basal bodies during division.

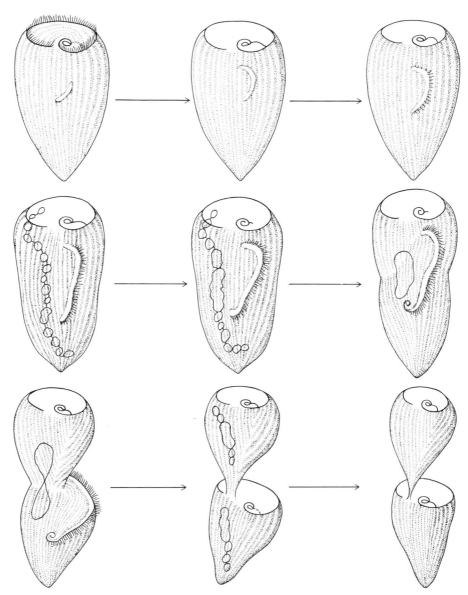

Figure 3.23 Stages in division of *Stentor,* showing formation and growth of new primordium leading to development of a complete system of kineties and cytostome in posterior half of the individual, accompanied by constrictive separation of anterior and posterior daughter individuals. [*After Tartar, 1962.*]

Cortical Inheritance

Although *Paramecium* is unsuitable for performing the sort of operations that have been so successful on *Stentor,* it has been possible by more indirect means to alter the precisely regular normal pattern of structure, to produce individuals with additional mouths, gullets, anuses, etc., without loss of viability. This is also true for certain other ciliates commonly employed in the laboratory, particularly *Tetrahymena* (Fig. 3.24). The altered structural pattern persists indefinitely, even through the sexual process of conjugation.

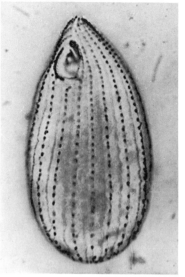

a

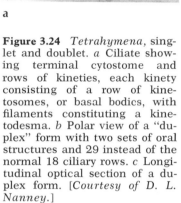
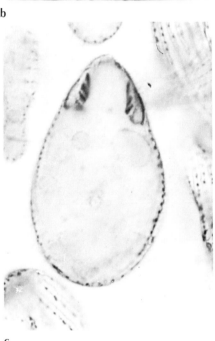

b

Figure 3.24 *Tetrahymena,* singlet and doublet. *a* Ciliate showing terminal cytostome and rows of kineties, each kinety consisting of a row of kinetosomes, or basal bodies, with filaments constituting a kinetodesma. *b* Polar view of a "duplex" form with two sets of oral structures and 29 instead of the normal 18 ciliary rows. *c* Longitudinal optical section of a duplex form. [*Courtesy of D. L. Nanney.*]

c

One of the simplest departures from the normal which has been induced is the inversion of one or more rows of the numerous longitudinal kineties, so that the inverted kineties show fibers emerging on the left and extending backwards, instead of emerging on the right and extending forwards. This partly deranged pattern has been perpetuated through several hundred generations, as the result of replication of basal units with the same orientation as those of the original inverted rows.

Doublet individuals are frequently seen in cultures of various ciliates, i.e., two apparent individuals virtually complete in total structure and organelles except that they are conjoined like Siamese twins and usually possess a single macronucleus between them. In cultures of *Paramecium* and *Tetrahymena,* when doublets turn up as a result of abnormal fission or of conjugation, the remarkable happening is that the doublets propagate as doublets by regular fission just as in singlets, and even undergo conjugative reproduction. Moreover, it is possible to mate doublets with singlets, so that a vast array of experimental possibilities is opened up.

Primarily, the question is the nature of the inheritable basis that enables a doublet to reproduce itself as a doublet and to behave generally as a single individual although with duplicated cortical systems, in contrast to the self-replicating singlet individual. The difference between the two forms is the same kind of difference seen between normal individuals and those with one or more inverted kineties, but is of a vastly more complex order. The question is essentially the same in the two cases: Is the inheritance of the new organization in any way under the control of, or determined by, the nucleus; or is the cortex as a whole, whether doublet or singlet, a truly self-perpetuating pattern, even though dependent on nuclear genes for the synthesis of some of its raw materials? We are concerned, in other words, with the nature of the inheritance of pattern as distinct from substance, and whether the innate tertiary or quaternary configurative potentials of the gene-determined proteins is a sufficient or an insufficient basis to work from. This question is crucial.

Paramecium, over the years, has been subject to intensive genetic experimentation and analysis, with not only gene markers but also the so-called kappa and killer traits used as cytoplasmic markers. Neither nuclear genes nor nuclear size, nor any components free to move as part of the fluid endoplasm, are found to have any bearing on the control of the difference between singlets and doublets. Only the cortex itself seems to be or to contain whatever genetic basis there may be. Such a conclusion, however, is so potentially important that positive evidence is required for its acceptance. Positive evidence, for example, could be the perpetuated transmission of a piece of special cortical pattern grafted into a normal cortical system, were it possible to make grafts such as have been done in *Stentor,* which is not the case. Nature, however, often performs a particular type of experiment which can be exploited.

In such an instance, following conjugation between a doublet and a singlet, the singlet carried away a piece of a doublet's cortex at the time of separation, and incorporated it as part of its own cortex. This particular freak was isolated and gave rise to a clone of like individuals, all of which were intermediates between singlets and doublets, with two sets of vestibules, two gullets, and the two ventral kinety fields, but with a single dorsal surface. That is, a piece of cortex pulled off from oral cortex of one cell and incorporated on the surface of another resulted in the inheritance and development of a complete additional oral region along the whole length of the animal on its ventral side. Accordingly, a small piece of cortex, as a natural graft, contains the genetic basis of a large but delimited part of the cell cortex.

In eggs, as in ciliates, there is reason to think that specific events of organelle replication may be controlled by the cell surface. This is less certain because the egg cortex lacks visible signs of polarity and organization. During the maturation of *Xenopus* eggs, however, breakdown of the germinal vesicle—which releases the egg from the premeiotic phase—can be induced by externally applied progesterone. This hormone has no effect when injected into the cell interior. It must produce its effect by interacting directly with the egg surface. Centrifugation experiments have shown that the cytoplasmic factor inducing germinal vesicle breakdown is predominantly localized in the clear (hyaline) ooplasm which contains the endoplasmic reticulum and a structureless ground substance. This is in keeping with the suggestion that the cell surface might affect the nuclear membrane of eukaryote cells by transmission of stimuli through the endoplasmic reticulum connecting them. Such continuity, without even any intervening reticulum, is reported in a plant cell (Fig. 3.25), where the plasma membrane and the outer layer of the nuclear membrane are clearly continuous with one another.

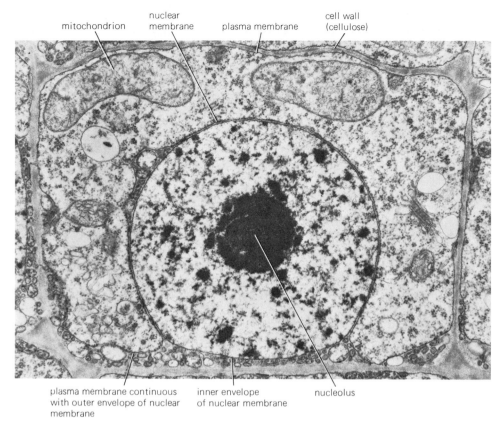

mitochondrion · nuclear membrane · plasma membrane · cell wall (cellulose)

plasma membrane continuous with outer envelope of nuclear membrane · inner envelope of nuclear membrane · nucleolus

Figure 3.25 A male reproductive cell of the plant *Blasia pusilla*, showing continuity of the nuclear membrane with the plasma membrane. Comparable continuities have been seen between plasma membrane and chloroplast membrane. [*Courtesy of Z. B. Carothers.*]

Cortical control of organelle replication in *Xenopus* is suggested by multipolar mitoses, lagging chromosomes, and chromosome bridges occurring in eggs with slight cortical injury. There is also evidence that the cell surface regulates the time of centriole replication as well as mitosis and cleavage.

Whether a cell is an egg, an organism, or a somatic cell, all components seem to be responsive to one another and constitute an open system with the immediate surroundings, with no part or property having a truly separate identity in the living state.

The cell is not a closed system whose properties are determined exclusively by its components. It is more than a "well-integrated chemical factory," although such a view of the cell may be necessary if we wish to investigate, e.g., an enzyme reaction within it. No cell, nor any organism, exists in isolation from its immediate environment and it cannot be conceived to do so in reality. In the case of cells, this becomes very clear when we consider the cell surface. Many cellular functions are directly influenced or controlled by macromolecules on the outside of the cell, either as components of the plasma membrane, as surface-associated materials, or as components of intercellular (extracellular) matrices. Many such macromolecules have been shown to have carbohydrate constituents (e.g., glycoproteins, mucopolysaccharides, proteoglycans, glycolipids). The Golgi apparatus functions both in synthesis or assembly of some of these carbohydrate-containing materials and in their transport to the cell surface as part of the secretory process. Such materials, with genetically controlled, specific carbohydrate groups, are involved in fundamental aspects of cellular function—recognition, motility, and association. For example, they are essential for recognition and adhesion between mating types in many unicellular organisms (probably for recognition by gametes of higher organisms) and in the structuring of multicellular forms and the association of embryonic cells during development.

Part of the Golgi apparatus function appears to be the assembly of membranes that have specific characteristics. It also plays an important role in the degradation of surface materials brought back into the cell by lysosomal enzymes, while secretion of lysosomal enzymes to the exterior results in the degradation of intercellular matrix materials.

The cycling and recycling of surface materials provide for the changing specificities in informational content essential for the control of differentiation and development. At both the cellular and the multicellular (supracellular) levels, various developmental phenomena may be guided by cell-to-cell and cell-to-environment interactions in which carbohydrate-containing materials act as determinants. The "informational potential" of such materials located at the cell surface may explain characteristics of cell movement, morphogenesis, and adaptability to enviromental stimuli during embryogenesis. Thus, altogether there is a close relationship between the genome and its regulators, the Golgi apparatus, the cell surface, the immediate external molecular and ionic environment, and the ultimate pattern of development and function of cells, both individually and collectively.

In this chapter we have dissected the cell into its most commonly found components and have described the most salient features of each. In a real sense, the cell is greater than the sum total of its parts, and an analytical approach can be misleading because it obliterates the interrelated nature of the structure and function of the organelles. Each organelle depends upon the continuing function of the other cellular components; they do not function in isolation. For example, a mitochondrion depends upon substrates provided by the cytoplasm, upon proteins coded for on nuclear-produced RNA, translated upon polyribosomes, and transported via cytoplasmic membrane channels. The cell's membranous components form a temporal and spatial continuum. Rough endoplasmic reticulum is believed to bud from the nuclear membrane; lysosomes and other membrane-bound vesicles form from Golgi membranes; plasma membrane in many cells is a mosaic formed, in part, by the fusion of cytoplasmic membrane and conversely is an important contributor (via pinocytosis) to the formation of internal cytoplasmic structure. The developmental phenomena with which this book is concerned depend upon the raw materials composing the cells. Differentiation, to a large extent, reflects specialized development of different organelles in different tissues, together with the accumulation of tissue-specific gene products.

READINGS

ALLEN, J. M. (ed.), 1967. "Molecular Organization and Biological Function," Harper & Row.

ALLEN, R. D., and N. KAMIYA (eds.), 1964. "Primitive Motile Systems in Biology," Academic.

BAXTER, R., 1971. Mitochondria, in J. Reinhart and H. Ursprung (eds.), "Origin and Continuity of Cell Organelles," Springer-Verlag.

BEAMS, H. W., and R. G. KESSELL, 1968. The Golgi Apparatus: Structure and Function, *Int. Rev. Cytology*, **23**:209–276.

BENNET, M. V. L., 1973. Function of Electrotonic Junctions in Embryonic and Adult Tissues, *Fed. Proc. Amer. Soc. Exp. Biol.,* **32**:60–64.

BRACHET, J., and A. E. MIRSKY (eds.), 1959. "The Cell," 6 vols., Academic.

DE REUCH, A. V. S., and M. P. CAMERON (eds.), 1963. "Ciba Symposium on Lysosomes," Little, Brown.

DE TERRA, N., 1974. Cortical Control of Cell Division, *Science,* **184**:530–539.

DuPRAW, E. J., 1968. "Cell and Molecular Biology," Academic.

FELDHERR, C. M., 1965. The Effect of the Electron-Opaque Pore Material on Exchange through the Nuclear Annuli, *J. Cell Biol.,* **25**:43–53.

FULTON, C., 1971. Centrioles, in J. Reinhart and H. Ursprung (eds.), "Origin and Continuity of Cell Organelles," pp. 170–221, Springer-Verlag.

GILULA, N. B., 1973. Development of Cell Junctions, *Amer. Zool.,* **13**:1109–1117.

HARRIS, H., 1970. "Nucleus and Cytoplasm," 2d ed., Clarendon.

HEUMANN, K. F. (ed.), 1973. Membranes in Growth, Differentiation, and Neoplasia, *Fed. Proc. Amer. Soc. Exp. Biol.,* **32**:19–108.

JAMIESON, J. D., and G. E. PALADE, 1967. Intracellular Transport of Secretory Proteins in the Pancreatic Exocrine Cell, *J. Cell Biol.,* **34**:577–615.

LEHNINGER, A. L., 1971. "Bioenergetics," 2d ed., Benjamin.

LIMA-DE-FARIA, A. (ed.), 1969. "Handbook of Molecular Cytology," North-Holland Publishing Company, Amsterdam.

LOEWENSTEIN, W. R., 1973. Membrane Junctions in Growth and Differentiation, *Fed. Proc. Amer. Soc. Exp. Biol.,* **32**:60–64.

LOEWY, A. G., and P. SIEKEVITZ, 1969. "Cell Structure and Function," Holt, Rinehart, and Winston.

MAZIA, D., and A. TYLER (eds.), 1963. "General Physiology of Cell Specialization," McGraw-Hill.

MITCHISON, J. M., 1971. "The Biology of the Cell Cycle," Cambridge University Press.

NASS, M. M. K., 1969. Mitochondrial DNA: Advances, Problems, and Goals, *Science,* **165**:25–35.

NOVIKOFF, A. B., E. ESSNER, and N. QUINTANA, 1964. Golgi Apparatus and Lysosomes, *Fed. Proc. Amer. Soc. Exp. Biol.,* **23**:1010–1022.

OLMSTED, J. B., and G. G. BORISY, 1973. Microtubules, *Ann. Rev. Biochem.,* **42**:507–540.

RAFF, R. A., and H. R. MAHLER, 1972. The Non-Symbiotic Origin of Mitochondria, *Science,* **177**: 575–582.

SINGER, S. J., and G. L. NICOLSON, 1972. The Fluid Mosaic Model of the Structure of the Cell Membrane, *Science,* **175**:720–731.

TARTAR, V., 1962. Morphogenesis in *Stentor. Advance. Morphogenesis,* **2**:1–26.

TEDESCHI, H., 1974. "Cell Physiology Molecular Dynamics," Academic.

TILNEY, L. G., 1968. The Assembly of Microtubules and Their Role in the Development of Cell Form, 27th Symposium, The Society of Developmental Biology, pp. 63–102.

VINCENT, W. S., and O. L. MILLER, JR. (eds.), 1966. Symposium on the Nucleolus, *Nat. Cancer Inst. Monogr.* **23.**

WENT, H., 1966. The Behavior of Centrioles and the Structure and Formation of the Achromatic Figure, *Protoplasmatologia,* **6**(G1):1–109.

WHALEY, W. G., M. DAUWALDER, and J. E. KEPHART, 1972. Golgi Apparatus: Influence on Cell Surfaces, *Science,* **175**:596–599.

WISCHNITZER, S., 1974. The Nuclear Envelope: Its Ultrastructure and Functional Significance, *Endeavour,* **23**:137–142.

WOLFE, S. L., 1972. "Biology of the Cell," Wadsworth.

CHAPTER 4

Gametogenesis

Gametogenesis is the prelude to sexual reproduction and encompasses two rather independent activities. In animals the end product of gametogenesis is the formation of a specialized reproductive cell, the egg or the sperm, by a complex series of events to be examined in this chapter. The other aspect of gametogenesis requires that the chromosome number be reduced from the diploid value to the haploid condition. Sexual reproduction involves the union of reproductive cells from two distinct organisms of the same species. If this is the case, either each reproductive cell must carry one-half the number of chromosomes of the parents or the chromosome number will double over each generation. The reduction in chromosome number is accomplished by the meiotic process, which results in one round of replication followed by two complete divisions rather than the single divisional event found in mitosis. Meiosis must therefore be incorporated into the steps leading to the final reproductive cell or gamete.

Sexual reproduction, by virtue of its requirement for a genetic contribution from two individuals, results in offspring with a new genetic identity distinct from that of either parent. To accomplish this end the reproductive cells have evolved as highly specialized cells with a surprising degree of similarity across the entire phylogenetic map. First we will examine *spermatogenesis,* the production of the male gamete, including meiosis, which can be applied to the female process as well. In the latter section of this chapter we will examine *oogenesis,* the formation of the female gamete.

SPERMATOGENESIS

In animals, with a few exceptions including nematodes and crustaceans, spermatogenesis produces a characteristic cell with a small, compact head and neck followed by a long, whiplike tail. The two principal functions of the sperm

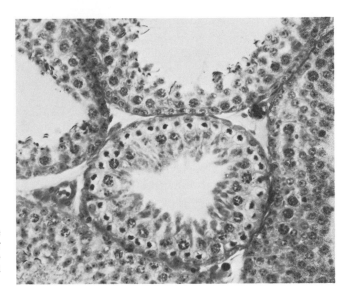

Figure 4.1 Cross section of a seminiferous tubule of a rat testis, showing outer enveloping cellular layer, basal layer of spermatogonia with dense nuclei, and inner layer of cells undergoing division and differentiation.

in sexual reproduction are to activate the egg to begin development and to contribute a haploid set of chromosomes to the diploid offspring. In addition the sperm typically provides a centriole to the fertilized egg, which is used in the mitotic divisions that follow fertilization.

The typical structural unit of the vertebrate testis, and of many invertebrate gonads as well, is the tubule. A cross section of a seminifcrous tubule is shown in Fig. 4.1. If the cells of the tubule are examined, obvious differences can be seen; these different cells are organized in a predictable way. There is a sequence that proceeds roughly from the outer edge of the tubule, where cells that have not yet begun spermatogenesis are found, to the inner cells where the process has been completed. The outer wall of the tubule is made of several layers (Fig. 4.2). It serves as an effective barrier to separate the developing

Figure 4.2 Semischematic figure showing small segment of the wall of an active seminiferous tubule. The sequence of events in the production of spermia is indicated by the numbers. A spermatogonium (1) goes into mitosis (2), producing two daughter cells (2a and 2b). One daughter cell (2a) may remain peripherally located as a new spermatogonium, eventually coming to occupy such a position as 1a. The other daughter cell (2b) may grow into a primary spermatoctye (3), being crowded meanwhile nearer the lumen of the tubule. When fully grown, the primary spermatocyte will divide again (4) and produce two secondary spermatocytes (5), (5). Each secondary spermatocyte at once divides again (6), (6), producing spermatids (7). The spermatids become embedded in the tip of a Sertoli cell (7a), there undergoing their metamorphosis and becoming spermia (8) which, when mature, are detached into the lumen of the seminiferous tubule. [*From Patten and Carlson, 3d ed., "Foundations of Embryology," McGraw-Hill, 1974.*]

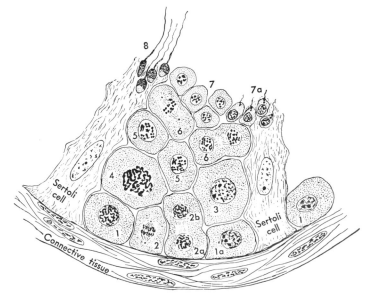

germ cells from the other body tissues and to provide the proper microenvironment for spermatogenesis to occur. For example, in sheep tubules there is less Na^+, more K^+ and Cl^-, much more glutamic acid, more aspartic acid, glycine, and alanine, but less of all other amino acids than in the plasma of the blood.

In the outer layer of cells are found the spermatogonia, cells that have yet to begin the process of meiosis; yet most of them are already irreversibly on the path leading to the final differentiated state. The spermatogonia arise from cells set aside very early during embryonic development, the primordial germ cells, which are destined to form the male gametes at a much later time. In many cases cytoplasm of the primordial germ cells can be traced back very early in development, in some cases back to the fertilized egg itself. These primordial germ cells divide mitotically, find their way into the gonad, and become the spermatogonia, the future stock of gametes for the animal.

In mammals, spermatogenesis typically proceeds in cycles of activity and the spermatogonia in one region of a tubule are typically at the same stage in this cycle. Adjacent regions are often in the next stage, and waves of spermatogenesis can be found along the length of the tubules of many mammals. At the start of the process in the rat, the spermatogonia can be identified as A_1 spermatogonia. This type of cell divides twice to form four A_2 spermatogonia. One of these four becomes a cell that remains dormant and does not divide again until another cycle of spermatogenesis commences. In a sense, therefore, this cell acts as a replacement for the cell that originated the cycle. The process of spermatogenesis usually continues throughout the adult life of the animal. Replacements must be set aside or all the potential germ cells will rapidly be exhausted and no new primordial germ cells will arise during the animal's lifetime.

The other three A_2 cells divide mitotically into six intermediate cells, which in turn divide mitotically into twelve B_1 cells and then into twenty-four B_2 cells. In man, seven distinct classes of spermatogonia are to be found. These different spermatogonia can be identified by their cytologic appearance and their diminishing size after each division. (Doubling of cell volume before mitosis does not occur as in most cell lines.)

After the last spermatogonial division, the nature of the cell changes; rather than prepare for another mitosis, it grows in volume and becomes a primary spermatocyte (no longer a spermatogonium); it has entered meiosis. Presumably some mechanism has kept track of the number of mitotic divisions that lead to the primary spermatocyte stage.

MEIOSIS

Cells remain in the primary spermatocyte stage for a period of time during which there is a sequence of events that make up the steps of the first meiotic division. The first step after the last mitotic division is the replication of the DNA, followed by a period recognizable as G_2. Then the prophase of the first meiotic division occurs, which can be divided into several stages. The events of meiosis described here for the primary spermatocyte are similar in the primary oocyte of the female. In meiosis two divisions follow one round of replication, and the chromosome number is reduced. Before meiosis each cell contains a pair of each of the homologous chromosomes, while after meiosis only one of each chromosome type is found per haploid cell.

The first stage in the meiotic prophase is called *leptotene* (Fig. 4.3). Since the chromosomes have been replicated, each must be composed of two iden-

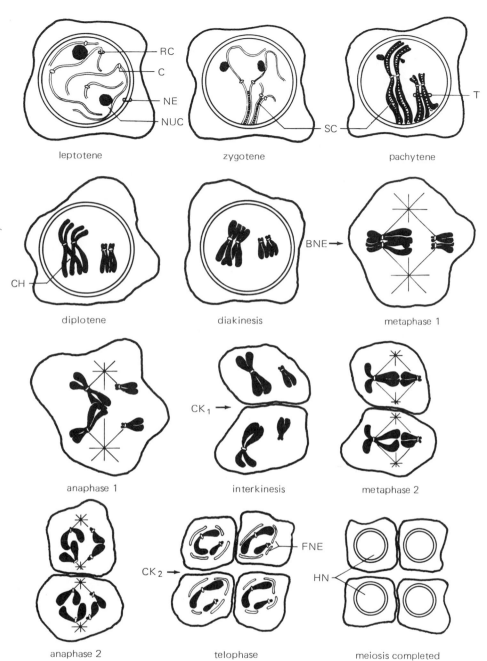

Figure 4.3 Stages of meiosis. BNE, breakdown of nuclear envelope; C, centromere; CH, chiasmata; CK₁ and CK₂, cytokinesis; FNE, formation of nuclear envelope; HN, haploid nuclei; NE, nuclear envelope; NUC, nucleolus; RC, replicated leptotene chromosomes; SC, synaptonemal complex; T, tetrad. [*After F. Longo and E. Anderson, 1974.*]

tical partners attached together by the centromere. Each of these is referred to as a chromatid and the complex is called a chromosome. In the leptotene stage, the very diffuse threads of chromatin that make up the interphase chromosome become thicker and thicker as a result of some process of contraction. As the chromosomes thicken and become visible, the homologous chromosomes—each consisting of the two identical chromatids—seek each other out in some unknown way.

The stage of the first meiotic prophase during which pairing occurs is zygotene; it is characterized by the close pairing of the homologous chromosomes. After the homologous chromosomes first make contact, a process termed *synapsis* occurs, in which the pair of homologues appear to become pressed together along their length, not unlike a zipper pulling both edges together. Since each chromosome is made of two identical chromatids, each of these zipped-up complexes consists of four chromatids called a *tetrad*. Another name for this is a *bivalent*. This condition persists through the next stage, *pachytene*, during which the bivalents appear to grow thicker. The number of tetrads in the cell will be equal to the haploid number of chromosomes in that species (23 in man).

A characteristic structure of pachytene chromosomes that is found in both spermatocytes and oocytes is called the *synaptonemal complex* (Fig. 4.4). When tetrads are examined in the electron microscope, they are seen to be closely intertwined with a ladderlike structure composed of three parallel bars with many cross fibers connecting the central bar with the two lateral ones. If the chromatin is digested away with DNase, the structure of the synaptonemal complex remains, suggesting it provides a structural framework in which the paired chromosomes are kept very close together for the required time. Though the exact function of the synaptonemal complex is unknown, presumably it is required for the events of the next stage to occur.

Figure 4.4 Electron micrographs of the synaptonemal complex. *a* Low-power micrograph showing the chromatin fibers of the pachytene chromosomes surrounding the ladderlike synaptonemal complex. *b* Higher-power micrograph of the synaptonemal complex after DNase treatment to remove chromosomal fibers. [*Courtesy of D. Comings and T. Okada.*]

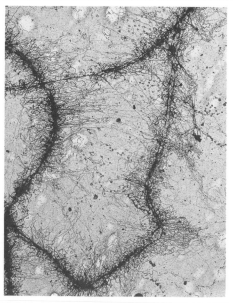 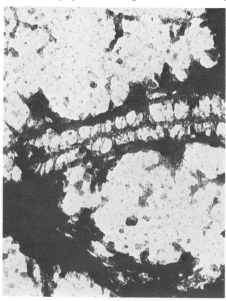

a   b

One of the important events of the first meiotic prophase is *crossing-over,* believed to occur during pachytene. In crossing-over there is actual breakage and exchange of chromosomal material. Crossing-over occurs between one of the two chromatids of each homologous chromosome of the tetrad. A piece of one chromatid of the maternally derived chromosome is transferred to the paternally derived chromosome in exchange for the identical piece from the other member of the pair. By this process there is a mixing of the genetic material (*genetic recombination*) that had originally come into the fertilized egg on different chromosomes. The end products of crossing-over are therefore chromosomes of mixed maternal and paternal genes. In this way the variation that can be passed on to the offspring, on which natural selection can act, is greatly increased.

If each of the products of meiosis is to have a complete set of all of the genes, it is essential that identical corresponding fragments of chromosomes are exchanged. In some cases mistakes are made; the result is one chromatid with extra genes, a duplication, and another chromatid with missing genes, a deletion. The manner in which this precision is achieved is unknown, but the synaptonemal complex may play an important role in the process.

After a period of tight apposition, the homologous chromosomes appear to separate and remain attached just at specific points called *chiasmata.* It is only at this *diplotene* stage, when the chromosomes have come apart from each other along most of their length, that the two chromatids of each chromosome are distinctly visible. The chiasmata of diplotene are thought to represent the points on the chromosome where crossing-over has occurred, though there does not appear to be a one-to-one correspondence between the number of chiasmata and the number of crossing-over events. During diplotene, in both spermatocytes and oocytes of many species, the chromosomes take on a distinct appearance and are called *lampbrush chromosomes.* This unusual chromosomal structure has been very important in genetic analysis and is discussed at length in a later section of this chapter. In both sexes, but particularly in the oocyte, the diplotene stage is an extended and an active one.

Following diplotene, the chromosomes become thickened and the chiasmata disappear by a sliding down the length of the chromosome. This is the last stage of prophase, called *diakinesis,* being completed with the disappearance of the nucleolus and the nuclear membrane and the movement of the tetrads to the metaphase plate.

The completion of the process of meiosis is as follows: During anaphase I the homologous chromosomes separate from each other. Since there is no interaction among the various tetrads, each one segregates into the two daughter cells in a manner independent of the other ones. It follows, therefore, that even in the absence of crossing-over there are a great number of genetically different gametes that can be produced. In man, with a haploid number of 23, there can be 2^{23} or nearly 10 million different gametes in one individual. Crossing-over with recombination raises this value to an essentially infinite possibility.

The first meiotic division produces two cells; each cell has only one of each of the original pair of homologous chromosomes, though at this point they have been greatly mixed together by crossing-over. Each chromosome at this stage is composed of two chromatids that are no longer identical with one another, as a result of the recombination of crossing-over. Telophase I occurs, and a short interphase termed *interkinesis* follows. These cells are now called secondary spermatocytes, a fleeting stage, and therefore they are rarely found in the tubules.

Interkinesis is followed by prophase II, a much simpler prophase than its predecessor. The chromosomes merely thicken and line up at the equatorial plane; the chromatids become separated in anaphase II as each centromere holding the pair is split in half. Four haploid cells, called *spermatids*, are produced from each primary spermatocyte and each will subsequently produce a mature spermatozoan.

A series of experiments by Stern and others have shed considerable light on certain of the molecular activities of the events occurring during the first meiotic prophase, and they pose numerous additional questions. In the above discussion it was stated that replication of the DNA occurred prior to prophase; this does not appear to be the complete truth. If one provides a population of meiotic cells (the best-studied are those of the lily) with ^{3}H-thymidine, the cells take up the isotope and incorporate it into ^{3}H-DNA during first meiotic prophase. This occurs after the period of premeiotic replication when all the DNA, according to dogma, should have been already synthesized. In the case of the lily, only about 0.3 percent of the total DNA is made during first meiotic prophase, the remaining 99.7 percent being synthesized during the S period preceding the first meiotic prophase.

This DNA synthesis, which is seen in autoradiographs to involve all the chromosomes, occurs during the zygotene and pachytene stages. These DNAs have been analyzed in several ways; Hotta and Stern (1971) conclude that the early DNA synthesis of zygotene represents synthesis of DNA that had not been previously replicated during interphase. In other words, for some reason a small amount of the DNA of the genome is left unreplicated until prophase. In contrast, the DNA synthesized during pachytene is DNA that had already been made during previous interphase and is now being made again. Pachytene DNA synthesis is unusual in that it is not a semiconservative replication as is the typical means of DNA synthesis; instead, it is similar to a repair type of replication where only one of the two strands is replicated in relatively short stretches. This latter type of replication is typically used by the cell to repair short damaged areas, such as those that occur after radiation.

The question of primary importance concerns the role of meiotic prophase synthesis of DNA in the meiotic process. If DNA synthesis is inhibited at various times during the prophase period, specific abnormalities are seen to arise. If the cells are treated with the inhibitor deoxyadenosine during early zygotene, the pairing of homologous chromosomes is arrested and the synaptonemal complex does not form. These results suggest that the process of association of meiotic chromosomes might require DNA replication at selected points on the chromosomes. If the inhibitor is not applied until midzygotene, meiosis proceeds, but is characterized by extensive chromosome fragmentation and other chromosome abnormalities. If DNA synthesis is allowed to proceed until late zygotene before deoxyadenosine is applied, chromosome breakage is not extensive until separation of the chromatids from each other (anaphase II), at which time severe abnormalities are seen. These workers speculate that the repair-type DNA synthesized during pachytene might be involved in the crossing-over process occurring at this time. Though definitive conclusions concerning causality are difficult to make from studies utilizing inhibitors, the mechanism of genetic recombination during meiosis is likely to be one of the key elements in this synthetic puzzle.

In related studies, other factors have been described that underlie basic events of meiosis in the lily. The decision to undergo meiosis can still be reversed in G_2 and mitosis can be made to occur, even though a small fraction of the DNA had not been replicated. In the first part of the G_2, the cells can be induced to undergo mitosis (they finish making their missing DNA first), but after a time they are capable of only a meiotic division. Some determining step seems to occur in the G_2 that excludes a nonmeiotic division.

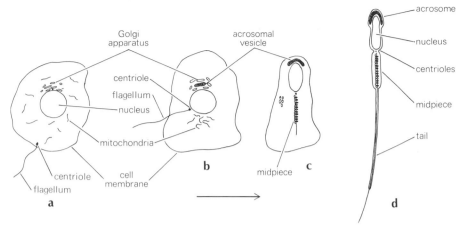

Figure 4.5 Spermiogenesis. *a* Activity involving the Golgi apparatus (acrosome) and special activity by one or both centrioles, both in flagellum formation and in movement to and from nucleus and cell membrane. *b* Localization and growth of mitochondria relative to flagellum axis, and acrosome formation. *c* Nuclear condensation, or compaction, and shoping by or of the cell membrane. *d* Discard of residual cytoplasm, resulting in final form of spermatozoon.

SPERMIOTELIOSIS (SPERMIOGENESIS)

We have followed spermatogenesis to a point where four relatively simple, spherical cells have been produced. The process that converts each spermatid into the characteristic structure of the sperm is called *spermioteliosis* or *spermiogenesis,* a subdivision of spermatogenesis (Fig. 4.5). The final product, the spermatozoan, is a marvelously constructed cell; it shows a remarkable uniformity of structure, with conspicuous exceptions, from lower invertebrates to mammals (Fig. 4.6). The main structural subdivisions are the head, midpiece, and tail. All are contained—as in living cells generally—by a continuous plasma membrane. Freeze-etch and electron micrographs of the surface and the structure of a sperm, respectively, are shown in Figs. 4.7 and 4.9. The whole cell is streamlined and pared down for action of a special sort and of limited duration. Its mission is to swim to the egg, to fuse with its surface, and to introduce its nucleus and centriole into the egg interior.

Structure and Formation of the Sperm

The sperm head contains two main parts, the *nucleus* and the *acrosome.* The nucleus of the sperm head is the ultimate in chromosome compactness. In going from the spermatid to the spermatozoon, the nucleus loses its entire fluid content, all its RNA, and most of its protein. Only one macromolecule escapes unscathed, its haploid amount of DNA. In some cases the proteins associated with the DNA are replaced by an unusual class of small, basic proteins called *protamines.* These molecules are characterized by high levels of one basic amino acid, arginine, as much as two-thirds of the amino acids in some cases. Presumably this type of protein helps in condensing the chromatin into the least possible space and therefore offering the least possible resistance to transport. In some sperm heads the DNA is actually in a near-crystalline state.

Evidence suggests that the chromosomes remain in small regions within the nucleus, rather than being spread throughout. For example, in the grasshopper, if the X chromosome, which replicates very late in the premeiotic S

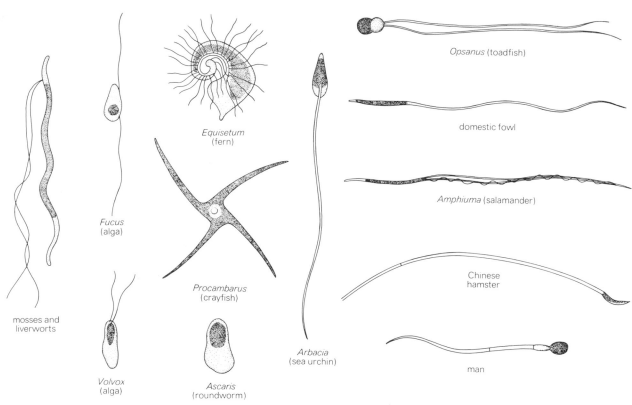

mosses and
liverworts

Fucus
(alga)

Volvox
(alga)

Equisetum
(fern)

Procambarus
(crayfish)

Ascaris
(roundworm)

Arbacia
(sea urchin)

Opsanus (toadfish)

domestic fowl

Amphiuma (salamander)

Chinese
hamster

man

Figure 4.6 Forms of spermatozoa. Plant sperm typically have two flagella, although in ferns and some others the flagella are numerous. Animal sperm typically have a single flagellum, occasionally two flagella, as in the toadfish, and in certain groups none at all, as in nematode worms such as *Ascaris*.

Figure 4.7 Surface replica after freeze-fracture treatment of a buffalo sperm. *a* Low-power micrograph showing acrosomal bulge (**Ac**) and the postnuclear sheath (**S**). *b* Higher magnification showing the postnuclear sheath, which fuses with the egg. [*Courtesy of J. Koehler.*]

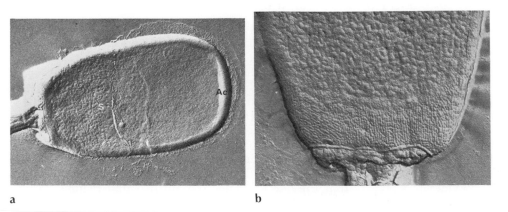

a

b

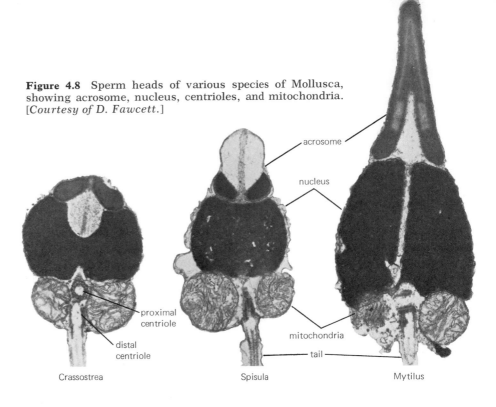

Figure 4.8 Sperm heads of various species of Mollusca, showing acrosome, nucleus, centrioles, and mitochondria. [*Courtesy of D. Fawcett.*]

acrosome

nucleus

proximal centriole

distal centriole

mitochondria

tail

Crassostrea

Spisula

Mytilus

phase, is labeled with ³H-thymidine, all the silver grains are localized in one region of the elongate sperm head. The acrosome of the sperm comes in various shapes (Fig. 4.8), but generally forms a cap over the sperm tip, as shown in Fig. 4.9. The acrosome forms by a complex process (described in most histology books) from the Golgi apparatus and contains a series of hydrolytic enzymes, much like the contents of a lysosome. The acrosome makes first contact with the egg in the act of fertilization. Behind the head is the midpiece, which varies greatly among different species. In rabbit spermatozoa, e.g., it consists mainly of a tightly coiled spiral of mitochondria surrounding the anterior part of the tail; in the sea urchin, a single mitochondrion wraps around the posterior part of the nucleus and adjacent part of the tail. Whatever the mitochondrial apparatus may be, it almost certainly supplies the energy required for the motility of the tail. This energy is limited and once expended, it apparently cannot be renewed. Spermatozoa are launched, so to speak, like torpedoes with limited range. If they do not reach the egg within the allotted time, they exhaust their supplies and die. In mammals they are aided in traversing the long distance through the female reproductive tubes by the contractions of the wall of the tube.

In the midpiece, within the mitochondrial ring, two centrioles are typically pressed against the posterior edge of the nucleus (Fig. 4.10). Centrioles usually are seen in pairs with one at right angles to the other. In the sperm the anterior centriole, or proximal centriole, typically is donated to the egg and helps in forming the first mitotic spindle after fertilization. The posterior centriole, or distal centriole, is responsible for the formation of the microtubules of the sperm tail.

Centrioles generally function as a site of the polymerization of microtubule subunits into long microtubules. The centriole itself shows the peripheral ring

89

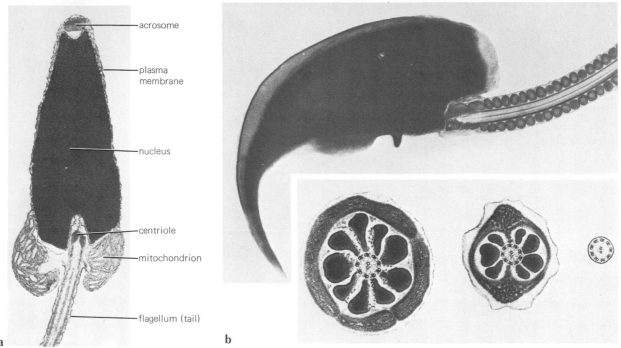

| acrosome |
| plasma membrane |
| nucleus |
| centriole |
| mitochondrion |
| flagellum (tail) |

a

b

Figure 4.9 Electron micrographs comparing sea urchin sperm (*a*) with mammalian sperm (*b*). Mammalian sperm shown as head with curved acrosome, nucleus, and middle piece surrounded by mitochondria, together with successive cross sections of tail, showing typical internal 9 + 2 tubule organization and outer ring of coarse fibers. [*Courtesy of D. Fawcett.*]

of nine triplets from which nine doublets and central pair of microtubules arise; this arrangement is imposed upon the structure of the tail. The manner in which the microtubules are put together into these long pipes is not completely known, but is currently the focus of considerable research. The sperm tail in cross section appears very similar to that of any other flagellum, although in the mammalian sperm and some other kinds, there is an additional outer ring of nine more fibers of a much thicker nature. The inner 9 + 2 group is called the *axial filament* or *axoneme*. The sperm tail provides the force for sperm

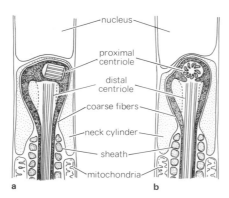

| nucleus |
| proximal centriole |
| distal centriole |
| coarse fibers |
| neck cylinder |
| sheath |
| mitochondria |

a   b

Figure 4.10 Vertical selections of snake spermatozoon, (*a*) parallel and (*b*) at right angles to the long axis of the proximal centriole. [*After C. R. Austin, "Fertilization," 1965. By permission of Prentice-Hall, Inc., Englewood Cliffs, N. J.*]

locomotion. One of the last events in this transformation is the elimination of the remaining unnecessary cytoplasm from the sperm.

If we reexamine the contents of the seminiferous tubule shown in Fig. 4.1, one type of cell is seen to stretch all the way from the outer to the inner edge. Cells of this type are found in many different groups of animals; in mammals they are called *Sertoli cells* (Fig. 4.2) after their discoverer. The Sertoli cells are the only ones within the tubule that are not derived from the primordial germ cells, and the reproductive cells are pressed tightly up against the wall of these special cells. The exact function of the Sertoli cells is not known, but they are generally assigned the role of support, protection, and/or nutrition for the developing gametes. Each germ cell passes up the length of a Sertoli cell as it goes from its earliest spermatogonial stage to its final differentiation into a mature spermatozoa.

Through much of spermatogenesis, distinct bridges exist between clusters of reproductive cells, i.e., actual physical openings between cells where no plasma membrane is found. These intercellular openings arise during the mitotic divisions of the spermatogonia by an incomplete separation of the cells at each telophase. As a result, all the members of a clone—i.e., those cells originally derived from one A_1 spermatogonium—remain in direct cytoplasmic contact with each other. No openings are seen to the Sertoli cells. It is believed that this direct communication between reproductive cells is responsible for the synchrony found for the differentiation of all the members of the clone. In other words, all the descendants of the primary spermatogonial cells go through the same steps at the same time.

In plants the final differentiation of the motile, male gamete is somewhat different. There is no acrosome, for the sperm cell does not have to make its way through specialized egg membranes. More striking, in ferns and cycads, is the development of a ciliated band around the cell. In the spermatid the centrioles multiply until a large number are formed; these become arranged in rows, and each then produces a cilium. As in animal sperm differentiation, however, the residual cytoplasm is shed after the general structure of the mature cell has been formed.

Although in animals meiosis always precedes differentiation of spermatozoa, in plants it may be far removed in time and phase. Accordingly we may conclude, provisionally at least, that although spermioteliosis follows meiosis during the production of spermatozoa, the two phenomena are essentially independent and meiosis as such has no causal relationship to sperm differentiation.

Nuclear Control of Spermioteliosis

Analysis of reproductive processes provides a unique opportunity for the study of chromosomal, and therefore genetic, activity. In mammals, for example, the female of the sex is XX and the male, XY. Presumably all genetic differences between the sexes can ultimately be traced to this single chromosomal difference. Since the male has all the genes, including those responsible for female reproductive structures, male development must occur in a way that represses female-specific genes. In contrast, development of male structures in the mammal could result from the fact that there is only one X chromosome (there are two in the female) or from the presence of male-specific Y genes. Because in humans, a person with one X chromosome and no Y chromosome develops as an immature female, it can be presumed that the presence of the Y chromosome is somehow responsible for male differentiations and therefore directly, or indirectly, for spermatogenesis.

What evidence of a direct nature exists linking the Y genes to spermatogenesis? The best information comes from studies on *Drosophila*. Presumably, similar principles hold in other cases. As mentioned earlier, in the diplotene stages of gametogenesis, the chromosomes may assume a very unusual configuration called the lampbrush state. Lampbrush chromosomes are fully described in the discussion of oogenesis, where they have been best studied. In brief, however, chromatin loops containing DNA are present along each chromosome; each loop apparently represents an actively transcribing set of genes (or gene present in numerous copies). Autoradiographs made of such chromosomes after administration of ^{3}H-uridine indicate that RNA synthesis is occurring on these genes. In *Drosophila hydei* the Y chromosome forms six giant loops in the primary spermatocyte stage. If any of these loops are absent, the end result is an abnormal, infertile sperm. This provides clear evidence that at least six genes on the Y chromosome are needed for the normal events of spermatogenesis to occur.

How can the genes of the Y chromosome be needed for spermiogenesis, when this process occurs after both meiotic divisions, a time when half the spermatids no longer possess the Y chromosome? To restate this paradox, X and Y chromosomes are separated in the first meiotic division; yet the spermatozoa that differentiate from the secondary spermatocyte receiving the X, not the Y, produce normal sperm. How, then, can the Y be needed? The answer to this puzzle seems to involve a phenomenon that will recur again and again in analysis of developing systems, that of stable, stored mRNAs. It appears that the protein synthesis going on during spermiogenesis uses mRNA templates that were made in the primary spermatocyte stage before the time the X and Y chromosomes were separated. This RNA is thus made at an early stage, stored for a considerable period of time, and then translated when the chromosome is no longer present. Studies with labeled RNA precursors suggest that RNA synthesis does not occur after the meiotic divisions.

OOGENESIS

The female gamete, the ovum or egg, arises by oogenesis; the process bears little relation to its counterpart in the opposite sex, apart from the meiotic process that occurs in both. The growing egg is known as an *oocyte,* or *egg cell.* To understand oogenesis, one must consider that the goal is to produce a cell capable of development after oogenesis has been completed. The events of oogenesis must be interpreted with the hindsight gained from the analysis of the postfertilization process.

The egg in all animals is large by comparison with the other cells of the body and is characterized by two important features, the presence of a blueprint for development and the means to construct an embryo from that blueprint. In other words, an egg has to be programmed and packaged during oogenesis. The *program* is in the form of molecular information somehow coded into the structure of the egg. It provides a potential for that cell to unfold—through a predictable sequence of changes—from a relatively simple, homogeneous-appearing cell into the complex preadult form. Since it is from the egg that this transformation springs, it must be within the organization of the egg that the directions are laid. The *packaging* refers to the presence within the egg of all the materials that will be needed to build the structures and provide the energy for the embryo up to the point where it can feed and therefore take in its own supporting nutrition.

Concerning the storage of developmental information, little is known in a direct sense, but many interesting observations have been made and experiments have been performed. A few of these will be discussed. The analysis of the storage of food reserves is an analysis of the biochemicals and of the microscopic structures involved; this opens the door to a very large array of macromolecules and ultrastructural observations made of oocytes of nearly every group. The cytoplasm of the oocyte is filled with many strange structures, and it is easy to become lost among all these forms.

As in spermatogenesis, the oocytes arise from primordial germ cells that are set aside very early in development and multiply by mitosis to form a population of oogonia, from which the oocytes will arise. In most chordates (the exceptions are among the amphibians and teleosts) all the oogonial divisions are completed and the meiotic prophase has begun before any of the oocytes become mature. In the human female, for example, all the potential future eggs of that individual have entered the meiotic prophase at approximately the time of birth, and no reserve oogonia remain. Many of these primary oocytes will remain in this stage of meiosis for several decades. Oogenesis, therefore, is not necessarily a continuous process as spermatogenesis is in the male. Rather, a primary oocyte population is maintained and a number of oocytes become mature as required.

Oogenesis in Amphibia

The mature amphibian egg is rather large (up to about 1.5 mm in diameter) and therefore must undergo a tremendous growth phase to carry it from its initially small size of less than 50 μm in diameter. The oocyte begins its development in a manner analogous to a primary spermatocyte by entering into the first meiotic prophase. In *Xenopus*, the widely used African clawed frog, e.g., the premeiotic S phase takes from 1 to 2 weeks, leptotene from 3 to 7 days, zygotene from 5 to 9 days, and pachytene about 20 days. The following stage, diplotene, is a very extended one during which most of the growth of both the nucleus and the cytoplasm of the oocyte occurs. If the diplotene stage nucleus is examined, the chromosomes are found to be in the lampbrush state. Lampbrush chromosomes are found in a wide variety of both invertebrates and vertebrates (including humans), though the basis for assigning this label to a given oocyte is not always clear. Figure 4.11 shows a micrograph of these chromosomes and representative diagrams.

Lampbrush chromosomes consist of an axial backbone from which pairs of loops extend out in opposite directions. Loops arise in pairs because each member of the pair is part of one of the two chromatids that make up each chromosome. The two homologous chromosomes remain attached to each other at the chiasmata. This is an unusual configuration for chromosomes to take, but it appears well-suited for the job at hand. The backbone of the chromosomes contains DNA and tightly associated protein and is transcriptionally inactive. The evidence suggests that the loops are made of one double-stranded DNA molecule, attached at both ends to the backbone at specific sites. At the base of the loops can be found a swelling (also containing DNA and protein) called a *chromomere*, from which the DNA is believed to be "spun out." Associated with the DNA is a considerable amount of RNA and protein, which give these loops a variety of appearances under the microscope. In the newt *Triturus* there are approximately 5,000 loops present at a given time of oogenesis per haploid set of chromosomes and, therefore, 20,000 per oocyte

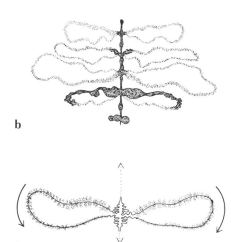

b

c

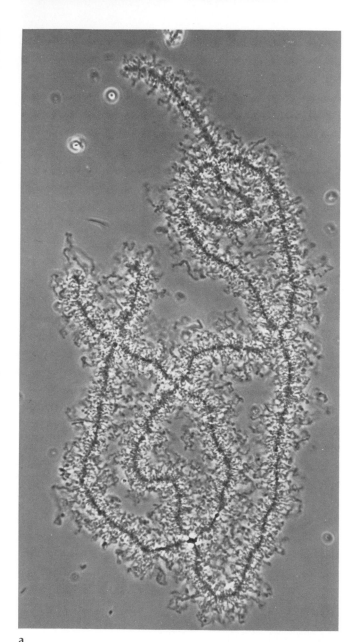

a

Figure 4.11 *a* Photomicrograph showing lampbrush chromosomes. [*Courtesy of J. G. Gall.*] *b* Diagrammatic representation of a section of a lampbrush chromosome showing paired loops emerging from the backbone. *c* Model of possible loop movement. A pair of loops extend from the chromosome axis, the chromomere uncoiling at one end and rewinding at the other, with RNA synthesis taking place along the loop axis as it unwinds. [*After Gall, 1963, and Wischnitzer, 1967.*]

nucleus. Each of these loops contains from 50 to 100 μm of DNA, an amount sufficient to code for many proteins. The question has been raised as to whether each loop is made of repeated copies of one or a few genes, or do they consist of an array of many different genes. We do not know for certain; but recent findings of the interspersion of repeated and unique sequences, the identification of the genes for messenger RNAs among those present in one or a very few copies, and the belief that the mRNA represents a small part of a much larger transcribed product add a much greater level of complexity to this question.

One investigative advantage of oocytes, amphibian in particular, is their size. It is a simple procedure to take an oocyte, place it in a depression on a slide, and—with a pair of fine forceps—break open both the oocyte and its nuclear membrane, thereby liberating the chromosomes into a drop of culture medium. If a radioactively labeled precursor of RNA (such as ^{3}H-uridine) is added, the sites of RNA synthesis can be determined by autoradiography (see Chapter 25). When this is done, the autoradiograph shows that the loop structures are the sites of intense incorporation of ^{3}H-uridine into RNA. As implied above, the backbone is unlabeled. Here, as in the electron micrographs of Miller, is an opportunity to observe directly the process of transcription. The presence of a loop appears to indicate gene activity. The question that is raised is: What part of the genome is actually being transcribed in these cells?

This is a basic question in the molecular biology of development. If the answer can be obtained, we are provided with a measure of how many genes are involved in programming the egg at the time of fertilization. Presumably, the transcriptional efforts of oogenesis provide the informational structure of the egg that will carry it through the early stages of development. Two approaches have been taken; the earlier one utilized an indirect analysis of the lampbrush chromosome, particularly by Gall, Callan, and coworkers; the other was a direct analysis of the oocyte RNA, particularly by Davidson and his colleagues.

Many species of salamanders have great quantities of DNA in their genomes, and as a result they have very large chromosomes that are easily studied microscopically. This extra DNA is present in the repeated fraction of the genome and presumably represents a greater number of copies of each of these genes. Results of the earlier investigations suggested that each loop of a chromosome was a continually moving strand of DNA. This DNA was believed to be spun out from the chromomere at one attachment point of the loop to the chromomere and to be reeled in at the other end (Fig. 4.11c). The average loop contains about 50 to 100 μm of DNA. It was estimated that it took about 10 days for a loop to be completely replaced with new DNA. The average lampbrush stage lasted about 6 months, and it was estimated that about 5 percent of the DNA of each chromomere was in the loop at any time.

If all these numbers are put together with the number of loops per set of chromosomes, the calculation can be made that approximately 9 m of DNA would be transcribed during oogenesis. This calculation fits very well with the known amount of DNA in these chromosomes; explicit in this view is that the entire genome in these amphibians is transcribed during oogenesis. This concept of total gene transcription during oogenesis has been integrated into a more general theory of gene organization (Callan, 1967), rather than being just a requirement for the programming of the amphibian egg.

Evidence derived from DNA-RNA hybridization in a different amphibian (described below) suggests that total transcription does not occur. If it does not, then the concept of extensive loop movement may be incorrect. If there were no movement, approximately 5 percent rather than 100 percent of the DNA would be transcribed. Presumably these represent the two extremes of possibility.

The other approach to this question has focused on the RNAs made during oogenesis in *Xenopus*. The genome of higher animals contains a repeated fraction (approximately 45 percent of total DNA in *Xenopus*) and a nonrepeated (unique) fraction (approximately 55 percent in *Xenopus*). Studies using DNA-RNA hybridization (see Chapter 25) have been performed with oocyte RNA and both fractions of DNA. It is estimated that the RNA present in the mature oocyte is complementary to at least 1.2 percent of the nonrepeated genes and up to about 7 percent of the repeated genes. DNA-RNA hybridization using the repeated fraction has inherent difficulties of interpretation, and therefore this latter value must be considered carefully. The reason is that among the repeated genes, one gene might be serving as a template for RNA synthesis, while during hybridization this species of RNA can bind to all the identical or related base sequences in the repeated DNA. The resulting hybridization value for repeated DNA may therefore be a greatly exaggerated one. If we consider only the value for nonrepeated DNA, this would represent a sufficient number of different genes to code for approximately 20,000 to 40,000 typical polypeptide chains.

A related question concerns the percentage of the RNA in the mature oocyte that might be utilized for the programming of the egg, as opposed to being part of the stockpile of ribosomal and transfer RNAs. Surprisingly, the percentage of RNA left over after these noninformational (nonheterogeneous) RNAs have been taken away is relatively small. Approximately 1 percent of the total RNA stockpile of the mature oocyte has a potential informational role. Of this 1 percent, from 90 to 99 percent has been transcribed from repeated genes, leaving a very small amount of RNA representing the nonrepeated DNA fraction. Because 1.2 percent of the unique DNA sequences is represented in this small amount of RNA, there must be relatively few copies of each sequence present in contrast with those transcribed from the repeated fraction of the genome. The bulk of the RNA of the oocyte, over 95 percent, is ribosomal.

Because rRNA synthesis is found only in conjunction with the nucleolus, we must examine the oocyte nucleoli to explain this accumulation of rRNA. Somatic cells of amphibians typically contain two nucleoli within the nucleus, one per haploid set of chromosomes. Since the growing amphibian oocyte remains for a long time in the prophase of the first meiotic division and, accordingly, is tetraploid, four nucleoli could be expected to be present. Yet in *Triturus, Siredon,* and *Xenopus,* there are up to 600, 1,000, and 1,200 nucleoli respectively.

If autoradiographs are made after incubation with ^{3}H-uridine, all of these hundreds of nucleoli are labeled, which suggests all of them are synthesizing rRNA. If each nucleolus is making rRNA, then presumably each nucleolus contains DNA that codes for this rRNA. Such DNA is termed rDNA. Several investigators have confirmed this hypothesis, and it appears certain that within these oocytes there is a selective gene amplification of the rDNA, as described on page 542.

Direct confirmation that the high-density DNA from oocyte nuclei is rDNA is its ability to hybridize with purified rRNA. Analysis of oocyte DNA from several other animals, including an echiuroid and a mollusk, similarly indicates a selective gene amplification for the ribosomal RNA genes. There is no corresponding increase in the numbers of copies of other genes, including the tRNAs; this case at present is the only example of selective gene amplification known to operate during differentiation.

Considering the rarity of selective gene amplification, can we justify the need for it in this present case? If we cannot, then presumably we do not understand the reason for its existence. During the period of growth, the amphibian oocyte has increased in diameter from about 50 μm to about 1.5 mm. This corresponds to an increased volume of about 27,000-fold. At the end of oogenesis, the cytoplasm of this giant cell is seen to contain a considerable complement of ribosomes, approximately 1.1×10^{12}. If no amplification were to occur, it has been estimated that the nearly 2,000 rDNA genes in a replicated set of chromosomes, working at maximum synthetic activity, would take approximately 500 years to accomplish this feat. Since the life span of a frog is well below this value, an alternate mechanism has evolved. Calculations suggest that no other species of RNA in these eggs is needed in sufficient numbers to require amplification of their DNA template.

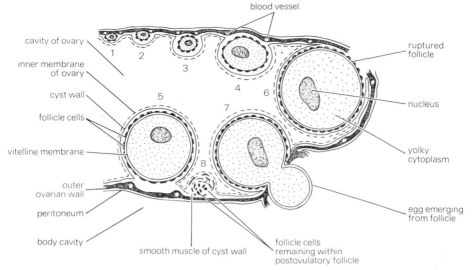

Figure 4.12 Lobe of frog ovary showing stages of growth of ovarian follicle, rupture of follicle, and ovulation. [*After C. D. Turner, "General Endocrinology," Saunders, Philadelphia, 1949.*]

Vitellogenesis It is during the lampbrush stage of oogenesis that the tremendous growth of the oocyte takes place (Figs. 4.12, 4.13). Oocyte volume increases about 100,000 times in *Rana* and 25,000 times in *Xenopus*. As the volume of the cytoplasm increases, the volume of the germinal vesicle increases as well, and the oocyte continues to stockpile the products of the nuclear activity described above. A point is reached where a new process begins, and the oocyte begins to deposit yolk in its cytoplasm as it continues to grow. Another point is reached where the lampbrush chromosomes retract their loops and condense; chromosomal RNA synthesis stops, though nucleolar rRNA synthesis and yolk deposition continue.

Yolk deposition, or *vitellogenesis*, in vertebrates usually is a process of the accumulation of material synthesized elsewhere in the body—particularly in

Figure 4.13 Growth of amphibian oocyte showing enormous accumulation of yolk granules proceeding from peripheral region inward. [*After Wischnitzer, 1966.*]

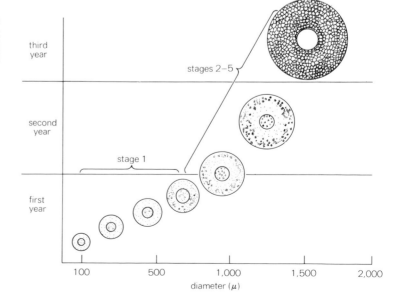

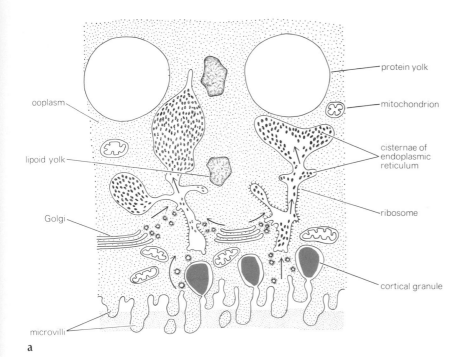

ooplasm

protein yolk

mitochondrion

cisternae of
endoplasmic
reticulum

lipoid yolk

ribosome

Golgi

cortical granule

microvilli

a

Figure 4.14 The processes involved in vitellogenesis. *a* Pinocytotic vesicles from the periphery fuse with the endoplasmic reticulum, and these are joined by vesicles from the Golgi apparatus. Material accumulates in the cisternae of the endoplasmic reticulum and eventually forms the protein spheres. [*After King, Bailey, and Babbage, 1969.*] *b* Freeze-etch replica of an unfertilized egg of the sea urchin egg of *Strongylocentrotus purpuratus.* Unfixed before freezing. In the upper part of the micrograph the plasma membrane, pm, is seen in surface view extending between and over the surfaces of the regularly spaced microvilli (mv) that project from the egg surface. In the lower part of the micrograph the fracture plane passes through the ooplasm, outlining the outer contour of a cortical granule (cg). × 64,000. [*Courtesy of W. J. Humphreys.*]

b

the liver—and transported by the blood to the oocyte. Yolk is a general term that covers the major storage material of the egg. Yolk can be mostly protein in content (proteid yolk) or mostly lipid (lipoid yolk) or both. Other materials are also included under the term "yolk."

Large protein molecules cannot directly penetrate the plasma membrane of the oocyte; therefore, some other mechanism must prevail. In the amphibians the yolk enters the oocyte by *micropinocytosis;* in this process, tiny regions of the plasma membrane move inward as vesicles that take the extracellular yolk macromolecules into the egg from the outside (Fig. 4.14). In amphibians the yolk macromolecule synthesized and secreted by the liver is a lipophosphoprotein, vitellogenin, which undergoes conversion in the oocyte into two molecules. One of these, phosvitin, is a protein with a high phosphate content (8.4 percent); the other, lipovitellin, is a lipoprotein with a lipid content of 17.5 percent. Together these molecules are organized into large crystalline structures called *yolk platelets.* Surrounding the crystalline portion of the platelet is a less dense material that may be polysaccharide. Associated with the yolk are enzymes that will be used after fertilization to break down these large storage molecules for use by the embryo. One of these enzymes, phosphoprotein phosphatase, splits off phosphate, thereby solubilizing the yolk protein. Another enzyme, a cathepsin, can then break down the protein. The deposition of yolk into the crystalline platelets begins in the periphery; the oocyte becomes filled from the outside to near the edge of the nucleus, where the process stops. At the end of oogenesis, the yolk platelets are larger and more tightly packed at one end of the egg, the *vegetal pole.* During this period, the oocyte is active in its own protein synthesis, though this contribution is small compared with that reaching the oocyte from the outside.

The nature of yolk formation and the general structuring of the cytoplasm vary greatly among animals (Fig. 4.15). Various cytoplasmic organelles—includ-

Figure 4.15 *a* Light micrograph of a thin section through molluskan oocytes. Note the large germinal vesicle (nucleus), the several nucleoli (each active in rRNA synthesis), the chromosomal material, and the cytoplasm, which has not yet begun to accumulate yolk. The small fraction of the much larger oocyte at the edge of the photograph illustrates the cytoplasm after it becomes filled with food reserve. [*G. Karp.*] *b* Electron micrograph of a portion of the cytoplasm of a hamster oocyte and adjacent follicle cell. In between these two cells the material of the zona pellucida is found being penetrated by the microvilli of the oocyte and the follicle cell. Clusters of mitochondria are seen within the cytoplasm of the oocyte. [*K. Selman.*]

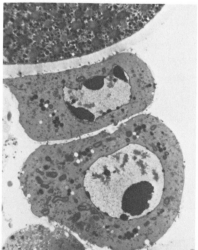

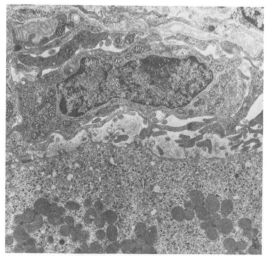

a   b

ing the endoplasmic reticulum, Golgi apparatus, and mitochondria—have been implicated in this process. As a result it becomes very dangerous to generalize these events for widely separated types of animals. One of the problems in analyzing results gained from the electron microscope is that one receives a series of completely static pictures of what we assume to be dynamic processes. As a result, we must attempt to put these various structures into action in our own mind's eye and to formulate a theory as to what they are doing. Objects from widely separated species, with a similar appearance in the electron microscope, become lumped together. If they are given the same name, the implication rapidly emerges that they have a similar function. This may not be justified.

In addition to yolk, other materials are included in the packaging. Carbohydrate is stored as glycogen and is present as dense cytoplasmic granules. Lipid accumulates with a thin, surrounding protein coat; these are termed *lipochondria*. Ribosomes are stored, using the rRNA made by the many nucleoli. Small pigment granules are incorporated into the surface layer of many amphibian eggs, though their distribution is not uniform. In addition, the cytoplasm contains a huge quantity of DNA—many times greater than that of the nucleus—which is associated, primarily at least, with the mitochondria. Mitochondrial DNA has become well known to cell biologists and, as in other types of cells, is presumably involved with mitochondrial function.

In those vertebrates that possess very large, yolky eggs— such as reptiles and birds—yolk deposition continues far beyond that of amphibians, until the true cytoplasm is only a very small fraction of the finished product.

We can follow all of these many examples of cytoplasmic packaging, but it is usually difficult to determine precisely the importance for development of each of these ingredients. In other words, at what point during embryonic development (if at all) does the stockpile become exhausted and the embryo become responsible for its own production of these materials? In the case of the store of ribosomes, an estimate can be provided. Mutants of *Xenopus* have been isolated whose chromosomes carry a deletion for the rDNA, have no nucleolus, and synthesize no rRNA. In the heterozygote condition, the cells produce normal quantities of rRNA. Heterozygous females produce oocytes with the typical number of ribosomes. After meiosis, half these oocytes will be left with the chromosome lacking the rDNA. If such an egg is fertilized by a sperm that is also a mutant, the embryo that develops will have no rDNA, i.e., it is anucleolate.

If these embryos that lack the ability to manufacture ribosomes are followed, an estimate can be obtained of the extent to which development can proceed solely on the ribosomes inherited from oogenesis. In the normal embryo, nucleoli appear and rRNA synthesis begins at gastrulation, 8 hours after fertilization. In these anucleolate mutants, development proceeds normally to the swimming tadpole stage (fourth day) and then they die. During this period, considerable protein synthesis and morphological changes occur in the absence of any new ribosomes; development proceeds well beyond the stage of gastrulation when new ribosomes normally appear.

Accessory Cells In most animals—though many exceptions exist—the development of the oocyte takes place with the aid of another type of cell, an *accessory cell*. There are two main types, the *nurse cell* and the *follicle cell*.

The nurse cell is found only in invertebrates, including some coelenterates, annelids, and insects. Nurse cells are derived from the same oogonium that gives rise to the oocyte. For example, in *Drosophila,* an oogonium undergoes 4 mitotic divisions, producing 16 cells. One of these becomes an oocyte and the remaining 15 become nurse cells. Nurse cells are connected to the oocyte by

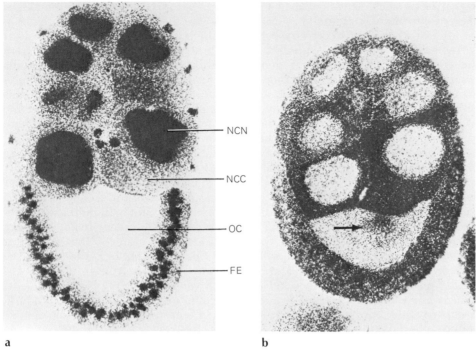

a   b

Figure 4.16 Autoradiographs of a follicle of the fly after incubation in ³H-cytidine. *a* Tissue fixed immediately after incubation with the label. Nurse cell nuclei are densely labeled, reflecting their role in providing newly synthesized RNA to the oocyte. The oocyte is unlabeled at this point. *b* A similar follicle fixed 5 hours after incubation with ³H-cytidine. Nurse cell nuclei no longer contain labeled RNA, which has moved out of the nucleus and has been replaced by newly synthesized RNA that is unlabeled. Labeled RNA is seen streaming into the oocyte cytoplasm through open channels between the two cells. NCN, nurse cell nuclei. NCC, nurse cell cytoplasm. OC, oocyte cytoplasm. FE, follicular epithelium. [*Courtesy of K. Bier.*]

direct cytoplasmic bridges, just as were the developing male reproductive cells. Through these openings, materials pass from the nurse cells into the oocyte, in which they are stockpiled. Nurse cells, therefore, bear much of the responsibility for the synthesis of materials of the unfertilized egg. If ³H-cytidine is provided to a female fly, it becomes incorporated into RNA. If autoradiographs (see Chapter 25) are made of the ovaries of these flies after a short exposure to this labeled RNA precursor, the nuclei of the nurse cells (Fig. 4.16) are strikingly labeled, indicating their intense RNA synthesis. The oocyte nucleus is unlabeled. If several hours elapse after the injection of an isotope, before the fly is killed, this labeled RNA has left the nurse cell nucleus and is found in the nurse cell cytoplasm, streaming into the oocyte through the intercellular bridges.

Such autoradiographs elegantly illustrate the advantage that can be gained through the use of an isotope. The injection of the ³H-cytidine provides a zero time for a process that normally is a continuum and has no starting point, and is therefore difficult to follow with only the microscope as a tool. This pair of micrographs tell clearly what is being made, where it is made, and what the fate of this material is. The longer we wait after injection, the farther the process has continued from our zero point, and we can easily follow the fate of the newly synthesized RNA molecules. In addition, if no new isotope becomes available, RNA synthesis will begin to produce molecules that are unlabeled. In this case we can then determine how long it takes to clear the old labeled RNA molecules out of the nucleus. This is clearly seen in Fig. 4.16, where grains are no longer present over nurse cell nuclei.

The other type of accessory cell, the follicle cell, is the accessory cell of vertebrates and many other groups. In vertebrates, these cells are derived from the germinal epithelium. They generally surround the oocyte; the materials entering the oocyte from the blood stream, such as yolk proteins, must presumably pass through the membranes of the follicle cells on the way. These cells, therefore, must in some way act as a screening influence to determine what materials will be allowed through. To facilitate this transfer process, there are projections reaching out from the surfaces of both the oocyte and the follicle cells. These *microvilli* interdigitate to some extent, thereby greatly increasing the surface area over which contacts, and thus exchange, can occur. It must be remembered that as a cell grows, its volume increases with the third power of its linear dimensions, while its surface area increases with the second power. As a result, unless there are compensating factors, the volume will increase disproportionately to the surface area. The amount of materials needed to pack the egg will be a function of the volume, while the amount of material that can enter the oocyte from its environment will depend upon the area in contact with the environment for exchange to occur. The microvilli and their interdigitation are clearly means to increase the exchange surface. In contrast with nurse cells, follicle cells do not arise from oogonia, are not in direct cytoplasmic communication with the oocyte, and generally transport rather than synthesize oocyte-bound materials, though this latter statement has numerous exceptions.

Oogenesis in Mammals

In the mammal, the presence of direct communication between the developing embryo and its maternal container makes the accumulation of cytoplasmic stores unnecessary. The mammalian oocyte remains a relatively small cell, in the order of 100 μm, though the surrounding region undergoes considerable change. The mammalian oocyte develops within connective tissue structure called a *follicle* (Fig. 4.17). As a given oocyte proceeds toward maturation, this follicle becomes larger, is filled with fluid (the *liquor folliculi*), and the oocyte becomes surrounded by more and more follicle cells. At the mature stage, the *graafian follicle*, the oocyte is suspended within the liquor folliculi. A thick membrane, the *zona pellucida*, separates it from a layer of follicle cells, the *corona radiata*, which is several cells thick. Follicle cells are also found surrounding the fluid cavity and are responsible for its secretion. During oocyte maturation, the germinal vesicle is actively synthesizing RNA, presumably responding to the same need for programming that is present in all other eggs.

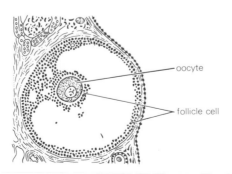

oocyte

follicle cell

Figure 4.17 A single follicle from a mammalian ovary. [*After C. D. Turner, "General Endocrinology," Saunders, 1949.*]

In the mammal, the maturation and subsequent steps are under the control of changing concentrations of hormones (Fig. 4.18). In the human, the maturation of the follicle is brought about by the combined presence of the anterior pituitary hormones, follicle-stimulating hormone (FSH) and luteinizing hormone (LH), and the hormone from the follicle cells themselves, estrogen. LH and FSH secretion are in turn responsive to neurosecretions from the tips of hypothalamic neurons that secrete controlling hormones into small blood

Figure 4.18 Diagram of the ovarian cycle showing levels of the four primary hormones (LH, FSH, estrogen and progesterone), the condition of the follicle, and the condition of the uterus. [*From Vander, Sherman, and Luciano, "Human Physiology," 2d ed., McGraw-Hill, 1974.*]

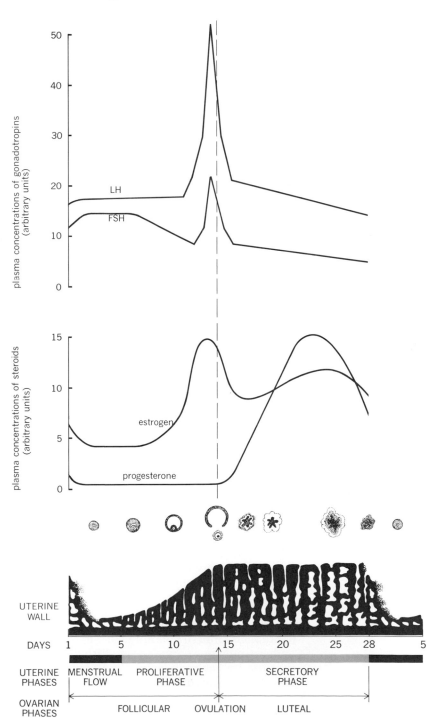

vessels bathing the anterior pituitary. At about the midpoint in the menstrual cycle, there is an abrupt surge of LH secretion that acts on the follicle—possibly by dissolving its surface layer—to cause the sudden release of the oocyte and its surrounding layer of follicle cells. This process is *ovulation*. After ovulation the follicle, now lacking an oocyte, transforms into an endocrine structure, the *corpus luteum*. This structure now secretes considerable quantities of estrogen and progesterone; they act on the hypothalamus, which in turn acts to shut down further synthesis of FSH and LH by the pituitary. The hormones of the corpus luteum act on the uterus to prepare it for the ovulated oocyte—now awaiting fertilization at the second meiotic metaphase—for implantation in the uterus several days later. If implantation does not occur, some mechanism (at present unknown) causes the corpus luteum to stop hormone production, and the uterine wall is sloughed as menstruation. FSH and LH secretions resume to begin a new cycle of follicle growth.

The invention of the birth control pill has been a direct outcome of basic research in reproductive physiology. These pills generally contain combinations of estrogen- and progesterone-like substances. The earlier group of pills contained sufficient quantities of hormone to inhibit follicle growth and ovulation by acting on the hypothalamic-mediated release of anterior pituitary hormones. With continued research, it was determined that smaller quantities of hormones could still prevent pregnancy without interfering so drastically with the ovarian cycle. It appears that a variety of targets, including the uterine wall and the cervical mucous, can be altered physiologically in some unknown manner to prevent fertilization and/or implantation.

MATURATION

The primary importance of the animal egg relates to its large size. Rather than producing four equal-sized cells, the meiotic divisions in the female produce one large cell and two or three small cells called *polar bodies*. The large egg size is retained by means of two extremely unequal meiotic divisions. They are produced by a meiotic spindle apparatus that is greatly displaced toward one side, the animal side, of the oocyte. If the spindle apparatus is caused to move by centrifugation to the center of the oocyte, the resulting division can be essentially equal, pointing clearly to the role of the apparatus in determining the relative volumes of the daughter cells. This inequality has the effect of maintaining the necessary large size of the principal oocyte despite the occurrence of the two meiotic divisions.

The question can be raised as to why meiosis is delayed until after oocyte differentiation in the female, unlike the male. No answer can be provided with certainty, though speculation concerning the basis for natural selection of a given adaptation can always be set forward. By delaying meiosis until after oocyte growth, the tetraploid amount of DNA can be utilized as a template for RNA synthesis rather than being restricted to one-fourth this amount. Another factor may relate to the DNA/cytoplasmic ratio. From several different examples, there is a significant relationship between the size of a cell and its DNA content. Under experimental conditions, amphibian embryos can be raised with haploid, diploid, triploid, tetraploid, or pentaploid amounts of DNA per cell. In these embryos there is a striking relation of DNA content to cell size. Tissues of a pentaploid embryo contain cells approximately five times larger than a haploid embryo, but approximately one-fifth the number (see Fig. 11.17). It is conceivable that the higher premeiotic DNA content of the germinal vesicle facilitates the greater cytoplasmic volume.

Figure 4.19 Maturation of *Nereis* egg. *a* Early prophase of first maturation division, beginning of breakdown of germinal vesicle (shortly after fertilization) showing nucleoplasm, nucleolus, and chromatin. *b* First maturation division (metaphase). Note spreading of fluid nucleoplasm into surrounding cytoplasm as the nuclear membrane of the germinal vesicle disappears, leaving behind the chromatin and nucleolus; also note the eccentric location of the maturation-division asters and spindle, which results in unequal division of the oocyte to form the first polar body. [*Courtesy of D. P. Costello.*]

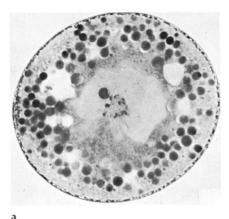

a

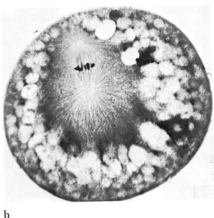

b

The term *maturation* describes the period from the end of the germinal vesicle stage to the fertilizable egg. The process of maturation that occurs at the termination of oocyte development includes more than just the meiotic divisions. The first maturational step is the breakdown of the germinal vesicle with the resulting mixture of what was previously restricted to either the nucleus or the cytoplasm (Fig. 4.19). In vertebrates, germinal vesicle breakdown and subsequent events can be induced in vivo or in vitro by hormones, either pituitary gonadotrophins or progesterone.

In amphibians, the hormonal induction of maturation stimulates a considerable burst of RNA synthesis as well as the morphological events of nuclear breakdown, ovulation, and meiosis. In vertebrates, the first meiotic division occurs, and the secondary oocyte proceeds to metaphase of the second division. It is at this point that maturation is arrested until after fertilization.

In conclusion, in this section on oogenesis we have reviewed the main features that relate specifically to the programming and packaging of the egg, so that the embryo can emerge from its organization. There are examples of considerable development in the absence of a sperm, clearly indicating the totality of the information contained within the egg. In one case, the anucleolate mutant, we have directly considered the consequence of malfunction during oogenesis. Two other examples (the direction of shell coiling in a snail and the o mutation in the axolotl) of the impact of oogenesis on development are presented in Chapters 6 and 8.

READINGS

BACETTI, B. (ed.), 1970. "Comparative Spermatology," Academic.

BIGGER, J. D., and A. W. SCHUETZ (eds.), 1972. "Oogenesis," University Park Press.

BROWN, D. D., and I. B. DAWID, 1968. Specific Gene Amplification in Oocytes, *Science*, **160**: 272–280.

————, and J. B. GURDON, 1964. Absence of Ribosomal RNA Synthesis in the Anucleolate Mutant of *Xenopus laevis*, *Proc. Nat. Acad. Sci.*, **51**:139–146.

CALLAN, H. G., 1967. The Organization of Genetic Units in Chromosomes, *J. Cell Sci.*, **2**:1–7.

CLERMONT, Y., and C. P. LEBLOND, 1953. Renewal of Spermatogonia in the Rat, *Amer. J. Anat.*, **93**:475–502.

COMINGS, D. E., and T. A. OKADA, 1971. Fine Structure of the Synaptonemal Complex, *Exp. Cell Res.*, **65**:104–116.

DAVIDSON, E. H., 1968. "Gene Activity in Early Development," Academic.

———, and B. R. HOUGH, 1971. Genetic Information in Oocyte RNA, *J. Mol. Biol.*, **56**:491–506.

FAWCETT, D. W., 1970. A Comparative View of Sperm Ultrastructure, *Biol. Reprod.* suppl. **2**:90–127.

———, 1975. Ultrastructural Aspects of Gametogenesis, 33rd Symposium, The Society of Developmental Biology, Academic.

GALL, J. G., and H. G. CALLAN, 1962. ^{3}H-Uridine Incorporation in Lampbrush Chromosomes, *Proc. Nat. Acad. Sci.*, **48**:562–570.

HESS, O., and G. F. MEYER, 1968. Genetic Activation of the Y chromosome in *Drosophila* during Spermatogenesis, *Advan. Genet.*, **14**:171–223.

HOTTA, Y., and H. STERN, 1971. Analysis of DNA Synthesis during Meiotic Prophase in *Lilium, J. Mol. Biol.*, **55**:337–355.

HOUGH, B. R., and E. H. DAVIDSON, 1972. Studies on the Repetitive Sequence Transcripts of *Xenopus* Oocytes, *J. Mol. Biol.*, **70**:491–509.

KIEFER, B. I., 1973. Genetics of Sperm Development in *Drosophila,* 31st Symposium, The Society of Developmental Biology, pp. 47–102.

KOEHLER, J. K., 1973. Studies on the Structure of the Postnuclear Sheath of Water Buffalo Spermatozoa, *J. Ultras. Res.* **44**:355–368.

LONGO, F. J., and E. ANDERSON, 1974. Gametogenesis, in J. Lash and J. R. Whittaker (eds.), "Concepts in Development," Sinauer.

MacGREGOR, H. C., 1972. The Nucleolus and Its Genes in Amphibian Oogenesis, *Biol. Rev.*, **47**: 177–210.

MOSES, M. J., 1968. Synaptonemal Complex, *Ann. Rev. Genet.*, **2**:363–412.

RAVEN, C. P., 1961. "Oogenesis: The Storage of Developmental Information," Pergamon.

ROOSEN-RUNGE, E. C., 1962. The Process of Spermatogenesis in Mammals, *Biol. Rev.*, **37**:343–377.

SMITH, L. D., 1975. Germinal Plasm and Primordial Germ Cells, 33rd Symposium, The Society of Developmental Biology, Academic.

———, and R. E. ECKER, 1970. Regulatory Processes in the Maturation and Early Cleavage of Amphibian Eggs, *Curr. Topics in Dev. Biol.*, **5**:1–30.

WALLACE, R. A., J. M. NICKOL, T. HO, and D. W. JARED, 1972. Studies on Amphibian Yolk. X. The Relative Roles of Autosynthetic and Heterosynthetic Processes during Yolk Protein Assembly by Isolated Oocytes, *Develop. Biol.*, **29**:255–272.

WILSON, E. B., 1925. "The Cell in Development and Heredity," 3d ed., Macmillan.

ZUCKERMAN, S. (ed.), 1962. "The Ovary," 2 vols., Academic.

PART II

BEGINNINGS OF DEVELOPMENT

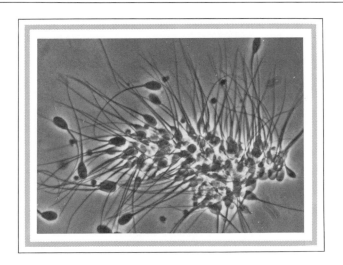

CHAPTER 5

Fertilization

Developmental phenomena have been most intensively studied in the frog and the sea urchin. Although frogs are suffering from overcollection, destruction of habitat, viral diseases such as cancer (renal adenocarcinoma) and red leg, they offer the following advantages: the animals are vertebrates, abundant, cheap, and easy to keep. They can be injected with hormones and caused to ovulate, and the eggs can be fertilized in vitro and raised synchronously in large numbers. Most frogs breed seasonally, though *Xenopus* can be induced to ovulate year round. The eggs are large and many intricate surgical experiments can be performed. One of the main difficulties is the impermeability of amphibian embryos to external molecules, which means that isotopes, drugs, etc., must be injected directly into the egg.

Of the many possible marine invertebrates, sea urchins have been most widely used for the ease of procuring large numbers of gametes. Spawning in ripe individuals is readily obtained either by injection of a solution of KCl or by stimulation with a weak electrical current. If it is a female, it is simply turned, oral side up, over a beaker of seawater and eggs come streaming out of the five gonopores to the bottom of the beaker. A large sea urchin can spawn many milliliters of packed eggs. If it is a male, determined by the white seminal fluid, it is turned over a small dish and great numbers of sperm become available. Eggs are readily fertilized and embryos are raised in large, synchronous cultures. The embryos are transparent, and internal processes can be observed. Unlike the amphibian, the embryos readily take up small molecular-weight materials and macromolecular metabolism is easily studied.

Generally, one must attempt to find the system that is best suited for the study at hand. Different embryos are obviously adapted to different experiments. If one is, for example, interested in developmental genetics, *Drosophila* is a likely choice, considering all the genetic background available on this one animal. If lampbrush chromosomes are desired, salamander oocytes are a good choice because of the size of these structures in these cells. Once a particular group of animals become widely studied, a background of information is built up that makes further study more profitable. The biggest difficulty with this approach is our tendency to generalize findings to all embryos when we have information about only a very few.

Mammals are very difficult to work with. They are hard to keep, their embryos are small and require very special conditions even for short periods, and a limited number of embryos can be obtained. One female is capable of providing only about 50 embryos after special hormone treatment, compared with the millions obtained from a large sea urchin. This makes it very difficult to perform biochemical studies on the early, small stages. It is a fairly safe assumption that if man were not a mammal, we would know next to nothing about mammalian embryonic development. At the molecular and cellular levels, however, there is a great similarity between the frog and sea urchin egg and that of a human. Large numbers of studies performed on the eggs of lower animals provide concepts of development that can then be tested in a defined way on embryos closer in evolution to ourselves.

STRATEGIES OF REPRODUCTION

Certainly one of the traits most strongly affected by natural selection is the ability of a population to fertilize its eggs. If the number of offspring that survive to reproduce diminishes, the future of that population is in obvious danger. The number of diverse, and often bizarre, reproductive strategies that have evolved illustrates this point. A species usually produces the number of eggs required to ensure its survival. In the case of some mammals, only one egg is produced at a time. To compensate for this drastically low fecundity, the sole egg is nurtured in the womb and protected after birth. On the other extreme are animals such as the parasites, many of which produce thousands of eggs per day. The chance for reproductive success is very remote and selection has favored high fecundity in these groups.

Fertilization requires the union of two cells from two different individuals, and mechanisms have evolved to ensure that the two will be present in the same place at the same time. For many animals, including mammals, internal fertilization clearly satisfies that role. Even here there is room for improvement and some mammals, including the prolific rabbit, delay the process of ovulation until copulation. This provides the necessary trigger for ovulation and virtually ensures fertilization. In many animals having external fertilization, complex physiological mechanisms have evolved to deliver large quantities of spermatozoa close to numbers of ripe eggs at the right time. The most primitive situation is probably that of many marine invertebrates, including the sea urchin, where communities of sexually mature adults shed (spawn) eggs and sperm freely into the surrounding water. The members usually become ripe in unison under the stimulation of common environmental cues of light and dark, tidal changes, and temperature of the water. To provide for simultaneous spawning, chemicals present in the fluid spawned by members of one sex will trigger release of the opposite gamete. Remember, these animals cannot see, touch, or hear each other; diffusible chemicals must provide the communication.

This phenomenon can readily be verified by a visit to a marine laboratory during the reproductive season, where one animal spawning in a tank will promptly set all the remaining members of the species into action. One of the most dramatic examples of reproductive timing is the palolo worm of Samoa. In these worms the posterior half develops ovaries or testes; this half then breaks off, swims to the surface of the water under the moonlight, and eggs and sperm are shed. Under the influence of photoperiod, tides, and neuroendocrine factors, the exact date (a particular night in November after the last quarter of the moon) when these worms reproduce can be predicted.

Another factor to be considered in the timing of reproductive activity between the two sexes is the limited life span of both gametes. Sea urchin sperm, for example, will remain fertile if kept in a concentrated state, in the cold, for more than a day. Once the sperm are diluted, however, their respiratory activity greatly increases and their life span is reduced to minutes or less. Similarly, sea urchin eggs will remain fertile for a few hours, but then rapidly deteriorate. Animals that live in freshwater face more severe problems as a result of the shortened life of spermatozoa in solutions of low salt. In these animals—including fish, amphibians, and invertebrates—sperm are delivered directly to the eggs at the moment of laying, if not before. In animals living on land, spermatozoa are generally stored in a physiological medium that maintains their life. In many forms, spermatozoa must be delivered internally via the insertion of a sexual appendage. Yet even in mammals, millions of sperm must be ejaculated in order that a sufficient number reach the upper end of the fallopian tube where one or more ripe eggs may be descending. In mammals, as in other animals, the life of the gamete is very limited. In humans, sperm remain fertile for about 2 days, and the egg is fertile for no longer than 24 hours. In rats, it is well established that the incidence of abnormal pregnancies rises sharply with the time elapsed between ovulation and fertilization. In man, one effect of fertilization of aging eggs is believed to be the production of triploid embryos, which account for approximately 20 percent of abortive pregnancies.

EGG ENVELOPES

Eggs are surrounded by a variety of extracellular covers with various names, origins, and functions. In an attempt to categorize these outer covers, we will divide them into structures formed (1) within the ovary, which can result from secretions of the oocyte, surrounding follicle cells, or both, and (2) within the oviduct. During the course of this chapter we will discuss the vitelline membrane and jelly coat of the sea urchin, the zona pellucida of the mammal, the chorion of a fish, the vitelline membrane of an amphibian, and the chorion of an ascidian. All of these are examples of the former type, produced by the egg and/or follicle cells.

The oviduct is responsible for such materials as the jelly in which amphibian eggs are wrapped and the majority of the contents of a chicken egg. In the case of the chicken, the product of the ovary, the ovum, consists of the yolk and a small area of cytoplasm on top of it, at which the sperm will enter and from which the embryo will begin to emerge. Surrounding this large cell is a thin membrane, the vitelline membrane, formed within the ovary. After fertilization, the egg passes through the oviduct and receives a covering of albumen (the egg white), the shell membrane (the thin membrane just beneath the shell), and the shell itself. Other examples of oviduct-derived envelopes are the shell membranes of reptile eggs and egg cases of mollusks and certain fish.

Whatever functions exist for external coats, jellies, or cell layers, these structures often present barriers to penetration of the ova by spermatozoa, and much of the biology of fertilization of eggs and much of the specialization of the spermatozoon itself relate to this circumstance.

CHEMOTAXIS VERSUS TRAP ACTION

If the eggs of a sea urchin, or any other animal, are placed on a slide and a tiny drop of a sperm suspension is added, in a short time a large number of sperm will have collected at the surface of the egg. These events can be followed under the microscope. The appearance suggests that the sperm have been attracted to the surface of the egg. If sperm are being attracted to the egg, the condition would be termed *chemotaxis,* implying that the sperm were responding to some chemical being liberated from the egg. Since the egg is a sphere, this chemical would be expected to diffuse outward in all directions. The result would be the production of a gradient of this chemical with its highest concentration at the egg surface and a diminishing concentration at greater distances from the source. If chemotaxis occurs, then the sperm must be able to recognize tiny differences in the concentration of the chemical to be directed to the egg surface by such a gradient. Another explanation can provide for the accumulation of sperm at the egg surface, that of *trap action.* This explanation states that the sperm swim in a nondirected random manner, but those that happen to reach the egg surface become trapped and remain. An analogy might be a group of persons wandering randomly around a large plot of land in the dark with a small well in the center of the area. By the break of day one would likely find a number of unfortunates at the bottom of the well, and chemotaxis could not be blamed for their fate.

The best way to determine if sperm are attracted to an egg is to track a series of sperm. If the sperm are moving randomly, they will move in the opposite direction as often as in the proper direction. For many years the conclusion had been that chemotaxis was present in ferns, liverworts, and mosses, but was absent among animals. At least two examples in animals, however, have been uncovered—one in a fish and the other in coelenterates. In the herring, as is typical of fish, there is a small opening called *the micropyle* (Fig. 5.14) in the outer cover of the egg. It is through the micropyle that the fertilizing sperm must enter, and if sperm in the vicinity of the opening are watched, they are seen to speed up and to be directed through the micropyle. In several coelenterates, such as the hydroid *Campanularia,* the eggs are kept within a vaselike structure, the *gonangium.* If sperm are followed, they are seen to be directed through the opening of the gonangium and down toward the egg in response to the diffusion of a specific molecule from the egg. These substances are of relatively low molecular weight and possess some species specificity.

SPECIFIC INTERACTING SUBSTANCES

Though chemotaxis has been found in rare cases, in the majority of animals, sperm appear to swim in a nondirected fashion. However, there are substances present in the surrounding region of the egg that have a dramatic effect on sperm. The history of this subject dates back to 1913, when Lillie found that sea urchin sperm clump together if dropped into a solution of seawater in which eggs of the same species have been shed. This solution, termed "egg water," contains macromolecules released from the jelly coat of the egg. Lillie called this substance *fertilizin,* which we now know as an acid mucopolysaccharide, a protein containing a very large amount of polysaccharide to which sulfate ions are esterfied.

The reason that sperm become clumped in the presence of fertilizin is that specific interaction occurs between the fertilizin molecules and a protein of complementary steric configuration, *antifertilizin,* present on the surface of the sperm. The formation of a clump requires that many sperm are brought together, and this requires more than one binding site on both reactants. In other words, each fertilizin molecule can attach to more than one sperm and each sperm can be attached to more than one fertilizin molecule. In this way fertilizin molecules serve as bridges between sperm, and sperm between fertilizin molecules; huge clumps can be formed.

These molecules on the two gametes are called *specific interacting substances,* and their interaction is often compared with antigen-antibody reactions. Sperm clumped by egg water are generally unable to fertilize eggs even after the clumps have completely dispersed, leaving them motile and fully normal in appearance. These unclumped sperm are believed to have retained a coat of fertilizin at their surface, which blocks their reactive sites and makes them infertile.

The obvious question arises as to why eggs possess substances that appear to inhibit the fertility of the sperm. Since fertilization occurs by the passage of sperm through a jungle of these molecules, the first assumption must be that under normal conditions the jelly coat does not destroy sperm function. However, we are still left with the question of what role it does perform. This area of research has been one of the more frustrating ones in developmental biology, and a clear answer to this question cannot be provided. Inherent in many studies is the belief that the interaction of these two substances somehow is required for sperm-egg attachment, a prerequisite for the fertilization event. However, the finding that eggs can be stripped of their fertilizin-containing jelly, and can still be fertilized, brings up the question whether they are needed at all. The possibility exists that sufficient fertilizin remains at the surface of the egg to accomplish the necessary task. One well-established property of fertilizin is its ability to activate the sperm, as evidenced by their increased respiration and motility as well as by an acrosomal reaction (discussed below).

The fertilization event is highly species-specific, and it is in this capacity that fertilizin may play a role. Invariably, an egg of a given species is capable of being fertilized most readily by a sperm of the same species. If cross-fertilization can occur, it is between gametes of related species. This suggests that species-specific chemicals are somehow involved in fertilization. Removal of the jelly coat of an echinoderm does tend to increase penetration by foreign sperm. In addition, there is a correlation between the strength of the antifertilizin-fertilizin reaction of two species and their ability to cross-fertilize. In other words, the more readily the foreign sperm are clumped by another species' fertilizin, the more readily cross-fertilization can occur between the two species. These results suggest that the fertilizin of the jelly coat acts to screen out sperm of foreign species, those with which it cannot specifically react.

In a few other species where it has been studied, other mechanisms exist to block cross-fertilization. In the hamster, for example, the zona pellucida appears to perform this function. Hamster eggs are capable of being fertilized by guinea pig sperm, but only after removal of this covering.

STATE OF EGG AT FERTILIZATION

Eggs of different species are typically fertilized at different times during the maturation process. As previously described, the eggs of vertebrates proceed to the second meiotic metaphase before sperm penetration. In the sea urchin, both meiotic divisions are completed before fertilization. At the other extreme there

TABLE 2   Stage of Egg Maturation at which Sperm Penetration Occurs
in Various Animals

Young Primary Oocyte	Fully Grown Primary Oocyte	First Metaphase	Second Metaphase	Female Pronucleus
Brachycoelium	*Ascaris*	*Aphryotrocha*	*Amphioxus*	Coelenterates
Dinophilus	*Dicyema*	*Cerebratulus*	Most mammals	Echinoids
Histriobdella	Dog and fox	*Chaetopterus*	*Siredon*	
Otomesostoma	*Grantia*	*Dentalium*		
Peripatopsis	*Myzostoma*	Many insects		
Saccocirrus	*Nereis*	*Pectinaria*		
	Spisula	Ascidians		
	Thalassema			

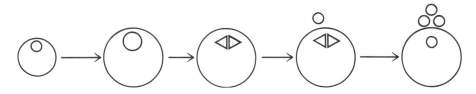

SOURCE: C. R. Austin, "Fertilization," © 1965. Reprinted by permission of Prentice-Hall, Inc. Englewood Cliffs, N. J.

are animals that have not begun meiosis at the time of fertilization. In these cases the sperm nucleus remains in the egg cytoplasm awaiting the maturation process before the subsequent events can occur. Table 2 lists representatives that are fertilized at the various stages.

All animal eggs are enveloped by one or more membranous or gelatinous layers, external to the plasma membrane. Such layers constitute barriers to penetration by the spermatozoon, and special enzymes must be incorporated into the sperm acrosome to facilitate its penetration. These "egg-membrane lysins" have been extracted from the sperm of a variety of invertebrates and vertebrates, including humans. In the mammal, when the oocyte is released from its follicle (Fig. 4.12) at ovulation, it is surrounded by a thick membrane, the *zona pellucida,* and by many layers of follicle cells called the *cumulus oophorus,* the innermost layer of which is the *corona radiata.* It is believed that the acrosome contains at least two enzymes that allow it to reach the egg. One is a hyaluronidase, which is capable of digesting the material that holds the follicle cells together, thereby allowing the sperm to pass through. The other is a proteolytic enzyme believed to be required for penetration through the zona pellucida. If rabbit ova are inseminated in the presence of inhibitors of proteolytic enzymes, fertilization is blocked.

ACROSOMAL REACTION

Fertilization requires mutual interactions between the sperm and the egg. The intact sperm as it emerges from the male is not capable of penetrating the egg. It must first undergo the acrosomal reaction in response to the egg environ-

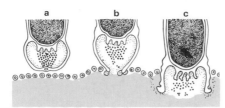
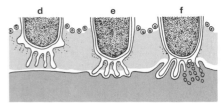
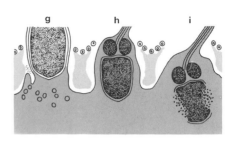
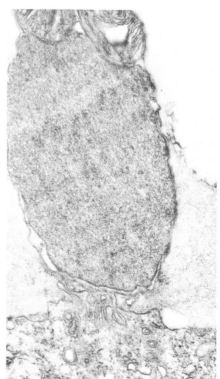

Figure 5.1 Stages of sperm-egg association (of polychaete *Hydroides*). *a* Unactivated spermatozoon at about the time of initial contact with the egg envelope. *b* Acrosomal reaction is beginning. The plasma membrane of the sperm and the acrosomal membrane have fused to one another to provide an outlet for the contents of the acrosome. *c* Contents of the acrosome (including lysins) are being released and the posterior wall of the acrosomal vesicle is beginning to evert to form acrosomal tubules, which will make the first contact with the egg. *d* Acrosomal tubules are leading sperm penetration through the outer egg covering. *e* Acrosomal tubules are initiating contact with the egg plasma membrane, which forms microvilli in response. *f* Plasma membranes of the sperm and egg have fused to form the zygote. *g–i* Successive stages in the engulfment of the sperm by the fertilization cone formed by the egg in response to sperm contact. [*After A. L. and L. H. Colwin, in C. B. Metz and A. Monroy (eds.), "Fertilization," vol. I, Academic, 1967.*]

ment. Early studies of the acrosomal reaction and of the early events of fertilization were performed on invertebrates, particularly by the Colwins on the hemichordate *Saccoglossus* and the polychaete *Hydroides*. More recently these events have been described for several mammals, and many of the basic processes are quite similar. We will first discuss the process in *Hydroides* (Figs. 5.1, and 5.2) and then contrast this with events in mammals.

Figure 5.2 *a* Electron micrograph of stage of initial contact of sperm and egg of *Hydroides*. Sperm plasma membrane meets egg envelope and ruptures, permitting the interior of acrosomal vesicle to open to outside. Egg plasma membrane is still separated from sperm cell by bulk of egg envelope. *b* Electron micrograph of contact stage of sperm and egg of *Hydroides*, showing acrosomal tubules indenting egg surface, and the beginning of the rise of the fertilization cone. The two gametes plasma membranes closely confront each other in the region of the interdigitation. [*Courtesy of A. L. and L. H. Colwin.*]

a

b

In *Hydroides*, the reaction begins when the sperm tip contacts the outer egg envelope. The first response is a fusion of two membranes, the outer cell membrane of the sperm head and the anterior membrane of the acrosomal vesicle (Figs. 5.1*b* and 5.2). Membranes are always continuous structures and are never found with free ends. If a membrane is split transversely, it appears to undergo immediate fusion. The fusion of membranes is a general method whereby cells release membrane-bound secretions. Once the fusion occurs, the contents of the vesicle are continuous with the external medium. Membranes derived from the Golgi vesicles, as in the case of the acrosome, seem to be particularly able to fuse with the outer cell membrane.

Once membrane fusion has occurred and the contents, including egg-membrane lysins, have been released, the posterior wall of the acrosomal vesicle is seen to form a number of small, rodlike projections (Fig. 5.1*b* and *c*). These grow in length (Fig. 5.1*d*) and make the first actual contact with the plasma membrane at the egg surface (Fig. 5.1*e*). Again a process of membrane fusion occurs, but this event involves the acrosomal membrane of the sperm and the plasma membrane of the egg. At this point we can consider the two gametes as one cell, the *zygote*. This latter fusion event provides an open channel to the interior of the sperm head (Fig. 5.1*f* and *g*), and the male nucleus and components of the midpiece gain entrance to the egg cytoplasm (Fig. 5.1*h* and *i*).

In the hemichordate *Saccoglossus*, as well as the river lamprey, a variety of echinoderms, and certain bivalve mollusks, the acrosomal reaction involves the formation of one long acrosomal tubule rather than the several small ones seen in *Hydroides*. In some cases this tubule forms at the edge of the jelly coat and extends a sufficient length, up to 75 μm, to make contact with the egg surface. Egg membrane lysins are released before the formation of the tubule and presumably aid in its penetration of the egg envelopes.

CAPACITATION

In the mammal, no filament is formed in the acrosome reaction, but the release of lytic enzymes is well established. The acrosomal reaction in mammals is only the last alteration in sperm morphology that allows it to penetrate the egg. The sperm that leave the testis proper are at least two steps from being fertile. One maturational step occurs in the tubules of the epididymis, though the nature of the changes is not known. A second maturational step occurs within the female reproductive tract and is termed *capacitation*. Again, the exact nature of the changes that occur during capacitation are not understood, though this event can occur in vitro in a completely defined medium. Capacitation may result from the removal of some inhibiting material from the sperm. One unusual technique for rendering mammalian sperm fertile is to mix them with Sendai virus, with which they agglutinate head to head (Fig. 5.3). Sendai virus is a common tool to bring about the fusion of membranes between two cells, and in this case the altered sperm are now capable of penetrating the ovum.

In mammals, as the sperm approaches the cumulus oophorus, the acrosomal reaction occurs. In contrast to invertebrates, this response involves the intermittent fusion of the plasma membrane and the acrosomal membrane. The result is a shroud of vesicles at the tip of the sperm and the early release of the acrosomal contents, which digest the intercellular cement of the follicle cells. By the time the sperm reaches the zona pellucida, there is little evidence

Figure 5.3 Head-to-head agglutination of live epididymal rabbit sperm after being mixed with Sendai virus. Fertilization occurs when rabbit ova are cultured in vitro with epididymal sperm to which Sendai virus is adsorbed. These sperm do not require capacitation in vivo in order to fertilize. Evidence of fertilization is penetration of sperm, the appearance of two polar bodies and pronuclei, and cleavage through the eight-blastomere stage. The viruses attach almost exclusively to the sperm acrosome, with resultant head-to-head agglutination of the sperm. [*Courtesy of R. J. Erisson, copyright © by the American Association for the Advancement of Science, 1971.*]

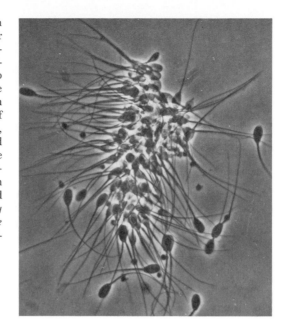

of any remaining acrosomal material. Yet, we know that the sperm must still contain a "zona lysin," which is clearly required for further penetration, and must be present within the remaining body of the sperm head. Penetration of the zona requires several minutes and leaves the sperm in virtual contact with the microvilli of the egg surface.

In contrast to invertebrates, membrane fusion between the two gametes does not occur at the posterior acrosomal membrane, which becomes the leading edge of the sperm's surface. Rather, fusion occurs between the egg membrane and the sperm membrane of the postnuclear cap region (Fig. 5.4) well behind the acrosomal tip. Presumably, those membranes that undergo the fusion process—regardless of which they happen to be—have acquired a special fusion-mediating property. In every case of successful fertilization in the an-

Figure 5.4 Electron micrograph of fertilization of hamster. [*Courtesy of R. Yanagimachi.*]

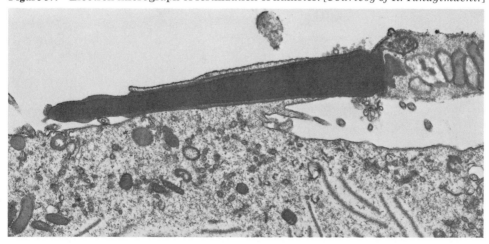

imals studied, the acrosomal reaction of the sperm is a prerequisite. In the sea urchin, sperm have been injected directly into the egg, bypassing the surface-mediated events. These injected spermatozoa do not activate the egg, but remain intact and mobile within the egg cytoplasm. In this case, at least, membrane fusion is the only means by which gametes can become united.

THE RESPONSE TO FERTILIZATION

Early Events

Fertilization is a critical stage in the life cycle of all animals, and the response of the zygote to fusion proceeds in many directions. Any discussion of the response to fertilization invariably centers around the echinoderm egg, since work on these animals has so dominated the field. The first visible response to sperm contact is the engulfment of the sperm by a protrusion of cytoplasm, the *fertilization cone* (Fig. 5.5). If sea urchin eggs are fertilized and immediately observed under a special dark-field illumination, a color change is seen to spread around the egg from the point of sperm penetration. Depending upon the species and the temperature of the water, this wave begins at about 30 seconds after sperm contact and is completed approximately 20 seconds later. This wave of color change is followed by the elevation of a membrane, the *fertilization membrane,* from the surface of the egg. As in the case of the color change, membrane elevation also begins at the site of sperm contact, as a small

Figure 5.5 Electron micrograph of *Arbacia* sperm being taken into the egg through the fertilization cone. [*Courtesy of E. Anderson.*]

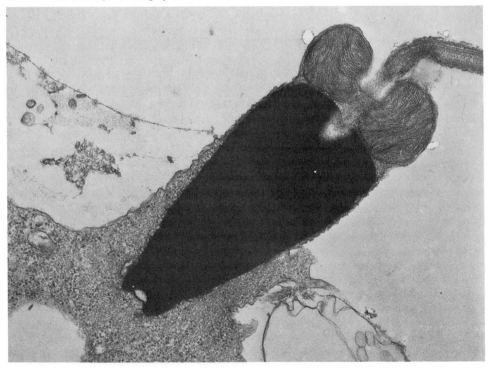

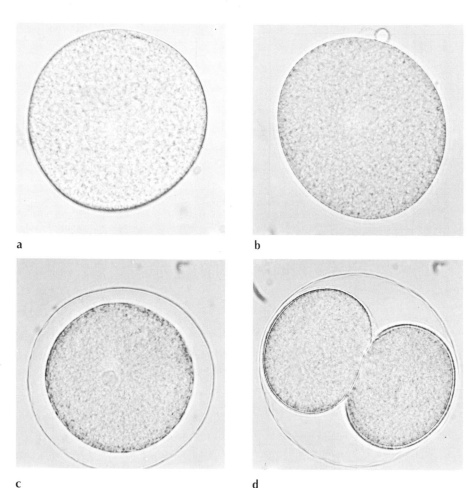

Figure 5.6 Maturation and fertilization in egg of sea urchin. *a* Egg showing metaphase of first maturation division. *b* Maturation complete, polar body evident, and pronucleus at center. *c* Fertilization membrane lifted off. *d* First cleavage. [*Courtesy of T. Gustafson.*]

blister, which continues around the egg. This process is shown in Fig. 5.7 and the completed membrane in Fig. 5.6c.

The morphological basis for this response is well established. If a section of an unfertilized egg is examined, a layer of small granules, the *cortical granules,* is found just beneath the plasma membrane (Figs. 4.14b, 5.7). The surface of the unfertilized egg is composed of two very tightly adhering membranes, the outer vitelline membrane and the inner plasma membrane. Within the first minute after sperm contact, the morphology of the surface region is completely altered. This alteration begins at the point of sperm contact by the fusion of the membranes of the cortical granules with the overlying plasma membrane (Figs. 5.7a, 5.8b and c). As this happens, the vitelline membrane detaches from the plasma membrane and lifts away from the egg surface. Once the cortical granule membrane has fused with the plasma membrane, the contents are released into the space formed between the two previously fused layers. The reaction of the cortical granules continues around the egg, leaving in its wake the formation of the fertilization membrane (Figs. 5.6, 5.8).

The contents of the cortical granules are used in several ways. A crystalline portion of the expelled material is seen to fuse with the underside of the fertilization membrane, forming lumps (Fig. 5.8c) that soon smooth out to form the

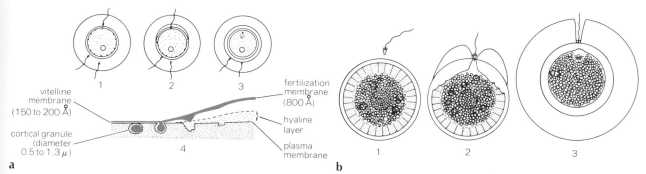

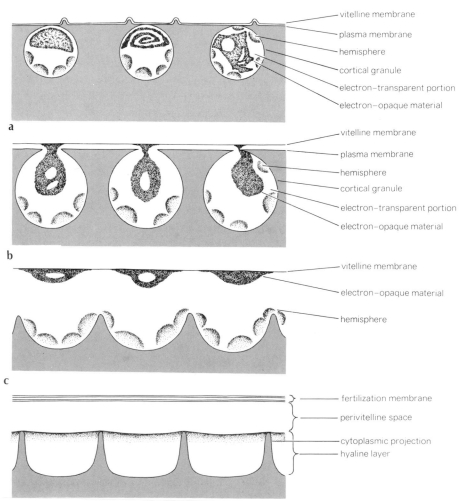

Figure 5.7 *a* Drawings 1 to 3 show the course of events in cortical granule breakdown and fertilization membrane elevation in the sea urchin egg. Drawing 4 illustrates the mechanism believed to underlie these events. *b* Reaction of the polychaete (*Nereis*) egg to sperm penetration. The cortex of the egg (drawing 1) contains many alveoli filled with fine granular material. At sperm penetration (drawings 2 and 3) the alveoli break down, and the granular material, apparently becoming strongly hydrated, swells to form a thick jelly coat that eventually surrounds the egg. [*After C. R. Austin, "Fertilization," 1965. Used by permission of Prentice-Hall, Inc., Englewood Cliffs, N. J.*]

Figure 5.8 Cortical reaction and fertilization membrane elevation in the sea urchin *Clypeaster japonicus*. *a* Unfertilized egg. *b* Fusion of egg plasma membrane and membrane of cortical granule with beginning of release of granule contents. *c* Adhesion of electron-opaque material to the vitelline membrane now lifted up; complete fusion of this material with the membrane will give rise to the fertilization membrane. Other material of the cortical granules is expelled into the perivitelline space, while other contents remain close to the egg surface to form the hyaline layer. *d* The egg surface upon completion of these events. [*After Endo, Exp. Cell Res.*, **25**:383 *(1961)*.]

final, complex surface layer. Another portion of the cortical granule material is seen to remain close to the egg surface, take up water, and form the hyaline layer. The hyaline layer consists primarily of acid mucopolysaccharide material; its formation requires the presence of calcium in the surrounding water. Still another contribution from the cortical granules is material that contributes to the fluid of the perivitelline space, including several known enzymes. The expulsion of cortical-granule material at fertilization is found in many groups besides the echinoderms, including fish, amphibians, and mammals. Many groups of animals, however, lack this phenomenon; even in sea urchin eggs, whose cortical granule breakdown has been inhibited, normal development can result.

If cortical breakdown is not essential, activation must result from a more basic response. The concept of an invisible, self-propagating, rapid "fertilization wave" as a primary response has been postulated, but has been difficult to demonstrate. The event most analogous to the proposed fertilization wave is the nerve impulse, and inherent in the theory is the concept that the wave would be accompanied by a change in the distribution of ions at the cell surface. Results of an early search for a change in membrane voltage is shown in Fig. 5.9.

Recent studies by Steinhardt and coworkers provide a probable physical basis for the fertilization wave in the echinoderm egg. The membrane potential of the unfertilized egg is approximately −8 mV (millivolt), with the inside negative. The Na^+ concentration within the unfertilized egg is kept very low relative to the environment, and the internal K^+ concentration is kept very high. Within 3 seconds after sperm and eggs are mixed, the membrane depolarizes and reaches a reversed membrane potential of about +10 mV. This depolarization results from the influx of Na^+ and is followed by a more gradual repolarization that takes about 1½ minutes to complete. This phase I response is followed by a near constant potential (phase II) for several minutes, and finally by an accelerating hyperpolarization that carries the membrane potential to −60 to −80 mV, at which it remains. The phase III hyperpolarization involves the movement of K^+ ions.

Figure 5.9 Membrane potential of the egg of *Asterias forbesii* and its changes following fertilization. Entry of the electrode into the egg causes a sudden appearance of a −60-mV membrane potential, which rapidly decreases to −30-mV. The previously steady potential decreases by 5 mV, as soon as the sperm contacts the egg. Subsequently, the potential again increases and remains steady at −40 mV, until the electrode is removed. [*After Tyler et al.,* Biol. Bull., **110**:*184 (1956)*.]

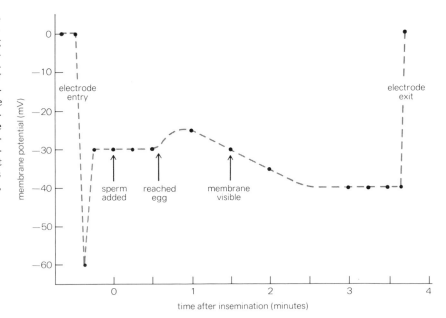

Rapid changes in membrane potential presumably involve rapid changes in the permeability properties of the membrane, at least toward Na$^+$ and K$^+$ ions. Slower changes in permeability following fertilization have been reported for several other molecules, notably phosphate, uridine, and amino acids.

The first changes, the membrane potential and cortical granule breakdown, are changes at the surface. Both appear to be propagated strictly at the surface rather than spreading through the endoplasm. Soon, however, the entire egg is drawn into the process; somehow the activation must spread inward toward the center of the egg. One of the responses of the cytoplasm to fertilization in the sea urchin is the marked increase in oxygen consumption. The unfertilized sea urchin egg is metabolically inert, awaiting an activation stimulus to begin energy consumption. The situation is one of returning the cell to a more typical metabolic activity rather than stimulating it to superhigh levels. The increase in oxygen consumption at fertilization is not universal; in fact, a few eggs are known to undergo a decrease after fertilization from a rather high, prefertilization rate. The unfertilized sea urchin egg is somehow in a maintained, inhibited state. This same condition extends to its protein synthetic activity, which is very low in the unfertilized egg and becomes activated about 7 minutes after fertilization. The underlying mechanism for this increased protein synthesis will be discussed in Chapter 9.

Morphological Changes at Fertilization

Simultaneous with the above physiological changes, numerous morphological changes accompany the fertilization event. In our earlier description we had left the sperm dangling at the point of its engulfment by the fertilization cone. The next series of events are quite similar in many animals. The following description is for the sea urchin *Arbacia*. Events are diagrammed in Fig. 5.10. Within a minute after contact, the entire sperm, with the exception of its membrane, is engulfed by the cytoplasm of the fertilization cone. In other animals a varying amount of the sperm is taken in. Once inside, the sperm rotates about 180° and begins to migrate toward the central region of the egg. The membrane surrounding the tightly packed sperm nucleus rapidly disappears, allowing the enclosed chromatin to begin a dispersion that will transform it from its nearly crystalline state into a more typical chromatin. Surrounding this chromatin, a new nuclear envelope forms by the fusion of membrane vesicles. As the male pronucleus migrates, microtubules become associated with the sperm centrioles to form the sperm *aster*. This structure will be responsible for

Figure 5.10 Fertilization in *Arbacia*. *a* The sperm head has entered the cytoplasm. *b–d* It turns through 180°. The sperm aster becomes evident, the midpiece is detached, and the aster seemingly leads the sperm nucleus toward the point of union with the female pronucleus. *e* Nuclear union appears to be complete and involves a male pronucleus that has not enlarged appreciably. The sperm aster divides to become the amphiaster for the first cleavage division. [*After C. R. Austin, "Fertilization," 1965. Used by permission of Prentice-Hall, Inc., Englewood Cliffs, N. J.*]

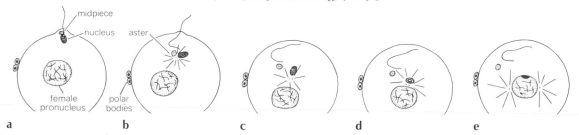

the formation of the first mitotic spindle apparatus in a short time. The fate of the egg centriole left over from the last meiotic division is unknown. Several electron microscopic studies have been performed, and this centriole has never been observed in the mature egg.

Pronuclei

While the above events are occurring, the female nucleus is also migrating toward the central region of the egg. During this period between fertilization and nuclear fusion, the male and female nuclei are called *pronuclei*. When the pronuclei are very near to one another they seem to respond to each other's presence. In *Arbacia,* the sides of the pronuclei facing each other flatten, projections are sent out, and the pronuclei fuse to become one cleavage nucleus. It is at approximately this point, or even before, that the DNA of the chromosomes in both pronuclei is replicated in preparation for the oncoming mitotic division.

The main variations in the above events seen in other animals relate to pronuclear activities. In many species the pronuclei do not directly fuse. Rather, they approach each other but each remains intact. Nuclear membranes of each pronucleus break down as first cleavage approaches; the chromosomes, which have previously replicated, are separated into the first two cells. It is in the telophase of the first mitotic division that nuclear membranes re-form to enclose, for the first time, both sets of chromosomes in each of the nuclei of the daughter cells.

Another major difference among animals is in the various stages of oocyte maturation at which fertilization can occur. In the mollusk *Mytilus,* for example, the sperm nucleus enters the egg cytoplasm at an early stage in its meiotic divisions. The male pronucleus begins its activities as the oocyte completes its maturation. An interesting observation in this case is that the two nuclei are engaged in contrasting types of activities. While the female set of chromosomes may be condensing as it approaches meiosis, the male set is dispersing. Similarly, nuclear membrane may be dispersing in one and re-forming in the other. These contrasting activities suggest that each nucleus is responding to specific factors that do not affect the other one.

The evidence suggests that the male and female pronuclei are in communication with each other. This can be illustrated by examination of salamander eggs, whose normal fertilization allows more than one sperm into the interior of the egg. In most animals, penetration by more than one sperm (called *polyspermy*) is a lethal condition, though in salamanders polyspermy is a normal state and only one of the male pronuclei actually fuses with the egg. Once this cleavage nucleus is formed, all the other male pronuclei degenerate (Fig. 5.11),

Figure 5.11 Polyspermy in the urodele *Triton. a* Entry of spermatozoa. The egg is in the metaphase of the second meiotic division. (Time, 10 minutes after insemination.) *b–d* For the first 2 hours and 20 minutes all pronuclei develop similarly; then, with one male pronucleus involved in syngamy with the female, the supernumerary male pronuclei begin to regress, the nearest one showing the change first. *e,* and *f* As the first cleavage mitosis proceeds, 3 hours and 20 minutes after insemination, suppression of all supernumerary male pronuclei is completed. [*After G. Fankhauser,* Ann. N. Y. Acad. Sci., **49:**684 (1948).]

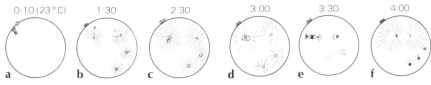

the ones closest to the cleavage nucleus deteriorating first. The impression gained from this series of events is that the process of pronuclear union results in the release of an inhibitory factor that spreads out in all directions, destroying unfused pronuclei in its wake.

Even though the male and female pronuclei communicate, each is capable of independent activity in the absence of the other. If, for example, either pronucleus is removed from the egg, the other will continue its migratory activity as if both were still present. Moreover, in artificially activated eggs, (see below) the egg pronucleus can migrate in the same manner as if it had been fertilized.

Experimental Activation

Considering the number of changes that occur during the first minutes after fertilization, it is very difficult to assign causal relationships in an attempt to explain the underlying basis for activation. A general theory must account for the initial surface events and the following chain reactions that carry the state of activation inward. Attempts to understand the underlying processes of the response of the egg have generally been based upon activation of the egg in the absence of a sperm, termed *experimental activation*. Development without benefit of a sperm is *parthenogenesis* and will be discussed below.

If the normal trigger mechanism, the sperm, is bypassed, then the experimental treatment must in some way connect with the primary activation event(s), since the entire activation syndrome results. It might be expected that the analysis of the agents that are capable of causing activation would point toward the nature of the normal triggers. The difficulty with this reasoning is the great variety of treatments that are capable of providing the needed trigger. These treatments range from physical damage, such as being pricked with a needle, to temperature shocks, to probably hundreds of chemicals, to salt solutions of different concentrations, etc. Theories of a highly unsubstantiated nature have been proposed, but are beyond the scope of this book.

One component that will have to be included in any general theory of activation of echinoderm eggs is the calcium ion. Experiments show that solutions of calcium chloride isotonic with, or hypertonic to, seawater are effective activators in many species of animals. Activation by other agents is dependent upon the presence of Ca^{2+}, and depriving eggs of Ca^{2+} sensitizes them to the subsequent action of Ca^{2+} when it is added back. Measurements suggest that most of the calcium of the unfertilized egg is bound to insoluble materials, but that fertilization results in a release of a significant percentage of this calcium into an unbound state. A recent report indicates that agents causing the release of intracellular Ca^{2+} are capable of fully activating the sea urchin egg. In this case release is accomplished by the addition of an ionophorous antibiotic that is capable of transporting Ca^{2+}.

Certain of the enzymes present in the sea urchin egg show marked increases in activity after fertilization. Several of these enzymes—ATPase, NAD kinase, and a protease—appear dependent upon calcium for their activity. The increased enzyme activities are believed to have a basic role in releasing the sea urchin egg from its metabolic inhibition, and they might be important in other basic cytoplasmic changes associated with fertilization. Whether the release of calcium from a bound state in the cortex (as first proposed by Heilbrunn) is sufficient to activate the entire program of events stored in the egg remains to be seen.

As described above, the activation of the sea urchin egg is followed by a sequence of physiological, morphological, and biochemical changes that are interrelated to one degree or another. Some of these changes occur rapidly upon fertilization or experimental activation, such as membrane depolarization, the cortical reaction, and elevation of the fertilization membrane. Other changes, such as the onset of DNA synthesis and the activation of protein synthesis, are delayed. It has recently been found that these latter events can be triggered in the absence of the very early events by treating unfertilized eggs with seawater to which ammonium hydroxide has been added. The result of such treatment is an egg in which DNA synthesis occurs, chromosomes are duplicated and split from one another, and protein synthesis can be demonstrated. In other respects, however, the egg remains unfertilized. The addition of sperm to ammonia-treated eggs renders them "fertilized"; they undergo membrane depolarization, the cortical reaction, and membrane elevation.

An important sidelight to the topic of experimental activation is the appearance of centrioles in these eggs when the egg appears to lack them at the time of activation. Since a sperm is not involved, the evidence suggests that they can arise in the cytoplasm in the absence of a preexisting centriole, a condition termed "*de novo* appearance." In many cases, experimental activation results in the *de novo* appearance of many more centrioles than are needed, and many asters (termed *cytasters*) can be formed (Fig. 5.12).

Parthenogenesis

As stated earlier, parthenogenesis is development of an egg in the absence of a sperm. In some species—primarily certain insects, crustaceans, and rotifers—parthenogenesis is a normal part of the adult life cycle, and adults

Figure 5.12 Double (*a*) and triple (*b*) asters of artificially activated sea urchin egg, after isolation by partial digestion of the egg. [*Courtesy of E. R. Dirksen.*]

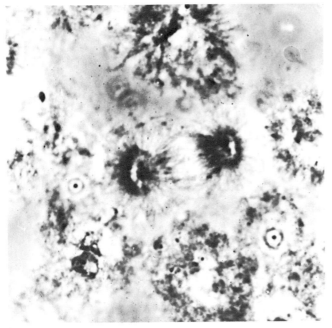 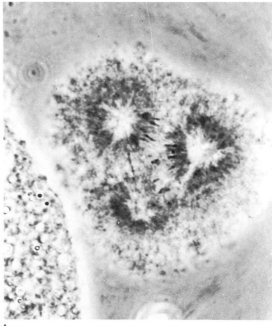

a   b

produced in this way contain a haploid chromosome number. The male drone of a bee colony is an example. Among vertebrates, a few subspecies of lizards have been discovered that develop parthenogenetically into females, and for which males are not found in the population.

Experimental activation starts the egg on the path of parthenogenesis. How far along that path a particular organism proceeds depends on a variety of factors, including the nature of the activating agent. A successfully developing parthenogenetic embryo would be expected to be haploid, but examination of such embryos indicates that this may not be the case. In fact, in nearly every case, those that develop under these conditions are diploid, and the question arises as to how this could happen. The process of becoming diploid requires the suppression of a division of chromosomes into two cells. One possibility is to suppress the second meiotic division, which can only occur in those eggs normally fertilized before the completion of meiosis. Another possibility is to suppress the first mitotic division, which normally occurs at first cleavage division.

The genetic consequences of these two processes are somewhat different, but the outcome in terms of chromosome number is the same. The fact that corrective events such as these can occur at all illustrates the importance of the normal diploid number of chromosomes. This is borne out by the lack of developmental success in vertebrate embryos that remain haploid. Even in amphibians, where a considerable imbalance of chromosomes is tolerated, the haploid condition is abnormal. In these haploid embryos, abnormalities appear as early as gastrulation and progress with age, so that very few ever reach metamorphosis. It should be kept in mind that regardless of the nature of the chromosomes of these embryos, the information for successful development is stored in the egg and the contribution from the sperm is not required in that capacity.

An important question arises with respect to the haploid amphibian embryos referred to above. Does their abnormal development result from the presence of randomly occurring lethal genes, which are now in an unchecked condition, or does it result from an improper number of chromosomes, which in itself would be lethal? Though the former explanation may contribute to the death rate, it does not appear to be the underlying problem. Under special conditions, amphibians can be obtained that are totally homozygous, but diploid. If the death of haploids is simply due to lethal genes that are not covered by a normal allele on the homologous chromosome, then these diploid homozygous embryos should share the same untimely death, which they do not. Similarly, in humans the extreme sensitivity to abnormal chromosome numbers is illustrated by the abnormalities resulting from trisomy, the presence of one additional chromosome. Down's syndrome (mongolism) is the condition resulting from trisomy of chromosome number 21. Trisomy of other autosomes produces either lethal or very severely abnormal conditions.

Treatments of mammalian eggs, including electric shock, heat, and cold, are also capable of activating the egg. The resulting development is almost invariably abnormal and arrested at very early stages. With the exception of a few early claims for rabbits, this is true even in those embryos that appear to have attained the diploid state; they die during early development, usually before gastrulation. Why these embryos should not develop is unclear, particularly since they arise from suppression of polar body formation, which would leave them partially heterozygous as a result of previous crossing-over. Mammals that are essentially homozygous can be obtained by extreme inbreeding, and such strains can be quite healthy. Some factor other than a genetic one may be responsible. The best development of parthenogenetic vertebrates has been found in turkeys; selection procedures have developed a strain that readily develops without a sperm, after suppression of the formation of the second polar body.

BLOCKS TO POLYSPERMY

In a variety of species, including the salamanders (as previously described), several sperm routinely enter the egg, though only one male pronucleus participates in formation of the cleavage nucleus. Where physiological polyspermy exists, it is usually among animals having large, yolk-laden eggs. Polyspermy in its pathological form is incompatible with normal development. If two sperm enter an egg, bringing with them two centrioles for use in division, a tripolar spindle apparatus generally forms and three cells are formed at first cleavage. If this were all, it might not matter. In such circumstances, however, the chromosomes of the nucleus formed by the fusion of three pronuclei, are distributed in a most irregular manner, and no daughter cell has a normal complement. This irregularity is passed on to subsequent cell generations. Considering the extreme sensitivity of normal activities to a proper balance of individual chromosomes, it is not surprising that this condition results in a premature death for these embryos. Most, if not all, species therefore have some sort of structural or physiological mechanism whereby fertilization is restricted to the active participation of a single spermatozoon.

The earlier work on the sea urchin (Rothschild, 1954) suggested that the block to polyspermy was a two-phased process. The first phase was postulated to occur rapidly (within a second or so) and to convey a partial block to further sperm penetration. It was calculated that after this rapid block, the egg was approximately one-twentieth as receptive to being entered by a second sperm. The basis for this partial block is unclear. At present the only known reaction to occur within this time frame is the change in membrane potential, which may therefore be involved in its formation. The first block rests on more theoretical grounds than the second, since it is based primarily on the calculation that sperm concentrations high enough to cause numerous collisions per second do not necessarily produce polyspermy. The second block is well established and is thought to be a direct result of the cortical reaction and subsequent membrane elevation. Once membrane elevation is completed, at approximately 1 minute, no additional sperm are capable of entering the egg. If cortical granule breakdown is inhibited in various ways in the presence of normal concentrations of sperm, the egg rapidly becomes polyspermic. If the membrane is removed after it is fully formed, additional sperm will readily penetrate the egg surface long after it had already been fertilized; i.e., it is refertilized.

Studies by various Scandinavian embryologists (reviewed in Runnstrom, 1966) suggested that protease release at fertilization might digest possible binding sites for the sperm on the vitelline membrane. This has now clearly been demonstrated by Epel and coworkers. If the fertilization process is stopped at various stages and the eggs are examined under the scanning electron microscope, it is seen that as the vitelline membrane lifts off from the surface of the egg, sperm previously attached to that membrane are detached (Fig. 5.13). The basis for sperm detachment is the release of proteolytic enzymes from the cortical granules. The proteases released by the cortical granules are inhibited by a substance extracted from soy beans, the soy bean trypsin inhibitor (SBTI). If

acrosome (discharged)   sperm nucleus   surface of egg membrane

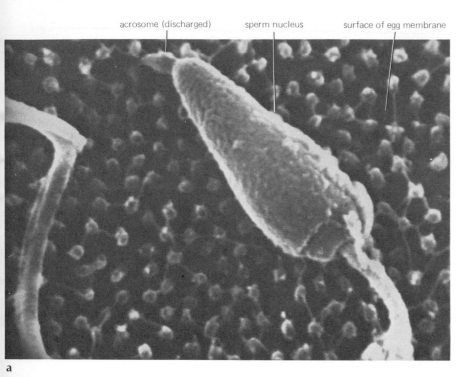

a

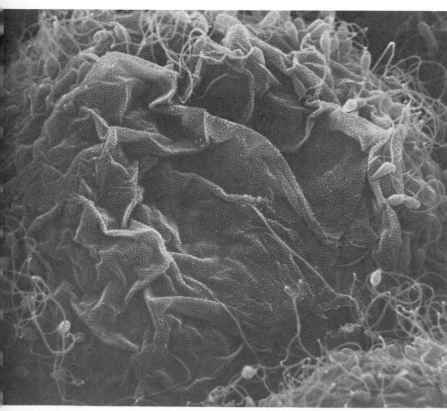

b

Figure 5.13 Scanning electron micrographs of fertilization in the sea urchin *Strongylocentrotus*. *a* The head of this spermatozoon has undergone the acrosomal reaction and is attached to the surface of the egg. The projections of the vitelline membrane are believed to reflect the locations of the microvilli projecting from the egg surface ($\times 31,000$). *b* Egg surface shown 30 seconds after fertilization. Vitelline membrane has lifted over a portion of the surface, detaching the sperm in the process. Remaining egg surface has yet to lose attached sperm whose tails are clearly visible. [*Courtesy of M. Tegner and D. Epel, copyright © American Association for the Advancement of Science.*]

eggs are fertilized in the presence of SBTI, the protease cannot function, and sperm that are able to attach cannot become detached. The result is polyspermy.

A method has been developed to obtain preparations of these enzymes. The procedure involves treatment of unfertilized sea urchin eggs with dithiothreitol (a reducing agent), which essentially eliminates the vitelline membrane. If these eggs are fertilized at a high egg concentration, the cortical granules rupture, expelling the contents into the supernatant (the "fertilization product"), which can be removed and studied. If unfertilized eggs are treated with this fertilization product, the sperm cannot attach because their binding sites have been digested; the eggs do not fertilize.

Results with other animals suggest that the basic processes described above are widespread. In frogs, the release of cortical granule material also causes an alteration in the nature of the vitelline membrane, making it impenetrable to other sperm. In the hamster, the parallels with the sea urchin are striking. Cortical granule breakdown in the hamster also releases a protease into the surrounding medium to act on the surface around it, the zona pellucida. In this case the alterations take a longer period, but they leave the zona impenetrable by other sperm. As in the sea urchin, this cortical product can be added before fertilization and can block the fertilization event. Soy bean trypsin inhibitor also inhibits the enzyme's activity. The hamster egg is used in these studies for the ease of its fertilization in vitro; presumably the same events occur in other mammals, including humans. Cortical granules, however, do not exist in many species. In certain eggs—including the surf clam—cortical granules are present, but they remain intact during the fertilization event. Even in those having a cortical granule breakdown reaction, the events may be quite dissimilar. In the fish, a tough, impenetrable membrane (*chorion*) exists over the entire unfertilized egg, except for a thin canal through it at the animal pole (Fig. 5.14). This opening is so narrow that only one sperm at a time can pass through. When the first has entered, a gelatinous substance flows up and plugs the canal; subsequently, a wave of cortical granule breakdown passes from the animal pole around the egg. The fish egg, as in amphibians, can be experimentally activated with a needle. After activation, the wave of cortical granule breakdown proceeds from that point regardless of where on the egg it occurs. If one waits 5 minutes after activation and adds sperm to the eggs, fertilization then occurs, indicating that the cortical response to previous activation has not placed the egg beyond the means of a subsequent sperm.

Fertilization, one of the critical events in the life of all sexually producing organisms, involves the union of two cells (one gargantuan in comparison with the other) from two individuals. Fertilization underlies the genetic variation found in all natural populations upon which natural selection can act, and it initiates a series of morphological and physiological changes within the zygote

Figure 5.14 Entry of the spermatozoa into the egg of the sturgeon. The micropyle traverses the three layers of chorion, and into its lower reaches projects a tongue of vitelline cytoplasm. Contact with and attachment to the cytoplasm appear to be necessary for the spermatozoon to complete its journey through the micropyle. After the first sperm has made contact, no other sperm can enter. [*After A. S. Ginsburg,* Cytologia, **1:**510 (1959).]

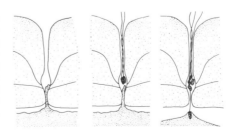

that begin development. Once activated, measurements of oxygen consumption, protein synthesis, DNA synthesis, and a variety of other parameters indicate that the fertilized egg is a very different cell, in a metabolic sense, than that found before its collision with the tiny sperm. In this chapter we have summarized the information available concerning the events prior to, during, and immediately following fertilization, as well as a variety of associated topics.

READINGS

AUSTIN, C. R., 1965. "Fertilization," Prentice-Hall.

BARROS, C., and C. R. AUSTIN, 1967. *In Vitro* Fertilization and the Sperm Acrosome Reaction in the Hamster, *J. Exp. Zool.,* **166**:317–323.

BEATTY, R. A., 1972. Parthenogenesis and Heteroploidy in the Mammalian Egg, in J. D. Biggers and A. W. Schuetz (eds.), "Oogenesis," University Park Press.

BEDFORD, J. M., 1972. An Electron Microscopic Study of Sperm Penetration into the Rabbit Egg after Natural Mating, *Amer. J. Anat.,* **133**:213–254.

COLWIN, L. H., and A. L., 1964. Role of the Gamete Membranes in Fertilization, 22nd Symposium, The Society for the Study of Developmental Growth, Academic.

DAN, J. C., 1970. Morphogenetic Aspects of Acrosome Formation and Reaction, *Advan. Morphog.,* **8**: 1–39.

EDWARDS, R. G., B. D. BAVISTER, and P. C. STEPTOE, 1969. Early Stages of Fertilization *In Vitro* of Human Oocytes Matured *In Vitro, Nature,* **221**:632–635.

EPEL, D., B. C. PRESSMAN, L. ELSAESSER, and A. M. WEAVER, 1969. The Program of Structural and Metabolic Changes Following Fertilization of Sea Urchin Eggs, in G. M. Padilla, G. L. Whitson, and I. L. Cameron (eds.), "The Cell Cycle: Gene-Enzyme Interactions," Academic.

ERISSON, R. J., D. A. BUTHALA, and J. F. NORLAND, 1971. Fertilization of Rabbit Ova in vitro by Sperm with Adsorbed Sendai Virus, *Science,* **173**:54–55.

FANKHAUSER, G., 1948. The Organization of the Amphibian Egg during Fertilization and Cleavage, *Ann. N.Y. Acad. Sci.,* **49**:684–708.

HINEGARDNER, R. T., B. RAO, and D. E. FELDMAN, 1964. The DNA Synthetic Period during Early Development of the Sea Urchin Egg, *Exp. Cell Res.,* **36**:53–61.

LILLIE, F. R., 1913. The Mechanism of Fertilization, in B. H. Willier and J. M. Oppenheimer (eds.), "Foundations of Experimental Embryology," Prentice-Hall.

LONGO, F. J., and E. ANDERSON, 1969. Cytological Aspects of Fertilization in the Lamellibranch, *Mytilus edulis, J. Exp. Zool.,* **172**:69–119.

———, ———, 1968. The Fine Structure of Pronuclear Development and Fusion in the Sea Urchin, *Arbacia punctulata, J. Cell Biol.,* **39**:339–368.

METZ, C. B., and A. MONROY (eds.), 1967. "Fertilization," 2 vols, Academic.

MILLER, R. L., 1966. Chemotaxis during Fertilization in the Hydroid, *Campanularia, J. Exp. Zool.,* **162**:23–44.

ROTHSCHILD, N. M. V., 1956. "Fertilization," Wiley.

RUNNSTROM, J., 1966. The Vitelline Membrane and Cortical Particles in Sea Urchin Eggs and Their Function in Maturation and Fertilization, *Advan. Morphog.,* **5**:221–325.

STEINHARDT, R. A., and D. EPEL, 1974. Activation of Sea Urchin Eggs by a Calcium Ionophore, *Proc. Nat. Acad. Sci.,* **71**:1915.

———, L. LUNDIN, and D. MAZIA, 1971. Bioelectric Responses of the Echinoderm Egg to Fertilization, *Proc. Nat. Acad. Sci.,* **68**:2426–2430.

TEGNER, M. J., and D. EPEL, 1973. Sea Urchin Sperm-Egg Interactions Studied with Scanning Electron Microscopy, *Science,* **179**:685–688.

TYLER, A., 1955. Gametogenesis, Fertilization, and Parthenogenesis, in B. H. Willier, P. Weiss, and V. Hamburger (eds.), "Analysis of Development," Saunders.

WILSON, E. B., 1925. "The Cell in Development and Heredity," 3d ed., Macmillan.

YAMAMOTO, T., 1961. Physiology of Fertilization in Fish Eggs, *Int. Rev. Cytol.,* **12**:361–405.

YANAGIMACHI, R., and Y. D. NODA, 1970. Ultrastructural Changes in the Hamster Sperm Head during Fertilization, *J. Ultras. Res.,* **31**:465–485.

ZANEVELD, L. J. D., K. L. POLAKOSKI, and W. L. WILLIAMS, 1973. A Proteinase and Proteinase Inhibitor of Mammalian Sperm Acrosome, *Biol. Reprod.,* **9**:219–225.

CHAPTER 6

Cleavage and Blastulation

Each cell in a multicellular organism has a limited role to play in the activities of that organism. It is estimated that a human as an adult is composed of several trillion cells. Each cell arises by mitosis, or by meiosis, from a previous cell. In a real sense it is the process of division (together with fertilization) that provides the link from generation to generation throughout evolution, back to primitive ancestral forms. Mitotic divisions build the animal, meiotic divisions provide for the next generation, which via fertilization leads to another round of mitotic divisions.

CLEAVAGE AND THE CELL CYCLE

The first mitotic divisions of each individual comprise the *cleavage* divisions; the cells produced are called *blastomeres*. The period of cleavage extends from fertilization to the formation of a characteristic developmental stage, the *blastula,* and is generally characterized by rapid, successive divisions without intervening periods of growth. By the end of cleavage, the embryo is provided with a sufficient number of cells with which to begin the task of organizing itself into a complex, multilayered structure.

Cleavage begins with a cell that has a greatly bloated volume and a distorted nucleus-to-cytoplasm ratio in comparison with cells of the adult body. The mitotic divisions of cleavage bring these properties in line with those of a more typical cell. In the sea urchin *Echinus,* for example, the nuclear/cytoplasmic volume ratio of the uncleaved egg is estimated to be 1:400, a drop from 1:7 during the previous oocyte stage that contains the large germinal vesicle. At the 4-cell stage the ratio is 1:18; it is 1:12 at the 64-cell stage and 1:7 in the blastula.

This transition is accomplished by the continuing division of the cytoplasm—without a period of growth as is generally found between mitoses—and by the continuing production of more and more nuclei. The increased cell number in itself has great consequences for development. The production of nuclei requires an equivalent amount of DNA and other associated macromolecules characteristic of the chromosomes and nuclear fluid. Membrane must be manufactured in great quantity to provide for these nuclei as well as for the increasing cell surface that necessarily accompanies a division. The formation of two spheres from one results in a 26 percent increase in surface area that must be covered. Similarly the materials required for division, such as the components of the mitotic apparatus, must also be manufactured. Since the period of early development is generally accomplished within a closed system, i.e., no external nutrition is taken in, these synthetic processes must occur at the expense of preexisting material. Nuclear material, membrane, spindle, etc., is built up with the stored reserves packaged into the egg during oogenesis.

The rate of cleavage is dependent upon the temperature, as are all biological processes, but is based primarily on the genetic nature of the organism.

In a typical population of rapidly dividing somatic mammalian cells, the time between divisions (*generation time*) is usually 15 to 20 hours at 37°C. In contrast, a sea urchin egg can reach a blastula stage of approximately 1,000 cells (ten generations) in a matter of a few hours at a much lower temperature. Not all eggs cleave this rapidly. For example, it takes a typical mammal about 12 hours to undergo its first cleavage, though other animals can develop to an advanced larval stage in barely a couple of days.

One measure of the rate of activity of the cleaving embryo is its level of DNA synthesis. In the sea urchin, replication begins either before or about the time of pronuclear fusion, in preparation for the first cleavage. This S period in the sea urchin *Strongylocentrotus* lasts approximately 10 minutes. The second S period, in preparation for the second cleavage, begins in telophase of the first mitosis, before the nucleus has even had a chance to completely re-form. The S_2 lasts approximately 13 minutes. If we extrapolate from 15°C, at which this sea urchin is developing, to 37°C, at which a mammalian cell would be kept, the S period shrinks to an equivalent of 3 minutes. In contrast, a rapidly dividing mammalian cell requires several hours in which to replicate its DNA. To replicate an entire set of sea urchin chromosomes in these times, it is estimated that there must be about 2,000 simultaneous sites of replication among the approximately 40 chromosomes. Embryonic cleavage appears to represent the biological ultimate in DNA synthesis.

Another measure of activity is the rate of respiration. Again, the best measurements were taken from sea urchins and show a general rise in respiration during cleavage. By means of very sensitive techniques, the oxygen consumed by one egg can be measured. After fertilization there is a six- to sevenfold increase over the unfertilized egg, reaching about one-trillionth of a milliliter of oxygen per egg per minute at the two-cell stage. By the 256-cell stage (after eight cleavage divisions), this value has increased fourfold.

YOLK DISTRIBUTION

A moment's comparison between a microscopic sea urchin or mammalian egg of approximately 100 μm and a frog egg of about 1.5 mm and the much larger chicken egg illustrates the range of variation that exists among eggs. As one might expect, eggs of such varying size do not cleave in an identical manner. Most important in determining cleavage properties is yolk content, which can be categorized as follows: Eggs whose yolk is minimal and therefore evenly distributed are called *oligolecithal* (or *isolecithal*). Sea urchins, *Amphioxus,* and

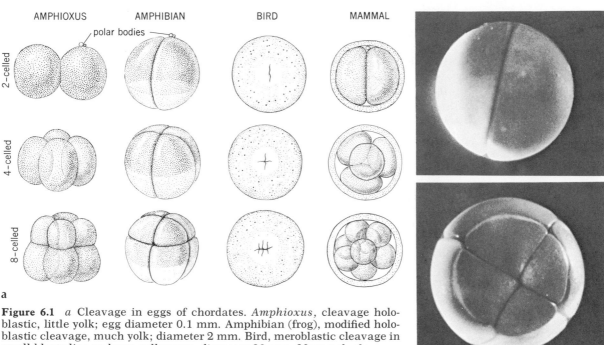

polar bodies

2-celled

4-celled

8-celled

a

b

Figure 6.1 *a* Cleavage in eggs of chordates. *Amphioxus*, cleavage holoblastic, little yolk; egg diameter 0.1 mm. Amphibian (frog), modified holoblastic cleavage, much yolk; diameter 2 mm. Bird, meroblastic cleavage in small blastodisc on large yolk mass; diameter 30 mm. Mammal, cleavage holoblastic, practically no yolk; outer trophoblast and an inner cell mass formed in blastula. *b* Two-cell and eight-cell stage of salamander egg, the third (equatorial) division having divided the egg into four small pigmented blastomeres located above four large yolky blastomeres.

mammals are oligolecithal. Eggs containing a greater amount of yolk that is concentrated at one end are *telolecithal*. Eggs such as those of reptiles, fish, birds, and amphibians are in this category, though some classifications separate less yolky eggs, such as amphibian, as *mesolecithal*. The eggs of many arthropods, particularly insects, have an unusual distribution of yolk. The non-yolky cytoplasm is confined to certain regions of the egg, namely, the center, the outer cortex, and the spokes that connect the center to the cortex. Such eggs are *centrolecithal*.

One manifestation of these differences in yolk distribution is the manner in which cleavage furrows pass through the egg (Fig. 6.1). Cleavage furrows, with a few exceptions, arise as a ring around the entire cell. The ring cuts through that cell by moving inward from all directions. In oligolecithal eggs, the entire egg volume becomes partitioned into blastomeres, i.e., cleavage furrows pass through the entire egg content. Cleavage furrows that are complete in this way are said to be *holoblastic*. Some telolecithal eggs, such as the amphibian, cleave holoblastically, but the yolk affects the rate at which furrowing can progress. In the frog egg the yolk is concentrated in the vegetal half and so cleavage is retarded in this region. As a result the animal half cleaves, often to produce a greater number of cells that are smaller in volume. In the telolecithal eggs with greater yolk content, cleavage is restricted to a disc of non-yolky cytoplasm at one end of the egg, the *blastodisc*. Cleavage furrows are thus incomplete and cleavage is *meroblastic*.

The importance of yolk distribution in determining whether furrows will be complete or not is shown by centrifugation of the normally holoblastic frog egg. After centrifugation, the yolk becomes packed even more densely in the vegetal half and cleavage furrows are not able to penetrate through it. The result is meroblastic cleavage and the animal half becomes divided into small cells.

In the centrolecithal eggs, nuclei divide in the central, non-yolky cytoplasm and then migrate through the spokes to the cortex. Once in the cortex, the nuclei, in the absence of surrounding cell membranes, spread themselves out along the periphery and then become separated from one another by the formation of surrounding membranes. Cleavage of centrolecithal eggs is termed *superficial cleavage*.

CLEAVAGE PATTERN

For a given species the relationship of one cleavage furrow to the next does not occur in a helter-skelter fashion, but rather is a carefully determined genetic trait. Several general patterns of cleavage are found, as well as numerous variations.

Before we can begin to describe these patterns, a few points must be understood. At first glance the eggs of most animals appear as spherical, rather homogeneous cells without any conspicuous differences at one end or the other. In every case, however, upon closer examination at least one axis can be found to be differentiated in some way. In other words, along one line of diameter we find a different structure at different places. This primary axis is called the *animal-vegetal axis* and marks the polarity of the egg. One feature, the site of polar-body formation, will always mark the location of the animal pole. The egg pronucleus begins its migration from this end of the egg. In those eggs with large amounts of yolk, as in amphibians, the yolk—being more dense than the cytoplasm—settles by gravity to one pole, the vegetal pole, opposite the egg chromosomes. In the frog egg, therefore, this axis of polarity is also the axis of gravity and the egg floats with its animal pole up. In oligolecithal eggs, such as those of the sea urchin, the yolk is evenly distributed and the manner in which the egg lies is unrelated to its animal-vegetal axis.

Cleavage, as described below, involves the separation of one cell into two by the formation of membranes in between the forming cells. The process of furrowing of the cytoplasm, cytokinesis, bears a strict relationship to the orientation of the mitotic spindle. A diagrammatic representation of a mitotic apparatus is shown in Fig. 6.2. The mitotic apparatus includes two centrioles that had originally been close together, but now have migrated to the opposite ends of the nucleus.

Centrioles are sites of the organization of spindle protein subunits into the microtubules that compose the spindle. The mechanism by which this occurs is unknown, but the centriolar influence appears to act at a small distance, since microtubules do not actually reach to the centriole itself. Emerging from near each centriole are short microtubular fibers, the astral fibers, that form a "sunburst" arrangement known as the *aster*. Between the two centrioles stretch the microtubular spindle fibers, some of which engage the chromosomes while others are continuous from pole to pole. The chromosomes lie between the two centrioles and are arranged along one plane of diameter of the cell. The long axis of the mitotic apparatus thus runs from centriole to centriole, and the cleavage furrow will always, under normal conditions, be perpendicular to this axis of the spindle. In other words, the cleavage furrow will be in the same plane in which the chromosomes previously had lain. It follows, therefore, that the cleavage pattern will ultimately be determined by the arrangement of the mitotic apparatus of the blastomeres.

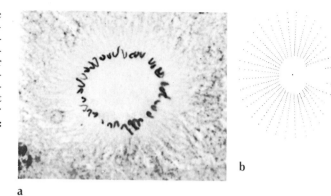

Figure 6.2 The mitotic spindle of the flatworm *Polychoerus*, showing chromosomal and centriolar orientation at metaphase. *a* Polar view of central spindle showing 34 chromosomes. *b* Centrioles with long axis at right angle to one another. [*After Costello*, Biol. Bull., **120:** 285 (*1961*).]

a

b

The orientation of the mitotic apparatus, in turn, depends upon the organization of the cytoplasm that dictates where it will form; this, in turn, depends upon the cytoplasmic package and program determined by oogenesis. We can push all of this back one more level, to the genetic material responsible for the activities of oogenesis, and conclude that the nature of cleavage is determined by genetic determinants acting upon cytoplasmic organization during oogenesis. This is clearly illustrated by cleavage in *Lymnaea*, described below.

The cleavage pattern of most animals falls roughly into three categories: radial, bilateral, and spiral. In radial cleavage the cleavage spindles are oriented with their long axis (centriole to centriole) either perpendicular or parallel to the axis of polarity (Fig. 6.3). In the first two cleavages the long axis is perpendicular to the animal-vegetal axis, and the furrow therefore is parallel to it. A division along this line is a vertical (or meridional) cleavage. Though the long axes of the spindle of the first two cleavages are both perpendicular to the animal-vegetal axis, they are at right angles to each other, as are the resulting planes of the furrows. The third cleavage, occurring in each of the four ex-

Figure 6.3 Development of radially cleaving egg such as those of echinoderms. *a–c* Early cleavage. *d–f* Conversion of morula to blastula. *g* Invagination of blastula to form a gastrula. *h* Evagination from the invaginated enteron to form a mesodermal or a coelomic pouch, thereby establishing the three primary germ layers: mesoderm, endoderm, and ectoderm.

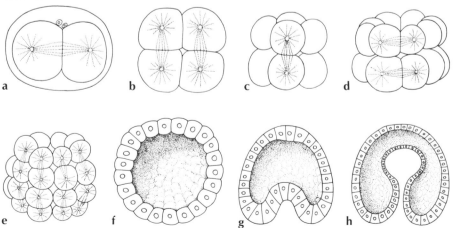

a

b

c

d

e

f

g

h

isting blastomeres, is generally a horizontal cleavage. In radial cleavage cells rest directly above one another as they cleave, forming tiers of cells (Fig. 6.1) and producing an embryo that has radial symmetry. Radial symmetry is the symmetry of a cylinder or a bottle or a star. One axis is differentiated along its length, i.e., the animal-vegetal axis, so that one end is different from the other. However, starting at any point on this axis and proceeding out in any direction, one encounters the same structures regardless of the direction. The consequence of radial symmetry is the anonymity of the blastomeres. No blastomere in a given tier of cells can be recognized from any other, since no distinguishing landmarks exist on any one meridian, much as one section of an orange becomes lost following a simple twirl.

In bilateral cleavage a right and left side become apparent, separated by a plane, the plane of bilateral symmetry. Cleavage activity on one side is mirrored by activity on the other side. Vertebrates cleave in an essentially bilateral manner, as does one class of mollusks, the cephalopods. In most cases, the plane of bilateral symmetry is established by the plane of the first cleavage furrow, and cleavage is bilaterally symmetrical.

In spiral cleavage an entirely different pattern is seen. In contrast with radial cleavage, the cleavage spindles lie at an oblique angle (some angle other than 90° or 180°) to the animal-vegetal axis (Fig. 6.4). The resulting tiers of cells come off in a spiral fashion to the right or the left and come to lie over the furrow of the underlying cell rather than squarely on top of it (Fig. 6.5). The consequences of such cleavage are that each cell is readily identifiable from one minute to the next from embryo to embryo. As a result many embryologists have painstakingly followed the fate of each cell of many of these embryos and have come to some remarkable conclusions. Animals with spiral cleavage, the spiralia, include members of such diverse groups as annelids, mollusks, turbellarian flatworms, some brachiopods, and echuroids; even nematodes have a type of such cleavage. If one follows the fate of individual cells (a cell lineage study) in the annelids, mollusks, and flatworms, the same cells are seen and their fate in many cases is identical among these three groups.

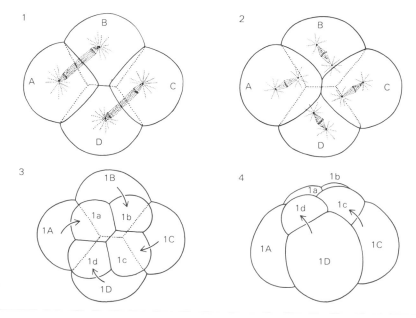

Figure 6.4 Spiral cleavage of egg of a mollusk. Last drawing is viewed from the side, others are seen from the animal pole.

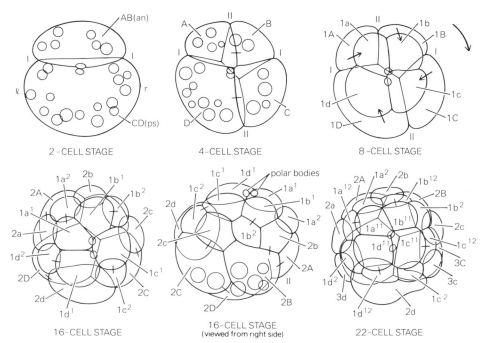

Figure 6.5 Spiral cleavage of the egg of the polychaete *Nereis*. All drawings are polar views except as noted for the 16-cell stage. The circles in the 2-, 4-, and 16-cell stages are oil droplets. [*After Costello*, J. Elisha Mitchell Sci. Soc., **61**:277 (1945).]

Discussion of specific examples involves some cell lineage terminology. In spiral-cleaving eggs, the first division produces two cells, the AB and the CD cells. After the second division there are the A, B, C, and D cells. Often there are differences in the sizes of these cells, which allow ready identification. At the third cleavage two tiers of cells are formed. The animal cells are *micromeres* and the vegetal tier cells are *macromeres*. Usually, as the name implies, the macromeres are larger, but among spiral eggs this term defines the animal and vegetal cells and the micromeres may be larger. The A cell gives rise to a macromere, the 1A, and a micromere, the 1a, and so on, for the B, C, and D cells. At the end of the third cleavage there are four micromeres (the first quartet of micromeres) and four macromeres. At the next division the 1A produces the macromere 2A and a micromere 2a, while the micromere 1a divides to form two micromeres, $1a^1$ and $1a^2$. At the next division (the fifth) the descendants of the A cell of the four-cell stage are the 3A, 3a, $2a^1$, $2a^2$, $1a^{11}$, $1a^{12}$, $1a^{21}$, and $1a^{22}$. Figure 6.5 shows cleavage part of the way through the fifth cleavage, i.e., some of the cells have divided but others have not. If we had followed the D cell rather than the A cell, we would have encountered cells with a more formative destiny. The large 2d cell (Fig. 6.5), for example, is responsible for a very large part of the ectoderm of the larva, and the 4d cell is responsible for nearly all the mesodermal structures.

The remarkable feature is that these same cells form essentially the same structures in many turbellarians, polychaete annelids, and mollusks (the main exception here being the cephalopods). All of these groups have been separated from each other for what probably approaches a half billion years; yet their early development, complex as it is, is virtually identical. This clearly illustrates the conservative nature of embryological development. Very little change appears to be tolerated in embryonic stages in species whose adult stages may bear no relation to one another. A similar result is found when the early postgastrulation stages of vertebrate development are compared, though the evolutionary separation time of the various classes is not nearly so great.

The cytoplasmic organization appears to determine the orientation of cleavage planes. In the spiralia, a cleavage can be a right-handed one, when the spindles are oriented so that the micromeres are formed to the right of the macromere, or a left-handed one. All the mitoses at one cleavage are either right (dextral) or left (sinistral) and the direction alternates at successive cleavage cycles. In other words, if one cleavage is left-handed (counterclockwise as viewed from the animal pole), then the next divisions of the cells will be right-handed (clockwise as viewed from the animal pole).

In snails with coiled shells, the direction of the coiling and therefore the entire viscera can be traced back to the direction of the third cleavage—whether it was dextral or sinistral. Among a population of the snail *Lymnaea*, both directions are found, and a single gene locus is responsible. Dextral coiling is dominant over sinistral. Therefore, one would expect that if a homozygous sinistral female is crossed with a homozygous dextral male, all the offspring would cleave dextrally, since it is dominant. The exact reverse is true, and all offspring cleave sinistrally. The reason for this apparent genetic paradox is that the cytoplasmic organization of the oocyte is produced under the guidance of the sinistral genes of the mother, and the cytoplasm becomes programmed for sinistral cleavage. In this case the sperm genome has no voice in the entire asymmetry of the individual's internal organs, which is dictated by the early cleavage pattern. In each case the embryo's cleavage is determined by the genes of its mother rather than by its own, and it is thus one generation behind in this respect.

CLEAVAGE OF THE SEA URCHIN EGG

The early stages of sea urchin cleavage are shown in the micrographs of Fig. 6.6 and the diagrams of Fig. 6.7. The first two divisions are vertical and at right angles to each other; the third is horizontal in each of the cells, producing an animal tier and a vegetal tier. In the fourth cleavage, the first indications are seen that different parts of the egg will have different properties. In the animal half, each cell divides with an equal vertical cleavage, producing one tier of eight cells of similar volume, the *mesomeres*. In the vegetal half, each cell undergoes a horizontal cleavage, which is also an unequal cleavage. It produces four small cells at the vegetal pole, the micromeres, and four large cells, the macromeres.

As in the case of *Lymnaea*, the unequal division at the fourth cleavage points to some underlying cytoplasmic program that will dictate where the mitotic apparatus will lie within each cell and where the cleavage furrow will strike. Not only does the program determine the place of micromere formation but it determines the time of this cleavage as well. One of the best ways to analyze the underlying mechanism of an event is to dissociate the event under scrutiny from other processes that normally accompany it. For example, if we are interested in what factors determine that an unequal fourth cleavage should occur in sea urchins, we can try to analyze which processes of the

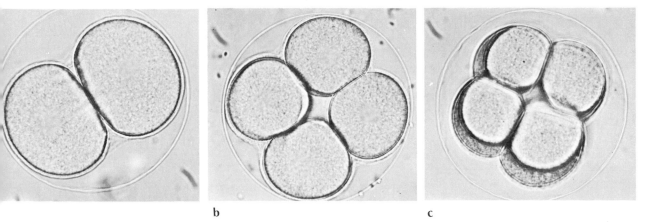

b

c

Figure 6.6 First three cleavages of sea urchin egg within fertilization membrane, showing hyaline layer, flattening of interface between adjoining cells, and curved free surfaces. [*Courtesy of T. Gustafson.*]

Figure 6.7 Diagram of first four cleavages of the sea urchin *Paracentrotus lividus*, showing the orientation of the spindle and the darkened pigment ring. Note the unequal division in fourth division, resulting in formation of micromeres.

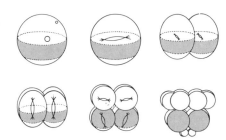

embryo can be separated from this unequal cleavage and which cannot. Presumably the latter may be related in a causal way to the unequal cleavage. Numerous treatments of a sea urchin egg are capable of suppressing cleavage divisions. For example, by the use of ultraviolet radiation or hypotonic seawater, the first one, two, or three cleavages can be inhibited. In any of these cases (Fig. 6.8), at the time when the fourth cleavage would normally have occurred (even if no prior cleavage had been allowed), an unequal horizontal cleavage takes place just as if no disruption had been inflicted on the egg. In some way the egg has kept track of the time after fertilization, and this "micromere clock" within the egg has determined that a horizontal, unequal cleavage should occur. In other words, since this cleavage has been dissociated from the three previous cleavages, we can conclude that its formation is not dependent upon any earlier cleavage. The elimination of what it is not related to tells us little about what it is dependent upon. The question then becomes: Are there any treatments that the egg can be subjected to that will selectively interfere with the micromere cleavage, and if so what else is coordinately inhibited? We may be able to answer this, but first a digression must be presented.

If sea urchin eggs are homogenized in distilled water, all the materials soluble in water will be extracted and those insoluble can be centrifuged to the bottom of the tube. If this pellet, after extraction in water, is then resuspended in 0.6 M KCl, a certain group of proteins that were not soluble in water are now solubilized in this salt solution. One of the amino acids that compose proteins, cysteine, has a sulfhydryl (—SH) group, and the amount of SH in the KCl ex-

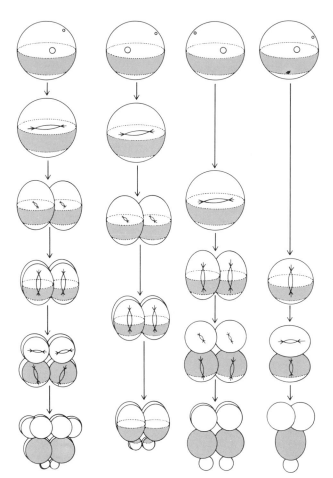

Figure 6.8 Normal and retarded cleavage in the sea urchin. The delays were induced by exposure to hypotonic seawater. The time elapsing between the stage seen at the top and the bottom is the same in all cases. [*After Hörstadius, 1939.*]

tract is easily determined. It has been found that if the amounts of SH present in the KCl extract are measured, using eggs of different stages of cleavage, there are striking changes that can be closely correlated with the cleavage cycle (Fig. 6.9). The maximum SH levels are found during cleavage and the minimum SH levels during mid-interphase. By the fourth cleavage there have occurred four SH cycles. How do these SH cycles relate to the micromere clock? If sea urchin eggs are irradiated with UV light or treated with the inhibitor 2,4-dinitrophenol (DNP) for a short time, the next cleavage is blocked, but the SH cycle continues. At the time when untreated eggs undergo their fourth cleavage, the treated eggs undergo their third cleavage (though their fourth SH cycle) and cleave unequally to produce micromeres at the vegetal pole in the eight-cell stage.

If cleaving sea urchin eggs are placed in seawater containing a bit of ether (0.6 vol percent), the SH cycle is blocked and the level of KCl-soluble SH remains constant until the eggs are removed. Even though the SH cycle is suppressed, nuclear division can continue. If these ether-treated eggs are returned to normal seawater and their cleavage is analyzed, it is found that the fourth cleavage (the third SH cycle) produces essentially an equal cleavage and no micromeres are formed, just as if it had been the third cleavage.

Figure 6.9 Lower curve illustrates the variation in SH content of extracted protein with time after fertilization. Maximum SH content coincides with mid-mitotic period through each of the first four cleavages. The upper two curves show the percentages of cells that have actually undergone division at each cleavage period. The very top graph illustrates a control culture undergoing the first four cleavages. The middle graph illustrates the effect of a one-minute exposure to ultraviolet radiation; the second cleavage is skipped, and the eggs wait until the time the controls are undergoing their third cleavage before they undergo their second. The second SH cycle continues unchanged in these irradiated eggs, even though the second cleavage has not occurred. At the time the controls undergo their fourth cleavage, the irradiated eggs undergo their third cleavage, which is now producing unequal micromeres at a premature cleavage stage. [*After M. Ikeda,* Exp. Cell Res., **40:**282, (1965).]

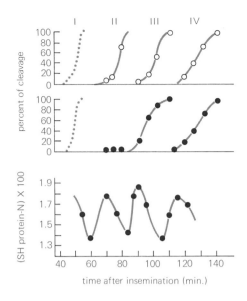

Many biological phenomena can be shown to occur with a predictable time interval, suggesting that mechanisms exist that are able of keeping some measure of time. Very little is known about these mechanisms—whether they relate to annual migrations of animals, monthly variations in reproductive activity, daily cycles of feeding behavior, or in this case rhythmic increases in cell number. The implications from the present study of micromere formation are that SH cycles keep track of cleavage number in anticipation of the fourth unequal cleavage. These two events cannot be dissociated from each other, in contrast with the dissociation that has been achieved between micromere formation and the number of nuclear divisions or cytokineses. Even though answers such as this one, if the interpretation of these results is correct, serve to push back the questions to a more basic level (i.e., what causes the cycles in SH level), they still serve to explain in a very real sense how complex developmental processes are controlled.

INTERCELLULAR COMMUNICATION

Among any group of closely applied cells there exists the potential for cellular interaction. Cleaving cells exhibit particularly clear evidence that some type of communication exists among the cells. This is most evident in the synchrony of the early cleavage divisions of many animals, in which all cells undergo division at the same time. The precision of this phenomenon is too great to be accounted for merely by built-in cytoplasmic signals present independently in each cell; there must be some communication among the blastomeres.

Two possible pathways exist for cells to inform one another. One route is via the extracellular medium, and thus the response must be mediated through the cell membrane itself. The other is by direct cytoplasmic continuity from one cell to another. Examples of the latter are the cytoplasmic bridges, such as those between spermatogonia, which are implicated in the synchrony of spermatogenesis. Other examples are the gap or low resistance junctions through which small molecules are able to pass directly in channels across the mem-

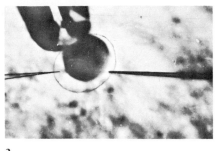

a

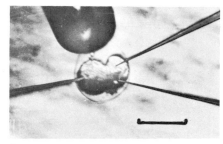

b

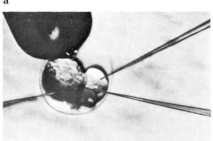

c

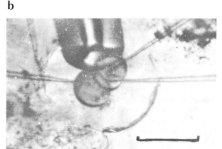

d

Figure 6.10 Intercellular electrical coupling at a forming membrane junction in a dividing egg of the starfish *Asterias forbesii*. *a* Fertilized egg impaled by two microelectrodes. *b–d* Various stages of cleavage with three microelectordes in intracellular position (calibration × 0.1 mm). Ion communication between the two blastomeres diminishes progressively during division as a cell-membrane junction forms at the plane of cleavage. [*Courtesy of W. R. Loewenstein.*]

branes of the two "coupled" cells. Cells communicating by this means are in a sense actually one giant compartment in terms of those molecules that can pass freely from one cell to the next. One measure of coupling is the flow of current, i.e., movement of ions between the cells, as measured by electrodes placed in two different cells.

Several embryos have been examined to determine the extent to which the cells are coupled. In the starfish *Asterias* (Fig. 6.10), the cells of the cleaving embryo become coupled only after the fifth cleavage, indicating this mechanism cannot be responsible for the synchrony observed in the first five cleavages. In *Xenopus*, studies taken up to the blastula (stage 7) show no evidence that the cells are capable of transferring molecules the size of fluorescein (molecular weight of 335) from one cell to the next. In contrast, during the early development of the fish *Fundulus*, all cells are coupled at the earliest stage examined, the four-cell stage, through at least gastrulation. The implication of the differences found from embryo to embryo is not clear, however, since studies of this type have just begun and the significance of cell coupling for development is not understood.

ALTERATIONS OF CLEAVAGE PATTERN

One of the most valuable means of learning about a developmental process is to attempt to disrupt the process by a specific treatment and then to explain the altered results in light of what that treatment is known to do. For example, x-radiation or ultraviolet radiation damages nucleic acids, and the effects of these agents on a process such as cleavage implicate nucleic acids in that process.

If the first two cells of a sea urchin are separated, each will continue to cleave. The next division of each isolated cell is a vertical one, and the next is horizontal (and equal). In other words, each isolated cell is cleaving just as if it had never been isolated; it does not begin its cleavage sequence over again. After two cleavages, each has two animal cells and two vegetal cells. At the next cleavage, the two animal cells divide vertically to form four mesomeres, and the two vegetal cells divide horizontally (and unequally) to form two micromeres and two macromeres. Each is cleaving just as if it were still half the original embryo; this pattern is called *half cleavage.*

However, a fertilized sea urchin egg, even before the first cleavage, can be cut in half with a fine needle right through its cytoplasm; each half will immediately heal over by formation of a membrane, and each half will cleave. The pattern of cleavage, whether it be half or whole, depends upon the time at which the operation is performed. If the egg is cut just after fertilization, each cleaves as if it were a whole egg, i.e., a whole cleavage pattern is seen in each. If the operation is delayed until just before the first cleavage, each cleaves in the half pattern. Intermediate times give whole patterns to some and half patterns to others. These results indicate that the cytoplasmic organization dictating the ordered cleavage pattern is not established in the unfertilized egg, but arises at some time between fertilization and first cleavage. Oogenesis, then, does not complete the program for cleavage in sea urchins. Another important conclusion from this experiment is the flexibility within the egg for a cleavage pattern other than its normal one.

The only way to determine such events as the time the cleavage program arises is to put the embryos under abnormal conditions and observe the results. This is the basic tenet of experimental embryology, and no other field of biology has used the "experimental state" with such far-reaching results.

IMPORTANCE OF CLEAVAGE

Even though much of the program for the cleavage pattern is contained within the cytoplasmic organization, mechanical factors can be demonstrated to play a role as well. For example, if a fertilized sea urchin egg is compressed between two cover slips so that its top and bottom become flattened, the spindles are forced to lie with their long axes parallel to the cover slips. In such a condition the ensuing cleavage furrow will be perpendicular to the planes of the cover slips. As long as the compression is maintained, the cleavages will continue to be vertical, producing one tier with an increasing number of cells. If the compression is removed, even as late as after the sixth vertical cleavage, normal development can result. This experiment indicates that the manner in which the cytoplasm is cleaved is not of utmost importance to the future development of the embryo, though this result does not necessarily pertain to all embryos.

Another type of experiment also suggests that certain developmental processes, at least, can continue in the absence of the typical cleavage pattern. For example, treatment of the polychaete egg *Chaetopterus* with a dilute solution of potassium chloride abolishes the ability of the egg to cleave. One might expect that blocking cleavage would leave the egg in the exact state as the typical uncleaved egg, but this is not the case (Fig. 6.11). Rather striking changes occur whose parallel can be found in the normally developing early embryo. Vacuoles and yolk take their place in a corresponding position and the surface becomes ciliated. The extent to which this process parallels normal development can be debated, but it appears that some developmental events can proceed independently of the parceling out of the cytoplasm. Again we have shown that the normally occurring processes can be dissociated from one another, presumably reflecting their different underlying mechanisms.

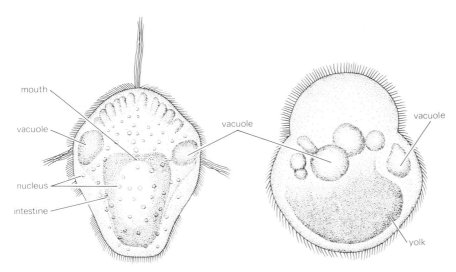

Figure 6.11 Differentiation without cleavage in the egg of the polychaete *Chaetopterus*. *a* Normal larva. *b* Unfertilized egg after treatment with dilute solution of potassium chloride in seawater for 24 hours. [*After Lillie*, Arch. Entwickl.-mech., **14**:477 (*1902*).]

mouth

vacuole

nucleus

intestine

vacuole

vacuole

yolk

Circumstantial evidence indicates that specific cleavage patterns reflect an underlying pattern of cytoplasmic differentiation. That is, the underlying organization of the moment causes the ensuing cell divisions to set apart cytoplasmic regions of different character. If for no other reason than this, cleavage patterns and cell lineage studies are informative. An example of this cause-effect relationship is seen in an experiment by Hörstadius on sea urchin eggs. If fertilized eggs are placed in hypotonic seawater, the rate of cell division is retarded, but the rate of cytoplasmic differentiation along the animal-vegetal axis is apparently unaffected (Fig. 6.8). Thus the first cleavage may take place at the time when the third cleavage usually occurs, and is equatorial; the second cleavage corresponds to the normal fourth, resulting in two animal blastomeres, one vegetal (macromere) and one micromere.

The conclusion that particular patterns of cleavage are unimportant in themselves (although they are informative in that they indicate underlying regional cytoplasmic differentiation of the egg) is strengthened when we consider later stages of development such as the blastula. In both sea urchin and frog, for instance, after nine or ten cleavages have taken place, it makes little difference in what order or pattern they initially occurred.

MECHANISMS OF CYTOKINESIS

The first mitotic division of the echinoderm egg has been the favored system for the study of the process of division itself. These eggs are essentially transparent, and the mitotic apparatus and progression of the furrow are easily observed in the living cell. The very high level of synchrony allows the investigator to obtain many cells at the same stage of mitosis. In addition the egg, in contrast with the average cell, is large; manipulations and measurements can be performed on it.

It is difficult even for the experienced observer to comprehend the ability of a structure that is a spherical mass at one minute to cleave itself in half the next minute, and to do so in a highly predictable time and manner. Many theories have been advanced to explain this event by placing the forces variously with the mitotic spindle, the cortex, or the plasma membrane itself.

In defense of these various theories, we have learned a considerable amount about the basic physical properties of the egg—values for its surface tension, its viscosity, its elasticity, etc.

In recent years, one of the theories has continued to gain favor: the contractile-ring theory proposed by Marsland. In this theory the force generated to cleave the egg resides in a thin strip of protoplasm just beneath the plasma membrane, the cortex, in the region of the furrow itself. Various types of experiments have supported this theory, and the finding of cytoplasmic filaments of 35 to 60 Å diameter in the cortex of the furrow region just before cleavage begins has indicated the means by which it occurs. These filaments have now been found in a variety of animals, including cephalopods, coelenterates, amphibians, annelids, mammals, and echinoderms (Fig. 6.12). The precise mechanism by which these filaments are capable of contraction is unknown. Since an individual filament does not thicken or become coiled, the suggestion has been made that shortening occurs by the sliding of filaments over each other, as in the actomyosin system of striated muscle. Whatever the mechanism, the effect of this contractile band of about 0.1 to 0.2 μm in thickness, completely encircling the egg, is analogous to the pulling of a purse string to narrow the diameter of its opening. A cortical layer of filaments has also been found in those animals, such as the jellyfish and the squid, whose furrow ad-

Figure 6.12 Photomicrographs of half-cleaved *Arbacia* eggs. *a* Light micrograph of an egg sectioned parallel to the long axis of the mitotic spindle. *b* Electron micrograph showing the cleavage furrow of a similar egg sectioned in the same plane as *a*. The layer of "dots" beneath the plasma membrane is the contractile ring, whose microfilaments are seen in cross-section when cut in this manner. The dark round body is a yolk granule. *c* Electron micrograph of a cleaving egg sectioned perpendicularly to those of *a* and *b*. This section is parallel to the furrow and, therefore, parallel to the contractile ring microfilaments. As a result, the filaments now appear as filaments and some spindle fibers are cut in cross-section. Three mitochondria are seen in addition to part of a yolk granule. [*Courtesy of T. E. Schroeder.*]

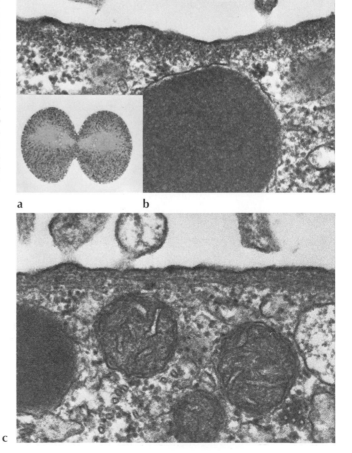

a   b

c

vances from only one end rather than as an encircling ring. As would be expected, cytochalasin B, which is capable of rapid dissolution of microfilaments, causes a rapid regression of a cleavage furrow even if added well after furrowing has begun.

The diameter of these filaments and their proposed contractile properties closely ally them in function with the well-studied filaments made of actin. Increasing evidence suggests that they are indeed made of this specific protein. One property of actin, regardless of where it is found, is its ability to bind to myosin extracted from vertebrate muscle tissue. The two proteins together form the actomyosin complex, which is identifiable in the electron microscope. If cleaving sea urchins are prepared with glycerin (a well-established procedure for observing muscle proteins), the filaments in the cortex of the furrow are visible. If myosin is added to these preparations, it is seen to be bound specifically by these filaments. To corroborate this finding, actin can be extracted from cleaving eggs. An alternate proposal for the chemical basis of cleavage has been proposed by Sakai (1968).

THE MITOTIC APPARATUS

Cytokinesis is one aspect of cell division. The other event invariably linked to it is nuclear division (mitosis), accomplished by the mitotic apparatus. Though these two processes appear to be causally linked, a surprising degree of dissociation is possible. Experiments by Hiramoto have shown that the furrowing events can occur after complete removal or disruption of the mitotic apparatus, but only if performed after the onset of metaphase. In other words, if the entire mitotic apparatus is sucked out of an anaphase cell, well in advance of the initiation of furrowing, cytokinesis will occur and in the same place it would have in the undisturbed cell. Figure 6.13 shows the furrow in a cell in which a large oil drop has been placed at anaphase prior to the onset of cytokinesis; it has completely displaced the spindle. In these eggs, the location of the furrow bears no relation to the displaced mitotic apparatus, but is along the same plane as if it had not been disturbed.

The conclusions emerging from a large-scale investigation of first cleavage (particularly by Rappaport) implicate the mitotic apparatus, and especially the asters, as the source of the stimulus for cleavage. The asters have been singled out as the source of the stimulus, since furrowing can be initiated between two asters even in the absence of the spindle and chromosomes. Presumably substances radiating from these two sources at each end of the spindle condition one part of the surface, namely, the equatorial region, for cytokinesis. This part of the membrane undergoes changes such as increased rigidity and a decrease in elasticity. This region of the surface will then develop the contractile ring of cortical filaments. It appears that the signals emanating from the mitotic apparatus have been emitted by late metaphase; after this time the furrow will form in the proper place regardless of the position or even the presence of the mitotic apparatus. If the spindle is displaced prior to metaphase, the furrow will occur in keeping with the new position of the mitotic apparatus, not the original position. Once the stimulus is received at the surface, the surface gains independence from other structures for the completion of its mission. Even pieces of furrow completely isolated from the remainder of the cell are still capable of undergoing contraction. Under normal conditions the plane of the furrow forms across the plane in which the chromosomes had lain. the appearance of the contractile ring of filaments, as well as their disappearance, is a very rapid phenomenon.

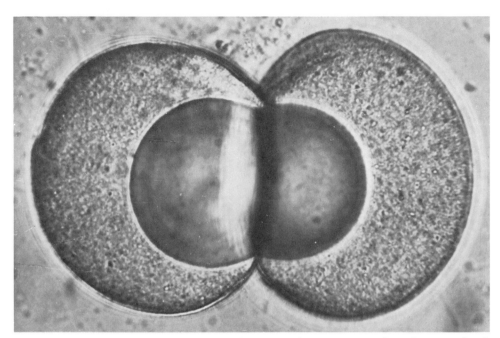

Figure 6.13 Injection of oil droplet into this sea urchin egg at anaphase has completely disrupted the mitotic apparatus, but has no effect on the position of the ensuing cytokinesis. [*Courtesy of Y. Hiramoto.*]

The materials needed for the division process, particularly the microtubule proteins of the mitotic spindle, account for a substantial (5 to 10 percent) percentage of the total egg mass. The question has been asked: When are these materials made in preparation for the first mitotic division? Studies during the 1950s and the 1960s demonstrated several methods to disrupt the echinoderm egg in a way that leaves the entire mitotic apparatus intact and capable of being studied. The early investigations established that the protein of the mitotic apparatus was composed for the most part of a single species (now known to be two molecular species, tubulin A and B) that could be isolated in a pure form. The analysis of the contents of the unfertilized egg revealed a considerable quantity of the protein component of the mitotic apparatus already present at that stage. This finding suggested that the bulk of the mitotic apparatus was preformed and awaited only the polymerization process to become incorporated into the structural machinery for division. This is typical of many types of morphogenesis within the cell. The precursors are not necessarily synthesized at the last minute, but may exist in a "precursor pool" well in advance of when they are actually needed.

Protein synthesis between fertilization and first cleavage is estimated to account for less than 0.5 percent of the total egg protein. However, the inhibition of protein synthesis during this period by the inhibitor puromycin blocks first division. Since the bulk of the mitotic apparatus for first cleavage is preformed, it is believed that some other protein component of the division process must be synthesized after fertilization before cleavage can occur. An alternate possibility, for which some evidence exists, is that puromycin is blocking cleavage by a side effect unrelated to its inhibition of protein synthesis. If this is true, it further demonstrates the care that must be taken in the interpretation of studies with metabolic inhibitors.

Though the basic mechanism involved in cleavage appear to be very similar in all animals, the patterns that are formed by the cleaving cells are dramatically dissimilar. The latter part of cleavage is marked by a decrease in the rate of cell division and the formation of the blastula. The blastula is generally a brief stage, awaiting a much more dramatic rearrangement of cells during gastrulation. The process of blastulation is so different among different animals that generalizations cannot be made and the student must learn by example. Most blastulas are characterized by an internal, fluid-filled cavity, the *blastocoel,* though a variety of animals possess a blastula completely filled with cells, a *stereoblastula.*

One of the better studied examples of blastulation is in the sea urchin, an embryo with an extremely spacious blastocoel, as is common among developing isolecithal eggs. In the sea urchin a cavity appears at a very early stage in cleavage (Fig. 6.6); this cavity continues to enlarge as the cells grow in number and decrease in thickness to form a thinner and thinner outer wall (Fig. 6.14).

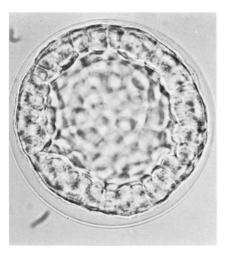

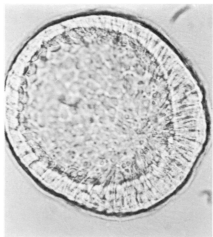

Figure 6.14 Early (*a*) and late (*b*) blastula of a sea urchin, showing blastocoel, single-cell-thick layer of the blastula wall, and external non-cellular hyaline layer. [*Courtesy of T. Gustafson.*] *c,d* Scanning electron micrographs of hatched sea urchin blastula. *c* bisected blastula showing blastula wall and blastocoel; *d* small area of external surface, each cell bearing a single cilium. [*Courtesy of W. J. Humphreys.*]

a

b

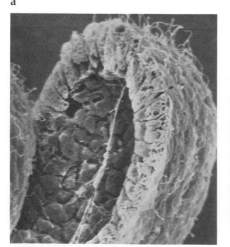

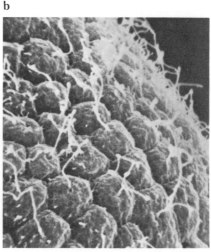

c

d

As each blastomere divides into two cells, one would expect that the large spherical egg would become chopped up into a mass of smaller cells, packed into the original volume; the formation of this entirely different structure is difficult to explain and presents formidable engineering problems. Why do the cells remain at the outer wall and allow the central region to become cavernous? Two theories have been presented to explain this formation. One of the basic premises of both theories is this: The reason the cells form an outer wall rather than a solid mass is that each cell is attached to the hyaline layer which tightly surrounds the entire embryo. In Dan's theory, the blastocoel forms and enlarges as a result of osmotic pressure of the blastocoelic fluid. This fluid contains a considerable quantity of macromolecules and might exert osmotic pressure via the osmotic uptake of water from the environment. If water were to move into the blastocoel, it could exert pressure on the cells attached to the hyaline layer and force them outward.

In the theory of Gustafson and Wolpert, blastocoel formation and expansion result from the manner in which the cells are packed. Just before each cell divides, the surface tension of the outer cell layer increases and the cells round up, divide, and produce two rounded cells. When one spherical cell divides into two spherical cells, the combined diameter of the two daughter cells exceeds that of the original cell. As long as the dividing cells remain in one layer and their outer surface remains attached to the hyaline layer, the layer of cells must inevitably push itself outward as a result of the increasing diameters of the cells. It is the radial pattern of cleavage that keeps the cells side by side rather than forming layers of cells. The rounding up of cells prior to their division suggests that changes occur in the surface tension of the membrane and in the adhesiveness of one cell to its neighbors. The importance of these factors is illustrated in Fig. 6.15. Transitions between *a, b,* and *c* are possible simply by changes in surface tension and cell-cell adhesiveness. Case *d* would require additional factors. The view of Wolpert and Gustafson, therefore, seems to explain echinoderm blastulation simply by changes in the mechanical properties of the cells and geometrical packing of an increasing number of cells, produced by radial cleavages, that remain attached to an elastic hyaline layer.

Figure 6.15 Possible configurations of the cross section of a tube comprising 24 cells in a single layer attached to a supporting membrane (H), with no change in cell volume. *a* Considerable contact between cells and no cavity. *b* Moderate contact, and a cavity is present. *c* Point contacts between the rounded-up cells. *d* Considerable contact with the supporting membrane. [*After Gustafson and Wolpert, 1967.*]

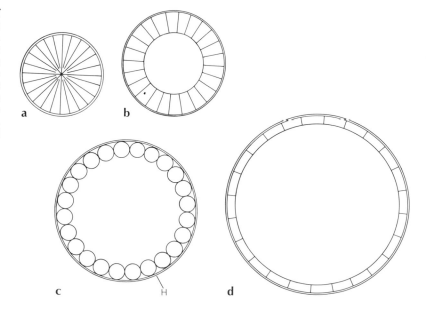

Blastocoel formation in the oligolecithal egg of *Amphioxus* (Figs. 6.1 and 6.16*a*) resembles that in the sea urchin. In embryos containing more yolk, blastula formation must be governed by different physical forces.

Not only is the amphibian egg larger than the invertebrate kinds just discussed but it contains proportionately more yolk. If a frog egg is centrifuged so that all the yolk is compacted toward one side, the yolk is seen to occupy about one-half the egg interior. Normally it is distributed as a gradient, so that the ratio of yolk to cytoplasm is least toward the animal pole and greatest towards the vegetal pole. As a result, the egg nucleus resides considerably above the equator. The relative concentration of yolk in the vegetal half of the egg and the location of the nucleus in the animal half have important consequences with regard to cleavage, blastula formation, and gastrulation (Fig. 6.16).

The first two cleavages are both in the plane of the polar axis, at right angles to each other. The mitotic apparatus, however, forms in conjunction with the eccentrically placed nucleus, so that the cleavage furrows first appear near the animal pole and progressively extend toward the opposite pole. The third, or horizontal, cleavage is also influenced by the position of the nucleus in each of the first four blastomeres; it divides each cell into a relatively small animal cell, or micromere, containing relatively little yolk and a relatively large, yolky, vegetal macromere (Fig. 6.1*b*). By so doing, it sets up a differential. From this time on, the micromeres divide relatively rapidly, free from the burden of cleaving through a yolk-dense region; the macromeres divide very slowly, since the cytoplasm is now loaded with yolk throughout. Yolk granules or platelets have the double effect of conferring physical inertia on the dividing

Figure 6.16 Schematic sectional diagrams comparing the blastulas of *Amphioxus*, frog, and chick. [*Modified from Huettner, "Fundamental of Comparative Embryology of the Vertebrates." By permission of The Macmillan Company, New York.*]

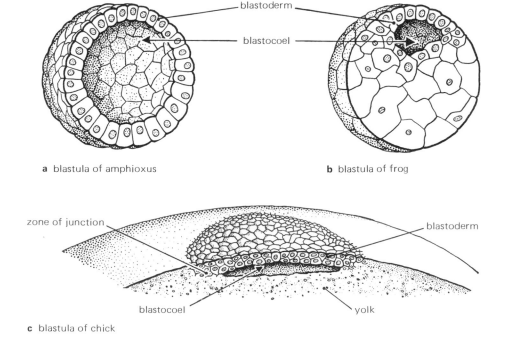

a blastula of amphioxus

b blastula of frog

c blastula of chick

mass and diluting the active cytoplasm with metabolically inactive inclusions.

As cleavage proceeds, a stage is reached that consists of an upper, animal region and a lower, vegetal region. The animal region is composed of numerous small, rapidly and synchronously dividing cells that cover a comparatively small blastocoel. The vegetal region is at least half the whole embryo and consists of relatively large, slowly dividing cells. In most amphibians—both frogs and salamanders—the cells constituting the roof of the blastocoel at first form an epithelium one cell thick; soon they establish a layer two cells thick, presumably because their rate of multiplication exceeds the capacity of the blastula to expand. In *Xenopus*, however, the blastula roof remains as a single layer. In meroblastic cleavage (Fig. 6.16) the yolk remains uncleaved; the thin, cleaving disc of cytoplasm becomes slightly elevated above the yolk to form a blastocoelic cavity.

In mammals an entirely different means of blastulation is seen. In the isolecithal sea urchin egg, the blastocoel can be found as soon as cleavage begins, as the cells remain in one peripheral layer. In the isolecithal mammalian egg, cleavage divisions are not radial and the embryos become a solid ball of cells, some of which are completely surrounded by other blastomeres. This solid intermediate state is the *morula,* and blastula formation results from a complete rearrangement of the blastomeres. The process, termed *cavitation,* is characterized by the uptake of fluid between the cells and therefore the formation of an internal cavity. As the cells become separated from each other, the embryo expands greatly in volume and a layer of cells forms around a central cavity (Fig. 6.1). Eventually the outer layer becomes thinner and more and more flattened; it is called the *trophoblast.* During this process of cavitation, not all the cells are incorporated into the thin, outer trophoblast layer. Instead, some of the cells collect in a clump (the inner cell mass) and are found within the blastocoel at one edge in contact with the trophoblast. In mammals this stage is called a *blastocyst,* but it corresponds to the blastula of other animals. The formation and development of the mammalian egg are described in more detail in Chapter 16.

Though some type of cleavage process is a prerequisite in the conversion of a single-celled egg into a multicellular embryo, the manner in which this takes place illustrates a remarkable diversity among animal groups. As a result of cleavage, the swollen cytoplasmic/nuclear volume ratio is corrected; the embryo is provided with a sufficient number of cells with which to begin the business of reorganization into a complex, multilayered structure. Though the process of cleavage is essential, the precise way it occurs is not always of great importance; in numerous cases the disruption of the normal series of cleavage furrows does not interfere with the embryogenesis of that individual. Cleavage is accomplished by a series of mitotic divisions whose study has provided insights into the mitotic process itself. The establishment of the contractile ring, as manifested in the contractile properties of its cytoplasmic filaments, has provided answers to questions that have been posed for many decades. In the following chapter we will return to the cleavage period with an eye to the informational organization of the early embryo.

READINGS

ARNOLD, J. M., 1969. Cleavage Furrow Formation in a Telolecithal Egg (*Loligo pealii*), I: Filaments in Early Furrow Formation, *J. Cell Biol.,* **41**:894–904.

BENNET, M. V. L., and J. P. TRINKHAUS, 1970. Electrical Coupling Between Cells by Way of Exracellular Space and Specialized Junctions, *J. Cell Biol.,* **44**:592–610.

BERRILL, N. J., 1961. "Growth, Development, and Pattern," Freeman.

BOYCOTT, A. E., C. DIVER, S. L. GARSTANG, and F. M. TURNER, 1930. The Inheritance of Sinistrality in *Limnaea peregra* (Mollusca, Pulmonata), *Phil. Trans. Roy. Soc., London, Ser. B,* **219**:51–131.

COSTELLO, D. P., 1955. Cleavage, Blastulation, and Gastrulation, in B. H. Willier, P. Weiss, and V. Hamburger (eds.), "Analysis of Development," Saunders.

DAN, K., 1960. Cytoembryology of Echinoderm and Amphibia, *Int. Rev. Cytol.,* **9**:321–367.

—— and M. IKEDA, 1971. On the System Controlling the Time of Micromere Formation in Sea Urchin Embryos, *Development, Growth, and Differentiation,* **13**:285–301.

GUSTAFSON, T., and L. WOLPERT, 1967. Cellular Movement and Contact in Sea Urchin Morphogenesis, *Biol. Rev.,* **42**:442–498.

HARVEY, E. B., 1956. "The American *Arbacia* and Other Sea Urchins," Princeton University Press.

HIRAMOTO, Y., 1965. Further Studies on Cell Division Without Mitotic Apparatus in Sea Urchin Eggs, *J. Cell Biol.,* **25**:161–167.

MARSLAND, D., and J. V. LANDAU, 1954. The Mechanics of Cytokinesis: Temperature-Pressure Studies on the Cortical Gel System in Various Marine Eggs, *J. Exp. Zool.,* **125**:507–539.

MIKI-NOUMURA, T., and F. OOSAWA, 1969. An Actin-like Protein of the Sea Urchin Eggs, I: Its Interaction with Myosin from Rabbit Striated Muscle, *Exp. Cell Res.,* **56**:224–232.

MITCHISON, J. M., and M. M. SWANN, 1954. The Mechanical Properties of the Cell Surface, *J. Exp. Biol.,* **31**:443–472.

NEEDHAM, J., 1942. "Biochemistry and Morphogenesis," Cambridge University Press.

RAPPAPORT, R., 1974. Cleavage, in J. Lash and J. R. Whittaker (eds.), "Concepts of Development," Sinauer.

SAKAI, H., 1968. Contractile Properties of Protein Threads from Sea Urchin Eggs in Relation to Cell Division, *Int. Rev. Cytol.,* **23**:89–112.

SCHROEDER, T. E., 1972. The Contractile Ring, II: Determining its Brief Existence, Volumetric Changes and Vital Role in Cleaving *Arabacia* Eggs, *J. Cell Biol.,* **53**:419–434.

SZOLLOSI, D., 1970. Cortical Cytoplasmic Filaments of Cleaving Eggs: A Structural Element Corresponding to the Contractile Ring, *J. Cell Biol.,* **44**:192–209.

WILSON, E. B., 1925. "The Cell in Development and Heredity," 3d ed., Macmillan.

CHAPTER 7

Organization of the Early Embryo

Epigenesis and Preformation
Polarity
Bilateral Symmetry
The Egg Cortex
Regulative Development and Physiological Gradients
Mosaic Development

> Ascidians
> Spiralia

Mosaic Versus Regulative Development
The Cephalopod Egg: Cortex and Pattern

EPIGENESIS AND PREFORMATION

One of the most profound questions of concern to biologists for several hundred years has been how the complex structure of an embryo and subsequent adult can develop from what appears to be the simple, unordered structure of the fertilized egg. As is most spectacularly conveyed by time-lapse cinematography, this simple, large cell becomes chopped into many cells and undergoes dramatic rearrangement; soon, complex structures begin to appear here and there as the entire embryo continues to be shaped according to some preexisting plan of construction. Each step along the way is predictable; little is left to chance.

Historically two theories were called upon to explain the events of development. One theory, *preformation*, simply denied that development results in an increase in order. The early preformationists of the seventeenth and eighteenth centuries held that a complete adult is present in each egg and development simply results in its growth and emergence.

As biologists began to look closer at the structure of the egg, no such preformed organization could be found; the theory of preformation became more untenable and was abandoned. The theory opposing preformation was *epigenesis*, a product of the eighteenth and nineteenth centuries. Epigenesis suggests that the structure of the embryo is able to emerge from what is a formless, protoplasmic mass. The foremost early proponent of this theory, Wolff, closely watched the development of plants and animals and saw from these studies that the particular organs developed in a gradual manner from more generalized embryonic parts.

By the end of the nineteenth century, experimental embryology had found its beginnings and each event demanded an explanation in a mechanistic fashion. One way out of the dilemma, in keeping with the newly emerging concepts, was to suggest that there was a type of preformation in the egg protoplasm that foreshadowed events to come; this preformation was not a morphological one but a molecular, biochemical one.

153

The current explanation for the emergence of the embryo from the egg is in a real sense a composite of these two opposing concepts, epigenesis and preformation: The information for total development is present in the egg in an unrecognizable form, not in the organization of the egg cytoplasm but in the genetic inheritance passed on by meiosis. If all the information for all processes of the organism is somehow present in the nucleotide sequence within the DNA, then the overall problem of development becomes one of information retrieval from this information storage bank. As discussed in the first chapter, the concept of sequential gene activation requires only that the proper initiating events occur. Once the first genes are expressed, then presumably part of that expression entails the activation of the next set of genes and so on, in an ordered and predictable fashion, until the program for development has run its course. The information is therefore present in a coded, preformed state, but the morphology of the embryo arises epigenetically from what is primarily unordered cytoplasm under the direction of the genetic material. The developmental biologist is left with the assignment of describing the multitude of steps that occur and of unraveling their underlying mechanisms.

Whatever the extent of molecular organization present in the cytoplasm of an unfertilized egg, it must result during oogenesis either from the activities of surrounding tissue or from synthetic activities of the oocyte itself. The difficulty in trying to separate information from these two sources is that the same genes are responsible for it whether they happen to lie in the oocyte or, for example, in the liver. How can we distinguish, once it is inside the egg, whether a given RNA has entered from outside or was synthesized from within? Some way is needed to distinguish between what is being made by the oocyte and what is made by the ovary, the liver, etc. Since different species have different observable properties, we need an animal in which the oocyte is of one species and the remainder of the tissue of another. Such a combination is known as a *chimera.*

Blackler has produced the necessary chimera by taking advantage of the following facts: (1) In amphibians, as in vertebrates in general, the gonad has two entirely different origins, the primordial germ cells and the remainder of the gonad. (2) The primordial germ cells can be identified very early within the endoderm of the amphibian embryo and can be removed. To make the chimera, the region of the primordial germ cells of one species, *Xenopus laevis* (*X.l.*), was removed and replaced with the primordial germ cells of another species, *Xenopus mulleri* (*X.m.*). When the ovary of this animal develops, all its oocytes will be from the *X.m.* donor and all the remaining ovarian cells will be from the *X.l.* host. Animals carrying the germ cells of another species are called *transmission hybrids.* When these transmission hybrids reach sexual maturity and produce eggs that can be fertilized, we can begin to analyze the resulting embryos with our original question in mind. If the eggs of this transmission hybrid are fertilized with the sperm from a *X.m.* male, then any deviation from the typical development of a *X.m.* embryo must be a result of the *X.m.* oocyte developing in a foreign environment. In this case, the resulting eggs, embryos, and adults were always completely *X.m.* in character and showed no effects of a developmental program arising from outside the oocyte during oogenesis. These results suggest that although the number of distinguishable properties between these two closely related species is limited, the oocyte in amphibians is responsible for its own program, to whatever extent such a program exists. If this conclusion is correct, the external tissue is left with the assignment of simply packaging the egg with necessary storage material.

If we begin with the assumption that oogenesis produces an egg with the beginnings, at least, of a developmental program, we should be able to find some evidence of its existence. The question is: What evidence has been obtained of a differentiation or heterogeneity in the structure of the egg? In the last chapter it was stated that all animal eggs have polarity, a differentiation along the animal-vegetal axis. Since polarity is not present in the very early stages of oogenesis (oogonia), it must arise during the growth and differentiation of the oocyte and must be imposed on the unpolarized oocyte from the outside. In the examination of a number of oocytes, such as those of echinoderms and mollusks, there is a predictable relationship between the position of the oocyte within the ovary and the future animal-vegetal axis. The point at which the oocyte is attached to the ovarian wall, and therefore the point of entrance of supplies to the oocyte from the outside, becomes the *vegetal pole*. In the ovaries of many animals, including mammals, oocytes are completely surrounded by follicle cells and there is no obvious relationship of any ovarian feature to polarity.

Among certain algae, the egg at the time of fertilization lacks polarity. This is the case in certain seaweeds, such as *Fucus,* in which polarity is expressed as a visible protrusion at about 12 hours after fertilization. The sequence of events is shown in the series of micrographs of Fig. 7.1. As a result of the protrusion at one pole, the egg becomes pear-shaped; it then divides unequally so that the

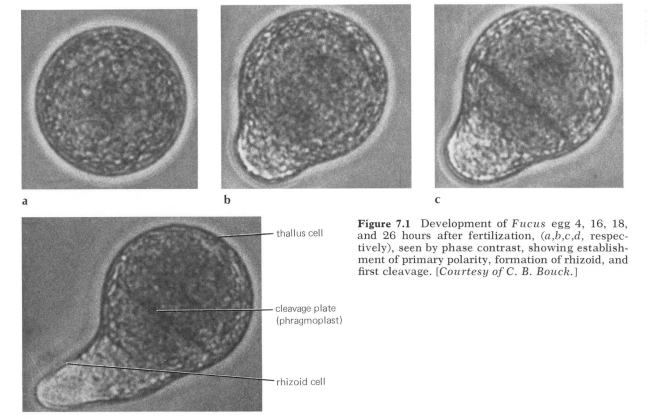

a

b

c

— thallus cell

— cleavage plate
(phragmoplast)

— rhizoid cell

d

Figure 7.1 Development of *Fucus* egg 4, 16, 18, and 26 hours after fertilization, (*a,b,c,d,* respectively), seen by phase contrast, showing establishment of primary polarity, formation of rhizoid, and first cleavage. [*Courtesy of C. B. Bouck.*]

protrusion remains as part of the smaller rhizoid cell, which will eventually form a holdfast to anchor the plant in the surf. The other cell, the thallus cell, will become the bulk of the plant. Though the first external sign of polarity is the rhizoidal protrusion, an underlying internal polarity is first observed as a concentration of RNA and cytoplasmic organelles at one side of the nucleus beneath the point where the rhizoid will form.

Since *Fucus* begins its development without an inherent polarity, the study of this egg provides information on the types of external stimulation that can affect the internal organization of an egg. It has been known for a long time that a variety of external factors can determine polarity in *Fucus*. If a light beam is focused on fertilized *Fucus* eggs, the rhizoid will form at the point away from the light source. If eggs are put in an electric current, the rhizoid forms toward the anode. In a group of eggs, the rhizoids of each develop toward the center of the cluster. Regardless of the specific manner in which the environment becomes polarized, this environmental differentiation becomes imposed upon the internal contents of the egg.

Jaffe, one of the principle investigators of polarity in *Fucus* and *Pelvetia* (both fucoid algae), has proposed that the basis of rhizoid formation is the development of loops of ionic current flowing into and out of each egg. If, for example, a number of eggs are placed in a small tube (Fig. 7.2) and light is shone in one direction, a current can be measured across these eggs, whose rhizoids will all be aligned. In contrast, if the eggs are simply allowed to develop rhizoids at random locations, no such current is detected. Jaffe suggests the reason for the current in the aligned eggs is that there is a flow of positive ions into the egg at the point where the rhizoid will form and out at the opposite end; the return through the medium forms a current loop (Fig. 7.2c) estimated at 9×10^{-10} amps per embryo. One consequence of the development of such a current is that charged molecules could migrate to different parts of the egg in response to its presence. There is evidence of migration of charged macromolecules to the site where the rhizoid will form. Jaffe calls this process *self-cataphoresis*. For the typical oocyte, polarity is established within the oocyte in an environment many times more complex than that of the sea in which *Fucus* polarity arises. Whether similar mechanisms exist whereby differentiations in the ovarian environment impose themselves upon the internal contents of the oocyte is not yet known.

More recently mass experiments employed nickel screens, each perforated with 25,000 holes, 75 μm in diameter. All were filled with fertilized *Pelvetia* eggs. Seawater containing a radioisotope of calcium ions (Ca^{2+}) was passed

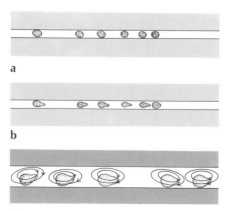

a

b

c

Figure 7.2 Measurement of electrical potentials in fertilized *Fucus* eggs. *a* Eggs drawn into glass capillary tube of diameter slightly less than that of the eggs. *b* A day later, all eggs have germinated in the same direction, dividing into a rhizoid and a thallus cell. *c* Suggested scheme of inferred current pattern in a tube. [*After Jaffe,* Proc. Nat. Acad. Sci. U. S., **56:**1102 (1966).]

through upper compartments, and unlabeled seawater was passed through lower compartments; illumination was directed from above in one set and from below in another. The rhizoid in each case grew toward the source of light. These experiments show that calcium ions enter the prospective growth pole of polarizing *Pelvetia* eggs faster than the opposite pole and leave this antipode faster than the growth pole. The resultant calcium current is greatest when first measured at 6 hours after fertilization and decreases as the time of final commitment to growth in a particular direction approaches. Jaffe considers the calcium current in the polarizing egg to be the creation of an intracellular gradient of free calcium ions, with the higher concentration at the leaking end. One way in which a calcium gradient might act to polarize such eggs is by producing an electric field across the cytoplasm; it may also be a regulator of microtubule polymerization within the cell.

Whatever the means of formation, the consequences of polarity are significant. The *animal pole* will generally form the anterior end of the animal and differentiate into the external covering of the embryo. The vegetal end typically is pushed into the interior of the egg at gastrulation and will differentiate into endodermal, and in some cases mesodermal, structures. As we saw in Chapter 6, the cleavage planes are formed in relation to the axis of polarity. The first and second planes of the sea urchin and frog, for example, coincide with the animal-vegetal axis, i.e., they are meridional; the third is perpendicular to it, i.e., it is equatorial. In the sea urchin the axis of polarity becomes the axis of radial symmetry during cleavage, while in the frog it comes to lie within the plane of bilateral symmetry.

When one examines the egg of the frog *Rana pipiens,* the polarity is obvious. Yolk is concentrated toward one end, the chromosomes lie at the opposite end where the polar bodies are given off, and there is a covering of black pigment over the egg in all regions except around the vegetal pole, which is unpigmented. These are the obvious markers of polarity, but they are not necessarily its primary features. The animal-vegetal axis of the frog egg, or of any egg, represents a basic structuring of the egg protoplasm. Many of the visible signs, such as yolk and pigment, are believed to have only secondarily responded to a previous, more basic differentiation. This is clearly illustrated by experiments in which these visible markers of polarity are displaced without disrupting the more fundamental organization of the egg.

One of the simplest and most effective methods of disturbing the visible organization of the egg is to place it in a centrifugal field. Under the influence of centrifugation, those components of the greatest density move fastest and become sedimented against the inner surface of the egg, facing the centrifugal pole (away from the center of the centrifuge rotor). Any materials less dense than the cytoplasmic fluid of the egg, such as oil droplets, float to the opposite end, the centripetal pole. Centrifugation produces an egg whose components are stratified into well-defined layers. Dense particulate materials (pigment granules, yolk granules, mitochondria, etc.) are in layers at one end, and above this is a clear zone containing the fluid cytoplasm in which the nucleus is generally found. This is capped by a collection of oil droplets. The eggs of the polychaete *Nereis*, after centrifugation, are shown in Fig. 7.3a.

The centrifugation experiments by Morgan on the sea urchin embryo indicate that the underlying basis of polarity is resistant to moderate centrifugal forces. In these pioneering experiments Morgan used the eggs of *Arbacia,* whose animal pole is marked by an indentation in its jelly coat that is easily identified in the presence of india ink. Upon centrifugation, sea urchin eggs do not orient with respect to gravity; i.e., they will settle with their animal-vegetal axis

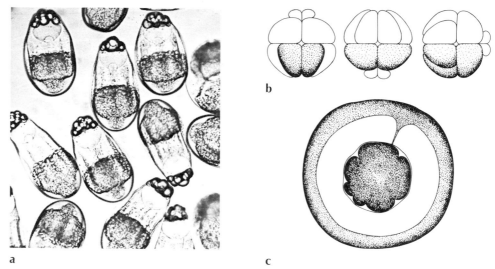

a   c

Figure 7.3 *a* Centrifuged unfertilized eggs of *Nereis,* showing zones of stratification, with oil drops at top, hyaline protoplasmic layer containing the nucleus, a zone of yolk spheres, a second hyaline zone, and a zone of jelly-precursor granules. [*Courtesy of D. P. Costello.*] *b* The fourth cleavage of centrifuged *Arbacia* occurs in keeping with the original animal-vegetal axis regardless of the stratification of the egg. The micromeres have formed at the centripetal pole, the centrifugal pole, and at the side, respectively. In *c* the method used by Morgan to identify the original animal-vegetal axis is shown. The india ink marks the position of the animal pole opposite which the micromeres are formed. [*After Morgan, 1927.*]

oriented randomly in the centrifugal field. Therefore, they will become stratified in all possible relations to their axis of polarity. If one observes the cleavage pattern in these eggs after centrifugation, the first cleavage furrow is usually perpendicular to the stratification (cuts across all layers), the second is parallel, and the third is at right angles to the first two cleavages. In other words, these three cleavages are now related to the stratification. Since the stratification is independent of the animal-vegetal axis, the first three cleavages must also be independent of the original egg polarity. Presumably the stratification imposes mechanical restraints upon the mitotic apparatus and establishes a new cleavage pattern.

When Morgan examined the fourth cleavage, he observed that the micromeres were formed at or near the original vegetal pole (across from the jelly funnel) regardless of how the first three cleavages had occurred (Fig. 7.3b). Similarly, gastrulation occurred at the original vegetal pole just as it would have in the uncentrifuged eggs. It is clear from these experiments that the visible components of the egg can be greatly disturbed and cleavage can be affected, but the underlying axis of polarity is resistant to these treatments. In numerous other animals stratification does not affect even the first cleavages, which continue to occur with respect to the axis of polarity.

BILATERAL SYMMETRY

In animals with a symmetrical body plan that is roughly bilateral such as vertebrates, three body axes can be defined: the anteroposterior, the dorsoventral, and the left-right. The anteroposterior axis is typically related to the axis of polarity and as such is established in the ovary. The other two axes become established simultaneously, though in a different manner among various animals. In some species, including the cephalopod mollusks and some insects, the unfertilized egg already possesses these three identifiable axes as a result of oogenesis. In some insects these axes become established within the oviduct. In other cases the point of fertilization is clearly related to the plane of bilateral symmetry, as in many mollusks, annelids, and amphibians; in other animals, such as the birds, reptiles, and mammals, these axes are not established until the end of cleavage.

This discussion concentrates on those cases in which the plane of bilateral symmetry (the median plane separating right and left halves of the embryo) becomes established at fertilization, as a result of the point of sperm penetration. The history of this subject can be traced back to 1885, when Roux was able to fertilize a frog egg at any desired point. He placed a fine silk thread on an egg and let a tiny drop of sperm creep along the thread to contact the egg at one identifiable point. Analysis of eggs fertilized at specific points indicates that the future plane of bilateral symmetry of the animal passes through the point of sperm penetration; in the majority of cases this also coincides with the plane of the first cleavage furrow. The conclusion is therefore reached that the point of sperm penetration establishes the entire bilateral organization of the future adult. Thus, as in the case of polarity, this axis is imposed upon the egg by an external factor.

Since the activation of a frog egg by temperature elevation or with a needle is perfectly capable of producing an embryo with a plane of bilateral symmetry—one that bears no relation to any point of activation—we can conclude that the unfertilized egg has at least inherent bilateral organization. If this were not true, why should one meridian become the plane of symmetry upon activation? Since the sperm establishes this plane upon fertilization, we can conclude that the inherent bilateralism is weak and is overridden by a stronger organizing force developed at the point of fertilization.

To understand the relationship between fertilization and symmetrization in the frog egg, we need to be familiar with a series of events that occur between

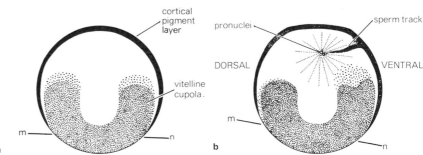

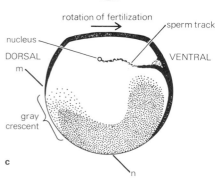

Figure 7.4 *a* Diagrammatic axial section of an unfertilized egg of *Rana fusca*, *m–n* representing the interior limit of the cortical pigment layer. *b* The reaction of the egg to the spermatozoon when it enters. Note in particular the 10° inclination of *m–n*, and that the vitelline horn has moved closer to the future dorsal side. [*After Ancel and Vintemberger*, Biol. Bull. *suppl.* **31**:377 (1948).] *c* An axial section through the center of the gray crescent of *R. fusca*, showing the modifications that have occurred in the egg after the rotation of fertilization (*rotation of symmetrization*). The arrow indicates the direction of the rotation of fertilization. The gray crescent, which marks the dorsal side, is formed. Within this dorsal area, only slight pigmentation remains after the pigmented cortical layer has receded. The vitelline horn on the dorsal side has moved nearer the cortex, and the line *m–n* has inclined through 30°.

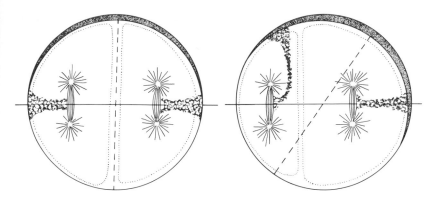

Figure 7.5 Equatorial section through dispermic frog egg showing that the gray crescent (position indicated by thin outline opposite thickest part of outline) forms at the midpoint between the two points of sperm entry. Broken line indicates plane of symmetry. [*After Herlant*, Arch. Biol., **26** (1911).]

the time of fertilization and first cleavage. The unfertilized frog egg outwardly consists of two regions: a dark animal region, which extends to below the equator (*m* to *n* of Fig. 7.4*a*), and a whitish vegetal region. The coloration of the animal region results from a layer of black pigment granules that lie in the cortex just beneath the plasma membrane. The vegetal region of the egg lacks these pigment granules. Internally a cup-shaped mass of white yolk granules occupies the vegetal region, with the central concavity opening toward the animal pole. Following fertilization, there is a rotation of the cortex relative to the internal endoplasm. In Fig. 7.4 this rotation of the outer "crust" is seen in the shift of the pigment from *m* to *n* of Fig. 7.4*a* to that shown in Fig. 7.4*c*. The cortex shifts toward the vegetal pole on the ventral side (the side of fertilization) and toward the animal pole on the dorsal side (opposite fertilization). The result of this shift is the appearance of a gray crescent on one side, just below the equator. The gray crescent is on the side of the egg where the cortex had moved toward the animal pole, in the position vacated by the pigmented part of the cortex. The midpoint of the crescent is on the meridian 180° from the point of fertilization. The gray crescent is middorsal, the meridian of sperm penetration is midventral; between these two meridians lies the plane of bilateral symmetry, which is usually marked by the first cleavage furrow. The gray crescent is a cortical structure and is of particular importance to later development. On occasion a frog egg is fertilized by two sperm; in such cases the gray crescent forms on the meridian midway between the two points of fertilization (Fig. 7.5).

THE EGG CORTEX

In the fertilized egg of the sea urchin *Arbacia* (after the cortical granules have expelled their contents) there are numerous red pigment granules whose position can be followed. Most of these granules are in the central endoplasm, though they are found in the cortex as well. If these eggs are centrifuged, the granules in the endoplasm move to the centrifugal pole of the egg, while those in the cortex do not. Why should the same type of granule behave so differently in these two locations? The most accepted answer is that the cortex of the sea urchin egg is a region of much higher viscosity, i.e., it is gelated with respect to the more fluid (more solated) endoplasm. As a result of this cortical gel, those granules located in that region are restricted from being displaced by the increased viscosity of their surroundings.

The gelated material that everyone is most familiar with is the gelatin gel, which differs markedly from the protoplasmic gel in the following ways. The protoplasmic gels increase their volume and absorb heat upon gelation, while a gelatin gel melts as it warms. These properties of protoplasmic gels cause them to become solated (made more fluid) by either an increase in hydrostatic pressure or a decrease in temperature, or a combination of both. This means that if a sea urchin egg is placed in a cylinder to which a piston is attached, and hydrostatic pressure is applied, the gelated regions of the egg will become solated. The greater the gelated state of the cytoplasm, the greater the pressure required to solate it. The invention of the pressure centrifuge allowed eggs to be subjected to hydrostatic pressure and to be centrifuged simultaneously. Marsland and Landau utilized this device to determine that cortical pigment granules as well as endoplasmic granules could readily be displaced by centrifugation as long as the eggs were first solated by the pressure. These findings provide convincing evidence of the gelated nature of the cortex.

It was Marsland's experiments with hydrostatic pressure treatments of eggs that led to his contractile ring theory of cleavage. It was found that if a cleaving sea urchin egg was subjected to high hydrostatic pressure, the cleavage furrow could be halted in its advance and forced to regress, presumably as a result of the solation of the contractile ring in the furrow region. As soon as the pressure is released, the furrowing begins again, unless the furrow is held back by pressure for more than 15 minutes. If the pressure is maintained for over 15 minutes and then released, cytokinesis does not occur, even though the nuclear division has been completed and there are two nuclei in the uncleaved egg. It appears that the surface has a limited time in which to contract; once this has passed, so has its furrowing capacity. Remarkably, at the time of the next division, these cleavage-inhibited eggs undergo double furrowing and four cells are produced. The cell has retained some trace of the missing cleavage and has now caught up to its number of nuclei.

Several other approaches taken to investigate the nature of the cortex illustrate the variety of techniques that can be brought to bear on one specific problem. One of the great traditions in developmental biology has been the micromanipulative procedure. The tools of the workers are delicate instruments: microneedles, micropipettes, fine scissors and forceps, and, in many cases, a micromanipulator. The needles and pipettes can be attached to the micromanipulator and their operation controlled by a system that translates the coarse movements of the hands into very small movements of the tips of the instruments. Various controls direct the instruments in the various possible directions, as the investigator observes their progress through the attached microscope. Inasmuch as the sea urchin egg and the mammalian egg are approximately 100 μm in diameter, the tasks that have been accomplished are impressive.

If a blunt-tipped microneedle is inserted into a sea urchin egg and pushed through to the opposite side, the tip of the needle does not come in contact with the very inner edge of the egg. Instead, when the tip reaches a position of about 3 μm from that edge, the surface begins to bulge and the needle moves no closer to the edge itself. Presumably there is some layer of approximately 3 μm resisting the penetration of the needle tip. If the needle is slowly withdrawn from the cortical layer back into the endoplasm, adhering gelled material can be seen flowing into the more fluid internal cytoplasm. Similarly, if an oil droplet is injected into the sea urchin egg, it never comes in direct contact with the inner edge of the cell membrane; rather it remains a few microns from the edge itself. Even when the cell divides, the advancing tip of the furrow is seen to be separated from the surface of the oil by a gap of several microns and remain at this distance as the droplet is split in two.

Not only has the existence of the cortex been indicated by the above techniques but it has been isolated in bulk after disruption of the eggs in 0.1 M $MgCl_2$, which lyses the cells and keeps the cortex gelated. By this technique large numbers of cells can be broken in a way that releases the internal contents, and the cell membrane and associated gelated cortex can be isolated. These isolated cortices are several microns thick, as would be expected; if they are isolated at different stages during cleavage, the SH content of the cortical proteins undergo the identical SH cycle described in connection with the micromere clock. It appears, therefore, that the micromere clock mechanism is a cortical phenomenon.

In contrast with the substantial evidence of the existence of the special cortical layer described above, the electron microscope has failed to provide any structural basis for these properties. In fact, in the one species of sea urchin that has been best studied, Mercer and Wolpert argue against the existence of a gelated cortex. These investigators find, for example, that centrifugation will pack granules directly against the inner edge of the membrane as if no gelled region were there to resist penetration. This controversy has not been resolved.

Evidence has accumulated that assigns to the cortex a very important role in the storage of developmental information. In the sea urchin, for example, the seat of polarity is capable of withstanding centrifugation, and it appears that the cortex is the only region of the egg for which the same can be said. One can still argue that the information is present in the endoplasm but is simply not connected to the particulate materials that are being displaced by the centrifuge. Even though it is difficult to conceive of an endoplasmic structure that retains its integrity in the midst of the centrifugal traffic, a more direct proof is needed. The best argument against the requirement of any cytoarchitecture of the endoplasm for polarity is that up to 50 percent of this internal cytoplasm can be indiscriminately removed with a micropipette without disturbing either the polarity or the course of normal development.

In the amphibian egg one particular cortical structure, the gray crescent, has been shown to be of vital importance for the normal development of the embryo. In a series of experiments that have largely been confirmed by other means, Curtis was able to transplant pieces of the cortex from one embryo to another (Fig. 7.6). In this procedure a small patch of the egg is cut with a fine tungsten needle and transferred into a small cut made at the surfce of a recipient egg. Only the outer crust (0.5 to 3 μm deep) is transplanted. Before fertilization, any small patch can be removed without effect upon development. The same is true for the removal of a piece of cortex after fertilization but before the cortical shift. Once the gray crescent has been formed, however, this piece of cortex is endowed with properties not shared by any other region. If the cortex of the gray crescent is removed, development comes to a halt prior to gastrulation.

If, instead of removing the gray crescent, another gray crescent is transplanted to the ventral side of an egg to produce two such regions, the resulting embryo undergoes gastrulation at both sites; it forms two archenterons and eventually an embryo that contains two sets of axial structures including notochord, spinal cord, somites, etc.

If these experiments are performed on embryos at the eight-cell stage rather than on the uncleaved egg, entirely different results are obtained. The gray crescent of the eight-cell stage still retains the ability to produce a second embryonic axis when grafted to younger stages, but the eight-cell stage itself no longer reacts to the graft of an additional crescent. Also, excision of the gray crescent at this stage no longer inhibits subsequent gastrulation and normal development. For a detailed account of amphibian gastrulation, see Chapter 11. These results suggest that a change occurs during the first several cleavages

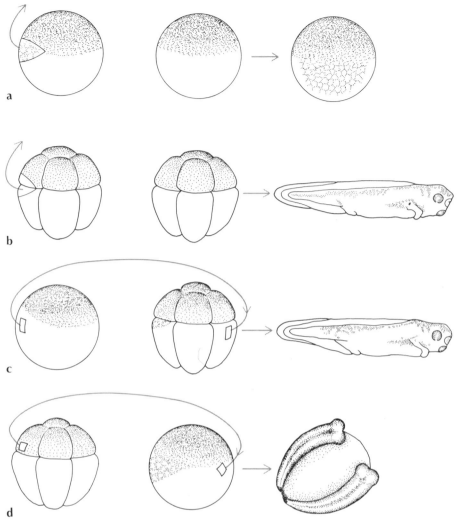

Figure 7.6 Experiments of Curtis in *Xenopus*. *a* Excision of the cortical gray-crescent area at the one-cell stage: no gastrulation. *b* Same experiment at the eight-cell stage: normal embryo. *c* Graft of the gray-crescent cortex of the one-cell stage to the ventral part of the eight-cell stage does not result in the induction of a secondary embryonic axis. *d* Graft of the gray-crescent cortex from the eight-cell stage to the ventral margin of the one-cell stage induces a secondary embryonic axis. [*After Curtis, 1962.*]

with respect to the localization of certain cortical powers. According to Curtis, a change in cortical organization spreads across the surface of the egg during the second and third cleavages, starting from the gray crescent; when this change is completed, interactions can take place among various parts of the cortex.

REGULATIVE DEVELOPMENT AND PHYSIOLOGICAL GRADIENTS

Development begins with one cell whose cytoplasm divides into many cells, each of which has a specific destiny, to give rise eventually to cells that have specialized differentiated properties. One of the basic questions in develop-

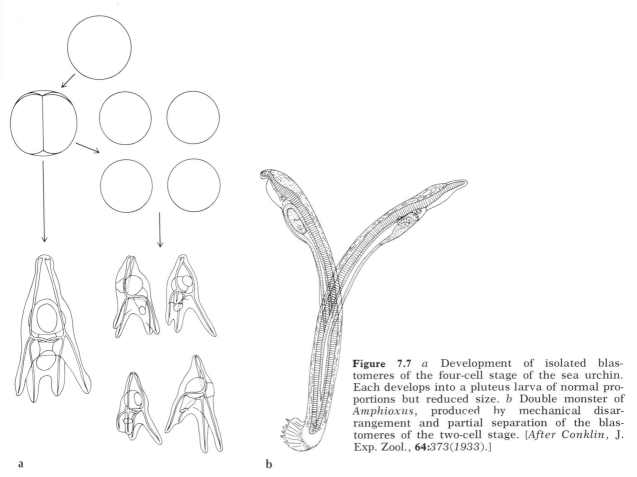

Figure 7.7 *a* Development of isolated blastomeres of the four-cell stage of the sea urchin. Each develops into a pluteus larva of normal proportions but reduced size. *b* Double monster of *Amphioxus*, produced by mechanical disarrangement and partial separation of the blastomeres of the two-cell stage. [*After Conklin*, J. Exp. Zool., **64**:373(1933).]

a

b

mental biology, and one of the first to be asked, is whether or not a cell can be made to develop into tissues other than that it would normally form.

The history of this question goes back to 1888, when Wilhelm Roux killed one of the first two cells of a frog egg with a hot needle. The embryo that resulted from the living member of this pair of cells resembled a half-embryo. The interpretation seems clear enough: each cell produced during cleavage will form the same structures it normally produces, regardless of what operations are performed on the embryo. A few years later (1892) Hans Driesch, working with the sea urchin, obtained opposite results.

Driesch separated the first two cells of the sea urchin embryo by vigorously shaking the embryos for several minutes until a few fertilization membranes had burst and the first two cells or four cells separated. He found that each of the first two or four cells could, in isolation, give rise to complete and normal larvae, though of reduced size (Fig. 7.7*a*). These results contradict those of Roux, and subsequent reinvestigations of the fate of the first two cells of a frog embryo supported the findings of Driesch. The original experiment had indicated each cell in the frog could form only a half-embryo because the dead cell remained as an influence on the activities of the living member. It seems that even though the cell was dead and therefore unable to differentiate, the living cell recognized its presence and was thereby limited in its own differentiation. Two-cell separation in *Amphioxus* also results in twins (Fig. 7.7*b*).

The striking regulation of blastomeres into whole embryos led Driesch to describe the egg as a *harmonious equipotential sytem*—equipotential because a part had a potency to form the whole, and harmonious because the parts work together so well. He defined the term *prospective significance* (or *prospective fate*) as the fate of an embryonic cell under normal conditions of development, and showed experimentally that the *prospective potency* of an embryonic cell is much greater than its prospective significance. He stated that *the fate of a cell is a function of its position in the whole.* In fact he not only emphasized the epigenetic and positional aspects of early development but spoke of both chemical and contact induction processes between cells and tissues, of polarity of the egg as an arrangement of polarized constituents, and of developmental controls mediated by nucleus and enzymes. The two foundation publications by Roux (1888) and Driesch (1892) can be read in English translation in "Foundations of Experimental Embryology," edited by Willier and Oppenheimer (1964).

These remarkable observations rank among the most important in the science of biology. How can a cell that is to form a part of an embryo suddenly form additional parts not in its normal repertoire? How can we view on the one hand the processes of development in a mechanistic fashion, and on the other hand conceive that an embryo can repair its own damage? What machine do we know that can be cut in half and both halves continue to function as if nothing had happened? How can a part have a sense of the whole? These are basic questions and we cannot yet provide definitive answers.

In sea urchin development, the third cleavage is the first horizontal cleavage and therefore the first time cells are found whose cytoplasm does not extend from the animal to the vegetal pole. This horizontal cleavage is seen to have a profound effect on the ability of the blastomeres to develop in isolation; they are no longer capable of differentiation in a totipotent manner.

The basis of this change in potency is clearly related to the separation of animal from vegetal materials. If the eight-cell stage is severed into two halves by a meridional operation, each group of four cells gives rise to an intact larva. In contrast, if the eight-cell stage is separated into two halves by a horizontal operation, neither the animal half nor the vegetal half can produce a normal embryo. The animal half differentiates into a hollow ball of cells with very long cilia; this abnormal embryo, called a *dauerblastula,* is devoid of endodermal and mesodermal differentiations. The vegetal half develops more normally but is characterized by the lack of arms, a more ovoid body shape, and the formation of an enlarged gut that is often evaginated outward (exogastrulated) rather than pushed within the embryo. The differentiations of the vegetal half reflect an exaggeration of endodermal differentiation at the expense of ectodermal structures. We do not have to wait, however, until the third cleavage to obtain embryos with these abnormalities. The unfertilized egg can be cut horizontally and each half fertilized. The animal and vegetal halves then develop as described for the eight-cell operation. An animal-vegetal differential with regard to prospective potency apparently already exists by the end of oogenesis.

The question that must be analyzed is how these two parts, the animal and vegetal halves, have become so different in their abilities to differentiate in isolation. A theory of gradients based on the work of Runnström and Hörstadius seems to explain this and many other results. According to this theory, the direction in which a given cell of a sea urchin embryo will differentiate is under the control of two influences acting coordinately throughout the embryo. One of these influences (activities or substances of unknown nature) is at its greatest concentration at the animal pole; the other is at its greatest level at the vegetal

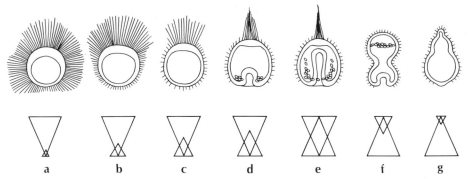

Figure 7.8 Sea urchin larvae of about the same age but varying in the animal and the vegetal tendencies. *e* Normal gastrula. *a–d* Larvae animalized to a varying extent. *f–g* Larvae vegetalized to a different extent. The hypothetical double-gradient system corresponding to each larva is indicated. Animalization can be brought about by a reduction of the amount of vegetal material, by treatment with various chemical agents such as SCN⁻ before fertilization, or by treatment with *o*-iodosobenzoic acid or 2,5-thiomethylcytosine during cleavage stages. Vegetalization can be brought about by lithium or chloramphenicol treatment during cleavage. [*After Gustafson , 1965.*]

pole. Each influence spreads out from its respective pole, decreasing until it has essentially disappeared in the region of the opposite pole. Since each diminishes in strength, each is considered to occur as a gradient and together they form a *double gradient*.

In this theory the nature of differentiation of each part of the embryo is based on the relative levels of each member of the double gradient. The concept is expressed diagrammatically in Fig. 7.8. In the lower row each factor is represented by a triangle: the broadest part represents the highest concentration and the narrow part, the lowest concentration. In Fig. 7.8*e* the normal condition is shown, in which both animal and vegetal influences are balanced and development is normal. If the embryo is placed under conditions that reduce the vegetal influence further and further (through an increasing imbalance), the animal develops more and more in an animal-half direction; i.e., it becomes animalized. If the reverse occurs and the embryo's vegetal influence predominates (Fig. 7.8*f* and *g*), the embryo develops as a vegetal half would and shows an enlarged gut that may exogastrulate; the embryo has been vegetalized. The differentiation of each region is believed to be directed by the specific animal/vegetal ratios of that region. Where the animal influence predominates, ectodermal structures are formed. Normally this is only near the animal pole, but if the vegetal influence is somehow depressed or the animal influence is increased, ectodermal differentiations will occur in a greater part of the embryo (Fig 7.8*a*). The reverse is true for the other gradient system. Techniques to alter the gradients are described below.

Physiological gradients have been invoked for a long time to explain a wide variety of developmental phenomena, including embryonic induction and nerve growth and regeneration. The underlying mechanism in a gradient hypothesis is that each part of the whole has a unique identity, a certain level of whatever is in the gradient. In a double gradient the important determinant is the relative value of each influence rather than its absolute amount. Runnström first proposed a double gradient mechanism underlying sea urchin development; Hörstadius, in a series of elegant microsurgical experiments (reviewed in 1939 and in 1974), is primarily responsible for providing evidence in its favor.

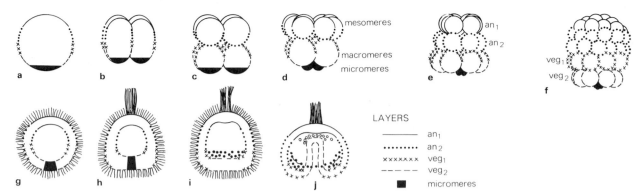

Figure 7.9 Development of sea urchin *Paracentrotus lividus* egg. *a* Uncleaved egg. *b* 4-cell stage. *c* 9-cell stage. *d* 16-cell stage formed by equal vertical cleavages in animal half and unequal horizontal cleavages in vegetal half. *e* 32-cell stage with two tiers of blastomeres (an_1 and an_2). *f* 64-cell stage. Macromere descendants form two tiers of blastomeres (veg_1 and veg_2). *g* Early blastula. *h* Later blastula, with apical organ, before formation of primary mesenchyme. *i* Migration of primary mesenchyme. *j* Gastrula: secondary mesenchyme shown at tip of archenteron and two triradiate spicules formed to the sides of it. [*After Hörstadius, 1939.*]

Before we describe the experiments of Hörstadius, the student must become familiar with the different cells of the early sea urchin and their prospective fates (Fig. 7.9). At the 16-cell stage there are eight mesomeres, four macromeres, and four micromeres ($8 + 4 + 4$ in the terminology of Hörstadius). At the 32-cell stage the animal half is composed of two rings of cells (eight per ring) called an_1 and an_2. By the 64-cell stage the macromeres have divided into two rings of 8 cells each, veg_1 and veg_2. The prospective fate of an_1, an_2, and veg_1 is the outer ectodermal covering of the embryo. Veg_2 will form the gut. The micromeres will differentiate into the skeleton. Hörstadius has isolated the various cells and clusters of cells of the cleaving embryo and recombined them in virtually every possible combination in an analysis of their prospective potencies.

If the double gradient theory is correct, differentiations should be predictable on the basis of the relative animal-to-vegetal influence of the part in question. An isolated animal half ($8 + 0 + 0$) differentiates in isolation into a hollow ciliated ball. If, however, four micromeres are added ($8 + 0 + 4$), a pluteus larva can develop; the micromeres provide the required vegetal influence to balance the animal half and restore the animal/vegetal ratios compatible with normal development. The isolated macromeres ($0 + 4 + 0$) represent a piece of the middle of both gradients; though they lack the extreme values of each influence, they retain the opposing concentrations. In isolation, the macromeres develop into a recognizable pluteus larva. It appears that the four macromeres are not required for the near-normal differentiation of the remaining 12 cells and vice versa. The animal half (eight mesomeres) greatly dominates one macromere ($8 + 1 + 0$), but if two mesomeres are combined with one macromere ($2 + 1 + 0$), a pluteuslike larva can form. An entire embryo can be shifted in its differentiation if its animal-vegetal balance is altered; this can be accomplished by the addition of 20 extra micromeres to an intact embryo ($8 + 4 + 24$). Under the influence of the greatly increased vegetal activity, the whole embryo develops as if it were a vegetal half.

167

These relative animal and vegetal activities can be essentially titrated, one against the other. If the layers of the 64-cell embryo are separated, their differentiation in isolation or after recombination with one, two, or three micromeres can be determined (Fig. 7.10). In isolation the veg_2 layer shows the most balanced differentiation. As micromeres are added to the veg_2 layer, a more and more vegetalized embryo will develop. In contrast, the an_1 layer can produce, in isolation, only the hollow ball of ciliated cells. Addition of micromeres to the an_1 layer begins to restore the necessary balance, and after four micromeres are added, a rather normal pluteus larva can be produced.

A chemical approach to the analysis of sea urchin development has gone hand in hand with the operative approach from the start. As early as 1892 Herbst discovered that lithium ions (from LiCl) added to seawater caused an increase in the amount of endoderm and led to exogastrulation (Fig. 7.11). Since it causes an entire embryo to develop as if it were a vegetal half, lithium is said to be a vegetalizing agent and to have vegetalized the embryo. Other agents, particularly thiocyanate (SCN^-) and trypsin, are capable of animalizing an embryo so that it will develop as an animal half. Superficially, it seems that lithium and micromeres have the same vegetalizing effect upon the embryo. In fact, experiments have indicated that alterations in differentiation that result from surgical disruption of the normal gradients can be balanced by a chemical disruption acting in the opposite manner. For example, treatment of an animal half with lithium will cause it to differentiate along nearly normal lines. This experiment indicates that the chemical treatments somehow interact specifically with the proposed double gradients and that study of their effects might provide information on the nature of the gradients themselves.

If gradients exist, there should be some way to demonstrate their presence. This appears to have been accomplished by the use of dyes that are capable of accepting electrons from the oxidative metabolism of the embryo in the absence

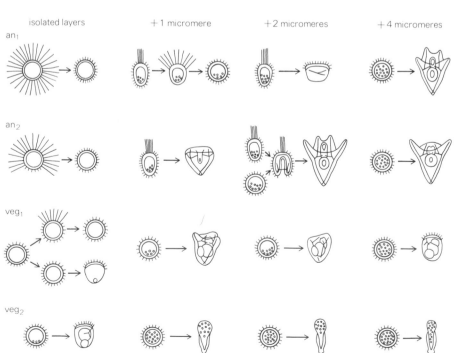

Figure 7.10 Development of the layers an_1, an_2, veg_1, and veg_2 in isolation (*left column*) and with one, two, and four micromeres implanted. [*After Hörstadius, 1939.*]

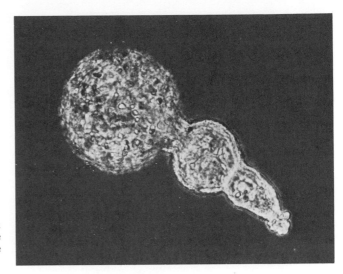

Figure 7.11 Exogastrulation of the sea urchin *Lytechinus*, due to the presence of lithium. Large bulb is a thin-walled ectodermal sac with the regions of the gut extending outward.

of oxygen. For example, if an embryo is placed in seawater with the dye Janus green, and the drop of stained embryos is sealed from the environment, the oxygen will eventually be exhausted as a means to accept electrons from the oxidative phosphorylation chain. When this happens the Janus green will become the electron acceptor and will be reduced in the process. The dye is colorless in the reduced state; therefore those regions of the embryo undergoing the highest level of oxidative metabolism should become colorless before less active parts. Under these conditions the vegetal pole loses its stain first, and the reaction spreads in an animal direction. As this reaction is proceeding, a second point of destaining at the animal pole spreads vegetally.

These results suggest that a correlation exists between a double gradient of metabolism and the double gradient of differentiation discussed above. The causal link between these two phenomena comes from the analysis of the metabolic gradients under conditions that are known to affect the morphogenetic gradients. The two appear to be linked. For example, lithium treatment abolishes the center of metabolic activity at the animal pole without affecting that of the vegetal region. Animalizing agents have the opposite effect and leave the embryo in possession of an intact animal gradient but lacking a counterbalance from the opposite pole. In each case the ratios of the two influences are greatly disturbed, and the expected abnormal differentiation results.

Micromeres, when added to the side of an intact embryo, initiate a new vegetal gradient at that point; the morphological outcome is the invagination of a secondary archenteron from that region. Addition of extra cells is an *implantation* experiment. Micromeres are said to have "induced" the formation of a secondary gut. The term *induction* specifies that the micromeres, in this case, have caused the surrounding tissue to differentiate in a way it would not have without this external influence. If the metabolic gradients of embryos are analyzed after implantation of micromeres, a third center of metabolic activity—in addition to that of the animal and vegetal poles—is seen within the added cells. Taken together, these results lend strong support for the double gradient hypothesis of sea urchin development, the developmental system most extensively analyzed to date. Hörstadius has presented this theory and has summed up his spectacular experimental investigations of half a century in his book "Experimental Embryology of Echinoderms" (1973).

169

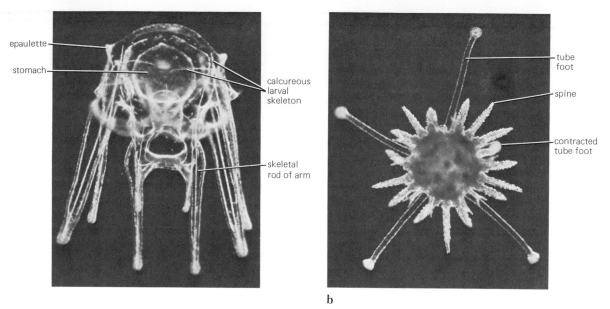

Figure 7.12 Photogrpahs of live stages of developing sea urchin *Echinus esculentus*. *a* Advanced 17-week-old bilaterally symmetrical pluteus larva with eight arms, ciliated epaulettes, and larval skeleton. *b* Young sea urchin soon after metamorphosis (7 weeks old, from fertilization) showing radial symmetry spines and tube feet. [*Courtesy of D. P. Wilson.*]

The foregoing analyses of the development of the sea urchin egg relate to two phases: (1) the early establishment of three primary germ layers represented by an outer ectodermal layer, and inner endodermal tubular layer confluent at each end into the ectoderm, and an intermediate mesoderm component; (2) the development of a specific type of larva capable of maintaining itself for a long period as a swimming, feeding, and growing planktonic organism.

Neither the symmetries nor the structures of the juvenile-adult type of organism—a radially symmetrical, crawling, and browsing sea-floor creature of great complexity—appear to be anticipated during the development of the egg to the pluteus stage. Only after a long period of growth as a pluteus larva does the profound metamorphosis of the adult pattern begin (Fig. 7.12). There is thus a dual quality to development: (1) the development of the egg as a specially programmed cell to become a particular type of transient larva and (2) the development of the egg as a totipotent cell capable of proliferation eventually sufficient to initiate the parental organization. A comparable dual system is seen in the development of ascidians.

MOSAIC DEVELOPMENT

We have seen that upon isolation of the first two or four cells of the sea urchin embryo, each is totipotent; development is regulative. If a similar operation is performed on a mollusk, annelid, ascidian, or one of several other groups, the result is different. To a lesser or greater degree the capability for differentiation of isolated cells of these embryos is restricted; i.e., their prospective potency may be little more than their prospective fate. The development of such embryos is termed *mosaic*.

An egg of this type is that of the ascidian *Styela*, in which a variety of distinct cytoplasmic regions are demarcated. The egg develops into a tadpolelike larva (Fig. 7.13), which subsequently metamorphoses into a sessile ascidian. In the unfertilized egg three distinct regions can be seen: a peripheral layer in which is embedded yellow lipid material in association with mitochondria, gray yolk material, and a germinal vesicle. Immediately after fertilization there is a dramatic shift in the egg contents that can be noted by the movement of the visible cytoplasmic materials (shown in the classical cell lineage study by Conklin, 1905). The germinal vesicle breaks down and its contents flow to the animal pole. The yellow plasm flows to the vegetal pole and forms a zone at that location. Above the yellow vegetal plasm is a thin clear zone, above which is the gray yolk that fills most of the egg. The egg contents do not remain in this position but are rearranged once more. At the future anterior side a gray crescent is formed. On the future posterior side two crescents have been described, a yellow crescent beneath the equator and a clear crescent above it. Most of the yolk becomes shifted to the anterior half of the egg. The bilateral organization of the egg is clearly defined by these visible regions.

The first cleavage plane always divides the egg in the plane of bilateral symmetry. As successive cleavages proceed, the material of the yellow crescent becomes segregated in two of the first eight blastomeres (Fig. 7.14); these continue to divide to form a total of 36 cells, the future muscle cells of the tadpole larva. Similarly the material in the anterior crescent becomes segregated as the 38 to 40 cells that differentiate as notochord cells. The gray yolky protoplasm forms the endoderm. The distribution of similar visibly distinct plasms in another ascidian, *Boltenia*, is shown in Fig. 7.15.

If the first two cells of an ascidian are isolated, each develops into a half-embryo. At the four-cell stage the anterior half can be separated from the posterior half; each develops in isolation into the same structures it would form in the intact embryo. In this latter case, for example, the anterior blastomeres form ectoderm, nervous system, notochord, and endoderm but not muscle

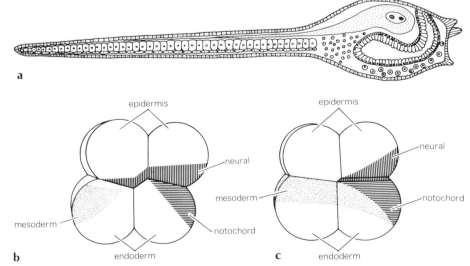

Figure 7.13 *a* Fully developed ascidian tadpole larva possessing notochord, dorsal nerve cord, and pharyngeal gill slits. This motile larva undergoes metamorphosis to form the sessile adult, which lacks the chordate characteristics of a notochord and dorsal nerve cord. *b* Fate map of eight-cell stage of ascidian embryo. *c* Fate map of eight-cell stage of *Amphioxus*, for comparison.

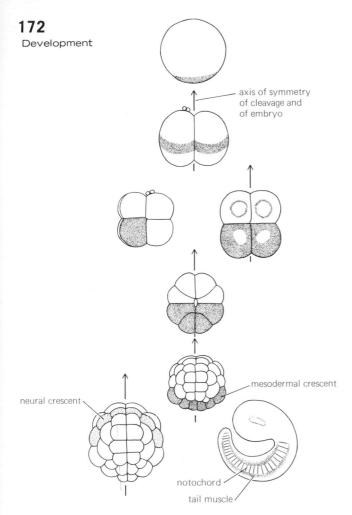

axis of symmetry
of cleavage and
of embryo

neural crescent

mesodermal crescent

notochord

tail muscle

Figure 7.14 Distribution of mesodermal crescent material (represented by naturally colored mitochondria in some species, and by vitamin C) in the cleaving ascidian egg, and the relationship between the embryonic axis and the symmetry of cleavage. Lowest two figures show distribution of crescent material in tail muscle of embryo (*right*), and (*left*) neural crescent cells. Arrows show embryonic axis.

tissue and mesenchyme. The prospective potency and the prospective fate are identical. If pairs of blastomeres are isolated at the eight-cell stage, the anterior vegetal pair, posterior animal pair, and posterior vegetal pair differentiate in keeping with their prospective fate. The anterior animal pair, however, do not differentiate into neural tissue as expected and require the presence of adjacent anterior vegetal blastomeres in order to differentiate.

The observation that different parts of the egg contain visibly different materials seems to be correlated with the restricted nature of their prospective potency. Are the various cytoplasmic components directly responsible for the differentiation of the cells in which they become segregated?

Conklin later established the causal relationship by centrifugation experiments. If *Styela* eggs are centrifuged after fertilization, the visible cytoplasmic regions (the yellow cytoplasm, the gray yolk, and the clear plasm) can be displaced in various ways. Under these circumstances development is always abnormal. He found that in ascidian embryos it is possible to recognize the endoderm, chorda, neural plate, and muscle cells by their colors, shapes, sizes, and histological characters even when these tissues are far from their normal positions. When egg substances have been dislocated by centrifuging, it is easy to see that the larval parts to which they typically give rise are also dislocated. Thus larvae may be turned inside out, with the endoderm, muscles, and chorda on the outside and the ectoderm, neural-plate cells, and sense organs on the inside. In other words, each type of cytoplasm differentiates into its expected tissue regardless of its position in the embryo.

These results have suggested that the ascidian contains materials, or morphogenetic factors, that become localized into different regions of the egg (Fig. 7.15). Each of these factors is in some way responsible for the path of differentiation taken by that cell in which these factors become localized. It must be reemphasized, however, that these precociously differentiating cells and tissues relate to the development of the special larval structures that constitute the distinctive chordate character of the larva—namely notochord, lateral bands of locomotory tail muscle, dorsal tubular nerve cord, and anterior brain vesicle with sense organs. None of these survive metamorphosis to become part of the adult ascidian.

At the time of fertilization the ascidian egg is essentially preprogrammed to develop into a tadpole larva. Although the special properties of the egg appear to be related to this production, not all of the egg is directed to the process, for some features of the permanent organism slowly develop during the rapid formation of the tadpole structure. When the period of tadpole larval activity comes to an end, however, and larval tissue is resorbed, the residual tissues rapidly complete their development to become a small but functional ascidian with beating heart, active gills, functioning gut, etc. In ascidian species where the tadpole larva has disappeared from development, the egg size, cleavage rate, time of gastrulation, time of hatching, and course of posthatching development remain the same as in closely related species that form a tadpole during the period between gastrulation and hatching.

In ascidians the visible components cannot be dissociated from the morphogenetic factors. This may not be the case in other forms. In many experiments it seems that the visible components reflect a more basic differentiation of the cytoplasm, one that remains in operation even after the visible components have been displaced. An example of this is described below.

Figure 7.15 *a* Flow of peripheral cytoplasm from animal pole to equator and from equator to vegetal pole at time of fertilization of ascidian egg. *b* Vegetal aspect of cleaving egg of ascidian *Boltenia echinata*, just before onset of gastrulation, showing segregation of different ooplasms within distinct cell groups, with colors and patterns as seen in living embryo.

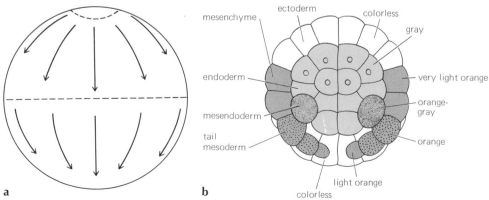

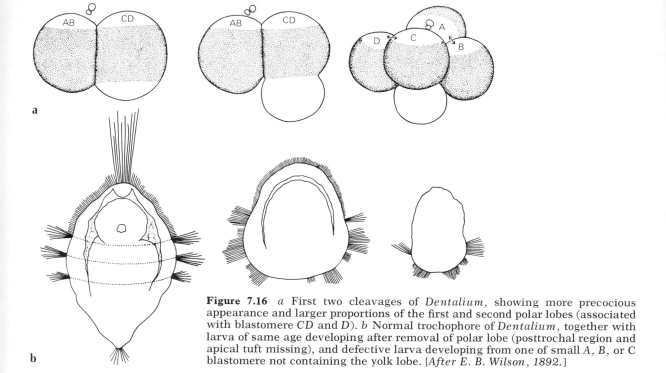

Figure 7.16 *a* First two cleavages of *Dentalium,* showing more precocious appearance and larger proportions of the first and second polar lobes (associated with blastomere *CD* and *D*). *b* Normal trochophore of *Dentalium,* together with larva of same age developing after removal of polar lobe (posttrochal region and apical tuft missing), and defective larva developing from one of small *A, B,* or *C* blastomere not containing the yolk lobe. [*After E. B. Wilson, 1892.*]

Spiralia

Many eggs, particularly those of the spirally cleaving molluskan species, are characterized by visible plasms that become shifted in various ways during the early postfertilization stages. This movement is termed *ooplasmic segregation*. In a number of mollusks, such as *Dentalium* and *Ilyanassa,* a specialized cytoplasmic component called the *polar lobe* has evolved as an apparent mechanism for the segregation of morphogenetic factors. The polar lobe appears as a large protrusion of cytoplasm at the vegetal pole prior to the first cleavage (Fig. 7.16). The first cleavage furrow then forms, cleaving an AB cell and a CD cell, with the polar lobe attached by a cytoplasmic bridge to the CD cell. The appearance, however, is of three cells and the stage is called the *trefoil*. After cleavage the entire content of the polar lobe goes into the CD cell. A second polar lobe reforms before the second cleavage and the process is repeated, with all the polar lobe material finding its way into the D cell of the four-cell stage. Several embryologists have investigated the function of the polar lobe; the most recent studies are those by Clement on the snail *Ilyanassa*. Clement has determined the effect of removing various blastomeres during the development of *Ilyanassa* to assign to each its developmental role. An experiment to determine the effect of cell removal on an embryo is called a *defect experiment*. If the missing cell contains some essential factor for the development of a structure or structures, it might be expected that its loss would leave the embryo unable to form that tissue. For example, removal of the first polar lobe of *Ilyanassa* results in the embryo's failure to develop an anteroposterior axis; it also lacks a velum, foot, shell, heart, intestine, and eyes. A typical larva is shown in Fig. 7.17. The most obvious conclusion is that the polar lobe contains morphogenetic factors that

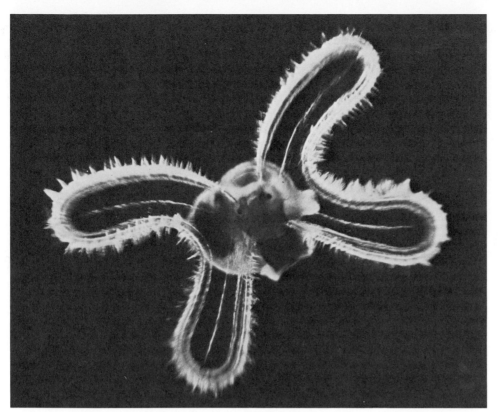

Figure 7.17 The planktonic veliger larva of a marine gastropod mollusk, the thick-lipped dog whelk *Nassarius incrustus*, swimming with fully extended velum. The velum is a transient larval structure that is resorbed during final metamorphosis. The essential structure of the adult-type organization is already present in the compact body within the velar larva; included, e.g., are the eyes, siphon, and shell gland. [*Courtesy of D. P. Wilson.*]

are in some way responsible for the differentiation of those structures in the cells in which the polar lobe materials become segregated.

The cytoplasm of the polar lobe will be distributed to various cells as cleavage proceeds. To determine when possible morphogenetic materials become segregated, Clement has removed the D macromere at different cleavages in different embryos. Removal of the D cell (leaves ABC) or removal of the 1D (leaves ABC descendants + 1d) or removal of the 2D (leaves ABC descendants + 1d + 2d) has essentially the same effect as removal of the polar lobe at the trefoil stage. If we wait until after the fourth cleavage and remove the 3D (leaves ABC descendants + 1d + 2d + 3d), the remaining embryo will now form velum, eyes, shell, and foot, but it still lacks the heart and the intestine. After the fifth cleavage the 4D can be removed, but the remaining embryo can form as an essentially complete larva. The 4D has no morphogenetic role. The conclusion from these experiments is that the factors in the lobe become segregated in two main steps. One step is in the formation of the 3d cell and the other in the formation of the 4d cell.

Evidence suggests that the influence of the polar lobe on the development of this snail is not contained in the endoplasm but, again, within its cortex. As might be expected, this conclusion is based upon centrifugation experiments,

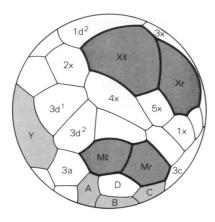

Figure 7.18 Silver-impregnated morula in *Teredo norvegica*, showing correspondence of local cortical differentiation and cleavage pattern. [*After Fauré-Fremiet and Mugard*, Acad. Sci. C. R., **227**:1400 (1948).]

as in the sea urchin. If the egg of *Ilyanassa* is held in an inverted manner and centrifuged, all the normal components of the vegetal endoplasm will be driven to the opposite pole. In this case the polar lobe which forms at the original vegetal pole has an entirely different composition; yet its effect on development (as determined by defect experiments) is unchanged. The undisturbed cortex must be held responsible.

The indication that such distinctive and precise patterns of cleavage are related to precocious regional specialization of the cortical region is supported by study of silver-impregnated preparations of the cleavage stages of the bivalve mollusk *Teredo norvegica* (Fig. 7.18). After expulsion of the second polar body, i.e., after fertilization but before cleavage starts, the surface of the egg is homogeneous. But after several cleavages have occurred, the two blastomeres X, derived from blastomere *D* (in cell-lineage nomenclature), which give rise to the shell gland of the larva, and blastomeres *M* and *Y*, which give rise to mesoderm-mesenchyme, show cortical silverline fine structure. Therefore, the differentiation of blastomeres is accompanied by or preceded by cortical events.

One of the basic questions in development concerns the cytoplasmic factors that direct specific gene expression. Virtually nothing is known of their nature, but the suggestion has been made that the polar lobe of *Ilyanassa* contains such factors. If RNA synthesis is compared in normal and lobeless embryos, the latter are far behind the controls. The basis for this reduced transcription level in lobeless embryos may well be the absence of specific gene activators segregated in the polar lobe.

MOSAIC VERSUS REGULATIVE DEVELOPMENT

The preceding discussion of the sea urchin, ascidian, and snail has led into a theoretical topic in which there is much difference of opinion. In the case of the ascidian and the snail, the prospect was considered that development may be controlled by the segregation of morphogenetic factors into different blastomeres. The development of embryos with such factors—assuming this concept is valid—is mosaic, a term that implies the egg is a patchwork of materials with morphogenetic influence. The fate of the cells that contain these factors is fixed as a result of their presence, i.e., their prospective potency is limited to their prospective fate. The term for fixation of fate is *determination*. A cell that upon isolation or after recombination can differentiate only into the structures that it normally forms is said to be fully determined. The ability to differentiate in isolation is called *self-differentiation*. Mosaic embryos are characterized by the early determination of their cells. Cells isolated from a mosaic embryo are typically capable of self-differentiation, and the remaining parts of the embryo are deficient in the structures normally formed by the missing cells. For example, if one of the first micromeres of a mollusk is isolated, it will divide twice to form four cilia-bearing trochoblasts. This is exactly its fate in the undisturbed embryo.

At the opposite extreme from the more highly mosaic embryos are the embryos whose cells are not determined until considerably later stages, such as the echinoderm and the vertebrate. These embryos are capable of adjusting, or regulating, to damage imposed upon them; they are classified as *regulative embryos*. In the sea urchin, for example, one can wait until the blastula stage and cut the embryo into two meridional halves, and each will form an entire larva. In another example discussed above, the macromeres can be removed and the remaining cells can form the pluteus. There is no evidence that morphogenetic factors become segregated in macromeres or in any other specific cell. The prospective potencies of the other 12 cells (at the 16-cell stage) include the formation of the gut, which is normally the prospective fate of the deleted macromeres. The other cells have regulated their activities to differentiate into structures they would not normally become.

Regulative development is characterized by a greater interaction of the embryonic parts. Two sea urchin embryos can be fused together and one giant larva will form. Each of the original embryos is now forming only one-half an embryo rather than the total product; this is another form of regulation. Each egg recognizes the presence of the other and adjusts its development accordingly. If two mosaic embryos are fused, each will continue to form one member of twins. Each cell acts independently of its neighbors.

Another way intercellular interaction manifests itself is in inductive contacts, i.e., contacts where one group of cells stimulates another group of cells to differentiate as it could not in isolation. Mosaic embryos tend to develop with a minimum of induction, i.e., tissues do not require specific contacts with other cells to differentiate; this is shown in their ability to self-differentiate.

The distinction between these two types of development is difficult to make; the view is generally accepted that the differences are relative ones and there is a continuous spectrum between the extremes. For example, we have pointed out that even in the highly mosaic ascidian, inductive interactions are required for normal development. We could have pointed out this same fact in our example of the mosaic development of *Ilyanassa*, since the ABC + 1d + 2d embryo lacks a foot. Normally the foot is derived from the 2d cell, as revealed by cell-lineage studies; this suggests that its failure to develop in embryos from which only the 2D is removed is due to a missing inductive influence from the 2D. It appears that in many of the so-called mosaic embryos, however, determination can be demonstrated at an early stage and the differentiation of the parts can be correlated with the localization of visible components.

The development of the frog illustrates the difficulty in assigning an embryo to a mosaic or a regulative position. If the first two cells of a frog are isolated, each can form an entire embryo. This indicates regulative development. However, if the ventral pair of cells is separated from the dorsal pair at the second cleavage, the former do not gastrulate while the latter can. This difference is directly related to the presence or absence of the gray crescent. Embryos without this cortical structure cannot develop. This clearly suggests that in the frog there is localization of morphogenetic factors; the egg is a mosaic. Similarly, in the frog egg there is evidence of the localization of material that is needed for primordial germ cell differentiation at a much later stage. In nearly every other way the frog embryo is highly regulative; it is only after gastrulation that the other parts are determined and are capable of self-differentiation. In the sea urchin, a change in the stage of determination can be shown by the isolation experiments of Hörstadius. At the 16-cell stage the isolated animal half forms the hollow ciliated ball. If this same animal half is isolated at the blastula stage, it is capable of forming a mouthlike structure, the apical tuft of cilia, etc., which are structures this region would normally develop. It appears that by the blastula stage, the animal half has been conditioned by the underlying mechanisms of determination so that it is now capable of self-differentiation; earlier it was not. Presumably, many of the same events in determination that take place by the blastula stage have occurred at a much earlier time in the mosaic embryo. In fact, even in the most strictly mosaic embryos an early change in determination can be demonstrated. For example, in several mosaic eggs—including the ascidian—if the egg is bisected before fertilization, each of the halves can form an entire larva; in these same species, if the first two blastomeres are separated, each develops into a defective larva.

When *unfertilized* eggs of *Ascidia* are fragmented into two equal pieces by equatorial, meridional, or oblique sections, and all fragments are then fertilized, each pair gives rise to twin tadpoles, although they are proportionately small. Not only are tadpoles formed from both haploid and diploid fragments (one having both egg and sperm nucleus, the other a sperm nucleus alone) but each fragment—whether haploid or diploid and whatever part of the original egg it represents—exhibits the normal, distinctive pattern of cleavage.

The problem, therefore, is by what means the specific programming is initiated. There are many unrelated instances where the tadpole organization has been entirely eliminated in the development of small, virtually yolkless eggs of ascidians living on the open sea floor, where the functional value of the tadpole larva is minimal; this suggests that a single mutation may be responsible for blocking, at least, such development.

Experiments with *Ciona* eggs that employ the cleavage-inhibiting drugs cytochalasin B (acting on microfilaments) and colcemid (acting on microtubules) have established a relationship between cytoplasmic segregation and differentiation of tissue-specific proteins. Ascidian larvae have two enzyme locations that occur relatively early in embryonic development: acetylcholinesterase in muscle cells of the tail and tyrosinase in the brain pigment cells. In the absence of cleavage, ascidian embryos develop acetylcholinesterase and tyrosinase in territories that match the known cell-lineage patterns for the two enzyme-containing tissues. This implies a differential segregation during cleavage, but independent of cleavage itself, of localized cytoplasmic information related to the development of these enzymes.

Since normal development occurs in at least some centrifugally stratified *Ciona* eggs, as well as in some from which up to half the egg cytoplasm has been removed, the segregated information is undoubtedly not located in the free cytoplasm of the egg. To be so faithfully segregated by cleavage, this information is probably positioned in a "two-dimensional" map on the egg surface, perhaps in either the plasma membrane or the cortical gel layer. The very strictly determinate cleavage pattern of the ascidian egg would then apportion these surface materials to the appropriate blastomeres and cells. According to Whittaker, no evidence excludes the intriguing possibility that such morphogenetic information might occur as stable conformations of ordinary cell surface components, and not be informational macromolecules in any orthodox sense.

Other experiments have employed colchicine and cytochalasin B, inhibiting nuclear divisions and cleavage respectively (in the ascidian *Phallusia mammillata*). This permitted ooplasmic segregation to proceed normally. Accordingly, both microtubules and microfilaments are eliminated as the structures responsible for ooplasmic segregation, leaving the cell membrane, or material associated with it, the probable basis for segregation control.

Figure 7.19 Direct development of the squid egg, from early morphogenesis to newly hatched stage. *a* Yolk mass of egg nearly enclosed by epibolic spread of cellular layer. The mantle and the pair of eyes are already observable as delimited areas in the cellular layer of the animal hemisphere. *b* Later stage showing primordia of much of the primary organization, i.e., shell gland, mantle, funnel, eyes, and arms. Much of the yolk vegetal hemisphere, now fully enclosed, will remain as the external yolk sac. *c* Progressive development of primordia already present. *d* Newly hatched stage with small external yolk sac still present. [*Courtesy of John Arnold.*]

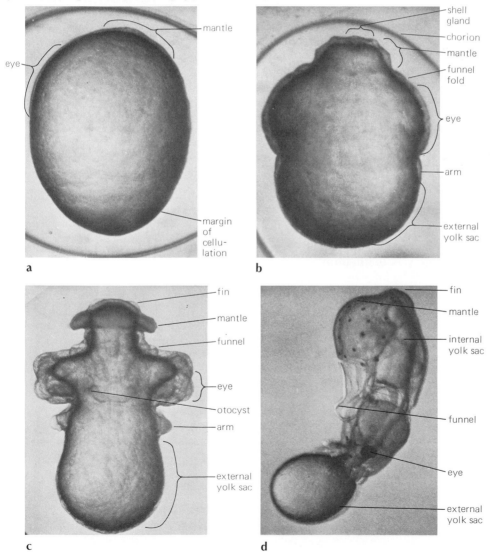

THE CEPHALOPOD EGG:
CORTEX AND PATTERN

There is little doubt that cephalopods, e.g., squid and octopus, evolved from a more primitive group of mollusks and at one time shared the spiralian inheritance. Adaptive changes, however, not only brought the cephalopods to the highest level of invertebrate evolution but resulted in the production of relatively large and yolky eggs. Development is direct, with no trace of either spiral cleavage or trochophore larva (Fig. 7.19).

Analysis of development in the squid has been made possible by culture techniques devised by Arnold (1965). The cephalopod embryo is well-suited for such a study since it is large, is telolecithal, and has bilateral cleavage; also, early development occurs on the surface of the large central yolk mass, so it is essentially a two-dimensional system. Cellulation of the egg proceeds by peripheral mitosis, and the blastoderm spreads over the egg surface from the animal pole to the vegetal pole with a minimum of cellular rearrangement. Thus specific locations remain relatively constant during development.

Three layers are eventually produced: an inner syncytial yolk epithelium or *periblast,* which digests the yolk and is also morphogenetically important, and two layers of outer cells, the inner one originally derived from a peripheral delamination (splitting) of the edge of the early blastoderm. These three layers spread peripherally and eventually enclose the entire central yolk mass about the time organogenesis becomes evident.

One of the earliest and most obvious organs to become recognizable is the eye. Experiments show that:

1   If the very early eye primordium is removed, leaving the yolk epithelium intact, the wound heals and a normal eye develops.

2   If the yolk epithelium is also removed and kept in isolation with the eye primordium, the isolate develops into an eye, while the donor fails.

3   Grafting dissociated and reaggregated tissues into isolated pieces of yolk epithelium results in the expected organ associated with the original site of the yolk epithelium.

From other extirpation and disruption experiments, Arnold concludes that informational pattern in the yolk epithelium at the onset of organogenesis is in accordance with a pattern already present in the egg cortex, at least at the time of the first cleavage. Further ligation experiments by another worker (Marthy, 1975), however, resupport an older concept, that the cellular material actually forming the embryo is the primary carrier of developmental information, and is accordingly self-organizing. Debate continues.

READINGS

ARNOLD, J. M., 1965. The Inductive Role of the Yolk Epithelium in the Development of the Squid, *Loligo pealii* (Lesueur), *Biol. Bull.,* **129**:72–78.

BERRILL, N. J., 1961. "Growth, Development, and Pattern," Freeman.

———, 1950. Size and Organization in the Development of Ascidians, in P. Medawar (ed.), "Essays on Growth and Form," Oxford University Press.

———, 1935. Cell Division and Differentiation in Asexual and Sexual Development, *J. Morphol.,* **57**:353–427.

BLACKLER, A. W., and C. A. GECKING, 1972. Transmission of Sex Cells of One Species through the Body of a Second Species in the Genus *Xenopus, Develop. Biol., 27*:376–394.

CATHER, J. N., 1971. Cellular Interactions in the Regulation of Development in Annelids and Molluscs, *Advan. Morphog., 9*:67–125.

CHAMBERS, R., and E. L. CHAMBERS, 1961. "Explorations into the Nature of the Living Cell," Harvard University Press.

CLAVERT, J., 1962. Symmetrization of the Egg of Vertebrates, *Advan. Morphog., 2*:27–60.

CLEMENT, A. C., 1962. Development of *Ilyanassa* Following Removal of the D Macromere at Successive Cleavages, *J. Exp. Zool., 149*:193–215.

CONKLIN, E. G., 1905. The Organization and Cell Lineage of the Ascidian Egg, *J. Acad. Nat. Sci., 8*:1–119.

CONRAD, G. W., 1973. Control of Polar Lobe Formation in Fertilized Eggs of *Ilyanassa obsoleta* Stimpson, *Amer. Zool., 13*:61–980.

CURTIS, A. S. G., 1962. Morphogenetic Interactions before Gastrulation in the Amphibian, *Xenopus laevis*, in the Cortical Field, *J. Embryol. Exp. Morphol., 10*:410–422.

DAVIDSON, E. H., 1968. "Gene Activity in Early Development," Academic.

DRIESCH, H., 1892. The Potency of the First Two Cleavage Cells in Echinoderm Development, in B. H. Willier and J. M. Oppenheimer (eds.), "Foundations in Experimental Embryology," 1964, Prentice-Hall.

GUSTAFSON, T., 1965. Morphogenetic Significance of Biochemical Patterns in Sea Urchin Embryos, in R. Weber (ed.), "Biochemistry of Animal Development," vol. I, Academic.

HÖRSTADIUS, S., 1973. "Experimental Embryology of Echinoderms," Clarendon Press, Oxford.

———, 1955. Reduction Gradients in Animalized and Vegetalized Sea Urchin Eggs, *J. Exp. Zool., 129*:249–256

———, 1939. The Mechanics of Sea Urchin Development, Studied by Operative Methods, *Biol. Rev., 14*:132–179.

HUXLEY, J. S., and G. R. DE BEER, 1934. "The Elements of Experimental Embryology," Cambridge University Press.

JAFFE, L., 1968. Localization in the Developing *Fucus* Egg and the General Role of Localizing Currents, *Advan. Morphog., 7*:295–328.

MARSLAND, D., 1956. Protoplasmic Contractility in Relation to Gel Structure: Temperature-Pressure Experiments on Cytokinesis and Amoeboid Movement, *Int. Rev. Cytol., 5*:199–227.

——— and J. V. LANDAU, 1954. The Mechanics of Cytokinesis: Temperature-Pressure Studies on the Cortical Gel System in Various Marine Eggs, *J. Exp. Zool., 125*:507–539.

MARTHY, H. J., 1975. Organogenesis in Cephalopoda: Further Evidence of Blastodisc-bound Developmental Information, *J. Embryol. Exp. Morphol., 33*:75–88.

MERCER, E. H., and L. WOLPERT, 1962. An Electron Microscope Study of the Cortex of the Sea Urchin (*Psammechainus miliaris*) Egg, *Exp. Cell Res., 27*:1–13.

MITCHISON, J. M., and M. M. SWANN, 1954. The Mechanical Properties of the Cell Surface, *J. Exp. Biol., 31*:443–472.

MORGAN, T. H., 1927. "Experimental Embryology," Columbia University Press.

NEEDHAM, J., 1942. "Biochemistry and Morphogenesis," Cambridge University Press.

OPPENHEIMER, J., 1955. Problems, Concepts, and Their History, in B. H. Willier, P. Weiss, and V. Hamburger (eds.), "Analysis of Development," Saunders.

PASTEELS, J. J., 1964. The Morphogenetic Role of the Cortex of the Amphibian Egg, *Advan. Morphog., 3*:363–388.

RAVEN, C. P., 1966. "Morphogenesis: The Analysis of Molluscan Development," Pergamon.

REVERBERI, G., 1961. The Embryology of Ascidians, *Advan. Morphog., 1*:55–101.

ROBINSON, K. R., and L. F. JAFFE, 1975. Polarizing Fucoid Eggs Drive a Calcium Current Through Themselves, *Science, 187*:70–72.

ROUX, W., 1888. Contributions to the Developmental Mechanics of the Embryo, in B. H. Willier and J. M. Oppenheimer (eds.), "Foundations of Experimental Embryology," 1964, Prentice-Hall.

STEARNS, L. W., 1974. "Sea Urchin Development," Dowden, Hutchinson and Ross.

WATTERSON, R., 1955. Selected Invertebrates, in B. H. Willier, P. Weiss, and V. Hamburger (eds.), "Analysis of Development," Saunders.

WHITTAKER, J. R., 1973. Segregation during Ascidian Embryogenesis of Egg Cytoplasmic Information for Tissue-Specific Enzyme Development, *Proc. Nat. Acad. Sci. U.S., 70*:2096–2100.

WILSON, E. B., 1925. "The Cell in Development and Heredity," 3d ed., Macmillan.

CHAPTER 8

Nucleus, Cytoplasm, and Cortex

EQUIVALENCE OF NUCLEI

In several places in this book the assumptions are made that all cells contain all the genes and that differentiation reflects selective gene expression in each type of cell. In other words, each cell contains *all* the genetic information but utilizes only what is relevant to its function. This view of differentiation has not always been held. In an earlier hypothesis, Weismann proposed that cells achieve a specialized state by retaining those parts of the chromosomes needed for that condition and by eliminating those parts they do not need. Thus, a liver cell would have within its nucleus only those genes needed for liver differentiation and function and would have lost the others. In this theory special consideration must be given to the germ cells, for they are responsible for producing a complete individual in the next generation and must retain all genes. Weismann's *germ plasm* theory provides that no loss of chromosomal material occurs in the cells leading to the gametes, in contrast with the loss in all other cells.

Chromosome Loss

One of the earliest studies examined the development of the nematode *Ascaris,* in which just such a loss of pieces of chromosomes occurs (Fig. 8.1). After the first cleavage (which is horizontal in *Ascaris*) the chromosomes in one of the two cells undergo fragmentation, and certain fragments are not passed on to the daughter cells at second cleavage. In the other cell, in which the germ-cell lineage is located, no fragmentation occurs and each daughter cell receives a total set of chromosomes. Chromosome loss, which is called *chromosome diminution,* continues in the succeeding divisions; but one line of cells is spared gene loss, namely, that line proceeding toward formation of the gametes.

Analysis of chromosomal elimination in *Ascaris* indicates qualitative differences in informational content of soma versus germ line. In comparison with the retained portion of the *Ascaris* genome, the eliminated DNA comprises few if any ribosomal genes but a large number of unique sequences. Thus an enormous amount of genetic information is lost through elimination. Chromosomal

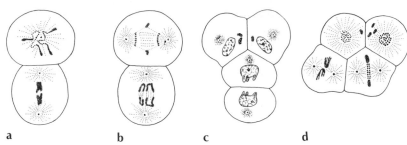

a   b   c   d

Figure 8.1 *Ascaris.* Development of an egg from the two-cell stage to the end of the four-cell stage. *a* Two-cell stage, upper cell undergoing chromosome diminution, lower cell showing normal chromosome behavior. *b* Two-cell stage, slightly later than in *a*, upper cell in side view. The ends of the diminished chromosomes remain in the center of the cell between the separating chromosome fragments. *c* Four-cell stage, resting nuclei. In the upper two cells, degenerating chromosome ends lie outside the nuclei. In the lower two cells, the undiminished chromosomes are recognizable by the irregular shape of the nuclei. *d* Four-cell stage, nuclei dividing. Upper cells show the earlier diminished chromosomes; lower right cell undergoes diminution; lower cells show normal chromosome behavior. The lower left cell corresponds to the lowermost cell of *c*, which has changed its position. [*After Boveri, 1899.*]

elimination also occurs in the somatic cell (non–germ cell) lines in certain insects. In two species of midge, induced chromosomal elimination in germ-line cells results in sterility in otherwise normal adults. Therefore at least some genetic information qualitatively different from that of the retained portion is contained in the eliminated chromatin, and this information is indispensable for normal gametogenesis.

Transplantation of Nuclei

The most direct approach to the question has been the nuclear transplantation experiment. This once again illustrates the potential for experimental manipulation in the study of development—if the biologist can clearly formulate the question, plan the necessary experiment, and overcome the technical difficulties inherent in any new probe at the subcellular level. The question is: Do irreversible (stable) changes in the genetic content of the nuclei occur during development? The experimental plan is to remove nuclei from cells of progressively older embryos, to insert these nuclei into uncleaved eggs whose nuclei have been removed, and to determine if these later-stage nuclei are capable of supporting the development of the recipient eggs.

A successful technique of embryonic nuclear transplantation, developed by

Figure 8.2 Enucleation of frog egg by means of capillary pipette or glass needle. Another method is to kill the egg nucleus by exposure to ultraviolet radiation. [*After Rugh, "Experimental Embryology,"* p. 180, Burgess, 1962.]

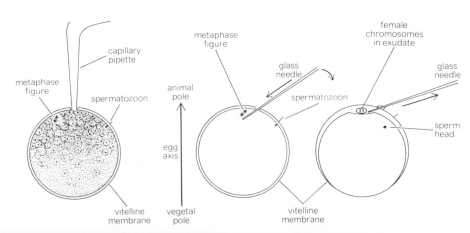

Briggs and King, used the frog *Rana pipiens*. In these studies the chromosomes of the recipient egg are removed from the animal region just after the egg is experimentally activated with a needle (Fig. 8.2). A substituted donor nucleus is obtained by using a micropipette with a diameter less than that of the donor cell so that the cell is ruptured. The isolated nucleus, together with a protective coat of surrounding cytoplasm, is injected into the cytoplasm of the already activated egg. Development proceeds, to whatever extent, under the direction of the newly acquired genetic material. Since the early work on *Rana,* a second system, using *Xenopus,* has probed the same question. There appear to be certain differences between these two series of investigations and considerable difference in interpretation. We will begin with a discussion of results in *Rana* and then consider the work on *Xenopus*.

The goal of the nuclear transplant studies is to determine if the nuclei remain equivalent to one another despite the alterations in the differentiating cytoplasm that surrounds them. To this end, nuclei from later and later stages are tested for their ability to support the development of the recipient, enucleated egg. It must be kept in mind that even if nuclei do become irreversibly altered, so that they can no longer support total development, this does not mean they have undergone gene loss. Other types of genetic alterations that cannot be reversed, that fall short of genetic deletion, not only are possible but are more likely.

When a nucleus from an early stage, such as blastula or early gastrula, is transplanted, a high percentage of the transplants develop into normal tadpole larvae. The interpretation is clear: no irreversible nuclear changes have occurred during this early period; the nuclei remain equivalent. This is a very important conclusion. By the early gastrula stage, thousands of cells of several different types have formed and have undergone considerable activity; yet there have been no stable alterations in their content.

When the nuclei are taken from the late gastrula or a later stage, the morphological development becomes restricted. As nuclei are taken from later- and later-stage *Rana* embryos, the resulting transplants are progressively more abnormal, and the percentage that develop into normal larvae is essentially zero by the neurula and tail-bud stages. Even the percentage of transplants that develop into blastulas becomes severely curtailed (65 percent from late gastrula, 33 percent from neurula, 17 percent from tail-bud when endodermal nuclei are donors). Several possible explanations could account for these findings: (1) that as the nuclei are taken from older stages, there is an increased risk of damage to the nuclei by the transplantation procedure; (2) that the nuclei are becoming differentiated in a stable, irreversible manner as development proceeds and they are no longer equivalent or totipotent; (3) that the nuclei are not irreversibly altered, but as they get older they are less able to manage in the egg cytoplasm, which becomes increasingly more distant from their own cytoplasmic state.

Before trying to decide among these explanations, we will present the overall results of the studies on *Rana*. Briggs, King, and DiBerardino have concentrated on two types of nuclei, endodermal and neural. Analysis of abnormal larvae from transplants involving both nuclear types shows that two characteristic larvae are formed. In the endodermal nucleus the larva is particularly deficient in ectoderm and mesoderm and much less so in endoderm (*endodermal syndrome*). In neural nuclear transplants, some larvae have the greatest deficiencies in endodermal and mesodermal structures. The technique of *serial transplantation* has shown that these nuclear restrictions are stable.

In a serial transplant (Fig. 8.3) the donor nucleus is injected into the egg, which is allowed to develop to the blastula stage; nuclei are then removed and are injected into new enucleated eggs, and so forth. In this way nuclei can un-

injection

fertilization

Figure 8.3 Serial transplantation of nuclei, from an embryo with nucleus derived from an egg arrested at the blastula stage. In each generation the development of the egg is arrested at the blastula stage, indicating that a permanent change has occurred, but it is not established whether the changes have occurred before or after transplantation. [*After Markert, "The Nature of Biological Diversity," p. 110, McGraw-Hill, 1963.*]

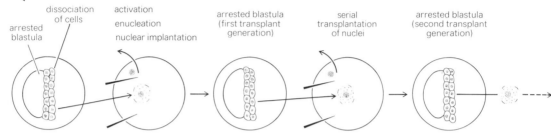

dergo many more divisions than they normally would if they were simply allowed to become part of deficient larvae that is arrested in its cells divisions. When nuclei with the endodermal syndrome are serially transplanted through up to five generations, there is no change in the type of deficiencies promoted. The nuclear alterations are stable and specific. The early conclusion from this finding was that these deficiencies revealed the nuclei were undergoing stable alterations as development proceeded, and that after a time an endodermal nucleus could no longer support mesodermal or ectodermal differentiation.

We now return to the three possibilities suggested above. The first one regarding damage can be ruled out; endodermal nuclei of the tail bud are no more sensitive than ectodermal nuclei of the early gastrula, yet the latter remain totipotent. The difference between the second and third possibilities relates to the time that the nuclear changes occur. In the second the changes occur before transplantation as a result of the normal course of development, while in the third they result *after* transplantation as a result of nuclear-cytoplasmic incompatibility. There is no doubt that the cytoplasm of the egg is very damaging; it is believed that essentially all nuclei from late embryonic stages sustain chromosomal damage, whether it is obvious under the microscope or not. This is not surprising; a nucleus from a late stage undergoes division, and therefore replication, in a much more leisurely fashion than it would in a newly fertilized egg with a cleavage regime demanding the most rapid replication. In the first cleavage cycles the later-stage donor nucleus seemingly cannot replicate fast enough, and it receives chromosomal damage. Therefore, damage must occur after transplantation, but the question remains: Are there changes prior to the transplantation? This group of investigators would argue that with development there must be nuclear modifications to explain the fact that endodermal and neural nuclei produce different types of deficient larvae. This cannot be explained by *random* damage to the chromosomes; it suggests that specific primary changes have occurred in the nuclei that lead to permanent, but predictable, differences as a result of specific chromosome damage. This implies that the primary changes make certain parts of chromosomes more sensitive to damage than others. One proposal is that parts of the chromosomes become more condensed (*heterochromatic*); these parts cannot replicate fast enough after transplantation and are lost. If

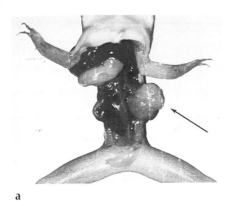

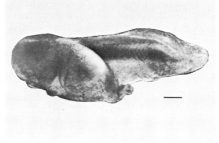

Figure 8.4 *a* Left renal tumor (arrow) of recently metamorphosed triploid frog. *b* Tadpole developed from egg with transplanted triploid tumor nucleus, with well-formed head, body, and tail (scale = 1 mm). [*Courtesy of R. G. McKinnell.*]

a   b

we assume there are primary changes in nuclei as development proceeds, two possibilities remain. The changes could be irreversible, such as gene loss or irreparable genetic repression, or they could be reversible ones that would require the proper environment for return to the original state. This environment is not provided by uncleaved egg cytoplasm. At the present time we cannot distinguish with certainty between these possibilities.

Although nuclei from late development stages of *Rana* show severe restrictions after transplantation, at least one type of adult nucleus is able to support development. These nuclei are derived from a frog tumor, a renal adenocarcinoma (Fig. 8.4*a*). The larvae that develop (7 of 143 became swimming tadpoles) from these transplants contain a wide variety of tissues (Fig. 8.4*b*). This indicates that these nuclei derived from an adult frog (although probably from an "abnormal" tumor cell), were capable of promoting the differentiation of entirely different tissues.

The other main series of nuclear transplantation studies, using *Xenopus* rather than *Rana*, has been carried out by Gurdon and his coworkers. In the early experiments nuclei from later and later embryonic stages were tested for their ability to support development. As in the experiments with *Rana*, when cells differentiate their nuclei are less able to support normal development after transplantation. In the studies of embryonic *Xenopus* donor nuclei, Gurdon has concentrated upon the larval intestinal epithelium cells of the tadpole. Because of their large size, it is relatively easy to obtain undamaged nuclei from these cells. Also, they represent a differentiated cell type, shown by a striated border and the capability of food absorption. In these experiments the majority of endodermal nuclei do not promote normal development, though approximately 20 percent produce tadpoles with functional nerve and muscle cells. In *Xenopus* the egg chromosomes cannot be removed mechanically and instead are destroyed by irradiation. The procedure used in these experiments is shown in Fig. 8.5. In a few cases transplanted nuclei promoted the development of normal, fertile adult frogs. To be certain that the transplanted nucleus is indeed providing the chromosomes, the donor nucleus carries an identifiable genetic marker. Donor nuclei are heterozygous for the nucleolar deletion and thus have only one nucleolus. The recipient egg that is irradiated contains the normal chromosome set. The resulting embryos that develop from the transplants contain cells with only one nucleolus rather than two, and it is proved the donor nucleus is responsible. One of the major points of controversy in these experiments is whether one can conclude there are no irreversible nuclear changes when only a very small percentage of the transplantations result in *completely normal* development (approximately 2 percent). Gurdon argues that as long as any of these nuclei can be proved to be totipotent, i.e., support total develop-

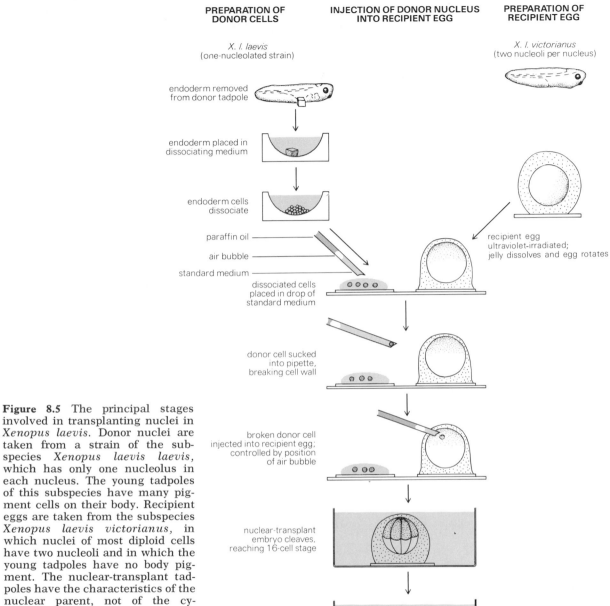

PREPARATION OF
DONOR CELLS

INJECTION OF DONOR NUCLEUS
INTO RECIPIENT EGG

PREPARATION OF
RECIPIENT EGG

X. l. laevis
(one-nucleolated strain)

X. l. victorianus
(two nucleoli per nucleus)

endoderm removed
from donor tadpole

endoderm placed in
dissociating medium

endoderm cells
dissociate

paraffin oil ————
air bubble ————
standard medium ————

dissociated cells
placed in drop of
standard medium

recipient egg
ultraviolet-irradiated;
jelly dissolves and egg rotates

donor cell sucked
into pipette,
breaking cell wall

broken donor cell
injected into recipient egg;
controlled by position
of air bubble

nuclear-transplant
embryo cleaves,
reaching 16-cell stage

nuclear-transplant
tadpole has *X. l. laevis*
pigmentation and one
nucleolus per nucleus

Figure 8.5 The principal stages involved in transplanting nuclei in *Xenopus laevis*. Donor nuclei are taken from a strain of the subspecies *Xenopus laevis laevis*, which has only one nucleolus in each nucleus. The young tadpoles of this subspecies have many pigment cells on their body. Recipient eggs are taken from the subspecies *Xenopus laevis victorianus*, in which nuclei of most diploid cells have two nucleoli and in which the young tadpoles have no body pigment. The nuclear-transplant tadpoles have the characteristics of the nuclear parent, not of the cytoplasmic one, showing that their nuclei are derived from the transplanted nucleus. [*After Gurdon*, Endeavour, **25**:96(1966).]

ment, we can conclude there are no irreversible (stable) changes along the path to the differentiated state. The transplants that do not have entirely normal development can simply be attributed to damage or to nucleocytoplasmic incompatibility. Even in many of these cases, the deficient larvae show a wide series of differentiations other than those in the cells from which the nucleus was taken (an intestinal type). That is, they clearly contain genetic material for a great variety of differentiated pathways.

In a more recent series of experiments, Laskey and Gurdon have successfully removed nuclei from cultured cells derived from adult skin; after transplantation these nuclei support the development of larvae that are nearly normal. As in *Rana,* these results indicate that nuclei from a specific cell type—in this experiment a normal adult cell—retain the genetic information for varied differentiations unrelated to the cell from which the nucleus was taken. In this case there is no doubt concerning the differentiated state of the donor cell because all these skin cells become keratinized within a week if they are left in culture.

Though there has been considerable disagreement between these two nuclear transplant systems (*Rana* and *Xenopus*), the interpretations have moved closer together. Clearly there are changes in nuclei during development: they get smaller, replicate more slowly, and are more easily damaged if nothing else. Disagreement may still remain as to how extensive and how reversible some of the nuclear changes might be among different cells, but there are no results from any of the experiments that suggest gene loss accompanies differentiation. As stated in several places in this book, all nuclei in most animals contain all the genes.

CYTOPLASMIC CONTROL OF NUCLEAR ACTIVITY

The nuclear transplantation studies with *Xenopus* by Gurdon and coworkers have clearly demonstrated cytoplasmic control over nuclear synthetic function. In the previous section we have described one type of recipient cell into which *Xenopus* nuclei have been transplanted, the activated, irradiated egg. The synthetic state characteristic of the early postfertilization stage is intensive DNA synthesis and negligible RNA synthesis (including the complete absence of rRNA synthesis and tRNA synthesis, which are not activated until much later). Nuclei transplanted into the activated egg undergo a predictable pattern of activities. These nuclei assume the synthetic activity characteristic of the nucleus they have replaced, regardless of their properties before transplantation. They become reprogrammed. A nucleus at the neurula stage is synthesizing all kinds of RNA, but is not likely to be making DNA. Within an hour after transplantation the synthesis of RNA has been suppressed and DNA synthesis has been activated to the typical early cleavage level. If the synthetic activity of the descendants of the transplanted nucleus is followed, we find that each type of RNA synthesis is sequentially reactivated at the same stage at which it occurs during normal development. Transfer RNA synthesis becomes reactivated at the blastula stage, and rRNA is reactivated at gastrulation. Such experiments suggest, but do not prove, that these kinds of nuclear expression are controlled independently by different cytoplasmic components.

The changing synthetic pattern after transplantation is accompanied by striking morphological changes in the donor nucleus that similarly reflect the expected state of an early cleavage nucleus. For example, the nucleus swells to the volume expected for that stage, an increase of over thirtyfold. The nucleolus of the transplanted nucleus disappears until its re-formation within the nuclei of the gastrula. The conditioning effect on nuclei by egg cytoplasm can be extended to injected nuclei from nonembryonic sources. If brain nuclei from adult *Xenopus* are injected into the activated egg cytoplasm, a marked swelling of these nuclei is found together with the activation of DNA synthesis in nuclei that had stopped making it before their differentiation into neurons (years earlier). Swelling appears to be a prerequisite for DNA synthesis; those nuclei that remain unswollen for whatever reason do not synthesize DNA.

What is there in egg cytoplasm that produces these rapid changes in injected nuclei? The answer is not known, but an interesting series of experiments indicates that proteins from the egg cytoplasm rapidly enter the nucleus as it swells. The evidence comes from injection of nuclei into eggs that had been "prelabeled" with ^{3}H-amino acids. The labeled amino acids are injected into the female body cavity at the same time hormones are administered that cause maturation, ovulation, and release of eggs (shed 12 to 16 hours after hormone treatment). Whatever label becomes incorporated into protein is made during the maturation period. When brain nuclei are injected into these prelabeled eggs, labeled protein is found in the nucleus in 10 minutes, which is prior to swelling or DNA synthesis. As the nuclei swell, the labeled protein accumulates within the nucleus to a concentration greater than that of the cytoplasm. It has been proposed that entering proteins become concentrated within the nucleus as a result of their specific attachment to the chromosomes. The most swollen nuclei accumulate the greatest concentration of labeled protein, and in turn these nuclei synthesize the most DNA.

In a related series of experiments, purified proteins of a known nature were made radioactive by attaching ^{125}I atoms to them (*iodination*); these proteins were injected into eggs containing transplanted nuclei. Does any injected protein become concentrated in the nucleus, or just proteins that would be expected to have a nuclear function? It appears that the latter possibility is the correct one. When ^{125}I-labeled histones are injected, the label accumulates in the nucleus, presumably as a result of the binding of the histones to the chromosomes. In contrast, if an unrelated protein such as ^{125}I-labeled bovine serum albumen is injected, it remains more concentrated in the cytoplasm.

The injection of an entire nucleus introduces a great number of different macromolecules, any number of which might be required for the response of the nucleus to the cytoplasmic signals. On the other hand, since the response is the synthesis of DNA, the enucleated egg may simply be deficient in DNA to replicate, and all that is needed is the presence of DNA. This can be tested by injecting purified DNA into the activated egg, together with a labeled DNA precursor (such as ^{3}H-thymidine). When this is done, new DNA is synthesized with the injected DNA as a template and the ^{3}H-thymidine as precursor. It appears that the cytoplasm contains all the necessary ingredients for replication to begin, and it may be that certain of these materials are among the substances that move into the swelling nucleus to cause it to begin to make DNA. If purified DNA can initiate the replication response, one might expect any type of nucleus to become activated in *Xenopus* cytoplasm. This appears to be the case. If mouse liver nuclei are injected into amphibian eggs, they become stimulated to synthesize DNA just as if they had been taken from a *Xenopus* neurula cell.

Whereas the cytoplasmic state of the activated egg dictates a stimulation of DNA synthesis and a cessation of RNA synthesis, the cytoplasmic state of a growing oocyte is just the reverse. Consider the synthetic activities of an amphibian oocyte in the midst of its lampbrush stage. It is making large quantities of RNA but has already replicated its DNA. What is the result of the injection of a blastula nucleus into the cytoplasm of a growing oocyte? In the blastula, nuclei are still making DNA at a fairly high rate but have not yet begun to make RNA at a significant level. Within a few hours after injection into oocyte cytoplasm, these nuclei have shut down their synthesis of DNA and are synthesizing RNA (Fig. 8.6a). If blastula nuclei had instead been injected into the activated egg, no RNA synthesis would have been initiated (Fig. 8.6b). The conditions for DNA synthesis are reversed (Fig. 8.6c, d). Oocyte cytoplasm does not activate DNA synthesis, while egg cytoplasm does. Swelling of transplanted

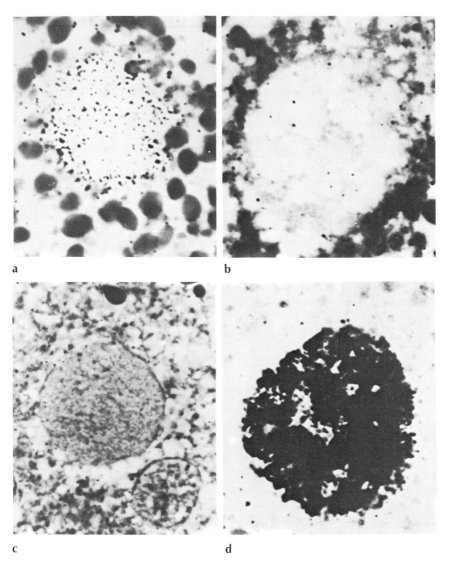

a   b

c   d

Figure 8.6 RNA and DNA of transplanted nuclei. Mid-blastula nuclei, which synthesize DNA but not RNA, are injected into (*a*) an oocyte and (*b*) an egg. Oocytes normally synthesize RNA but not DNA; eggs normally synthesize DNA but not RNA. Nuclei injected into the oocyte synthesize RNA, but similar nuclei injected into the egg do not. Black granules are silver grains showing incorporation of ³H-RNA precursors. *c, d* Results following injection of brain nuclei into oocyte and egg, respectively. Frog brain nuclei synthesize RNA but rarely DNA. In the oocyte where RNA synthesis is progressing, brain nuclei do not synthesize DNA, but in the egg the injected brain nuclei switch from RNA to DNA synthesis in response to conditions in the host-cell cytoplasm. [*Courtesy of J. B. Gurdon.*]

blastula nuclei in eggs versus oocytes is shown in Fig. 8.7. Though they do swell considerably in egg cytoplasm, they enlarge many times more in oocyte cytoplasm, as would be expected if the transplanted nucleus is to mimic the large germinal vesicle. Injection of purified DNA into growing oocyte cytoplasm does not cause this DNA to become replicated as it did in the activated egg. There are two possible explanations to explain why injected DNA should not be replicated in oocyte cytoplasm. Growing oocyte cytoplasm may lack certain necessary materials for replication, or growing oocyte cytoplasm might contain an inhibitor of DNA synthesis. We cannot clearly decide between these possibilities on the basis of experiments with only one type of cytoplasm. We will reconsider this question below.

Growing oocyte cytoplasm activates RNA synthesis and shuts off DNA synthesis; activated egg cytoplasm does the reverse. In between these two stages is sandwiched the mature, unfertilized egg. This stage is characterized by the lack of both DNA and RNA synthesis; therefore, if the rules apply, a nucleus injected into these cells should stop both synthetic activities. If brain cell nuclei are injected into maturing oocytes, RNA synthesis comes to a halt (they were previously inactive in DNA synthesis and remain so). They are rapidly converted into condensed chromosomes typical of the meiotic chromosomes normally found at this stage.

These very important experiments give us a look at one of the most basic processes in cell biology, the cytoplasmic control of nuclear activity. Another series of experiments relates directly to this question, though the cells employed are not usually embryonic. The technique, termed *cell fusion,* involves the association of two cells, the dissolution of the membranes separating the cells, and the subsequent fusion of their cytoplasms. In experiments by Harris, fusion is brought about by the addition of an inactivated (therefore noninfective) virus. The virus attaches to the cell membranes and makes the cells "sticky" so that they fuse. For a period of time, fused cells contain two or more nuclei; they are multinucleate. If the mixed cells are derived from different types of tissue, or even from different species of animals, they are still capable of fusing and of forming multinucleate cells (*heterokaryons* if from two species) that contain a mixture of both cytoplasms. Various fates can befall these hybrid cells, one of which is the formation of a population of healthy, dividing cells with mixtures of both types of chromosomes within each nucleus. For two sets of chromosomes to fuse into one nucleus, an intervening mitosis must occur. As the nuclei within the fused cell prepare for mitosis, the nuclear membranes break down, the chromosomes line up in a metaphase plate containing both types of chromosomes, the chromatids separate into daughter cells, and a nuclear membrane re-forms in each cell, enclosing a mixed population of chromosomes. Cell fusion has been an invaluable tool in the study of several aspects of cell function, including the

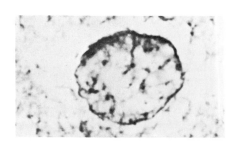

a

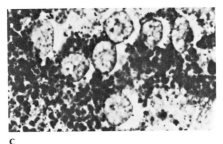

c

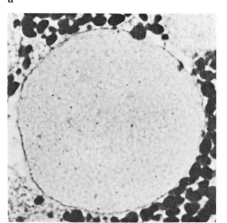

b

Figure 8.7 Blastula nuclei, which synthesize DNA but no RNA, swell following their injection into (*a*) an egg or (*b*) an oocyte and commence a prolonged period of RNA synthesis. The nucleus in the oocyte enlarges 200 times. *c* Blastula nuclei of normal dimensions. [*Courtesy of J. B. Gurdon.*]

nature of the malignant state and human cell genetics. The present discussion is concerned with the effects of mixing cytoplasm from two cells upon the synthetic activities of the nuclei.

We will consider just one case of cell fusion from the standpoint of reprogramming nuclear activity, the fusion of the hen erythrocyte with the malignant human cell HeLa. (Other examples can be found in Harris's "Nucleus and Cytoplasm," 1970). The chicken erythrocyte is a circulating red blood cell, the terminal stage in a series of differentiation steps. The nucleus of this cell is synthetically inactive; it makes no DNA and no RNA and its chromatin is tightly condensed. The HeLa cell is a rapidly dividing, active cell that makes RNA continuously and DNA during its periodic S phases. When these two cells are fused, there is a rapid enlargement of the erythrocyte nucleus (a twenty- to thirtyfold volume increase), a loosening of the condensed chromatin into a more "synthetic" state, the accumulation of cytoplasmic materials, and the reactivation of both RNA and DNA synthesis (Fig. 8.8). The chicken erythrocyte nu-

Figure 8.8 The reactivation of the erythrocyte nucleus. *a* A heterokaryon containing one HeLa nucleus and one hen erythrocyte nucleus, on the first day after fusion. The nuclear bodies are visible in the erythrocyte nucleus. *b* A heterokaryon containing one HeLa nucleus and one hen erythrocyte nucleus which has now begun to enlarge. The nuclear bodies are more diffuse and stain less deeply. *c* A heterokaryon containing one HeLa nucleus and one hen erythrocyte nucleus at a later stage of reactivation. The nucleus is now very much larger and the nuclear bodies are not visible. *d* Autoradiograph of a heterokaryon from a 24-hour culture exposed for 20 minutes to tritiated uridine. The autoradiograph was developed after exposure for 3 days. The cell contains four HeLa nuclei and four hen erythrocyte nuclei. All the nuclei are synthesizing RNA. [*Courtesy of Henry Harris.*]

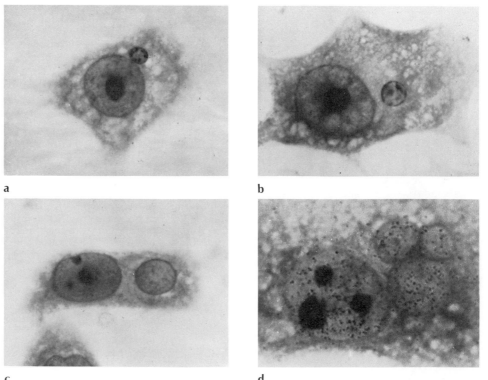

a   b

c   d

cleus is quite dormant, yet it can be rapidly reprogrammed under cytoplasmic influence to a full synthetic capacity.

In addition to dormancy, another feature of chicken erythrocytes makes them even more suitable for cell fusion studies: they can be fused either with or without the cytoplasm. If adult hen erythrocytes are treated with the fusing virus, the cells are lysed and cytoplasm leaks out. Remaining to fuse with the other cell are a cell membrane and a nucleus; therefore, after fusion the total cytoplasm is essentially donated by the HeLa cell. In contrast, when an embryonic chick erythrocyte is used, the cytoplasm is not lost and the fused cells have both chick and human cytoplasm. In either case the erythrocyte nucleus is completely inactive prior to fusion and is reactivated following fusion. If we consider the chick erythrocyte-HeLa first, we have a heterokaryon with both nuclei and both cytoplasms; the result is an activation of the erythrocyte nucleus rather than an inactivation of the HeLa. This is always the case regardless of the types of cells that are fused, i.e., these nuclear control signals are positive (they turn syntheses on) rather than negative signals that would be expected to turn syntheses off. The adult hen erythrocyte-HeLa gives us additional basic information. The erythrocyte nucleus must be responding to a signal from the human cytoplasm, since the bird cytoplasm had leaked out prior to fusion. There is no evidence of species specificity for these activation signals. It must be kept in mind that we are speaking of general activation (RNA synthesis) rather than specific activation (specific mRNA synthesis). The activation of the general RNA or DNA synthetic state may not require highly specific macromolecules but may instead simply require a specific ionic composition or other rather general cytoplasmic state. The induction of specific species of RNA is presumably a much more complex process. Cell recombinations involving separation and combination of nucleus and cytoplasm are further facilitated by causing cells to extrude their nuclei, so that the two components may be variously manipulated. This is done by treatment with cytochalasin B (Fig. 8.9).

With a few exceptions, during embryonic development the entire store of genetic information is passed on to all the cells, and differentiation stems from selective utilization. The overall conclusion from the transplantation experiments is that stable, irreversible changes have not been established. Certainly

Figure 8.9 A fibroblast cell extruded its nucleus, resulting from treatment with cytochalasin B. [*Courtesy of S. B. Carter.*]

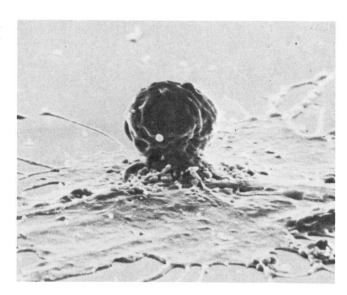

in a transcriptional sense the differentiated state is stable. However, this can be rapidly overcome (as illustrated by the nuclear reprogramming experiments) by a new cytoplasmic state. The question of differential gene expression is discussed in Chapter 17.

NUCLEUS, CORTEX, AND DETERMINATION IN INSECT DEVELOPMENT

Insect eggs, even the smallest, are relatively rich in yolk. The nucleus lies in a central position, embedded in a small island of cytoplasm from which fine strands extend to the periphery of the egg, where they form the cortical layer of cytoplasm (Fig. 8.10). This layer is called the *periplasm.* As the nucleus undergoes successive divisions, the daughter nuclei move apart, in which stage they have been termed *energids.* The process continues through eight divisions, by which time the nuclei enter the periplasm, and cell boundaries form between them for the first time. The single layer of cells now surrounding the yolk is the blastoderm. Subsequently, a *germ band* appears in the blastoderm as the first visible differentiation of the embryo. It first appears in the presumptive prothorax region of the embryo-to-be and continues to differentiate anteriorly and posteriorly from this region.

The eggs of insects vary greatly among the different insect groups, ranging from eggs with great regulatory powers (e.g., those of the dragonfly, which can be made experimentally to produce twin embryos, by dividing the germ band longitudinally during early cleavage) to those of dipterans (e.g., *Drosophila,* in which determination of the presumptive embryonic parts is already set at the time of fertilization).

Mosaic eggs of this sort are typical of higher Diptera and of Lepidoptera (i.e., holometabolous insects that undergo drastic, complete metamorphosis). In these eggs the main regions of the body appear to be already mapped out in the cortical plasma at the time of laying, before the egg nucleus has begun to divide. Since elimination of some of the migrating nuclei by ultraviolet irradiation at a sufficiently early stage of development does not affect morphogenesis, their place being taken by other nuclei arriving in the cortical region, the subsequent fate of the cleavage cells is evidently determined by the regional nature of the cortical plasma. The nuclei are clearly equivalent. The general conclusions are that in the absence of nuclei in the cortical region, the cortical

nuclei (energids)   periplasm

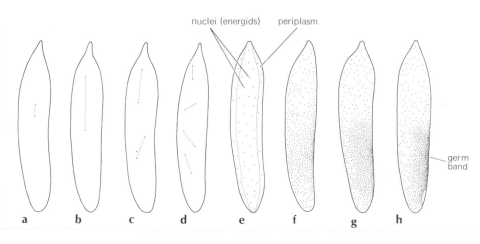

germ band

a   b   c   d   e   f   g   h

Figure 8.10 Early development of the dragonfly *Platycnemis,* showing the first three divisions of the nucleus, the spreading of the daughter nuclei through the egg cytoplasm (the two sister nuclei from a division are joined by a dotted line), the multiplication of the nuclei to form a blastoderm, and their aggregation to produce the germ band. [*After Seidel,* Arch. Entwickl.-mech., **119:**322 (*1929*).]

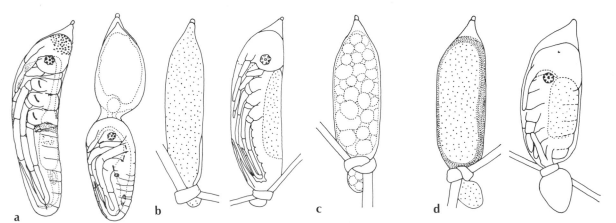

Figure 8.11 Regulation in the insect egg. *a* Normal embryo of the dragonfly *Platyc-nemis penipes,* seen from the left side, and dwarf embryo, obtained by partial constriction of the egg at the four-nucleus stage. The dwarf is normally proportioned and developed, and its organs have arisen from regions the presumptive fate of which was quite different; their fates were therefore not irreversibly determined at the stage operated upon, and regulation has been possible. *b* The operation of the formation center. If a very small part of the posterior of the egg is constricted off at an early stage, an embryo can develop. *c* If the constriction lies a little further forward, no embryo forms. *d* After the formation of the blastoderm, an embryo is formed even if the constriction lies well forward, since the formation center has by that time completed its action. [*After Seidel,* Arch. Entwickl.-mech., **119**:322 (*1929*).]

plasma or periplasm has become chemically differentiated and that the nuclei are later subject to this chemodifferentiation. In the egg of a hemimetabolous insect such as the dragonfly, however, which undergoes an incomplete metamorphosis, the determinative chemodifferentiation of the cortex is not attained until some time after the cleavage nuclei have reached the cortical layer. If a substantial portion of the anterior region of the egg at this stage is removed by ligation, a well-proportioned but reduced embryo differentiates in the remaining posterior part of the egg (Fig. 8.11).

Extrinsic Control of Regional Development

During the embryonic development of holometabolous insects such as *Drosophila,* a remarkable segregation takes place. One population of embryonic cells becomes determined for forming the larval body; i.e., the cells differentiate so that at the time of hatching, the organs and systems of the first-instar larva (the stage before the first molt) are ready to function. A second system is set apart within this primary embryonic system as small isolated territories, the *imaginal discs* (Fig. 8.12), which individually undergo some growth during larval existence but do not otherwise proceed with further development until metamorphosis. Differentiation is postponed in this second system, but cell division is not; for the discs, which are so small in the embryo that they are hardly recognizable, each consists of thousands of cells when they reach their final size at the beginning of metamorphosis.

At metamorphosis most of the larval organs break down within the pupal case and their cells disintegrate. Simultaneously the cells of the imaginal discs begin to differentiate into specific cell types, and the cells of each disc collectively develop a structure characteristic of the location of the disc on the body wall. Thus three pairs of anterior discs together form the head (with its special

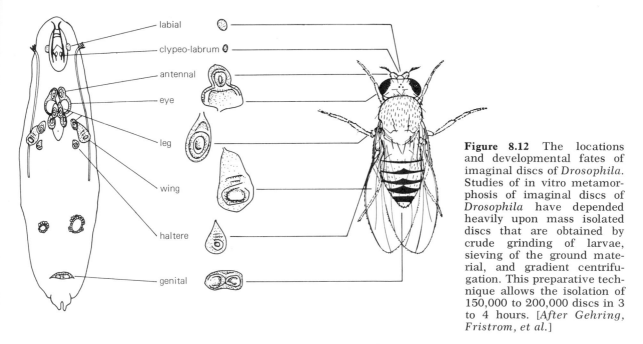

labial

clypeo-labrum

antennal

eye

leg

wing

haltere

genital

Figure 8.12 The locations and developmental fates of imaginal discs of *Drosophila*. Studies of in vitro metamorphosis of imaginal discs of *Drosophila* have depended heavily upon mass isolated discs that are obtained by crude grinding of larvae, sieving of the ground material, and gradient centrifugation. This preparative technique allows the isolation of 150,000 to 200,000 discs in 3 to 4 hours. [*After Gehring, Fristrom, et al.*]

mouth parts and sense organs), three pairs of thoracic discs give rise to the six legs, two pairs of more dorsal thoracic discs form the wings and specialized wing rudiments (halteres), and a posterior bilobed disc gives rise to the genital structure. Each disc accordingly develops into a structural complex that eventually connects with neighboring complexes; together they construct the complete adult. Each disc is therefore specifically determined with regard to its destiny relative to the whole organism, and this determination must occur some time before the differentiation of the disc becomes evident.

Development of Imaginal Discs

Analytical genetic studies have long established the fruit fly *Drosophila melanogaster* as the classical material for such experimental investigation. Its small size, life cycle, and ease of culture have been assets. Larger insects have been more suitable for operative procedures. Now that these techniques have been refined for use on the smaller organism, *Drosophila* has become the primary subject for all kinds of investigation, mainly because its genetic constitution is the best known. It has four major developmental stages, as in *Cecropia* and other holometabolous insects. Embryonic development persists for about 22 hours; then the larva hatches, grows for about 4 days, forms a pupa, and in 4 days undergoes metamorphosis to an adult.

In *Drosophila melanogaster*, during the prepupal period the imaginal discs (Fig. 8.13) are converted in a matter of hours into the basic form of the adult insect. There are extensive gross morphological changes involving the evagination of the discs, fusion of the discs into a continuous sheet of tissue, and formation of the cuticle. Discs, invaginated in pockets during larval life, evaginate at the onset of metamorphosis. Evagination and RNA synthesis in the discs can be evoked in vitro by the hormone ecdysone.

Each disc is a small nest of cells, set aside early in embryogenesis, which is determined to develop during metamorphosis into a particular adult structure

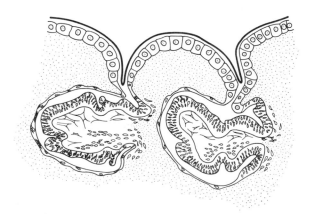

Figure 8.13 Longitudinal section of invaginated imaginal discs of the wings of an ant. The discs evaginate during pupation (metamorphosis). [*After Wigglesworth, 1954.*]

such as wing, leg, antenna. At the time of determination, each disc consists of about 10 to 40 cells. During the following three larval stages (*instars*) the cells of the discs proliferate, and by the third instar the discs consist of several thousand cells. Despite this proliferation the cells remain undifferentiated during larval growth, yet maintain the determined state.

Imaginal discs can be cut out of an insect larva with a fine tungsten needle and then implanted by means of a micropipette into the body cavity of other larvae, i.e., tissue culture in vivo. The hosts pupate, and the implanted discs also undergo differentiation, each according to its original fate; i.e., an eye disc gives rise to an eye, a leg disc to a leg, etc. Such discs therefore lend themselves to a variety of experimental procedures.

While an implanted disc usually differentiates only according to its original prospective fate, under certain conditions it can give rise to more and different structures, although generally as duplication of structures typical of the particular disc. Each remains district-specific, but within the district significant regulation can take place. Even so, regional determination is apparent within a particular disc well before disc activation begins. A leg disc, for instance, contains cell subdistricts that develop into claws, tarsal parts, tibia, femur, trochanter, coxa, and adjoining parts of the thorax, each such district having bristles and hairs in specific numbers and patterns. Similarly the genital disc (male) is a mosaic of subdistricts more or less determined as prospective sperm pump, penis, anal plates, and hind gut, and each of these in turn is a mosaic of still smaller subdistricts (Fig. 8.14). If the disc is subdivided before any differentiation becomes evident, however, each part reorganizes to form a harmonious whole of proportionate size.

The final differentiation of the discs (indicated by the onset of metamorphosis) is controlled by hormones. Throughout larval life the discs are exposed to a high level of juvenile hormone, secreted by the corpora allata, which has the combined effect of sustaining the larval organization and inhibiting disc differentiation. When metamorphosis begins, the level of this hormone drops and disc differentiation is allowed to proceed, each according to its initial determination. The specificity of this determination is at least sufficient to allow localization in the leg disc, for example, of such organs as transverse rows of bristles, claws, groups of sensilla, and even a single bristle in the trochanter. The primordia for the segments of the adult leg are arranged in concentric annuli in the disc, and these annuli are converted to tubular structures when the disc everts.

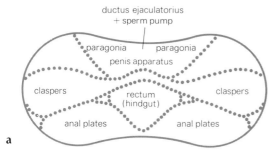

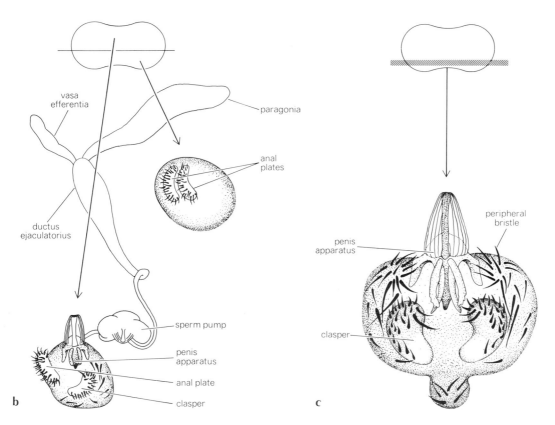

Figure 8.14 *a* A map of the anlagen (presumptive areas) in a male genital disc of *Drosophila melanogaster*. *b* Result of a fragmentation experiment; below, the metamorphosed structure obtained by the anterior half (*left*) and the posterior half (*right*). *c* Result of a localized irradiation indicated by hatching; below, the metamorphosed implant in which no anal plates are differentiated. [*After Hadorn, 1965.*]

Initiation of Discs

The discovery that imaginal discs are essentially determined with regard to their prospective fate in 2½ to 4 hours of development raises the question of their origination. Do they arise in the earliest stages of embryonic development from single epidermal cells or from groups of cells? Is the single cell the source of a specific cell population, or does the initial definitive area usually embrace a group of cells, large or small, and therefore relate to a supracellular agency of some kind? The technical problem here is a familiar one, namely, to trace particular cell populations to their source or to the structures they ultimately form. Concerning the so-called determinate-type eggs of many invertebrates, the early studies of cell lineage yielded descriptive mappings of regional cellular differentiations, from the uncleaved egg onward.

The same principle has been applied by different methods to the development of *Drosophila* in relation to the pattern of differentiation. The technique employed is the x-ray induction of somatic chromosomal crossing-over, whereby single cells in the imaginal discs are caused to become homozygous for recessive marker genes that remain heterozygous elsewhere in the body. These marked cells give rise to generations of daughter cells that are also homozygous for the marker; the clones thus produced are recognizable as patches of mutant tissue on the surface of the adult, notably as clones bearing both the bristle markers, yellow and singed.

The center of attention in these experiments was the differentiation of the leg. The most striking feature of the cell lineage of leg discs is that clonally related cells come to occupy long, narrow stripes in the longitudinal direction of the leg. The numerous somatic crossing-over experiments indicate that the number of cells initially destined to give rise to the leg is about 20, and that these cells are present as a group of prospective leg cells in developing eggs less than 3 hours old. This group of cells apparently remains static during the remainder of the embryonic period; further cell division does not commence until the second half of the first larval instar. Results show that determination of the leg disc into regions does not occur until after the third larval instar. These findings suggest that a certain area of the egg surface is destined to give rise to the leg disc (similarly with all other types of disc) and that this localization of prospective leg or other organ tissue is independent of the particular cellular state at any given time. In fact, the whole early blastoderm appears to function as a "morphogenetic field" within which presumptive imaginal discs become specified as to location and character. Each disc in its turn behaves like a field; the disc borders may function as reference points specifying the location of the organ districts, or district fields, of which all discs are probably made. Each of these districts will form a specific part of the pattern of adult structures formed by the disc as a whole. The "field" concept is discussed on page 310.

Transdetermination

In the foregoing experiments, predetermined but undifferentiated disc tissue implanted into a larval host received full exposure to the insect metamorphic hormone during the pupation of the host. In further experiments, pieces of imaginal discs were inserted directly into the abdomen of the adult fly. Ordinarily the disc cells would stop dividing and begin to differentiate as soon as the host pupation begins. In this circumstance they continue to grow and divide indefinitely, as long as a sample of proliferating cells is transferred to a new adult abdomen every 2 weeks, i.e., as long as they are regularly subcultured as in typical tissue-culture procedure. By this means the cultured disc cells live for years, from fly to fly, without undergoing any observable differentiation (Fig. 8.15). Since cell populations cultured in this way have been maintained for several years, passing through hundreds of adult fly generations, there have been ample time and opportunity to check on cell potentialities.

The starting point of these experiments by Hadorn was a male genital disc. Half of such a disc, the stem piece, is implanted in the abdomen of an adult fly; the other half, the test piece, is implanted in a larva where it will differentiate during pupation. After 2 weeks the stem piece is recovered and divided into two; one piece is again inserted in an adult abdomen as the stem piece, and the other into a larva as the test piece, to see if it still differentiates as before. At first the test pieces continue to differentiate into typical genital structures. Then, as time and transfers continue, test pieces develop into the leg parts or

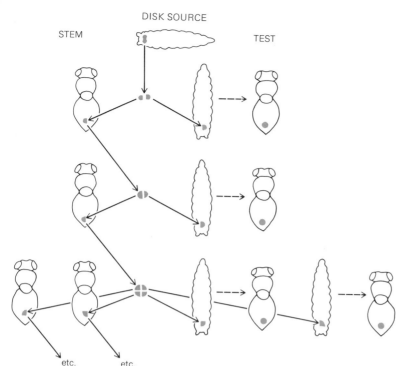

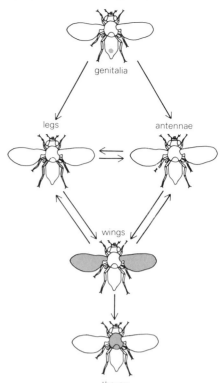

Figure 8.15 Method used for permanent cultures in vivo. Stem-line fragments grow but remain undifferentiated; test fragments pass metamorphosis and develop into adult structures. [*After Hadorn, 1965.*]

Figure 8.16 Transdetermination sequence undergone by seven kinds of imaginal-disc cells is shown by arrows. Genital cells, for example, may change into leg or antenna cells, whereas leg and antenna cells may become labial or wing cells. In most instances the final transdetermination is from wing cell to thorax cell; the change to thorax appears to be irreversible.

head organs, switching from the original determined path to another, a change that has been termed *transdetermination* (Fig. 8.16). Evidence that it is not due to somatic mutation is provided by the discovery that transdetermination occurs in groups of contiguous cells not clonally related and is too frequent to be due to mutation.

Transdetermination can proceed from state to state. In a particular transfer series, for instance, genital-disc cells gave rise to head and leg structures in the eighth transfer generation, or after about 4 months. After the thirteenth transfer they gave rise to wings. After nineteen transfers, a thoracic type of structure appeared. In other words, genital-disc cells may give rise to head or leg cells, which may give rise to wing cells, which may give rise to thoracic cells, but apparently the genital cells cannot transform directly to wing cells. Haltere discs (*halteres* are a segmental pair of rudimentary wings modified to serve as flight stabilizers) transdetermine directly to wing but not to leg or genitalia. Leg discs transdetermine directly to wing but not to haltere. In some sense haltere is closer to wing than to leg and genitalia. Both can transdetermine to wing but not to each other. Moreover the transdetermination may become stabilized at any stage and need not proceed to a specific end point.

Each type of transdetermination—from genital to antennal structures or

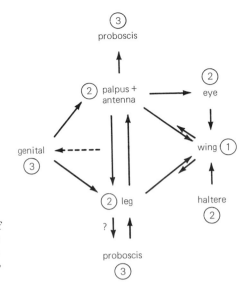

Figure 8.17 Flow pathway diagram of transdetermination. [*After Gehring, in "The Stability of the Differentiated State," W. Beerman, J. Reinart, H. Ursprung, (eds.), Springer-Verlag, 1968.*]

from leg to wing structures, for example—occurs with a characteristic probability per transfer generation from adult to adult (Fig. 8.17). The new state of determination is clonally heritable in the transdetermined tissue line. The determined state must therefore be a self-maintained state. A speculative and sophisticated discussion of the possible controls for determination and transdetermination in *Drosophila,* by Kauffman, can be read in *Science,* 1973. Ongoing investigations are for the most part published in volumes of "The Biology of Imaginal Discs, Results and Problems in Cell Differentiation" (Springer-Verlag).

READINGS

Nucleus and Cytoplasm

BRACHET, J., and E. HUBERT, 1972. Studies on Nucleocytoplasmic Interactions during Early Amphibian Development, *J. Embryol. Exp. Morphol.,* **27**:121–145.

BRIGGS, R., 1973. "Developmental Genetics of the Axolotl," pp. 169–201, 31st Symposium, Society of Developmental Biology, Academic.

DAVIDSON, R. L., 1973. "Control of the Differentiated State in Somatic Cell Hybrids," pp. 295–328, 31st Symposium, Society of Developmental Biology, Academic.

DıBERARDINO, M. A., and N. HOFFNER, 1970. Origin of the Chromosomal Abnormalities in Nuclear Transplants, A Reevaluation of Nuclear Differentiation and Nuclear Equivalence in Amphibians, *Develop. Biol.,* **23**:185–209.

EPHRUSSI, B., 1972. "Hybridization of Somatic Cells," Oxford University Press.

FLICKINGER, R. A. (ed.), 1966. "Developmental Biology" (readings), Wm. C. Brown.

GORDON, S., 1973. Regulation of Differentiated Phenotypes in Heterokaryons, pp. 269–294. 31st Symposium, Society of Developmental Biology, Academic.

GURDON, J. B., 1974. "The Control of Gene Expression in Animal Development," Harvard University Press.

——, 1968. Transplanted Nuclei and Cell Differentiation, *Sci. Amer.,* December.

——, and H. R. WOODLAND, 1968. The Cytoplasmic Control of Nuclear Activity in Animal Development, *Biol. Rev.,* **43**:233–262.

——, 1964. The Transplantation of Living Nuclei, *Advan. Morphog.,* **4**:1–43.

HARRIS, H., 1970. "Nucleus and Cytoplasm," Oxford University Press.

LASKEY, R. A., J. B. GURDON, and L. V. CRAWFORD, 1972. Translation of Encephalomyocarditis Viral RNA in Oocytes of *Xenopus laevis*, *Proc. Nat. Acad. Sci. U.S.*, **69**:3665–3669.

McKINNELL, R. G., R. A. DIGGINS, and D. D. LABAT, 1969. Transplantation of Pluripotential Nuclei from Triploid Frog Tumors, *Science*, **165**:394–396.

TERRA, N. DE., 1969. Cytoplasmic Control over the Nuclear Events of Cell Reproduction, *Int. Rev. Cytol.*, **25**:1–29.

TOBLER, H., K. D. SMITH, and H. URSPRUNG, 1972. Molecular Aspects of Chromatin Elimination in Ascaris, *Develop. Biol.*, **27**:190–203.

Nucleus and Cortex

BEERMANN, W., 1966. "Cell Differentiation and Morphogenesis," North-Holland Publishing Company, Amsterdam.

BODENSTEIN D., 1955. Progressive Differentiation: Insects, in B. Willier, P. Weiss, and V. Hamburger (eds.), "Analysis of Development," Saunders.

———, 1953. Embryonic Development, Postembryonic Development, in K. D. Roeder (ed.), "Insect Physiology," Wiley.

BRYANT, J. P., and G. SCHUBIGER, 1971. Giant and Duplicated Imaginal Discs in a New Lethal Mutant of *Drosophila melanogaster*, *Develop. Biol.*, **24**:223–264.

——— and H. A. SCHNEIDERMAN, 1969. Cell Lineage, Growth, and Determination in the Imaginal Leg Discs of *Drosophila melanogaster*, *Develop. Biol.*, **20**:263–290.

GARCIA-BELLIDO, A., and J. R. MERRIAM, 1969. Cell Lineage of the Imaginal Discs in *Drosophila* Gynandromorphs, *J. Exper. Zool.*, **170**:61–75.

GEHRING, W., 1967. Clonal Analysis of Determination Dynamics in Cultures of Imaginal Discs in *Drosophila melanogaster*, *Develop. Biol.*, **16**:438–456.

HADORN, E., 1968. Transdetermination in Cells, *Sci. Amer.*, **219**:110–123.

HOLLIDAY, R., and J. E. PUGH, 1975. DNA Modification Mechanisms and Gene Activity during Development, *Science*, **187**:226–232.

KAUFFMAN, S. A., 1973. Control Circuits for Determination and Transdetermination, *Science*, **181**:310–318.

LEWIS, E. B., 1964. Genetic Control and Regulation of Developmental Pathways, in M. Locke (ed.), "The Role of Chromosomes in Development," 23d Symposium, Society of Developmental Biology, Academic.

OUWENEEL, W. J., 1972. Determination, Regulation, and Positional Information in Insect Development, *Acta Biotheor.*, **21**:115–131.

POODRY, C. A., P. J. BRYANT, and H. A. SCHNEIDERMAN, 1971. The Mechanism of Pattern Reconstruction by Dissociated Imaginal Discs of *Drosophila melanogaster*, *Develop. Biol.*, **26**:464–477.

STERN, C., 1968. Developmental Genetics of Pattern, pp. 135—173, in "Genetic Mosaics and Other Essays," Harvard University Press.

URSPRUNG, H., 1967. *In vivo* Culture of *Drosophila* Imaginal Discs, in F. W. Wilt and N. K. Wessells (eds.), "Methods of Developmental Biology," Crowell.

———, 1966. The Formation of Patterns in Development, in M. Locke (ed.), "Major Problems in Developmental Biology," 25th Symposium, Society of Developmental Biology, Academic.

———, 1963. Development and Genetics of Pattern, *Amer. Zool.*, **3**:71–86.

WADDINGTON, C. H., 1962. "New Patterns in Genetics and Development," Columbia University Press.

WIGGLESWORTH, V. B., 1966. Hormonal Regulation of Differentiation in Insects, in W. Beermann (ed.), "Cell Differentiation and Morphogenesis," North-Holland Publishing Company, Amsterdam.

CHAPTER 9

Molecular Biology of
Early Development

Preformed, Maternal RNA
Embryonic Transcription
Preformed RNA Versus Embryonic RNA
Protein Synthesis during Early Sea Urchin Development
Preformed Proteins

The preceding chapters dealt with information present in the egg and early embryo as revealed by nonbiochemical means. This chapter is concerned with the same period of development with an emphasis on molecular biology. This is a vast topic whose horizons are continually expanding. The discussion is accordingly restricted to informational macromolecules and their synthesis and role in early development. Particular emphasis is placed on the nature and role of the molecular information passed on from oogenesis as well as that supplied by the embryonic nuclei.

PREFORMED, MATERNAL RNA

As discussed in several earlier chapters, the egg receives a considerable store of informational RNA from the activities of oogenesis. This RNA can be extracted from a batch of unfertilized eggs and analyzed in a variety of ways. Two of the most important measurements concern the variety and quantity of different RNAs. Questions of variety (or diversity) of nucleic acid are best answered by hybridization experiments to determine the percentage of the DNA that can hybridize to a population of RNA (see page 550). When this experiment is performed with RNA from an unfertilized *Xenopus* egg, it is found to be complementary to 1.2 percent of the nonrepeated genes and to a maximum of 7 percent of the repeated gene fraction. A similar experiment with the spiralian egg *Urechis* gives a value of 8.5 percent of the nonrepeated sequences. If all these RNAs complementary to the nonrepeated DNA sequences were templates for proteins, they would be diverse enough to produce approximately 20,000 to 40,000 different polypeptide chains (of average size range) in either the amphibian or *Urechis*. The actual number of RNAs that become translated in either embryo is not known. The genome of *Urechis* is much smaller than *Xenopus* and, therefore, a correspondingly higher percentage of the DNA produces an equivalent variety of RNA species.

The above procedure tells us of the diversity but not of the quantity of informational RNAs in the egg. The term *informational RNA* is used to exclude those RNAs that we know for certain are not translated, in particular the rRNAs and the tRNAs. Another, more widely used, term is *DNA-like RNA*. This reflects the great diversity of RNA species that bind to a wide fraction of the genome and therefore have nucleotide base composition (percentage of G + C) very similar to the DNA. Another term for these RNAs is *heterogeneous,* indicating the great diversity of molecular weight reflected by their distribution throughout the typical sucrose gradient. The use of all these vague and ambiguous terms (DNA-like, heterogeneous, informational) simply reflects our ignorance of their function. The messenger RNAs are certainly in this fraction, but what percentage they constitute is not known. To prepare an RNA fraction that is to be essentially pure messenger RNA, the method of preference is to extract the RNA from a purified preparation of polysomes after removal of the ribosomes. Other than the ribosomal RNAs, there are no known RNA molecules besides mRNA in the polysomes. In the present experiment the total RNA of the egg is used. Whether all informational RNAs that can be extracted from the egg are translated is not known, but it is believed that they can be translated in an in vitro system of protein synthesis (see page 552). The use of such a system provides a straightforward measure of the quantity of template-active RNA that has been extracted.

When RNA from the unfertilized sea urchin egg is tested in this manner, approximately 4 to 5 percent *can* direct amino acid incorporation into proteins. However, this provides no estimate of the number that are actually translated in the embryo and no estimate of the number of *different* protein chains being made; it is simply the total absolute number.

EMBRYONIC TRANSCRIPTION

We can conclude from the above results that development of the egg begins with a legacy of template information, but when does the embryonic genome begin to be expressed? There is a variety of related questions to be considered. When does RNA synthesis begin in the embryo? What types of RNA are made and at what stage? When does the RNA made by the embryo become translated into proteins? When does the RNA made by the embryo become necessary for continued normal development? Though these questions are obviously related, each is distinct, each requires a different analytical approach, and each provides a different answer. As might be expected, the answers to all these questions depend entirely upon the animal chosen for investigation. During the past years many studies have been made of a wide variety of species, and a comparative discussion could be presented. Rather than attempt this, we will concentrate on the sea urchin and the frog and bring in a few other animals to illustrate the variety of approaches that have been taken.

When does transcription begin and what types of RNA are made? In the sea urchin and frog, RNA synthesis can be demonstrated during the early cleavage period. The method employed is described on page 553. The incorporation of radioactively labeled precursors into RNA has been demonstrated in virtually every animal examined by the time of gastrulation.

In the following brief examination of the types of RNA made by the embryo, we will consider only rRNA, tRNA, and mRNA, assuming that mRNA is made from what is originally a much larger molecule. In the sea urchin and frog the level of RNA synthesis per embryo remains low during the preblastulation period, and the only type of RNA made at these times appears to be DNA-like. In *Xenopus* there is a rapid activation of RNA synthesis at the mid- to late-blastula period, which is also the time at which tRNA synthesis is first detected. Soon after, at the beginning of gastrulation, rRNA synthesis begins, following the appearance of nucleoli in which it is synthesized. That different types of RNA are activated at different times indicates synthesis of each type is controlled independently. Presumably each has its own activation signals. We know from the study of the anucleolate mutants that in the absence of rRNA synthesis, development can proceed well past gastrulation; this suggests rRNA synthesis begins well before it is absolutely necessary for new rRNA.

The pattern in the sea urchin is similar to that in *Xenopus*. Messenger RNA synthesis occurs during early cleavage and tRNA synthesis is activated before gastrulation, while rRNA synthesis is first found at gastrulation. In the sea urchin there also exists a major activation of RNA synthesis before gastrulation. It is believed that the pregastrulation activity provides both these embryos with the necessary templates to make proteins needed for the subsequent events of gastrulation.

This picture of early mRNA synthesis and delayed rRNA synthesis is not universally found. For example, in both the nematode *Ascaris* and the mouse, rRNA synthesis begins soon after fertilization. Presumably the stage at which a particular RNA is made, whether it is rRNA or mRNA, is related in some way to the activities of that embryo. We have described in detail the packaging of the amphibian egg with ribosomes; as a result the embryo is able to delay its own ribosome production until gastrulation or later. On the other hand, a mammalian embryo begins its life with a scarcity of cytoplasmic ribosomes, and this deficiency is reflected in the activation of rRNA at an earlier stage of development.

In *Xenopus* different parts of the embryo become activated at different times, suggesting that the activation signals do not act across the entire embryo, but rather each part (or maybe each cell) is responsible for its own actions. In contrast, in certain other embryos there is also an activation prior to gastrulation, but all cells appear to undergo the stimulation simultaneously.

With the technique of DNA-RNA hybridization, some indications of the nature of the RNAs made a different stages can be ascertained. Are the RNAs made during development the same species that were present in the unfertilized egg or are they different ones? The procedure to answer such a question involves the competition experiment described on page 551. In the sea urchin, with respect to the RNAs complementary to the *repeated DNA*, it appears that the species of RNA made during the blastula period are the same species that were present in the unfertilized egg (Fig 25.1*a*). However, when the RNA made after gastrulation is examined (Fig. 25.1*b*), a significant percentage (approximately 40 percent) appear to be RNAs that were not present at an earlier stage. That is, the RNAs activated from the repeated genes at gastrulation include a large number that were not transcribed before gastrulation or during oogenesis. Evidence from many different analyses points to gastrulation as the time when large-scale new synthetic activities (both RNA and protein) occur.

PREFORMED RNA VERSUS EMBRYONIC RNA

The embryo begins as an egg and rapidly becomes transformed into a multicellular form whose activities carry it toward an increasingly complex morphology. From what we know of the role of proteins in all the various cellular activities, we would predict that these changes require a continual input of newly synthesized proteins. This is readily confirmed by the use of substances that inhibit protein synthesis. Inhibitors such as puromycin or cycloheximide rapidly bring all the outward signs of development to a halt. The need for new proteins is clearly established; but on which RNA templates, maternal or embryonic, are they being translated? In other words, to what extent do the preformed, maternally derived RNAs direct development as opposed to those RNAs made by the embryo after fertilization? How can these two sets of RNAs be distinguished? In a sense we are back to a similar dilemma posed about the information stored in the oocyte—whether it was derived from the oocyte nucleus or from the surrounding tissue. Again, there are certain ways of probing the relative roles of the maternal and embryonic RNAs.

Blackler's technique to determine the source of the stored information was to produce a chimera. A similar approach has been used to distinguish between maternal and embryonic templates. Eggs of one species can often be fertilized with the sperm of a related species, even though safeguards against this occurrence are widespread. The formation of interspecies hybrids generally requires higher concentrations of sperm or the removal of outer egg barriers. Once the foreign sperm is inside, development is essentially normal for a predictable time and in a number of cases can proceed to the adult stage. The mule, a hybrid between a horse and a donkey, is a case in point.

Even the development of closely related species shows observable differences. Such differences might concern the rate of development, e.g., the time after fertilization when various cleavages occur or the time of hatching. The differences might be morphological—the appearance of the blastula, the nature of gastrulation, the number of mesenchyme cells, or the type of skeleton. Certainly biochemical differences that reflect the different genetic composition of the two species must exist. DNA-RNA hybridization techniques can distinguish between RNAs made by different species and can provide another means to analyze the activities of the interspecies hybrid.

Once a foreign sperm has entered an egg, the effect of a set of foreign chromosomes can be observed. As soon as development of the hybrid deviates from that of the maternal species toward that of the paternal species, we know that paternal genes have been transcribed. In a normal embryo there is no way to point to a period when the embryonic genes have been active, since we cannot tell which events in development involve maternal templates and which utilize embryonic templates. The introduction of the foreign genes of the sperm allows such an analysis. Studies of interspecies hybrids in frogs and sea urchins indicate that early development uses maternal RNAs. In the sea urchin it is generally found that the first evidence of paternal gene involvement occurs at gastrulation or beyond; in the amphibia the paternal characteristics generally appear after gastrulation is complete. In the ascidian, development of hybrids resembles a strictly maternal pattern throughout the formation of the complex ascidian tadpole, even in hybrids where the maternal chromosomes have been removed and all genes in the embryo are derived from the sperm.

The morphological analysis of hybrids calls for numerous assumptions and tells us only about RNAs that result in visible or measurable effects. It is entirely possible that many RNAs made by the embryo are being translated at early stages but are not being detected in the hybrids as a paternal trait. Since we know the embryonic genome is active soon after fertilization, it seems quite suspect that it is not until gastrulation that its effects are seen. In fact, other analyses of more sophisticated molecular nature suggest that RNAs made by the embryo are translated and that the resulting proteins do have an important role in early development.

Several lines of evidence point to the necessity of embryonic transcription if development is to proceed to any significant extent. One approach is to abolish embryonic transcription and let the embryo show whether it needs this transcription by revealing how far it can develop in its absence. Several techniques can be used for this destructive analysis. One can obtain an activated frog egg that lacks functional chromosomes. The technique involves sperm irradiation, which destroys its chromosomes but does not affect its fertilizing capacity. These chromosomes are irreversibly damaged and do not participate in any subsequent events. Once the egg is activated by such a sperm, the egg chromosomes move very close to the animal pole surface to complete meiosis, and they are removed with a needle. Since the egg chromosomes have been removed and the sperm chromosomes have been destroyed by irradiation, there are no chromosomes available on which transcription can occur. These enucleated frog embryos cleave and develop into a seminormal blastula, at which time development is arrested. There is no indication of gastrulation.

The removal of the entire chromosomal material of an embryo certainly deprives it of its genetic inheritance, but how many other problems does it cause? We need only consider the case of an extra chromosome number 21 in humans (the cause of Down's syndrome) to realize the sensitivity of cellular activities to the proper chromosome number. How can we be sure that development in these enucleated embryos is arrested by a transcriptional deficiency rather than by some side effect?

An alternate means to abolish transcription and corroborate the results of physical enucleation is to inject the amphibian egg with actinomycin D and achieve a "chemical enucleation." When this is done, development proceeds to the blastula stage and stops there. As in the above technique, we cannot be certain that the embryo is stopped as a result of the inhibition of RNA synthesis rather than by an unrelated side effect. From both experiments, however, we can conclude that development in the frog can proceed *at least* to the blastula stage in the absence of embryonic RNA synthesis.

It is not surprising that gastrulation does not occur in the absence of RNA synthesis. As previously described, gastrulation is foreshadowed by a general activation of transcription that includes the appearance of new species of RNA not found in the unfertilized egg. It is believed that these RNAs produced before gastrulation are needed for this event to occur. It would be expected that gastrulation would not occur if transcription is blocked. The development of the sea urchin under conditions of enucleation (chemical or physical) is very similar to that of the frog, i.e., development proceeds to the blastula and stops (Fig. 9.1). The most resistant embryos in terms of continued development in the presence of actinomycin D are the spiralian embryos that illustrate mosaic develop-

Figure 9.1 Effect of actinomycin D on sea urchin development. *a* Normal *Arbacia punctulata* pluteus larva. *b* Arrested *Arbacia* blastulas after continuous treatment with actinomycin D. [*Courtesy of C. H. Ellis.*]

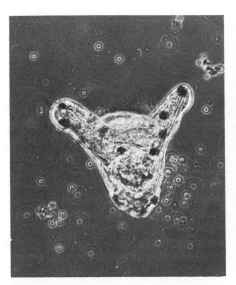 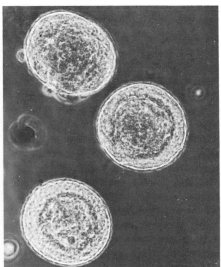

a   b

ment. This suggests that these embryos might be more dependent on preformed mRNA templates than is the regulative development of the mammal, sea urchin, and frog. The conclusion is corroborated by several independent lines of evidence, and the proposal has been made that embryonic determination is reflected at the molecular level by the presence and localization of tissue-specific mRNAs. In mosaic development, the early determination of the cleaving embryo would be ascribed to the localization of specific RNAs within specific blastomeres.

In order to decide exactly how far an embryo can progress before it must call on its genes to continue its development, we need a less damaging technique than those described above. The most suitable genetic damage to utilize in the study of gene function is the genetic mutation. Most mutations involve a very small part of one gene and therefore act to produce a template RNA that codes for a polypeptide with an altered, and thus nonfunctional, amino acid sequence. Since only one gene is being affected, we can assume that any observable deficiency in development is a direct result of the absence of one correct RNA that cannot be made by the embryo.

In the mouse a mutant with an extremely early effect on development has been isolated. When this mutant, known as t^{12}, is present in a homozygous condition (t^{12}/t^{12}, derived from mating of two heterozygotes), it produces visible effects on development as early as the two- to four-cell stage. Development is arrested at the morula, a few cleavages later. The defect manifests itself in several abnormalities, but it is difficult to be sure when dealing with a mutant exactly where the defect lies. An elegant technique (beyond the scope of this book) that deals with this problem can be found in Hotta and Benzer, 1973. Since mouse development is disturbed by the two- to four-cell stage, we can conclude that this gene is normally active by *at least* that stage. It appears from this and other findings that mammalian development relies most heavily upon the transcriptive activity of its own genes and less on its content of preformed RNA than do many other embryos, including the frog and the sea urchin.

As one might expect, the analysis of development employing genetic mutations has reached its most sophisticated level in *Drosophila*. Early studies had indicated that embryos beginning life with missing pieces of chromosomes could expect to undergo developmental arrest during cleavage or blastulation. Presumably, certain genes are required (and missing in the deleted chromosome fragments) to support development even to the early blastula stage. In the past several years extensive studies by Suzuki and coworkers have provided information on a variety of genes that act during the development of *Drosophila*. In these studies Suzuki has taken advantage of a special class of mutations, the temperature-sensitive (TS) mutations. Flies carrying a TS mutation will appear perfectly normal if raised at a lower temperature (e.g., 17°C, termed the permissive temperature) but will show the mutant phenotype, which is usually death, if raised at a higher temperature (e.g., 29°C, termed the restrictive temperature). Why should the mutant phenotype show up only at the elevated temperature? The answer lies in the physical chemistry of proteins. Increased temperature places certain stresses on protein molecules that tend to disrupt their three-dimensional structure and thus their function. In the normal (wild-type) protein these elevated temperatures are not sufficiently destructive to alter protein function. However, we can assume that the mutant protein is more sensitive to disruption due to its altered amino acid sequence; when the temperature is raised, the protein cannot function and the mutant phenotype results.

Gene function can be described at several successive steps: (1) the period

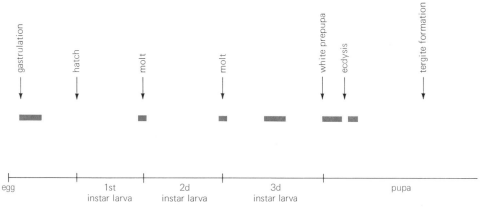

Figure 9.2   The temperature sensitive periods for a gene (shi[s1]). Elevation of the temperature during any of the periods blocked out in the above figure causes the death of the organism. It appears that this gene is active in an on-and-off manner throughout early development. [*After D. Suzuki, 1974.*]

during which the gene is transcribed, (2) the period of RNA translation, (3) the period of protein function, and (4) the stage when a detectable effect is first seen. No set time separates these steps; it depends upon the particular gene and its cytoplasmic environment. Analysis of TS mutants tells us about the last two steps. The period during which the protein is functioning is the temperature-sensitive period (TSP), which is determined by raising and lowering the temperature (Fig. 9.2). If the fly is living at the elevated temperature during a significant part of the TSP of its mutant gene, it will show the mutant phenotype (death, a missing structure, a different morphology). The time between the TSP and the stage at which the mutant phenotype is observed can vary from minutes to hours or even longer. Certain genes act early in development and others act late; certain genes act one time, others two times, still others several times; some act in an on-and-off manner while others act continuously. There are even established differences in the same gene in the different sexes. The studies on TS mutants in *Drosophila* have provided considerable information on the timing of gene function and have corroborated what would have been predicted by other means.

PROTEIN SYNTHESIS DURING EARLY SEA URCHIN DEVELOPMENT

As was described in Chapter 5, there is considerable activation of protein synthesis in the sea urchin beginning a few minutes after fertilization. The rate of protein synthesis climbs steeply through the early cleavage period and drops off at the blastula stage to begin a second rise prior to gastrulation. By the end of the first cleavage cycle the rate of protein synthesis is estimated to be 10 to 70 times that of the unfertilized egg. The translation of RNA occurs on polyribosomes that are best analyzed by sucrose-density-gradient centrifugation (see page 540). This serves to separate polyribosomes from one another on the basis of the number of attached ribosomes. The greater the number of ribosomes attached to a mRNA strand, the faster it will move through the gradient and therefore the closer it will be to the bottom of the tube at the end of the centrifugation.

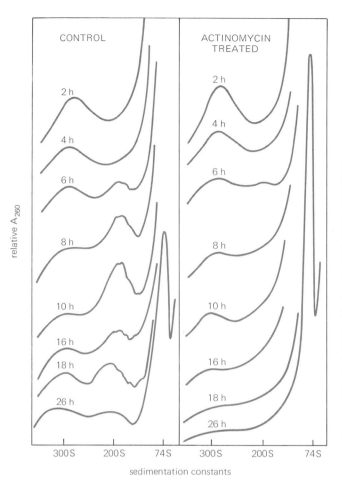

Figure 9.3 Sedimentation profiles of polyribosomes from sea urchin embryos at various times after fertilization in the absence (*left*) and presence (*right*) of actinomycin D, which blocks the synthesis of RNA by the embryo. The first polyribosome peak to appear after fertilization (none are present in the unfertilized egg) occurs toward the bottom of the tube (far left of each gradient is the bottom). This peak represents the r-polyribosomes that sediment rapidly. The peak appears equally as well in the presence of actinomycin D, indicating that it forms as a result of the recruitment of preformed maternal mRNA and is not dependent upon newly synthesized embryonic messages. By 6 hours after fertilization, the control embryos are showing a second peak, toward the top of the centrifuge tube. This peak represents the smaller, slowly sedimenting s-polyribosomes that increase in amount during the next hours. These are the histone-synthesizing polyribosomes and their accumulation is sensitive to actinomycin D (compare the 10-hour control and drug-treated). [*After A. A. Infante and M. Nemer,* Proc. Nat. Acad. Sci. U.S., **58**: *681, 1967.*]

Figure 9.3 shows the polyribosome profiles of sucrose gradients at various times after fertilization. The rate of protein synthesis in the unfertilized egg is low and there are correspondingly few polyribosomes; over 90 percent of the ribosomes are present in an unattached state. This distribution changes slowly after fertilization as two distinct classes of polyribosomes appear in the gradients. By 2 hours after fertilization, the heavier polyribosome class is seen as a major peak toward the bottom of the gradient. These are the heavier r-polyribosomes (r denoting rapid sedimentation), which contain an average of 23 attached ribosomes and have an average molecular weight of nascent (being synthesized) protein of 57,000. By 6 hours after fertilization, a second, lighter class of polyribosomes is clearly visible. These are the s-polyribosomes (s denoting slow sedimentation), which have an average number of 9 ribosomes and average nascent protein molecular weight of 9,300.

To determine which of the polyribosomes are most active in the incorporation of amino acids into protein, the embryos are given radioactively labeled amino acids just prior to homogenization. This label will be taken up and incorporated into the growing polypeptide chains that remain attached to the polyribosomes (nascent chains) within the gradient. By the distribution of the labeled amino acids in the gradient, it can be determined which polyribosomes are most active in protein synthesis (Fig 9.4a). The results suggest that all the polyribosomes are engaged in protein synthesis to an approximately equivalent degree. The smaller polyribosomes have less label, but this is expected since they are making smaller proteins; therefore, each ribosome will have smaller labeled nascent chains.

The use of labeled amino acids tells us about protein synthesis but nothing about the nature of the mRNA threads by which the ribosomes are held together. How can we distinguish polyribosomes with preformed RNA from those with embryonic RNA? There are two ways. One approach is to provide the cells with radioactively labeled RNA precursors, such as ^{3}H-uridine, prior to

Figure 9.4 Sucrose-density-gradient profiles showing polyribosomes of the sea urchin during cleavage. Embryos were incubated in radioactive precursors as described below, washed, homogenized, and the homogenate centrifuged at 15,000 g to remove cell organelles. The supernatant containing the ribosomes and polyribosomes was then centrifuged through the gradient. In both of these curves the solid line represents the absorbance of each fraction from the centrifuge tube. Since absorbance reflects amount of material present, this curve indicates the amount of ribosomes present throughout the gradient. The peak on the right-hand side of the graph (close to the top of the gradient) indicates the monoribosome peak, i.e., those not present in polyribosomes. The hatched part of the curve shows the region of the s-polyribosomes. The area to the left of the shaded part is the region containing the r-polyribosomes. The dotted line in each graph shows the radioactivity present in each of the fractions of the gradient.

a Embryos were incubated in a ^{3}H-amino acid for 10 minutes before homogenization. The dotted line, therefore, reveals the newly forming protein chains that remain attached to the polyribosomes as they sediment through the sucrose. The r-polyribosomes are seen to incorporate much more radioactivity than the s-polyribosomes. If, however, the incorporation is corrected for the smaller size of the s-polyribosomes, all the different-sized polyribosomes are found to be equally active in protein synthesis.

b The embryos were incubated in ^{3}H-uridine for 90 minutes prior to homogenization. During this period the ^{3}H-uridine is incorporated into RNA, which leaves the nucleus and becomes recruited into polyribosomes. Only those polyribosomes using RNA synthesized by the embryo will be labeled. Polyribosomes made up with preformed, maternal RNA will contribute to the absorbance (line without dots) of the fractions in which they occur but they will not contribute to the radioactivity (dotted line) of those fractions. The curve of the radioactivity of b indicates that the s-polyribosomes are composed of newly synthesized embryonic RNA to a much greater extent than r-polyribosomes. [*After Kedes and Gross, 1969.*]

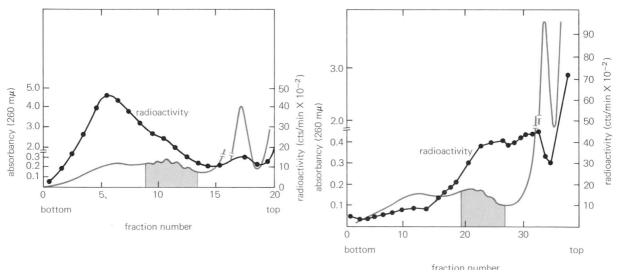

a   b

homogenization. This label will be incorporated into RNA in the nucleus, some of which will enter the cytoplasm as mRNA and become rapidly attached to polyribosomes. During early sea urchin development, since synthesis of tRNA and rRNA has not yet begun, we can be certain that all the label on the polyribosomes, after ^{3}H-uridine application, is in mRNA. Polyribosomes made with preformed mRNA will remain unlabeled, while those with embryonic mRNA, which had been synthesized during the time the label was available, will be radioactive. In this experiment (Fig. 9.4*b*) the label occurs in all sizes of polyribosomes, but the lighter class (s-polyribosomes) is preferentially labeled. Since the labeled mRNA is found throughout the gradient, we can conclude that the embryo is synthesizing a wide variety of sizes of mRNA and thus is providing templates for many different proteins.

A radioactive label can always be employed to examine a substance, such as embryonic RNA, which has just been synthesized; it is more difficult to examine substances that are already present, such as preformed, maternal RNA. One method is to block the formation of new RNA (using actinomycin D) and then follow the polyribosome profiles after fertilization. If polyribosomes appear in the presence of actinomycin D (and thus in the absence of embryonic RNA synthesis), we know they are forming by using maternal, preformed mRNA as a template. The right-hand column of Fig. 9.3 shows the polyribosome profiles at corresponding times after fertilization, in embryos that had been treated with actinomycin D from before the time of fertilization. The r-polyribosome peak at 2 and 4 hours forms similarly to the controls. These polyribosomes are using maternal mRNA as a template. The most significant effect of the drug is to greatly decrease the formation of the s-polyribosome peak (Fig. 9.3), indicating its dependence, to a larger extent, upon newly synthesized mRNA. Neither class of polyribosomes is using only one or the other class of mRNA; each is a mixed group.

These results tell us something of the distribution of preformed versus embryonic information and how it is used, but little of the nature of the specific proteins involved. Several studies by Gross and coworkers have recently provided important data on the more specific properties of these polyribosomes. The s-polyribosomes appear to be totally responsible for the synthesis of histones. These small, highly basic proteins are found closely associated with the DNA as part of the chromosomes. Any substance closely associated with the DNA should increase in proportion to increasing DNA levels. Cleavage is a time of intense DNA synthesis, and the synthesis of histones must keep pace if chromosomes are to be produced. The appearance of the s-polyribosomes as a major peak by 6 hours, its rise to contain about 35 percent of the embryo's ribosomes by the 10-hour early blastula, and its relative decline after 20 hours reflect the relative need for chromosomal proteins at each of these times. Histones are not necessarily of greater importance for development than other proteins, but they have received more attention because of special properties that make them more amenable for biochemical analysis.

If the histones are extracted from a sea urchin embryo and are fractionated by electrophoresis (see page 547), five distinct groups are found (Fig. 9.5). These five classes of histones differ from each other in molecular weight and amino acid composition. If labeled amino acids are given to the embryo prior to homogenization and histone preparation, all five classes become labeled; this indicates that all these proteins are being made by the embryo rather than simply being selected from a pool of histones already present at fertilization. Are they being translated from preformed or embryonic mRNA? To answer this question we can examine the effect of actinomycin D upon histone production. Since, as already indicated, the s-polysomes are significantly reduced in the presence of actinomycin D and these are the polyribosomes making histones,

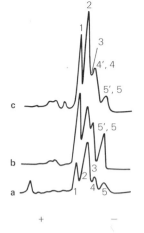

Figure 9.5 Patterns of histones extracted from three stages of sea urchin development and fractionated by electrophoresis. Five main classes of histones are separated by this technique, and the relative quantities of each class are shown for (a) 32-cell stage, (b) mesenchyme blastula stage, and (c) postgastrulated prism stage. Class 2 is very low in the 32-cell stage but predominates later in development. Class 3 histone is the major peak at the 32-cell stage but is not longer evident as a distinct peak after gastrulation. The numbers 4′,4 and 5′,5 indicate that in these cases the peak can be shown to consist of two separate peaks under other conditions. [*After L. C. Benttinen and D. G. Comb*, J. Mol. Biol. **54**: 355, 1971.]

we would expect to find an effect. In fact there is a considerable reduction in histone synthesis. However, all five classes of histones continue to be produced in the absence of embryonic RNA synthesis. This clearly indicates that preformed mRNA for all these histones is present in the unfertilized egg. Calculations suggest that during early cleavage more than two-thirds of the histone production occurs on maternal template, while at the blastula stage this figure has dropped to below one-third.

Even though all five classes of histones are made at all stages of development, there are changes in their relative proportions as development proceeds. Histone class 2 is barely visible at the 32-cell stage but dominant at the gastrula. In one case a complete change in the manufacture of the specific class 1 histone occurs during development. In *Lytechinus*, the cleaving embryo makes a species of histone in the F1 class that is referred to as F1-m (m for morula). If the histones are examined at the gastrula stage, this histone species is missing and is replaced by F1-g (g for gastrula), which migrates in a slightly different way in the electrophoresis apparatus. This appears to be a clear example of the synthesis of a new protein during development, although by the gastrula stage many new proteins may be expected.

An entirely different approach confirms these findings. As already indicated, morphological criteria show that the development of sea urchin hybrids resembles the maternal species up to the point of gastrulation. A biochemical analysis of the F1 histones in a sea urchin hybrid, however, points to the translation of RNAs transcribed from the paternal genome by at least the mid-

Figure 9.6 Patterns of histones after electrophoresis in acrylamide gels. The five classes of histones are labeled F1, F3, F2b, F2a2, and F2a1. The four gels represent the patterns of histones from the hatched blastula stage of sand dollar embryos (DeDe), sea urchin embryos (DD), and hybrids having a sea urchin egg fertilized by a sand dollar sperm (DDe) and vice versa (DeD). Sand dollar embryos give one band of F1 class histone while sea urchin embryos give two bands, both of which migrate differently than the sand dollar band. In both hybrids all three bands are present by the hatched blastula stage, indicating the activity of the paternal chromosomes prior to this stage. [*Courtesy of D. Easton.*]

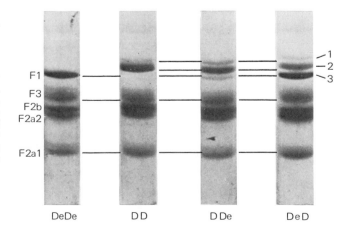

blastula stage. In this case the F1 histones from each of the parent species migrate at a different rate under electrophoresis, i.e., the proteins of each parent can be recognized. In the hybrid, by mid-blastula both proteins can be detected (Fig. 9.6), proving the existence of embryonic mRNA that is translated. In addition, the relative amount of the paternal protein (18 to 30 percent) is consistent with the presence of three sources of mRNA for histones: maternal preformed, maternal embryonic, and paternal embryonic.

The above indicates that the s-polyribosomes are responsible for histone synthesis. On what evidence is this based? The experiments that prove the s-polyribosomes are responsible for histone production reflect the level of sophistication attained by the molecular biology of development in at least a few cases. Once the polyribosomes are separated on the sucrose gradient and collected into different tubes, the mRNA from each class of polyribosome can be extracted and purified. If this purified RNA from the light polyribosomes (s-polyribosomes) is run on a sucrose gradient (Fig. 9.7), a peak of RNA sedimenting at about 9S is found. This particular RNA can be isolated in a test tube just as the s-polyribosome from which it was derived had been isolated in the earlier step. The 9S RNA appears to be essentially pure histone mRNA. It can be separated by electrophoresis into several fractions that are believed to be the mRNAs for the different classes of histones.

The purified histone mRNAs can be translated in vitro by using a cell-free protein synthesis system (see page 552). When this is done with the 9S RNA from unfertilized eggs of *Lytechinus,* histones are made in the test tube. In fact, the F1-m histone can be identified. This indicates that mRNA for histones, including the F1-m histone, is present in a preformed state in the unfertilized egg. If the 9S RNA from the s-polyribosomes of the gastrula stage is added to a cell-free protein synthesis system, histones are also made but the F1-m species is not among them. This mRNA is no longer present in the gastrula; in its place is the F1-g mRNA, since the F1-g histone is now found among the protein products directed by the gastrula 9S RNA. All the evidence agrees that this class of proteins is translated from both maternal and embryonic mRNAs.

Several other specific proteins have also been examined to determine whether or not they are translated on preformed mRNAs. These include the

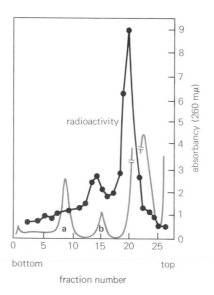

bottom   top

fraction number

Figure 9.7 Sucrose-density-gradient profile of the RNA extracted from the s-polyribosomes. Embryos were incubated in ^{3}H-uridine for 90 minutes, homogenized, and a polyribosome gradient prepared as described in the legend of Fig. 9.4. Those fractions containing the s-polyribosomes (hatched area of Fig. 9.4) were taken and the RNA was extracted from these polyribosomes. Several types of RNA are extracted in this procedure: the two species of rRNA, the tRNAs, and the mRNA. Only the mRNA that had been synthesized during the 90-minute incubation in ^{3}H-uridine will be radioactively labeled. In this graph the solid line is a measure of the amount of RNA (determined by absorbance) in each part of the gradient; the two peaks (A and B) are the two ribosomal RNAs, neither of which is labeled. The dotted line shows the radioactivity of the various parts of the gradient and the profile is dominated by one large peak near the top of the tube. This peak contains the mRNAs for all the histones, as can be demonstrated by using this RNA as a template for histone synthesis in a cell-free system. [*After Kedes and Gross, 1969.*]

microtubule proteins, which are synthesized at all times after fertilization; the enzyme ribonucleotide reductase, which first appears about one hour after fertilization; and the hatching enzyme, which is made by the mid-blastula stage to destroy the fertilization membrane and release the embryo from this container. The evidence indicates that all three of these proteins are made on preformed mRNAs. The microtubule proteins are made in enucleated halves of eggs that have been artificially activated; the hatching enzyme is strictly maternal in interspecies hybrids; and the ribonucleotide reductase appears in actinomycin-D-inhibited embryos.

The ability of embryos to operate on preformed mRNA is a remarkable biochemical feat. We conceive of the egg as filled with a massive number of different messengers; yet it appears that specific mRNAs are selected at specific times for translation. At the time of fertilization the mRNA molecules and the ribosomes are unattached to one another; each is readily isolated independently from the other. During the first hour following fertilization, there appears to be selective recruitment of specific mRNAs into polyribosomes for translation. At one hour the ribonucleotide reductase is translated, and after a while it appears to be shut off (or at least its level drops). At a later time the hatching enzyme must be translated. The histones are made in response to the chromosomal need for them. Though we know virtually nothing of these mechanisms, the study of transcription and translation in the early embryo is revealing more and more of the complexity of information utilization within the cell.

PREFORMED PROTEINS

In the previous section the relative roles of preformed and embryonic RNAs were discussed. The embryo begins development with another preformed, macromolecular store, i.e., the proteins synthesized during oogenesis and inherited by the embryo for use after fertilization. Information on this subject is scarce, but there is one well-studied case. The Mexican axolotl has primarily been used because it is the most genetically defined amphibian available. This study exploits the o-mutant strain, in which the o exerts a maternal effect that results in a deficiency in the egg cytoplasm.

The o gene is a recessive factor that determines a complex of abnormalities, including a reduced capacity for hind-limb regeneration, subnormal development of secondary sexual characters in the male, and deficiencies in various other tissues and organs, together with a reduction in the vigor and life span of this genotype. In embryos obtained from axolotls homozygous for gene o, development is always arrested during gastrulation.

The eggs of o/o females cleave normally until mid- to late-blastula stages, when cell division rate slows down. Embryos then enter gastrulation with cells somewhat larger than normal and later invariably become arrested prior to neurulation. Cytological studies of such embryos show a very sharp drop in mitotic frequency in all parts of the late blastula, although chromosomal constitution of cells during the critical period remains normal.

The cytoplasmic deficiency responsible for the o effect at gastrulation can be corrected by injecting eggs of o/o females with cytoplasm from normal eggs. Recipient eggs then develop beyond gastrulation and may attain larval stages. The corrective component is found within the nucleus, the germinal vesicle, of large oocytes, i.e., in the nucleoplasm or in the egg cytoplasm thereof following germinal-vesicle breakdown. Comparable extracts of blastulas show a reduced corrective activity. The corrective material, presumably a product of the normal allele of o, is a protein produced during oogenesis that later plays an indispensable role in early organogenesis.

In summary, certain genes are transcribed during oogenesis and provide an information store for the egg. Other genes are activated by the embryo and provide new information. Both these populations are interwoven into the biochemical affairs of the early embryo, and the translational process reflects the presence of both populations of mRNA. At this point it is difficult to generalize from the results presented; the limited evidence suggests that different embryos time their biochemical events in different ways. The next few years are certain to produce a considerable extension of our knowledge in this field.

READINGS

BACHVAROVA, R., and E. H. DAVIDSON, 1966. Nuclear Activation at the Onset of Amphibian Gastrulation, *J. Exp. Zool.*, **163**:285–295.

BADMAN, W. S., and J. W. BROOKBANK, 1970. Serological Studies of Two Hybrid Sea Urchins, *Develop. Biol.*, **21**:243–256.

BELL, E. (ed.), 1965. "Molecular and Cellular Aspects of Development," Harper & Row.

BRIGGS, R., 1973. Developmental Genetics of the Axolotl, 31st Symposium, Society of Developmental Biology, pp. 47–102, Academic.

CRIPPA, M., and P. R. GROSS, 1969. Maternal and Embryonic Contributions to the Functional Messenger RNA of Early Development, *Proc. Nat. Acad. Sci. U.S.*, **62**:120–127.

DAVIDSON, E. H., 1968. "Gene Activity in Early Development," Academic.

EASTON, D. P., J. P. CHAMBERLAIN, A. H. WHITELEY, and H. R. WHITELEY, 1974. Histone Gene Expression in Interspecies Hybrid Echinoid Embryos, *Biochem. Biophys. Res. Comm.*, **57**:513–519.

FANKHAUSER, G., 1955. The Role of Nucleus and Cytoplasm in Development, in B. H. Willier, R. Weiss, and V. Hamburger (eds.), "Analysis of Development," Saunders.

GLISIN, V. R., M. V. GLISIN, and P. DOTY, 1966. The Nature of Messenger RNA in the Early Stages of Sea Urchin Development, *Proc. Nat. Acad. Sci. U.S.*, **56**:285–289.

GRAHAM, C. F., 1973. The Necessary Conditions for Gene Expression during Early Mammalian Development, 31st Symposium, Society of Developmental Biology, pp. 201–224, Academic.

GRANT, P., 1965. Informational Molecules and Embryonic Development, in R. Weber (ed.), "The Biochemistry of Animal Development," Academic.

GROSS, P. R., and COUSINEAU, G. H., 1963. Macromolecule Synthesis and the Influence of Actinomycin D on Early Development, *Exp. Cell Res.*, **33**:368–395.

HUMPHREYS, T., 1969. Efficiency of Translation of Messenger RNA before and after Fertilization in Sea Urchins, *Develop. Biol.*, **20**:435–458.

HOTTA, Y., and S. BENZER, 1973. Mapping of Behavior in *Drosophila* Mosaics, 31st Symposium, Society of Developmental Biology, pp. 129–167, Academic.

INFANTE, A. A., and M. NEMER, 1967. Accumulation of Newly Synthesized RNA Templates in a Unique Class of Polyribosomes during Embryogenesis, *Proc. Nat. Acad. Sci. U.S.*, **58**:681–688.

KARP, G. C., C. MANES, and W. E. HAHN, 1974. Ribosome Production and Protein Synthesis in the Preimplantation Rabbit Embryo, *Differentiation*, **2**:65–73.

KEDES, L. H., and P. R. GROSS, 1969. Synthesis and Function of Messenger RNA during Early Embryonic Development, *J. Mol. Biol.*, **42**:559–575.

NEMER, M., 1974. Molecular Basis of Embryogenesis, in J. Lash and J. R. Whittaker (eds.), "Concepts in Development," Sinauer.

RAFF, R. A., H. V. COLOT, S. E. SELVIG, and P. R. GROSS, 1972. Oogenetic Origin of Messenger RNA for Embryonic Synthesis of Microtubule Proteins, *Nature*, **235**:211–214.

RUDERMAN, J. V., and P. R. GROSS, 1974. Histones and Histone Synthesis in Sea Urchin Development, *Develop. Biol.*, **36**:286–298.

SCHULTZ, G. A., and R. B. CHURCH, 1975. Transcriptional Patterns in Early Mammalian Development, in R. Weber (ed.), "The Biochemistry of Animal Development," Academic.

SLATER, D. W., and S. SPIEGELMAN, 1966. An Estimation of Genetic Messages in the Unfertilized Echinoid Egg, *Proc. Nat. Acad. Sci. U.S.*, **56**:164–170.

STEPHENS, R. E., 1972. Studies on the Development of the Sea Urchin *Strongylocentrotus droebachiensis*, III: Embryonic Synthesis of Ciliary Proteins, *Biol. Bull.*, **142**:489–504.

SUZUKI, D. T., 1974. Developmental Genetics, in J. Lash and J. R. Whittaker (eds.), "Concepts in Development," Sinauer.

WHITELEY, A. H., B. J. McCARTHY, and H. R. WHITELEY, 1966. Changing Populations of Messenger RNA during Sea Urchin Development, *Proc. Nat. Acad. Sci. U.S.*, **55**:519–525.

PART III

DEVELOPMENT OF THE CHORDATE EMBRYO

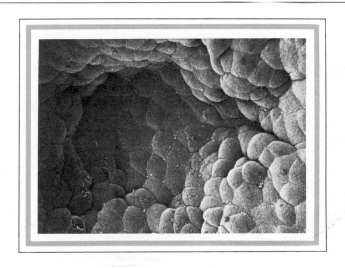

CHAPTER 10

Morphogenesis

The Development of Amphioxus
The Development of the Ascidian Tadpole Larva

Morphogenesis is the progressive attainment of bodily forms and structures during development. It has been called the quintessential problem of the developmental biologist. The phenomenon is the most easily observed, the most easily described, and probably the least understood process of development. In spite of recent advances in the understanding of the behavior of macromolecules and consequent reexamination of the classic problems of development, the problems remain. The questions persist because the new analytical methods—which involve extraction, purification, degradation, and identification of the macromolecular constituents of living matter—are intrinsically destructive. There is no opportunity for the observation of *development* as an ongoing life process that requires the integrity of cellular function. Only static "time slices" are provided. Wilde (1974) has recently emphasized that the student of development can never afford to neglect the *flow of time,* that we are concerned not only with *what happens* but also *when it happens* in both morphogenesis and differentiation.

The very essence of development is continuous change, and it is difficult to come to grips with it. It has to be seen to be appreciated. One can easily see great changes from day to day in the development of the comparatively large eggs of fish, frogs, and salamanders, but only stop-action speeded-up films can properly portray the steady, continuous process of change. Many such films are now available for presentation and study.

The full impact of the living developmental process in its totality, however, is best experienced by observing the development of the very small translucent eggs of certain marine animals. In particular, the holoblastic eggs of echinoderms (starfish, sea urchin, sand dollar) and of protochordates (ascidian, *Amphioxus*) offer an ongoing spectacle of great beauty and wonder within a matter of hours, with perhaps one sleepless night for the observer. Depending on the temperature, a sea urchin egg fertilized early one morning may develop into a pluteus larva by late the following day, with changes observable hour by hour. Ascidian eggs become swimming tadpole larvae (Fig. 7.14) during the same time, the smallest doing so between dawn and dusk. These forms are readily obtained and studied at any of the marine biological laboratories scattered around the world, and even in inland laboratories during this age of jet delivery. *Amphioxus,* however, the very prototype of chordate development and therefore of vertebrate development that has grown out of it, is less amenable, since it spawns during only a few days in the year and is not commonly abundant. Nevertheless its development has been well described, most recently by Conklin.

In *Amphioxus* and the other forms just mentioned, the egg is about 0.1 mm in diameter. At a given temperature all such eggs develop at much the same rate and undergo cleavage in the early stages about every half hour. Cleavage proceeds either until cells are about the same small size as the somatic cells of the species or, in certain parts, until cell division is replaced by precocious cell differentiation. In most cases eggs of this type divide to form several thousand cells. Cleavage rate is rapid at first but steadily slows to a standstill, as though approaching a state of equilibrium. During and immediately following this period, the community of cells must have attained a morphological structure and a cellular differentiation capable of serving as a self-supporting functional organism. *What happens when* during this whole process is the focus for students of morphogenesis. The transformation of the egg into a blastula, together with a molecular approach to the process of gastrulation, have been described in Chapter 6. Here we are concerned with the events that follow.

Gastrulation is the most critical phase of early embryonic development. During the development of small holoblastic eggs, the single-layered hollow sphere of cells, the blastula, infolds to form two and then three layers of cells that constitute the gastrula. The outermost layer becomes the *ectoderm,* the innermost layer the endoderm, and the intermediate layer the mesoderm. (Similarly, although by ingrowing rather than by infolding, the single-layered blastodisc of meroblastic eggs becomes the three-layered blastoderm.) Each of the three germ layers thus established continues to develop morphologically and histologically along its own special path. Gastrulation is the whole event during which the three layers are established. It can be approached from several standpoints or, stated differently, it raises several very different problems. What are the means, in cellular terms, by which the various morphogenetic movements are effected? What instigates such movements? What is accomplished by these movements? How is the timing controlled? Questions of this sort apply to morphogenetic phenomena generally, not only to gastrulation.

THE DEVELOPMENT OF AMPHIOXUS

Cleavage in *Amphioxus* results in a blastula that consists of a single layer of columnar cells surrounding a large blastocoel (Fig. 10.1). The greater the number of cleavages before gastrulation begins, the larger both the blastula and the blastocoel become and the smaller the constituent cells. Gastrulation in *Amphioxus* occurs when about 800 cells have been formed, between the ninth and tenth cleavages. It begins as a flattening of the blastula wall at the vegetal pole, followed by invagination of the whole vegetal half of the blastula so that double-walled cup-shaped gastrula forms. As a result the blastocoel becomes completely obliterated. The internal layer constitutes the *archenteron;* the opening is the *blastopore.* As cell division continues, the gastrula elongates and the blastopore becomes progressively smaller as its dorsal, lateral, and ventral lips converge.

During this process the cells derived from the chordal crescent and those derived from the mesodermal crescent of the egg, at first widely separated from one another, are brought into juxtaposition. As a result the presumptive notochord is now flanked by presumptive mesoderm. At the same time the presumptive neural material that initially lay anterior to the chordal crescent is in effect stretched over the notochord as the neural plate.

There is no evidence that the constituent cells in different territories of the *Amphioxus* gastrula or the neurula are dividing at different rates. In other words, neither the process of gastrulation nor that of neurulation can be ex-

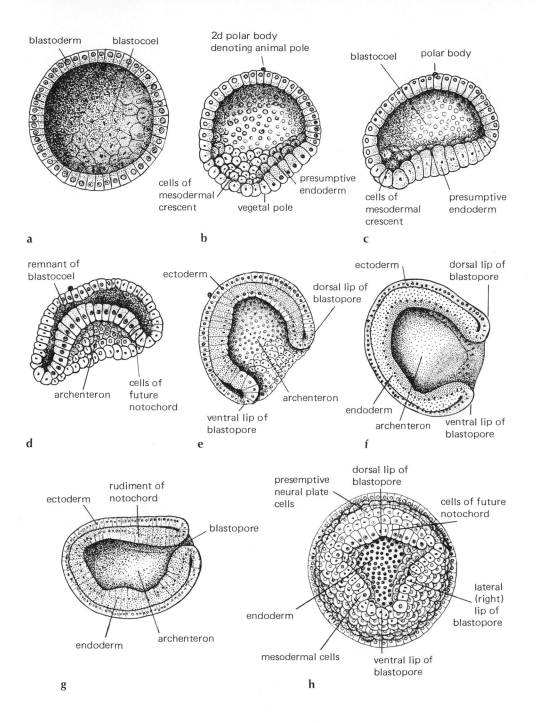

Figure 10.1 Stages of gastrulation of *Amphioxus*. The embryos in *a-g* are represented as cut in the median plane. *a* Blastula. *b, c* Beginning of invagination. *d* Invagination advanced, the embryo attaining the structure of a double-walled cup with a broad opening to the exterior. *e, f* Constriction of the blastopore. *g* Completed gastrula. *h* Middle gastrula, whole, viewed from side of blastopore. [*From Conklin, 1932.*]

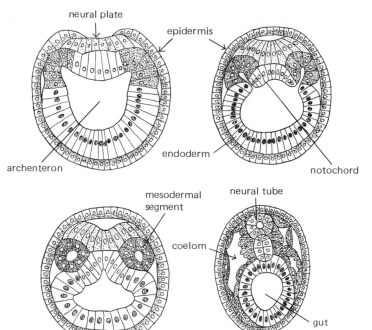

plained, with validity, as the result of differentials in cell division rates between one territory and another—e.g., between prospective neural plate and prospective epidermis. At the same time it may be highly significant that cell division is out of phase in the various recognizable and distinctive territories of the developing embryo (Fig. 10.2). This suggests that in each prospective territory the cells are at least beginning to take a special, presumably biochemical, path that is distinct. With continuing elongation and cell division, the flattened neural plate rolls up on itself to form a neural tube, open in front as a *neuropore.* Simultaneously ectodermal folds along its side stretch over the neural tissue to fuse together as a continuous sheet (Fig. 10.3). This phase of development is known as the *neurula.*

Meanwhile further development has occurred within the embryo. When fully formed, the archenteron develops ridgelike outgrowths as the result of outpushing, or evagination, from the middorsal and from each dorsolateral region. These slowly constrict from the archenteron proper to become the rudimentary notochord and the lateral mesoderm tissue respectively (Fig. 10.3). The notochord separates as a continuous middorsal rod immediately below the developing neural tube. The mesoderm on each side separates from the archenteron as a series of pocketlike evaginations, each of which becomes a mesodermal segment, or *somite,* with its own cavity. The series does not arise simultaneously throughout its length; the outpocketings appear at first anteriorly and then in quick succession toward the posterior end of the embryo. At a particular moment, before completion of the process, there is accordingly a *gradient* with regard to the stage of formation of mesodermal pouches along the anteroposterior axis, i.e., an axial gradient. The remainder of the archenteron, after outpocketing, persists as the endoderm proper, from which most of the digestive system derives. A large evagination from its ventral side becomes the liver

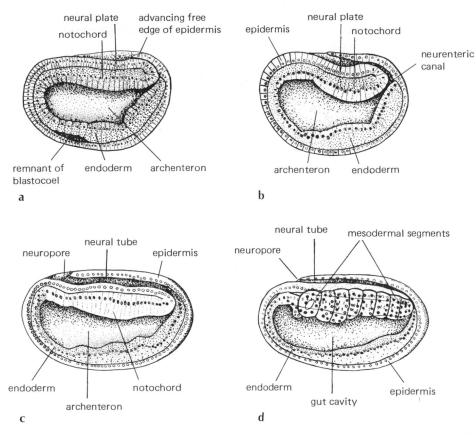

Figure 10.3 Stages of neurulation of *Amphioxus*. In *a*, *b*, and *c* the embryos are represented as being cut in the median plane. *a* Earliest stage of neurulation. *c* Almost completed neurula. *d* Slightly later stage than *c* but cut paramedially so that the right row of mesodermal segment can be seen. *e* Completed neurula whole, seen from the dorsal side. The transparency of the embryo allows one to see at the same time the various parts superimposed over one another (neural tube, notochord, mesodermal segments and gut). [*From Conklin, 1932.*]

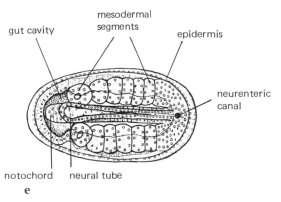

diverticulum. An invagination from the anterior end of the ectoderm of the embryo extends posteriorly to fuse with the anterior end of the archenteron, thus forming the mouth. In an apparently simple and direct manner, a spherical epithelial envelope one cell thick transforms, by means of stretchings and foldings, into an elongate chordate organism. It is complete, with a digestive tube open at both ends, with a supportive notochord and a tubular nerve cord, and with a series of mesodermal somites on each between gut and epidermis.

223

In contrast with the above, although essentially similar in pattern, the embryo of the ascidian undergoes gastrulation between the sixth and seventh cleavages; i.e., it begins and completes the process between the 64-cell and 128-cell stages (Fig. 7.14). The overall effect, however, is the same as in *Amphioxus,* namely, to bring the chordal and mesodermal territories together as prospective tail, while neural plate dorsal to the notochord transforms into a neural tube. The whole development closely resembles that of *Amphioxus,* except that the morphogenetic process appears to be accelerated, or condensed, relative to the course of cleavage (Fig. 7.15). Fewer cells are present at each morphogenetic stage. It should be noted, however, that in the ascidian the mesoderm does not subdivide to form segments nor does it develop a coelom (Fig. 10.4).

The first major morphogenetic event in the development of most animal eggs is gastrulation. The sweeping transformation of a blastula into a gastrula is essential to further development and presents a challenge at several levels. The process is described in the following chapter in terms of cell and tissue movements and mechanics. Apart from the molecular control of the event, initiated or at least activated following fertilization, the primary question is: Are such movements independently prepared for in earlier stages or are they the

Figure 10.4 Neurula stage of development of ascidian. *a* Dorsal view (*left*) and side view (*right*) of neurula of *Styela,* and cross section of open-neural-plate stage of younger embryo. [*After E. G. Conklin, 1905.*] *b,c* Early and late neurula of *Clavelina* from side, showing neuropore, neural tube, notochord (stippled), and superimposed tail mesoderm and mesenchyme. [*After Van Benedin and Julin,* Arch. Biol., *2:317 (1884).*]

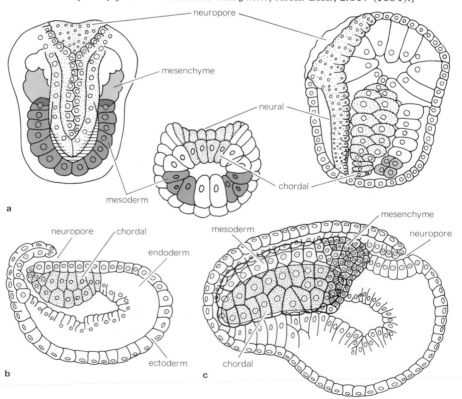

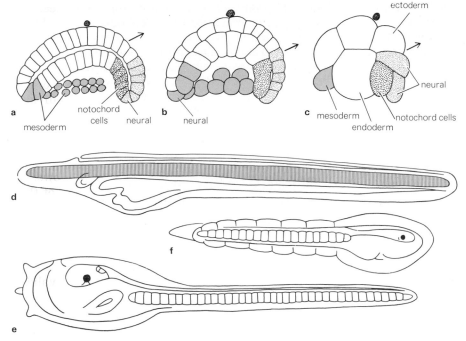

Figure 10.5 Gastrulas and larvae of *Amphioxus*, an ascidian, and a larvacean tunicate, showing effect of varying ratios of differentiation and cleavage rates. *a,d* Gastrula and larva of *Amphioxus*. *b,e* Gastrula and larva of ascidian *Ciona*. *c,f* Gastrula and larva of *Appendicularia*.

inevitable response to processes of cell differentiation already occurring? Are the gastrular changes responses to differentiation or are they responsible for differentiation?

In this connection a comparison of the development of three lower chordates is informative. These are *Amphioxus* and the tunicates *Styela* (an ascidian tunicate) and *Oikopleura* (a larvacean tunicate). All three have translucent eggs of roughly the same size (about 120 μm in diameter); all develop the basic chordate organization including notochord, dorsal tubular nerve cord, lateral tail musculature, and gill slits (Fig. 10.5). In all three, at or before fertilization, a flowing cytoplasm establishes crescentic zones in relation to the egg cortex, imposing bilateralism on the egg. Crescentic zoning, bilateral cleavage pattern, the association of the anterior crescent with chordaneural tissue and of the posterior crescent with mesoderm (muscle) indicate a fundamental relationship between the three.

In each of the three forms, cell division within the crescentic zones ceases as histological differentiation becomes visible. In all three there is a close correlation between the rates of differentiation of notochordal and mesodermal tissues. There is also a correlation between this and the time of onset (in terms of cleavage) of gastrulation. *Amphioxus* gastrulation occurs between the ninth and tenth cleavages, in *Styela* between the sixth and seventh, and in *Oikopleura* between the fifth and sixth. Correspondingly, the number of notochordal and muscle cells in the *Amphioxus* embryo is 300 to 400, representing from eight to nine divisions of the initial territory; in *Styela* there are about 40 cells in each, representing from five to six divisions; and in *Oikopleura* the number of each kind of cell is 20, or from four to five divisions.

In each form the size of the cells produced is inversely proportional to their number. Differentiation relative to cleavage rate is accelerated in ascidians compared with *Amphioxus,* and in *Oikopleura* compared with ascidians. Thus, cell division in the crescent-derived tissues ceases three divisions sooner in the ascidian than in *Amphioxus* and one division sooner in *Oikopleura* than in the ascidian. The onset of gastrulation is advanced to exactly the same degree. This correlation strongly suggests gastrulation is a response to the already advancing differentiation of the cleavage embryo into sharply delineated histogenetic territories.

In spite of the minute scale of these overall events, we are confronted with the primary problem of development—no less in *Amphioxus* and ascidian than in mice and humans—namely, the emergence and nature of pattern or organization. The great advances in molecular biology at the level of the individual cell have yet to illuminate this fundamental phenomenon of multicellular development in any truly satisfactory way.

Throughout development we find an interplay between cellular differentiation and multicellular morphogenesis. We also find two opposite points of view concerning the relative role of individual cell character and the role of possible supervising agencies. These viewpoints may be briefly stated as follows: (1) Cells and tissues tend to acquire locations according to the character of their individual or collective differentiation. (2) Cells and tissues tend to differentiate according to their location in the organized system. Both concepts are prominent in contemporary developmental biology, although both were formulated by Driesch at about the turn of the century. We do not necessarily have to choose between two such apparently conflicting concepts. It is a common experience for biologists to find that when a question is posed to nature as a choice between one interpretation and another, the response is that both are valid in varying degree in varying circumstances. This is true of the concepts we have just stated, which implies that we are faced with an intriguing but difficult intellectual problem. A similar situation is found in the brain-mind relationship.

The framing of a question in science, at whatever level, is of the utmost importance because the answer, if any, will be in the same terms of reference. If the question or experiment concerns the role of the genes or transcription, the answer will further our understanding of that role. If the question relates only to cytoplasmic or cortical events during development, something may be discovered concerning those events but little will be learned about related gene activity. In view of the multilevel organization of organisms and the developmental transformations, such limitations need to be kept in mind.

At one end of the developmental scale is the cell. Everything necessary for the emergent expression of the mature multicellular organism of whatever kind is present in the cell. The molecular approach begins with the genome. At the subcellular level it has been fantastically informative. At the level of the whole cell we are left with a vague dissatisfaction, for we do not have the key to a full understanding. An eminent molecular biologist, Erwin Chargoff (1971), has said that he cannot rid himself of the feeling that we still lack an entire dimension that is necessary for the understanding of a living cell. In the case of eggs, especially the human egg, which has the capacity to become a thinking organism, this caution should never be forgotten.

CHARGAFF, E., 1971. Preface to a Grammar of Biology, *Science,* **185**:637-642.

CONKLIN, E. G., 1933. The Development of Isolated and Partially Separated Blastomeres of *Amphioxus, J. Exp. Zool.,* **64**:303–375.

———, 1932. The Embryology of *Amphioxus, J. Morphol.,* **54**:69–119.

———,1931. The Development of Centrifuged Eggs of Ascidians, *J. Exp. Zool.,* **60**:1–80.

JOHNSON, K. E., 1974. Gastrulation and Cell Interactions, in J. Lash and J. R. Whittaker (eds.), "Concepts of Development," Saunders.

REVERBERI, G., 1961. The Embryology of Ascidians, *Advan. Morphog.,* **1**:55–103.

TRINKAUS, J. P., 1965. Mechanisms of Morphogenetic Movements, in R. L. DeHaan and H. Ursprung (eds.), "Organogenesis," Holt, Rinehart and Winston.

WEISS, P., 1950. Some Perspectives in the Field of Morphogenesis, *Quart. Rev. Biol.,* **25**:177–198.

WILDE, C. E., 1974. Time Flow in Differentiation and Morphogenesis, in J. Lash and J. R. Whittaker (eds.), "Concepts of Development," Saunders.

Gastrulation

Gastrulation is the first and most crucial step in the transformation of the cleaving egg into some semblance of the embryo-to-be. As a morphogenetic process (introduced in the preceding chapter), gastrulation is a highly integrated activity that involves the embryo as a whole and takes place in markedly different ways in different types of developing eggs. It is therefore preferable to describe and analyze the event separately as it occurs in small holoblastic eggs (those of echinoderms and *Amphioxus*, Figs. 11.1 and 11.2), in larger relatively yolky holoblastic eggs (of amphibians especially), and in meroblastic eggs (particularly of teleosts and birds).

When in position, the cells or tissues of the three primary layers differentiate along different lines. In the development of regulative eggs, groups of cells transplanted from one layer to another at an early stage differentiate according to their new location. Therefore, since the differentiation of each layer depends on its position relative to the others, the primary function of gastrulation appears to be the morphogenetic movement whereby the three layers become established. The specific differentiation within each layer occurs subsequently and depends upon the tissue location. Nevertheless, in normal development, regions of the blastula are displaced by gastrulation into radically different locations; in this sense gastrulation can be said to be a process of rearrangement of parts.

Conversely, in more mosaic development, regional differentiation is evident even in cleavage and blastula stages, and gastrulation actually brings such regions into proper mutual topographical association. Morphogenetic move-

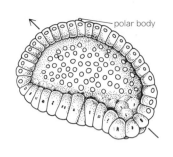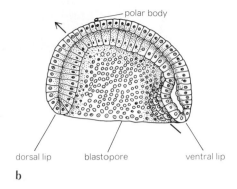

Figure 11.1 Gastrulation in *Amphioxus*. *a* Flattened vegetal plate stage. *b* Complete invagination with obliteration of blastocoel. Arrow indicates anteroposterior axis of embryo. Polar body marks original animal pole. [*After Conklin, 1932.*] **a**

b

polar body

dorsal lip   blastopore   ventral lip

ment reflects the zoning of the egg or blastula into specialized areas. Yet it is not likely that two very different cause-and-effect relationships actually prevail, each exclusive of the other, in a particular species. It is more likely that in all cases some degree of regional differentiation takes place during development preceding the onset of gastrulation. In more or less regulative eggs, the prospective potency of cells in various locations in the blastula is greater than their prospective fate; i.e., any incipient differentiation preceding gastrulation is reversible and cells can respond to the new circumstances implied by new locations.

GASTRULATION IN HOLOBLASTIC EGGS

Gastrulation in Small Holoblastic Eggs

Gastrulation in small holoblastic eggs has been studied mainly in echinoderms, particularly starfish, sea urchins, and sand dollars. Cell division proceeds regularly to form a blastula with an increasingly thin wall that is one cell thick, surrounding an increasingly large blastocoel. Following the tenth division, the cells develop cilia at their outer surface (Fig. 6.14). The blastula rotates within the fertilization membrane and by means of a hatching enzyme soon escapes to begin a free-swimming existence.

About 24 hours later one side of the spherical blastula flattens, corresponding to the original vegetal pole region. The flattening signals the onset of gastrulation; in the middle of the flattened area an invagination of small diameter soon appears, the aperture of which is the blastopore (Fig. 11.2*a*). As the invagination proceeds (and apparently from its beginning), cells are extruded from the invaginating surface into the blastocoel (Fig. 11.2*b*). These are termed *primary mesenchyme cells*. The gastrula grows in length as the invagination proceeds, changing its shape from a hemispherical to a more cylindrical form.

We are concerned here with the cell and tissue mechanics responsible for the actual performance, particularly the initial flattening of the vegetal region of the blastula to form the vegetal plate and the inpushing of the center of the plate as an invagination.

Many attempts have been made in this century to explain how the invagination is accomplished. The early interpretations were based on the following assumption: the forces that bring about gastrulation result from the pressure of dividing cells acting in a plane of the polar axis so that the cells of one hemisphere are turned in. This concept was tested by Moore in a series of direct operational experiments on echinoderm embryos, principally by cutting away parts of the embryo above the vegetal plate.

229

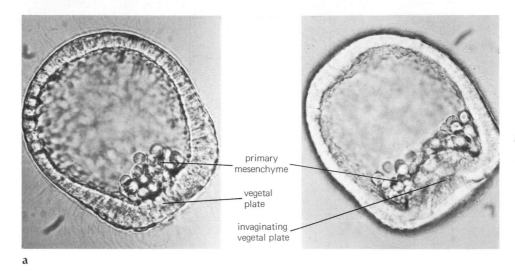

primary
mesenchyme

vegetal
plate

invaginating
vegetal plate

a

"upper corner"

animal plate
archenteron-tip
pseudopodia
secondary
mesenchyme cells
main ciliated band
around ventral side
ventrolateral chain
of primary mesenchyme
ventrolateral cluster of
primary mesenchyme
"arm bud"
ring of primary mesenchyme

b

Figure 11.2 *a* Early gastrulation (invagination) in sea urchin. [*After Gustafson and Wolpert, 1967.*] *b* Advanced gastrula showing distribution of primary and secondary mesenchyme cells.

The surprising result of excising the vegetal plate is the continuation of the process of invagination in the isolated plate. The inpushing deepens, and the rim of the isolated plate rolls up and closes over the central invagination to form a comparatively small gastrula (Fig. 11.3). Experiments such as these show that the forces producing gastrulation act in the plane of the vegetal plate to produce an inward movement of the center, rather than through the vertical, or median, plane. If a radial cut is made, passing from the periphery to the center of the isolated plate, the cut edges spring apart; this suggests that the whole plate is normally under tension. It is also noteworthy that in such small, reconstituted gastrulas, the periphery of the plate, which normally would become invaginated as endoderm, is changed into functional ectoderm. Moore concluded that the forces having to do with invagination exist in the endodermal plate; in intensity and direction they are disposed from the center outward in the form of a radial gradient. He suggested that differential cohesion of cells may be an important factor in producing pocketing.

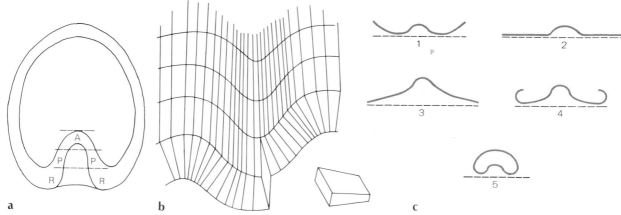

a   b   c

Figure 11.3 *a* Outline of normally invaginating gastrula. *A*, the originally active zone derived from the central spot of the gastral plate; *P*, the active zone derived from the plastic zone of the plate, which formed the periphery of the plate surrounding *A*; *R*, the new active ring. *b* Changes in cell shape associated with folding of columnar epithelium. *c* Horizontal view of the positions assumed successively by the gastral plate of starfish *Patiria miniata* during the hour following excision. [*After Moore, 1941.*]

Gustafson and Wolpert have also illuminated the primary phase of gastrulation with the aid of time-lapse cinemicrography. The films show that during the first phase of invagination the columnar cells of the vegetal plate have reduced contact with one another and a rounding-up of their inner borders, but they retain full contact with the outer hyaline layer at the egg surface. Their rounded inner borders show pulsating activity.

Micrographs by Tilney, Gibbins, and Porter show large numbers of microtubules distributed parallel to the long axis of the filopodia of primary mesenchyme cells. After the filopodia fuse to form a "cable" of cytoplasm (Fig. 11.4), microtubules become aligned parallel to the long axis of the cable and parallel to the cytoplasmic stalks connecting the cell bodies to the cable. When colchicine and hydrostatic pressure (which cause microtubules to disassemble) are applied to gastrulae, the microtubules disappear and the primary mesenchyme cells tend to spherulate. When D_2O (which tends to stabilize microtubules) is applied, the microtubules persist and the cell asymmetries remain unaltered. From these results it is concluded that microtubules are influential in the development of the filopodial form of primary mesenchyme cells.

Figure 11.4 Distribution of microtubules at each stage in the sequence. Note that these elements parallel the long axis of the asymmetry of the cell. When the cell is spherical (stage 3) they radiate radially from a central spot. [*After Gibbins et al., 1968.*]

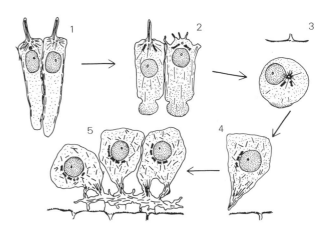

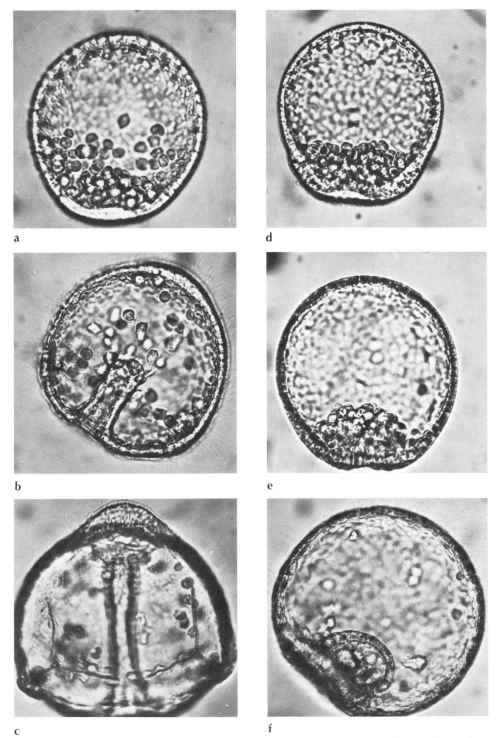

Figure 11.5 Photomicrographs of living embryos of sea urchin *Lytechinus pictus* from early to late gastrulation. *a–c* Control embryos raised in complete seawater at 29, 38, and 68 hours after fertilization. *d–f* Embryos raised from prior to fertilization in sulfate-free seawater at 29, 38, and 68 hours after fertilization respectively. × 400. [*After Karp and Solursh, 1974.*]

Another aspect of primary mesenchyme cell activity that has come under study is its apparent requirement for sulfate ions in the seawater. If embryos of the sea urchin *Lytechinus* are reared in seawater lacking sulfate, development proceeds normally to the stage of primary mesenchyme cell migration, and the cells pile up within the blastocoel rather than migrate along its walls (Fig. 11.5). If the primary mesenchyme cells of embryos raised in sulfate-free seawater are examined in the scanning electron microscope, they are found to have a smooth surface as opposed to the control embryos whose mesenchyme cells are covered by an irregular coat of material. This irregular surface has been shown to reflect the presence of sulfated mucopolysaccharide, which is required for cell migration.

The first phase of gastrulation takes the tip of the invaginating tube about one-third of the way through the blastocoel. There is a pause, followed by vigorous pseudopodial formation at the tip of the archenteron. These pseudopodia attach to the inner surface of the gastrula wall (Fig. 11.6), and their subsequent contraction pulls the archenteric tip forward. As pseudopodia reach for the gastrula wall ahead, similar pseudopodia reach toward them from the anterior gastrula wall (ectoderm). They at least aid in drawing in the mouth invagination, an inpocketing similar to that in the first phase of gastrulation, which meets and fuses with the tip of the archenteric tube to form a continuous tube, the intestine (Fig. 11.7). It is significant that the archenteric pseudopodia extend toward a particular region of the gastrula wall where the mouth invagination is destined to appear; at the same time pseudopodia from cells of the future mouth region, followed by actual invagination, extend toward them. The effect is clearly seen at a distance, but it is not known whether one region is stimulating the other or whether there is a mutual reaction between two innately active regions. It is uncertain whether the contractile force of the pseudopods is sufficient to draw the invaginations toward each other, or whether increased cell number or cell stretching in the invaginating tubes is responsible.

With further development, the tip of the archenteron buds off the secondary mesenchyme and coelom. Following this an ingrowth from the oral-field area of the outer wall, or ectoderm, forms the stomodaeum, which fuses with the tip of the archenteron to form a continuous digestive tube through the interior of the larva.

Figure 11.6 *a* The time course of invagination of the gut during gastrulation. Ordinate, extent of invagination, in microns; abscissa, the time scale, in film frames. The time between frames is 20 seconds. The arrow indicates the time when pseudopodia were formed. [*After Gustafson, 1967.*] *b* The pseudopodal attachments of the primary mesenchyme cells to the ectoderm wall. The wall has been stretched, and the pseudopodal contacts at the cell junctions are clear. A triradiate skeletal spicule (in black) is forming among a cluster of primary mesenchyme cells. [*After Gustafson, 1967.*]

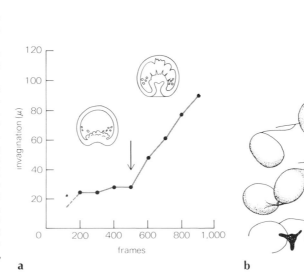

a

b

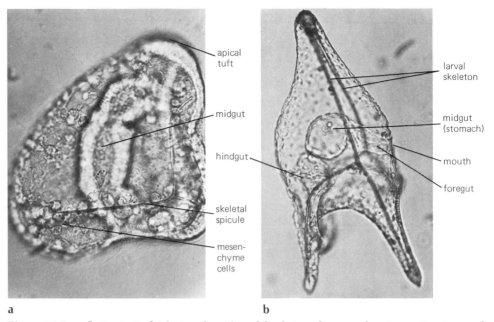

a   b

Figure 11.7 *a* Late gastrula (prism larva) and *b* pluteus larvae, showing extension and subdivision of invaginated digestive tube, its union with the stomodaeal invagination, and the relation of tips of larval skeleton to location of outgrowth of pluteus arms. [*Courtesy of T. Gustafson.*]

When pseudopodia are torn loose after the archenteron has already elongated to about one-half the blastocoelic diameter, the archenteron everts to the outside so that the larva becomes an exogastrula, presumably as a result of the change in tension or related mechanical stress.

Gastrulation in Large Holoblastic Eggs

The eggs of amphibians, of certain fish, and of the jawless vertebrate, the lamprey—all of which are laid in freshwater—represent what may be called the primitive vertebrate egg. Such eggs are larger than those of the sea urchin, the ascidian, or *Amphioxus* and have a diameter from 1 to 3 mm. Moreover these eggs contain proportionately more yolk. When a frog egg is centrifuged, so that the relatively heavy yolk granules are thrown toward one side, half the egg is seen to be packed with yolk. In the normal egg this yolk is distributed as a gradient, increasing from the animal to the vegetal pole. Nevertheless such eggs undergo total cleavage, i.e., they are holoblastic. Cleavage to form a blastula continues until thousands of cells are present, with the blastocoel located within the animal hemisphere. Only then does gastrulation begin.

It is possible to distinguish three main regions in the blastula—an upper part around the animal pole, a lower part around the vegetal pole, and an intermediate or marginal zone between the others that extends around the equator. In many amphibian species the animal region is most deeply pigmented, while the marginal zone, also pigmented, is typically grayish in contrast with the commonly white vegetal region. The marginal zone includes the gray crescent, which has already been discussed in connection with the establishment of bilateral symmetry in the fertilized egg. The three regions approximately represent the future three primary germ layers.

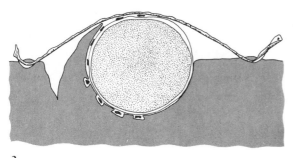
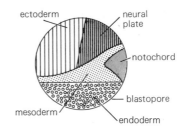

a

b

Figure 11.8 *a* Mapping of movement of various areas of salamander egg and embryo by means of vital-dye staining devised by Vogt. [Arch. Entwickl.-mech., **106** (*1925*).] The egg is held against pieces of agar stained with Nile blue or neutral red. *b* Map of amphibian egg showing prospective areas and site of future blastopore.

The animal region constitutes the presumptive outer germ layer (ectoderm), the vegetal region forms the future inner layer (endoderm), and the marginal zone becomes the middle layer (chordamesoderm). Because of the large number of cells (50,000 to 100,000) constituting the blastula as a whole, the differentials in yolk content and cell numbers between the two hemispheres, and other factors, a full comprehension of the gastrulation movements has been difficult to obtain. Cells of the blastula seem predestined to move inward or to remain outside, and apparently to develop into particular tissues and organs, as a consequence of their relative positions in the blastula. Do cells or cell sheets move inward because they are already becoming different from those that remain outside, or do they become different because they have moved inside to a different environment?

Much of what is known comes from Vogt's vital-dye method of analysis, in which small pieces of agar impregnated with various kinds of vital dye, particularly neutral red and Nile blue sulfate, are pressed against the surface of the blastula (Fig. 11.8); subsequent shape changes and migrations of the stained patches of the blastula are followed. Vogt was able to construct a fate map showing the future ectoderm, mesoderm, and endoderm—the ectoderm comprising the presumptive central nervous system and epidermis, the mesoderm including the material for the notochord, with myotome and other material on each side, and the endoderm comprising the primitive gut and its derivatives. Such a map shows the prospective or presumptive fate of the various territories of the blastula.

GASTRULATION PROCESS

The first indication of the onset of gastrulation in amphibian development is an infolding that starts on the border line of the vegetal region exactly below the center of the gray crescent area; i.e., it is in the marginal zone at a point lying on the axis of bilateral symmetry, so as to form a narrow groove or slit (Fig. 11.9). The fold above the groove represents the upper, or dorsal, lip of the developing blastopore and is derived directly from the gray crescent.

The formation of the dorsal slit marks the initiation of a process that underlies the entire phenomenon of amphibian gastrulation, namely the inrolling, or *involution*, of tissue. Cells at the rim of the blastopore undergo a change in shape (described below) that causes them to sink into the slit. Those cells that

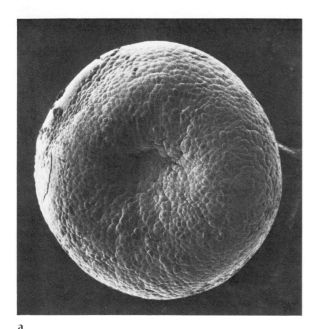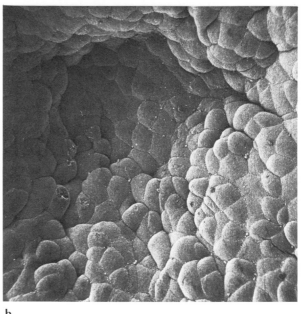

a   b

Figure 11.9 Scanning electron micrographs of the onset of gastrulation in the frog (*Rana*). *a* Gastrula showing blastoporal depression with inrolling dorsal rim (*top left*). *b* Enlargement of detail of blastopore, with middorsal region at the upper left. [*Courtesy of Judy Clark.*]

involute are replaced by new cells that are moved from their original position on the surface of the embryo to the blastoporal lip. As a result there is a flowing or streaming movement of the cells toward and around the blastoporal lip, as shown by the elongation of dye spots that were initially round in shape. The lip of the blastopore is, therefore, a continually changing structure.

Once inside the embryo the involuted cells move away from the blastopore and deeper into the interior forming the walls of an increasingly spacious cavity, the archenteron. The archenteric tube remains open to the outside via the blastopore. In the early stages of gastrulation the tissue of the lip represents anterior archenteric tissue destined to become foregut and mesoderm of the head (prechordal mesoderm). At later stages of gastrulation increasingly more posterior internal structures are found undergoing involution at the lip.

At first the blastopore is just a slit on the dorsal surface and it is over the dorsal lip that the involution of the chordamesodermal cells destined to form the dorsal axis of the embryo occurs. As the inward movement of tissue continues, the two ends of the blastoporal groove extend horizontally around the embryo (Fig. 11.10*a*). The extension of the slit results from the involution of tissue in an increasingly greater arc, forming what are termed the lateral lips of the blastopore. Eventually they meet on the ventral side of the embryo, forming the ventral lip opposite the starting point, and consequently complete the circle of the blastopore. The formation of a ring of involuting tissue occurs by surrounding the bulk of the large, yolk-laden cells of the vegetal hemisphere. As gastrulation proceeds the ring moves slowly in a vegetal direction sweeping down over the yolky endoderm and enclosing it within the interior.

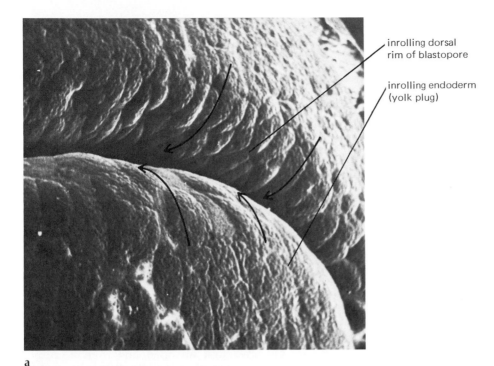

inrolling dorsal
rim of blastopore

inrolling endoderm
(yolk plug)

a

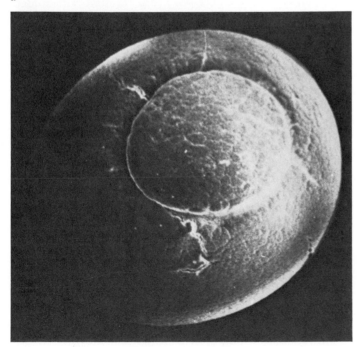

b

Figure 11.10 Scanning electron micrographs of late gastrulation (yolk-plug stages) of
the African clawed frog *Xenopus* from vegetal pole. *a* Inrolling of blastopore rim around
the diminishing margin of the yolk plug of *Xenopus*. *b* Epibolic enclosure of large, yolky
vegetal cells by pigmented, ectodermal cell layer. [*SEM courtesy of David Tarin.*]

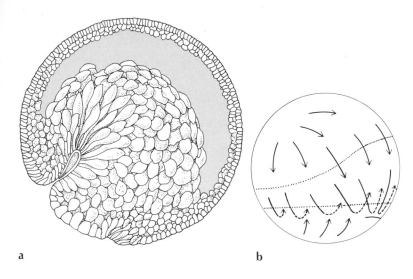

a

b

Figure 11.11 Bottle (flask) cells seen during invagination in amphibian egg. *a* Slightly schematized section through an advanced gastrula, showing active extension of cells. [*After Holtfreter, 1943.*] *b* Gastrulation movements as seen from the side.

Meanwhile the upper, ectodermal layer of cells, inrolling along its edge, appears to extend progressively over the lower, vegetal region. This process, called *epiboly,* is particularly apparent in frog embryos, where animal-pole cells are deeply pigmented and vegetal cells are white. The ectodermal sheet does in fact expand, as the cells continue to divide and to spread out; eventually the originally sickle-shaped blastopore becomes first an open and then a closed circle of steadily diminishing size. Finally a *yolk plug* (Fig. 11.10*b*) surrounded by dark ectoderm is all that remains of the mass of vegetal cells. At last only a narrow vertical slit denotes the blastopore and the termination of gastrulation. At this time the ectoderm alone covers the surface of the embryo. However, some involution (rolling-under) continues in the lips of the blastopore.

The apparent epibolic growth of an expanding pigmented ectoderm over a seemingly passive unpigmented vegetal region is, to some extent, an illusion. The vegetal region is actually as dynamically involved as the animal region (even though the constituent cells are comparatively large, few, and yolky). Simultaneously with the flowing-downward and -inward stream of presumptive notochord and mesoderm around the extending rim of the blastopore, the presumptive endoderm streams upward and inward in a similar but grosser manner, the upper and lower streams rolling in together in a marvelously integrated motion (Fig. 11.11). The full impact and beauty of this event can be conveyed only by time-lapse cinematography, for in nature the process is too slow to be visually appreciated and neither words nor still pictures can adequately portray the reality.

Primary Germ Layers

Internally gastrulation includes the movement of the chordamesoderm and the endoderm into their final positions. As the first shallow groove of the blastopore deepens, the archenteron, or primitive gut, begins to form. During the continuing process of involution the archenteron lengthens, somewhat in the manner of the lengthening of the archenteric tube in the sea urchin gastrula. It does so until the blind end reaches the inner surface of the ectoderm opposite the blastopore, where later a small invagination of the ectoderm fuses with the archenteron. The ectodermal invagination forms the mouth cavity or stomodaeum; the adjacent endoderm becomes the pharynx.

238

As the archenteron begins to elongate, its anterior roof is formed by material of the prechordal plate that rolls over the dorsal lip of the blastopore, advancing in front of the anterior end of the notochordal material. Its floor and sides consist of endoderm. Most of the mesoderm invaginates by rolling over the lateral and ventral lips of the blastopore. The notochord and the mesodermal material at this stage form one continuous sheet, the chordamesodermal mantle. It lies between the ectoderm and the endoderm; the lateral parts grow downward between the ectoderm and the free margin of the endoderm. The three germ layers are then in their definitive positions (Figs. 11.12, 11.13).

Integration of Gastrulation

Various theories have been proposed to account for the orderly integrated movement of cells responsible for amphibian gastrulation. Principally the debate is whether some supercellular agency acts to produce the overall movement, with individual cells caught up and passively carried along, or whether the whole action can be explained as the sum of the parts, as stated by Holtfreter in his classical account of the process (1943). Much of this interpretation rests on

Figure 11.12 Gastrulation and the establishment of the germ layers, as seen in sagittal sections. [*From Patten and Carlson, "Foundations of Embryology," Fig. 5.5, p. 119, based on Vogt, 1929.*]

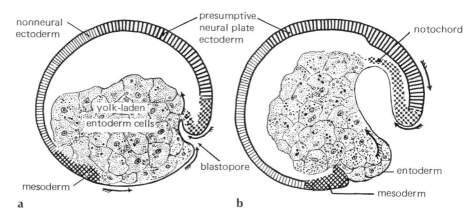

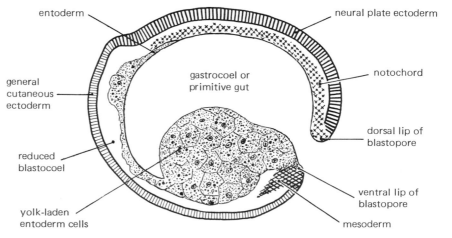

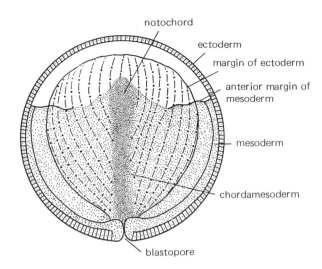

notochord

ectoderm

margin of ectoderm

anterior margin of mesoderm

mesoderm

chordamesoderm

blastopore

Figure 11.13 Germ-layer relationships in the late gastrula of the frog, from dorsal side. The neural plate is not indicated. [*From R. Rugh, "The Frog," p. 110, McGraw-Hill.*]

the properties of a surface coat of the egg and embryo comparable with the hyaline layer of the echinoderm blastula. It is an integral part of the egg surface and it persists as the outer surface of the cells, at least through cleavage and blastula formation. Positive evidence for the existence of such a coat comes from focused ultrasonic treatment, which has been used to isolate a coat from young frog embryos. Later, it cannot be isolated without attached cells.

Summing up, Holtfreter describes the roles of cells and surface coat as follows: (1) The shape of individual cells reflects the direction of their movement; (2) invagination is everywhere associated with a temporary transformation of the constituent cells into flask shapes; (3) the boundaries of the inner cells are not continuous like the wax in a honeycomb, but each cell is a discrete unit, interconnected with its neighbors only by slender processes; (4) all peripheral cells are firmly held together by a common surface coat of plastic elasticity.

The question of whether a "surface coat" truly exists, however, remains topical and in any case is somewhat semantic. Much depends on the definition, that is, whether it refers to the cell membrane proper and an underlying layer of peripheral cytoplasm or to a supra- or extracellular layer consisting of mucopolysaccharides that have a low electron density.

Taken as a whole, the blastoporal cells look like a bunch of radishes arranged in such a way that by a variation of the length and width of the neck, every space within the bunch is occupied by a cell body. Thus short cells are interlocked with long ones (Fig. 11.14).

Bottle Cells

The surface cells of the dorsal zone that become flask-shaped as they approach the blastopore are the *flask cells* or *bottle cells*. These prospective endodermal cells continue to attenuate until the bulk of each cell has moved completely into the interior, although they rarely lose their connection with the surface even when the neck of the cell has been greatly stretched. Electron micrographs show that long microvilli protrude at the distal surface of the bottle cells and interdigitate with adjacent cells, which may anchor the cell to the archenteron surface.

Strongly elongated cells appear along the line of the ventral blastopore lip as well as the dorsal lip. Some are endodermal but most are mesodermal. The mesoderm of the dorsal and lateral marginal zone invaginates at first as a continuous layer; but the cells become less mutually cohesive and tend to stick more closely to the overlying prospective neural ectoderm than to the adjacent endoderm. Thus the invaginating mesoderm does not penetrate the endoderm but glides into the interior on the surface of the deep endoderm and so contributes to the enlargement of the archenteron.

Holtfreter emphasized that the connection of the bottle cells to the surface is essential for invagination, that otherwise they would pass into the interior as individuals and their combined pulling force would be vitiated. He demonstrated this elegantly: When endoderm cells covered with surface coat are placed on a mass of inner uncoated, blastocoelic endoderm, the coated cells spread over the uncoated (Fig. 11.15a). In contrast, if an aggregate of uncoated endoderm is placed on uncoated endoderm, it becomes incorporated (Fig. 11.15b). If, however, an endodermal graft is covered with ectoderm, the endodermal component sinks into the endodermal substrate but the ectoderm at first spreads on the surface and then becomes isolated (Fig. 11.15c). Finally, if a grafting of blastoporal cells that are partly covered by surface coat is placed on an endodermal substrate, the graft invaginates and forms a blastopore, with bottle cells adhering to the coated area (Fig. 11.15d). Accordingly, bottle cells and the surface layer to which they adhere are responsible for the onset and continuation of invagination. The tight coherence of the surface layer serves not only to integrate the pulling activity of independently moving bottle cells into a coordinate system; it also communicates the pull to adjacent endoderm and mesoderm cells.

While bottle cells may be important for the initiation of invagination, what forces are responsible for its continuation? The cause seems to be in the marginal blastopore zone itself. Pieces of the blastoporal rim, especially the dorsal rim, invaginate wherever they may be transplanted elsewhere in the embryo. It must be remembered, however, that the rim of the blastopore is a location only and that cells are continuously moving from the external surface into the interior, throughout the relatively long gastrulation process.

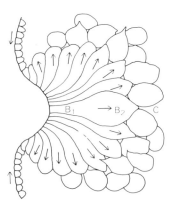

Figure 11.14 Bottle cells extending from blastopore.

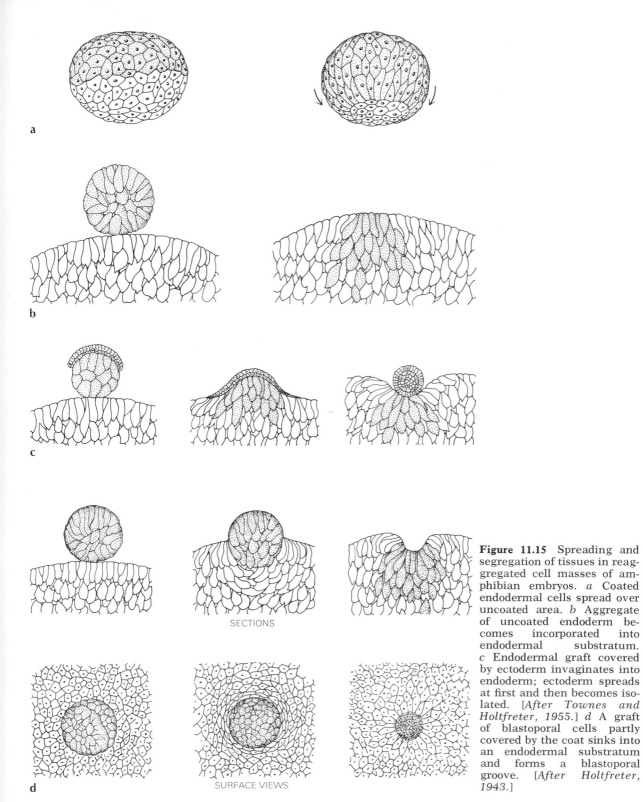

a

b

c

d

SECTIONS

SURFACE VIEWS

Figure 11.15 Spreading and segregation of tissues in reaggregated cell masses of amphibian embryos. *a* Coated endodermal cells spread over uncoated area. *b* Aggregate of uncoated endoderm becomes incorporated into endodermal substratum. *c* Endodermal graft covered by ectoderm invaginates into endoderm; ectoderm spreads at first and then becomes isolated. [*After Townes and Holtfreter, 1955.*] *d* A graft of blastoporal cells partly covered by the coat sinks into an endodermal substratum and forms a blastoporal groove. [*After Holtfreter, 1943.*]

A primary question is whether cells, individually or collectively, change in character as they pass into the marginal zone because they occupy that location, or whether cells inroll at that site because they have already become significantly different from those still at the surface. The latter is probably true, although precise experiments to show this have not yet been performed. There is no doubt, however, that once segregated into the outside, inside, and in-between portions characteristic of the ectoderm, endoderm, and mesoderm respectively, the three layers have very different properties.

In a classical series of experiments, Holtfreter (1939) separated the germ layers of the amphibian gastrula and reunited them in various combinations. Two pieces of pure endoderm fuse to form a smooth sphere. Prospective ectoderm and endoderm at first fuse closely but later move apart with only a thin bridge of tissue uniting them. In mixtures of ectoderm, endoderm, and mesoderm, the mesoderm adheres to both endoderm and ectoderm, thereby uniting two nonadherent layers. Mutual adhesion is highly selective and is more than mere difference in stickiness. Cellular affinities are clearly of great importance in gastrulation, just as they are in tissue organization generally.

Exogastrulation

Exogastrulas are readily produced by maintaining embryos in hypertonic saline solution. The archenteron is everted and the endoderm encloses the chordamesodermal tissues, while the ectodermal layer survives as an empty, crumpled envelope attached to the posterior endoderm by only a narrow stalk (Fig. 11.16). Even in its exogastrulated position, the marginal zone proceeds with its characteristic movements of dorsal convergence and anteroposterior elongation; at the same time it becomes embedded in the mass of endoderm. The displaced marginal zone develops into an axial notochord associated with somites and pronephric (renal) rudiments, together with various other mesodermal structures. In other words, the chordamesodermal sheet behaves as a self-differentiating unit in contrast with the isolated ectoderm.

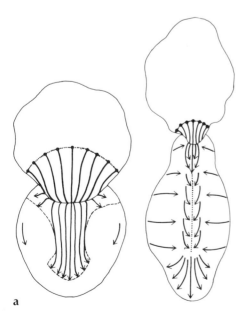

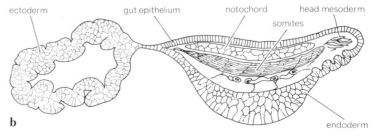

Figure 11.16 Exogastrulation. *a* Mass movements of tissue during exogastrulation in amphibian embryo. Ectoderm above, mesendoderm below. Compare with normal tissue movement during gastrulation shown in Fig. 10.1. *b* Main differentiations in an exogastrulated embryo. [*After Holtfreter, 1933.*]

ectoderm   gut epithelium   notochord   head mesoderm

somites

endoderm

a   b

Tissue Spreading during Gastrulation

During gastrulation every cell and every part of the embryo participate. The total event consists of three simultaneous movements. The future ectoderm expands and covers the whole surface of the gastrula stage, partly by continuing cell division but especially by thinning or spreading of the epithelial layer. This spreading tendency is inherent in the cells of both the superficial and the inner ectoderm. A grafted piece spreads in all directions over a surface, and the expansion of the presumptive ectoderm in normal development is readily explained as a spreading that merely follows the path of least resistance, replacing the mesoderm and endoderm as they move inward.

One layer thus imposes direction of movement on another. The endoderm also has an innate tendency to spread, although its spreading capacity is limited by the spreading ectodermal sheet to the amount required for normal gastrulation. The general picture of amphibian gastrulation that emerges may be summarized as follows:

1   The superficial endodermal cells of the marginal zone sink into the deep endoderm as bottle cells. Since their outer ends cohere tightly together, the surface begins to pocket and the archenteron begins to form.

2   Prospective mesoderm, which already has an inherent tendency to stretch in the anteroposterior direction, follows and, once inside, spreads on the highly adhesive lower surface of the overlying ectoderm.

3   At the same time the spreading ectoderm cells expand as a sheet over the invaginating mesoderm and replace it as it disappears from the surface.

Cell Division and Morphogenesis

The role of cell division appears to be mainly permissive rather than directive, in much the same way that the number of bricks available for building limits what may be built. Nevertheless morphogenetic processes may proceed more or less normally in spite of notable departure from normal cell numbers. Thus in salamander larvae with nuclei that are haploid, diploid (normal), and pentaploid respectively, cell size in various tissues varies directly with the degree of ploidy. Although the overall size of the eggs, embryos, and larvae is essentially the same in all, and constituent organs in the larvae are similar in size and form, the cellular makeup of tissues and organs is numerically very different. Larger and fewer cells are produced as the degree of ploidy increases. For example, cross sections of kidney tubules of haploid, diploid, and pentaploid larvae show eleven, six, and three cells respectively; yet all tubules have the same diameter and wall thickness (Fig. 11.17). A similar situation is seen in sections of the lens epithelium of corresponding larvae. In all of these cases, normal morphogenesis occurs.

Further evidence that embryonic organization is notably independent of cell number comes from experiments involving suppression of mitosis. When early blastulas of *Xenopus* are exposed to the drugs colcemid or mitomycin C, the mitotic cycle of the cells is blocked, with the result that normal increase in cell number is prevented from that time on. Such blockage is complete either immediately or after one further cell division. If blockage is begun as late as the stage of dorsal-lip formation, essentially normal morphogenesis ensues up to tail-bud stages, including differentiation of ectodermal structures, notochord, and twitching somitic muscle. Blockage induced at earlier stages results in developmental arrest, possibly because the smaller number of cells present is too small to permit the various morphogenetic tissue movements to take place.

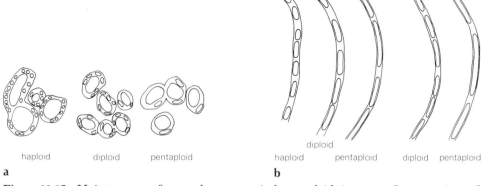

Figure 11.17 Maintenance of normal structure in heteroploid tissues. *a* Cross sections of pronephric tubules from a haploid larva (35 days old), from a diploid, and from a pentaploid. Size of tubules and diameter of wall remain approximately the same, in spite of differences in cell size, through changes in cell shape. *b* (*Left*) Small portions of lens epithelium of the same haploid, diploid, and pentaploid larvae. Thickness of epithelium remains nearly constant. (*Right*) Corresponding portions of lens epithelium of an older diploid larva and of a pentaploid of the same age and stage. Cells and nuclei of the pentaploid again flattened to about same diameter as in the diploid. [*After Frankhauser,* Quart Rev. Biol., **20**:20 (1945).]

GASTRULATION IN MEROBLASTIC EGGS

The Teleost Blastoderm

The cleavage differential seen along the animal-vegetal axis in the amphibian egg is carried to an extreme in the eggs of bony fishes and of the truly terrestrial vertebrates. These two groups are believed to have evolved from primitive freshwater fish with amphibian-type eggs and embryos. In both cases, irrespective of egg size, yolk is so densely packed and so fills the interior of the egg that only a cap of polar cytoplasm, or *blastodisc*, containing the nucleus, is capable of division. The first cleavages consequently produce blastomeres that are separate from one another where they adjoin, but are continuous with the underlying mass of yolk. Subsequent mitoses segregate them entirely, as a cellular cap called the *blastoderm,* from the undivided yolk region of the egg. Early cleavage is therefore partial, and development is *meroblastic.* The blastoderm that develops on top of the yolk increases by continued cell division and gradually envelops the yolk, although the embryo forms from only a part of it, the so-called embryonic shield. The remainder forms the extraembryonic tissue. Gastrulation in these forms is therefore, at least in large part, the process of overgrowth, or epiboly, whereby the undivided yolky region of the egg is engulfed by the spreading margin of the blastoderm to form the *yolk sac.*

In meroblastic eggs the cleavage and blastula phase is a period during which a cell size characteristic of the species is being established in the blastoderm. The blastoderm, consisting of the layer or mound of cells now completely separated from the underlying yolk, is anchored to the yolk at its margin by the *periblast.* This is a peripheral continuation of the epithelial cellular layer (the blastoderm) on to the yolk syncytium, where partial division of the egg cortex continues. In the teleost the rapid spreading of the blastoderm is combined with thickening and invagination of material at the peripheral edge, where the blastodermal cells roll inward above the periblast.

Both the blastoderm and the periblast have an intrinsic capacity to spread. Normally the blastoderm and the periblast spread over the yolky sphere toward the vegetal pole, the periblast extending ahead of the blastoderm. In fact the periblast can complete epiboly in the total absence of the blastoderm. The blastoderm, however, ordinarily completes its epiboly by spreading over the periblast and catching up with the periblast margin. Finally the whole yolk is enclosed by the two layers that constitute the yolk sac. The periblast substratum, in fact, appears to be essential for spreading of the blastoderm. The thickened edge of the blastoderm advancing over the yolk is known as the *germ ring* (Fig. 11.18).

Gastrulation in Amniotes

Birds and Reptiles As in the teleost, cleavage in the meroblastic eggs of birds and reptiles is initially confined to a cytoplasmic blastodisc, or *germinal disc,* at the animal pole of the egg. Radial and circumferential cleavage furrows continue to divide the disc superficially, leaving the cells still continuous with undivided yolk below (Fig. 11.19). Then horizontal furrows cut away the superficial cells except at the disc margin, leaving a slitlike space, the blastocoel, above the yolk. The blastodisc is thereby converted into the blastoderm.

Horizontal divisions further divide the early blastoderm into three or four layers. The central cells overlying the blastocoel constitute the clear *area pellucida.* The marginal cells adjoining the yolk are darker and form the *area opaca.* The outermost marginal cells, connecting the blastoderm with undivided cytoplasm of the yolk surface (the periblast), form the *germ wall.* These early stages of development occur while the fertilized egg is still passing down the oviduct of the hen. At the time of laying, about 60,000 cells are present in the chick blastoderm. The upper and lower layers of the blastoderm are known as the *epiblast* and *hypoblast* respectively. In contrast with the teleosts, the embryo-forming area lies inside the margin of the blastoderm.

In the chick the two aspects of gastrulation, namely, the advance of the blastodermal margin and the establishment of a visible embryonic axis, are regionally separate processes. The growth of the blastoderm margin is exclusively concerned with enclosure of the yolk within a yolk sac, while a *primitive*

Figure 11.18 *a* Blastodisc of fish, with embryonic axis established, seen from above. *b* Fish embryo above yolk surface, from side. Arrows show stages of tissue movement toward the axis and the vegetal pole (*After W. W. Ballard*).

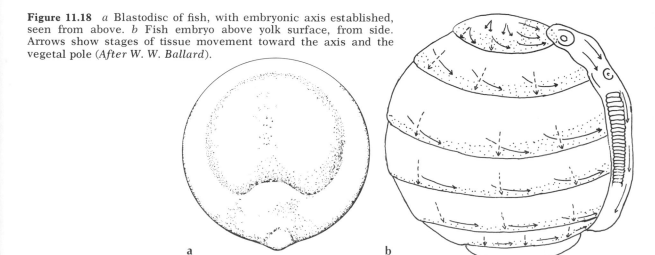

a   b

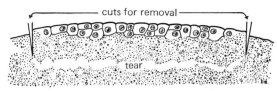

cuts for removal

tear

morula of chick on yolk

Figure 11.19 Schematic diagrams comparing chick and amphibian morula stages. By removing the chick morula from the large yolk sphere and pulling the margins together, its basic similarity to the amphibian morula is made evident. [*From Patten and Carlson, "Foundations of Embryology," Fig. 4.5, p. 102, McGraw-Hill.*]

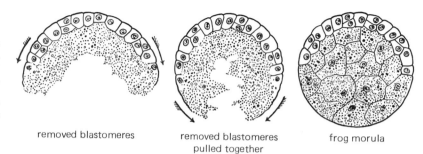

removed blastomeres

removed blastomeres pulled together

frog morula

streak, corresponding to the primitive shield of the teleost, first appears at some distance from the edge of the blastoderm and extends toward the center (Fig. 11.20). The primitive streak first appears in the midline at the posterior region of the area pellucida and then elongates anteriorly and becomes constricted. The elongated axis of the primitive streak foreshadows the anteroposterior axis of the future embryo.

It has often been suggested that streak elongation is due to an incorporation of new material, added to one end or the other. Markers added to the anterior as well as the posterior tip, however, remain closely associated with these two ends of the streak. *Streak lengthening therefore results essentially from a very active stretching of the area in which the streak has appeared.* This is confirmed by the use of tritiated thymidine. The lengthening is due to an active pushing forward as well as backward, which would explain how the circular

Figure 11.20 Chick. Surface views of embryonic disc. *a* Early gastrula stage. *b* Mid-gastrula (definitive streak) stage. *c* Late gastrula (head process) stage. Full arrows indicate surface tissue movements; dotted arrows, movements of cells below surface. *d* Sagittal section of stage *c,* showing node, neural plate, and notochord. [*After Deuchar, 1965.*]

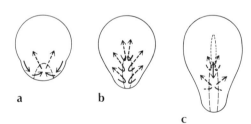

a　　b

c

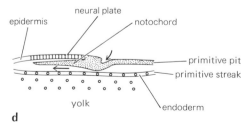

epidermis　　neural plate　　notochord

primitive pit

primitive streak

yolk　　endoderm

d

area pellucida becomes gradually pear-shaped and why an early primitive streak already possesses bipolarity, since both halves of the younger streak are remodeling in opposite directions.

The morphogenetic movements leading to the formation of the primitive streak begin as soon as the incubation temperature rises to the normal level (38.5°C). They begin as a movement of cells toward the posterior median end of the blastoderm. Much of the posterior half of the area pellucida at the pre-primitive-streak stage enters the primitive streak and becomes mesoderm. To what extent this tissue is replaced from the anterior end of the blastoderm is not known. Marking experiments indicate that some forward movement takes place in the midline as the primitive streak forms. As soon as the streak appears, it is characterized by a typical bipolarity; that is, the anterior half yields endoderm as well as mesoderm, whereas the posterior half yields only extraembryonic mesoderm.

As the definitive streak is formed a groove appears along its length, and it is toward this groove that cells migrate and via this groove that cells reach the interior. The thickening of the blastoderm that constitutes the primitive streak corresponds to the dorsolateral margins of the amphibian blastopore, here fused as a single structure. The thickened anterior end of the streak, known as the *primitive knot* (Fig. 11.21) or *Hensen's node,* corresponds to the dorsal lip. The primitive ridges correspond to the lateral lips. As in the amphibian the lips are continually changing structures, being composed of cells in the process of turning in from the surface layer (epiblast) and moving into the interior. The movement of cells toward the streak and down into it is termed *immigration* (Fig. 11.21).

Gastrulation in birds and reptiles is closely related to the whole story of the primitive streak, since the mesoderm as well as the endoderm invaginate through it. The lower cellular layer of the blastoderm, however, comes from more than one source. Large blastomeres become progressively detached from the upper layer at a very early stage, while embryonic endoderm later invaginates from the primitive streak to a lower layer position.

Detailed marking studies by Spratt and Haas, employing carbon and carmine particles (Fig. 11.22), and by Vakaert, using vital dyes, have shown that the primitive streak forms as a result of convergence of epiblast cells to the midline of the blastoderm. Here they sink in and migrate out laterally between the epiblast and the hypoblast to form the *mesoblast.* Rosenquist labeled epiblast cells with tritiated thymidine, a much more precise form of marking, and grafted them to unlabeled blastoderms. This showed conclusively that some endoderm, as well as the mesoderm, originates from the epiblast, invaginating at the primitive streak. Migration of both presumptive mesodermal and endodermal cells laterally outward and away from the primitive streak is a continuing process. Either new cells must enter by immigration from the epiblast or they must result from a relatively high rate of cell division within the streak. The evidence is conflicting. However, mesoblast cells are seen to be connected to each other and to cells of the primitive streak by junctional contacts (Fig. 11.23), especially along their trailing surfaces. They do not break away from the primitive streak as free cells and migrate as individuals, but form a loosely connected network.

In general, tissue sinks in along the center line of the streak. It then moves laterally and forward beneath overlying ectoderm and above subjacent endoderm to form the chordamesoderm, which is equivalent to the chordamesodermal sheet of the amphibian embryo. The presumptive notochordal

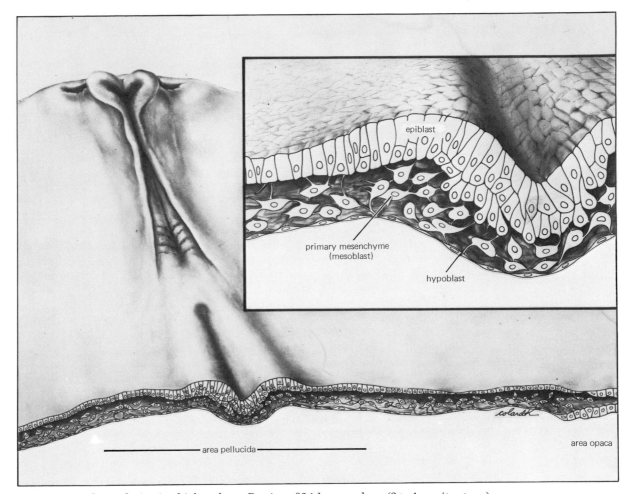

Figure 11.21. Gastrulation in chick embryo. Portion of 24-hour embryo (3 to 4 somite stage) showing embryo with head fold, open neural groove and neural folds, somites, the node, and primitive streak. The blastoderm has been transected about midway along the length of the primitive streak to show the cellular constitution of the area pellucida and area opaca. Inset, an enlargement of the primitive streak showing the cells of the epiblast invaginating and migrating laterally as the mesoblast. The hypoblast is seen as a thin underlying epithelium. Compare with the invaginative dorsal lip process of the amphibian embryo seen in Fig. 11.15. Epiblast, mesoblast, and hypoblast correspond to the three primary germ layers, ectoderm, mesoderm, and endoderm. [*From E. D. Hay, "Epithelial-Mesenchymal Interactions," Williams and Wilkins, 1968.*]

tissue of the chick underlies the midline of the embryonic axis, with lateral mesoderm at each side (Fig. 11.22). As this continues, with such tissue moving forward to the limits of the embryo-to-be, the primitive-streak tissue undergoes a corresponding attrition at its anterior end. In effect, the streak becomes progressively shorter and seems to shift posteriorly.

The shortening of the primitive streak is accomplished by the posterior regression of Hensen's node, which consists primarily of chordamesoderm in the process of turning inside. Once inside, the tissue of the prospective notochord

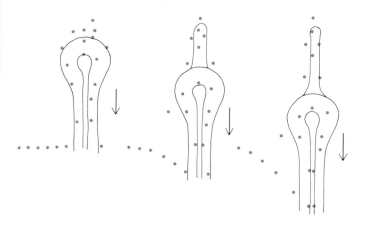

Figure 11.22 Convergent movement of epiblast of chick embryo toward the primitive streak, where the tissue sinks at the midline. The dots illustrate the changing positions of carbon-marked epiblast (ectoderm) cells. Later changes in the primitive streak are shown in Figure 12.14. [*After Spratt, 1946.*]

moves to underlie the epiblast in the region that will become the neural plate. As the most anterior parts of the embryonic axis are formed, the node progresses down the streak to produce more posterior parts (see Fig. 12.14). This process is further discussed in the next chapter.

The search for underlying causative factors in early chick development has been a difficult and controversial area of research. The principal questions relate to the formation of the epiblast and hypoblast of the early blastoderm and the formation and orientation of the primitive streak.

Upon incubation of the egg outside the body, differential growth occurs in the blastoderm, which exhibits radial and polarized patterns of differential rates of cell multiplication in various regions of the cell population. The outcome of this differential growth is a ring-shaped, lower-level *cell-population-density gradient* with maximal density on one side where the primitive streak is normally initiated (Fig. 11.24).

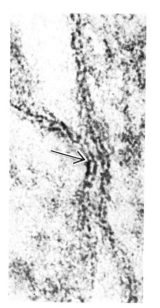 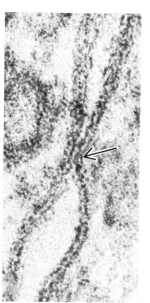 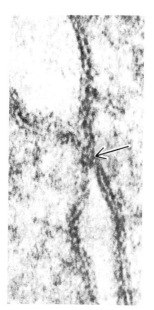

Figure 11.23 High-magnification electron micrographs showing junctions between dissimilar tissues in a stage-4 embryo near the primitive streak. *a* Close junction between plasmalemmas of mesoblast and presumptive endodermal cells (hypoblast). The arrow points to the outer leaflet of the trilaminar surface membrane of one of the cells. *b* Tight junction between mesoblast and epiblast. *c* Tight junction between mesoblast and hypoblast. Magnification: × 280,000. [*Courtesy of R. L. Trelstad, E. D. Hay, and J. P. Revel.*]

a   b   c

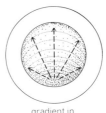

gradient in
cell density

lower-surface
movement
pattern

Figure 11.24 Properties of the unincubated blastoderm of the chick. The upper-left diagram shows a gradient in cell density with an eccentrically located region of rapidly dividing cells where the embryo normally will be initiated. The upper-right diagram illustrates the tendency of the lower-layer cells to spread radially and symmetrically below the upper layer. Other blastodermic properties are indicated below. The lower-left diagram represents a gradient in the growth potential of the marginal zone of the blastoderm, foreshadowing the spreading of the margin over the underlying yolk, which it eventually encloses. The lower-right diagram indicates the presence of a gradient in the capacity of various parts of the blastoderm, when isolated, to form an embryo. [*After Spratt and Haas, 1960.*]

gradient in
marginal-zone
growth potential

gradient in
embryo-forming
capacity

According to Spratt there is a gradient in the embryonic-axis-forming capacity of isolated pieces that is congruent with the bilaterally symmetrical gradient in cell-population density and growth potentiality. He considers the important property of the blastoderm to be the presence of a group of rapidly dividing cells located eccentrically. Here the embryo body is initiated. The cells of this growth center tend to spread out radially as a lower cell layer (hypoblast) along the underside of the radially symmetrical and immobile upper layer (epiblast). The spreading lower cells form a coherent sheet that moves like a viscous fluid away from its source until it reaches the marginal zone of the blastoderm; then the cells at the edge move circumferentially to the right and to the left. The course or pattern of movement of the lower sheet of cells is accordingly like a fountain, and it appears to be entirely a consequence of the geometry of the blastoderm.

In normal development, the axis of symmetry of the lower-layer movement pattern and the position of the head-tail axis of the future embryo coincide. If the main axis of the movement pattern is experimentally shifted, the head-tail axis is correspondingly shifted. If the lower-layer movement is blocked, no embryo develops.

The concept of a single, embryo-initiating, growth center is in question. The dominance of a particular area of the blastoderm may be due to the coordination of cells throughout the entire area pellucida rather than to a high rate of mitosis and density of cell population.

Both the area pellucida endoderm and also the mesoderm arise from the primitive streak. Endoderm formation rapidly outstrips that of the mesoderm, so that an endodermal layer is complete when the mesoderm is still only partly invaginated. This premature formation of the endoderm determines the orientation of the primitive streak. If the endoderm is removed from a blastoderm at an early primitive-streak stage and is then replaced at right angles to its original position, the streak continues to form, but bends at its anterior end toward the original anterior end of the endoderm. Therefore, the endodermal layer at least plays a part in directing primitive-streak formation and the cell movements of the upper layer.

Mammals Cells of the mammalian blastula (blastocyst) wall accumulate at the inner surface at one pole to form an inner cell mass. The small mammalian egg has almost certainly evolved from a large, yolky meroblastic egg as seen in reptiles and birds. The developmental phase corresponding to germ-layer formation is represented by processes of cell segregation and delamination. The early development of mammals is separately discussed in Chapter 16.

Multiple Embryo Formation

The potentiality and lability of the chick blastoderm preceding the establishment of the primitive streak have been demonstrated, as in fish, both by environmental conditioning and by operative procedures. Because development of a bird egg normally proceeds at a high incubation temperature, the system is comparatively sensitive to temperature change. Cooling the developing egg of a chick at the critical pre–primitive-streak stage retards or arrests the developmental process. Such cooling may be followed by a simple physical change such as cytoplasmic gelation; in any case it is reversible. Following the return to normal incubation temperature, two or three primitive streaks commonly appear on the blastoderm in place of the one that would have developed normally. Consequently two or three well-formed embryos develop. However, since they are associated with the same yolk sac, they become abdominally conjoined at hatching, as in fish, where partial or complete twinning also is induced by critical temperature changes during a particular phase of blastodermic development (Fig. 11.25). Operative procedures in chicks offer a wider range of experiments:

1   If the early blastoderm is cut into two pieces while it is still on top of intact yolk, twins develop (Fig. 11.26).

2   If the blastoderm is cut into four pieces by two crosscuts and grown on a culture medium, each piece develops a well-formed embryo with its head toward the original center of the blastoderm (Fig. 11.27).

3   Conversely, if three blastoderms, each having had its posterolateral parts cut away, are joined so that the three prospective organization centers unite in the middle of the fused disc, three embryos form, each with its head toward the middle; i.e., the original blastodermal polarity is reversed.

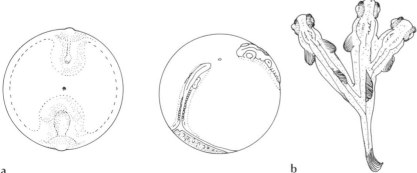

Figure 11.25 *a* Twins and *b* triplets in teleost development.

a   b

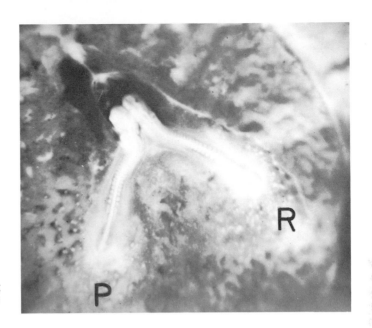

Figure 11.26 Chick twins produced by cutting unincubated blastoderms. [*Courtesy of Nelson T. Spratt, Jr.*]

In all such cases, embryos are formed from cell populations that otherwise would have contributed either to the formation of extraembryonic tissues or to entirely different parts of the embryo. The blastoderm is evidently a two-layered disc of tissue that is essentially undetermined with regard to specific embryonic axes until after considerable growth or expansion. The establishment of an axis or axes appears to be a consequence of a dynamic flow or spreading of the lower-level cell sheet; the sheet represents a more or less equipotential system

Figure 11.27 Potentiality and polarity in chick blastoderm. Four individuals resulting from division of blastoderm into four segments. [*After Spratt and Haas, 1960.*]

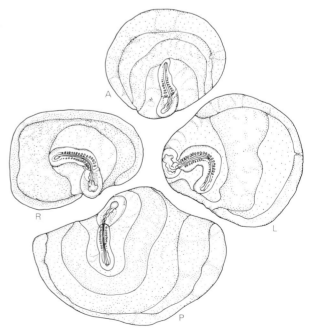

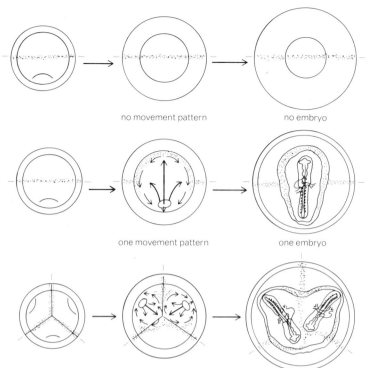

no movement pattern — no embryo

one movement pattern — one embryo

two movement patterns — two embryos

Figure 11.28 Bilateralizing role of the lower-layer movement pattern (as shown by movements of applied carmine particles), which gives rise to single or twin individuals as the case may be. [*From "Introduction to Cell Differentiation" by N. T. Spratt, copyright © 1964 by Litton Educational Publishing, Inc., by permission of Van Nostrand Reinhold Publishing, Inc.*]

as long as movement persists. Each portion, if large enough, possesses the capacity to form a whole when isolated from the rest. Spratt has shown, by means of applied carmine particles, that multiple axial induction depends on the presence of independent fields of fountainlike movements of the lower-layer cells (Fig. 11.28). These are in place of the single fountainlike movement characteristic of normal development, which establishes the embryonic axis.

DISPERSION AND REAGGREGATION OF THE BLASTODERM

Certain teleosts known as annual fish hatch, grow, shed eggs, and die in a season and bridge the year only as eggs arrested at an early stage of development. Blastomeres, however, disperse and reaggregate during the process. Normal development of annual fish eggs is characterized as follows: (1) After cleavage produces a certain number of blastomeres, a striking event occurs. The cells enter a stage of complete dispersion and become scattered around the egg, after which they reaggregate before embryogenesis can begin. (2) Annual fish eggs are capable of undergoing diapause, or developmental arrest, at one or all of several distinct embryonic stages.

According to Wourms, who worked with the eggs of *Austrofundulus myersi,* two populations of blastomeres form during cleavage. They segregate at the flat, hollow blastula stage, in the typical manner of teleostean development (Fig. 11.29). By the early flat blastula stage there are flattened periblast cells adjacent to the yolk, continuous with a surface-enveloping layer, and a

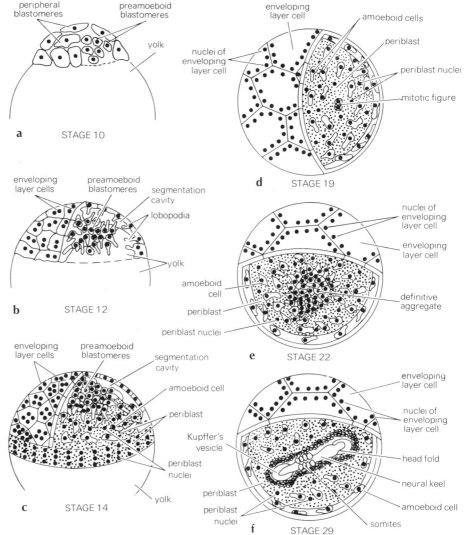

Figure 11.29 Dispersion and reaggregation in *Austrofundulus myersi*. Chorion removed; surface view of the egg with enveloping layer intact on one side; on the other side, the enveloping layer is removed to illustrate underlying amoeboid cells and periblast; periblast stippled; cell numbers reduced for clarity; oil droplets not illustrated. [*After Wourms, 1967.*]

compact mass of amoeboid, more or less spherical, blastomeres (Fig. 11.29*a,b*). The enveloping cell layer apparently does not participate in the formation of the embryo but goes on to form an extraembryonic membrane that is shed at the time of hatching. As epiboly commences, the amoeboid blastomeres consolidate into a mass and then migrate away from that mass as individual cells. They move into the space formed when the enveloping layer and periblast advance over the yolk. When epiboly is completed, the amoeboid blastomeres of the 3-day egg, which will later form the embryo, are completely dispersed (Fig. 11.29*c,d*). At this stage no germ ring or embryonic shield is present; this would be an obvious impossibility. Both cell contact and, presumably, consequent intercellular communication are essential for a cell population to express collective potentiality.

During the late dispersed phase, cell contacts increase in number and duration until, after a few days, these cells come together to form a definitive aggregate within which embryogenesis occurs (Fig. 11.29e). In 10 days a solid ridge has formed in the aggregate, while development of a typical teleostean embryo follows (Fig. 11.29f). The development of five other genera of annual fishes appears to be essentially similar. The reaggregation mass may therefore be considered identical to the embryonic shield of nonannual teleosts.

Whatever developmental processes may have been proceeding in the egg and the blastomeres at the molecular level, they must be of a general nature affecting all cells. With such complete disorientation of the blastomeres that constitute the prospective embryo and adjoining tissue, the organizational or morphogenetic processes inevitably begin only after reaggregation, i.e., in a reconstituted blastoderm. At this time the prospective potency of the contributing cells must be maximal, since the position of any given cell in the aggregate is random.

In recent experiments by Oppenheimer, portions of *Fundulus* embryonic shields, usually posterior or anterior halves, were partially dissociated into cell clumps and separate cells by exposure to salt solution lacking magnesium and calcium ions. The dissociated cells and cell clumps were reaggregated in salt solution containing these ions. They were immediately grafted to extraembryonic regions of host gastrulas. Complexes associated with grafts derived from posterior shield portions frequently formed typically differentiated tails. Complexes associated with grafts derived from anterior shield portions frequently formed, among other structures, highly differentiated eyes, often with normal retinal stratification and sometimes accompanied by lens, cornea, iris, or optic nerve.

Why, for instance, are eyes rather than other organs most frequent in the secondary complexes of anterior origin? Why is the differentiation of the eyes superior to that of the brain in these complexes? These questions are unanswerable with the present evidence. While it may represent only a restatement of the questions raised by these results, rather than an answer to them, the conclusion seems inescapable that a tail field of importance is operating in the posterior shield and an eye field of principal importance in the anterior shield. These fields, whatever fields may be, either survived the drastic experience they have undergone or reconstructed themselves—if that is a more reasonable possibility—to accomplish the dramatic and consistent regulation for which these experiments provide evidence.

It may well be that what are already "set in their ways" in early *Fundulus* gastrulas are a set of fields rather than cells programmed to form specific structures. When Spemann first defined the organizer, he defined it in terms of fields: "Such a fragment of an organizing center can briefly be called an 'organizer'; it creates for itself in the indifferent material in which it lies, or into which it is transplanted, a 'field of organization' of definite orientation and extent."

MACROMOLECULAR CONTROL

All available evidence indicates that every embryonic and somatic cell contains the whole genome. Those that do not become either transformed or moribund. In other words, despite its special fate in the multicellular organization, each cell has the nuclear constitution necessary to recreate the whole organism. The question is: How do individual cells in a developing system recognize their particular situation in that system and respond accordingly? This question confronted Driesch long ago as a result of his classical investigations of sea urchin development. Finding no satisfactory answer, he retreated into a philosophical corner and assigned an "entelechy," a sort of individual intelligence, to each cell. This concept was generally rejected, although it does have something in common with our contemporary outlook. In place of an ephemeral guiding principle, we think the cell has a repertoire of appropriate responses to appropriate clues, acquired through long ages of evolution and now stored. This is essentially the meaning of selective gene activity, and it assigns a managerial function to the genome of every cell.

Experiments with eggs and embryos of the teleost fish *Fundulus heteroclitus*—mainly by Oppenheimer, Wilde, and Crawford—have shown this material to be outstanding for developmental study, particularly for combinations of molecular biology techniques and those of classical descriptive morphology and teratology (abnormal development). Synchronous development of a very large number of fertilized eggs can be established by timed external fertilization controlled by the experimenter. This makes it possible to take large samples at any desired stage or time for chemical and macromolecular analysis and also to make continuous observations of both normal and abnormal development. Moreover, the passage of various drugs through the egg membrane can readily be observed. By knowing how and when a particular inhibitor drug acts and by understanding how a particular defect develops and what parts are affected, it is possible to estimate any direct causal relationship between the event and the effect of the drug. The harmful effect of a drug on the course of development is termed an *insult*. When the insult is chemical, we can associate the resultant morphogenetic defect with the mode and time of action of the chemical.

A drug used in this connection is pactamycin, an inhibitor of protein synthesis in mammalian and bacterial systems. The site of action is at the binding site of aminoacyl-transfer RNA to ribosomal subunits. Its effect on protein synthesis is reversible by removal of the drug. In *Fundulus*, the administration of precisely timed pulses of pactamycin inhibits protein synthesis at every stage. When the inhibitor is applied within seconds or minutes after fertilization, cleavage is inhibited. Since actinomycin D, which prevents transcription of RNAs from DNA by binding to guanine in the DNA, does not affect cleavage, we may conclude that proteins synthesized during this period and required for cleavage are made upon maternal templates.

A series of experiments employed these two types of inhibitor drugs. Applied at successive stages of development, they caused strictly time-controlled insults to the genetically controlled macromolecular chemistry. The experiments give us a catalog of morphogenetic events and the time at which they begin. The genomic control of gastrulation apparently begins at the second minute after fertilization and is established by the fifth minute. The anteroposterior axis of the body is determined by macromolecular synthesis at the third minute and is complete by the sixth minute. The whole set of mechanisms concerned with the formation of the head is determined soon after, while evidence exists for a subserial ordering of determination of the individual organs of the head.

Accordingly there seems to be an obligate order of synthesis of morphogenetically meaningful macromolecules, i.e., nucleic acids and proteins. The early biosynthesis of these macromolecules, probably in strict temporal order, is essential for normal morphogenesis. It cannot be disturbed without resulting in specific morphogenetic failure or permanent defect. Even though relief of the inhibition may allow for all the essential syntheses to proceed, some of these will be out of proper sequence and proper relationship to the ongoing development. Consequently they cannot play their proper morphogenetic role. Yet development under such circumstances still continues, carrying unchangeable defects such as notochord without nervous system, nervous system without somites, etc.

Crawford and Wilde conclude that the morphogenetic process entered into at fertilization behaves as though all cells and their progeny are committed and are cognizant of time flow and position. Only those cells that are open targets of the inhibitor during—and only during—the pulse, or period of the drug, fail in their morphogenetic commitment and behavior. They emphasize that the morphological event of gastrulation in *Fundulus* is preceded by 40 hours of essential macromolecular synthesis, without which gastrulation is aborted. The most important initiating and controlling events appear to be confined to the period immediately following fertilization and well within the first cleavage period while the zygote is a single cell.

There is evidence that cells of the blastula do not become significantly different from one another up to the time that gastrulation (primitive-streak formation) begins. This has been shown both by experiments and by the natural occurrence of disaggregation of the blastula. The question consequently is: How can the conclusion (based on analysis of early macromolecular events) that crucial processes are initiated during the one-cell stage and the conclusion (based on disaggregation and multiple embryo formation) that the blastoderm is equipotential be reconciled? The organizational process that determines the scale and symmetry of the embryo-to-be clearly is not firmly set until a late blastoderm or blastocyst stage. The long-preceding synthetic events must therefore be concerned with a different aspect of development. We do not know the answer; the first step is to formulate the question, as above. An analogy can be made with the construction of a house. Materials such as bricks, stone, steel, cement, lumber, and glass have to be accumulated before a building can be assembled. Whether one or more buildings of a certain design are to be built is a decision more or less independent of the diversity of the materials available and depends on quantities, available space, etc. But any earlier event that harmfully affects the quality or results in the absence of certain materials will have a deleterious effect on the subsequent construction, even though construction may still continue, although imperfectly or incompletely.

The problems of pattern or design of the embryo-to-be—the siting and the scale of it—appear to be unrelated to the facts we possess concerning the biochemical changes in the early blastoderm or blastocyst, or to the incipient signs of cytodifferentiations. As in the developing limb, the phenomenon of emergent organismal pattern exhibits the process of self-assembly and self-organization in its most challenging form.

READINGS

BELL, E., 1960. Some Observations on the Surface Coat and Intercellular Matrix Material of the Amphibian Ectoderm, *Exp. Cell Res.*, **20**:378–383.

BELLAIRS, R., 1969. Experimental Twinning and Multiple Monsters in Chick Embryos, in E. Bertelli (ed.), "Teratology," Excerpta Medica.

BENNETT, M. V. L., M. E. SPINA, and G. D. PAPPAS, 1972. Properties of Electronic Junctions between Embryonic Cells of *Fundulus, Develop. Biol.*, **29**:419–435.

BLUEMINK, J. G., 1972. Cortical Wound Healing in Amphibian Eggs, *J. Ultrastruct. Res.*, **41**:95–114.

BRUMMETT, A. R., 1968–1969. Deletion-transplantation Experiments on Embryos of *Fundulus het-eroclitus*, I: The Posterior Embryonic Shield, *J. Exp. Zool.*, **169**:215–253. II: The Anterior Embryonic Shield, *J. Exp. Zool.*, **172**:443–463.

CHILD, C. M. 1940. Lithium and Echinoderm Exogastrulation: with a Review of the Physiological-Gradient Concept, *Physiol. Rev.*, **13**:4–41.

CRAWFORD, R. B., C. E. WILDE, JR., M. K. HEINEMANN, and F. J. HENDLER, 1973. Morphogenetic Disturbances from Timed Inhibitions of Protein Synthesis in *Fundulus*, *J. Embryol. Exp. Morphol.*, **29**:363–382.

GIBBINS, I. R., L. G. TILNEY, and K. R. PORTER, 1968. Microtubules in the Formation and Development of the Primary Mesenchyme of *Arbacia Punctulata*, *Develop. Biol.*, **18**:523–539.

GUIDICE, G. 1973. "Developmental Biology of the Sea Urchin Embryo," Academic.

GUSTAFSON, T., and L. WOLPERT, 1967. Cellular Movement and Contact in Sea Urchin Morphogenesis, *Biol. Rev.*, **42**:442–498.

HOLTFRETER, J., 1944. A Study in the Mechanics of Gastrulation, II: *J. Exp. Zool.*, **95**:171–212.

——, 1943. Properties and Functions of the Surface Coat in Amphibian Embryos, *J. Exp. Zool.*, **93**:251–323.

——,1943. A Study in the Mechanics of Gastrulation, I: *J. Exp. Zool.*, **84**:261–318.

HÖRSTADIUS, S., 1973. "Experimental Embryology of Echinoderms," Oxford University Press.

KARP, G. C., and M. SOLURSH, 1974. Acid Mucopolysaccharide Metabolism, the Cell Surface, and Primary Mesenchyme Cell Activity in the Sea Urchin Embryo, *Develop. Biol.*, **41**:110–123.

MOORE, A. R., 1941. On the Mechanics of Gastrulation in *Dendraster excentricus*, *J. Exp. Zool.*, **87**:101–111.

NICOLET, G., 1971. Avian Gastrulation, *Advan. Morphog.*, **9**:231–262.

OPPENHEIMER, J. M., 1972. Regulation of Partially Dissociated and Reaggregated Portions of *Fundulus* Embryonic Shields, *J. Exp. Zool.*, **179**:63–80.

SPRATT, N. J., and H. HAAS, 1960. Integrative Mechanisms in the Development of the Chick Embryo, I: *J. Exp. Zool.*, **145**:97–137.

TRELSTAD, R. L., E. HAY, and J. P. REVEL, 1967. Cell Contact during Early Morphogenesis in the Chick Embryo, *Develop. Biol.*, **16**:78–106.

TRINKAUS, J. P., 1969. "Cells into Organs," Prentice-Hall.

WOURMS. J. P., 1972. Developmental Biology of Annual Fishes. II. Naturally Occurring Dispersion and Reaggregation of Blastomeres during the Development of Annual Fish Eggs, *J. Exp. Zool.*, **182**:160–200.

——, 1967. Annual Fishes, in F. H. Wilt and N. K. Wessells (eds.), "Methods in Developmental Biology," Crowell.

CHAPTER 12

Neurulation and Induction

The Event: the Neurula
The Process: Neurulation

> Cell shape and cell adhesion
> Microtubules and microfilaments
> Neural crest

The Cause: Neural Induction

> Induction in the chick: the node
> Competence

The Problem: Chemical Nature of Induction

Toward the end of gastrulation in amphibian embryos, when the yolk plug is disappearing and the blastopore is becoming a dorsoventral slit, the embryo is still almost spherical. At this time faint streaks appear on the dorsal side, extending from the dorsal edge of the blastopore to the anterior end of the embryo (Fig. 12.1). They are the first external signs of the *neural plate*. A median streak represents the future neural groove; the marginal streaks represent the neural fold of each side. *Neurulation* is primarily the process whereby a flattened neural plate transforms into a hollow *neural tube*.

Figure 12.1 Neurulation in the salamander. *a* Early stage, with yolk plug still evident, showing shallow neural groove and neural folds. *b* Middle stage, showing great difference in width of prospective brain and prospective spinal cord.

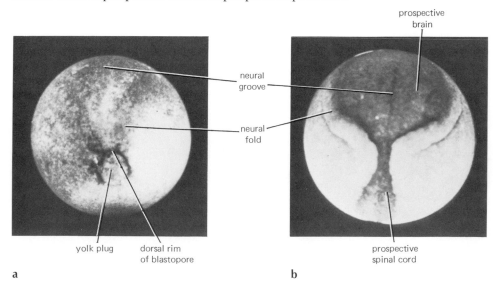

a

b

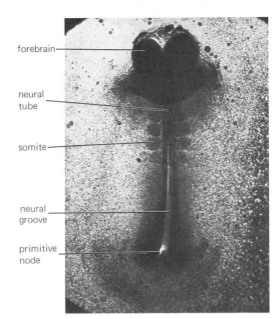

forebrain

neural
tube

somite

neural
groove

primitive
node

Figure 12.2 Neurulation in the reptile embryo (an amniote embryo). Compare with chick embryo in Fig. 11.21. Here is a four-somite turtle embryo, showing head fold and developing brain, neural tube open posteriorly as a neural groove, four pairs of mesodermal somites with lateral mesodermal plate extending posteriorly on each side of the neural groove, and primitive node.

Neurulation continues until the whole neural tube, representing the brain and the spinal cord and their outgrowths, has been entirely segregated from the overlying surface ectoderm. In amphibians and other lower vertebrates, or anamniotes, the enclosure of the neural tube is completed at much the same time throughout its length. During the whole process the stage is known as the *neurula*. In the land vertebrates of all classes, the process of neurulation occurs in a progressive manner from the anterior to the posterior part of the embryo. For example, in the embryo of Fig. 12.2, neural-tube formation has been completed anteriorly, stretching as far back as the region of the third somite. At this stage the embryo contains a well-infolded brain, the trunk region has a fused neural tube anteriorly and an open neural plate posteriorly, and the most posterior part of the embryo is still undergoing gastrulation. Therefore, although the neurula stage is precisely definable in amphibian development, neurula and neurulation are terms that apply in a temporal succession to the stage and process seen along the embryonic axis. They are associated with an axial gradient with regard to time and stage of axial development.

Neurulation, though specifically the process of neural-tube formation, is also the phase of development during which mesoderm and endoderm undergo primary differentiation into particular structural entities, as already noted in *Amphioxus*. During neural-plate formation, the mesoderm, which is already separated from the endoderm of the archenteric roof, demarcates into five strips of tissue representing the median dorsal notochord and, on each side, the band of somites and the lateral plates.

THE EVENT: THE NEURULA

The cells of the neural plate become elongated and constitute a columnar epithelium, so that the plate thickens: the adjoining ectodermal cells remain more or less flattened. The edges of the neural plate rise as ridges. As they continue to do so, they become the neural folds. The neural plate between them

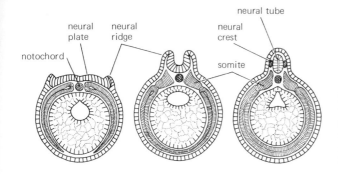

Figure 12.3 Three stages in urodele neurulation in transverse section, showing open neural plate, neural groove with neural folds, and closed neural tube covered by epidermis, respectively. The notochord, mesoderm, and endoderm are also seen in all three stages, in progressive differentiation.

tends to narrow, forming a wide neural groove. At the same time the embryo begins to lengthen along its anteroposterior axis. The neural folds then meet in the dorsal middle line and fuse, thus forming a tube (Fig. 12.3). For a time the folds are still separated anteriorly. Consequently there is a temporary anterior opening into the tube, which is called the *neuropore*.

Finally the lateral ectoderm (epidermis) of each side, which has been spreading dorsally as the neural ectoderm (*neurectoderm*) narrows, also meet and fuse at the middorsal line. The neural tube is thereby cut off and lies beneath the completed epidermal layer. As the neural folds fuse middorsally and separate from the covering epidermis, a mass of cells called the *neural crest* migrates out of the dorsolateral region of the neural tube into the surrounding tissue. The cells of the neural crest are derived from the transition zone between the neural plate proper and adjacent presumptive epidermis. These migratory neural-crest cells will differentiate into a great variety of tissues.

During gastrulation in amphibian embryos, the invaginating endodermal and mesodermal tissue extends progressively toward the anterior end of the embryo, as long as the blastoporal involution continues. A gradient is thereby set up with regard to the length of time the invaginating tissue has been exposed to the internal environment during this period.

As the roof material of the archenteron rolls inward, the first mesoderm to invaginate is in advance of the anterior end of the notochordal material and forms the prechordal plate, cells that will later become the mesoderm of the head. The notochordal material rolls over the dorsal lip of the blastopore to form the middorsal strip of the chordamesoderm. As it does so, it begins to elongate longitudinally and contract laterally. It separates at its anterior end from the prechordal plate and laterally on each side from the remainder of the mesoderm to become the somite and lateral-plate mesoderm (Fig. 12.4). During the period of late gastrulation and neurulation, the overlying roof of the archenteron is composed of the mesoderm that has invaginated over the dorsal lip. After a period, endoderm closes below the dorsal mesodermal tissue so that the archenteron (or future embryonic gut) becomes completely bounded by endodermal cells.

Each tissue of the neurula thus constituted proceeds with its own characteristic patterns and processes of morphogenesis. These several phenomena, which are integrated into the development of the embryo as a whole, are briefly described below but will be considered in greater detail in later pages of this chapter and the next. One pervasive phenomenon that should be emphasized here, however, is the changing shape of the embryo. The whole embryo begins

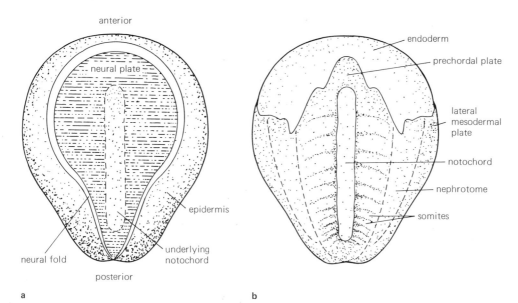

Figure 12.4 Dorsal view of amphibian neurula, to be compared with somewhat earlier stage seen in Fig. 11.13. *a* Surface view showing neural plate and position of underlying notochord. *b* Deeper view of same, showing notochord, extent of lateral mesoderm and prechordal mesodermal plate, and regions of segmenting somitic mesoderm and unsegmented nephrotomic or intermediate mesoderm.

to grow in length as neurulation proceeds. At least some of this extension appears to depend on extension of the notochord, but whether this is solely responsible is debatable.

THE PROCESS: NEURULATION

In amphibians the neural tube forms from as much as 50 percent of the ectoderm. In this group especially, the topographic aspects of the folding and stretching movements of the neural plate during neural-tube formation, as well as the fate of each part of the neural plate during development, have been so well studied by means of vital dyes and tissue transplantation that, descriptively, neurulation is thoroughly understood (Fig. 12.5). It is easy to see what happens. How the morphogenetic movements are brought about and what controls or determines the various processes involved are, however, frustrating problems. Moreover, the whole event may take a very short time. In the comparatively large egg of the salamander it takes about 2 days, but in the smaller egg of *Xenopus* it is remarkably rapid and is complete within about 3 hours after the neural plate begins to infold.

This rapid action by itself appears to rule out one of the earlier proposed explanations. In 1874 His suggested that form changes in the cells, and eventually in the neural plate as a whole, result from growth pressure (tissue expansion) due to excessive mitosis in the neural ectoderm within a confined area. More than half a century later, Gillette showed that while there is a 23 percent increase in the number of cells present in the whole ectoderm during neurulation, there is no increase in its total volume; cells are simply becoming smaller.

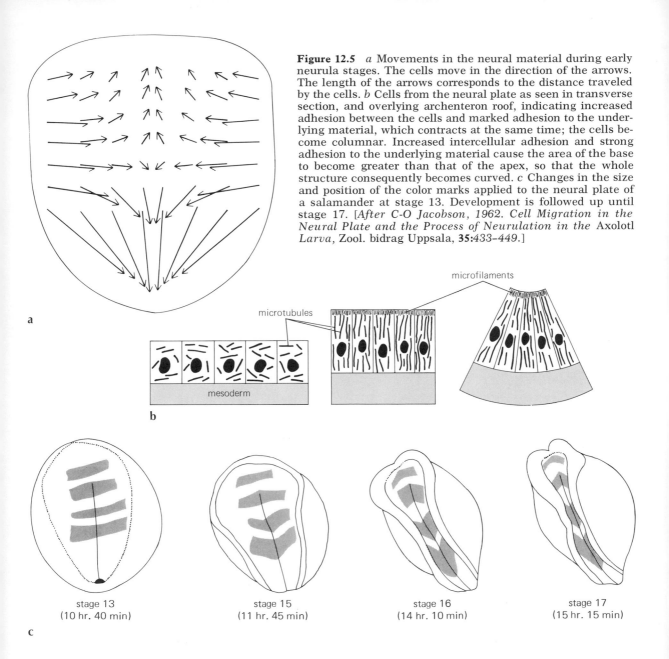

Figure 12.5 *a* Movements in the neural material during early neurula stages. The cells move in the direction of the arrows. The length of the arrows corresponds to the distance traveled by the cells. *b* Cells from the neural plate as seen in transverse section, and overlying archenteron roof, indicating increased adhesion between the cells and marked adhesion to the underlying material, which contracts at the same time; the cells become columnar. Increased intercellular adhesion and strong adhesion to the underlying material cause the area of the base to become greater than that of the apex, so that the whole structure consequently becomes curved. *c* Changes in the size and position of the color marks applied to the neural plate of a salamander at stage 13. Development is followed up until stage 17. [*After C-O Jacobson, 1962. Cell Migration in the Neural Plate and the Process of Neurulation in the* Axolotl *Larva,* Zool. bidrag Uppsala, **35**:433–449.]

microfilaments

microtubules

mesoderm

a

b

stage 13
(10 hr. 40 min)

stage 15
(11 hr. 45 min)

stage 16
(14 hr. 10 min)

stage 17
(15 hr. 15 min)

c

Further, he showed that there are no detectable differences in either cell number or cell size between the neural and the nonneural ectoderm. Differences in cell shape are another matter.

Neural folds do not meet simultaneously throughout their length, although closure of the whole may be complete before final separation from the epidermal ectoderm. As a rule, the narrower the neural plate is to begin with, the sooner the folds come together. The wider the plate the longer it may take, probably for the simple reason that there is more ground to cover. In any case we are faced with the fact that a neural plate has a particular shape, typically wide in front where it becomes the brain and narrow behind where it becomes the spinal cord (Fig. 12.1). Both shape and size of the neural plate call for explanation apart from the question of tissue mechanics involved in the conversion of a plate into a tube.

Cell Shape and Cell Adhesion

Attempts to analyze the process of neurulation, as in the study of most problems of development, go back to the nineteenth century, in particular to Roux (1885). He maintained that events resulted from certain changes in the neural plate itself rather than from the effects of outside forces such as expansion, and therefore pushing, by the surrounding ectoderm. Because the cells of the neural plate, beginning with those of the neural ridges, become taller and then flask-shaped, their basal and free surfaces necessarily become smaller (Fig. 12.5b). Since the free outer surface becomes more constricted than the basal surface, the layer of cells tends to curve inward. These two changes in cell shape have been held responsible for the neurulation process, as described on the following pages. On the other hand, the cells of the nonneural ectoderm flatten to some extent and the tissue therefore tends to expand as a sheet.

The ectoderm lateral to the plate moves toward the plate, and this has been regarded as an important factor in initiating the contractile forces. However, portions of neural plates, when cleanly excised from salamander embryos and maintained in vitro, have been observed to undergo infolding movements without the aid of neighboring tissue. Elongation of the neural-plate cells involves an active rather than a passive change in cell shape, i.e., the capacity to elongate is intrinsic to the neural-plate cells themselves. This is shown by the fact that single, isolated, urodele neural-plate cells retain their columnar shape and continue to elongate in culture (Holtfreter, 1947).

Microtubules and Microfilaments

In the salamander, at the end of gastrulation the entire ectoderm consists of a simple, low, columnar epithelium in which the cells of the neural portion are indistinguishable from those of the epidermal portion. As neurulation proceeds, the presumptive neural cells first elongate dramatically to form the high columnar epithelium of the neural plate. The neural-plate cells then constrict apically, thereby becoming flask-shaped as the plate rolls up to form the neural tube. In urodeles the neural ectoderm remains a simple epithelium throughout neurulation, and the process is simpler than that seen in the more complex neural ectoderm of anuran amphibians. During neurulation the elongating cells of the neural ectoderm contain both oriented microtubules and apical cytoplasmic filaments. In the cell apex the tubules are oriented with their long axes parallel to the free surface, the apical microtubules; in the elongated body of the cell they are oriented with long axes parallel to the axis of elongation, the paraxial microtubules. During this period of neural cell elongation, the presumptive epidermal cells gradually flatten to form a squamous epithelium. A developing basement membrane appears beneath the basal surface of both types of cells during the period of neurulation.

One possible mechanism for the formation of the elongated cells of the neural plate is an active extension of the microtubules by addition of subunits, i.e., growth, which in effect pushes at the apical and basal ends of the cell. Either paraxial microtubules extend the full length of the cell or shorter, overlapping microtubules are stabilized in position by lateral interactions with closely adjacent microtubules. Rather than the cell's continual production of additional microtubule subunits for growth, it seems more likely that some paraxial microtubules are broken down and their subunits used for the extension of others in the elongating cell.

Ectoderm in *Xenopus* and other anuran amphibia is two-layered, the superficial and the deep layers, and neurulation is accordingly somewhat more complex. The cell shape changes associated with neurulation are principally those of the deep layer. Initially cuboidal cells of the median strip of the deep layer of the neural ectoderm undergo elongation and apical constriction to become flask-shaped. During elongation each cell possesses about 150 microtubules oriented parallel to the elongating axis of the cell (Fig. 12.6*b*). Both before and after the period of cell elongation, the same cells possess only a few nonrandomly oriented microtubules.

The active role of both microtubules and microfilaments in neurulation is supported by experiments exposing neurulas of *Xenopus* and the chick to a number of agents known to interfere with the assembly or maintenance of these structures. In *Xenopus,* vinblastine was used to disrupt microtubules, thus preventing neurulation from proceeding and also reversing changes in cell shape associated with neurulation that may already have taken place. At the least, microtubules appear to be necessary to maintain the elongated shape. In the chick, elongate neurula cells round up when treated with colchicine and lose their constricted state when exposed to cytochalasin (a microfilament disruptive agent). Both treatments prevent neurulation from proceeding. In the presence of cytochalasin the neural folds of the chick embryo come away from each other, eventually falling back and flattening, although the neurula cells remain wedgeshaped. Microtubules are still present in these cells but microfilaments are mostly lacking.

According to Schroeder, the dynamically significant factors operating during neurulation include:

1   Microtubule-dependent cell elongation

2   Microfilament-dependent cell contraction

3   Swelling and consequent extension of the notochord by intracellular vacuolation

4   The capacity of flask cells to realign

5   Epidermal spreading

The nature of the coordinating mechanisms of the morphogenetic process of neurulation remains a basic problem. Two questions are involved: Is the interpretation in terms of cell shape, microtubules, and microfilaments a valid explanation of how an epithelial cell sheet can roll up into a tube? Is this process essential to the formation of a neural tube in all vertebrates? This explanation of tube formation may well be valid for some but not for others. The mode of formation of a hollow tube in fish, however, is very different. The neural tube forms as a solid rod of cells that separates from the ectoderm and subsequently somehow acquires a hollow interior. This suggests that the common method of plate and tube formation characteristic of most vertebrates is not essential to neural differentiation as such, but represents one of possibly several means by which one kind of tissue can separate from another.

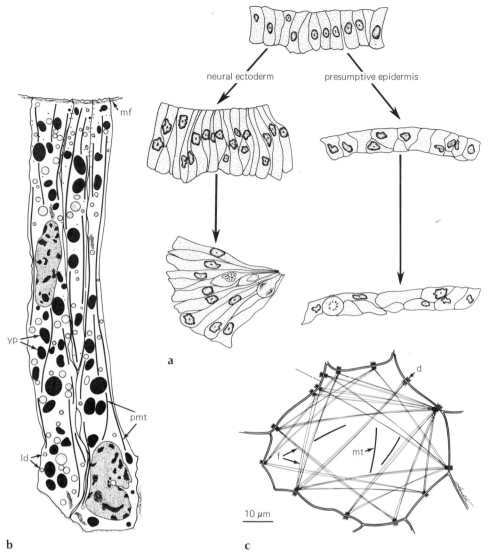

Figure 12.6 *a* Two possible routes of ectodermal differentiation; the tall columnar cells of the neural tube and the flattened cells of the epidermis. *b* Orientation of microtubules and microfilaments in elongating neural-plate cells. The microtubules (pmt) are aligned parallel to the axis of the cell, while the microfilaments (mf) are arranged in a circumferential bundle around the apex in purse-string fashion. *c* A flattened epidermal cell. Microtubules are randomly oriented, but the microfilaments (f) are arranged in discrete bundles, often seen in continuity with desmosomal fibers (see Fig. 3.5) and are thought to span the cell from desmosome to desmosome (d). [*After B. Burnside,* Develop. Biol., **26:**434, *Academic Press, 1971.*]

Neural Crest

The neural crest forms from the dorsal ectoderm along each side of the neural plate during the final stage of neural tube closure and is at first continuous anteroposteriorly. From the first, the neural crest consists of a mass

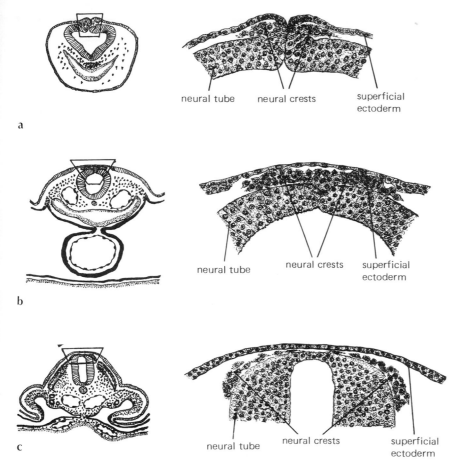

neural tube   neural crests   superficial
                                 ectoderm

a

neural tube   neural crests   superficial
                                     ectoderm

b

neural tube   neural crests   superficial
                                 ectoderm

c

Figure 12.7 Transverse sections to show the origin of neural-crest cells. The location of the area drawn is indicated on the small sketch to the left of each drawing. *a* Anterior rhombencephalic region of 30-hour chick. *b* Posterior rhombencephalic region of 36-hour chick. *c* Mid-dorsal region of cord in 55-hour chick. [*From Patten and Carlson, "Foundations of Embryology," McGraw-Hill, 1974.*]

of loosely aggregated cells at each side of the dorsal midline of the embryo. Cell migration begins almost immediately after the aggregations are evident. Cells migrate by the advancing ruffle-edge process seen in fibroblasts. Streams of neural-crest cells appear in the anterior region of the embryo before they begin to scatter toward their final destinations (Fig. 12.7). In the trunk they tend to scatter from the start of the general migration. The supply of cells from this source is impressive both in quantity and in the diversity of eventual differentiation.

Many neural-crest cells become localized in segmentally arranged clusters alongside the neural tube. They form the ganglia of cranial sensory nerves anteriorly and the dorsal root ganglia of spinal nerves more posteriorly. Some become ganglionic cells of the adrenal medulla and sympathetic nervous system. Others become the nonneural nerve-sheath cells (Schwann cells). Some become mesenchyme. A large group of cells disperses widely beneath the ectoderm to form pigment cells in various locations, often in striking patterns: the melanophores of the higher vertebrates and the carotenoid and silvery pigments of lower vertebrates. Neural-crest cells also assume a mesenchymal character. They contribute to connective tissue and most notably supply the cartilage of the visceral skeleton (jaw, hyoid and gill arches) together with part of the skull. They do not contribute to the axial skeleton (trunk vertebrae and limb skeleton). A general account and analysis of this remarkable diversity has been presented by Weston (1970).

Many questions arise concerning the whole neural crest phenomenon:

1   Are neural-crest cells already differentiating at the time of their segregation from the dorsal ectoderm of the late neurula? In other words, is this segregation the result of crest tissue becoming cytochemically different from the adjoining presumptive neural and epidermal tissue?

2   Do cells of the neural crest migrate at random into other parts of the embryo from the vicinity of the neural tube, or do they travel along determined pathways?

3   Do the cells reach particular target areas and, if so, do they recognize their destinations on arrival?

4   Do cells disperse into regions where they play no part or become cytolyzed?

5   What determines the specific type of differentiation that a particular group of neural-crest cells undergoes?

In spite of much effort over many years, none of these questions could be answered until a cell-specific, nontoxic, long-term cell marker became available, namely, tritiated thymidine. Tritiated thymidine is provided to a donor embryo for incorporation into the DNA of its cells. At the appropriate stage, before the neural-crest cells have emigrated, a piece of the labeled neural tube is excised and transplanted in place of a comparable region of an unlabeled host embryo. The labeled cells migrate into the surrounding unlabeled tissues of the host; they can readily be identified by autoradiography against the unlabeled cellular background. Employing this technique, Weston showed that trunk neural-crest cells emigrate in two fairly well-defined streams that (1) move ventrally into the mesenchyme between the neural tube and the myotomes to form segmental spinal and sympathetic ganglia and (2) move dorsolaterally into the superficial ectoderm (rather than the dermis as had previously been thought). The cells follow definite pathways and, for causes yet unknown, cease to move and accumulate rapidly at precise destinations; i.e., there is no random migration followed by selective survival at appropriate locations.

The direction of the ventral stream is independent of the nature of the mesenchyme through which it moves, but is oriented with respect to the neural tube. Thus when a neural tube with attached neural crest is inverted, the crest cells continue to migrate but move dorsally instead of ventrally, i.e., in inverse direction, retaining their direction relative to the tube itself. The tritium-marking experiments also show that the neural-crest cells migrate to their particular target locations without getting lost on the way.

The more basic questions remain unsolved. It is probable but so far entirely unproved that a single, extensive population of neural-crest cells gives rise to several kinds of pigment cells or melanoblasts (depending on the species), to various sensory and autonomic ganglia, to the adrenal medulla, and to certain skeletal and connective tissues. If this view is correct, we are not only left with the questions concerning the determination of the pathways and the oriented movement of the cells; we are also left with the all-pervading problem of how cells and tissues interact with one another and with their immediate intercellular environment to select particular paths of cytodifferentiation. These problems are considered further in Chapters 17 and 20 on cytodifferentiation and tissue patterns and differentiation.

That epidermal pigmentation arises from a class of migrating neural-crest derivatives has allowed investigators to examine the basis of complex pigment patterns to determine whether they result from information carried by the environment into which the melanoblasts migrate or rather are inherent in the pigment cell itself. The basic design of these experiments is to surgically replace a section of the neural tube of one animal with a portion of a neural tube donated by an embryo of another species. If this operation is performed prior to the stage at which neural-crest cells have emigrated from the neural tube, donor melanoblasts will migrate into the surrounding tissue of the host. The subsequent pattern formed by donor cells can be analyzed with respect to the characteristics of each species involved. In these experiments it is generally found that the pigmentation patterns reflect the donor species in those regions into which donor cells have migrated.

The most complex pigmentation patterns are found in bird feathers and result from the differentiation of melanoblasts into specifically colored melanocytes during feather differentiation. It is generally believed that the stem pigment cells are capable of a variety of overt cytodifferentiations; the specific one expressed is a result of the microenvironment that each cell finds itself. For example, if a feather pattern is composed of a striped arrangement of red and brown, those melanoblasts that migrate into the developing feather at a time when a red stripe is being formed will produce red pigment granules as a result of some unknown stimulus in that region at that time. At a later stage, that same melanoblast might have differentiated in an entirely different direction.

Presumably the environmental signals are sufficiently nonspecific so they can evoke patterns in cells that have achieved a state of differentiation allowing them to respond in their own way as dictated by their own genotype. The phenotype expressed is that of the donor species, but the environmental influence is reflected in the nature of the donor pattern that is observed. Donor colors and patterns remain in keeping with the anatomical region into which they have migrated. For example, neural tube taken from the leg region of the donor species and inserted into the wing region of a member of a second species will produce the *wing* color and pattern of the donor species, regardless of the region of the embryo from which it was originally taken. Similar results are found when transplants are made between members of the opposite sex in species having sexually dimorphic pigment patterns. Melanoblasts derived from male embryos produce male plumage patterns in those regions of the female bird in which they find themselves.

Anterior to the neural crests proper, the tissue intermediate between presumptive neural tube and lateral presumptive epidermis is known as the *sense plate*. This arises mainly from the transverse neural fold at the anterior end and it gives rise to a variety of structures associated with the development of sense organs. The same problems of determination and destiny arise as in the neural crest proper. This is not surprising, since the tissue involved is essentially a continuation of the neural crest around the anterior end of the neural tube.

THE CAUSE: NEURAL INDUCTION

Treatment of amphibian embryos at the onset of gastrulation with hypertonic medium results in exogastrulation. Apart from the effect on cell and tissue movement, the striking feature is that the inverted chordamesoendoderm proceeds with self-differentiation, but the ectoneuroderm merely survives as an

Figure 12.8 Dorsal blastopore lip of an early newt gastrula, transplanted into the blastocoel of another, induces a complete secondary embryo. [*Courtesy of L. Saxén and S. Toivonen.*]

undifferentiated crumpled envelope (Fig. 11.16). This suggests that at least the initiation of neural differentiation and neurulation depends on the presence of adjacent, perhaps adjoining, tissue. Neural differentiation needs to be triggered or induced. The early embryonic ectoderm appears to be neutral, or entirely unspecialized, and may be directed by other tissues or by various agents to take one path of differentiation rather than another. Many experiments support this conclusion. Although the first analysis of induction, by Spemann between 1901 and 1912, concerned the development of the eye—specifically the induction of a lens by the optic-cup rudiment—the classical experiments upon which the concepts of "embryonic induction" and "organizer" were founded came later. In 1924 Spemann and Mangold discovered that the dorsal blastopore lip tissue from a salamander gastrula turns inward when transplanted into a ventral or lateral position on another gastrula and that it induces the host to form a secondary embryo (Fig. 12.8). The significant feature of this discovery is that chordamesodermal tissue can induce neural differentiation in ectoderm that would ordinarily differentiate as epidermis.

Most of the spectacular experiments on the amphibian embryo have been those of Spemann and his coworkers, particularly Mangold and Holtfreter. Spemann summarized much of this work in a series of lectures published in 1938 but now reissued. Two of the most important papers, by Spemann and Mangold (1924) and by Holtfreter (1939), are to be seen in English translation in "Foundations of Modern Embryology," edited by Willier and Oppenheimer (1974).

The question of critical importance is whether all the components of the secondary axis are simply differentiating from the donor tissue or whether some of the host tissue of the ventral flank region is being differentiated into some of these axial structures that it would not normally form. If the latter possibility is found to be true, an induction has occurred. The crucial experiments by Spemann and Mangold showed that both the transplanted dorsal lip and the tissue of the host embryo contribute to the formation of the secondary embryo, the graft forming most of the chordamesoderm and the host supplying the nervous system. The source of the two sets of tissue, graft and host respectively, could be determined by employing embryos of different species whose tissues are distinguishable. These and similar experiments showed that (1) uncommitted ectoderm responds to underlying chordamesoderm by undergoing neurulation and (2) the dorsal-lip territory of the blastopore has a high capacity for self-differentiation and serves also as an organization center, although the nature of the organizing influence or agent still remains elusive.

One of the first questions to be answered concerns the time of induction of the neural system. When pieces of the prospective neural plate, the dorsal ectoderm, of the *early gastrula* are transplanted to the ventral region of another gastrula, they develop according to their new position, i.e., they become belly epidermis. Pieces removed from a *late gastrula* and transplanted to a ventral position develop according to their original position; i.e., they become neural plate (Fig. 12.9). Induction evidently occurs during the time when the material initially present in the dorsal lip moves inward and forward to the anterior region of the embryo. The vital-staining experiments of Vogt showed that the material successively forming the dorsal blastoporal lip moves forward as the archenteric roof. Transplants taken from the roof of the archenteron are also able to induce a secondary embryo on the belly of a new host; i.e., the archenteron roof acts as an inductor in essentially the same way as does the dorsal-lip tissue proper. The nature of the induction is dependent upon the relative position of inducing tissue along the anteroposterior axis. Pieces of anterior roof tissue usually induce secondary embryos with more or less complete head structure, whereas pieces of posterior roof tissue generally induce outgrowths with tail structure. A more direct approach to the specific question of neural induction by transplants has been made since 1950 by Nieuwkoop and coworkers in Holland and by Toivonen and Saxén in Finland. In these experiments various portions of the archenteron roof, taken at different periods, have been combined with ectoderm of various ages in the so-called sandwich technique outside the

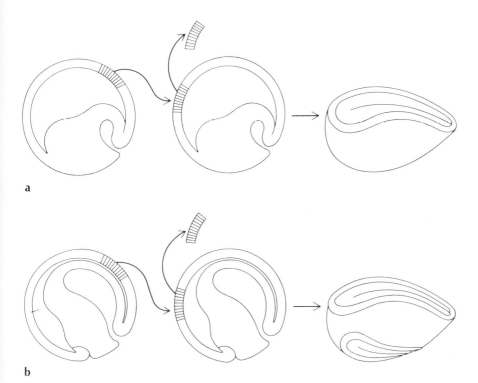

a

b

Figure 12.9 Removal and substitution of regions of neural plate at different stages of development. *a* Piece of presumptive neural plate removed from an early newt gastrula, and grafted onto the ventral side of another of the same age. No induction occurs, but the graft develops in accordance with its new surroundings. *b* A corresponding piece removed from a late gastrula develops in the new surroundings according to its original fate. [*After Saxén and Toivonen, 1962.*]

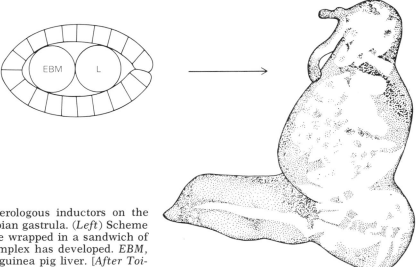

Figure 12.10 The effect of two heterologous inductors on the undetermined ectoderm of an amphibian gastrula. (*Left*) Scheme of the experiment: both inductors are wrapped in a sandwich of ectoderm. (*Right*) An embryolike complex has developed. *EBM*, extract of bone marrow; *L*, piece of guinea pig liver. [*After Toivonen and Saxén, 1955.*]

embryo (Fig. 12.10). Other experiments have interrupted the normal neural inductive process. The results of these diverse and numerous experiments have been utilized by these two laboratories as a foundation for hypotheses concerning the formation of the embryonic central nervous system. In the model by Toivonen and Saxen it is proposed that two inducing substances are present within the embryo. When acting alone, one of these substances, a neuralizing inductor, induces forebrain structures while the other, a mesodermalizing inductor, induces posterior structures (trunk and tail) in competent ectoderm. It is proposed that these factors are present as gradients. The neuralizing substance would have its highest concentration across the mid-dorsal section of the embryo and its level would decrease in a ventral direction. The mesodermalizing factor would be most concentrated in the posterior embryonic regions, decreasing in an anterior direction. The nature of the differentiation displayed by a given ectodermal region would reflect the relative influences of these two inductors. Anteriorly, forebrain structures would form; posteriorly, tail tissue, while intermediate positions would form mid-brain, hind-brain, and spinal cord. Much of this theory is based on the extraction and purification of substances that have neuralizing or mesodermalizing inductive influences on uncommitted ectoderm. Guinea pig liver and guinea pig bone marrow, for example, have provided such substances, respectively. When present together in an ectodermal sandwich (Fig. 12.10), tissues characteristic of the entire anterior-posterior dorsal axis differentiate, much more than will form from the influence of these substances when present by themselves.

The theory of Nieuwkoop proposes that the process of neural induction is a biphasic event (Fig. 12.11). This is shown by operational experiments that interrupt the normal induction process. These experiments demonstrate that during gastrulation the inductive activities spread through the overlying ectoderm in a caudocranial, or posteroanterior, direction as two successive waves. The first wave travels ahead and farther than the second. The shape of the neural plate is said to be determined by the spreading spatial distribution of the first wave, or activating agent. The second wave, or transforming agent, only changes the regional character of part of the neuralized region.

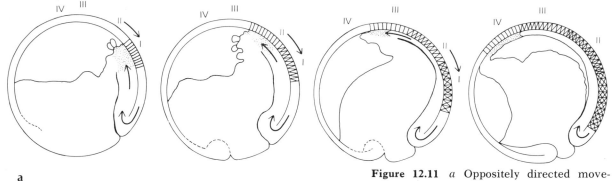

a

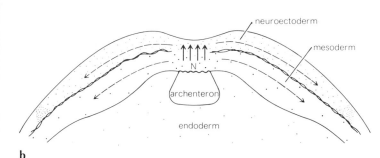

b

Figure 12.11 *a* Oppositely directed movements of invaginating archenteron roof and epibolically extending ectoneuroderm at four successive stages of the gastrulation process. The interaction of both layers leads to a caudocraniad spreading of an activating inductive principle in the ectoderm when it overlies the prechordal portion of the archenteron roof. This primary action is followed by a caudocraniad spreading of a superimposed transforming inductive principle emanating with increasing intensity from successively more caudal regions of the archenteron roof. *b* Mediolateral spreading of an inductive action within the mesoderm and a similar spreading of the neuralizing action in the overlying ectoderm. Parallel vertical arrows indicate the main site of the neuralizing inductive action (*N*) in the area of intimate adhesion of the two germ layers. [*After Nieuwkoop, 1966.*]

Induction in the Chick: the Node

The inductive processes in chick and presumably other amniote embryos appear to be essentially the same as those in amphibians and other anamniotes. If the anterior end of the primitive streak (*Hensen's node*) is extirpated, stripped of all adhering endoderm, and implanted beneath the ectoderm at the side of the area pellucida, it induces a secondary embryonic axis consisting of neural tube, notochord, and somites (Fig. 12.12). This ectoderm does not contribute to the neural tube of the normal embryo. A similar experiment with the same result has been performed in mammalian (rabbit) embryos. As in the case of experiments on amphibian embryos, however, many tissues and substances have been found to induce axial embryonic structure when implanted beneath responsive ectoderm. Nevertheless, in both cases the power of inducing neural tissue is greater in the anterior end of the normal inductor, i.e., the dorsal lip of the blastopore of the amphibian and the node of the primitive streak of the chick.

In amphibians the dorsal lip of the blastopore persists as such throughout the process of gastrulation, in spite of the diminishing size of the blastopore. It represents a location where chordamesodermal material continues to inroll and to move anteriorly beneath the ectoderm. As it does so, it changes in inductive capacity, inducing a head when taken from an early gastrula and inducing a tail when taken from a late gastrula (Fig. 12.13). In the chick, as described in the preceding chapter, the node progressively regresses posteriorly down the

274

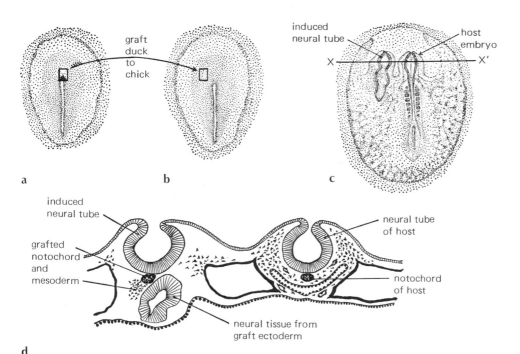

Figure 12.12 Semischematic drawings showing the induction of an accessory neural tube as a result of grafting notochordal tissue from a duck donor into a chick host. *a* Duck embryo showing the location from which the graft was taken. *b* Chick host showing the location where the graft was implanted. *c* Embryo cultivated for 31½ hours after implanting of the graft, showing the location of the induced accessory neural tube. *d* Section at level of the line *X-X'* in *c*. [*From Patten and Carlson, "Foundations of Embryology," McGraw-Hill, 1974.*]

Figure 12.13 *a* Implantation of the margin of the blastopore lip from an early gastrula (head inductor) into another of the same age causes development of a secondary head (above). *b* The margin of the blastopore lip of a late gastrula (trunk inductor) induces a secondary trunk and tail when implanted in an early gastrula. [*Courtesy of L. Saxén and S. Toivonen.*]

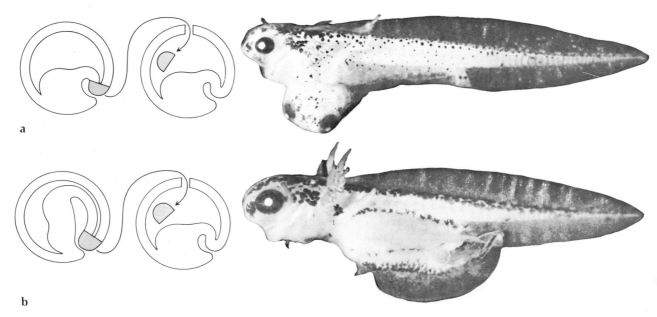

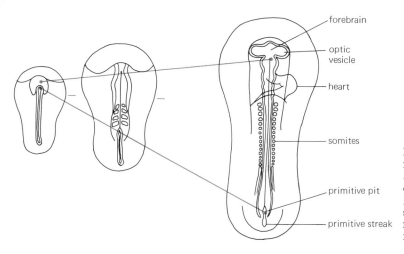

Figure 12.14 General relationship of the regressing node center to the elongating axial parts of the chick embryo. Time increases from left to right in the diagrams. Note the more rapid and extensive regression of the primitive streak relative to marked areas lying lateral to it. [*After Spratt, 1946.*]

forebrain
optic vesicle
heart
somites
primitive pit
primitive streak

primitive streak. That is, as the streak shortens, the node persists as a center of activity comparable with the amphibian dorsal lip.

When the primitive streak is at its original full length, the presumptive notochord is situated in the mesoderm in and around the node. The notochord with the remainder of the embryonic axis differentiates immediately in front of the node and is continuously added to posteriorly as the node retreats (Fig. 12.14). In amphibians the presumptive chordamesoderm is laid out *in situ* beneath the presumptive neural plate during the process of invagination and archenteron formation; in the chick and other amniotes the laying down of the chordamesoderm has become separated from the main events of gastrulation.

The problem posed by embryonic induction is complex. Whatever the nature of inductive agents in the inductor tissue may be, the result of any induction is affected by the location of the reacting tissue as well as by that of the inducer. For instance, transplants of posterior archenteron roof tissue of the amphibian gastrula, the so-called tail organizer, induce tail structure when implanted in posterior regions of another gastrula; they induce a secondary head when inserted in the anterior region. In the chick, however, the situation is different. There is no evidence that grafts taken from the posterior end of the primitive streak can induce a trunk or tail.

The success of operative experiments of the kind we have been discussing has depended greatly on technical progress. An amphibian embryo that has received a graft will survive—if not otherwise injured and under suitable conditions—even beyond the stage of hatching. In the beginning, however, it took many years for Spemann to perfect the technical operational skill of grafting fragments from the dorsal lip of one embryo to the flank of another, and to train his students accordingly. In chick embryos the problem has been even greater because such experiments are virtually impossible in the intact egg, and chick embryos removed from the egg rarely live for more than a day. New methods have therefore had to be developed. One of these combines ectoderm and mesoderm from different levels of the chick blastoderm and grows them as sandwiches within the coelomic cavity of older embryos. Another overcomes the difficulty of working within the egg by taking grafts of Hensen's node from full-length primitive-streak blastoderms. The grafts are inserted beneath the ectoderm of blastoderms of the same age lying *in situ* on the yolk.

In both sets of experiments, forebrain, midbrain, and hindbrain were induced. From these and other experiments, the conclusion was reached that the

277
Neurulation and
Induction
node is initially a head organizer, but as it retreats it becomes successively a trunk and then a tail organizer. (Compare with amphibian blastopore in Fig. 12.13.) In other words, the differences in the regional character of the induced neural tissue are to a large extent dependent on the position of the node (Fig. 12.14).

Chordamesoderm for all regions derives entirely from the node; i.e., it was part of the node at an earlier stage. Moreover, both the node and the anterior end of the streak possess a certain autonomy. If the node and anterior streak are cultured either in vitro or on the chorioallantoic membrane, the node will regress down the streak and an embryonic axis will differentiate. This whole process, however, is very poorly understood. Yet it holds the key to so much that is characteristic of the development of the higher vertebrates. It is frustrating that the process and consequences of node activity are phenomena normally hidden from direct observation and analysis by confinement within a shelled egg or an inaccessible womb.

Competence

Competence is defined as the physiological state or capacity of a tissue that permits it to react in a morphogenetically specific way to determinative stimuli. Whatever it may be, competence is always related to particular stimuli and particular corresponding responses. With regard to primary induction, therefore, we may speak of neural differentiation as a *primary competence* of the ectoderm.

It has long been known that ectoderm of amphibian embryos transplanted from various developmental stages from blastula to early neurula gradually loses neural competence. As the ectoderm ages it gradually loses its capacity to respond to the inductive stimulus of the chordamesoderm by becoming neural tissue. Similarly dorsal-lip tissue transplanted under ventral ectoderm at various stages of development shows that neural competence of nonneural ectoderm drops sharply near the end of gastrulation and is lost by the onset of neurulation. Isolated ectoderm unexposed to neural induction and ectoderm exposed to a neural inducer at too late a stage differentiate into epidermis.

The decrease in neural competence with aging of the tissue has been tested by isolating fragments of gastrula ectoderm, maintaining them in isolation for various lengths of time, and then transplanting them into different locations in a neurula where various strong inductors are present. Competence to form brain structures markedly decreases at an age corresponding to the late gastrula stage of control embryos. Ectoderm corresponding to the late neurula stage is completely without neural competence; yet the two neural-crest derivatives, namely, mesenchyme and pigment cells, can still be evoked in ectoderm of the tail-bud stage. Older ectoderm, already differentiating as epidermis, is entirely without competence to do anything but proceed toward its intrinsic epidermal destiny.

At the same time, the aging of the ectoderm does not merely restrict its neural competence; it can also bring about new responsiveness not present before. This is known as *secondary competence*. Late neurula epidermis, no longer convertible into neural tissue, becomes competent to respond to other inductors. Under the influence of eye vesicle, hindbrain, and forebrain, respectively, it differentiates into lens, ear vesicle, and nasal pits during postneurula stages of development. Successive states of competence appear synchronously with the succession of primary and secondary inductors (Fig. 12.15).

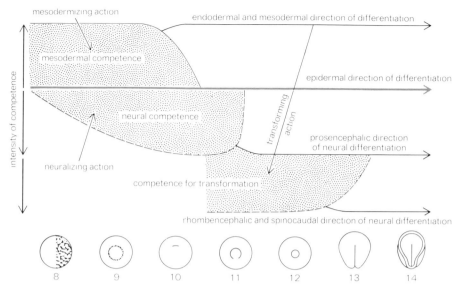

Figure 12.15 Diagrammatic presentation of the successive phases of competence for, respectively, endodermal and mesodermal differentiation, prosencephalic neural differentiation, and rhombencephalic and spinocaudal neural differentiation of the presumptive ectoneuroderm. In the absence of any inductive action, the ectoderm develops exclusively in an epidermal direction. On the abscissa, stages are given according to Harrison. [*After Gebhardt and Nieuwkoop,* J. Embryol. Exp. Morphol., **12** (*1964*).]

THE PROBLEM: CHEMICAL NATURE OF INDUCTION

The discovery of the primary-inductor quality of the dorsal lip of the amphibian blastopore, the "organizer" of Spemann, led to concerted attempts by teams of embryologists and biochemists throughout the 1930s to identify its chemical nature. Sterols, protein, nucleoprotein were all implicated. The massive effort faded before the indigestible discoveries that whereas the only live tissue that could evoke primary embryonic structures was dorsal-lip material, almost any tissue from the whole animal kingdom could do so if killed, i.e., denatured, by heat or alcohol (Fig. 12.16). Finally inorganic agents such as iodine and kaolin, and then even local mechanical injury, were found to be effective. All that

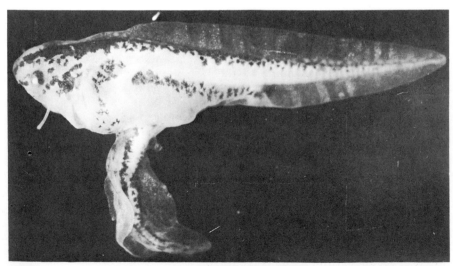

Figure 12.16 Implantation of a piece of alcohol-treated guinea pig kidney tissue into the blastocoel of a gastrula induces tail outgrowth with myotomes, notochord, and spinal cord. [*Courtesy of L. Saxén and S. Toivonen.*]

remains of the early grand concept of a master-chemical embryonic organizer is Holtfreter's sublethal cytolysis, namely, the idea that reversible cell injury liberates the neural inductor. In all cases membrane destruction occurs. However, the main outcome of this early search for the chemical nature of the organizer has been the view that the answer to the problem must lie in the tissues being "organized."

The inductor becomes an evocator. That is, it does not induce a pattern or a particular differentiation, but rather it evokes or triggers a particular response among the many that a cell or a sheet of cells may have in its repertoire. Responses are specific. Evocators of a given response may be widely diverse and may not be chemically related in any significant way to the event called forth, even though different responses may be made to closely related stimuli.

The analysis of chemicals capable of evoking preprogrammed responses is less dramatic than the search for inducing molecules that contain the information upon which the response is based. However, the determination of the nature of the chemicals that operate in vivo in carrying inductive messages from one tissue to another remains a major task in developmental biology. The search for the inducers has followed several avenues.

One of the problems apparent from the earlier work was the need to be certain that the response observed was a direct consequence of chemicals being released by the supposed inducing tissue rather than a nonspecific response to sublethal cellular damage. Toward this end, in vitro culture conditions were developed that would maintain small pieces of tissues in a healthy state for long periods to allow differentiation to take place. One of the key studies in this subject was that of Niu and Twitty, who continued the investigation of naturally occurring embryonic inducers. Using a hanging drop culture, they maintained a small piece of embryonic mesoderm in the drop for approximately 1 week. After this period a small piece of early gastrula ectoderm was introduced into the drop (either in the presence of the mesoderm or after its removal), and its fate was followed for the next several days. The result of this procedure is the differentiation of the ectoderm into branched pigment cells and neurons. Ectoderm placed into similar drops in which no previous inducing tissue has been growing does not differentiate. It appears that embryonic mesodermal tissue has released inducing substances into the drop that are then capable of stimulating undetermined ectoderm to differentiate, even after the mesoderm has been removed. No contact between the two tissues is required. The media in the drop has been "conditioned" by the inducing tissues. If the mesoderm is allowed to remain in the drop for a longer period (14 to 18 days) before the introduction of the ectoderm, muscle cells are also found among ectodermal derivatives. This latter observation suggests that the inductive specificity of the chemicals in the drop changes with the age of the inducing tissue.

Studies such as this provide information about the inductive process but little about the chemical nature of the substances involved. Chemical analyses cannot be performed on tiny pieces of tissue or small conditioned drops. Another branch of research on this topic has taken advantage of the findings that a variety of tissues, both embryonic and adult, are capable of causing undetermined ectoderm to differentiate along predictable paths. Guinea pig liver tissue, for example, acts as an archencephalic inducer (nose, eyes, forebrain formed) while guinea pig kidney is a spinocaudal inducer causing a predominant formation of trunk and tail structures. Two sources have been found of a mesodermal inducer that causes the formation of muscle, notochord, and kidney tubules, i.e., mesodermal structures. These latter substances are extracted from either 9- to 11-day chick embryos (by Tiedemann and colleagues) or from guinea pig bone marrow (by Yamada and colleagues). The advantage of the study of these nonembryonic (heterologous) inducing tissues is the opportunity to obtain large amounts of material with the capability of purifying and characterizing the active substances. The disadvantage is the uncertainty as to whether there is any meaningful relationship between these substances and those operating normally during embryonic induction (Fig. 12.10).

Analysis of the nature of heterologous inducers has been a subject of great controversy. Studies of the mesodermal inducing substances indicate they are of a protein nature; they appear in protein fractions upon extensive purification and their activity is destroyed by proteolytic enzymes.

The foremost proponent of a nucleic acid basis for inducing molecules has been Niu. In recent experiments, for example, he has tested the inductive potentiality of germ-cell RNAs, as compared with RNAs of somatic origin, upon postnodal portions of chick blastoderm at the definitive primitive-streak stage. Heart and kidney RNAs often induced cardiac and tubule differentiation, respectively, but rarely any neural differentiation; brain RNA induced neural differentiation but rarely any other. Germ-cell RNA (extracted from calf testis) induced what resembled a secondary axis. Niu has concluded that germ-cell RNA can alone evoke the whole range of embryonic axial differentiations.

In their stimulating book "Primary Embryonic Induction" (1962), Saxén and Toivonen summarized the chemical analysis of inductors as follows:

1   It has been shown that most of the inductively active tissues can be separated chemically into fractions yielding different inductive actions.

2   Correspondingly, chemical analyses have shown that fractions which yield archencephalic (forebrain, eye, nose) inductions are chemically different from preparations inducing spinocaudal (spinal cord, tail) or mesodermal structures (muscle, kidney, cartilage).

3   Some chemical or physical treatments of "combined" inductors (deuterencephalic or spinocaudal) will always destroy selectively the capacity to induce caudal structures, and following these treatments the tissues yield a pure archencephalic inductive action.

In 1968 L. G. Barth and L. J. Barth, long associated with the problem of primary-inductor analysis, clarified a different concept. In their own words: "While a wide array of unrelated chemical compounds and tissue extracts have been found to act as stimuli for induction of new cell types in the ectoderm of *Rana pipiens* gastrula, their primary site and mechanism for action are still unknown. A release mechanism as the basis for primary induction was looked for several decades ago in the form of gradients in energy-yielding systems within the early gastrula, and competition among the various regions of the gastrula. Current thinking tends to express the problem in terms of regional differential release of factors responsible for gene activation and derepression. The search now as before is directed, as we can see it, toward understanding how simple physiological factors, such as local change in ion concentration or pH, can alter energy-yielding systems and gene function in a manner meaningful for cellular differentiation."[1]

Their own working hypothesis is that the actual process of induction may be initiated by release of ions from bound form, representing a change in ratio

[1] L. G. and L. C. Barth, The Sodium Dependence of Embryonic Induction, *Develop. Biol.,* **20**:236 (1967).

between bound to free ions within the cells of the early gastrula. Experimentally, induction of nerve and pigment cells in small aggregates of prospective (presumptive) epidermis of the frog gastrula has been found to depend on the concentration of the sodium ion, that is, in the absence of other tissue; also, normal induction of nerve and pigment cells by mesoderm in small explants from the dorsal-lip and lateral marginal zones of the early gastrula is dependent on the external concentration of sodium. Nerve and pigment cells are induced when the culture medium contains 0.088 M NaCl; at 0.044 M NaCl the mesoderm differentiates into muscle and mesenchyme but nerve and pigment cell induction does not occur The interpretation is that normal embryonic induction depends on an endogenous source of ions and that an intracellular release of such ions occurs during late gastrulation.

Cations Li^+, Na^+, or Ca^{2+} all can induce differentiation of neurons from presumptive epidermis. Such neurons can be further induced to differentiate into pigment cells by later treatment with the same ions. In fact, three types of neurons or pigment cells are produced by sequential inductions. Ectodermal cells cultured in vitro must be treated with an ion that can trigger them to become neurons before they are competent to become pigment cells, although the same inducer (such as lithium ions) can effect both inductions. Moreover, great changes in concentration and proportions of cations occur in vivo during inductions of nervous tissue.

Transplantation of tissues between different genera and even orders of amphibians demonstrates the complexity of the interacting system of inductors, fields, and, in this procedure, genetic competence. These experiments exploit certain morphological differences between various amphibian larvae. Most salamander larvae possess a pair of rodlike temporary lateral head structures known as *balancers,* each consisting of a core of cartilage covered by epidermis. Anuran tadpole larvae have no such structure but do possess a pair of purely epidermal adhesive suckers below the mouth. If competent frog ectoderm, from a site remote from the ventral suckers, is grafted to a site on a salamander embryo corresponding to the sucker location of the frog, an epidermal sucker develops. Conversely, if competent salamander ectoderm, on a site remote from the balancer location, is grafted to a site on a frog embryo corresponding to the balancer location of the salamander, a balancer develops. In each case the transplanted tissue responds to *a position* on the host embryo and develops the structure appropriate to that position as though the host were of the same species as itself, although in each case the host cannot develop such a structure. It is as though the transplant says, "I recognize my new position but I must respond in my own way."

The guidelines are recognized by implanted tissue even from a different order, but the response is dictated by the specific genomic constitution of the explant. In other words, unstructured tissue recognizes position in the system; for example, it forms a balancer or not, or a ventral sucker or not, depending on whether the implant is urodele or anuran. Position, implying local specific circumstances, is recognized, but the positional properties as such do not carry the precise instructions for the formation of any particular structure. They merely enable a group of uncommitted cells to self-organize, or self-assemble, into one particular pattern of the many permitted by their genomic constitution. Wolpert (1969) has termed this guideline property *positional information*, discussed further in Chapter 24 in relation to *Hydra*. The persisting problem is the physical or chemical nature of the system supplying positional information; i.e., what cues of the environment do cells respond to? This may be approached both at the field phenomena level and at the cellular or molecular substrate level.

The concept of positional information is defined by Wolpert as that variable, whatever its nature, which is perceived by cells and which supplies at each point within a field a measure of *relative* position within that field. It is clearly derived from the morphogenetic field and gradient system concepts. At the least, however, it serves to focus attention on the main problem, which is the nature of the coordinating developmental system.

READINGS

BARTH, L. G., and L. J. BARTH, 1967. Competence and Sequential Induction in Presumptive Epidermis of Normal and Hybrid Frog Gastrulae, *Physiol. Zool.,* **40**:97–103.

—— and ——, 1968. The Role of Sodium Chloride in Cells of the *Rana pipiens* Gastrula, *J. Embryol. Exp. Morphol.,* **19**:387–396.

—— and ——, 1974. Ionic Regulation of Embryonic Induction of Cell Differential in *Rana pipiens, Develop. Biol.,* **39**:1–23.

BURNSIDE, B., 1971. Microtubules and Microfilaments in Newt Neurulation, *Develop. Biol.,* **26**:416–441.

CALLERO, J., 1971. Primary Induction in Birds, *Advan. Morphog.* **8**:149–180.

HOLTFRETER, J., 1968. Mesenchyme and Epithelia in Inductive and Morphogenetic Processes, in Fleischmajer (ed.), "Epithelial-Mesenchymal Interactions," Williams and Wilkins.

—— and V. HAMBURGER, 1955. Embryogenesis: Amphibians, in B. H. Willier, P. A. Weiss, and V. Hamburger (eds.), "Analysis of Development," Saunders.

KARFUNKEL, P., 1972. The Activity of Microtubules and Microfilaments in Neurulation in the Chick, *J. Exp. Zool.,* **181**:289–302.

——, 1971. The Role of Microtubules and Microfilaments in Neurulation in *Xenopus, Develop. Biol.,* **25**:30–56.

LEE, H., and M. C. NIU, 1973. Studies on Biological Potentiality of testis-RNA, in M. C. Niu and Segal (eds.), "The Role of RNA in Reproduction and Development," North-Holland Publishing Company.

NIEUWKOOP, P. D., 1973. The "Organization Center" of the Amphibian Embryo: Its Origin, Spatial Organization, and Morphogenetic Action, *Advan. Morphog.,* **10**:1–39.

NIU, M. C., and V. C. TWITTY, 1953. The Differentiation of Gastrula Ectoderm in Medium Conditioned by Axial Mesoderm, *Proc. Nat. Acad. Sci. U.S.,* **39**:985–989.

SAXÉN, L., and S. TOIVONEN, 1962. "Primary Embryonic Induction," Prentice-Hall.

SCHROEDER, T. E., 1973. Cell Constriction: Contractile Role of Microfilaments in Division and Development, *Amer. Zool.,* **13**:949–960.

SPEMANN, H., 1938. "Embryonic Development and Induction," Yale University Press (reissued 1968).

—— and H. MANGOLD, 1924. Induction of Embryonic Primordia by Implantation of Organizers from a Different Species, in English translation, in B. H. Willier and J. M. Oppenheimer (eds.), "Foundations of Experimental Embryology," 1964, Prentice-Hall.

TARIN, D., 1971. Histological Features of Neural Induction in *Xenopus laevis, J. Embryol. Exp. Morphol.,* **26**:543–570.

TIEDEMANN, H., 1967. Biochemical Aspects of Primary Induction and Determination, in R. Weber (ed.) "The Biochemistry of Animal Development," vol. 2, Academic Press.

WESTON, J. A., 1970. The Migration and Differentiation of Neural Crest Cells, *Advan. Morphog.,* **8**:41–110.

WOLPERT, L., 1969. Positional Information and the Spatial Pattern of Cellular Differentiation, *J. Theoret. Biol.,* **25**:1–47.

YAMADA, T., 1962. The Inductive Phenomenon as a Tool for Understanding the Basic Mechanism of Differentiation. *J. Cell. Comp. Physiol.,* **60** (suppl.): 49–64.

Organogenesis

Organogenesis begins with the neurula stage in amphibians and other lower vertebrates. The neurula stage ends with the closure of the anterior and posterior neuropores and the fusion of the ectodermal (presumptive epidermal) sheet above the neural tube. In higher vertebrates the neurula state is reached at different times along the embryo's anteroposterior axis.

VISUALIZATION OF THE EMBRYO

It is difficult to visualize the entire ongoing development even during gastrulation and neurulation, because we are confronted during each phase with a three-dimensional organization of cells and tissues that changes continuously. Postneurula development becomes increasingly complex, and four-dimensional visualization (three spatial dimensions plus time) calls for both concentration and practice. Cinematography is a great aid. For example, in films on salamanders and on fish, weeks of continuous development, from egg to feeding larva, are condensed to 40 minutes. A brief description of the external form of early amphibian development must suffice here. We must emphasize, however, that the developmental changes are all part of a continuing process. Dividing this process into time or structure stages such as blastula, gastrula, neurula, and postneurula is arbitrary and more a convenience than a reflection of the evident quality of flow of the entire phenomenon.

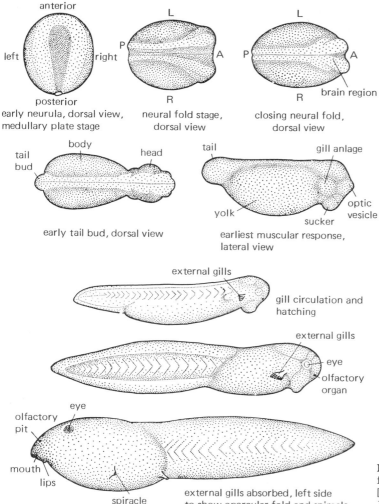

anterior

left — right

posterior

early neurula, dorsal view, medullary plate stage

L

P — A

R

neural fold stage, dorsal view

L

P — A

R

brain region

closing neural fold, dorsal view

tail bud

body

head

early tail bud, dorsal view

tail

gill anlage

yolk

sucker

optic vesicle

earliest muscular response, lateral view

external gills

gill circulation and hatching

external gills

eye

olfactory organ

olfactory pit

eye

mouth

lips

spiracle

external gills absorbed, left side to show opercular fold and spiracle

Figure 13.1 Postneural development of frog, from neurula to second-stage tadpole. [*From R. Rugh, "The Frog," McGraw-Hill, 1953.*]

Perhaps the most obvious change, beginning with the onset of neurulation and extending long into postneurula development, is the elongation of the embryo. The amphibian neurula, at first almost spherical, elongates along its anteroposterior axis (Fig. 13.1). With further development the anterior region of the embryo protrudes as the head, while a small tail bud forms at the posterior end. During this period various internal developments are visible as external prominences, in particular the bulging of the optic vesicle and gill rudiment on each side of the head (Fig. 13.1).

The harmonious flow or progression of developmental change, however, can only be observed in a superficial way. The related internal events cannot be observed directly. They require disassembly and reassembly to be understood even in terms of anatomic description, as though one were taking a watch or engine apart and putting it together again to know what has to be explained. A three-dimensional picture of a complex embryo is usually obtained by cutting the embryo into a series of two-dimensional sections, studying them individually, and putting them together again mentally or graphically. Embryos may be

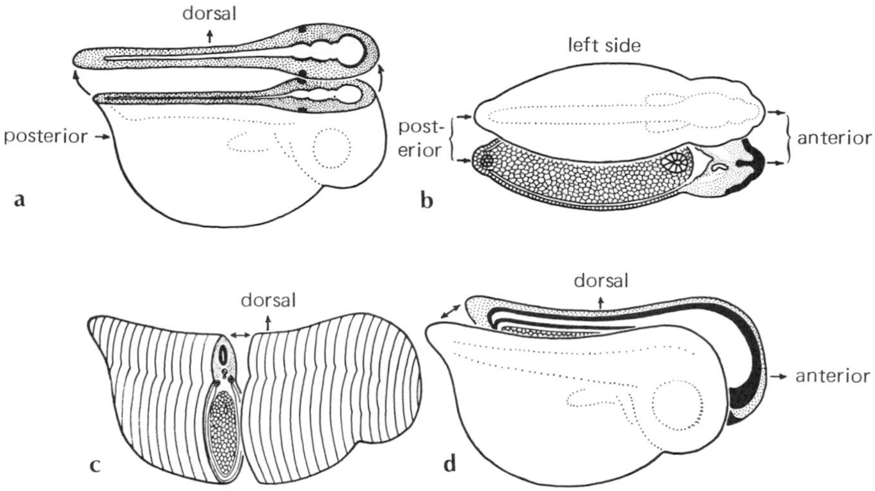

Figure 13.2 Planes in which the embryo may be cut or sectioned, showing the shape and internal structure of the early postneurula stage of the frog embryo: *a* lateral view of frontal section; *b* dorsal view of frontal section; *c* lateral view of transverse serial section; *d* lateral view of sagittal section. [*From R. Rugh, "The Frog," McGraw-Hill, 1953.*]

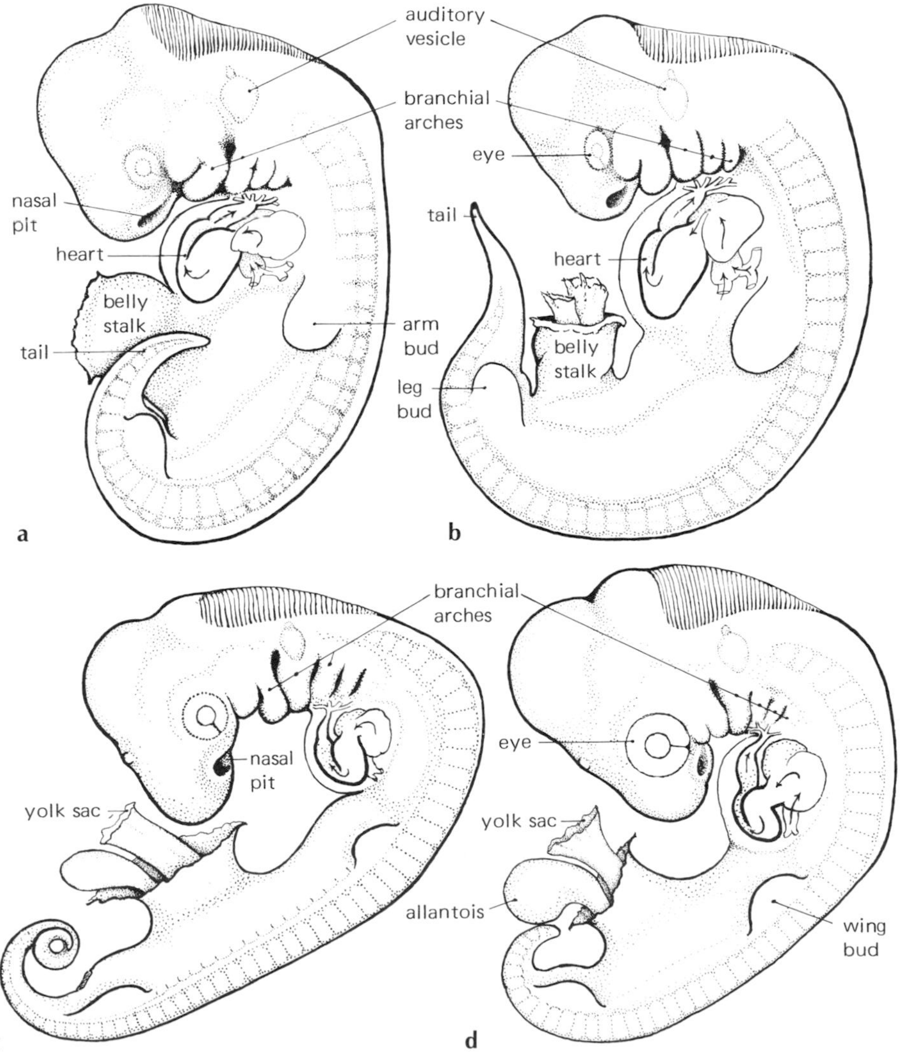

Figure 13.3 Embryos of (*a*) man, (*b*) pig, (*c*) reptile, and (*d*) bird at corresponding developmental stages. The striking resemblance of the embryos to one another indicates the fundamental similarity of the processes involved in their development. [*From William Patten, "Evolution," Dartmouth College Press, Hanover, N.H., 1922.*]

sliced in any one of the three spatial dimensions to yield a series of frontal, transverse, or sagittal sections (Fig. 13.2). This tedious process becomes more so as embryos are examined at successively later stages. The problem is not conceptual but is simply the need to visualize happenings not directly observable. We have already had a comparable example in the vital-staining experiments with eggs and blastulas to discern various cell shiftings otherwise difficult to detect.

The primary differentiation of the embryo into ectodermal, mesodermal, and endodermal regions represents fieldlike distributions of corresponding territorial tendencies already existing in the blastula. The differentiation tendencies for notochord, originally distributed over a wider area than the presumptive rudiment, are gradually restricted to the later rudiments. Somite mesoderm develops on both sides of the notochord. The presumptive nephric rudiments appear lateral to the somitic mesoderm, and lateral and ventral portions of the mesodermal mantle give rise to lateral plate and, in the chick, to blood islands, respectively. Each of these structures is believed to form within a certain range of intensity of the influence from the notochordal rudiment. Several of these structural components again show a differentiation into smaller units.

Altogether the developmental process clearly exhibits progression from the general to the particular (epigenesis). This is seen in the overall appearance of advanced embryos of higher vertebrates, namely, reptiles, birds, and mammals (Fig. 13.3). They are remarkably alike even though they become widely different in final form.

THE POSTNEURULA EMBRYO

The Brain

In amphibians and other vertebrates the brain is the first major organ to differentiate into distinctive parts. The rudimentary brain, consisting of the large anterior end of the neural tube, becomes somewhat constricted into forebrain (*prosencephalon*), midbrain (*mesencephalon*), and hindbrain (*rhombencephalon*). The last merges posteriorly with the spinal cord. The cavities are known as the *diocoel, mesocoel, rhombocoel,* and *neurocoel*. This may be seen in the amphibian embryo in Fig. 13.4*a* and in the chick embryo in Fig. 13.4*b*. It is followed almost immediately, or is even accompanied, by local evaginations demarcating the optic rudiment on each side of the forebrain, together with the epiphysis (pineal body) from the roof of the midbrain and the infundibulum (pituitary component) from its floor. These three evaginations (one paired and two median) result in a segregation of prospective specializing tissues of greatly different territorial dimensions (Fig. 13.4*b*). The developmental sequence is again from the general to the particular, not only with regard to regional territorial limits but in relation to emergent localized cytochemical differentiations.

Lateral-plate Mesoderm

Simultaneously with this early appearance of pattern in the neural system, the mesodermal sheet of each side of the embryo extends laterally and downward toward the midventral region as the *lateral plate*. It splits into an outer, somatic layer adjacent to the ectoderm and an inner, visceral or splanchnic layer close to the gut endoderm. The right and left parts of the somatic layer

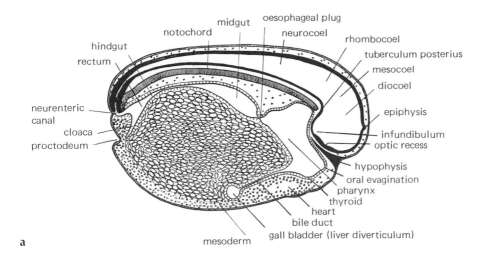

a

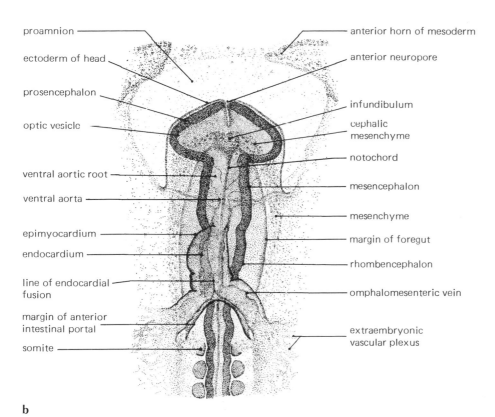

b

Figure 13.4 *a* Longitudinal section of 3-mm frog embryo. [*From R. Rugh, "The Frog,"*
McGraw-Hill, 1953.] *b* Ventral view of cephalic and cardiac region of chick embryo of
9 somites (about 29 to 30 hours incubation). [*From Patten and Carlson, "Foundations*
of Embryology," 3d ed. McGraw-Hill, 1974.]

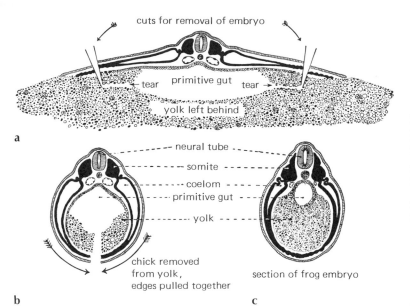

cuts for removal of embryo

tear — primitive gut — tear →

yolk left behind

a

neural tube

somite

coelom

primitive gut

yolk

chick removed
from yolk,
edges pulled together

section of frog embryo

b

c

Figure 13.5 Comparison of chick and frog embryo in transverse section. *a* Diagram showing how the usual method of removing chick embryos from the yolk in order to prepare them for microscopic study makes the sections appear as if the primitive gut had no ventral boundary. *b* and *c* show how removing a chick from the yolk and pulling its edges together ventrally facilitates comparisons with forms that do not develop with their growing bodies spread out on a large mass of yolk. [*From Patten and Carlson, "Foundations of Embryology," 3d ed., McGraw-Hill, 1974.*]

fuse midventrally as do the right and left parts of the splanchnic layer. The cavity between the two layers is the body cavity or *coelom*. The lateral-plate mesoderm, which lines the coelom, will form the peritoneum, pericardium, and pleura. The lateral-plate mesoderm also extends into the head region, ventral to the pharynx, as mesenchyme, i.e., as loosely connected cells. There it will form the connective tissue of the head. The situation is essentially the same in frog and chick embryos in spite of the development of the chick on the virtually flat upper surface of the yolk mass; this is in contrast with the frog embryo, which is able to enclose its relatively much smaller, yolky region. Figure 13.5 shows a comparison of equivalent stages of chick and frog, including the procedure for removing a chick embryo from its underlying yolk. Somatic and splanchnic mesoderm is also known as parietal and visceral mesoderm.

The Gut

In a comparable manner, in late neurula and early postneurula development in amphibians, the digestive tube also undergoes primary regional differentiation (Fig. 13.6). The endoderm invaginates to form the archenteron or primitive gut. At the anterior end of the elongating neurula, the adjacent anterior ectoderm invaginates as the stomodaeum and fuses with the anterior, blind end of the archenteron to form an oral plate of both ectoderm and endoderm. A proctodaeal invagination of ectoderm, or anal primordium, forms at the site of closure of the ventral part of the blastopore to fuse with the posterior end of the archenteron. A continuous digestive tube, eventually open at both ends after rupture of the oral and anal plates, is thus formed. It continues to develop more or less as a self-contained entity. It differentiates into various regional territories along its anteroposterior axis, primarily into foregut (pharynx), midgut, and hindgut, together with the stomodaeal and proctodaeal tissue at the two ends. This tissue exhibits epidermal histological characteristics as distinct from endodermal.

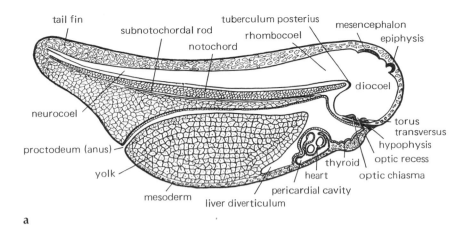

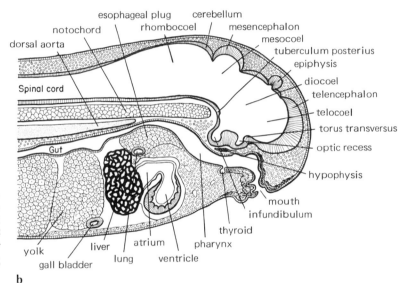

Figure 13.6 *a* Longitudinal section of 5-mm frog, showing differentiation of brain and gut with primary regions. *b* Development of the brain and anterior structures in 11-mm frog tadpole. [*From R. Rugh, "The Frog," McGraw-Hill, 1953.*]

A prominent liver diverticulum from the midventral region of the midgut appears almost immediately; it represents the major separation or segregation of the massive and specialized liver complex from the digestive tube. The pancreas evolves from the developing intestine at the same level as the liver diverticulum as three buds that fuse into a single glandular mass. At the same time a very small area anterior to the opening of the liver diverticulum begins to evaginate toward the midventral side of the embryo to become the thyroid gland.

At least in some degree the anteroposterior differentiation of the endoderm depends on external influences. Endoderm taken from the foregut, destined to become pharynx, differentiates as intestine if experimentally surrounded by posterior ectomesodermal tissue. Midgut endoderm grafted into the anterior ectomesoderm instead produces pharynx, together with other structures. Liver tissue rarely develops in other than its normal location. It seems probable that regional differentiations of the endoderm, as in neural structure, depends on the mesoderm.

289

The Heart

The heart is the first organ to become functional during embryonic development. Whatever the final shape and structure of the heart may be, the organ consists of three basic components: (1) the innermost lining, or *endocardium,* which is continuous with the endothelial lining of blood vessels; (2) the *myocardium,* or heart muscle; and (3) the *pericardium,* a tough cellular membrane enclosing the myocardium. In all vertebrates the heart begins to function when it is little more than a straight tubular structure.

In amphibians mesenchymal cells from each side of the embryo, close to the midventral wall of the pharynx, move together to form a midventral strand that will give rise to the endocardium.

In the amphibians the mesenchyme beneath the pharynx in the anterior region organizes into sheets that become continuous posteriorly with the lateral-plate sheets of somatic and splanchnic mesoderm. The split between these two layers in the trunk forms the coelom, i.e., cavity. Extending anteriorly into the heart-forming mesoderm, the split becomes the pericardial cavity. Three layers of tissue thus lie between the ventral pharyngeal endoderm and the adjacent ectoderm (Fig. 13.7). With further development the endocardial layer becomes an endothelial tube, while the two-walled epithelial mesoderm below folds upward around it. As these two layers meet above the endocardium, each layer on one side fuses with its counterpart on the other, thus producing two separate envelopes around the endocardium. The outermost remains epithelial and forms the pericardium. The inner layer, in contact with the endocardium, becomes the myocardium. The short, straight tubular heart then begins to lengthen.

In birds and mammals heart development is essentially similar; but as the result of the flattening of the amniote embryo compared with lower vertebrates,

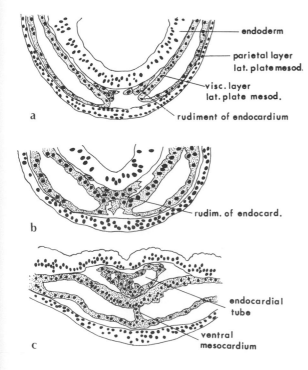

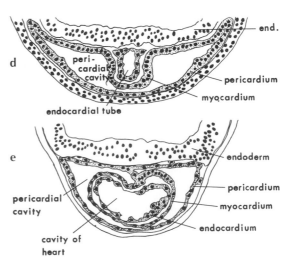

Figure 13.7 Development of the heart in amphibian embryos (urodeles). [*From B. Balinsky, "Introduction to Embryology," 3d ed., Saunders, 1970.*]

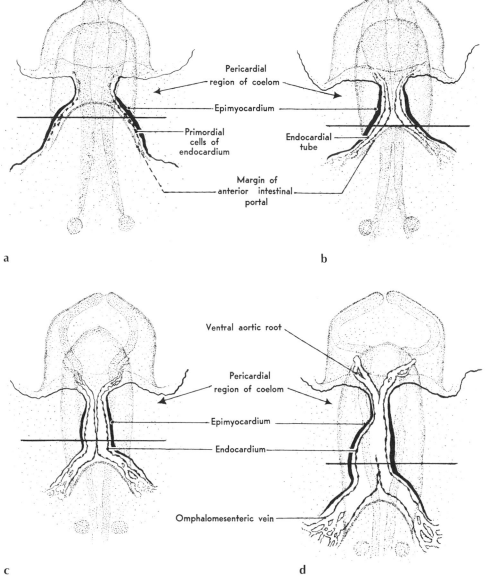

Figure 13.8 Ventral-view diagrams to show the origin and subsequent fusion of the paired primordia of the heart. Horizontal lines indicate successive stages of left-right proximation of endocardium and epimyocardium. *a* Chick of 25 hours. *b* Chick of 27 hours. *c* Chick of 28 hours. *d* Chick of 29 hours. [*From Patten and Carlson, "Foundations of Embryology," 3d ed., McGraw-Hill, 1974.*]

the developing heart not only is more amenable to experimentation, it shows its bilateral origin more clearly. As the embryo is completed ventrally, by folding-off processes, the paired primordia of the heart are brought together in the midline and become fused. Anteriorly and posteriorly they remain paired as the ventral aorta and vitelline vein, respectively. For heart and other ventral organs and tissues, this process is studied best by careful examination of a series of transverse sections in the laboratory. The chick heart begins to beat at the nine-to ten-somite stage, at first slowly and then rapidly. At this time the heart begins to loop outward toward one side. This folding of the heart into an S-shaped tube appears to be due in part to its growth in length between two fixed points within the less rapidly growing pericardium and in part to greater growth along one side of the tube than the other (Fig. 13.9).

The heart develops from a combination of a left and right rudiment (Fig. 13.8); but these rudiments are not fully determined. Early studies showed that if the two parts of the early chick heart are prevented from fusing by the insertion of a barrier, two hearts are formed. Similarly, if a lateral half is removed, the remaining half becomes a whole heart. Further, if one rudiment is surgically split lengthwise, each part becomes a whole heart complete with its own circulatory vessels. Almost any part or any combination of parts of the heart rudiment stage can form a functioning heart. An anterior half rudiment can do so, and so can combinations of two anterior half rudiments or of two posterior half rudiments. This is true also for the mammal.

Although the heart develops from a pair of rudiments uniting in the midventral line of the body, it is an asymmetrical organ with regard to its left and right sides. If the rudiments are prevented from fusing, so that two hearts develop, the left heart develops with the normal asymmetry whereas the right heart has a reversed asymmetry, a mirror image. This condition is known as *situs inversus*. A similar situation with regard to the left-right asymmetry of the whole abdominal region—i.e., heart, liver, and gut—is often seen in human identical twins, derived from one egg.

SEGMENTATION AND EMBRYONIC ELONGATION

One of the most outstanding features of vertebrate organization is the segmentation of the dorsal region of the body into a series of more or less repeating parts, in both neural and mesodermal tissue. During neurulation the lateral mesodermal sheets extend laterally and ventrally to fuse with each other in the midventral line of the embryo. Simultaneously the most dorsal portion of the mesoderm, at each side of the notochord, undergoes successive constrictions beginning anteriorly and progressing posteriorly to form a series of segmental blocks, the *somites* (Fig. 13.9).

Mesodermal segmentation, in conformance with accompanying neural segmentation, is also characteristic of two invertebrate phyla, the annelids and the arthropods. The unique feature in vertebrates is that the segmentation process affects only the dorsolateral band of mesoderm at each side of the notochord. The lateral-plate mesoderm on both sides of the body remains unsegmented even though it is still continuous with the segmenting tissue.

Segmentation of a neuromuscular system into a number of units acting in series appears to be a much more effective locomotor mechanism than a single extended muscle sheet system. The positive value of segmentation of certain portions of the body seems clear enough. In vertebrates the unique association of segmented and nonsegmented tissue throughout the length of the body combines advantages of both conditions. The locomotory apparatus is a highly differentiated segmental system, while the sustaining systems concerned with digestion, circulation, excretion, and reproduction are primarily those of the nonsegmented body. The renal system, deriving from the band of intermediate mesoderm between dorsal and ventral mesoderm, partakes in the embryo of both segmental and nonsegmental features.

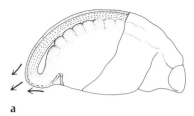

Figure 13.9 *a* Side view of postneurula of urodele showing somite formation (ectoderm removed in posterior
half of embryo) and outgrowth of tail bud, mainly by
tissue extension. *b* Chick embryo of 29 somites (about
55 hours incubation) showing caudal fold overlying tail
bud, together with differentiating brain, sense organs,
heart, and yolk blood vessels. Note that anterior portion
of embryo is twisted so that left side of head faces the
yolk and only the right side is seen. [*From Patten and
Carlson, "Foundations of Embryology," 3d ed.,
McGraw-Hill, 1974.*]

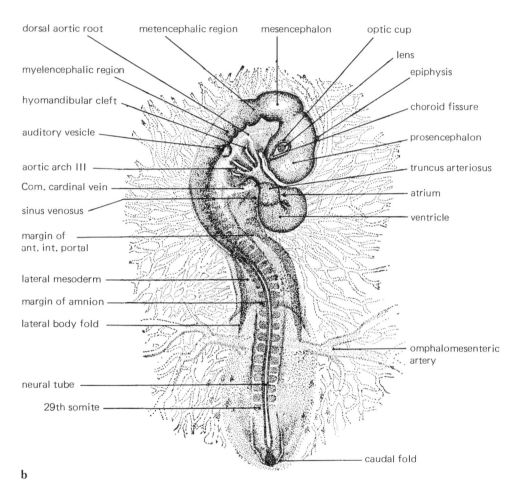

Somites

Somites are first formed as almost solid masses of cells derived from the
dorsal mesoderm. Progressive segregation is shown in Fig. 13.9. From the first,
the cells constituting a somite show radial arrangement. A central cavity appears and the radial orientation of the outer zone of cells becomes more definite. The central cavity is filled by a core of irregularly arranged cells shown by
radioautographic studies to arise from the somitic wall. Somewhat later the
ventromesial part of the somite loses its originally precise boundaries and

merges with the central core. This combined aggregation of loosely connected cells, i.e., now exhibiting mesenchymal character, extends toward the notochord from the somite of each side. It is known as the *sclerotome,* later to give rise to a segment of the axial skeleton. Four stages in somite differentiation are shown in Fig. 13.10.

During the formation of the sclerotome, the outer cell zone of the somite retains its firm outline and its more or less epithelial character. Part of this zone lies parallel to the ectoderm and is known as the *dermatome.* It contributes to the *dermis* (connective tissue layer), although this layer is known to receive cells from the somatic mesoderm generally.

The most dorsal part of the somite becomes the *myotome,* which shifts from its original position near the neural tube to a somewhat more ventral position. For a while the original cavity of the somite persists between the dermatome and the mytotome as the *myocoel.* The myotomes give rise to the skeletal musculature of the body with the exception of muscle tissue in the head and gill region, which develops from head mesenchyme.

The Trunk

Throughout the trunk and tail regions of vertebrates, segmentation clearly involves the spinal cord in addition to the mesodermal segmentation. Each pair of somitic segments and their derivatives is supplied by a corresponding pair of spinal nerves and ganglia. The question is whether the mesodermal segmentation induces the neural segmentation, or vice versa, or even whether both are induced by some external embryonic property. The question, however, is readily answered.

The neural crest is at first a continuous column of cells along each outer side of the closing neural folds. From the start the neural-crest cells appear to have an intrinsic tendency to break up into small groups. The segmental localizations of these groups, which give rise to the segmental sensory ganglia and nerves, are determined by the segmental arrangement of the myotomes. Experimental removal or disarrangement of adjacent myotomes abolishes or correspondingly disarranges the segmental array of the ganglia.

The Head

A comparable relationship between mesoderm and neural components of the trunk almost certainly prevails during the development of the head. The situation, however, is complicated and confused by the varying degrees of fusion of the embryonic segments that together constitute the integrated entity we call a head. This developmental and evolutionary phenomenon, seen in vertebrates, annelids, and arthropods alike, presents a major subject for experimental analysis. Little has been done in this connection, although the regional patterning of brain and sense organs has received considerable attention (Chap. 15).

Notochord and Embryonic Elongation

The embryo continually lengthens during neurula and postneurula stages. In amphibians the lengthening of the notochord is considered the chief motivative force underlying the accompanying lengthening of the neural plate and dorsolateral mesoderm. This conclusion is based on the following considerations: (1) Isolated parts of the neural system fail to elongate. (2) Notochordal rudiments stretch and form elongated rods even if cultivated in vitro. (3) The notochord accordingly changes its shape actively, whereas the neural plate or tube is pulled in length by the adjacent notochord.

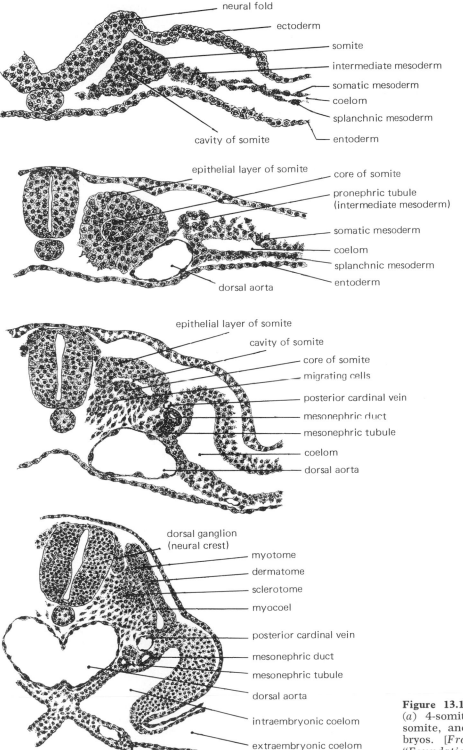

neural fold
ectoderm
somite
intermediate mesoderm
somatic mesoderm
coelom
splanchnic mesoderm
entoderm
cavity of somite

epithelial layer of somite
core of somite
pronephric tubule
(intermediate mesoderm)
somatic mesoderm
coelom
splanchnic mesoderm
entoderm
dorsal aorta

epithelial layer of somite
cavity of somite
core of somite
migrating cells
posterior cardinal vein
mesonephric duct
mesonephric tubule
coelom
dorsal aorta

dorsal ganglion
(neural crest)
myotome
dermatome
sclerotome
myocoel
posterior cardinal vein
mesonephric duct
mesonephric tubule
dorsal aorta
intraembryonic coelom
extraembryonic coelom

Figure 13.10 Transverse sections of (*a*) 4-somite, (*b*) 12-somite, (*c*) 30-somite, and (*d*) 33-somite chick embryos. [*From Patten and Carlson, "Foundations of Embryology," 3d ed., McGraw-Hill, 1974.*]

Extension of the notochord is effected by the enlargement of the notochordal cells, through vacuolation, within a confining sheath enclosing the notochordial rod as a whole. In the protochordates (*Amphioxus* and ascidians) this process and circumstance cause the embryonic chordal cells to interdigitate until a column of single cells is attained. The thrust of the collective enlargement of the chordal tissue is accordingly linear, particularly toward the posterior end of the embryo. The situation is similar in the lower vertebrates; however, because of the greater size of the egg, embryo, and notochord, a number of vacuolating and vacuolated cells are present in a cross section of the notochord rather than a single-cell layer. The same extension mechanism holds for the embryos and larvae of amphibians. In amniote embryos, where a notochord is formed but its cells do not enlarge, body lengthening must take place through other means, such as by polarized cell proliferations or by tissue stretching that changes cell shape.

The Tail

The above considerations should be kept in mind in an examination of tail formation, in amphibian development especially. Whatever the mechanical basis of stretching may be, the embryo as a whole undergoes considerable stretching, particularly in its posterior half. Coinciding with this, a remarkable transformation of the posterior part of the neural plate and tube takes place; they elongate to a greater extent than the ventral part of the embryo. Since the hindmost end of the neural tube is attached to the blastopore, the neural tube becomes bent over and forward, whereby the apex of the bend becomes the tip of the *tail bud* (Fig. 13.9a). The neural tube is present in the tail bud as one tube above another, conjoined at the bud tip. These two limbs of the neural tube have very different developmental fates. The dorsal part continues into the growing tail as presumptive spinal cord. The other forms muscle tissue.

Vital-staining experiments with salamander embryos, however, show that the posterior one-fifth of the neural plate is destined to form segmental muscular tissue. Extirpation of posterior neural plate results in deficiencies in somitic mesoderm of the tail and hind end of the trunk. According to Ford (1948) the production of the tail by the tail bud does not depend on cell proliferation but is the result of stretching. The whole posterior trunk region from the tenth somite back is put in position by this stretching, with some eight or nine pairs of somites being added. The role of stretching in the process of mesodermal segmentation may be basically important. It is also notable that neural-tube formation does not necessarily imply prospective neuralization, since in the tail it forms muscle; nor, as in fish, is neuralization dependent on neural-tube formation.

In amniotes the rapid growth in the length of embryo coincides with the period of regression of the primitive streak. This growth is not due to contributions from the cephalic end of the primitive streak, as was widely believed, but to growth of the embryo in front of the streak. This was indicated in Fig. 12.14. In the chick, by the end of the second day, little more than the node and a very short portion of the streak remain. This remnant is the tail bud (Fig. 13.9b). At this stage there are about 24 pairs of somites. Nevertheless the posterior portion of the embryo anterior to the tail bud continues to extend. During this extension additional pairs of somites are added sequentially until about 50 have been formed. Both cell proliferation and tissue stretching are probably involved.

There are other questions apart from the intriguing ones about the presumptive fate of the various regions of a differentiating somite. The nature of the underlying process that results in the initial segmentations and the nature of the agency that determines how many pairs of somites will be produced remain unknown. Yet there are also minor problems. The formation of more or less repeating parts in an organism is a morphological event of very great value that has been exploited to its fullest extent in several animal phyla and in plants as well. The answers to these two questions—i.e., what determines the formation of segments and what determines the number produced—almost certainly are closely related. The problem has long been recognized, but only a few experiments have been performed on vertebrate embryos. One such experiment by Spratt, showed that if the area pellucida of the chick embryo is cut about 3 mm posterior to the primitive pit, somites fail to be formed in the posterior portion. This finding led him to conclude that such failure was due to severance of contact between prospective somite mesoderm posterior to the cut and an anterior "somite center" responsible for serial somite organization.

Another proposal has been that the notochord directly induces somites from presumptive mesoderm. Inasmuch as there are many reports of somite formation in notochordless embryos, while grafts of notochord merely induce a nonspecific clumping of cells, the notochord cannot be held responsible for segmental induction. Similarly, somite formation can occur in the absence of neural tissue, although claims have been made for a controlling role for neural-plate tissue.

The remaining concept is that of Bellairs, based on the results of experiments. In one set the blastoderm was transected across the presumptive somite region, leaving a very narrow strip of primitive streak (0.1 mm wide) attached to the posterior portion. The strip, which was made as narrow as possible to exclude possible "somite centers," was retained in order to promote regressive movement down the primitive streak. In most cases somites formed in the posterior piece; but in control experiments, where no part of the anterior primitive streak was included, regression did not occur and somites did not form. These and other experiments not only speak against the presence of somite induction centers; they support the conclusion by Bellairs that regression movements of the streak are essential for somite formation and that cell shape and surface properties, associated with a process of tissue stretching, are involved.

There are but few facts to go on. Somites on each side are formed one by one in a posterior direction, as though constricted successively from the front end of the unsegmented mesodermal band on each side of the notochord. Successively formed somites in a series are approximately the same size at the time of demarcation. The interval between the recognizable initiation of successive somites is also approximately the same throughout the succession. The existence of some kind of counting mechanism has been proposed to explain the precision in number produced in a particular species. The number of somite pairs produced is species-specific. This feature is associated, for instance, with the relatively small number of vertebrae characteristic of neck and trunk of amphibians, birds, and mammals and with the large number typical of snakes. The vertebrate embryo, however, is far from being the most conducive to an experimental approach to the segmentation phenomenon. Mesodermal segmentation is much more amenable to observation and analysis in annelids, especially in polychaetes. An understanding of the process, which is similar in principle to that of vertebrates, is more likely to come from studies of this material, particularly in the case of regenerative development.

Renal System

On each side of the body a band of intermediate mesoderm lies between the somite-forming dorsal mesoderm and the unsegmented lateral-plate mesoderm, which encloses the coelom and persists in part as continuous sheets. This intermediate zone is the *nephrotomic plate,* or intermediate mesoderm (Fig. 13.10). It gives rise to a series of segmental pronephric tubules, the *pronephros* (the most anterior and first-formed kidney unit in the vertebrate embryo). Later in development a second and more posterior series of excretory tubules is formed, the *mesonephros,* which will serve as the excretory organ of the embryo. In birds and mammals a third and even more posterior set develops, the *metanephros.* The pronephros is a functional organ only in some of the lower fishes, which never develop more posterior tubules. In higher fishes and in amphibia the pronephros degenerates and the mesonephros becomes the excretory organ of the adult. In birds and mammals the mesonephros also degenerates and the metanephros, the last to appear, becomes functional toward the end of embryonic life. Nevertheless pronephros, mesonephros, and metanephros together are a continuous series of segmental structures that develop in anteroposterior time sequence from the intermediate mesoderm of each side of the embryo in the higher vertebrates.

In each segment the nephrotome is the stalk of the somite. Each tubule arises as a solid bud of cells from this tissue. A cavity within each bud, at first continuous with the myocoel dorsally and the coelom ventrally, is the *nephrocoel.* The dorsolateral wall of each nephrotome unit thus formed becomes drawn out as a hollow tube. These will empty into a common duct on each side of the body, the *pronephric* or *primary nephric duct,* which later extends posteriorly as the *mesonephric duct* (Fig. 13.11).

The primary nephric duct is primitively a segmental duct, inasmuch as it originates by the junction or fusion of the distal extremities of the most anterior segmented nephric units in the most primitive vertebrates. This probably represents the evoluntionary origin. In most vertebrates, including some fish and most amphibians and amniotes, however, the duct arises as a thickening of the dorsal side of the intermediate mesoderm, which becomes folded off or delaminated. Once inaugurated in the region of the ninth to thirteenth somites (chick), the duct begins to extend posteriorly until it reaches the cloacal region. Evidence indicates that this elongation results from free terminal growth. As it grows, the nephric duct is joined by mesonephric tubules that appear later. Experimental evidence indicates that differentiation of the mesonephric units depends upon induction by the primary nephric duct (Fig. 13.12). This relationship certainly seems to be true of the metanephros. The ureteric bud or outgrowth, which arises from the posterior end of the nephric duct, clearly induces the formation of the numerous nephric units (metanephroi) constituting the chick and mammalian kidney. When the two components of a kidney unit (nephrogenic mesenchyme and a ureteric bud of the nephric duct) are separated by the membrane filter, inductive action still occurs, i.e., the signals or stimuli pass through the filter. In fact, the nephrogenic mesenchyme will still produce secretory tubules if pieces of the dorsal side of the embryonic spinal cord are substituted for the normal derivative of the mesonephric duct. This is a morphogenetic response, therefore, to an inductor that is not tissue-specific, just as primary neural induction in the early embryo is not tissue-specific. After

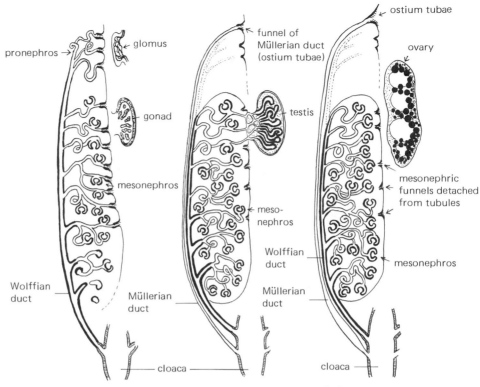

Figure 13.11 The transition from the indifferent stage of the urogenital system (*a*) into the male condition (*b*) and the female condition (*c*) in the frog. Note that the Müllerian duct is present in both sexes although it becomes functional (as the oviduct) in the female. [*From B. Balinsky, "Introduction to Embryology," 3d ed., Saunders, 1970.*]

Figure 13.12 Early development of renal structure. [*After A. L. Etheridge, J. Exp. Zool., 169:33, 1969.*]

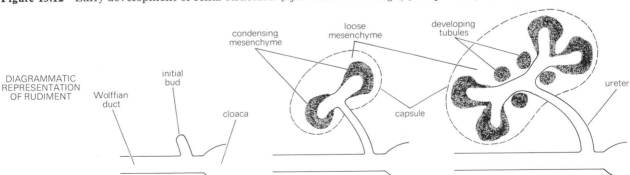

an initial response is made, continued exposure to the inductive agent is necessary to stabilize the event. This leads to the concept that a primary commitment, or determination, phase is followed by a secondary support.

Reproductive System

Eventually the nephric duct separates longitudinally into two ducts that relate to both the renal and the reproductive systems. The gonad—whether destined to become male or to become female—is represented at first by the *genital ridge*, an outgrowth of the viscera of the lateral plate, which projects into the dorsal coelom at each side of the midline. The ridge lies between the dorsal mesentery of the abdomen and the kidney rudiment on either side. The primordial sex cells, however, originate elsewhere, in the endoderm, in the frog, chick, and mammal. They migrate by means of ameboid movement and blood circulation. Primordial germ cells contain large amounts of alkaline phosphatase at a time when this enzyme is absent from other cells of the embryo. By means of a specific stain for this enzyme, the migration of the germ cells from this source into the genital ridges has been followed. Without the immigration of primary germ cells (when destroyed by radiation, e.g.), the gonads still undergo differentiation but remain sterile. In the chick, if a blastoderm whose germ area has been excised is joined in culture with a normal blastoderm in such a way that yolk-sac blood vessels anastomose, the gonads of the former will be colonized by the germ cells of the latter. With this remarkable technique it has been possible to form various chimeric gonads. Chick gonads, for example, have been populated by the germ cells of a duck.

Normally the primary germ cells become embedded in the epithelium of the germinal ridge, while the ridge thickens and bulges out toward the coelomic cavity (Fig. 13.13). This constitutes the outer *cortex* of the gonad. At the same time the dorsal side of the ridge hollows out and is filled by mesenchyme cells arranged in strands. These strands, or *primitive sex cords*, constitute the inner *medulla* of the gonad.

The gonad thus formed is the *indifferent gonad*, a stage that is the same in both sexes. Subsequently, in the male the primordial germ cells migrate from the cortex into the primitive sex cords, which become hollowed out and are converted into the *seminiferous tubules*. Spermatogonia arise from the primary germ cells, while Sertoli cells arise from the sex-cord tissue. The original cortex of the indifferent gonad is reduced to a thin epithelial layer covering the juvenile testis (Fig. 13.14). In the female the medulla of the indifferent gonad becomes reduced. The primordial germ cells remain in the cortex and greatly increase its thickness. Masses of cortical cells on the inner surface of the cortex divide into groups of cells surrounding a number of primary germ cells. These then become the primary oocytes. Primary germ cells nearer the surface of the cortex remain undifferentiated and serve as a reserve throughout the fertile phase of the female life span.

Proximity of the gonad to the renal organ has resulted in the exploitation of the nephric ducts as the means of conveying sperm or eggs to the cloaca. The longitudinal splitting of the primary nephric duct relates to this. That part of the primary duct associated with the pronephros—on the site thereof—survives as the *oviduct*, or *Müllerian duct*, and in the frog persists in both sexes. In the male the duct associated with the mesonephros, the *mesonephric* or *Wolffian duct*, performs double duty as ureter and sperm duct. Ripe sperm transfers to the sperm duct by way of small ducts connecting with the anterior mesonephric tubules (Fig. 13.11).

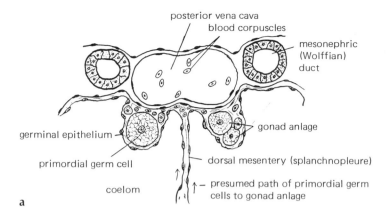

posterior vena cava
blood corpuscles

mesonephric
(Wolffian)
duct

germinal epithelium

gonad anlage

primordial germ cell

dorsal mesentery (splanchnopleure)

coelom

presumed path of primordial germ
cells to gonad anlage

a

Figure 13.13 *a* Gonad primordia (anlagen) in 11-mm frog tadpole, showing probable path of germ-cell migration [*After R. Rugh, "The Frog," McGraw-Hill, 1953.*] *b* Section through midbody region of chick embryo, illustrating the manner in which the primordial germ cells originate in the yolk-sac endoderm and migrate thence to the developing gonad. [*From Patten and Carlson, "Foundations of Embryology," 3d ed., McGraw-Hill, 1974.*]

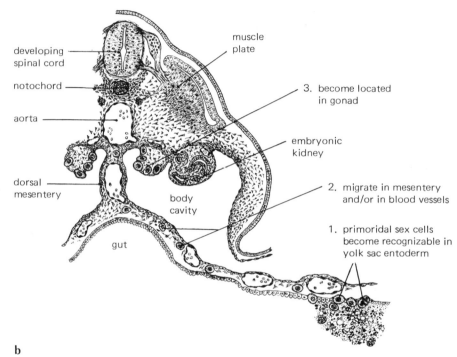

muscle
plate

developing
spinal cord

notochord

3. become located
in gonad

aorta

embryonic
kidney

dorsal
mesentery

2. migrate in mesentery
and/or in blood vessels

body
cavity

1. primordial sex cells
become recognizable in
yolk sac entoderm

gut

b

At the start of sexual differentiation the gonads are ambisexual, having the potentiality to develop in either the female or the male direction. The direction is controlled by the sex genes, associated with the sex chromosomes, which determine the predominance of either cortex or medulla of the primordial gonad. Every individual possesses, simultaneously, feminizing and masculinizing genes necessary to orient sexual differentiation, but in each case there is a prevalence of one or the other, a particular genic balance.

Various experiments with amphibians demonstrate, however, that the sexual form of the gametes (spermatozoa and oocytes) is not a necessary consequence of the genotype of the primordial germ cells but is the result of the nature of the gonadal territory in which they develop. In other words the cortex

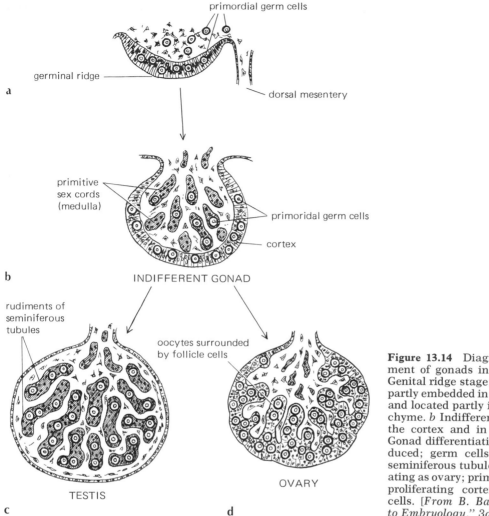

Figure 13.14 Diagram showing development of gonads in higher vertebrates. *a* Genital ridge stage; primordial germ cells partly embedded in epithelium of the ridge and located partly in the adjacent mesenchyme. *b* Indifferent gonad, germ cells in the cortex and in primary sex cords. *c* Gonad differentiating as testis; cortex reduced; germ cells in sex cords (future seminiferous tubules). *d* Gonad differentiating as ovary; primary sex cords reduced; proliferating cortex contains the germ cells. [*From B. Balinsky, "Introduction to Embryology," 3d ed., Saunders, 1970.*]

and medulla serve, respectively, as gynogenic (female) and androgenic (male) vector territories. Individuals (amphibians and fish) with a female genetic constitution can undergo spermatogenesis just as genetically male individuals can undergo oogenesis.

Treatment with the male hormone testosterone causes prevalence of medulla in developing gonads, with consequent spermatogenesis, while the female hormone estradiol or estrone causes prevalence of cortex, with consequent oogenesis, irrespective of the genetic constitution. A classical example is the so-called freemartin in cattle, analyzed long ago by F. R. Lillie, whose account is reprinted in "Foundations of Experimental Embryology." If a pair of twin cattle of opposite sex develop in such a way that there is fusion of their extraembryonic blood vessels and intermingling of the fetal blood, the male develops normally but in the female there is an extensive reversal of many sexual structures. Lillie's theory was that male hormones overcame the normal female sexual development. Whether a hormonal mechanism normally operates in connection with the primordial indifferent gonad remains uncertain. It is known, however, that the primordial germ cells play no part in the sexual differentiation of the gonads, since prevention of the germ cells from populating the gonad does not prevent differentiation of the gonad into cortex and medulla.

The differentiation of the reproductive ducts, mammary glands, etc., in mammals is better understood. During the indifferent or neutral stage of development, the primordial structures for both sexes develop together, independent of influences from the gonads. The Müllerian ducts (oviducts) can develop autonomously unless inhibited by male sex hormones. In a female, therefore, they proceed to form the adult reproductive tract. The mesonephric ducts on the contrary require the stimulus of male sex hormones in order to form the male reproductive tract. This occurs only after the male gonad has differentiated sufficiently to produce male hormone, which at the same time causes regression of the female tract. In a female, such hormones are absent and the mesonephric ducts regress.

AXIAL GRADIENTS

In the foregoing description of embryonic systems, we have drawn attention to a time sequence in the attainment of various stages of differentiation along the embryonic or anteroposterior axis. Head structure appears before trunk and trunk appears before tail. The sequence is always from head to tail and is especially evident in the serial formation of somites. Gradients of this kind are known as *axial gradients*. Once the process of axial growth in the posterior parts comes to an end—irrespective of whether such growth is cell proliferation, cell enlargement, or tissue stretching—the more recently established embryonic regions eventually catch up with the more precociously formed regions. In other words, the term axial gradient is purely descriptive of the differences in the stage of development of various structures located sequentially along the main axis. It reflects the stage of development at a particular time. It denotes only differences in the time at which some process begins, first becomes evident, or completes a certain phase of development; it does not indicate differences in rate of development. The term says nothing about the process underlying the lag in initiation time along the anteroposterior axis.

EXTRAEMBRYONIC STRUCTURES

Evolutionary changes in egg size, yolk content, egg envelopes, maternal association, etc., all have impact on the course of development. The developing system itself has to adapt to any changes that affect its circumstances. For example, a mass of condensed yolk in the egg in effect calls for the formation of an enclosing yolk sac during early development, so that the developing system comprises both an embryonic and an extraembryonic component. In fish, the yolk sac is the only extraembryonic structure. In terrestrial vertebrates, the extraembryonic structures consist of yolk sac (for enclosure of yolk), allantoic sac (for enclosure of waste material from the embryo), and amnion (for protection of the embryo within the confines of the shell) (Fig. 13.15). The terrestrial vertebrate egg is known as the amniote egg by virtue of the amnion, a unique structure.

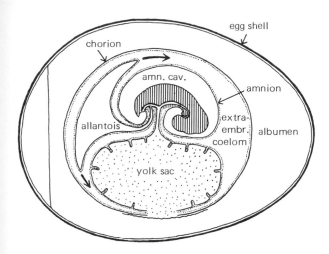

Figure 13.15 Egg of chick complete with shell, albumen, yolk, embryo, chorion, amnion, allantois, and yolk sac. [*From B. Balinsky, "Introduction to Embryology," 3d ed., Saunders, 1970.*]

The amnion forms in relation to the process that segregates the body of the embryo from the spreading yolk sac; this results in the appearance of a yolk stalk uniting the two, in fish as well as in amniotes. During this process in amniotes, the head of the embryo and, a little later, the tail each become covered by a fold of the ectomesodermal layer, which is external to the embryo proper and is continuous with the corresponding tissue of the yolk sac. These are the head fold and tail fold, respectively. With further development of the whole, the head and tail folds extend toward one another and fuse. Each fold is in effect a doubled layer of ectomesoderm. Fusion results in an outer layer of ectomesoderm with ectoderm facing the exterior, and an inner layer of ectomesoderm with ectoderm facing the embryo. The outer layer is the *chorion*, continuous with the external layer of the yolk sac, and the inner layer is the *amnion*. The space between the amnion and the embryo is the fluid-containing amniotic cavity or chamber. In humans, loose embryonic cells may be withdrawn by hypodermic needle during various stages of pregnancy and examined for sex and certain other genetically determined characteristics, a procedure known as *amniocentesis*.

During the development of all amniotes the allantoic sac, forming from the posterior end of the renal system like an everted bladder (Fig. 13.16), fuses with the investing outermost layer, or *chorion*, of the extraembryonic tissues to form the chorioallantois. This structure, richly vascularized, serves the embryo as the primary respiratory surface and the embryologist as an ideal site for the culture of transplants from other embryos.

In placental mammals the maternal system supplies all needs; there is neither yolk in the yolk sac nor accumulating wastes in the allantois. The chorioallantoic tissue together with the trophoblast constitute the *placenta* (Fig 13.17), which is united with the wall of the maternal uterus. The stalk of the allantois survives as the umbilical cord. It contains the blood vessels of the embryo, which supply the placenta, and returns the enriched blood to the embryo or fetus until birth do them part. The amnion persists unchanged from that seen in the chick as the fetal sac or membrane.

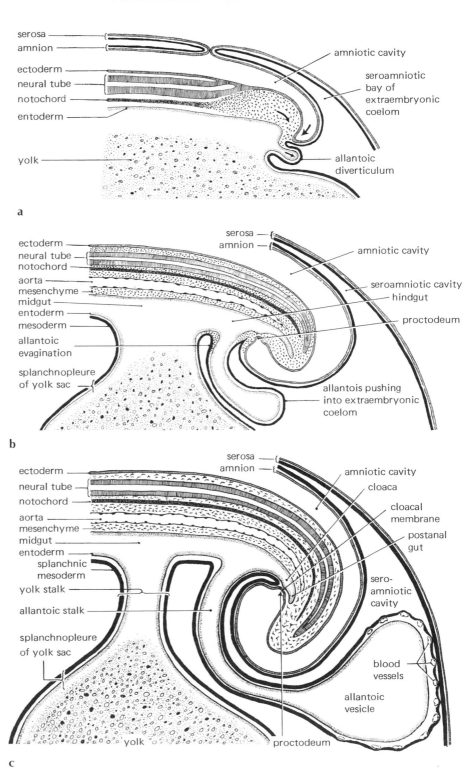

Figure 13.16 Three stages in diagrammatic sections of caudal end of chick embryos to show development on amnion and allantois. [*From Patten and Carlson, "Foundations of Embryology," 3d ed., McGraw-Hill, 1974.*]

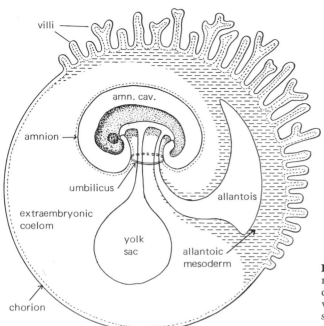

villi

amn. cav.

amnion

umbilicus

extraembryonic
coelom

yolk
sac

allantois

allantoic
mesoderm

chorion

Figure 13.17 Embryo and membranes of a placental mammal, showing placental development from fused chorion and allantoic wall, extending as fingerlike villi that interlock with uterine tissue. [*From B. Balinsky, "Introduction to Development," 3d ed., Saunders, 1970.*]

The amniote egg may be regarded as a remarkable evolutionary invention enabling development to proceed in a nonaquatic external environment. It primarily involves a massively increased yolk content and the confinement of the egg within a liquid-containing, nonexpansible calcareous shell impermeable to water.

READINGS

BELLAIRS, R., 1971. "Developmental Processes in Higher Vertebrates," Prentice-Hall.

DEHAAN, R. L., and H. URSPRUNG, (eds.), "Organogenesis," Holt, Rinehart and Winston.

FORD, P., 1950. The Origin of the Segmental Musculature of the Tail of the Axolotl, *Proc. Zool. Soc. London,* **119**:609–632.

JOHNSON, L. G., and E. P. VOLPE, 1973. "Patterns and Experiments in Developmental Biology," W. C. Brown.

PATTEN, B. M., and B. M. CARLSON, 1974. "Foundations of Embryology," McGraw-Hill.

SAXEN, L., 1971. Inductive Interactions in Kidney Development in "Control Mechanisms of Growth and Differentiation," 25th Symposium, Society of Experimental Biology, Academic.

WILLIER, B. H., P. A. WEISS, and V. HAMBURGER, 1955. "Analysis of Development," Saunders.

CHAPTER 14

Limb Development

The developing vertebrate limb has been intensively analyzed experimentally as a nearly independent interacting system of epithelial ectoderm and mesenchymal (loose mesoderm) components. The initiation stages have been studied both in salamander and chick embryos; tissue interaction has been more successfully analyzed in the developing wing of the chick. Reconstruction, or regeneration, of the differentiated limb has been mainly followed in larval and juvenile amphibians.

THE LIMB DISC

The first sign of a developing amphibian limb is a small mound of tissue on the flank at the site of a prospective limb. It consists of two primary components, namely an accumulation of mesenchyme cells overlaid by a cap of ectoderm. This disc of tissue is large enough to be subdivided, rotated, or transplanted before it develops into any sort of structure. The area involved, at least in amphibians, is circular and extends over 3½ somites in diameter (Fig. 14.1), although the mesodermal somites as such do not contribute to limb development. In a normally developed limb, which is a complex and asymmetric structure, the anterior and posterior sides are clearly recognizable, and so are the dorsal and ventral, corresponding to the anteroposterior and dorsoventral axes of the body. In addition the limb has a proximodistal organization. In the early stages of limb development, the form of the developing limb bud and the pattern of skeletal rudiments emerging within it are remarkably similar in all land vertebrates. The disc grows out to give an elongated stem region, slightly narrower at its base, and later an expanded distal paddle. The mesenchyme cells are uniformly distributed at first; they become locally condensed to produce the characteristic pattern of cell accumulations that give rise first to the cartilages and later to the bones of the limb.

The important questions concern the establishment of the several axial

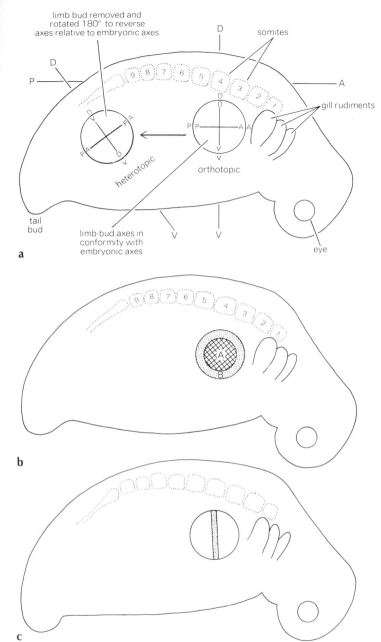

Figure 14.1 Experiments on limb-bud differentiation in salamander (*Ambystoma*) during tail-bud stage. *a* Transplantation of limb disc from normal (orthotopic) site to another (heterotopic) site. The limb differentiates normally. *b* Presumptive limb area (*A*) and limb field (*A* + *B*). If limb area is removed, peripheral-limb-field territory replaces it; if all of limb field is removed, no replacement occurs. *c* If limb disc is split and the two parts are prevented from re-fusing, two limbs develop. [*After F. H. Swett, 1937.*]

polarities, the nature of the limb disc itself in relation to its immediate surroundings, and the relative roles of ectoderm and mesoderm and their interaction. The pioneering experiments in this field were made by Ross Harrison during the first quarter of this century.

As in virtually all developing systems—even though limb rudiments first appear relatively late in the development of the embryo—the area of tissue forming the limb disc constitutes an equipotential system, as defined by Driesch in 1905. This was shown by the following experiments on the earliest limb-bud stage of the salamander (Fig. 14.1).

1   If half a limb bud is destroyed, the remaining half gives rise to a completely normal limb.

2   If a limb bud is slit vertically into two or more segments, while remaining an integral part of the embryo, and the parts are prevented from fusing again by inserting a bit of membrane between them, each may develop into a complete limb.

3   If two limb buds are combined in harmonious orientation with regard to their axes, a single limb develops that is large at first but soon is regulated to normal size.

The relation of limb polarities to those of the embryo as a whole is shown by inversion experiments. In these a limb-disc area was cut out, turned through 180°, and reimplanted; i.e., nothing was changed except that the anteroposterior and dorsoventral axes of the prospective limb were turned around. If these were fully determined at the time of operation, a limb should develop that is entirely normal except that it is turned backwards and upside down relative to the body. If there was no determination at this time, however, a limb should develop that is normal in every respect. In actuality a limb develops that is normal in that dorsal structure is still dorsal and ventral structure is still ventral, but anterior and posterior sides are interchanged. In other words, the anteroposterior polarity of the disc tissue was already established, presumably as part of the primary axial polarity of the embryo as a whole, but the dorsoventral polarity was still reversible.

PROSPECTIVE LIMB AREA AND THE LIMB FIELD

The first sign of limb-bud development becomes evident in the somatic layer of the lateral-plate mesoderm. At this stage the somatic layer is an epithelium; it becomes thickened where the limb bud will appear. Mesenchyme cells migrate from this area and sever their connections with the mesoderm, although the mesoderm never loses its own continuity as an epithelial sheet of tissue. The mesenchyme cells accumulate external to the lateral mesoderm. They become firmly attached to the inner surface of the epidermis, which in turn becomes slightly thickened as the result of cell elongation. In amphibians two pairs of limb discs appear from the first, separate from each other. In fish they are similar except for an initial extension along the anteroposterior axis of the embryo. In amniotes the combined epidermal-mesenchymal thickening extends as a horizontal ridge along each side of the body (the Wolffian ridges). The intermediate part of the ridge later disappears, leaving anterior and posterior regions as the definitive limb areas.

In amphibians, at least, limb-bud determination occurs very early indeed. If pieces of prospective limb mesoderm of the lateral plate are cut out very soon after the closure of the neural tube, and are then transplanted elsewhere under the epidermis of the head or the trunk, a limb develops, although in an abnormal site (i.e., heterotopically). The epidermis everywhere responds to the presence of the underlying prospective limb mesoderm and becomes the epithelial component of the limb bud. Experiments performed in the chick show that properties in the limb mesoderm responsible for the tissue interactions that lead to outgrowth and elaboration of complex limb form are transitory. They are lost at a definite stage in the process of active cytodifferentiation in a proximodistal sequence. These so-called morphogenetic properties are also lost at the same temperature-dependent rate when limb mesoderm cells are cultured in vitro and then tested for inductive activity.

Two terms have commonly been used with respect to the capacity of limb-bud territory to develop into a limb. In the salamander, if the *prospective limb area* and only that area is extirpated at an early stage—i.e., all the area that will normally give rise to the limb—a limb will still develop after a short delay. If, however, a somewhat larger circular area—i.e., an additional ring of tissue surrounding the prospective limb area—is included, no limb develops. In the first case, after extirpation of the prospective area, adjoining tissue moves in to replace it and the limb disc is reconstituted. In the second, the replacement tissue has also been removed. This larger area, which represents the whole prospective limb-bud potential, is called the *limb field*.

The term *field* may best be described by a collection of properties exhibited by a region of the embryo in which a particular tissue or organ will develop. A basic property of a field is the regulative power of cells to form the given structure in the periphery of the area. The individual parts (presumably the individual cells) possess some recognition of what is happening in other parts of the area. That is, they recognize their position within the whole. If the field is split or another field is added to it, the parts recognize the disruption as some change in information about their new position; they can respond accordingly. This is described by Wolpert as *positional information,* already briefly discussed. Another basic property of a field is the gradual, progressive nature of the determinations. In the development of a structure, there is an early period during which small parts are totipotent and can form the entire organ. Later their potency becomes restricted and they can form but a small part of the whole. The primary field has become subdivided into smaller fields. Eventually a point is reached where the parts are fully determined and therefore capable of forming only the structures they would have if left undisturbed. The problem is the nature of the mechanism whereby cells in the field recognize their relative position with respect to all other parts that will form other tissues of the final structure.

ECTODERM-MESODERM SYSTEM

The limb grows as a result of rapid multiplication of cells within the limb disc rather than by migration of cells or tissue from outside the disc area. The limb-forming material is clearly localized in the mesoderm (mesenchyme); no limb develops if the disc mesoderm is completely removed, leaving only the prospective limb ectoderm in place, nor does a limb develop where prospective limb ectoderm is transplanted to a new site. A limb does develop where prospective limb mesoderm is transplanted beneath ectoderm in other places (Fig. 14.1a). Limb mesoderm transplanted to the flank with a covering of flank ectoderm gives rise to a limb with normal asymmetry if the mesoderm is oriented with its anterior side forward. It gives rise to a limb with reversed asymmetry if the mesoderm is oriented with its anterior side facing backward. On the basis of these early experiments, the concept of mesodermal determination of limb development seems to be a good working hypothesis. Nevertheless, an assumption that the prospective limb ectoderm plays no important role is by no means justified. Isolated mesoderm from limb-disc stages cannot form limb structures in the absence of ectoderm.

The analysis of limb development and determination, in contrast with limb regeneration, has shifted over the years from amphibian material—in which limb rudiments although readily accessible are inconveniently small—to the chick. The chick offers larger territories to work with but has required more sophisticated techniques, mostly devised by Zwilling. His studies form the foundation for most of the modern work on limb development. The shift in attention has also been from the initial limb-disc stages to the more or less advanced limb bud.

THE ECTODERMAL RIDGE

In the chick the prospective mesoderm of the wing bud becomes finally localized at the two-somite stage. Grafting experiments show that the anteroposterior axis becomes determined at the 5-somite stage, the dorsoventral axis at the 13-somite stage. The limb-forming areas, however, do not become morphologically distinguishable until the 14-somite stage. The wing rudiment is represented at this time by a slight condensation of mesenchyme and a little later by a thickened ridge of ectodermal tissue, the ectodermal apical ridge (Fig. 14.2).

In the chick embryo the only tissue that seems to foster continued limb development is the ectodermal cover (apical ectoderm) of the limb bud. Neither ectoderm from other regions of the limb donor's body nor ectoderm from younger embryos seems capable of influencing the limb mesoderm so that it will complete its distal development. Apical ectoderm, in these experiments, has no other specificity than eliciting limb outgrowth; it does not influence the type of limb formed, i.e., leg or wing.

Ectoderm in early chick consists of an outer layer of flattened cells called the *periderm,* which degenerates before hatching, and a basal layer of cells resting on the basement membrane that covers the mesoderm. In the limb bud these basal cells are tall and columnar with wide spaces between except at the basement membrane. If the ectoderm is removed and cultured in vitro, the cells become mixed up in the operation and then rearrange themselves to re-form this typical structure. Apical growth of the wing in the chick embryo is suppressed when the thickened apical ectodermal cap or ridge of the limb bud is extirpated. Excision of this apical ectodermal ridge results in the development of partial limbs, lacking distal structures (Fig. 14.3). The amount of distal

Figure 14.2 *a* Chick embryo, stage 21. Limb buds appear as prominent swellings on the body wall. *b* Cross sections of chick embryos, stages 17 and 19, at the wing-bud level. There are differences in thickness of the ectoderm between ventral and dorsal faces of the wing bud. [*After R. Amprino, 1965.*]

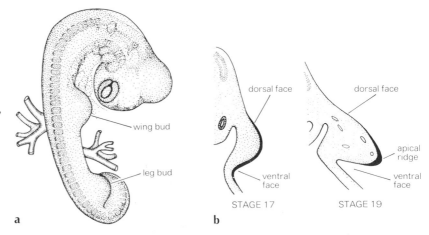

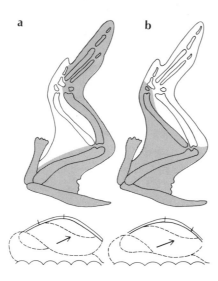

a

b

Figure 14.3 Effects on the development of the wing bud of the removal of (*a*) the cranial or (*b*) the caudal half of the apical ridge of ectoderm (lower schemes). Wing parts which form are shaded. *After J. W. Saunders, J. Exp. Zool.,* **108**:363 (1948).]

deficiency depends on the stage subjected to the procedure. Early limb buds, deprived of the apical ectodermal ridge, develop only girdle elements, humeral stumps, etc. (Fig. 14.4). Later limb buds are less affected. The ectodermal ridge is formed partly by cell proliferation but also by ectodermal cells moving distally up the limb bud over the mesoderm on its dorsal and ventral surfaces. These cells pile up at the apex to form a ridge in which the basal cells are compressed so that they become pseudostratified and are arranged fanwise in cross section. Saunders showed that only those presumptive regions destined to form the most proximal parts of the limb exist in the earliest stages; the remainder are added in proximodistal sequence as the bud grows outward (Fig. 14.5). He postulated that this sequential process depends upon an *inductive activity* of the thickened ridge of ectoderm at the apex of the bud.

The apical ridge, however, does not determine the axial level of the underlying mesenchyme. This has been demonstrated by Rubin and Saunders. They exchanged ectodermal caps between limb buds of different ages; each

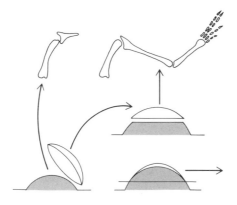

Figure 14.4 Induction by the apical cap. (*Left*) Differentiation of a limb bud after removal of the apical cap. Only the femur and a part of the tibia are differentiating. (*Right*) Graft of an apical cap on the basal part of the leg, after the distal half has been severed. The basal mesenchyme is induced by the apical cap to form the distal components. [*After A. Hampé*, J. Embryol. Exp. Morphol., **8**:247 (1960).]

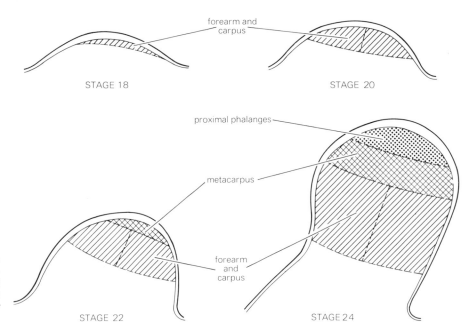

Figure 14.5 Maps of prospective wing segments in four embryonic stages. The apical ridge of the ectoderm is shown covering the mesodermal (shaded) tissues in each stage. [*After R. Amprino, 1965.*]

STAGE 18

STAGE 20

forearm and carpus

proximal phalanges

metacarpus

forearm and carpus

STAGE 22

STAGE 24

composite limb then developed into a normal limb. In terms of their model, the apical ectodermal ridge is needed to keep the mesenchyme labile at the tip but does not direct the path of progress there. The ridge issues a general permit rather than specific instructions. The level pattern specificity must therefore be programmed intrinsically within the mesoderm. This and other features of limb development are discussed at length by Wolpert and others, in connection with positional information in chick limb morphogenesis, in "Foundations of Experimental Embryology."

There is a difference in the behavior of ectoderm in the chick compared with amphibians. Ross Harrison showed long ago that ectoderm from any part of the body of a salamander embryo whose neural folds have not closed is capable of participating in limb formation. Ectoderm taken from the head of an embryo *subsequent* to neural-fold closure and placed over limb-bud mesoderm *suppresses* limb development. Up to the tail-bud stage, however, trunk ectoderm is still capable of participating in limb formation.

An apical ridge has been said not to exist in amphibian limb buds, although it has been described for mammalian limb buds. The scanning electron microscope, however, demonstrates its presence (Fig. 14.6) in *Xenopus laevis* (Tarin and Sturdee, 1971). The course of the ridge is consistently related to a marginal sinus in the underlying mesenchyme; other features of limb morphogenesis, such as formation of a paddle (Fig. 14.7) and the sequence of condensation of skeletal rudiments in the mesenchyme, correspond closely to those seen in other vertebrates (Fig. 14.12a). In chick and amphibian, the limb bud is at first equipotential. For example, if a wedge of wing bud is cut out and implanted into an incision in another wing bud of the same stage, a normal wing develops from the composite bud (Fig. 14.8); the donor tissue is integrated.

313

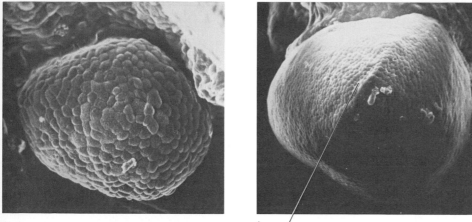

a

b

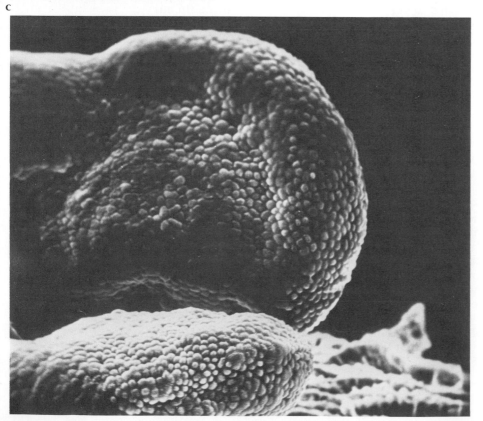

apical
ectodermal
ridge

basement
membrane

mesenchyme

c

Figure 14.6 Development of the apical ectodermal ridge during limb-bud development in amphibian (*Xenopus laevis*). *a* SEM (×4400) of apex preceding ridge formation. Note difference in dimension of the dorsoventral and anteroposterior transverse axes of the limb bud. *b* SEM (×1300) of apex of later stage with ridge well formed. *c* Section through same stage as *b*, showing thickened apical ridge ectoderm separated from underlying mesenchyme by basement membrane. [*Courtesy of David Tarin and A. P. Sturdee.*]

Figure 14.7 SEM of paddle stage of *Xenopus laevis*, seen broadside and edgewise. [*Courtesy of D. Tarin and A. P. Sturdee.*]

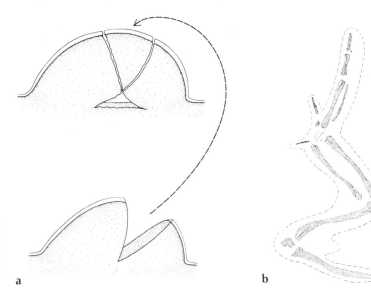

Figure 14.8 Chick wing bud. *a* Large wedge-shaped sector (arrow), isolated from a donor wing bud (*bottom*), and implanted into a host wing bud. *b* Normal wing developed from the composite wing bud. [*After R. Amprino, 1965.*]   a   b

ROLE OF EXTRACELLULAR MATRIX

In anuran amphibian embryos, mesenchyme cells of the prospective hind limb leave the lining of the coelomic cavity, migrate to nearby epidermis, and accumulate there to form the limb bud. In *Xenopus laevis*, about 40 hours elapse between the appearance of detectable limb mesenchyme and the formation of a semicircular limb bud. A basement membrane lies between the epidermis and the mesenchyme. It consists of a basal lamina and an organized network of collagen fibrils that constitute the basement lamella, to which mesenchyme cells add mucopolysaccharides. This complex of cells and fibers persists throughout most of the body, but beneath the prospective limb epithelium the extracellular matrix components undergo degradation and reorganization. This is followed by a closer connection of mesenchyme with the ectodermal epithelium and its associated basal lamina (Fig. 14.9). At the same time specialized junctions appear between the mesenchyme cells.

During the early stages of limb development, a continuous and uniform basal lamina is present beneath the limb epithelium. Filopodia (fine protoplasmic extensions) of mesenchymal cells establish intimate associations with the basal lamina, especially during the period of ectodermal ridge formation. In other words, degradation of collagenous lamellae permits direct association of mesenchyme cell surfaces (filopodia) with surface-associated products of epithelial cells (organized into the basal lamina). According to Kelley and Bluemink, if basal laminae and other components of extracellular material control interacting embryonic cells, as suggested by Grobstein and others, the observed contact between cell surfaces and the basal lamina may mediate intercellular signals having morphogenetic significance (positional information). Development of low-resistance pathways for intercellular ions and metabolite transport may functionally integrate the mesenchyme and coordinate events (such as cell division and changes in cell position specific to the spatial patterns that underlie morphogenesis in the amphibian limb).

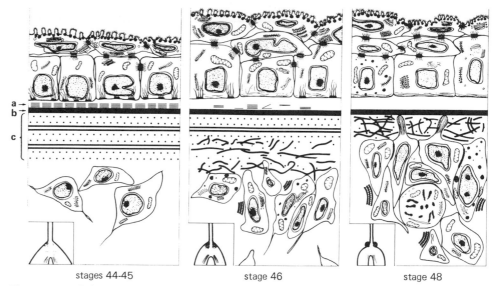

stages 44-45   stage 46   stage 48

Figure 14.9 Schematic diagram illustrating progressive alterations in extracellular matrix, intercellular contacts and junctions, and epitheliomesenchymal association during stages 44–45, 46, and 48 in *Xenopus laevis*. Epithelial (above) and mesenchymal cells (below) are separated by phospholipid-containing adepidermal granules (fine-lined squares; *a*), a basal lamina (solid black band; *b*) and the basement lamella of collagen (lines and dots of same diameter; *c*). Note progressive disorganization of basement lamella, delamination of adepidermal granules, and loss of hemidesmosomes at basal surface of epithelium. Epithelial cell contacts (desmosomes) are stable during this period. In contrast, mesenchymal cells acquire focal right junctions and gap junctions by stage 48, maintaining the close associations characteristic of earlier stages. Filopodia exhibiting microfilaments penetrate the disrupted matrix by stage 48 and abut the overlying basal lamina. [*After Kelly and Bluemink, 1974.*]

MESODERMAL MAINTENANCE FACTOR

The Saunders-Zwilling theory has a mesodermal maintenance factor acting on the ectodermal ridge (Fig. 14.10). When the ridge is separated from its underlying mesoderm by a very thin sheet of mica, or if limb mesoderm is replaced by nonlimb mesoderm, the ectodermal ridge degenerates. Conversely, thickened ectodermal ridge always appears wherever there is a limb-mesoderm outpushing. Crucial questions are: Does the ridge form independently and then induce mesodermal outgrowth, or do the thickened regions of the ectoderm form in relation to some pattern present in the mesoderm? If the thickest regions from two or three ectodermal ridges are placed in tandem along the distal edge of one limb mesoblast, do they all remain thick and active as outgrowth inducers, or do they become modified under the influence of the mesoderm?

The result of experiments was that in every case the composite ectodermal ridge fused to form a single ridge, which gradually acquired a typical normal configuration that gave rise to a normal limb. Much the same results were obtained when limb-bud ectoderm was rotated 180° in relation to the mesoderm and when wing-bud ectoderm was placed on leg-bud mesoderm and vice versa.

Figure 14.10 Distribution of the maintenance factor in the wing-bud mesoderm (shaded), according to (a) Zwilling and (b) Saunders et al. c Reciprocal interactions between limb-bud mesoderm and ectoderm, and vice versa, according to the Saunders-Zwilling theory. The activity of the mesodermal factor on the ridge is indicated by the lower arrows. The outgrowth activity exerted on the mesoderm by the activated and thickened apical ridge is represented by the upper arrows. [*After H. Amprino, 1965.*]

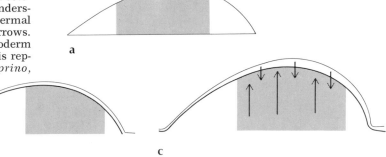

Ectodermal ridge pattern conformed to the expected normal mesodermal pattern. Moreover, essentially similar results were obtained when genetically normal ectodermal ridges were combined with mesoderm from limb buds of polydactyl mutants: a preaxial thickening of the ridge persists in regions where flattening normally occurs, and accessory distal structures develop there as in the limb buds of polydactyl controls.

Chick limb mesoderm, if grafted under the embryonic flank ectoderm, can induce in the latter an apical ectodermal ridge that will condition outgrowth of a supernumerary limb. This happens, however, only if the flank ectoderm is deliberately torn. This could mean that interruption of the basement membrane is essential. In summary, the evidence suggests that the mesodermal-ectodermal interaction is a reciprocal one (Fig. 14.10), with the respective influences acting across, and possibly mediated by, the intervening extracellular matrix.

AXIAL GROWTH SEQUENCE

The later course of limb development appears to be essentially the same in amphibians, birds, and mammals, and it exhibits a precise proximodistal sequence of growth and differentiation. When mesodermal components of successively older limb buds were isolated and grown in the emptied eye orbits of older hosts, the mesoderm from younger buds formed proximal parts. More distal parts appeared only as older buds were used. Experiments consist of marking the mesoderm of various parts of chick limb buds with insertions of small masses of fine carbon particles, and similarly marking both ectoderm and mesoderm with finely powdered colored chalk. Following the fate of the labeled regions clearly demonstrates the general sequence. Basal (proximal) tissue differentiates first, and successively more distal regions of the limb are added as distal growth of the limb bud continues. This is also shown by experiments in which, for instance, a piece of tissue is cut out from the distal end of a leg bud and inserted in the distal end of a wing bud. In such a case, a normal wing develops, except that a toe forms at the tip of one digit.

In the mammal the early development of the limb bud appears to be essentially like that of the chick, although it has been less studied experimentally because of the mammalian developmental circumstances. It has, however, been more intensively studied histologically, particularly with regard to the formation of skeleton. In the mouse embryo, the first demonstrable activities connected with limb morphogenesis take place in the mesoderm, as a lateral crest of tissue, although ectoderm is still thin and shows no cytochemical pecularity. Yet even at this stage the limb mesoderm cannot grow and chondrify without ectodermal covering. By the eleventh day, the limb bud of a rat embryo is longer than it is wide; an apical ectodermal ridge is already present, covering the distal third of the bud. At this stage, femoral precartilage has already individuated, while more distally the presumptive mesoderm of the tibia and fibula has condensed as a common precartilaginous plate. In the distal third the mesoderm is still undifferentiated; it forms a thick marginal layer, rich in RNA, beneath the ectodermal ridge, representing the presumptive material of the distal limb segment. A little later, as the result of simultaneous gradients of morphogenesis, different precartilaginous masses of mesoderm condense successively from the tarsal element to the distal phalanx in each digital ray.

A gradient in rate of cell division becomes established along the primary limb axis for any particular stage. Mitotic indices in the limb bud decline from an initial 10 percent (at stage 18) to about 2 percent (at stage 30), but the decline is most rapid proximally so that the gradient along the proximodistal axis is established. The cell density in the bud mesoderm varies in a very regular manner and is closely correlated with mitotic index: mitotic index is inversely proportional to cell density. This finding is important not only in its own right because it may be the first demonstration of density-dependent growth control in vivo; it is important also because it provides a new mechanism for the control of growth and pattern formation in limb morphogenesis. The correlation between mitotic index and cell density may have important implications for control of growth of the mesenchyme. If we assume that such a causal relationship does in fact exist, so that increasing density inhibits mitosis, a model of growth control of the mesenchyme can be formulated that also has important implications for the role of the apical ectoderm ridge and pattern formation. If mesenchyme cells show contact inhibition of movement and tend to move into any free space, and the ectoderm grows uniformly, then free space becomes available faster at the distal tip and the density will be reduced there. This could lead to increased cell division at the tip.

It is possible to think of the apical ectodermal ridge as exerting its influence on the mesenchyme not by an inducing action but by controlling the growth of the ectoderm, and thus mitosis, in the underlying mesoderm. The skeletal pattern is laid down in the proximodistal direction. This appears to involve a mechanism whereby the positional information of the cells is specified along this axis. We do not know what mechanism is involved, but it is clear that the amount of cell proliferation will affect a cell's position along the axis and that distal cells divide relatively more often.

CELL DEATH AS A MORPHOGENETIC AGENT

As limb development proceeds, whether in amphibian, bird, or mammal, a sculpturing process results in the particular form of the limb. This sculpturing is not entirely a matter of relative regional growth but is also a truly erosive process involving cell death, i.e., necrosis. In the chick, an opaque patch of tissue appears in a 5-day limb bud at the site of the future knee joint. The patch consists of degenerating cells that will in some way be eliminated from the system (Fig. 14.11).

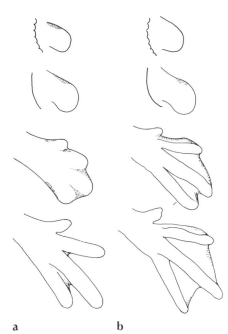

Figure 14.11 The pattern of necrosis (cell death) in leg primordia of (*a*) chick and (*b*) duck, in relation to webbing. Shaded areas are necrotic. [*After Saunders and Fallon, 1966.*]   a   b

Following this earlier discovery, Saunders has made an extensive study of cell death as a positive morphogenetic agent responsible for shaping a number of regions of the chick wing, such as the shoulder. Precartilage tissue, for example, may go on to produce cartilaginous matrix or may fail to do so and soon die; the two processes together help to mold the form of the limb skeleton. Cell death may thus play a role in the separation of radius and ulna, and autophagocytosis may indicate a change in the differentiation path of the mesenchyme cells lying between the radius and the ulna. Similarly, tissue regresses between the digits of the chick foot but remains as webbing in the duck foot. Yet tissue cells doomed to die if left in place may survive if transplanted before a critical stage to another site; they degenerate when moved a little later. Studies by Saunders have indicated that the cells of the limb bud between the forming digits become programmed (determined) to die at a stage (65 hours in the chick) well in excess of the time that necrosis occurs (95 hours). If the tissue is removed at the earlier stages and is transplanted to a neutral region of the embryo, or cultured in vitro, cell death results at approximately the same time it would have if the cells had not been explanted. These results suggest that a stage of differentiation is reached by 65 hours of development in the early limb bud. This sets in motion a condition that proceeds to death at a later stage. The mechanism has been referred to as a *death clock*.

Cellular death as a regional phenomenon has been widely observed in embryonic development. It is clearly a useful process inasmuch as it removes unwanted tissue whose substance usually can be reutilized elsewhere, as in the metamorphosis of many animals, notably amphibians and insects. Local removal of cellular material clearly facilitates many processes, such as separation of tissue layers, but how essential it may be to normal development is still somewhat in doubt. Death clocks and their genetic programming do seem to function in establishing shape in both insect and vertebrate morphogenesis.

Limbs are particularly susceptible to developmental toxic agents, notoriously so in the case of thalidomide, a chemical commonly prescribed in Europe in the 1950s for pregnancy disturbances. It caused thousands of babies to be born without limbs. This susceptibility appears to be due to the fact that a developing limb, from the moment of its inception as a limb disc and throughout the period of elongation of the limb bud, is a relatively rapidly growing mass of tissue. Anything that interferes, directly or indirectly, with the growth process will inhibit or alter its development. Since growth of the limb bud occurs mainly at the distal end of the bud as long as the apical mesoderm remains undifferentiated, this part of the bud continues to be the most susceptible region.

During mammalian development many chemical agents are known to pass readily across the placenta, while the absence of various drug-metabolizing enzymes predisposes the fetus to toxic drug effects that may lead to abnormal embryogenesis. Thalidomide inhibits limb development. In both fetal and maternal tissues of the rat, thalidomide accelerates the biosynthesis of nucleic acids but has only a slight effect on the biosynthesis of proteins. Acceleration of the synthesis of DNA suggests an acceleration of cell proliferation that could alter the temporal course of differentiation.

Recent experiments on 5- to 8½-week-old aborted human embryos exposed to thalidomide in vitro suggest that the site of action of this drug in producing limb defects is not upon the limb itself. By means of radioactive thalidomide and autoradiography, the primary binding site was found to be the mesonephric tissue. There is always a direct anatomic connection between limb development and nephric tissue, even when supernumerary limbs are induced in salamanders. Earlier observations had indicated that the mesonephros of 2- to 3-day-old chick embryos undergo chondrogenesis if cultured on nutrient agar. When thalidomide was used, the tentative conclusion was that mesenchymal tissue associated with the mesonephros at a specific stage of development has a positive influence upon subsequent limb chondrogenesis (possibly by influencing cell migration), and that thalidomide reacts with the mesonephric tissue to inhibit the nephric tissue. No other chondrogenic tissue was found to be inhibited by thalidomide treatment, not even isolated limb tissue.

Many drugs known to damage, or suspected of damaging, the fetus have their effect during the early stages of pregnancy when the woman may not yet be aware that she has conceived. By the end of 6 weeks the embryo has essentially been formed. The general rule is that most drugs affecting metabolism affect development in some degree, and at any particular stage of development those structures or organs at a critical stage of morphogenesis and differentiation are the most susceptible. All stages can be adversely affected, however.

Among drugs known to damage the human fetus are the antibiotics streptomycin, tetracycline, and sulfonamides, during late stages of pregnancy; excessive amounts of vitamins A, D, B_6, and K; certain barbiturates, opiates, and other central nervous system depressants when taken near the time of delivery; and the synthetic hormone progestin, which can masculinize the female fetus.

In addition, animal studies have implicated such common drugs as aspirin, antinausea compounds, phenobarbital, and the tranquilizer chlorpromazine as possible causes of fetal abnormalities.

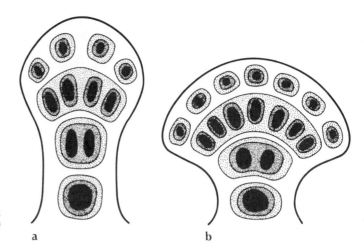

Figure 14.12 Diagrams to show chondrification centers in (*a*) normal limb development and (*b*) in talpid mutation. [*After Ede, 1971.*]

a   b

MUTATION AND MORPHOGENESIS

A chick mutation now being exploited is the talpid mutant, caused by recessive lethal genes that are possibly alleles. In this form the development of the limb is distorted dramatically. In early stages the limb bud is broad and fan-shaped. In embryos that survive to later stages, the cartilage skeleton of the limb shows a tendency to fusion of the proximal elements and at the same time excessive distal elements, thereby producing a broad, shovel-shaped polydactyl limb (Fig. 14.12). A generalized defect in the embryo in the process of mesenchymal condensation, wherein the distinction between condensed and noncondensed regions is blurred, appears to be responsible. Experiments show that such cells are less motile than normal ones and also that cell death is remarkably reduced. The anterior and posterior necrotic zones are absent, while stripping off the apical ectodermal ridge does not lead to a wave of cell death. Ede has proposed that the talpid gene primarily affects the adhesive properties of limb-bud mesenchymal cells; the talpid allele results in limb mesodermal cells more strongly adhesive than corresponding cells in wild-type embryos. This hypothesis has been tested by the technique of cell sorting in aggregates of normal and mutant cells. Thus if the talpid and the wild-type cells are equally adhesive, they should mix at random; if talpid mesodermal cells are more adhesive than wild-type cells, cell rearrangement should take place in mixed aggregates. Cell sorting did not occur. Adhesive differences may exist but are too small to be revealed by cell sorting. The question remains unsettled.

Chondrogenesis in Limb Development

Chondrogenesis (formation of cartilage) occurs in mesenchyme cell aggregations within the developing limb; i.e., a pattern of cartilage rudiments prefigures the limb skeleton. There are, accordingly, two types of patterns to consider: the arrangement of chondrocytes within the rudiments and the arrangement of the rudiments within the limb bud. The talpid gene affects both. In the talpid mutant the condensations are more numerous and smaller and are grouped in larger areas. Only a few cells, and perhaps only a single cell, are necessary to initiate chondrogenesis in cultures of somitic mesenchyme. A huddling of cells at the center of any small mesenchymal aggregation in the limb bud may do the same. Fusion of proximal cartilage elements in the talpid mutant may occur simply because sluggishness (as distinct from adhesiveness) causes the failure of aggregation movements to separate neighboring rudiments.

In the intact limb an additional spacing marks off blocks of tissue from its base to its apex, indicating the upper limb, lower limb, metapodial, and digital regions. Thereafter the simpler rules exhibited in the aggregates will give a rough approximation to the basically pentadactyl pattern of cartilage rudiments. A single rudiment is at the base, where the limb is narrowest; two are next distally, where it is slightly broader; there are four or five digits distally at the expanded limb paddle. The talpid limb is fan-shaped. Proximally the cartilage rudiments are fused, but in the very extended distal region excess digital condensations are formed, presumably because the rules governing condensaton distribution are unchanged.

The development of the limb as a part, or an organ, exhibits all the basic phenomena associated with the development of the egg and the organism as a whole: genomic control, morphogenetic field, sequential inductions, self-assembly, polarities, histodifferentiation, and cytodifferentiation. In one important way it is a simpler system for analysis than developing eggs. Most eggs may be assumed to be preprogrammed to proceed with at least some developmental processes, and in many cases to a very great extent. It is generally difficult to determine to what degree and in what manner an egg might develop without having undergone any preparation at all apart from the attainment of large size as a cell. Limb discs or limb buds clearly are not preprogrammed. Their axial polarities, however, are derived from those of the whole embryo, and they receive some signals designating them as "limb" and "forelimb" or "hind limb." This last property may be regarded as some form of positional information. Or it may be thought of as a component of the elusive, invisible pattern preceding and underlying the visible organization of the whole embryo. That pattern is the quintessential problem of developmental biology. Once initiated, the presumptive limb is a self-organizing system, comparable with the regeneration blastema that forms and develops from amputated salamander limbs (see Chap. 23).

READINGS

AMPRINO, R., 1965. Aspects of Limb Morphogenesis in the Chicken, in R. L. DeHaan and H. Ursprung (eds.), "Organogenesis," Holt, Rinehart and Winston.

DAVID, D. S., and J. H. HINCHLIFFE, 1971. Cell Death in the "Opaque Patch" in the Central Mesenchyme of the Developing Limb: a Cytological, Cytochemical and Electron Microscopic Analysis, *J. Embryol. Exp. Morphol,* **26**:401–424.

EDE, D. A., 1971. Control of Form and Pattern in the Vertebrate Limb, *Symposium, Soc. Exp. Biol.,* **25**:235–254.

FABER, J., 1971. Vertebrate Limb Ontogeny and Limb Regeneration: Morphogenetic Parallels, *Advan. Morphog.,* **9**:127–149.

HARRISON, R., 1921. On Relations of Symmetry in Transplanted Limbs, *J. Exp. Zool.,* **32**:1–136.

KELLY, R. U., and J. G. BLUEMINK, 1974. An Ultrastructural Analysis of Cell and Matrix Differentiation during Early Limb Development in *Xenopus laevis, Develop. Biol.,* **37**:1–17.

RUBIN, L., and J. W. SAUNDERS, 1972. Ectodermal-mesodermal Interactions in the Growth of Limbs in Chick Embryo, *Develop. Biol.,* **28**:94–112.

SAUNDERS, J. W., and J. F. FALLON, 1966. Cell Death in Morphogenesis, in M. Locke (ed.), "Major Problems in Developmental Biology," 25th Symposium, Society of Developmental Biology, Academic.

SINGER, R. H., 1972. Analysis of Limb Morphogenesis in a Model System, *Develop. Biol.,* **28**:113–122.

SUMMERHILL. D., J. H. LEWIS, and L. WOLPERT, 1973. Positional Information in Chick Limb Morphogenesis, *Nature,* **244**:492–496. Reprinted in B. H. Willier and J. M. Oppenheimer (eds.), "Foundations of Experimental Embryology," 1964, Prentice-Hall.

SWETT, F. H., 1937. Determination of Limb Axes, *Quart. Rev. Biol.,* **12**:322–339.

TARIN, D., and A. P. STURDEE, 1971. Early Limb Development in *Xenopus laevis, J. Embryol. Exp. Morphol.,* **26**:169–179.

ZWILLING, E., 1961. Limb Morphogenesis, *Advan. Morphog.* **1**:301–329.

CHAPTER 15

Sense Organs and Nervous System

The three primary sense organs, nasal (*olfactory*), auditory (inner ear or *otic*), and eye (*optic*), develop as paired structures from or in close association with various regions of the developing brain. Their location in relation to the basic divisions of the embryonic fish and mammal brains is shown in Figs. 15.1 and 15.2. In each case we are concerned with the course of development, or developmental event, and with the nature of the agencies involved in the initiation and location of the organ rudiment.

The development of vertebrate sense organs as virtually independently forming complexes is shown in thought-provoking experiments with amphibian

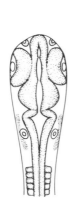
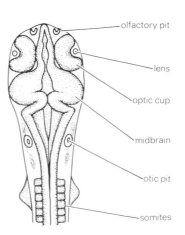

Figure 15.1 Development of brain and sense organs of fish embryo.

olfactory pit

lens

optic cup

midbrain

otic pit

somites

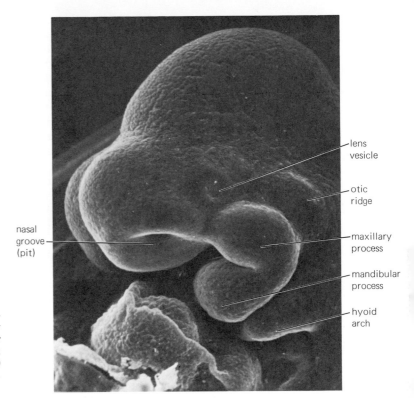

nasal
groove
(pit)

lens
vesicle

otic
ridge

maxillary
process

mandibular
process

hyoid
arch

Figure 15.2 Scanning electron micrograph of embryo hamster, stage (9½ day embryo) showing lens vesicle over center of underlying optic vesicle, together with nasal invagination (olfactory or nasal pit) and the mandibular and hyoid arches. [*Courtesy of S. M. Meller.*]

embryos by Holtfreter. The experiments are described under the title "Tissue affinity, a means of embryonic morphogenesis" (in English translation in "Foundations of Experimental Embryology," Willier and Oppenheimer). Anterior neural plate is induced by underlying prechordal endomesoderm. Following the initial stimulus, pieces of anterior neural plate together with some adjoining epidermis, but without any subjacent inductor tissue, show a surprising capacity for independent and unorthodox development. Such a piece is shown in Fig. 15.3. The original piece in this case consisted, in part, of the lateral portion of the neural plate and, to a larger extent, of adjacent epidermis. Located between them is a portion of the neural crest, the source of mesenchyme, pigment cells,

Figure 15.3 Development and differentiation of neural tube, eye with lens, and nasal organ from small portion of combined ectodermal and neuroectodermal salamander embryonic epithelium. [*Courtesy of J. Holtfreter.*]

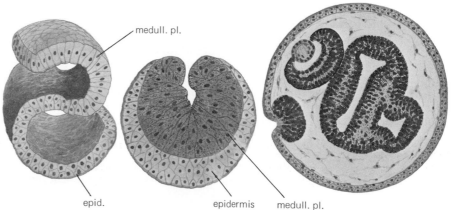

medull. pl.

epid.

epidermis

medull. pl.

325

and also of ganglia and cartilage. Shortly after isolation, the epidermis turns upward and envelops the neural material, while the latter contracts and sinks inward to form a groove. A day later involution of the neural plate is complete. Subsequently the epidermal vesicle expands, and mesenchyme and pigment cells develop from the neural crest. The inner neural mass of cells then develops into a hollow brain structure complete with a developing optic cup. A lens develops from the epidermis in conjunction with the optic vesicle, while an olfactory or nasal pit develops independently from the epidermis. With the exception of the olfactory pit, all the neural material is separated from the epidermis by mesenchyme. An overall patterning of the isolated piece of neurectodermal epithelium clearly takes place, in accordance with available territory. It involves separation of the three types of tissue initially present (neural, neural-crest, and epidermal) and regional responses between adjacent tissues. In a remarkable manner it is a self-organizing system or entity.

NASAL ORGAN

Of the three sense organs, nasal organs are by far the most simple in structure and development. The nasal rudiment is first evident as a slight thickening of the ectoderm, the *nasal placode*, on each side of the anterior end of the embryo adjacent to the neural folds of the forebrain. The placode invaginates to form a *nasal sac*. The lining of the sac differentiates as olfactory neurosensory cells located among supportive epithelial cells, with axons passing inward to the forebrain. Differentiation of the nasal rudiment begins at an early stage. Transplantation experiments indicate that it does not wait until formation of the neural plate and neural folds; in amphibians it may even start during gastrulation. During and after neurulation the rudiment acquires greater capacity for self-differentiation. Extirpation of the rudiment is followed by replacement from adjoining ectoderm, as in limb rudiments; this capacity is subsequently lost, in keeping with a general decrease in ectodermal competence.

AUDITORY ORGAN

In amphibians both *auditory placode* and nasal placode areas are underlaid by chordamesoderm during late gastrular stages. Auditory ectoderm comes to lie next to the myelencephalic part of the neural tube. Determination of the rudiment at these early stages of development is not fully completed, however, since it can be reversed by explanting to other regions. During neurulation the rudiment becomes a more independently developing unit. In the chick the auditory placode is evident at the seven-somite stage.

Shortly before the ear placode has formed, the prospective ear ectoderm has the characteristics of an equipotential system; a whole ear can form from a part and a single normal ear can form from two fused rudiments. As in the development of the nasal rudiment, the placode invaginates, as the *auditory pit*, which then pinches off to form a vesicle. By this time the capacity of the parts to become a whole has been lost. The vesicle, by means of epithelial outgrowth and ingrowth, becomes compartmentalized, forming the endolymphatic duct and the utricle and saccule chambers. Later the three semicircular canals form the dorsal lining of the utricle (Fig. 15.4). The auditory vesicle has the capacity to draw mesenchyme cells toward it, as shown by transplanting vesicles to abnormal sites in the embryo. This mesenchyme, whether from normal or ab-

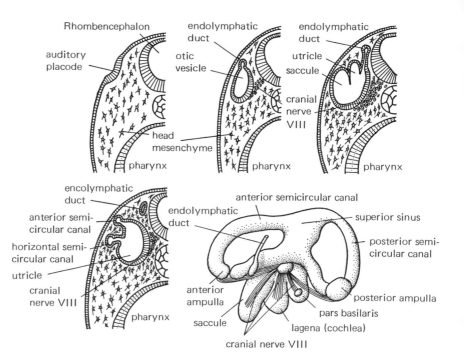

Figure 15.4 Development of the auditory apparatus of frog, from auditory (otic) placode and vesicle. [*After Krause, from R. Rugh, "The Frog," McGraw-Hill, 1953.*]

normal source, differentiates as the cartilaginous capsule and closely envelops the epithelial compartments and tubes formed from the sensory vesicle.

The developing ear vesicle is a very strikingly asymmetric structure. Extensive experimental analysis of the polarity determination was conducted by Ross Harrison over a generation ago. He found that before and during the determined, or mosaic, phase of development in the salamander, the rudiment becomes irreversibly polarized along both its anteroposterior and its dorsoventral axes. The experiments consisted of transplanting rudiments into the ear region of donors of equivalent developmental stage, in one or another of the four possible orientations relative to the axes of the host embryo. Further experiments showed that expression of polarity depends in part on the strength of the polarization within the rudiment and in part on the intensity of the polarizing factors in the host environment.

Both the anteroposterior axis and the dorsoventral axis, which are evidently the initial guide lines for the establishment of the basic pattern of ear vesicle development, are apparently derivative. In other words, the embryo as a whole acquires a polarization of tissue along both its A-P and D-V axes, which is secondarily imposed upon the ear rudiment. This is shown in amphibian embryos by the direction of beat of the cilia covering the external surface; it becomes fixed during gastrulation and is very evident in the neurula, preceding the time of polarity fixation in the ear vesicle. In both ear vesicle and limb disc, however, the anteroposterior axis becomes determined earlier than the dorsoventral axis. In both cases reversal of the rudiment at a critical stage may result in a structure with reversed anterior and posterior features, but with normally oriented dorsal and ventral features.

Certain other experiments present a puzzling and challenging problem. The amphibian ear vesicle has been rotated experimentally after it becomes a mosaic and its axes are fixed; under some imperfectly known circumstances

327

the vesicle develops in its newly oriented position, but in others it tends to turn back to its normal position. By what means we do not know.

THE EYE

Of all the organs of the vertebrate body—apart from the brain—the eye is the most complex, particularly in terms of cell diversity, component tissues, and parts that are unified to form an optical instrument of amazing proficiency and efficiency. The course of development has been fairly well worked out, although it is replete with problems at every stage. The evolution of the vertebrate eye, however, and therefore the evolution of the development of the eye have hardly been considered. The challenge is great. The greatest individual contribution to our understanding of the eye, particularly in relation to its adaptive evolution and development, has been that of George Walls.

Unlike the nasal and auditory organs, which originate in neurectoderm external to the neural tube, the *sensory layer* or *retina* of the eye develops directly as outpushings from the lateral walls of the cephalic neural tube (Fig. 15.5). These protrusions are the *optic vesicles;* they are in fact specially differentiated parts of the brain. As they constrict from the remainder of the forebrain wall, they retain a connecting *optic stalk,* which later serves for the development of the optic nerve. In the subsequent development of the eye, three very different components cooperate to become the whole organ. These are the optic vesicle, which gives rise to the retina and the pigment layer; the *lens placode,* situated in the ectoderm overlying the optic vesicle; and mesenchyme adjacent to the vesicle. The overall development has been well reviewed by Coulombre, who has also contributed experimentally to analysis of lens and corneal development especially. In brief, a large number of tissues assemble during the vertebrate

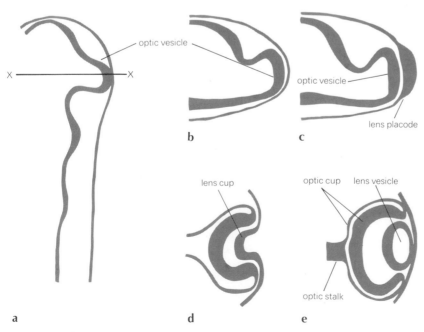

Figure 15.5 Development of the optic cut, lens, and cornea. *a* Dorsal aspect of the embryo at the stage at which the optic vesicle makes contact with the overlying ectoderm. *b* Transverse section through the level *X-X* at the same stage as that represented in *a. c* Transverse section at the same level following induction of the lens placode by the tip of the optic vesicle. *d* Invagination of the optic cup and optic vesicle. *e* Separation of the lens vesicle from the surface, and reunion of the surface ectoderm to form the presumptive anterior corneal epithelium. [*After A. J. Coulombre, 1965.*]

eye development in such a way that their size, shape, orientation, and relative positions meet the precise geometrical tolerances required by the optical function of this organ. The cells that make up these tissues are contributed by the ectoderm and the mesoderm. They become highly specialized to fulfill the diverse functional requirements of the eye. For example, both the cellular and extracellular portions of the dioptric media (cornea, lens, vitreous body) become highly transparent. The intrinsic musculature of the eye (protractor lentis, retractor lentis or ciliary musculature) is appropriately oriented and attached to alter the position or shape of the lens and to focus the visual image in the plane of the retina. The outer tips of the visual cells are specialized to transform the light energy of these images into coded trains of nerve impulses. The neural retina, which is a peripherally developed portion of the central nervous system, develops a cytoarchitectural organization, enabling it to reorganize the output of the visual cells into a form suitable for transmission to the brain. It is important that the eye maintain constant shape during visual function. The scleral and corneal cells construct an outer eye wall that maintains its shape in the face of intraocular pressure and the pull of the extrinsic muscles.

The morphogenesis of the whole can be subdivided into several phases. In the first phase, inductive effects separate the specific material of a particular rudiment, such as the retinal rudiment within the neural plate and the lens and cornea within the surface ectoderm. In the second phase, cell differentiation occurs within each rudiment, e.g., the differentiation of optic-vesicle cells into pigment and retinal epithelia and the differentiation of the lens. The third phase, of a supracellular character, is concerned with the formation of the ciliary body and corneal curvature, the differentiation and growth of sclera and cornea, and the general growth of the eye.

The outpocketing of the optic vesicle usually begins before the time of closure of the neural folds. To what extent differential mitosis is involved and to what extent apical microfilaments of the cells are involved is not known. Once the anterior neuropore has closed, internal accumulation of fluid plays a part in expanding the optic vesicle. If optic vesicles fail to reach the adjacent ectoderm, no lens is induced. If only the tip of the optic vesicle contacts the surface ectoderm, a perfect eye develops but it is comparatively small. Coinciding with the period of lens induction, the optic vesicle invaginates to form the optic cup, the outer layer of which becomes the pigmented epithelium and the inner wall, the neural retina.

Determination of the Eye Rudiment

The first question concerns the events that precede the evaginative process: What determines the establishment of the pair of prospective retinal outgrowths and when does this occur? Vital-staining experiments have shown that the material destined to become the optic vesicles and their optic stalks and chiasma region lies well forward in the neural plate. The same procedure has also shown that the area from which the future lens develops lies outside the presumptive neural plate, lateral to and in front of the presumptive-eye rudiment (Fig. 15.6a). Primarily, the eye develops as the result of these two areas being brought together and interacting. Identification of these areas, however, is merely a mapping process that says nothing about the state of the tissues, i.e., whether or not they are still indifferent, whether in some way they have yet to be determined.

One method that shows when retinal determination becomes irreversibly established is to constrict a developing egg in the sagittal plane—the plane of

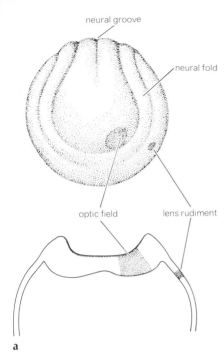

neural groove

neural fold

optic field

lens rudiment

Figure 15.6 *a* The position of the presumptive optic cup and presumptive lens in the neurula stage. *b* Neurula with a rectangular piece of the neural plate excised and inverted. (See text for description of results.) [*After Spemann, 1938.*]

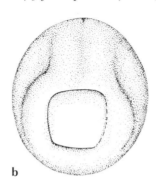

a

b

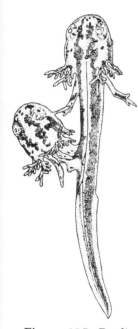

Figure 15.7 Duplication of head, including eyes, brain, etc., following partial constriction of developing egg. [*After Fankauser,* Ann. N.Y. Acad. Sci., **49**:684.]

the embryonic axis. When this is done, an embryo develops as a double-headed monster, with two brains, two pairs of eyes, etc. (Fig. 15.7). This holds true in the newt up to the commencement of gastrulation; until this stage, determination of eye and lens is labile or absent, since two additional eye rudiments can still form. The determinative process may accordingly be assigned to the gastrulation or early neurulation periods.

A number of experiments have been made in this connection, with regard to the eye rudiment proper. One is to explant the presumptive-eye rudiment of the open-neural-plate stage into the flank of another embryo to test for its capacity for self-differentiation. When this is done, an optic cup develops in the new position.

Other experiments made with the early neurula stage consisted of excising a rectangular piece of neural plate and subjacent mesoderm and replacing it after rotating through 180°. In his classical experiment Spemann cut transversely through the prospective-eye rudiment, thereby leaving a portion in place and displacing the other portion to a more posterior location on the opposite side (Fig. 15.6*b*). Optic cups developed from each portion—the size depending on how the prospective area was divided—so that diagonal pairs resulting from a divided rudiment were complementary in size. Accordingly the optic-cup rudiment has already been determined in the early neurula, to the extent of its general destiny to form optic cup; yet it is still labile with regard to any regional determination within it, since any part when isolated attempts to form a whole. This labile state continues for some time.

In certain circumstances one median eye (cyclopia) forms instead of a pair of laterally placed eyes. The presumptive-eye area, as already stated, is located in a median position in the extreme anterior part of the neural plate. In normal development the area divides into right and left components, the definitive optic-vesicle areas. Cyclopia appears, however, if developing eggs are chemi-

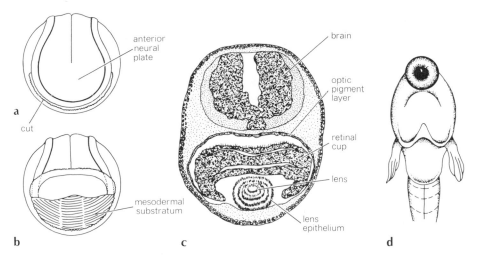

Figure 15.8 Cyclopia in the newt, produced by mechanical defect. Excision of the mesodermal substratum of the anterior part of the medullary plate in the early neurula stage has entailed median fusion of the eyes into a single ventral eye. *a* Neurula prepared for operation by cutting around the anterior border of the medullary plate. *b* Anterior part of medullary plate is lifted. The mesodermal substratum thus exposed is then excised and the medullary flap is put back in position. *c* Cross section through the head, showing the ventral eye with a single median lens. *d* Fish larva with cyclopean eye induced by magnesium (or lithium) chloride treatment of early embryo.

cally treated (with lithium chloride, alcohol, chloretone, etc.) or morphologically altered so that the two lateral parts of the prospective retinal area fail to become separated by an intruding wedge of median neural plate and mesoderm. Thus excision of the mesodermal substratum of the anterior region of the neural plate in the early neurula stage allows the prospective-eye rudiments to remain as one, and a single large median eye develops (Fig. 15.8).

Intimate association with mesenchyme is a general condition, however, for the continuing development of the optic vesicle. This is shown when vesicles evaginating from the neural tube are isolated in vitro without access to the matrix of mesenchyme that normally surrounds them. They attain only a very rudimentary level of organization.

Under normal circumstances the optic vesicle continues to grow; its distal region, after making contact with the lateral head epidermis, invaginates. By this means a single-layered vesicle transforms into the two-layered optic cup, the inner layer becoming the retina and the outer layer becoming the pigmented layer of the eye.

Lens Induction

The investigation of lens induction has had a confusing history. Spemann and later investigators reported different results from experiments, depending on which species frog was used. In *Rana sylvaticus* and *Rana palustris,* transplanted optic vesicles induce a lens from the overlying ectoderm of any part of the body. In *Rana esculentes,* only the normal prospective-lens ectoderm responds to the presence of the optic vesicle, although the *R. esculentes* vesicle evokes lens development anywhere in *R. sylvaticus* and *R. palustris;* this indicates that the vesicles are generally inductive but that ectodermal competence is variable. In *R. catesbiani* the lens is completely dependent upon the

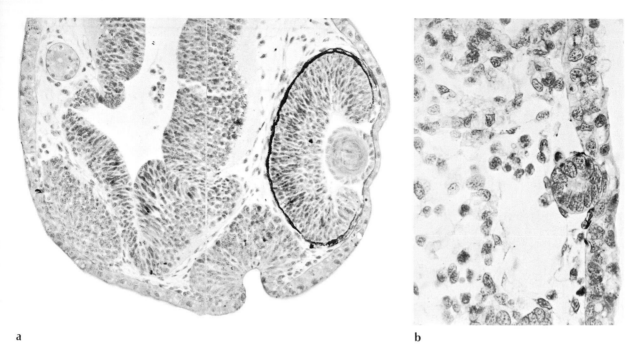

a   b

Figure 15.9 *a* Transverse section of a 12-mm salamander larva in which a lens has developed in the absence of the retina. The embryo was reared at 13°C until the early neurula stage, when the right retinal anlage was excised. *b* Section of an explant of presumptive-lens epidermis combined with the subjacent endodermal wall of the archenteron and the anterior portion of the lateral-plate mesoderm. A lens has been induced from the epidermis. [*Courtesy of A. G. Jacobson.*]

optic vesicle, even though the ectoderm is generally responsive. In *R. esculentes* and *R. fusca* the lens develops in the normal position even in the absence of the optic vesicle. Results such as these show that:

1   All optic vesicles are lens-inductive, even to ectoderm of other species, genus, or order.

2   A lens can develop independently of induction by optic vesicle (Fig. 15.9).

3   Ectodermal competence to form lens may be local or general.

The overall inductive processes involved in lens development are shown graphically in Fig. 15.10.

    To sum up, most regions of the early embryonic ectoderm are competent to form lens when properly stimulated, but this competence rapidly becomes restricted to that region overlying the optic vesicle or optic cup. The competent region is induced to become lens by a succession of interactions: first with the underlying endoderm of the foregut, then with portions of the presumptive-heart mesoderm, and finally with the tip of the optic vesicle.

    In some species the endodermal and mesodermal influences are alone sufficient in strength and duration to initiate ectodermal lens differentiation. In others they at least prepare the ectoderm by lowering the threshold to optic-vesicle induction. In all, the optic vesicle plays an important role—whether or not it is the principal inductor—in determining the final phase and in aligning the lens precisely with the rest of the eye. The nature of the inductive influ-

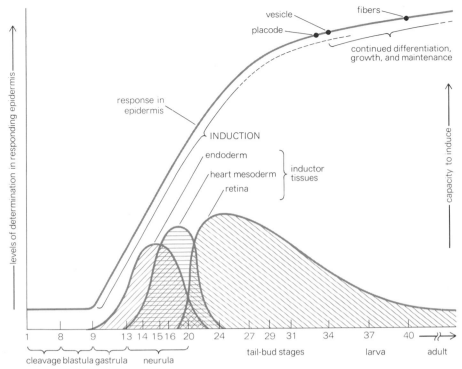

Figure 15.10 Lens induction in a salamander. The abscissa, representing time, is marked off in arbitrary stage numbers and names. The relative amount of time between stages is illustrated; actual time varies greatly with the temperature. At 17°C, the time between stages 9 and 40 is 3 weeks in the West Coast newt. The ordinate for the response curve is logarithmic, the level of response being a function of the sum of all past inductions. The ordinate representing the capacity of inductor tissue to induce is linear. [*After A. G. Jacobson, 1966.*]

ences remains unknown; embryonic optic vesicle and guinea pig thymus, for instance, can also induce and sustain lens development in competent ectoderm. The terminal induction requires proximity between vesicle and ectoderm, although not full cell contact. In fact, an acellular layer develops between the two epithelia. It is several microns thick and results from fusion of the basement membranes of the two layers. Nevertheless the intervening distance is very small, and the barrier has been shown experimentally to pose no difficulty to the diffusion of molecular substances.

Even when lens ectoderm has been committed to lens differentiation, the commitment is by no means an all-or-none affair. Removal of the lens at various stages of development into a neutral environment, such as the body cavity, shows that it only gradually becomes independent of the optic cup. This influence persists even in some adult salamanders. In any case, as the lens vesicle pinches off from the ectoderm, the basement membrane of the placode envelops the vesicle and gives rise to the lens capsule. The cells constituting the back of the lens vesicle continue to elongate and, under the influence of the neural retina, produce the lens fibers, as described in the following section. As the fibers grow, they obliterate the lens cavity, while cells of the front side of the vesicle form the lens epithelium.

Lens Differentiation

The lens of the vertebrate eye is an aggregate of fibers, each formed during terminal differentiation of an epithelial cell. At the end of this differentiation process, the lens-fiber cell lacks a nucleus and becomes filled with a distinctive collection of proteins. Lens function depends upon the refractive index of its components, so that light impinging upon the eye can be bent to focus upon the retina. The proteins of the lens that give it this property are called *crystallins*, of which there are several types. Crystallins are classified as alpha, beta, delta, or gamma, depending upon their electrophoretic mobility. They are best studied with immunological techniques.

The lens is first induced as the lens placode (Fig. 15.5*c*), a disc-shaped thickening of the ectoderm in contact with the distal surface of the optic vesicle, which invaginates to form the lens vesicle. The orientation of the lens with regard to the optic axis is continuously controlled by a mechanism operating throughout development. Experimental alteration of normal lens orientation (e.g., inversion) is followed by remarkable reorganization changes, which return the lens to a normal orientation. This property is controlled by an agent diffusing from the neural retina but not from the cornea or optic sclera.

Morphologically the mature lens lacks blood vessels and is composed of an outer, single layer of epithelial cells; a zone of cellular elongation, or equatorial region, composed of cells in the process of developing into fiber cells; and the inner fiber cells. After the embryonic lens has been formed, fiber cells are continuously laid down throughout life in the zone of cellular elongation, where cuboidal epithelial cells continually transform to the elongated fiber cell characterized by gamma-crystallin protein. Finally, since the fiber cell loses its replicative activity, it essentially enters a permanent stationary phase and can only proceed to death. In contrast with the fiber cells, the epithelial cells of the central region retain their ability to replicate and are in a reversible stationary phase (Fig. 15.11).

The time for the cell cycle of the lens epithelial cells in newborn mice has been calculated to be 56 hours, the G_1 phase taking up three-quarters of this time. In the 3-day-old mouse most of the cells undergo DNA synthesis, but in the 12-day-old mouse only the cells of the germinative epithelium do so. The differentiation phase, however, is very long. The time taken for cells moving from the germinative region to differentiate into an elongated fiber cell is 6 months. In the chick the length of time required for cells of the lens ring, or annular pad, to develop into a fully differentiated fiber cell is 2 years.

The situation in the lens is typical of that in many other tissues in the body. Each kind of tissue represents a cell population of a certain sort. Each kind

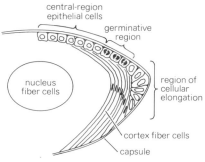

central-region epithelial cells
germinative region
nucleus fiber cells
region of cellular elongation
cortex fiber cells
capsule

Figure 15.11 The lens of the adult vertebrate. The lens is surrounded by an external noncellular capsule. Beneath the capsule are the lens epithelial cells. In the peripheral area is the transitional region of cellular elongation, where the epithelial cells begin to elongate into fiber cells. The fiber cells that are newly laid down constitute the cortex region; those laid down during the early growth period of the lens compose the nucleus region of the adult lens. The internal, posterior side is below. [*After Papaconstantinou,* Science, **156**:338 (1967). *Copyright © American Association for the Advancement of Science.*]

must in some way be maintained throughout the life of the organism. In fact, aging and death of the organism as a whole may be essentially the progressive, inevitable, collective failing of the tissue-maintenance mechanisms. In the lens, new fiber cells continually form from the peripheral equatorial zone of elongating epithelial cells; these in turn derive from the adjoining germinative region of the lens epithelium. Thus fiber cells are systematically laid down, layer upon layer, throughout life. Eventually those fiber cells forming the central or nucleus fiber cells of the lens lose their cell nuclei and remain permanently entombed in the center of the lens. Inevitably the lens ages and dies at the center, although it is renewed at the edge. Its life course and destiny therefore depend on the relative rates of progression toward cell death and of peripheral cell birth. This situation is complicated by the fact that the aging or dying cells in the center, or their equally aging protein products, cannot be sloughed off to make way for new cells or material. As the protein ages, it loses its elasticity and becomes steadily more rigid so that accommodation decreases. Finally the protein loses its transparent quality and the lens becomes milky-white as cataract develops.

Lens Regeneration

A lens is readily regenerated in some vertebrates, notably in salamanders, though rarely in frogs and toads. This is in keeping with the exceptional capacity of urodele amphibians, especially species of the newt *Trituris,* to regenerate whatever part may have been lost—even the front part of the head, including the jaws. The great interest in the regeneration of the lens comes from the discovery made by Colucci and Wolff in the late nineteenth century that it regenerates from the dorsal rim of the iris (Fig. 15.12), a source remarkably different from its epidermal origin in the embryo.

Figure 15.12 Histological location of the proliferating zone at the representative stages of Wolffian lens regeneration. Each figure shows a section through the middorsal pupillary margin of the lens regenerate, oriented perpendicular to the main body axis. The cornea (external "anterior") side is above, the retina (internal "posterior") side below, the dorsal side toward the left, and the ventral side toward the right. *a* Regeneration stage II. *b* Stage V. *c* Stage VIII. *d* Stage XI. White circles denote cells in the proliferating zone; black circles, cells which are in proliferation. White cells are depigmented; black cells are pigmented. Lines indicate cell boundaries. [*After Papaconstantinou,* Science, **156**:338 *(1967). Copyright © American Association for the Advancement of Science.*]

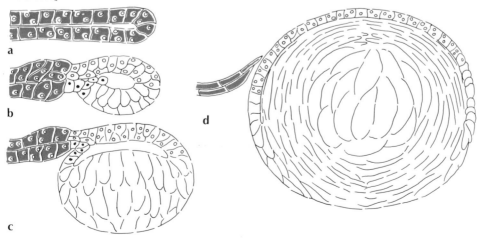

a

b

c

d

The capacity to regenerate a lens in this way is generally absent during embryonic development; it first appears in the young larval stages when tissues have already attained a high degree of functional differentiation. In the newt, removal of the lens from the larval or adult stages is followed by regeneration of a lens from the iris epithelium.

As a rule a regenerative process follows injury to the tissue. Here, lens regeneration occurs without injury to the iris, since it still occurs if the lens is removed through the roof of the mouth instead of through the cornea. Moreover, if a lens is removed and replaced, no regeneration occurs. Neither does it occur if the lens of an adult is replaced by a much smaller lens from a younger individual. Instead, the small lens grows rapidly to the size appropriate to the host. Evidently a lens has an influence, presumably chemical, which inhibits adjacent tissue from regenerating a lens as long as it is present.

The lens exerts its own influence on the development of the eye. It is principally responsible for the induction and maintenance of the cornea, although this capacity is gradually lost as development proceeds, while anterior corneal epithelium becomes progressively more independent of its inductor.

The lens also controls the accumulation of the material forming the expanding semifluid vitreous body behind the lens; this in turn generates mechanical forces important in the construction of the skeletal wall of the eye, the sclera. Scleral cartilage develops in the first place from mesenchyme that condenses around the expanding optic cup. Although the inductor of scleral cartilage has not been identified, circumstantial evidence suggests that the neural retina or the pigmented epithelium, or both, may be the inductors; for the neural tube is known to induce vertebral cartilage, while scleral cartilage corresponds precisely in area with the underlying pigmented epithelium of the retina. It is of general interest that the cells of precartilaginous scleral mesenchyme, once their fate has been determined, form flat plates of cartilage in tissue culture, after being disaggregated and reaggregated. Similary treated precartilaginous mesenchyme from chick embryo limbs form rods of cartilage. Such properties assume great significance in connection with processes of regeneration.

Cornea

Competence to form corneal epithelium is present in most of the early embryonic ectoderm, although the cornea normally arises only over the embryonic eye and in a size, shape, and orientation appropriate to the eye. The optic cup alone is able to induce corneal anterior epithelium from ectoderm in amphibians, but the lens is mainly responsible for the induction and maintenance of the cornea. Collagen is intimately involved in corneal structure and development.

During early development in the chick embryo, the cornea becomes progressively opaque but undergoes reversal and is transparent after 14 days of incubation. Partial dehydration of the cornea is a necessary condition for the development of this transparency.

In the adult, the corneal stroma is made up mostly of water, collagen, glycosaminoglycans, and stromal fibroblasts. The collagen fibrils of each layer are oriented in the same direction, but at right angles to the fibrils of the two adjacent layers, to form an orthogonal ply with all layers roughly parallel to the corneal surface (Fig. 15.13). A combination of mechanical stress and matrix self-assembly may produce an orthogonal matrix that undergoes a gradual angular displacement, which is the same in both eyes. How the spatial pattern in the primary corneal stroma is passed on to the secondary stroma is unknown.

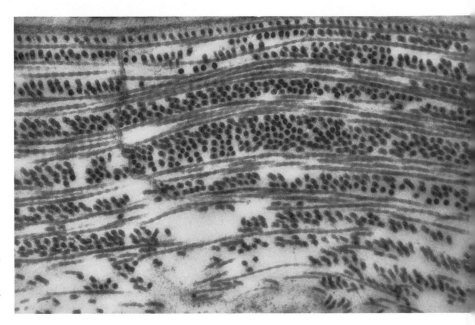

Figure 15.13 Ply layers of collagen fibrils characteristic of corneal stroma. Alternate layers appear at right angles to one another. [*Courtesy of Marie Takus.*]

The primary corneal stroma may orient the mesenchymal cell; the mesenchyme may then influence the orientation of the collagen it produces. Alternatively, the primary stroma may serve directly as a nucleus or template around which mesenchymally derived collagen becomes precipitated.

These few components are assembled in time and space in such a manner that the cornea develops a large number of strikingly different functional characteristics: avascularity, tensile strength, deturgescence, a tissue-specific population of ions, regenerative capacity, a characteristic interference pattern in polarized light, an appropriate refractive index, a precisely controlled curvature that contributes to its refractory power, and transparency. Simultaneous development of such diverse properties sets strict limits on the manner and sequence in which the corneal components can be compatibly assembled during development.

Whole-eye Regeneration

The capacity of the urodele eye to regenerate completely following removal of all except a very small remnant has long been known. As a rule, cornea, sclera, and retina are renewed from corresponding components of the eye fragment as a process of coordinated self-assembly. The whole event is a spectacular performance, but the particular interest is in the regeneration of the sensory retina following its surgical removal. This layer readily separates from the adjoining pigmented epithelium and can be forced or flooded out of the vitreous chamber through a slit in the eyeball. A new retinal layer is then replaced by the pigmented epithelium, a phenomenon thoroughly investigated by Stone and his students. The pigmented epithelium not only can regenerate the neural retina early in embryonic life in most kinds of vertebrates, as long as a small piece of neural retina is present, but even when the pigmented epithelium is from one class (chick) and the retinal fragment from another (mouse).

Development of Retinal Architecture

The neural retina is one of the most complex tissues in the vertebrate body. This thin sheet of tissue is composed of several different cellular layers. They include various types of sensory cells, the cell bodies (containing the nuclei) of the neurons of the optic nerve, interconnectives between these two types, and associated structural cells. The visual image in the optic region of the brain results from the patterns of light that fall upon the sensory cells of the retina, which is dependent upon the development of an impressive cytoarchitecture of this layer.

During early phases of development, cell division is confined mainly to the margin of the optic cup. In embryos, radioautographic analysis of retinas labeled with tritiated thymidine shows that immature retinal cells migrate to the outer surface of the layer as they divide; the daughter cells then migrate back to their appropriate locations within the differentiating retinal layers. Increase in thickness and complexity is accompanied by waves of cell death, which are probably related in some way to the orderly establishment of the precise neurosensory network. The innermost layers of the retina (i.e., those nearest the center of the eye) differentiate first and the sensory layer of rods and cones last. Once differentiation has begun, the intricate and interrelated processes leading to the final cytoarchitecture apparently constitute a self-directing and self-sustaining complex (Fig. 15.14).

The sequence of retinal-cell differentiations is as follows:

1 Glial cells, which become Müller's fibers and will envelop the retinal neurons, develop cytoplasmic processes connecting the inner and outer surfaces of the sensory retina; the terminals of these processes combine to form the internal and external so-called limiting membranes.

2 Ganglion cells, which form the innermost layer of neurons, send out axons, which together grow to form the optic nerve by way of the optic stalk. Dendritic processes of the ganglion cells form synapses with axons from the next layer to differentiate, i.e., the inner nuclear layer, which contains at least three kinds of neurons.

3 The outer nuclear layer, which is the outermost layer of the neural retina, is the last to differentiate after local cell division ceases. There, axons synapse with the dendrites of the bipolar cells of the inner nuclear layer.

4 The light-sensitive rods and cones develop from the outer ends of the cells of the outer nuclear layer. Each cell produces a cytoplasmic bud at its outer end, which protrudes through a pore in the external limiting membrane. Here again, further differentiation is sequential and centrifugal. The inner segments of the rods and cones are first formed, and from them the outer segments later arise. Various organelles are formed (Fig. 15.15). One, a basal body or centriole, elaborates a noncontractile cilium that has nine peripheral filaments but no central filaments, and is otherwise typical. It takes part in the development of the outer segments of the rods and cones. Rod or cone sacs fold in from the plasma membrane close to the tip of the cilium, which may induce them, and become arranged like a stack of coins.

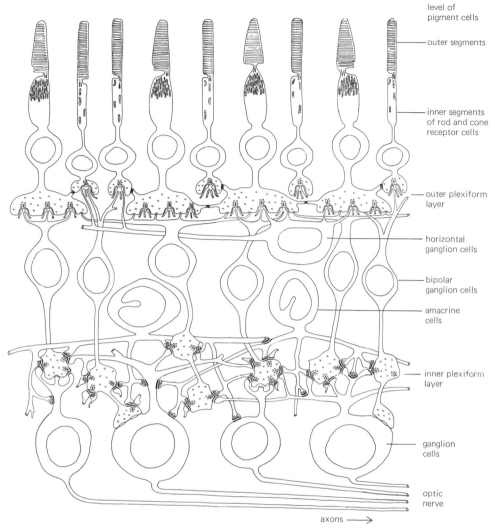

Figure 15.14 Summary diagram of synaptic contacts between the principal types of retinal cells in the human retina. The upper layer consists of rods and cones, the outermost segments of which are more or less embedded in the retinal pigment cell layer (not shown). These sensory cells make synaptic contact with their neighbors and with a complex layer of bipolar and horizontal ganglion cells. These in turn make synaptic contacts with the inner ganglion cells whose axons constitute the optic nerve. [*Courtesy of B. B. Boycott, 1974.*]

5 Finally, pigmented epithelial cells, whether differentiating from the outer layer of the embryonic optic cup or from the reconstituted layer during retinal regeneration, extend fine cytoplasmic processes. They interdigitate with the emerging outer segments of the rods and cones, thus locking the two layers together.

6 Electron micrograph observations following injection of tritiated leucine have shown that the stacked folds of the outer segments of both rods and cones in mammals are continuously shed and re-shed from the new segments. The shed material is phagocytized by cells of the pigment layer.

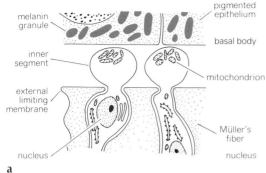

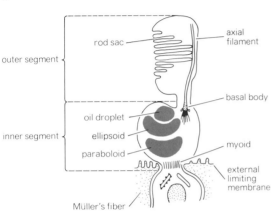

a

Figure 15.15 Rod and cone cytogenesis, illustrating the successive stages in the maturation of the cone or rod. [*After A. J. Coulombre, 1961.*] *a* Cells differentiating between pigmented retinal epithelium and the external limiting membrane of the sensory retina, forming a bulbous inner segment of the prospective rod or cone. *b, c* Two later stages showing development of outer segment, the folding of the plasmalemma to form a stacked series of membrane plates, and the axial filament, which is essentially a noncontractile cilium complete with basal body.

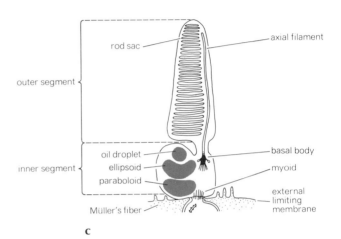

b   c

NERVOUS SYSTEM

The problems in understanding the development of the nervous system will be a center of research in developmental biology for many years to come.

Nerve Growth Factor

There is much evidence that nerves can respond to specific chemical stimulation. The best examples of such effects come from studies of hormones and of a particular protein, nerve growth factor (NGF). The endocrine and nervous systems are closely interrelated groups. In some cases neurons are known to secrete hormones (neurosecretory cells), and there are many examples of neuron function being mediated by circulating hormone levels.

NGF participates in the growth, development, and maintenance of certain parts of the nervous system; it may even be involved in processes such as cancer induction and wound healing. The nature of its participation is unclear, but the protein is now known to resemble insulin both structurally and functionally and is therefore hormonelike in its activity.

The investigations into nerve growth factor have had a long, interesting history. The first indication of a factor that could specifically affect the differentiation of certain types of neurons occurred in experiments with a mouse tumor. The tumor was grown on the chorioallantoic membrane of the chick, a favorite site for the growth of a variety of tissues. The chorioallantoic membrane is chosen for its ease and accessibility. If a window is cut in the shell of a chick of the appropriate age, a piece of tissue from a mammalian or avian source can be dropped into the hole, where it will land on the chorioallantoic membrane and become penetrated with blood vessels that nourish the cells as the tissue grows. If a mouse sarcoma (a cancerous tissue that is nonepithelial) is grown in this way, it is found that there is a striking enlargement of the sympathetic and sensory ganglia of the chick. Some substance, NGF, enters the circulation of the chick from the mouse tissue and has a specific effect upon these neural-crest derivatives. Exposure of a mammalian fetus to nerve growth factor can result in up to a twelvefold enlargement in the sensory and sympathetic ganglia. Increased size results from both increased cell number and cell size.

One technique for learning about the nature of an unknown factor is the determination of which enzymes it is sensitive to. One source of particular hydrolytic enzymes is snake venom; attempts to determine the sensitivity of nerve growth factor to snake venom hydrolases had a surprising effect, namely, the stimulation of nerve growth rather than its destruction. The reason for this paradoxical finding was the presence of a nerve growth factor within the venom at much higher concentration than that in the malignant tissue. More recently another source of nerve growth factor has been found, the submaxillary salivary gland of the mouse, in which the concentration is manyfold greater than in snake venom. Why this particular gland contains the factor is not known; its presence is not required for nervous system differentiation, since it can be removed without any effect upon neural development. From this gland, sufficient quantities of the protein have been purified to permit amino acid sequence determination.

The physiological source of NGF has puzzled investigators since it was shown that the submaxillary gland could not be the sole source in mice. In the male mouse, this gland contains large quantities of NGF—approximately ten times that in the submaxillary glands of females and up to 1,000 times more than in other tissues, including the heart, spleen, and kidney. It is unclear whether NGF is synthesized by male mouse submaxillary glands or merely stored there. After removal of these glands, the concentration of NGF in plasma decreased at first but then gradually increased until it returned to normal after about 2 months. Thus, other tissues must also synthesize it.

Among the candidates for this role are glial cells and fibroblasts. Glial cells are found in close association with neural-cell bodies in ganglia and the brain. Their exact function is unknown, but they are generally thought to support and maintain neuronal function. Glial cells could either be the source of NGF required by neurons, or the NGF could somehow facilitate the activities by which neuroglia support and maintain neurons. Fibroblasts also secrete NGF, and these cells may be a physiological source of the polypeptide.

Nerve Outgrowth

One of the first questions to be considered concerned the mechanism whereby a single nerve cell can span the distance between the central nervous system in which its nucleus is found and the peripheral muscles and organs that it supplies. The question was resolved by Ross Harrison in what is considered the first tissue-culture experiment. Harrison removed a small part of the neural tube from a frog embryo, placed it in a tiny drop of lymph fluid on a cover slip to provide the cells with nutrition, and inverted the cover slip over the depression on a slide to form a "hanging-drop" culture in which the piece of presumptive neural tissue could differentiate. Within the next few days he

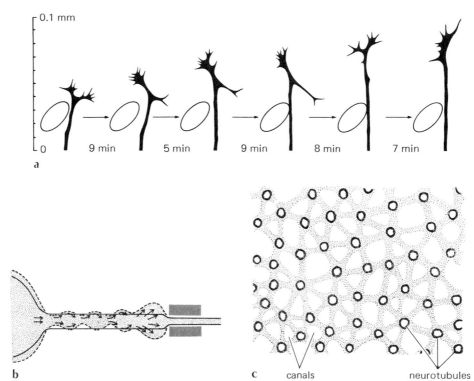

Figure 15.16 *a* Six successive views of the end of a growing nerve fiber, showing its change of shape and rate of growth. The sketches were made with the aid of a camera lucida at the time intervals indicated. The red blood corpuscle, shown in outline, marks a fixed point. The average rate of elongation of the nerve was about 1μm per minute. The total length of the nerve fiber was 800 μm. The observations were made upon a preparation of frog embryo ectoderm, isolated in lymph, 4 days after isolation. [*From R. G. Harrison, J. Exp. Zool.* **9:**787–846, 1910.] *b* Axonal flow. The mature neuron is in a state of perpetual, rapid growth; it grows forth mainly as an axon, consuming its substance on the way. The axonic substance flows as a whole. The solid content of each central nerve-cell body (of a mammal) is renewed almost once a day, the daily inflow into the axon being close to 10 percent. *c* The axon substance, consisting of neurotubules and intertubular canals, advances as a semisolid mass exhibiting a succession of semisolid waves traveling over the axonal surface away from the cell body. [*After Weiss, 1969.*]

found that axons emerged from the embryonic nerve cells, or *neuroblasts*, and grew out into the medium just as they would have emerged from the neural tube of the embryo to penetrate into the surrounding tissue (Fig. 15.16*a*). From this experiment it appeared that the nerve tracts, many feet long in the larger vertebrates, are the result of outgrowths from cells in the central nervous system.

What mechanism is responsible for enabling the tip of a cell to extend itself for such long distances? Recent studies on nerve outgrowth in tissue culture indicate that both microtubules and microfilaments are responsible. Thus, if the growing tip of a neuron is followed, numerous pseudopodial processes are found that contain minute pointed extensions at their tip. Electron micrographs indicate that these microspikes (filopodia) are filled with microfilaments whose contractile activity presumably provides the motile force for pulling the tip of the neuron forward. Treatment of these cells with cytochalasin B produces a rapid disappearance of the microspikes and a cessation of neuron advance. In addition, if the main body of the growing axon is examined with the electron microscope, bundles of microtubules are found running parallel to the long axis of the neuron; they apparently aid in giving support to the extended process. Treatment of cultured neurons with colchicine results in disassembly of the microtubules and, after a short period, the withdrawal of the axon process.

The mature neuron generates neuroplasm continuously in its cell body and then conveys it into the nerve fiber as a cohesive column advancing at a daily rate of about 1 mm (axonal flow). This has been established in experiments by Weiss that resulted in "damming" of flow in constricted nerve (Fig. 15.16*b*). His findings were supplemented by electron-microscopic and cinematographic data. Neurotubules and neurofilaments extend in linear, latticelike arrangement down the length of the axon. Employing tritiated hydrogen as a radioactive marker, both Leblond and Weiss have followed the course of labeled amino acids as a crest of protein traveling down the length of an axon. This is not a stream of substance *inside* a stationary axon but a movement of the *whole axon itself* as a semisolid column. These and many other experiments have led to the concept that *the mature neuron is in perpetual growth and grows forth as axon, consuming its substance on the way.* In fact, from 6 to 11 percent of the cell protein moves out daily from the cell body, amounting to an average renewal rate of the whole solid content of each central nerve-cell body almost once a day.

Nerve Guidance

A related question, and one of the most basic, is what mechanism is responsible for guiding the original nerves from their point of origin to their specific synaptic locations. This complicated question has both anatomical and physiological aspects.

The basic circuitry of the nervous system has a predictable and therefore a genetic arrangement. Each nerve cell, as it emerges from a particular ganglion in the brain or spinal cord, proceeds to a predictable location in the body, which may be a great distance from its origin. Are the original neurons guided to their final destination by some inherent information within the nerve cell, or does the environment through which they migrate lead the advancing tip? If the environment does play a critical role, what types of cues does it provide the growing neuron and what mechanisms within the neuron are operating to sense the environment? At the present time we have very little information.

One of the early observations concerning nerve outgrowth was made by Weiss in his analysis of axonal extension in tissue culture. He found that the direction the growing tip took depended upon the contour of the physical substrate over which growth occurred. A particularly well-suited substrate for culture and observation is a blood clot. It is composed of fibrous proteins that become oriented when stretched or under physical tension.

When differentiating neuroblasts are cultured on this medium, the axons tend to grow along the oriented components. Weiss termed the response of the nerve to the substratum "contact guidance"; he suggested that the direction axons grow in vivo reflects a similar physical pathway through which they are directed to their final, genetically determined site. Contact guidance could then explain the anatomical relationships of the nervous system, but physiological questions then arise. Nerves carry impulses from one place in the body to another. They provide the communication system whereby one tissue informs the central nervous system (via the sensory neurons) of its condition. The central nervous system, in turn, directs the activity (via the motor neurons) of the peripheral organs. The important question is whether the specific function of a neuron is established before its connection with the tissue to be innervated or only after. In other words, does the function of a motor nerve growing from the spinal cord to a muscle—in the hand, for example—become determined by the muscle cells with which it makes contact? The alternative would be that the neuron had already been specified as to where it was going and what it would do before it reached its destination.

Inherent in the concept that neural circuitry is a result of contact guidance is the principle that nerve outgrowth is an anonymous process—anonymous in the sense that the growing axon does not have a specific identity. The physical factors of the environment lead each nerve to its proper synaptic connection, and only afterward does that nerve become specified.

Alternatively, a neuron could be directed to a specific site by the chemical nature of the environment in conjunction with existing nerve-cell specialization. If the tissues through which the various neurons migrate is heterogeneous, so that different pathways result in different chemical stimulation, any given neuron could be directed in any particular route. In such a mechanism, the neurons must have some particular chemical identity so that each can recognize a particular set of chemical cues. This does not imply that every single neuron need be biochemically unique at its inception, but rather that the neurons of each major route would have at least a collective identity. However, in at least a few cases where precise connections must occur (as in the optic nerve described below), each neuron seems to be specified at a very early stage.

Optic Nerve Specificity

The most sophisticated developmental neurology has concerned the outgrowth of the optic nerve of lower vertebrates. As with the olfactory and auditory nerves, neurons of the optic nerve arise in the sense organ and grow to specific locations in the brain. In fish and amphibians the visual center is in the *tectum*, the optic projection center in the brain, and the locations to which each part of the sensory retina sends its neurons can be mapped.

Retinotectal mapping involves the simultaneous stimulation of selected sites on the retina and the measurement of electrical activity in the brain. The sensory cells of the retina can be stimulated either by shining a very fine beam of light upon a small retinal area or by implanting an electrode. The corresponding site, or projection, on the tectum is measured by determining which parts of this brain region become electrically active. It is found that there is a predictable point-to-point correspondence between the retina and the tectum; a dorsal sensory cell in the right retina projects to the left side of the left tectum, etc. (Fig. 15.17). The question to be considered is: How does each of these optic neurons arrive at the correct site within the brain?

It is difficult to conceive of a purely physical mechanism able to direct closely grouped growing neurons to selective tectal points. Experiments on regenerating optic nerves makes this even more unlikely. If the optic nerve of a goldfish, for example, is severed, the initial responses involve the degeneration of the parts of the axons on the tectal side of the cut. The cell nuclei of these neurons are located within the retina; the portion of the nerves from the retina to the cut remains alive and capable of regeneration. If these cut nerves are allowed to regenerate and their retinotectal projection is mapped, it is found that the exact same point-to-point correspondence is regained, even if the viable

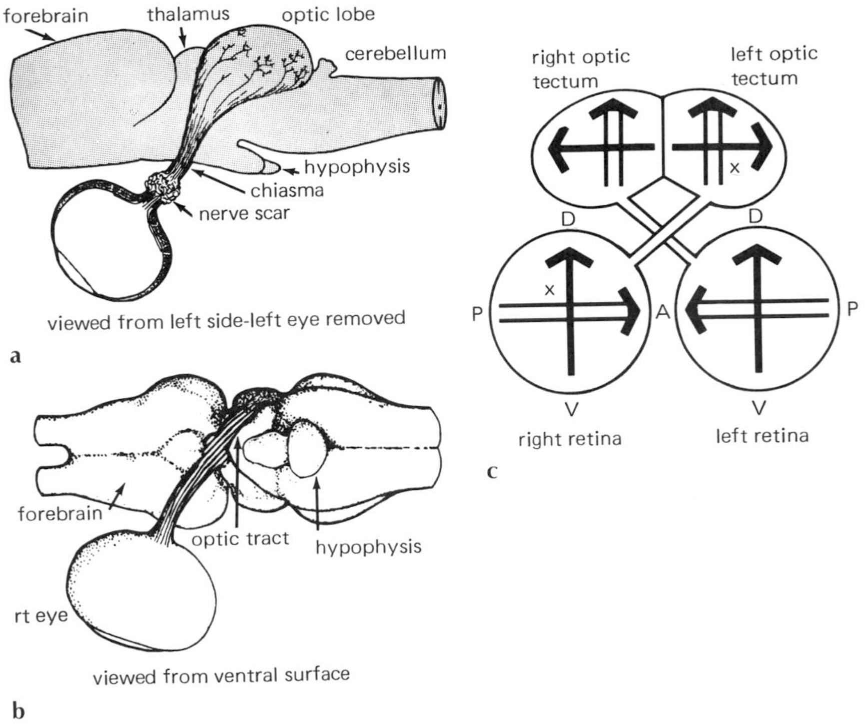

Figure 15.17 Visual pathways of the amphibian. In *a* the right eye with optic nerve is shown after section and regeneration. The left eye and optic nerve are not shown. The right optic pathway crosses at the optic chiasma to form the left optic tract that is distributed to the left optic lobe or tectum as shown in *b*. [*From Sperry, 1951b.*] In *c* are shown diagrammatically the orderly maplike projections from the right and left retinas to the left and right optic tecta. P, A, D, and V on the retinas signify posterior, anterior, dorsal, ventral. [*After J. C. Eccles, 1973.*]

nerve portion is displaced to a new site after the initial surgery. It appears, therefore, that as in the original outgrowth period, each neuron is capable of precise directional regrowth, even from a foreign location. It has been concluded that for such a precise regeneration to occur, some chemically directed mechanism must be responsible.

The analysis of the initial optic nerve outgrowth in fish and amphibians by Stone, Sperry, Jacobson, and their coworkers corroborates the theory of a chemical basis of guidance. The question then arises: When do these neurons attain this identity?

An approach to this question has been made by analysis of behavior after various surgical operations on the retina. If the retina of the salamander *Ambystoma* is rotated at a very early stage in eye development, there is no effect upon the visuomotor responses of the adult salamander (Figs. 15.18 and 15.19). If, however, the retina is rotated at a later stage, still well before the optic neurons make contact with the brain, the visuomotor responses are inverted to the same extent of the original rotation. The neurons have been specified prior to rotation. For example, if the retina is rotated 180° at the later stage, the adult salamander that develops will strike 180° away from a food object swung into its visual field. This condition is never corrected. Responses remain completely abnormal unless the retina is rotated back to normal in adult life. Inverted visual behavior indicates that each neuron is growing out to the same site in the tectum that it would have if the retina had never been disturbed. At some point during the outgrowth process, well before the axons have reached the brain, each neuron gains an identity that dictates to which part of the tectum it will proceed. This is determined by the retinal part from which it grows. If rotation is performed after

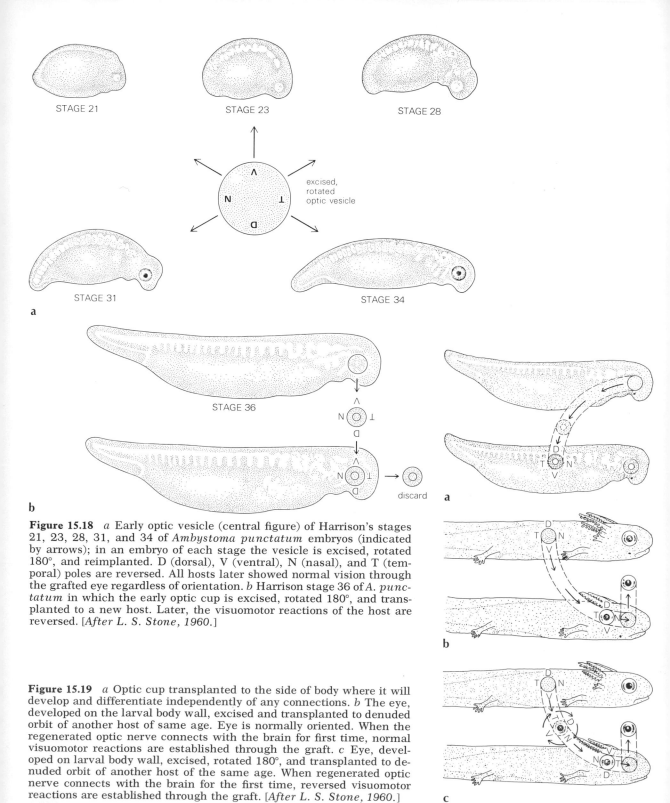

Figure 15.18 *a* Early optic vesicle (central figure) of Harrison's stages 21, 23, 28, 31, and 34 of *Ambystoma punctatum* embryos (indicated by arrows); in an embryo of each stage the vesicle is excised, rotated 180°, and reimplanted. D (dorsal), V (ventral), N (nasal), and T (temporal) poles are reversed. All hosts later showed normal vision through the grafted eye regardless of orientation. *b* Harrison stage 36 of *A. punctatum* in which the early optic cup is excised, rotated 180°, and transplanted to a new host. Later, the visuomotor reactions of the host are reversed. [*After L. S. Stone, 1960.*]

Figure 15.19 *a* Optic cup transplanted to the side of body where it will develop and differentiate independently of any connections. *b* The eye, developed on the larval body wall, excised and transplanted to denuded orbit of another host of same age. Eye is normally oriented. When the regenerated optic nerve connects with the brain for first time, normal visuomotor reactions are established through the graft. *c* Eye, developed on larval body wall, excised, rotated 180°, and transplanted to denuded orbit of another host of the same age. When regenerated optic nerve connects with the brain for the first time, reversed visuomotor reactions are established through the graft. [*After L. S. Stone, 1960.*]

Figure 15.20 The relationship between visual field, retina, and tectum in *Xenopus* with normal retina, double-nasal compound retina, and double-temporal compound retina. Normally, points *A, B, C* in the visual field project in the same order rostrocaudally on the tectum. In the compound retina the projection from each half-retina has spread over the whole contralateral tectum. The order of tectal projection from the compound retina is correct for the original half of the retina, but is reversed for the grafted half-retina. [*From R. M. Gaze, M. Jacobson, and G. Székely*, J. Physiol. (London), **165**:484–499 (1963).]

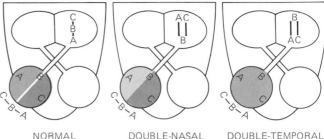

NORMAL   DOUBLE-NASAL   DOUBLE-TEMPORAL

this stage has been reached, the neurons continue to behave as if they were derived from the original site.

Although genetic and developmental processes presumably determine the selective connections of optic nerve fibers, we have little insight into the nature of these processes. Two alternative hypotheses have been proposed. Sperry suggests that matching maps of biochemical specificities develop independently in retina and tectum, and each optic nerve fiber has a unique biochemical specificity that permits it to connect only with tectal cells having a matching specificity. The other hypothesis is that only retinal ganglion cells become specified, and they carry their specificities to the tectum.

Most recent analysis has been performed on *Xenopus* (Fig. 15.20). The results suggest that:

1   Specification occurs very rapidly, since vision, if affected, is always affected to the same degree of early rotation

2   A point is reached (stage 30 of *Xenopus*) in which one axis is specified but the other is not. In other words, the retinal projection is normal in the dorso-ventral axis but inverted in the anteroposterior axis, resulting in a visuo-motor response correspondingly abnormal in only one direction.

Before stage 30, rotation of the retina does not result in any visuomotor disturbance, suggesting that specification has not occurred before this point. If, however, a stage-28 eye is removed and cultured in vitro for a period of a day or two and is then transplanted into the socket of a suitable host, it is found that the resulting behavior is normal only if the eye is grafted in the same anatomical position it had in the donor. The eye was originally removed at a time when it was not completely specified; in tissue culture it gained specification at a time corresponding exactly to the period it would have become specified had it been left alone. This result suggests that some determinative influence is present in the retina at stage 28; otherwise a more complete specification on the same terms would not have occurred in tissue culture. That rotation can overcome this preliminary influence suggests it is readily reversible. Once stage 32 is reached, specification is essentially irreversible as measured by simple rotation experiments, since behavioral activity is disturbed to the same degree of rotation. Under special conditions, however, it appears that specification can be modified even after stage 32. Surgical techniques have allowed Jacobson and coworkers to construct composites of retinas derived from two sources. For example, a retina can be made with the left half of one and the ventral half of another. In such a composite, one-quarter of the original retinal architecture would be absent (the right-dorsal quadrant) while another quarter (the left-ventral quadrant) would be represented twice. If retinal projection is completely specified at stage 32, a composite such as this made after that stage should produce a tectum without connections in one quarter and doubly innervated in another. Such is not the case and a much more normal retinotectal projection is found, which indicates that specification before stage 32 is still to some extent reversible.

Other experiments also indicate there is no fixed map of coordinate specificities built in the retina and the tectum. Compound eyes made of two nasal or two temporal retinas make a double projection to the contralateral tectum, so that each half of the compound eye spreads its fibers over the whole of the available tectal surface (Fig. 15.20). The absolute position of each optic-nerve-fiber terminal in the tectum becomes fixed only later in development. How the elastic properties of the retinotectal map in the embryo become a system of fixed-place specificities in the adult has yet to be discovered.

Two aspects of retinal cell biology have been recorded that can be correlated with the time of specification at approximately stage 32. One of these is the cessation of cell division in the cells of the central part of the retina. The second is their uncoupling, typical of cells proceeding in different biochemical directions. Whatever the change from an unspecified to a specified state may be, it occurs rapidly and does so before the development of photoreceptors (rods and cones) or of synaptic connections within the retina or between the retina and the visual centers of the brain. DNA synthesis ceases in all but the most peripheral retinal ganglion cells at this time, and the cells probably complete their terminal mitosis before they become specified. This may signify that DNA synthesis stops before synthesis of specific macromolecules starts.

An entirely different explanation of the development of retinotectal connections, which does not require biochemical identification of either retinal ganglion cells or tectal cells, has been given by M. Jacobson. According to this alternative, the temporal order of developmental events during formation of the retinotectal projection becomes translated into orderly connectivity. To achieve an orderly point-to-point map from retina to tectum, all that may be required is that retinal ganglion cells cease DNA synthesis and start axonal outgrowth in a predetermined spatiotemporal order. The developmental timetable will then determine the spatiotemporal pattern of arrival of axons and formation of their connections in the tectum. In this hypothesis, the specificity of the retinal ganglion cells would be an expression of differences in timing of their differentiation and growth, rather than a matter of selective biochemical labeling. However, Jacobson's group also devised several experiments in which the time developing optic nerve fibers in the frog contacted their targets was later than normal. For example, they transplanted an eye from one embryo onto the body of another embryo or grew it in a tissue culture. They let the eye grow for two weeks and then transplanted it back to its original host. At this time, all the normal connections between the optic nerve fibers and the tectum were made, although the arrival of fibers in the tectum had been delayed by the experimental procedure. Additional evidence against such a temporal hypothesis was obtained by Cowan in experiments with chick embryos. His experiments showed that optic nerve fibers grow across the surface of the tectum in search of their targets; they do not make connections with the first part of the tectum they encounter.

A direct assay for retinal-tectal cell-cell recognition was devised by Roth. He found that retinal cells from the top (dorsal) half of a pigeon's eye will bind to the bottom (ventral) half of its tectum but not to the top half, and that retinal cells from the bottom half of the eye will behave conversely. This effect is consistent with the fact that nerve fibers from the top half of the eye will connect with the bottom half of the tectum and vice versa. In order to determine the basis of the specificity of the binding of retinal cells to tectum, he exposed the tectal cells to various enzymes. Thus far, two sugar-degrading enzymes—a galactosidase and a glucosaminidase—are found to affect binding of retinal cells from the bottom half of the eye to cells from the top half of the tectum; they will not affect binding by retinal cells from the bottom half of the eye. Roth suggests that these sugar molecules in the cell membranes may play a key role in recognition.

DEVELOPMENT OF BEHAVIOR

The nature of the components that contribute to the development of behavioral patterns is one of the most complex questions of all. The analysis of behavior in most animals indicates that it can be coded within the genetic material. In some way, information in the form of DNA nucleotide sequence must become manifest in the neural circuitry and neuromotor activity. Very little is known of how this is accomplished, but a few studies have begun to describe the parameters. Basic questions are to what extent behavior is determined by a period of trial-and-error learning and to what extent it automatically follows the proper neural connections.

One approach is to block all muscular activity during the period when neuromotor connections are being formed and trial-and-error activity would be occurring. Salamander embryos raised in the presence of chlorobutanol during the formative period are immediately capable of completely normal swimming movements when the drug is removed, even in the absence of any previous muscular function. In lower vertebrates, therefore, it seems that once the proper nervous connections are made, specific behavior follows without the need for instruction to develop correct neural circuits.

In a comparable series of studies on the chick, Hamburger has analyzed the nature of the nervous system and its relation to muscular activity. The first movements in the chick embryo occur at about the fourth day of incubation with movements of the head. In human embryos a similar initial movement occurs at about the eighth week. In the chick this activity results from the completion of motor circuits from the trigeminal nerve to cervical neck muscles. During the next few days an increasing number of muscles become active as more and more motor innervation takes place. Until the eighth day there are no functional sensory nerves, and therefore all movements occur in the absence of sensory stimulation. In other words, nervous activity responsible for this movement originates within the central nervous system and is unrelated to environmental stimulation. Analysis of movements up until the seventeenth day suggest that there is no trial-and-error learning period in the chick. Movements through this period remain uncoordinated, and in many cases antagonistic muscles are undergoing contraction at the same time. Only after the seventeenth day do integrated behavioral movements take place, and Hamburger concludes that they do not result from previous muscular activity.

The behavioral machinery as a whole apparently works according to how it is built. For the organism to function at all, many responses have to be ready to act appropriately upon the first demand. Nevertheless, especially in mammals, much of the response system matures after birth in relation to sensory stimuli. This is particularly the case with vision, as shown from experiments with kittens by Hubert and Wiesel. In this connection, however, we must remember that the bulk of the optic nerve fibers project to the visual cortex comprising the posterior portion of the cerebral cortex of each side. Relatively few fibers now project to the geniculate bodies, which represent the optic tectum of the lower vertebrates. During early postnatal development in the cat, mainly in the 1- to 2-month-old kitten, and in humans, probably in the 2- to 4-year-old child, there is a visual-sensitive period of remarkable developmental plasticity. The experiments involve so-called feature-detectors, which are of two kinds: those that are found in many creatures and those that are specific to a particular species. The latter usually enable an animal to flourish in its behavioral environment. For example, the frog has visual cells that react when an object the size of a fly enters its field of vision. One can argue that these specific feature detectors are programmed genetically, but it is also possible that their development may at least be partially determined by environmental influence.

The feature detectors of an adult cat, located by means of minute electrodes inserted in the brain, turn out to be orientation-selective. They respond to, or are specific to, any line or edge moving across the animal's visual field along a particular orientation or angle. Any one cell is specific to a particular orientation, but all angles through the entire range of 360° are covered by the population of nerve cells in this area of the brain. Most of the cells are binocular, wired up to both eyes. In contrast, the very young kitten has almost no feature detectors. The cells destined to become feature detectors have not yet become specified for this function. The situation is comparable to *Xenopus* at about stage 30.

When kittens reared in visual environments consisting of only vertical stripes, or of only horizontal stripes, but not both, were later brought into the natural world, the "horizontal" cats were perfectly capable of jumping on a chair. When walking on the floor, they kept bumping into the chair legs as though they were invisible. The "vertical" cats avoided the chair legs but never attempted to jump on the chair, as though the seat did not exist. Brain examinations showed that the vertical cats had no horizontal-feature detectors and consequently, and literally, could not see anything composed of horizontal lines, such as the seat of a chair. Horizontal animals had no vertical detectors and so could not see vertical chair legs.

Other workers have measured the speed at which the character of the feature detectors is specified, with the astounding discovery that as little as 1 hour of visual experience can change the nature of feature detectors, much as though it were a learning experience. All these discoveries have important bearing on human development. Infants with uncorrected squint or severe astigmatism will grow up with permanent defects because it is the brain that is affected, not the eyes. Correction must be made while the brain is still plastic, during the visual-sensitive period of the first 2-to-4 years. What is true of vision probably applies to our other senses as well. We all know that infants go through a period of intense curiosity. This may be a behavioral expression of the brain's most sensitive period for acquiring knowledge and learning techniques. Unless the specific sensitive periods in the development of the brain are exploited to the full at the right time, their potential may be lost forever.

ADELMANN, H. B., 1936. Problems of Cyclopia, *Quart. Rev. Biol.*, **11**:161–304

COULOMBRE, A. J., 1965. The Eye, in R. L. DeHaan and H. Ursprung (eds.), "Organogenesis," Holt, Rinehart and Winston.

—— and J. L. COULOMBRE, 1965. Regeneration of Neural Retina from the Pigmented Epithelium in the Chick Embryo, *Develop. Biol.*, **12**:78–92.

DEHAAN, R. L., and H. URSPRUNG (eds.), 1965, "Organogenesis," Section II: The Nervous System, Holt, Rinehart and Winston.

ECCLES, J. C., 1973. "The Understanding of the Brain," McGraw-Hill.

GAZE, R. M., 1970. "The Formation of Nerve Connections," Academic.

GOTTLIEB, G., 1973. Behavioral Embryology, vol. I, "Studies on the Development of Behavior and the Nervous System," Academic.

HAMBURGER, V., 1968. Emergence of Nervous Coordination, in M. Locke (ed.), "The Emergence of Order in Developing Systems," 27th Symp. Soc. Devel. Biol., Academic.

HOLTFRETER, J., 1939. Tissue Affinity, A Means of Embryonic Morphogenesis, in English translation, in B. H. Willier and J. M. Oppenheimer (eds.), "Foundations of Embryology," Prentice-Hall.

HUNT, R. K., and M. JACOBSON, 1974. Development of Neuronal Locus Specificity in *Xenopus* Retinoganglial Cells after Surgical Eye Transsection or after Fusion of Whole Eyes, *Develop. Biol.*, **40**:1–15.

JACOBSON, M., 1970. "Developmental Neurobiology," Holt, Rinehart and Winston.

LEVI-MONTALCINI, R., and P. V. ANGELETTI, 1965. The Action of Nerve Growth Factor on Sensory and Sympathetic Cells, in R. L. DeHaan and H. Ursprung (eds.), "Organogenesis," Holt, Rinehart and Winston.

SPERRY, R. W., 1965. Embryogenesis of Behavioral Nerve Nets, in R. L. DeHaan and H. Ursprung (eds.), "Organogenesis," Holt, Rinehart and Winston.

STONE, L. S., 1960. Polarization of the Retina and Development of Vision, *J. Exp. Zool.*, **145**:85–93.

TRELSTAD, R. L., and A. J. COULOMBRE, 1971. Morphogenesis of the Collagenous Stroma of the Chick Cornea, *J. Cell Biol.*, **50**:840–858.

WEISS, P., 1955. Nervous System, in B. H. Willier, P. A. Weiss, and V. Hamburger (eds.), "Analysis of Development," Saunders.

YNTEMA, C. L., 1955. Ear and Nose, in B. H. Willier, P. A. Weiss, and V. Hamburger (eds.), "Analysis of Development," Saunders.

CHAPTER 16

Early Mammalian Development

The mammalian egg and its development are noted for several outstanding characteristics. The egg is very small (about 0.1 mm in diameter) and apparently yolkless, and it develops within the maternal uterus. Yet it quickly develops the various features of the amniote embryo, namely, blastoderm, yolk sac, amnion, and allantois. At a very early stage in development, the embryo invades the uterine lining and establishes itself as a graft that grows with all the avidity of a tumor. It develops into a placenta, which is a transformation of the allantois and chorion as seen in the chick into a unified structure interlocking with uterine tissue. This structure (Fig. 16.1), which in its original form in birds and reptiles served for waste storage and for respiratory exchange, now functions as a selective organ for all metabolic exchange between embryo and mother. The stalk of the allantois, containing the artery and the vein that supply the placenta, persists as the umbilical cord.

As in reptiles and birds, eggs are fertilized in the region of the funnels of the oviduct. In mammals the small egg is transported down the oviduct by the ciliated epithelium of the duct; during this time it undergoes at least the first stages of cleavage (Fig. 16.2). The mechanism of embryo transport is thought to involve a combination of ciliary action and muscular peristalsis. Only the epithelium of the upper part of the oviduct is ciliated, so ciliary action may be mostly concerned with passage of the unfertilized egg into the tube after ovulation, and with maintaining fluid currents there during the fertilization period. From fertilization, through the whole preimplantation period of development, the mammalian embryo remains relatively independent of the mother. This fortunate circumstance provides experimental embryologists with a great opportunity. But from implantation on, the embryo is almost entirely at the mercy of the mother and perishes swiftly if her hormonal, physiological, and immunological adaptations to pregnancy are inadequate.

MIGRATION AND FATE OF GERM CELLS

As in other vertebrates the primordial germ cells originate in the endoderm and later migrate to the genital ridges of the rudimentary gonad of the embryo. In

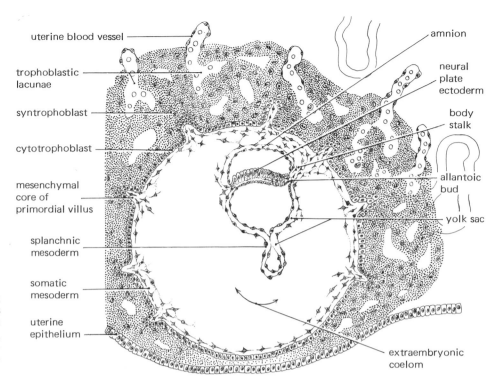

Figure 16.1 Human embryo of about 13 days fertilization age. [*From Patten and Carlson, "Foundations of Embryology," McGraw-Hill, 1974.*]

Labels (clockwise from top left): uterine blood vessel, trophoblastic lacunae, syntrophoblast, cytotrophoblast, mesenchymal core of primordial villus, splanchnic mesoderm, somatic mesoderm, uterine epithelium, amnion, neural plate ectoderm, body stalk, allantoic bud, yolk sac, extraembryonic coelom

Figure 16.2 Development of the human embryo in the reproductive tract, from fertilization to implantation. [*After H. Tuchmann-Duplessis, G. David, and P. Haegel, "Illustrated Human Embryology," vol. I, Springer-Verlag.*]

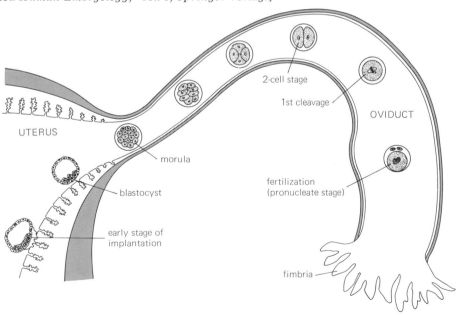

Labels: 2-cell stage, 1st cleavage, OVIDUCT, fertilization (pronucleate stage), fimbria, morula, blastocyst, early stage of implantation, UTERUS

mammals they are first recognizable in the early, presomite embryo, where they arise in the endoderm of the yolk-sac stalk, the allantois, and the gut. The cells are distinguishable because of their large size, numerous pseudopodiallike protrusions, and highly undifferentiated cytologic characters. The primordial germ cells migrate from their place of origin mostly by means of active amoeboid movements. On arrival in the embryonic genital ridges, they not only give rise to all the definitive germ cells but also act as inductors in the development and future organization of the gonads. The primordial germ cells multiply actively to give rise to oogonia, which leave the surface of the developing ovary by breaking through the basement membrane of the germinal epithelium. The oogonia occupy the cortical region of the ovary and continue to multiply.

In the human, the many cells thus produced by the time of birth constitute the sole source of ova throughout the life of the female. Of these, only about 400 will be ovulated and descend the oviduct between puberty and menopause. Yet, the period of ovarian storage is long compared with that of virtually all other mammals. Sperm are stored in the male for relatively very short periods and by nature are comparatively short-lived. Yet they, too, may be less than perfect. Normal sperm carry either an X or a Y sex chromosome. Those with an X chromosome yield a genetic female, since the zygote then has the XX constitution. Those with a Y chromosome yield males, since the zygote then has the XY constitution. Occasionally, however, sperm form that have neither an X or a Y chromosome, probably the result of nondisjunction during meiosis. A zygote produced in such a case has two complete sets of autosomal chromosomes but only a single sex (X) chromosome, constituting an imbalance. The effect of this condition is known as Turner's syndrome. In the mouse there is no effect. In the human the XO individual, although female, will be somewhat stunted physically and mentally, with various organic deficiencies, and will be sterile. Most XO fetuses are naturally aborted, but about 1 in every 1,000 human births has the XO constitution. In these individuals, no germ cells migrate into the genital ridges. Neither oocytes nor ovarian hormones are produced, resulting in sterility and the absence of the secondary sexual characteristics associated with puberty.

EARLY MOUSE DEVELOPMENT

The mature mouse ovum has a diameter of 95 μm. It has five to ten times as much mitochondrial DNA as normal diploid somatic cells. It is surrounded by a noncelluar secretion produced by follicle cells and oocyte known as the *zona pellucida*, which plays an important role in the fertilization process. Cleavage is total (holoblastic), as might be expected in such a small and almost yolkless mammalian egg. The timetable of the early developmental events, up to the establishment of the primary embryonic structures, is shown in Table 3.

CLEAVAGE AND BLASTOCYST

Although in size and general appearance the mammalian egg (Fig 16.3) closely resembles the small eggs of many marine invertebrates and the protochordates, its development, except for the return to holoblastic cleavage, differs in important ways. Eggs do not all cleave at the same time intervals, nor are all the cleavages in each cell of a single egg completed at the same time, so that in many cases there may be uneven numbers of cells. Cleavage takes place much

Days of Gestation	Stage
1	One- to two-cell, in uppermost part of oviduct
2	Two- to sixteen-cell, in transit to uterus
3	Morula (solid ball of cells), in upper part of uterus
4	Free blastocyst in uterus, shedding of zona pellucida
4½	Beginning of implantation
5	Inner cell mass elongating, primitive streak evident, and proamniotic cavity
6	Implantation complete, extraembryonic parts developing
7	Ectoplacental cone, amniotic folds, primitive streak, heart and pericardium forming, head process evident
7¼	Early neurula, neural plate, chorioamniotic stalk, allantoic stalk beginning, inner cell mass with three cavities, somites beginning to differentiate, foregut present
8½	Neural tube formed, embryo established
9–19	Growth of fetus
19–20	Birth

SOURCE: C. R. Austin, "Fertilization," © 1965. Reprinted by permission of Prentice-Hall, Inc. Englewood Cliffs, N.J.

Figure 16.3 Cleaving egg of rabbit fertilized and cultured in vitro, about 0.15 mm diameter. [*Courtesy of R. J. Erisson, copyright* © American Association for the Advancement of Science.]

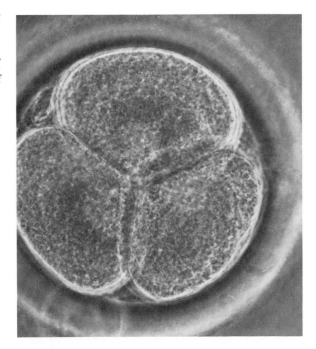

more slowly than in most lower vertebrates or invertebrates. Whereas frog eggs cleave about once an hour, and goldfish eggs and sea urchin eggs once in 20 to 30 minutes, the mouse egg takes 24 hours for its first cleavage division and 10 to 12 hours for each succeeding division. We do not know the reason for the difference.

By the two- to four-cell stage in the mouse, and the morula in the rabbit, nucleoli have become prominently active centers of RNA synthesis. The morula becomes a blastula or *blastocyst,* in the 32- to 64-cell stage, by acquiring an eccentrically placed cavity filled with fluid (Figs. 16.4 and 16.5). The blastocyst, however, differs from the blastula seen in the sea urchin or in *Amphioxus* and shows kinship with meroblastic development. A single layer of lining cells, the *trophoblast,* encloses the cavity of the blastocyst except at one side, where a knob of cells forms the *inner cell mass.* The inner cell mass represents the embryo-to-be and certain extraembryonic membranes, while the trophoblast is primarily responsible for making contact with the maternal circulation.

The blastula shortly becomes the free blastocyst, escaping or "hatching" from the enclosing zona pellucida, a process that includes both an enlargement and a rhythmic undulating movement. However, if the zona pellucida is digested off with pronase, normal hatching behavior still occurs in vitro inasmuch as lobes extrude from the trophoblast cells at the appropriate time. The function of the zona pellucida is believed to include maintenance of the normal cleavage pattern and prevention of egg fusion.

Figure 16.4 Early development of the mouse egg. *a* Four-cell stages, each enclosed in thick zona pellucida (micro-injected silicone droplets, here seen in two cells in each case, are employed as cell tracers in subsequent development). *b* Blastocyst showing differentiation into inner cell mass and trophoblast, with large blastocoel. Hatching from the zona has already occurred. The end of a micropipette used for injection of droplets or of cells into the developing system. [*Courtesy of I. B. Wilson.*]

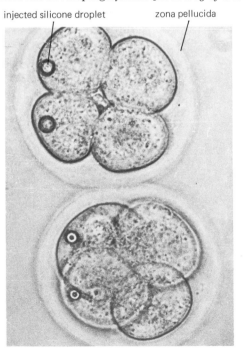
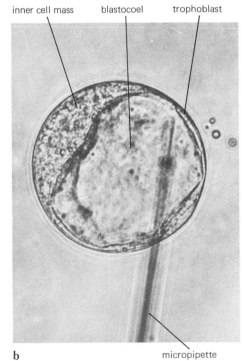

injected silicone droplet   zona pellucida   inner cell mass   blastocoel   trophoblast

a   b   micropipette

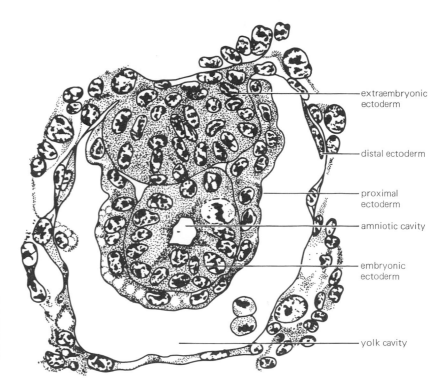

Labels on figure (top to bottom, right side):
extraembryonic ectoderm
distal ectoderm
proximal ectoderm
amniotic cavity
embryonic ectoderm
yolk cavity

Figure 16.5 Section of a mouse blastocyst soon after implantation, at about 5 to 6 days after fertilization. [*From Snell and Stevens, "Early Embryology of the Laboratory Mouse," McGraw-Hill, 1966.*]

IMPLANTATION

Implantation begins shortly after hatching, during which the trophoblast cells in contact with the uterus transform to giant cells, while the inner cell mass changes in form and size. Similar changes in the rabbit are thought to be initiated and controlled by a protein, named *blastokinin,* which is secreted by the uterus into the uterine cavity.

During implantation the trophoblast cells aggressively invade the uterine tissue (Fig. 16.6), ceasing about the ninth day in the mouse, when maternal blood vessels are reached and breached. When implantation is in extrauterine sites such as kidney, spleen, and testes, the period of invasion, which becomes extremely destructive, is much extended. Implantation occurs in the absence of ovarian hormones in extrauterine sites. In some locations, such as abdominal mesentery (particularly in rabbits), abnormally sited implantations of an entire litter may develop to term, although delivery of the young may be impossible and fetal death follows. The uterus is prepared for implantation by the action of the ovarian hormones progesterone and estrogen. When the uterine endometrium is in an appropriately sensitized condition, a decidual or implantation reaction can be induced not only by the blastocyst as a stimulus, but by an artificial stimulus such as the scratching of a needle.

GASTRULATION

During implantation the inner cell mass undergoes gastrulation, inasmuch as the part nearest the blastocoel splits off to form the endoderm, while the remaining cells form the ectoderm. The situation resembles that in the chick

357

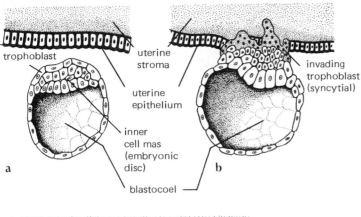

trophoblast

uterine stroma

uterine epithelium

inner cell mas (embryonic disc)

blastocoel

a

invading trophoblast (syncytial)

b

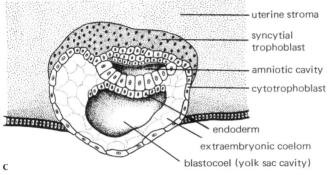

uterine stroma

syncytial trophoblast

amniotic cavity

cytotrophoblast

endoderm

extraembryonic coelom

blastocoel (yolk sac cavity)

c

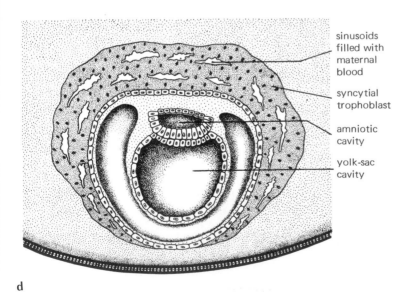

sinusoids filled with maternal blood

syncytial trophoblast

amniotic cavity

yolk-sac cavity

d

Figure 16.6 Implantation of the human embryo. *a* The blastocyst is not yet attached to the uterine epithelium. *b* The trophoblast has penetrated the epithelium and is beginning to invade the uterine stroma. *c* The blastocyst has sunk further into the stroma and the amniotic cavity has appeared. *d* The uterine epithelium has grown over the implantation site, so that the blastocyst is entirely enclosed in maternal tissue, and irregular spaces, the sinusoids, filled with maternal blood, have appeared in the syncytial trophoblast. [*After H. Tuchmann-Duplessis, G. David, and P. Haegel, "Illustrated Human Embryology," vol. I, Springer-Verlag.*]

blastoderm, where there are upper- and lower-level sheets of cells. A short primitive streak becomes evident as a thickening of the embryonic ectoderm in the posterior half of the blastoderm (Fig. 16.7). Mesoderm forms from cells moving sideways from the streak between ectoderm and endoderm. Having given rise to the mesoderm and the notochord, the streak disappears. Formation of the embryo proceeds anteriorly from the primitive streak in much the same way as in the chick, with formation of chordamesoderm, neural plate, and somites. There is a strong general resemblance between, for instance, a 29-somite chick embryo and a 28-somite pig embryo. The course of development of the head, heart, somites, limbs, sense organs, etc., is very similar.

CULTURE OF EGGS AND EMBRYOS

Mammalian oocytes, which normally mature in the ovary, can be induced to mature in a culture medium. Even human oocytes, obtained from ovaries, have been brought to maturation, fertilized, and cultured in vitro to the blastocyst stage. Such mammalian eggs may then be introduced into the uterus, where they implant in the normal manner.

Attempts to maintain developing mammalian embryos in culture beyond the blastocyst stage have been mostly unsuccessful. It was thought that further development depended on contact with the uterus. This barrier to differentiation, at least in the mouse, has been overcome by (1) the use of reconstituted rat-tail collagen as the substrate for implantation, which fixes the inner cell mass and induces polarity on the mouse embryos, and (2) a factor or factors contained in fetal calf serum used for cultivation. Under these circumstances mouse embryos have been raised in vitro to the early somite stage, corresponding to 8½ days of normal gestation (Fig. 16.8) or nearly halfway through the usual gestation period as a whole. Frequent changes of the culture medium are necessary. These results imply that (1) the rapid removal of metabolic waste from the embryo is critical for the differentiation of the embryo proper or

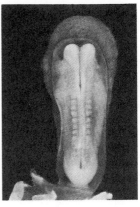

Figure 16.7 Human embryo at 8-somite stage (probable age 18 days from fertilization) within amnion, showing large neural folds anteriorly, somites in trunk region, and primitive streak posteriorly. [*From B. M. Patten and B. M. Carlson, "Foundations of Embryology," McGraw-Hill, 1974.*]

Figure 16.8 Scanning electron micrograph of mammalian embryo, removed from amnion. Neural development in the hamster at open neural-fold stage (7¾-day embryo), showing early optic evagination internally from each side of the open brain cavity. Compare with SEM of older embryo, Fig. 14.6 [*Courtesy of R. E. Waterman.*]

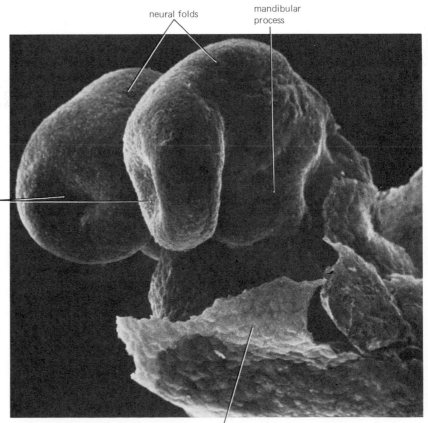

neural folds

mandibular process

optic evaginations

torn amnion

(2) the culture medium contains some unstable factor or factors essential for embryo differentiation that must be supplied constantly. Rabbit blastocysts also can develop beating hearts, somites, and neural structures in tissue-culture medium supplemented with well-circulated and oxygenated serum.

REGULATION AND DETERMINATION

Experiments of many kinds concerning the question of regulation versus determination in early mouse development have been conducted on both sides of the Atlantic, notably by Garner, Tarkowski, Mintz, Wilson, Hillman, and Moustafa, together with their coworkers. These experiments all contribute to a single, general concept known as the inside-outside concept.

The position of microdrops of inert silicone, placed at various locations of the egg periphery or centrally at the interface between the first two blastomeres, can be followed in subsequent development (Fig. 16.5). The eventual locations of the droplets have an apparent random distribution with regard to trophoblast and inner cell mass. There is no constant relationship between the initial site of a droplet and any particular topographic destiny; this indicates there is no bilateral symmetry or polarity inherent in the cleaving egg. Physico-chemical positional effects must determine whether cells become trophoblast or inner cell mass.

Two-celled eggs usually show abnormal cleavage patterns in vitro after the zona is removed; this appears to be due to inadequately developed cell adhesiveness. As a result the blastomeres form loosely bound flat plaques or random arrangements. They may, however, round up and form a morula, which continues development. Eight-celled eggs deprived of the zona pellucida progress in vitro in a completely normal fashion to the blastocyst, when they may be reimplanted into the uterus of a foster mother for further development. Blastomeres of naked eggs during all stages of cleavage tend to remain in contact with their neighbors, though they may be separated with versene, a compound that binds Ca^{2+} and Mg^{2+}. Surfaces of eggs from which the zona pellucida has been removed are considerably stickier than they are when the membrane is still present, and the eggs tend to adhere to each other. The fusion is greatly accelerated at 37°C; this fact has served as the basis of a method for synthesizing genetic mosaics (Fig. 16.9). The composites will develop when transferred to a foster mother. Both Tarkowski and Mintz obtained living chimeric animals by fusing synchronously cleaving mouse embryo (Fig. 16.10). When fusions are made at the eight-cell stage, almost 100 percent normal blastocysts develop, of

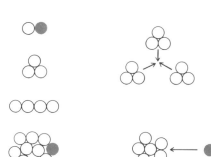

Figure 16.9 Experimental combinations of mid-cleavage eggs. Each circle represents an entire, denuded egg. Black circles are eggs preincubated in ³H-thymidine before aggregation. Arrows show a second step in aggregation. [*After Mintz*, Proc. Nat. Acad. Sci., **58**:344, 1967.]

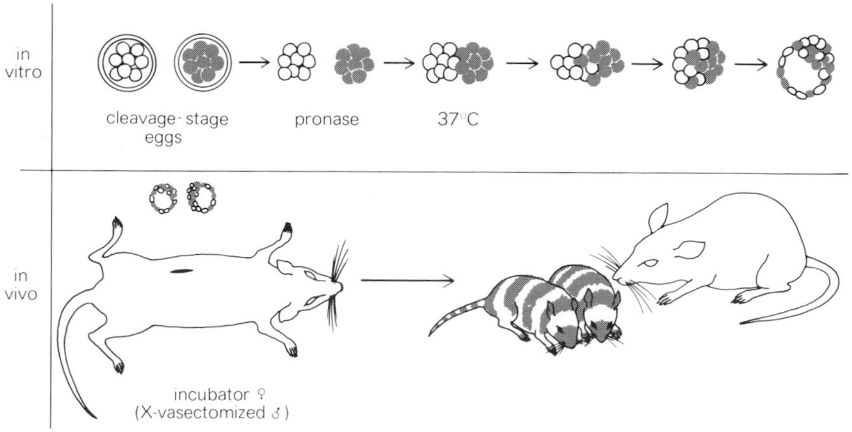

Figure 16.10 Experimental procedures for producing allophenic mice from aggregated eggs. Cleavage stages are denuded of external membrane and are fused together. The combined eggs are then introduced into the uterus of a foster mother, where they implant and develop. [*After Mintz, 1967.*]

quadruple parentage. To follow contributions made by cells from each egg, blastomeres from one member are prelabeled for autoradiographic analysis by incubation with tritiated thymidine before fusion.

In other experiments that used the same technique, double-size, genetically mosaic blastocysts were obtained by fusing cleavage stages of embryos of dissimilar genotypes. As in the case of all giant blastocysts obtained through fusion, normal embryo size is restored during implantation in the foster mother. This is true even when as many as 16 have been united to form one enormous blastocyst, which begins with a correspondingly large inner cell mass. According to Mintz, the basis for this size regulation may lie in the origin of the embryo from a small, fixed number of cells (possibly as few as three) in the inner cell mass, regardless of the total number of cells in the blastocyst. The assumption is that the size of the embryo at each stage, including birth, is a direct expression of the number (mass) of cells initially destined to form the embryo proper, irrespective of the total number of inner-cell-mass cells.

Fusion of cleaving eggs to give rise to normal, though large blastocysts is possible even when the fused embryos are at different stages. Fused eight-cell and four-cell stages (i.e., 12 hours out of phase) and eight-cell and late morula stages, fused in pairs of labeled and unlabeled components, showed that trophoblast from the early blastocyst can be incorporated into the inner cell mass. All develop into normal blastocysts.

Not only do complete asynchronous early developmental stages combine to develop normally as a single system, but when eight-cell and late blastocyst stages are dissociated into their constituent cells, reaggregation masses can develop into normal blastocysts even though the aggregated cells derive from the two different stages.

In another series of experiments, embryos and parts of embryos were combined during early preimplantation development; they were followed by means of tritiated DNA or by using cells with different electrophoretic variants of glucose phosphate esterase. Results showed that each blastomere of a four-celled embryo can form both trophoblast and inner cell mass and that there is no evidence for segregation of morphogenetic factors at the four- or eight-cell stage. Moreover, one blastomere of an eight-celled embryo (in the rabbit) can form a complete adult after the other seven have been killed with a needle.

Single mouse embryonic cells have been successfully transplanted into preimplanted mouse blastocysts; some of these blastocysts developed into chi-

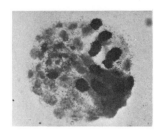

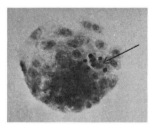

a

b   c

Figure 16.11 Transplanted mouse blastomeres. *a* A recipient blastocyst with labeled synchronous cells 40 hours after transplantation of the labeled cells. *b* A recipient blastocyst 40 hours after cell transplantation with five labeled cells. *c* Litter of five fetuses typical of chimeras produced when either embryonic synchronous or asynchronous cells are transplanted into preimplanted mouse blastocysts. At birth and during postnatal development, chimerism is expressed in coat color, eye pigmentation, and germ cells. [*Courtesy of L. A. Moustafa.*]

meric young. When one or more single labeled cells from an inner cell mass of one blastocyst are injected by means of a micropipette into another mouse blastocyst, large parts of the developing host embryo are colonized by descendants of the labeled cell (Fig. 16.11). This implies that very few cells in the host blastocyst are truly embryonic, for otherwise a single additional cell could not contribute so much to the future embryo. Accordingly, embryonic determination is not initiated until the blastocyst is well established.

INSIDE-OUTSIDE CONCEPT

According to the inside-outside concept, embryonic cells differentiate according to their position in the system. Therefore: (1) a cell will form only part of the inner cell mass if it has previously been on the inside of the morula; (2) a cell will form only trophoblast if it has previously been on the outside of the morula; and (3) the cell should remain in these positions for at least 8 hours if it is to acquire the properties of either of these two cell types. This has been tested by Hillman and Graham (1971) who found that:

1   If blastomeres of a four-cell embryo are labeled with tritiated thymidine and placed on the outside of another intact four-cell embryo, the labeled cells are almost always found in the trophoblast part of the blastocyst, which develops 2 days later. The whole eventually becomes a typical embryo. Under normal circumstances, these labeled cells would form both inner cell mass and trophoblast whereas now they form only trophoblast because of their peripheral location in the composite embryo.

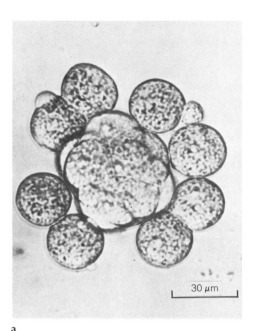

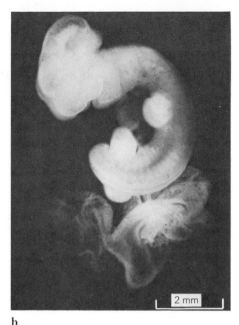

30 μm

2 mm

a b

Figure 16.12 The effect of cell position on cell determination in mouse embryos. *a* The whole of one embryo outside another. A 4-celled embryo was disaggregated and each blastomere allowed to divide once. All the blastomeres were then arranged on the outside of another 8- to 16-celled embryo, and the composite was implanted in a foster mother. The cells placed on the outside generally form yolk sac and trophoblast, although contributing to fetus formation; the inside cells form fetus primarily. *b* A 13-day embryo formed from a composite of sixteen 8-cell stages. [*Courtesy of N. Hillman.*]

2 If a whole morula is marked with tritiated thymidine and is surrounded on all its surfaces by a total of 15 unlabeled morulas (Fig. 16.12), all the cells of the enclosed embryo form part of the inner cell mass of the giant composite that subsequently develops; none form trophoblast cells as they normally would.

3 If the central cells are isolated from these composites after 2 days, it is found that they have irreversibly lost the ability to form trophoblast vesicles. That is, all the cells of the embryo had acquired the properties of the inner cell mass by enclosure inside other cells for the previous 2 days. The surrounded morula must be inside the composite for more than 8 hours if its ability to differentiate into trophoblast is to be suppressed.

4 Restriction of developmental capacities of the blastomeres has occurred by the blastocyst stage. Cells on the outside of the blastocyst (trophoblast) are unable to form part of the postimplantation fetus (derived from the inside) either as a group of cells or as a single cell injected into another blastocyst. Cells on the inside of the blastocyst (inner cell mass) cannot by themselves continue to develop when implanted into the uterus of a pseudopregnant (hormonally prepared) animal.

5 According to the concept, a cell differentiates solely because of position with regard to the rest of the embryo. To repeat, outside cells become trophoblast, inside cells become inner cell mass.

Once the blastocyst has become fully implanted and differentiated, development proceeds, sustained by metabolic exchanges across the boundary between the placenta and the uterine blood vessels.

EMBRYO AND FETUS

Apart from the hazards of implantation, the crucial period in human development is the third and fourth week following fertilization, when a woman first begins to wonder whether she is pregnant. At the end of this time an embryo is recognizable, with virtually every feature present, even though the whole is only about one-third of an inch long. There is a head, complete with rudimentary eyes, ears, and brain, and a body with a digestive tract, heart and bloodstream, simple kidneys, and a liver. There are two pairs of small, budlike bulges representing the future arms and legs (Fig. 13.3). By the end of the second month, often still unnoticed or ignored, the embryo has grown to about 1 inch in length and weighs about a gram, small enough to sit upon a postage stamp. Yet it is already recognizably human, with nose, lips, tongue, milk teeth buds, a rounded body, and all the internal organs at work. The embryo, as it is called up to this stage, is complete. The worst mistakes, if any, have been made, with a price yet to be paid. What is left to be done is mainly the tremendous growth and further elaboration of what is already constructed, a process that continues to adulthood and is only momentarily interrupted by birth. After 6 weeks the embryo ceases to be called an embryo and is known as the fetus, in order to emphasize that another phase of existence has been reached. By the end of the second month, therefore, we can say with some assurance that the person in the womb is present, with all the basic equipment and some sensitivity, but with a long, long way to go to be fully human. Whether a single individual or two identical twins or more are produced, however, was a developmental decision made soon after the completion of implantation. This question is taken up in the following section.

TWINNING IN MAMMALS

Twins can be monozygotic (one-egg, identical) or dizygotic (two-egg, fraternal). Dizygotic twins are formed when two eggs are shed in a single ovulation period and are fertilized by two separate spermatozoa. The resulting young resemble each other genetically no more than do any other brothers and sisters. Injection of gonadotrophic hormones can induce multiple ovulations and hence promote dizygote twinning. This technique finds practical application in cattle breeding, while in women multiple births are an undesirable side effect of the use of gonadotrophins to combat sterility.

The production of two or three embryos from a single blastoderm is not infrequent in fish, reptiles, and birds, but the offspring are fated to an early death. In all of these, the two or more embryos developing from the single blastoderm inevitably share one and the same yolk sac. When the yolk is finally resorbed, the embryos become united at their abdominal surface as Siamese twins. In mammals the situation is different because the yolk sac is a small remnant, empty of yolk, and plays no part in later development. Mammalian identical (monozygotic) twins are united only in that they share a common placenta, although each has its own umbilical cord and amnion. Inasmuch as the cords are in any case broken at birth, the offspring are set free from one another.

True twinning cannot be studied in most mammals because the event itself cannot be anticipated and is known only after the critical process has occurred. Various species of the armadillo, however, produce identical twins as the normal routine; the offspring number two, four, and commonly, eight, according to the species.

The nine-banded Texas armadillo, *Dasypus novemcinctus,* produces four monozygous offspring routinely. The study of normal development in this species is inevitably the study of quadruplet formation. The basic studies are by Patterson (1913). These are discussed at length in "The Biology of Twins" (Newman, 1917) and were recently reexamined by Storrs and Williams with regard to biochemical and anatomical variation within sets of quadruplets. Analysis of this development strongly confirms the conclusion that the mammalian egg is completely labile until well after implantation of blastocyst in the number of embryos that can be initiated.

The armadillo blastocyst is similar to that of the mouse, except for a very much larger vesicular cavity. It consists of an outer trophoblast and an inner cell mass that segregates into ectoderm and endoderm cell mass. At the time of this segregation, the inner cell mass has eleven cells, six of which (with larger nuclei) will form embryonic ectoderm; the remainder become endoderm. As in other mammals, the ectoderm forms a hollow vesicle that becomes both the embryonic ectoderm proper and the amnion.

In nontwinning mammals the embryo first appears as a primitive streak in a thickened area, or apical pole, of ectoderm forming the floor of the vesicle, thereby establishing bilateralism (the embryonic axis). In the armadillo, after a period of growth of the blastocyst, two embryonic ectodermal thickenings appear. These are located at two ends of the same bilateral axis, each with its head toward the apical pole (Fig. 16.13a). They are the primordia of the two *primary embryos*. According to Newman, the original bilateralism of the vesicle, which determines this primary axis, has been secondarily imposed by the preexisting bilateralism of the uterus; no other explanation of the coincidence between uterine and embryonic axes is apparent.

Secondary embryos first appear as shorter secondary outgrowths of the ectodermal plate on an axis at right angles to the primary axis, after the primary embryonic areas are already identifiable (Fig. 16.13b). In another species (*Dasypus hybridus),* however, the typical number of monozygous embryos produced ranges from seven to twelve, with a preponderance of eight. In this species one or two tertiary axes probably form across the blastodermic ectoderm between the primary and secondary axes.

It is evident that in the mammal—as in fish, reptile, and bird—there is no preprogramming of the egg for a specific development of an embryo and no definitive determination; any part of the ectodermal blastocyst disc can establish an embryonic field capable of self-directed development into a typical embryo.

Quadruplets derived from a single zygote presumably have identical genes. Nevertheless such quadruplets are only approximately identical, and recent

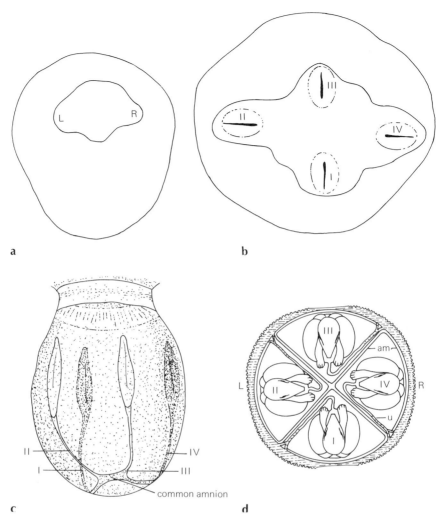

Figure 16.13 Quadruplet production in the armadillo. *a* Blastocyst with outline of ectodermal vesicle developed from an inner cell mass. One axis of the vesicle is longer than the other and a left and right "primary bud" form at the ends of the longer axis. *b* Later stage showing four embryos at late primitive-streak stage, resulting from two "secondary buds" forming between the two primary buds, at the ends of the shorter axis; all four are oriented toward the center of the complex or common amnion. *c* Later stage showing that the primary embryos (II and IV) are in advance of the secondary embryos (I and III). *d* Full-term quadruplets seen from one pole, occupying four quadrants with partitions. (*After Patterson*).

biochemical analyses have shown that a remarkable degree of variation actually exists.

It was observed that enormous physiological variations exist within very closely inbred rats, fowl, etc. The question arose whether unknown factors, aside from the gene pool itself, also control the intricate process of differentiation, particularly *the extent to which each of the numerous types of differentiated cells proliferates.* During the production of the four primordial buds in the armadillo in two stages, small variations in initial size and cell constitution (apart from chromosomal content) are inevitable. These could in turn lead to varying differences in the sizes of organs and in biochemical parameters related to these varying organ sizes. Analyses show that differences are always present and are detectable for 20 parameters measured. It was concluded that such differences are due to inescapable, accidental differences in the makeup of the cytoplasms of the four primordial buds. How many of each kind of cell and how much of each tissue will be produced during development are of paramount importance, because they may govern the most fundamental and important characters of the organism. Much of human variability, accordingly, may be the result of circumstantial quantitative differences arising during the initial phase of embryo establishment, in addition to those from genetic variability.

READINGS

AUSTIN, C. R., and R. V. SHORT (eds.), 1972. "Reproduction in Mammals." Book 2. "Embryonic and Fetal Development," Cambridge University Press.

BERRILL, N. J., 1968. "The Person in the Womb," Dodd, Mead (and Apollo).

BLANDAU, R. J., 1975. Fetal-Maternal Interactions, 33rd Symposium, The Society of Developmental Biology, Academic.

———, 1971. "The Biology of the Blastocyst," University of Chicago Press.

DANIEL, J. C., 1972. "Methods in Mammalian Embryology," W. H. Freeman.

FLANAGAN, G. L., 1962. "The First Nine Months," Simon and Shuster.

GARDNER, R. L., 1975. Analysis of Determination and Differentiation in the Early Mammalian Embryo Using Intra- and Interspecific Chimaeras, 33rd Symposium, The Society of Developmental Biology, Academic.

GRAHAM, C. F., 1973. Early Mammalian Development, 31st Symposium, The Society of Developmental Biology, Academic.

———, 1971. The Design of the Mouse Blastocyst, Symposium, *Soc. Exp. Biol.,* **25**:371–378.

HILLMAN, N., M. I. SHERMAN, and C. F. GRAHAM, 1972. The Effect of Spatial Arrangement on Cell Determination during Mouse Development, *J. Embryol. Exp. Morphol,* **28**:263–278.

HSU, Y. C., 1973. Differentiation *in vitro* of Mouse Embryos to the Stage of Early Somite, *Develop. Biol.,* **33**:403–411.

McLAREN, A., 1972. The Embryo, in C. R. Austin and R. U. Short (eds.), "Reproduction in Mammals," Book 2, Cambridge University Press.

MANES, C., 1975. Genetic and Biochemical Activities in Preimplantation Embryos, 33rd Symposium, The Society of Developmental Biology, Academic.

MARKERT, C. L., and J. PAPANCONSTANTINOU (eds.), 1975. "The Developmental Biology of Reproduction," Academic.

MINTZ, B., 1967. Mammalian Embryo Culture, in F. H. Wilt and N. K. Wessells (eds.), "Methods in Developmental Biology," Crowell.

———, 1964. Synthetic Processes and Early Development in the Mammalian Egg, *J. Exp. Zool.,* **157**:85–100.

MOUSTAFA, L. A., and R. L. BRINSTER, 1972. The Fate of Transplanted Cells in Mouse Blastocysts in vitro, *J. Exp. Zool.,* **181**:181–192, 193–202.

MULNARD, J. G., 1971. Manipulation of Cleaving Mammalian Eggs with Special Reference to a Time-lapse Cinematographic Analysis of Centrifuged and Fused Mouse Eggs, *Advan. Biol. Sci.,* **6**:255–274.

NEWMAN, H. H., 1917. "The Biology of Twins," University of Chicago Press.

PATTERSON, J. T., 1913. Polyembryonic Development in *Tatusia novemcineta, J. Morphol.,* **24**:599–684.

RUGH, R., 1968. "The Mouse. Its Reproduction and Development," Burgess.

SHERMAN, M. I., 1975. The Relationships between the Early Mouse Embryo and its Environment, 33rd Symposium, The Society of Developmental Biology, Academic.

STERN, S. M., AND I. B. WILSON, 1972. Experimental Studies on the Organization of the Preimplantation Mouse Embryo, *J. Embryol. Exp. Morphol.,* **28**:247–261.

STORRS, E. E., and R. J. WILLIAMS, 1968. A Study of Monozygous Quadruplet Armadillos in Relation to Mammalian Genetics, *Proc. Nat. Acad. Sci.*, **60**:910–914.

TARKOWSKI, A. K., 1975. Induced Mammalian Parthenogenesis and Early Development, 33rd Symposium, The Society of Developmental Biology, Academic.

———— and J. Wroblewska, 1967. Development of Blastomeres of Mouse Eggs Isolated at the 4- and 8-celled Stage, *J. Embryol. Exp. Morphol.*, **18**:155–180.

WILSON, I. B., E. BOLTON, and R. H. CUTLER, 1972. Preimplantation Differentiation in the Mouse Egg as Revealed by Microinjection of Vital Markers. *J. Embryol. Exp. Morphol.*, **27**:467–479.

PART IV

CELL DIFFERENTIATION AND TISSUE ASSEMBLY

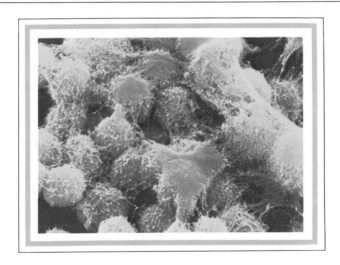

Cytodifferentiation

Cytodifferentiation is the process whereby cells acquire those biochemical and morphological properties necessary to perform their specialized functions. The transformation from the *undifferentiated* to the fully *differentiated* state is a gradual one. It begins with a shift in developmental potential from the totipotent to the more restricted. As development proceeds, the repertoire of types into which a given cell can differentiate becomes gradually limited. In vertebrates there is no evidence of truly undifferentiated cells that can be directed into any morphogenetic pathway under the appropriate environmental conditions. Rather, the process of cytodifferentiation in the embryo and the continual process of tissue renewal in the adult are accomplished by a diverse population of *stem cells,* each capable of providing the organism with a limited variety of specialized cells.

In this chapter we will examine the process whereby a variety of precursor cells (stem cells) undergo the terminal steps in the differentiation of each cell line. Though each differentiated cell type has reached this stage via a predictable and unique series of events, developmental biologists have sought to uncover principles that can be applied to many, if not all, of these cytodifferentiations. Questions of general importance considered in this chapter include: What mechanisms are responsible for shifting a cell along one path of specialized differentiation rather than another? What is the nature of the primary events leading to differentiation and at what stage do they occur? At what stages in the differentiation process can specialized gene products, such as hemoglobin or myosin, be identified? To what extent is cytodifferentiation determined by interactions with the cellular and noncellular environment as opposed to internal factors? To what extent is the continuing cycle of mitotic divisions involved in the cytodifferentiation process? How stable is the differentiated state and under what conditions, if any, can it be reversed? To what extent can cytodifferentiation be explained in terms of a sequential series of self-assemblies?

CELL SPECIFICITY

An outstanding feature in a multicellular organism, whether a hydra or a mammal, is that each differentiated cell type falls into a clearly recognizable discrete category, sharply set off from other cell types.

The various types of cell specialization appear to be accentuations of the properties of the unspecialized or undifferentiated cell, such as plasma membrane, intracellular organelles, cilia or flagella, microfibrils and microtubules, etc. Secretory cells like those of the pancreas show extreme development of the endoplasmic reticulum-Golgi system, produce specific zymogen proteins, and have a sharply polarized internal organization. Nerve cells combine localized axoplasmic growth and terminal secretion with considerable development of the electrochemical features of the plasma membrane. In retinal cells stacks of infolded plasma membrane form the pseudocrystalline rods. Schwann cells produce excessive plasma membrane that becomes wrapped around nerve axons as the myelin sheath. Contractile cells have hypertrophied systems of actomyosin microfibrils. Spermatozoa are primarily condensed cells with extreme development of the microtubule system characteristic of all cilia or flagella. All such specializations are recognizable in the general features of the undifferentiated cell, although each may be unique in having certain proteins not present in others. In a sense the general properties of the cell represent the keyboard on which various types and patterns of selection are made (Fig. 17.1).

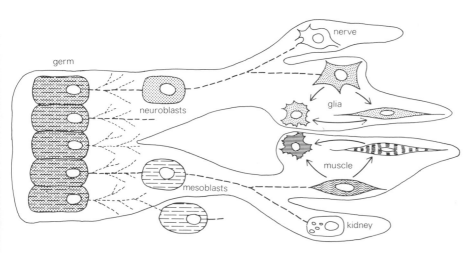

Figure 17.1 Differentiation of cells in steps, from unspecialized embryonic cells through stem cells such as neuroblasts and mesoblasts to differentiated nerve, glia, muscle, and kidney cells. [*After Weiss, 1953.*]

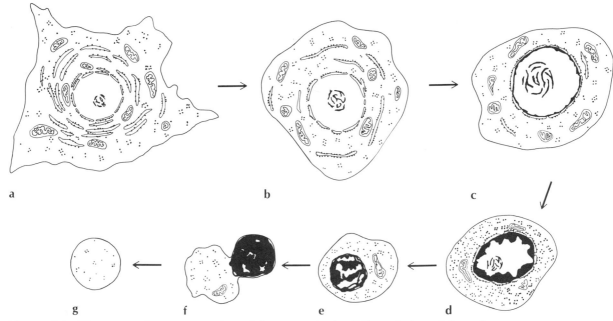

Figure 17.2 Diagrammatic representation of the stages in the differentiation of the red blood cell. *a* The hypothetical pluripotent mesenchymal cell, which can give rise to more than one type of stem cell. *b* The hemocytoblast, the stem cell of the erythroid line. These cells are identifiable and determined but do not show overt erythroid differentiations. *c* The proerythroblast; a stage of active RNA synthesis in preparation for differentiation. *d* The basophilic erythroblast, characterized by chromosomal condensation and concomitant reduction in nuclear activity. Hemoglobin synthesis is believed to begin in these cells. *e* The polychromatophilic stage, characterized by increasing synthesis and accumulation of hemoglobin and decreasing levels of RNA synthesis. *f* The orthochromatic erythroblast, characterized by an inactive nucleus and hemoglobin-filled cytoplasm. These cells are no longer capable of cell division. *g* The reticulocyte, which has lost its nucleus and is found circulating in the bloodstream, continues to synthesize hemoglobin for a day or two. The final stage is the terminally differentiated erythrocyte, or red blood cell, characterized by the absence of protein synthesis. [*After R. A. Rifkind, in J. Lash and J. R. Whitaker, "Concepts of Development," Sinauer, 1974.*]

ERYTHROPOIESIS

Erythropoiesis is the formation of erythrocytes (red blood cells). It is a sequential, stepwise series of changes whereby a determined precursor cell, a *hemocytoblast,* fills with hemoglobin, shuts down all RNA and protein synthesis, and is released to the circulation to transport oxygen (Fig. 17.2). Analysis of erythropoiesis centers on the synthesis and accumulation of hemoglobin, a well-characterized metalloprotein found only in cells of the erythrocyte line. Each hemoglobin molecule consists of a protein, globin, composed of four polypeptide chains—of which several different species are encoded within the genome—and four iron-containing porphyrins known as heme. In the mouse and in man the prenatal period is characterized by two sites of erythrocyte formation, first in the yolk sac and then in the liver. The yolk-sac erythroblasts form clusters of erythroid cells, termed *blood islands,* from which they enter the fetal circulation. There they complete their maturation in synchrony.

The erythrocytes that arise in the yolk sac contain several different hemoglobins (together termed *embryonic hemoglobin),* each distinct from the adult variety. The adult hemoglobin molecule contains two alpha and two beta poly-peptide chains; the embryonic hemoglobins contain the alpha chains but have substitutes for the betas.

Erythropoiesis in the yolk sac becomes joined and is soon replaced by another site of erythrocyte formation, the fetal liver. The liver is the primary site for the production of erythrocytes for the fetus but is replaced after birth by the bone marrow, which is the definitive site for the tremendous lifetime production of circulating red blood cells. Thus, as with numerous other cells—skin cells, lymphocytes, pigment cells, etc.—the process of erythropoiesis, first initiated in the embryo, continues throughout the life of the individual. In man there are three types of hemoglobin produced: embryonic hemoglobin by yolk-sac erythroblasts, fetal hemoglobin by fetal liver erythroblasts, and the adult variety produced after birth, primarily by bone-marrow erythroblasts. Fetal hemoglobin is characterized by a greater affinity for oxygen than the adult molecule and ensures oxygenation of the fetal blood.

Erythropoiesis is under the control of a hormone, erythropoietin, a glycoprotein produced by the kidney in response to lowered tissue oxygenation. Erythropoietin both in vivo and in vitro specifically induces an erythroid precursor cell (one already determined toward erythropoiesis) to proliferate and differentiate via a series of steps into the mature erythrocyte. Terminal differentiation is characterized by the condensation and inactivation of the chromatin along with increasing use of the protein-synthesizing machinery for globin synthesis.

MELANOGENESIS

Vertebrate pigment cells, or *melanocytes,* derive from two sources. Most pigment cells of the body arise from the neural crest after extensive migration. Melanogenesis does not begin until the precursor cells have migrated to their definitive location. The melanocytes of the retinal pigmented layer derive from a different source: cells descendant from the original optic vesicle. The coloration of melanocytes derives from a polymer of L-dopa, which is formed from the amino acid tyrosine by the enzyme tyrosinase. This polymer, termed *melanin*, is believed to be associated with protein and is found in an organelle called the melanosome (Fig. 17.3). The formation of melanosomes by melanoblasts is the terminal step in the differentiation process by which the melanocyte is formed. The melanosomes are complex cell organelles. They are formed by dilations of the endoplasmic reticulum and are composed of subunits of fibrillar protein that form a sheetlike matrix in which tyrosinase is normally embedded. Tyrosinase arises in the Golgi and reaches the melanosome by fusion of the two vesicles. Melanin is then deposited on these protein structures until the melanosome is fully pigmented and enzymatic activity is lost. The number and distribution of the melanocytes, the morphology of the cell, and the color of the melanin are all influenced by identified genes, some of which act primarily within the melanoblast. Others function within the surrounding cells that make up the tissue environment.

Melanocytes, like most terminally differentiated cells, do not normally divide. Throughout the life of the animal they must be replenished through differentiation from a pool of melanoblasts. Melanoblasts do undergo mitotic replication, but with increasing age their supply diminishes, evident in the white hair of aging humans. The genetic control of pigmentation, whether acting within the melanocyte or through the tissue environment, is modified by the changing conditions brought about by age. This is perhaps simply another

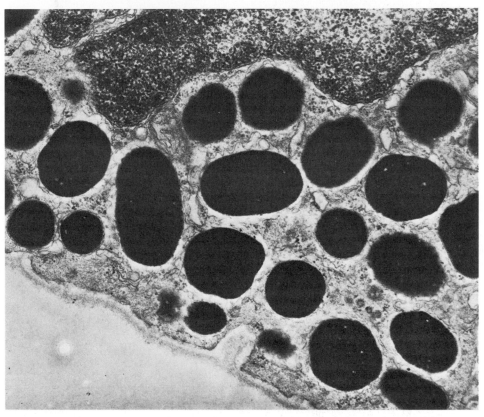

a

Figure 17.3 *a* Electron micrograph of a region of a cell from the pigmented iris epithelium. The cytoplasm of these pigmented cells is filled with melanin-containing organelles, melanosomes. [*Courtesy of J. Dumont and T. Yamada.*] *b* Development of melanosomes in melanocyte. Vesicles (V) containing "protyrosinase" budded off from Golgi (G). Vesicles develop into "premelanosomes" (PMS) in which protyrosinase molecules have become organized into characteristic patterns. Melanin is polymerized on protein matrix in PMS until melanosomes (MS) are dense particles without tryosinase activity. [*Modified from Seiji et al., 1963, by permission of the New York Academy of Sciences.*]

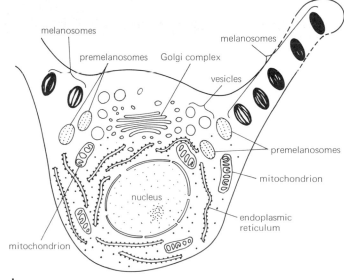

b

expression of the fact that the cell's genome is sensitive to the state of cell differentiation and is also the major contributor to the state of differentiation.

An interesting experiment that relates to the genetic state of the pigment cell and its cytoplasmic environment used cell hybridization between pigment cells and connective-tissue fibroblasts. Two types of pigment cells were used, diploid and essentially tetraploid. A hybrid formed by the diploid pigment cell and the fibroblast was unpigmented and lacked enzymes essential for pigmentation. Presumably cytoplasmic factors in the fibroblast shut down specific gene activity needed for the phenotypic expression of the pigmented state. If the tetraploid pigment cells were used, some of the hybrids were pigmented and produced both pigmented and unpigmented progeny. The remaining hybrids were unpigmented and produced only unpigmented progeny. Several interpretations are possible. Regardless of which is correct, these results illustrate the complex nature of the relationship between the cytoplasmic factors that control gene expression and the state of the genome.

CHONDROGENESIS

The primary characteristic of cartilage is the presence of large amounts of extracellular *matrix*. It surrounds the living cells, is secreted by them, and provides rigidity and elasticity to the tissue. The study of chondrogenesis centers on the synthesis and secretion of matrix, of which there are two major components: collagen and chondromucoprotein, which consists of chains of sulfated polysaccharides (primarily chondroitin sulfate) attached to a protein core. The synthesis of chondroitin sulfate and collagen is not restricted to cartilage cells (chondrocytes). Unlike the terminally differentiated myocytes or erythrocytes, terminally differentiated chondrocytes cannot be recognized solely by the molecules they synthesize.

The most widely used criterion for the occurrence of chondrogenesis is the incorporation of sulfate into chondroitin sulfate. Even though other types of cells make this molecule, cartilage cells manufacture much greater amounts and can be identified. Similarly, the collagen made by chondrocytes has a different polypeptide chain from that in the collagen of other tissues. Determination of this specific collagen, as opposed to other types, requires considerable material and analysis. In other words, criteria for the mature chondrocyte, which is actively producing matrix, are established but they do not lend themselves to the analysis of the very earliest and most important stages of cytodifferentiation, when matrix formation is occurring at very low levels.

Chondrocytes are the differentiated cells that arise primarily from two sources of chondroblasts: the neural crest and the sclerotome of the somites. The first histologic sign of chondrification in the precartilaginous mesenchyme of a developing embryo is the close apposition of rounding cells to form precartilaginous mesenchyme. The cell-mass effect and cell cohesion appear to be the most important factors among the various recognized conditions for cartilage formation. Amphibian neural-crest cells in culture emigrate and disperse as a predominantly single layer of flattened cells. The majority differentiate into polymorphic mesenchymal cells, while others become pigment cells or neurons. But within this layer of spreading cells, matrix-encapsulated cartilage cells appear. This cytodifferentiation is associated with an aggregation and piling up of the cells into nodules, with cell numbers varying from about ten to several hundred.

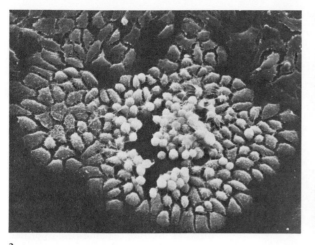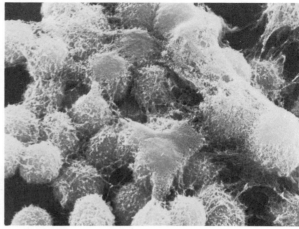

a   b

Figure 17.4 Scanning electron micrograph of a single cartilage colony (clonally derived). *a* Low-power micrograph showing the morphology of the colony. Cells most actively engaged in matrix production are found in the center of the colony. *b* Higher magnification of the central cells showing the nature of the extracellular matrix (composed of chondromucoprotein and collagen) and its effect on cell shape on the dish. [*M. Solursh and G. Karp.*]

Chondrogenesis has attracted much attention because the massive secretion and chemical complexity of cartilaginous matrix constitute a challenging and available target for biochemical investigation. The problem of elucidation, however, has been unexpectedly difficult. Under suitable nutritive conditions and given sufficient time, somite tissue will form cartilage without additional stimulation. Lash has shown that somite tissue produces cartilage sooner and in greater amounts if it is exposed to notochord or spinal cord or to extracts thereof. The essential feature is the synthesis of chondroitin sulfate. In the 3-day chick embryo, various tissues besides cartilage are able to synthesize this substance, but in older embryos (10 days) the synthesis occurs mainly in cartilage. This indicates that such synthesis becomes restricted during development. Lash suggests that when somites are exposed to various inducers in cultures—e.g., to notochord and spinal cord extracts—no new metabolic pattern is elicited, but a preexisting pattern seems to be enhanced.

Like several other types of cells, cartilage cells can be removed from the embryo and placed in culture at low cell density; under proper conditions clones of cartilage cells will differentiate. The scanning electron micrographs of Fig. 17.4 illustrate such a clone. The entire colony in this photograph has developed by the proliferation of one cultured cell. As with other types of cells, the initial phase of culture is marked by proliferation and is followed by a second phase, overt cytodifferentiation. The activities of a particular cell reflect the position of the cell within the colony; those within the center are most actively engaged in matrix production. This is reflected in their increased incorporation of sulfate into chondroitin sulfate, demonstrated autoradiographically (Fig. 17.5). As a result of their biosynthetic activity, the more centrally located cells of the colony become covered with matrix, as shown in the scanning electron microscope (Fig 17.4*b*).

Differentiating cells exist in complex environments, the components of which can dramatically affect the metabolism within the cell. Intracellular

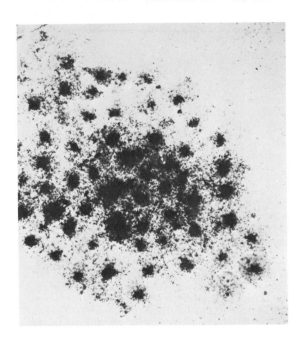

Figure 17.5 Autoradiograph of a cartilage colony (unstained) incubated
in radioactive sulfate ($^{35}SO_4$) for 10
minutes. Sulfate becomes incorporated
into chondroitin sulfate of the chondromucoprotein and thus provides an
indicator of relative matrix production
by the cells of the colony. Central cells
are much more active than peripheral
ones. [*M. Solursh and G. Karp.*]

activities can be modified by contact with the surface of other cells as well as by
contact with substances of large and small molecular weight in the medium.
Materials of large molecular weight can be present in a soluble or an insoluble
state. In the latter case the material is termed a matrix, typically composed of
collagen and/or acid mucopolysaccharide, such as chondromucoprotein, which
have increasingly been implicated as external substances capable of regulating
internal events.

The importance of the extracellular matrix is clearly illustrated during
chondrogenesis. Destroying chondromucoprotein with the enzyme hyaluronidase serves to depress the synthesis of additional chondromucoprotein,
suggesting the existence of a feedback loop between the substance on the outside of the cell and its synthesis on the inside. Addition of this material to the
medium in which the cells are growing stimulates its intracellular production.

Not only does sulfated-acid mucopolysaccharide affect the synthetic activities of chondrocytes, it seems to be of prime importance in calling forth the
chondrocyte character in the first place. In the above discussion it was stated
that the notochord stimulates the cells of the somite to become chondrocytes.
Recent evidence suggests that the ability of the notochord to provide this stimulation depends upon an acid-mucopolysaccharide covering that surrounds those
structures. If the acid-mucopolysaccharide coat is removed from the notochord,
its stimulatory activity for chondrogenesis by somite cells is greatly diminished.

MYOGENESIS

The differentiation of muscle tissue has been widely studied, though considerable controversy on certain aspects remains among the workers in this field.
Muscle tissue is well suited for studies of cytodifferentiation. It is characterized
by both a highly specific morphology, centered around the presence of a well-

organized fibrillar structure, and a specialized biochemistry, centered around the presence of myosin and several specific enzymes. In this discussion myosin is considered a protein specific for muscle cells, as it has been regarded over the years by investigators in this field. Recent evidence has indicated that myosin may be present in a wide variety of cells; this should be taken into account in our discussion. In this section we will consider primarily the differentiation of striated muscle, though many of the biochemical events may be similar to those in smooth and cardiac muscle tissue as well. Striated muscle tissue consists of highly elongate, multinucleate *myotubes* containing long *myofibrils* lattice-spaced in the cytoplasm (*sarcoplasm*). The organization of actin and myosin filaments, of which there are millions in each myofibril, is illustrated in Fig. 17.6.

Figure 17.6 Actomyosin. *a* Diagrammatic representation of part of a myofibril showing overlapping array of actin- and myosin-containing filaments. [*After Huxley, copyright © 1969 by the American Association for the Advancement of Science.*] *b* Electron micrograph of a cross section of a myofibril showing hexagonal arrangement of actin filaments around each myosin filament. [*Courtesy of H. Aldrich.*]

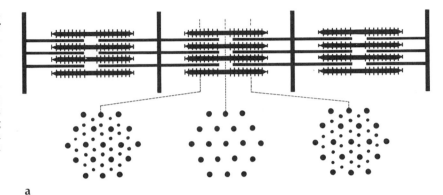

a

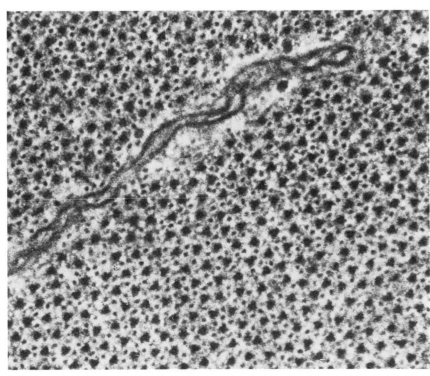

b

Cytodifferentiation

The differentiation of striated muscle tissue can be considered to occur in two primary steps. The *presumptive muscle cell* is derived from the mesoderm of the lateral plate and the myotome region of the somite, except in the head and neck, where it is derived from nonsomitic, mesenchyme cells. These presumptive myoblasts, though determined to form muscle, appear in the electron microscope as typical undifferentiated mesodermal cells and contain no evidence of their future transformation. The presumptive myoblasts proliferate to form a collection of myoblasts which stop dividing and fuse together to form the elongated myotube containing many nuclei within a common cytoplasmic compartment.

The process of myoblast fusion and that of myotube elongation appear to be relatively independent events, since they can be dissociated from one another under suitable conditions in vitro. The supernatant fluid from homogenized chick embryo cells (embryo extract) contains factors that stimulate muscle differentiation in culture. One factor from embryo extract promotes myoblast fusion, but in the absence of a second factor the syncytium formed remains as a globular structure. If the second factor is added, the globular mass becomes elongated into the myotube shape. The elongation is believed to require the presence of microtubules, whose formation may be promoted by this second factor from embryo extract.

The stage between the proliferation of presumptive myoblasts and the fusion has received the most attention and is the most controversial. Cells undergoing fusion are in the G_1 phase (pre-DNA synthesis) of the cell cycle. Once fusion has begun, no further DNA synthesis will occur within those nuclei; DNA synthesis is never detected within nuclei of the myotube. With the appearance of the myotube comes the synthesis in rapidly increasing levels of the muscle-specific proteins, myosin and several enzymes. The contractile filaments appear in the cytoplasm. The presence of very low levels of myosin is detected by its binding with antimyosin antibodies. The binding between antibody and antigen (myosin in this case) is followed visually by tagging antibody molecules with a fluorescent marker. Cells that fluoresce in the fluorescence microscope contain myosin.

Myosin is a large protein believed to be synthesized on polyribosomes containing as many as 50 to 60 ribosomes. Newly synthesized myosin is believed to organize by self-assembly into thick filaments containing approximately 200 molecules of myosin. The myosin filaments together with thin actin filaments are organized into the pattern illustrated in Fig. 17.7*b*. The thin filaments form a hexagonal array around each thick filament. The earliest myofibrils have a relatively small number of filaments, to which is added an increasing number until millions of filaments are found in the mature myofibril. Filaments are added at the circumference of the thickening myofibril, which probably serves as a nucleation site for the recruitment process.

In the second chapter the question was raised to what extent the intracellular contents might be generated strictly by processes of self-assembly. Muscle cytodifferentiation provides an opportunity to examine this question because there is considerable information on the biochemistry of the principal structural components and a highly ordered morphology. Though convincing evidence of self-assembly in vivo is difficult to obtain, the general belief is that the geometric lattice of the myofibril can arise in this manner. The hexagonal array of thin filaments around each thick filament reflects the actin-binding cross-bridges that project from the myosin molecules to dictate a stable sixfold symmetry. Evidence that the filament lattice pattern forms by self-assembly in vivo comes from studies of embryonic cardiac muscle cells that have already differentiated, but whose filaments are secondarily dispersed following dissociation of the cells in trypsin. In these cells the filaments are capable of reorganizing themselves in the presence of inhibitors of protein synthesis. This study takes advantage of the dissociation of the synthetic and assembly process; all the structural proteins needed have already been manufactured, and the assembly process can be studied without confusion by continuing muscle protein synthesis. That protein synthesis is not required for assembly indirectly suggests the pieces can be put into place noncatalytically, i.e., by self-assembly.

Another aspect of myoblast differentiation is the formation of receptors for the neurotransmitter substance, acetylcholine. These receptors are identified by their specific binding of radioactively labeled neurotoxins from snake venom. Binding occurs only at the cell surface and only after cell fusion, under normal conditions, indicating that the appearance of these receptors accompanies the intracellular cytodifferentiation.

Myoblast Fusion

The requirement that tissue should normally develop from the fusion of its component cells is unusual and has a history of some disagreement. The alternative, now disproved, was that myotubes formed by continuing mitoses without subsequent cytokineses. Some evidence that myotubes arise by fusion (Fig. 17.7) follows: Radioactively labeled thymidine is never incorporated into nuclei of the myotube. Similarly, quantitative determination of the DNA content within the nuclei of myotubes shows that they invariably contain the diploid amount and therefore must be in the G_1 phase of the cell cycle. If mitosis were occurring, S phase and G_2 phase cells would also have to be present.

Allophenic mice, formed by the fusion of two early embryos, have been used to examine numerous basic questions in developmental biology, one of which is that of fusion during myogenesis. In this study mouse embryos differing at the locus for one enzyme were fused. The enzyme, NADP-isocitrate dehydrogenase, is composed of two identical subunits, the subunits being genetically different between the two parental strains of mice. Allophenic mice offer a biochemical means of detecting cell fusions at the differentiated tissue level. If each myotube contains nuclei descended from an original nucleus that divided without cytokinesis, all nuclei of each myotube will be identical. If the multinucleate condition results from the fusion of myoblasts, the myotubes of mosaic mice will contain nuclei from both parental strains. If the former is the case, muscle should display only two types of enzymes, corresponding to each parental type. If the latter is the case, muscle should contain three types of enzymes, corresponding to each parental type and a hybrid formed by the production of two different subunits in the same common cytoplasm (Fig. 17.8). Analysis shows that the hybrid enzyme exists in skeletal muscle and not in any other tissues. Therefore the myotubes are formed in vivo by myoblast fusion.

In Vitro Analysis of Myogenesis

Myoblasts can be grown in culture under conditions where colonies derived from a single cell (a clonal colony) will undergo fusion, myotube formation, and cytodifferentiation, as described above. Using this system, a number of environmental parameters can be studied for their effect on muscle cell differentiation, though uncertainties always exist concerning whether cell behavior is the same

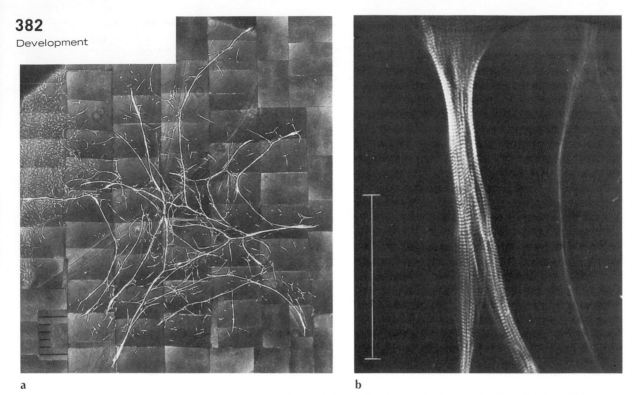

a b

Figure 17.7 *a* A muscle colony 18 days after its origin from a single cell. Most of the cells have fused to form long myotubes, though numerous single myoblasts are still present. *b* An area of the colony at higher magnification seen through polarized light to demonstrate the presence of cross-striated myofibrils typical of striated muscle. [*Courtesy of I. R. Konigsberg.*]

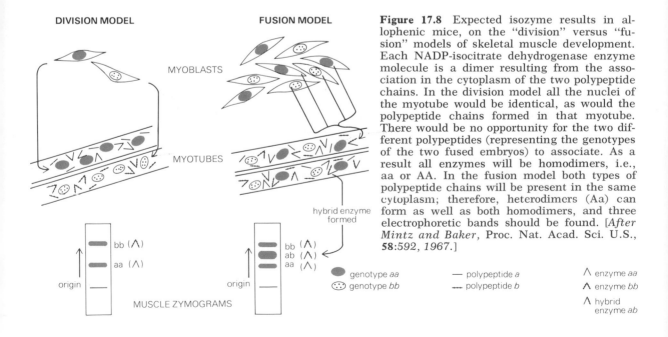

Figure 17.8 Expected isozyme results in allophenic mice, on the "division" versus "fusion" models of skeletal muscle development. Each NADP-isocitrate dehydrogenase enzyme molecule is a dimer resulting from the association in the cytoplasm of the two polypeptide chains. In the division model all the nuclei of the myotube would be identical, as would the polypeptide chains formed in that myotube. There would be no opportunity for the two different polypeptides (representing the genotypes of the two fused embryos) to associate. As a result all enzymes will be homodimers, i.e., aa or AA. In the fusion model both types of polypeptide chains will be present in the same cytoplasm; therefore, heterodimers (Aa) can form as well as both homodimers, and three electrophoretic bands should be found. [*After Mintz and Baker*, Proc. Nat. Acad. Sci. U.S., **58**:592, 1967.]

in vivo as in the culture medium. It has been observed, for example, that in vitro differentiation is characterized by a more rapid and extensive cell fusion and by the formation of myotubes that are much more branched than those within the body.

Cell culture has shown that myogenesis requires a particular substrate for the cells to attach. Collagen, secreted by fibroblasts, provides the necessary surface. A wide variety of factors in the medium, including hormones and many unknown materials, have been shown to have a marked effect on myotube formation and differentiation. Differentiating cells typically condition the medium in which they find themselves with substances that promote that differentiation.

One of the most important questions that has been studied in culture is the nature of the change in the myoblast cell preceding its fusion. Controversy exists as to whether or not events occur during the preceding cell cycle that remove that cell from the pool of dividing cells and render it "postmitotic" and capable of fusion, and whether or not the G_1 phase preceding fusion has been extended and fusion promoted by factors in the medium. Discussions of these important questions can be found in Holtzer et al., 1973; O'Neill and Stockdale, 1972; Konigsberg and Buckley, 1974; Doering and Fischman, 1974.

In vitro experiments allow the investigator to construct a variety of conditions that cannot be found within the genetically determined environment of the organism. The interaction of cells that normally would never find themselves together has been a favorite and informative in vitro experimental design. When chick and mouse myoblasts are mixed, fusion occurs between these cells, indicating that the process shows little regard for species-specific cell surface markers. If, however, chick cardiac and striated muscle myoblasts are mixed, fusion between these two cells does not occur, indicating that recognition of tissue-specific markers is of prime importance in the fusion process.

EMBRYONIC DETERMINATION

In the first part of this chapter we described a few events that take place during the terminal steps in the differentiation of some cell types that have been studied. During the terminal stages the cells become visibly differentiated; they have attained a phenotypic expression. These stages have received the most attention because they are the most readily examined. It is the earlier stages, of which little is known, in which a cell's fate becomes fixed. We have paid considerable attention to the change in prospective potency of cells in vertebrate embryos during gastrulation. Following gastrulation, cells transplanted to new environments would differentiate in the foreign surroundings into the same tissues they would normally have formed if left undisturbed. The onset of determination marks the first step in the differentiation process; the cells of the embryo are no longer equivalent with respect to the tissues each can form. The term differentiated, which expresses the fact that cells have become different from one another, is as suitably applied to the earlier stages as it is to those cells in which visible morphological evidence can be found.

The specific nature of the changes that accompany determination is unknown. The changes are believed to reflect the differential expression of the genome among the cells of the embryo. Convincing evidence shows that differentiated cells are engaged in differentiated synthetic programs. RNA populations extracted from different tissues contain widely different RNA species. Chromatin isolated from one tissue synthesizes RNA in vitro not made by chromatin from other tissue. Fetal liver chromatin, for example, produces globin mRNA in vitro while chromatin from brain does not. Selective gene activation has been studied in the stage-specific puffing patterns of the giant chromosomes of insect larvae. RNA synthesis—which can be followed by the incorporation of labeled RNA precursors—occurs only at specific genetic loci, which must first undergo an untangling process to produce a puffed appearance. Each stage of development is characterized by particular puffs in each larval tissue; the puff pattern can be modified in predictable direction by insect hormones. These observations are considered in more detail with the general topic of determination during insect development in Chapters 8 and 22.

The first steps in differentiation might be expected to follow the selective activation of a battery of genes. The genes restrict the potential of the cell and its progeny by directing it along certain pathways and away from others. Differential gene activity in embryonic cells presumably reflects differential stimulation in the embryonic nuclei, which, in turn, reflects the position of each cell within the embryo.

It is generally assumed that the transition from the undifferentiated to the fully differentiated state is a gradual one with many steps. Indirect evidence for this comes from many sources. Inherent in the concept of the embryonic field is that the cells of the field are capable of forming other parts of the organ but not parts of some tissue of a foreign field. As later and later stages are reached, the ability of a given part of the field to form peripheral structures becomes progressively limited. During the early development of the hemopoietic tissues, cells can be found that are *pluripotent:* they can form a variety of specialized cells of the lymphoid, erythroid, and granulolytic series. At a later stage the pluripotent cell is no longer found and each of these individual lines has its own precursor. The pluripotent cell has become *unipotent.* Similarly the exocrine, endocrine, and duct cells of the pancreas are believed to differentiate from a common precursor cell in the initial pancreatic rudiment. Another example of progressive differentiation is in the somite cells. They differentiate into cartilage, muscle, and connective tissue. As development proceeds, each of these tissues has its own precursor cell—the chondroblast, myoblast, and fibroblast, respectively. In the initial stages of somite formation all cells appear indistinguishable; there is no reason to suspect that any given cell cannot form all three fully differentiated cell types.

The intermediate in the sequence from the undifferentiated to the cytodifferentiated is the stem cell. A given stem cell is committed to differentiate along a path from which one or a few closely related cell types can emerge. Stem cells appear in the embryo, but in many tissues they remain throughout the life of the animal to provide the pool of precursors from which the terminally differentiated cells will arise.

The basal layer of cells in the epidermis, for example, consists of actively proliferating cells that are cytologically and biochemically unspecialized. Individual cells of the basal layer lose their attachment to the basement membrane and appear to be forced up by crowding into the more superficial layers of the epidermis. During this outward movement, the cells synthesize the specialized protective molecule, keratin. In the final stage, the keratinized cells die and are eventually sloughed off to be replaced by the newly formed cells differentiating from the basal layer of stem cells.

The differentiation of the basal stem cells into keratinizing cells is a response to the change in environmental circumstances. Even at this stage their fate can be changed. If these cells are exposed to vitamin A, the keratinizing epidermis differentiates instead into a mucoid-secreting epithelium.

We are obviously a great distance from understanding the mechanism by which cells become determined and differentiate along one path or another. One of the most important aspects of this problem concerns the nature and time of appearance of tissue-specific molecules, whether they are mRNAs, proteins, or some other substance. When do molecules appear that are characteristic of one type of cell relative to the stage at which overt cytodifferentiation takes place? Are some or all of the RNA templates for cytodifferentiation produced long before the event itself? If they are, then later stages of differentiation can be thought of as being primarily controlled at the posttranscriptional level. Or, rather, is there progressive gene expression so that the availability of new mRNAs limits the nature of the events that can take place? In other words, is the cell waiting for new RNAs and therefore being governed by transcriptional control mechanisms? These are greatly simplified and extreme alternatives, but the question as to what levels of control of information transfer are at work during each stage of the differentiation process is basic to our understanding of development. Recent studies have provided some facts concerning the temporal nature of gene expression in several differentiating systems. We will consider three of these: myogenesis, pancreas formation, and erythropoiesis. We are still at the stage where we must consider individual cases rather than present one scheme, if such exists, that can be adapted for all cells. However, recent advances in nucleic acid methodology have allowed biologists to move from the analysis of differentiation as seen in the microscope, and even from the analysis of specific proteins, toward the analysis of specific species of RNA, i.e., toward the expression of the genome itself.

Cytodifferentiation is generally accompanied by the appearance of highly specific, characteristic proteins, including myosin during myogenesis, globin during erythropoiesis, and hydrolytic enzymes and insulin during pancreogenesis. Three major techniques have been employed to determine whether the mRNA that codes for a given protein, such as those above, has been synthesized at any given stage of development.

In the first, actinomycin D is administered and the synthetic activity of the tissue followed. If the mRNA for the protein being studied had already been synthesized at the time the inhibitor was added, that protein should appear regardless of the application of the drug. If, instead, the gene coding for that protein had not been activated at the time of actinomycin D application, the given protein will not appear.

In the second technique, the presence of a specific mRNA is determined by its ability to direct the synthesis of the corresponding protein in a cell-free system. In this case the RNA populations must be extracted from the cells at the stage in question and this RNA added to the appropriate protein-synthesizing system. If the specific mRNA is present, the corresponding protein will be produced; if the mRNA is absent, there is no condition under which that protein can appear. This method is discussed on page 552.

In the third technique, the presence of a specific mRNA is determined by its ability to hybridize to a complementary, radioactive DNA molecule. With the identification and purification of the enzyme, reverse transcriptase, it has become possible to synthesize, in the test tube, highly radioactive DNA molecules having the complementary base sequence to any given species of RNA that can be purified. Reverse transcriptase is an enzyme that uses RNA as a template to construct a complementary copy of DNA. The virus uses this enzyme to allow its genetic information to become integrated into the host chromosomes; biologists have used it to prepare highly radioactive DNA copies, termed *cDNA*, of specific mRNAs. Once the labeled DNA is made, it can be used to probe preparations of RNA in a search for the species of mRNA used as the template. The ability to synthesize labeled cDNA probes depends on techniques that allow one to isolate a sufficient quantity of one mRNA species. Because at the present time only a limited number of such mRNA species are available, only a limited number of probes have been utilized. General aspects of the hybridization techniques are discussed in Chapter 25.

Genetic Regulation of Myogenesis

Biochemical analysis of muscle cell differentiation is centered upon myosin and certain enzymes characteristic of muscle tissue. When are these proteins, and the mRNAs that code for them, first detectable? One difficulty that must be considered before this question can be answered is that there may be considerable differences in various types of muscle cells among different animals. It appears, for example, that myosin synthesis may be initiated at considerably different times during myogenesis.

Analysis of the myoblasts in the early stages of chick somite development reveals that the prefusion myoblast contains myosin, as detected by its binding to antimyosin antibodies. The presence of visible myosin filaments is shown in electron micrographs. Studies of myoblasts from older chick embryos, however, indicate that myosin synthesis occurs only after cell fusion. The significance of this stage-dependent difference is not clear.

Studies of rat myoblasts in culture suggest that the mRNAs for myosin synthesis are present in the mononucleated myoblasts prior to fusion, though myosin synthesis is not detected until hours after the fusion event. This finding is based on the observation that actinomycin D administered prior to fusion does not prevent the event nor does it prevent the postfusion activation of myosin synthesis. Though these findings do not indicate at what stage these mRNAs are synthesized, they suggest that the appearance of these proteins during cytodifferentiation occurs upon RNA templates synthesized some time prior to that at which myoblast fusion takes place.

Genetic Control of Erythropoiesis

The terminal differentiation of erythrocytes is characterized by the increasing synthesis and accumulation of hemoglobin, which accounts for over 95 percent of the protein of the mature red blood cell. For this reason, erythropoiesis is well suited for the analysis of control mechanisms governing protein synthesis during differentiation. The search for the time at which the globin mRNA can first be detected has employed sophisticated molecular techniques, but as in myogenesis, the definitive answers are not yet available.

In the chick, the beginnings of a vascular network appear in the morphogenesis of the blood islands just beyond the edge of the area pellucida, which becomes known as the *area opaca vasculosa*. Blood-island formation occurs between the definitive primitive-streak stage and the head-fold stage (18 to 24 hours of incubation). It results from the aggregation of mesodermal cells into clusters, which become induced by the underlying endodermal cells to form the endothelial wall of the blood vessels and the enclosed erythrocytes.

The time at which hemoglobin can be detected in the developing chick embryo depends upon the sensitivity of the technique by which it is measured. Earlier studies using a fairly sensitive staining assay found the first indications of the presence of hemoglobin in the six- to eight somite stage. This was approximately 10 hours after the head-fold stage and the formation of the blood islands, and approximately 10 hours after its appearance became insensitive to actinomycin D. Actinomycin D added prior to the head-fold stage will block the appearance of hemoglobin at the six- to eight-somite stage, while application after the head-fold stage does not block subsequent hemoglobin synthesis. These results suggest that the mRNA for hemoglobin is made by the head-fold stage, after which the inhibition of RNA synthesis does not affect the appearance of the corresponding protein. The question raised by these results concerns the apparent delay between the synthesis of the mRNA and its translation into the polypeptide chains of the globin protein. Does the mRNA lie dormant in the cytoplasm for 10 hours before some translational control mechanism causes it to be translated? More recent studies used isotopic tracer methods capable of detecting very small quantities of newly synthesized hemoglobin. They indicate that translation of the globin mRNAs begins soon after their transcription and, therefore, that complex translational control mechanisms need not be invoked. These results illustrate an ever-present difficulty: The interpretation of data depends upon the limitations of the methods used. Some methods of detection are more sensitive than others; all have a defined limit below which detection cannot be made and conclusions cannot be drawn.

The preoccupation of the maturing erythrocyte with hemoglobin synthesis has permitted investigators to isolate and purify the mRNAs that code for the polypeptide chains of globin. From this mRNA fraction, highly radioactive cDNA probes have been synthesized and utilized in several ways. Probes of nuclear RNA being synthesized in hemoglobin-producing cells have indicated that the globin message is originally contained within huge RNA molecules, much larger than the message itself. These large RNAs are termed *transcriptional units*, from which the cytoplasmic, polysomic mRNA is carved.

When is the globin mRNA first detected? Two hemoglobin-producing systems have been analyzed. In one case the cells under study are malignant leukemia cells that can be induced to undergo erythroid differentiation in culture. These cells are called *erythroleukemia cells;* the inducing agent is an artificial substance, dimethylsulfoxide, not erythropoietin. Probes of RNA from uninduced cells have failed to reveal the globin message, which is found to accumulate rapidly after induction with dimethylsulfoxide. Similarly, the addition of actinomycin D prior to stimulation blocks the inductive process. These results suggest that the uninduced erythroleukemia cell is not engaged in globin mRNA synthesis and that its stimulation to differentiate requires transcriptional level control.

In another study, erythroid precursor cells, prior to hemoglobin synthesis, were isolated from liver of fetal mice. These cells were found to lack globin mRNA, as tested by the ability of their RNA to direct the synthesis of globin in a cell-free system. If, however, these precursor cells were stimulated with erythropoietin to undergo differentiation, the presence of the globin mRNA was detectable by 10 hours and rapidly accumulated. These results also suggest that transcriptional activation—in this case of the message for hemoglobin—occurs just prior to the synthesis of the protein itself, rather than being present much earlier in a nontranslated state.

Even though synthesis of hemoglobin accounts for up to 90 percent of the proteins synthesized by erythroblasts, there is no evidence of any increase in the number of globin genes to allow for increased transcription. Analysis of the

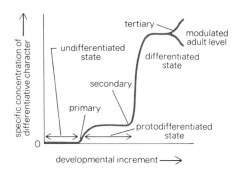

Figure 17.9 Possible regulatory stages in cyto-differentiation. [*After W. Rutter, et al.,* Exp. Biol. Med., **1:***110, 1967.*]

erythroblast genome indicates that no more than an estimated two copies of globin DNA exist in each genome, the same approximate number as in any other type of cell. The limited amount of globin DNA available for use as a template at any given time is illustrated in studies of the template activity of isolated chromatin. Chromatin prepared from differentiated cells will direct the synthesis of RNA from those genes that are open for transcription, i.e., the same genes that were being expressed at the time within the cell. Chromatin from erythroblasts, for example, produces globin mRNA; that from brain will not. Of the total RNA transcribed from erythrocyte chromatin, only 0.007 percent of the RNAs made represent globin mRNA. It appears that 0.007 percent (less than 1 in 10,000) of the exposed DNA sequence can account for over 90 percent of the proteins being synthesized at the most active stages. These figures dramatically illustrate the effectiveness of the cell's regulatory machinery. In the test tube, the hemoglobin gene is just one of the thousands in the chromatin that is capable of being transcribed. In the cell, however, this small number of genes produces RNAs that may be selectively synthesized, selectively accumulated, and selectively translated to account for these relative values. These figures further illustrate that two genes per cell can, under the appropriate conditions, account for a cell's becoming packed with one type of protein. Gene amplification is not necessary in these cells. The only established case of selective gene amplification is that for ribosomal DNA, which is necessary as a result of the tremendous volume of the egg being packaged.

Genetic Control of Pancreas Formation

The pancreas is also an excellent system for study at the biochemical level. Its differentiation is characterized by the synthesis of a variety of proteins that have been studied. The proteins of the pancreas are of two types, produced in different cells and secreted into different vessels. One group of proteins, a wide variety of hydrolytic enzymes secreted into the ducts leading to the intestine, is the product of the bulk of the pancreatic cells, the *exocrine acinar cells.* The other proteins are hormones, insulin and glucagon, products of islets of endocrine cells embedded within the pancreas.

The exocrine acinar cells have a distinct ultrastructural morphology reflecting their high rates of protein synthesis and their extensive secretory activity. Fully differentiated pancreas cells have an extensive rough endoplasmic reticulum where the enzymes are synthesized, an elaborate Golgi complex where they are packaged, and a great number of secretory, or zymogen, granules in which the enzymes are prepared for release. Insulin is produced by the β (or beta) cells, which can be readily distinguished from the glucagon-producing α (or alpha) cells. Beta cells are characterized by their dense cytoplasm and the presence of beta granules.

In the mouse, pancreas morphogenesis begins approximately halfway through the gestation period by the bulging of a group of cells of the dorsal endoderm (roof of the archenteron) into the surrounding mesenchyme. The intimate association of an epithelium, in this case derived from the gut, and a mesenchymal tissue is important in the formation of a number of organs including the salivary gland, lung, kidney, thyroid, mammary gland, pituitary, and liver. It is generally found that a mesodermal factor acts as an inducing agent to promote the differentiation of the epithelium. As a result of this epithelial-mesenchyme interaction, a bulbous pancreatic rudiment is formed.

Biochemical analysis of the cells of the pancreatic rudiment on the twelfth day of mouse development indicates that the enzymes characteristic of the mature exocrine pancreas, as well as insulin, are present at a low level. The low level of these proteins is maintained until the fourteenth day, after which it begins to rise to reach the high levels characteristic of the fully differentiated pancreas cell. Insulin and lipase, for example, are present in at least a 10,000-fold greater concentration in the cells of the pancreas rudiment compared with the cells of the embryo in general. The presence of these proteins prior to the fourteenth day is clear indication that the cells have achieved a tissue-specific differentiated state; yet morphologically they remain relatively unspecialized. The acinar cells lack the highly differentiated rough endoplasmic reticulum, Golgi, and zymogen granules; the beta cells lack the beta granules. Rutter has termed this the *protodifferentiated state* to distinguish it from an earlier period where these proteins are absent and a later period where they are present at much greater concentration (Fig. 17.9).

The first transition (to the protodifferentiated state) is accompanied by the activation of a large battery of pancreas-specific genes. The primary transition, therefore, must be considered a major transcriptive event leading to cytodifferentiation, which is delayed for several days. The primary transition can be considered a change from a precursor cell to one with a pancreatic phenotype, even though the phenotype is not that of the fully differentiated cell.

The protodifferentiated phase is accompanied by a great change in the appearance of the pancreatic rudiment. At its start, the epithelial-mesenchymal rudiment is little more than a bulge of the wall of the intestine. At its termination, cell proliferation has resulted in a great increase in the cell number and morphogenesis has produced a convoluted epithelium. The cytologic appearance of the cells, however, remains unspecialized.

A second transition step (occurs after day 14 in the mouse) converts the protodifferentiated cells to the fully cytodifferentiated state. Enzyme levels after the second transition range from 1,000 to 10,000 times that of the protodifferentiated state. Since many, or all, of the specific messenger RNAs must already be available within the cells to account for the presence of all the pancreatic enzymes, the secondary transitional step may reflect primarily a translational control mechanism. This does not mean that additional transcriptional regulation is not required for this second transition as well. Actinomycin D administered during the protodifferentiated phase will block the development of the fully differentiated state, suggesting that additional RNA synthesis is required. Once the protodifferentiated state has ended, however, actinomycin D is no longer effective in blocking the subsequent cytodifferentiation.

Indications have been found that the biphasic accumulation of specific proteins characteristic of the pancreas occurs in other cells, including cartilage, thyroid, and mammary gland tissue. No evidence of such a series of steps has been found in the previous examples of the erythroblast or myoblast. The general applicability of this model in the regulation of differentiation remains to be determined.

The analysis of the differentiation of the pancreas by Rutter and coworkers has recently centered upon the interaction of a protein produced by the mesenchyme with the cells of the pancreatic epithelium. This protein, termed *mesenchyme factor* or *MF*, has been extracted from the membranous fraction of the mesodermal cells in high salt solutions and has been greatly purified for use in studies of differentiation. The presence of MF is an absolute requirement for the growth and differentiation of the pancreas, and the evidence strongly suggests that it has its effect by interaction with the cell surface.

As has been shown for hormones and nerve growth factor, the ability of regulatory molecules to act at the cell surface of a responding cell is revealed by demonstrating the effect when that molecule is prevented from being taken up by the cells. Mesenchyme factor can be covalently linked to inert beads of Sepharose, which blocks MF entry into the epithelial cells but does not prevent it from promoting cellular growth and differentiation. In fact, in response to the presence of these beads, the responding cells become tightly pressed against the bead surface, attached by the bridges of mesenchyme factor. Autoradiographs of these cells after exposure to ^{3}H-thymidine indicate that nearly all the cells that are synthesizing DNA are directly attached to the coated beads. It appears that the interaction of MF with the cell surface greatly stimulates the DNA synthetic capacity of these cells. Not only are the attached cells stimulated to divide, they can undergo cytodifferentiation into mature pancreas cells, with the basal side of the cell attached to the bead and the microvilli in the opposite direction.

One event that seems to occur in a wide variety of differentiating tissues is the stabilization of mRNAs for the tissue-specific proteins at some stage during differentiation. For example, in the cases of hemoglobin, myosin, and the pancreatic enzymes, a point is reached where the mRNAs for these proteins become highly stable. That is, they remain within the cytoplasm for relatively long periods of time. The general test for messenger stabilization is the continuing synthesis of the specific protein in the absence of the synthesis of the mRNA. In each of these cases once a certain stage is reached, inhibition of RNA synthesis by actinomycin D is without effect upon the continuing accumulation of these proteins; the mRNAs have become stable in the cytoplasm.

NATURE OF THE INDUCTIVE INTERACTION

In Chapter 12 considerable attention was paid to the process of embryonic induction as a means whereby a responsive tissue was directed along a particular path of development. The nature of the inductive interaction has remained one of the least understood events despite a long history of investigation. The intervention of an inducing molecule into the activities of a reacting tissue has been considered in two ways. The earlier view emphasized an "instructive" role of the inducing substances in which the inducer carried some specific information that was directly utilized by the responding tissue to cause it to differentiate. Inducers of this type might be expected to interact with the genome in some highly specific manner to activate the synthesis of one or more RNAs that code for tissue-specific proteins.

An alternate concept gives the inducing substances a "permissive" role, one which provides a favorable environment in which the phenotypic expression is promoted. In this view the competent state of the responding tissue at the time of induction is emphasized, suggesting that the inducer releases a preprogrammed sequence of events rather than supplying information needed for the differentiation process. This latter view stresses the background of the responding tissue and its previously determined potential. It has come primarily from recent work in tissue-culture differentiation where the importance of the environment has been emphasized.

Cartilage, for example, has been a favorite tissue for in vitro culture and can be used to illustrate these points. The early evidence, gained from both in vivo and in vitro studies, suggested that the differentiation of somite tissue into cartilage required an induction by substances emanating from either notochord or spinal cord tissue. Extracts from these, and only these, cells were found to be active among a wide variety of types that were tested. In other words, there appeared to be a high degree of specificity associated with these inducing tissues; specificity is generally interpreted as reflecting an instructive interaction.

Several lines of evidence, however, suggest that even in this case, the inducing substances are having a permissive role. With the development of more favorable culture media, it was discovered that somite tissue could differentiate into cartilage by itself, in culture isolation. Such differentiation is termed "spontaneous cartilage." It indicates cartilage formation does not require some extraneous piece of information that must be provided from its environment. Rather it suggests that the notochord or spinal cord provides a particularly favorable environment, but not an essential one, for the expression of the cartilage phenotype. The inducing substances are believed to enhance a chondrogenic bias already preprogrammed into these cells. Cells not having this bias are not induced. Even cartilage-forming cells from other parts of the embryo, such as the limb, are not stimulated by notochord or spinal-cord tissues. The specificity is as much a property of the responding tissue as it is of the inducing cells.

The induction of cartilage by notochord is like the induction of myogenesis by collagen, neurogenesis by nerve growth factor, pancreas formation by a mesenchyme factor, erythropoiesis by erythropoietin, etc. In each of these cases the responding cells are already determined, at least partially, toward their definitive course. In cases such as these, a permissive interaction may be more understandable than in the case of primary induction seen by the roof of the archenteron on the presumptive neural ectoderm. In the latter case this inductive interaction may be the first step in differentiation, i.e., the original determinative event; and as such an instructive role for the inducing substances seems more appropriate.

MODULATION OF THE PHENOTYPE IN CULTURE

The effect of the culture medium upon differentiation can be shown with a wide variety of cells. It has been generally found that if a differentiated tissue is removed from the body, dissociated into single cells, and cultured in vitro, these cells rapidly assume an undifferentiated appearance. Cartilage cells, for example, cease the production of matrix materials, pigment cells lose their melanosomes, etc. In the earlier literature these cells are considered to have *dedifferentiated*. This term has generally been avoided in recent years, or at least carefully defined, since it carries the implication that the differentiated cell has in some way reverted to a more primitive, undifferentiated state. Such is not the case. Analysis of the capability of these cells reveals that in many respects they are no less differentiated than the state from which they were derived. Cartilage cells, for example, when placed into culture, retain the enzymes needed for matrix production, even though matrix is no longer synthesized; some other factor has intervened to shut production down.

Whether previously differentiated cells remain undifferentiated in appearance or regain their original phenotype depends to a great extent upon the culture conditions. The phenotype of cartilage cells, for example, depends upon numerous factors including the nature of the substrate the cells grow upon, the density at which they are growing, and the chemical nature of their environment. Under certain conditions the cells become polygonal-shaped, are seen to be incorporating large quantities of sulfate, and to be accumulating matrix, as those shown in Fig. 17.4. If the medium is changed by the addition of substances of high molecular weight from an embryo extract, the cells undergo a change in shape to a stellate, fibroblastlike cell with a much greater surface area. They lose the characteristics of the cytodifferentiated state. If the substances from the embryo extract are removed in a suitable period, the cells will regain the cartilage phenotype; they can revert to the fully differentiated cartilage state, but no other. Cells that have lost their overt differentiation are in a state of covert, or hidden, differentiation. The oscillation between the overt and covert state is termed *modulation*.

THE STABILITY OF THE DIFFERENTIATED STATE

One of the most important questions in the analysis of differentiation is whether the events that lead to the mature terminal cell are such that the fate of that cell is forever restricted. In the previous section, the modulation of a cell between its fully expressed phenotypic state and some covertly differentiated cell was described. The underlying difference between these two states is apparently subtle even though their phenotypes are highly diverse. The question presently under consideration is whether the cell that once was fully differentiated and has lost these properties can be shifted into any other path of differentiation. This question is a complex one and has had a long and turbulent history; unambiguous examples in vertebrates are very difficult to find. This reflects either the infrequency with which it occurs or the difficulty in arranging for the proper conditions in which it can be observed. The most generally cited example of a change in differentiation is in Wolffian lens regeneration, where the dorsal part of the iris (a neural ectoderm derivative) can dedifferentiate and redifferentiate into a lens (an epidermal ectoderm derivative). The essence of the transformation in Wolffian lens regeneration is the extrusion from the iris cell of all its melanosomes, the activation of DNA and RNA synthesis and division, and the reprogramming of the dedifferentiated cell into the entirely different phenotypic pathway of the lens cell. Some investigators argue that if one clear-cut example can be found, the irreversibility of the differentiated state has been proved. Others take the alternate view—that one or two cases reflect peculiarities with respect to that particular tissue. One can argue that cytodifferentiation in iris cells occurs at a state prior to the terminal determinative stages typical of most tissues. The resolution of this question awaits more examples. The eye has been the source of another example of metaplasia, that involving the interconversion of the pigmented and sensory layers of the retina. Though these are much more closely related with respect to their embryonic origin than are lens and iris, they are very different in the components that make up their cytoplasm, and each is a highly complex cell. The interconvertability of the two layers of the retina appears to be responsible for a disease in man. Retinitis pigmentosa is characterized by the pigmentation of the sensory layer of the retina, suggesting that some defect in the stabilization of the differentiated state has occurred in these cells.

The greatest claims for metaplastic transformations have been made for regenerating tissues, though the extent to which this occurs is highly debatable. Most investigators in this area would agree that at least with respect to the cells of muscle, cartilage, bone, and connective tissue, interconvertability can occur. Each of these cells is highly specialized, with many tissue-specific molecules. Yet after a process of dedifferentiation, redifferentiation into another cell type seems to be able to occur.

CELL DIVISION AND DIFFERENTIATION

There is a background of controversy about the relationship between cell division and cytodifferentiation. Tissue differentiation, both in vivo and in vitro, is characterized by an initial period of proliferation followed by the cytodifferentiation of a nondividing population of cells. It has been argued that the transition to the overtly differentiated state is accompanied by a loss of proliferative capacity. For a while mitosis and cytodifferentiation were thought to be mutually exclusive phenomena. Though a highly structured cytoplasm would be expected to interfere at least mechanically with division, there are numerous examples of a cytodifferentiated cell capable of DNA synthesis and subsequent cytokinesis. Cardiac myoblasts, for example, containing ordered myofilaments, have been seen to divide; cartilage cells with surrounding matrix are readily shown to incorporate both ^{3}H-thymidine into DNA and ^{35}SO$_4$ into matrix-bound chondroitin sulfate (Fig. 17.10).

The role of mitosis in differentiation is unclear at this time. In the studies by Holtzer of a variety of differentiating systems, including chondrogenesis, myogenesis, and erythropoiesis, mitosis as a causative event for differentiation is stressed. In this concept, mitosis facilitates the differentiation process whereby two daughter cells attain reactive states not in the repertoire of the mother cell. The cell cycle, in this view, can lead either to duplication of the mother's phenotype or to one or two daughter cells with pathways very different from those active in the mother cell. The former is a *proliferative cell cycle;* the latter is a *quantal cell cycle.* Proliferative cell cycles lead to increased numbers of similar cells. Quantal cycles are postulated to be the means whereby diversity via genetic reprogramming is introduced into replicating systems. If mitosis is suppressed either by adding inhibitors or by culturing cells at high cell density, differentiation does not occur. Accordingly, myoblasts just before cell fusion are considered "postmitotic" and no longer a member of the pool of dividing cells. Some event has occurred that has rendered them incapable of division and ready for cytodifferentiation. The contrasting view is that a terminal myoblast, i.e., one with full potential for fusion, is still capable of further rounds of division provided the proper environment can be created. According to Holtzer, the transition to the terminal generation capable of cytodifferentiation can be coupled to one particular round of DNA synthesis. The

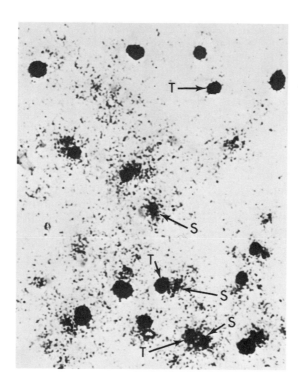

Figure 17.10 Autoradiograph showing a few cells of a cartilage colony (unstained) after incubation for 2 hours in ^{3}H-thymidine and 10 minutes in ^{35}SO$_4$. Some cells are seen to incorporate both these isotopes, indicating the simultaneous activities of replication and matrix synthesis, the characteristic of the fully differentiated cartilage phenotype. T refers to thymidine-labeled nuclei; S to sites of ^{35}SO$_4$ incorporation in the cytoplasm. [*M. Solursh and G. Karp.*]

actual expression of the quantal cycle leading to full phenotypic differentiation may occur immediately. Alternatively, the altered state may be covertly transmitted through several subsequent proliferative cycles, to be expressed many generations later in response to environmental factors. If mitosis is suppressed before the quantal cycle, by inhibitors or by high cell density, differentiation cannot occur. Studies aimed at resolving this question are now in progress.

The Effect of 5-Bromodeoxyuridine

One compound, 5-bromodeoxyuridine (BrdU or BUdR), has been found to have an anomalous effect on a wide variety of differentiating cells. This compound generally blocks the development of a cytodifferentiated phenotype, though the precise effects vary with the cell type under study and the stages at which the compound is applied. BUdR is incorporated into DNA. Its incorporation can be blocked by excess thymidine, with which it competes. In certain cases the presence of BUdR in the genome is mutagenic. This is not the basis for its effect upon differentiation, since in many cases its effects can be readily reversed by removing it from the medium. Reversibility would not occur if stable genetic changes (mutations) were being promoted.

The mechanism of action of BUdR remains a mystery, though several theories have been put forth. In some manner it appears to repress the expression of genetic information that is characteristic of the specialized cell, i.e., the nonessential information, without disrupting the genetic expression for the metabolism required for life itself. As a result, RNA synthesis, protein synthesis, cell division, etc., generally continue in a normal manner. The effect of BUdR generally requires its incorporation into DNA during an S phase. One such exposed cycle is sufficient, though evidence exists that BUdR effect may also be directed at the cell surface in some cases. Examples of inhibition by BUdR include myosin synthesis and fusion during myogenesis, matrix production during chondrogenesis, zymogen granule formation during pancreas development, antibody synthesis by lymphocytes, hemoglobin synthesis during erythropoiesis, and numerous others. The ability of BUdR to selectively suppress specialized functions with minimal disruption to "housekeeping" activities has suggested that the development of these specialized differentiating properties involves a separate regulatory mechanism, one which may have many common features among all the cell types. As such, BUdR is an important probe into the nature of differentiation. Its mechanism of action is being intensively investigated.

ISOZYMES

Enzymes often exist in multiple molecular forms, each form catalyzing the same reaction but with varying kinetic properties. They are called *isoenzymes*, or *isozymes*, and are most easily explained by example. The isozyme most often encountered in the literature is lactate dehydrogenase, or LDH, which catalyzes the conversion of pyruvate to lactate. LDH is made up of four subunits, of which there are two varieties, A and B. The subunits, A and B, are coded by two different genes. Five possible enzymes can be formed from a tetramer containing two different subunits (AAAA, AAAB, AABB, ABBB, and BBBB), and all are active and can be found within the various tissues. The composition of a given LDH molecule has an important relationship to its enzymatic properties; the greater the number of A subunits in the tetramer, the more resistant the enzyme is to inhibition by pyruvate and the more suited for anaerobic metabolism.

Since the association of the subunits into active enzyme is a random process, the relative proportion of each of the five possible enzymes reflects the relative synthesis of the A and B subunits. For example, if there is a much greater synthesis of the A subunit in a particular cell, there will be a greater proportion of the tetramers AAAA and AAAB. Since the A and B subunits have differing electrical charge, the various isozymes can be readily separated from one another. If all five are present, five distinct bands will be seen. The relative amounts of protein in each band reflect the relative synthetic rates of the two subunits.

Certain tissues will show characteristic patterns regardless of the animals from which they are taken. This is so in the heart and those muscles that undergo vigorous but noncontinuous contraction. Heart muscle shows high percentages of B, while biceps show high percentages of A. In the liver there are great variations of A and B, depending on the source. In some animals embryonic life is characterized by a much larger proportion of A subunits; in others the B form predominates. In each case there is a gradual increase in the concentration of the other subunit until the adult patterns are reached. Shifting isozyme patterns during development reflect changes in gene expression; as such they are an important tool in the study of differentiation, even if the specific nature of the shifts is not always understood.

MASS EFFECTS

The importance of the chemical nature of the microenvironment has been stressed in the previous sections. Another important factor is the number and proximity of surrounding cells. Experiments with isolated, "undifferentiated" vertebrate pigment cells showed in no case did a single isolated cell undergo cytodifferentiation in a minute hanging drop of nutrient culture medium. However, when two cells were present together in a microdrop, one underwent dif-

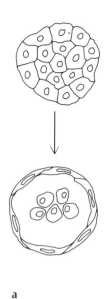

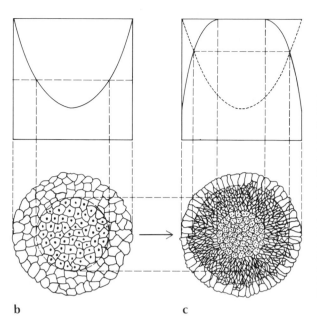

Figure 17.11 Gradient systems within a cell cluster. *a* An equipotential cell cluster segregates into an outer envelope and an inner residual cluster, the two components now having different microenvironments. *b* A resultant gradient of composite conditions relating to inward and outward diffusion of metabolites. *c* Changes in cell type and cell shape resulting from release of reactant products of cells responding to the initial diffusion gradients. [*After Weiss, 1953.*]

a   b   c

ferentiation. Apparently there is an exchange of cues into the microenvironment, extending to the neighbor cell, so that one of the two cells is able to initiate differentiative processes.

Similar contrasting cell systems, differing only by one cell, responded in a variety of ways, but in each case the single isolated cell merely survived, while one cell of the double isolate differentiated. As the number of cells isolated together increased up to 15, the rate, degree, and numbers of cells differentiating also increased. It was concluded that an exchange of a metabolic nature takes place between cells and medium, and the altered medium is thus made more suitable for support of cellular differentiation in the isolated small group of cells. Metabolic gradients within cell clusters are illustrated (Fig. 17.11).

Explants of presumptive head mesoderm from a single early gastrula of the urodele *Triton* form only muscle; larger masses, consisting of identical cells derived from the fusion of several of these same primordia, form muscle, notochord, brain, sensory primordia, and epidermis. Similarly, in cultures of small numbers of cells from *Xenopus* embryos, whereas as few as five to ten mesoderm cells are capable of carrying out neural induction, many more responding cells are required to become induced. Thus no neural differentiation is seen in culture groups of less than 100 cells, while brain tissue is formed in that of greater mass.

In summary, we have tried in this chapter to bring together information about a variety of aspects relating to the transformation of cells from the undifferentiated to the fully differentiated state. The processes of differentiation remain poorly understood. Analysis with the electron microscope has provided an in-depth description of the events of cytodifferentiation in a great number of cell types, but very little is known concerning the underlying controlling mechanisms. The study of the molecular biology of cytodifferentiation is providing increasing descriptive information about which macromolecules are present at each stage in a variety of cell types, but very little information about the events responsible for their synthesis or the nature of the determination process. The development of more suitable in vitro culture conditions has provided developmental biologists with the opportunity to study differentiation independently of the multitude of systemic influences to which a cell is normally subject in vivo. The environment in which the cultured cell is growing and differentiating can be manipulated at will, and the importance of such factors as cell density, cell adhesion, and cell division can be studied. In the first section we posed a variety of questions. Some of these have been answered, at least partially, in the pages between; others cannot be answered now, but they are being currently investigated.

READINGS

DAWSON, D. M., T. L. GOODFRIEND, and N. O. KAPLAN, 1964. Lactic Dehydrogenases: Functions of the Two Types, *Science*, **143**:929–933.

DeHAAN, R. L., and H. URSPRUNG (eds.), 1965. "Organogenesis," Holt, Rinehart, and Winston.

DOERING, J. L., and D. A. FISCHMAN, 1974. The *In Vitro* Cell Fusion of Embryonic Chick Muscle Without DNA Synthesis, *Develop. Biol.*, **36**:225–235.

DUMONT, J. N., and T. YAMADA, 1972. Dedifferentiation of Iris Epithelial Cells, *Develop. Biol.*, **29**:385–401.

ELLISON, M. L., and J. W. LASH, 1971. Environmental Enhancement of *In Vitro* Chondrogenesis, *Develop. Biol.*, **26**:486–496.

FLEISCHMAJER, R., and R. E. BILLINGHAM (eds.), 1968. "Epithelial-Mesenchymal Interactions," Williams and Wilkins.

HERRMANN, H., S. M. HEYWOOD, and A. C. MARCHOK, 1970. Reconstruction of Muscle Development as a Sequence of Macromolecular Syntheses, *Curr. Topics in Develop. Biol.*, **5**:81–234.

HOLTZER, H., 1974. More to Muscle than Myosin, *Nature*, **249**:106–107.

——, H. WEINTRAUB, R. MAYER, and B. MOCHRAN, 1972. The Cell Cycle, Cell Lineages, and Cell Differentiation, *Curr. Topics in Develop. Biol.*, **7**:229–256.

KAFOTOS, F. C., 1972. The Cocoonase Zymogen Cells of Silk Moths: A Model for Terminal Cell Differentiation for Specific Protein Synthesis, *Curr. Topics in Develop. Biol.*, **7**:125–191.

KONIGSBERG, I. R., and P. A. BUCKLEY, 1974. Regulation of the Cell Cycle and Myogenesis by Cell-Medium Interaction, in J. Lash and J. R. Whittaker (eds.), "Concepts in Development," Sinauer.

——, 1963. Clonal Analysis of Myogenesis, *Science*, **140**:1273–1284.

KOSHER, R. A., and J. W. LASH, 1975. Notochordal Stimulation of *In Vitro* Somite Chondrogenesis Before and After Enzymatic Removal of Perinotochordal Materials, *Develop. Biol.*, **42**:362–378.

LEVITT, D., and A. DORFMAN, 1974. Concepts and Mechanisms of Cartilage Differentiation, *Curr. Topics in Develop. Biol.*, **8**:103–149.

LOCKE, M. (ed.), 1963. "Cytodifferentiation and Macromolecular Synthesis," 21st Symposium, The Society of Developmental Biology, Academic.

MARKS, P. A. and R. A. RIFKIND, 1972. Protein Synthesis: Its Control in Erythropoiesis, *Science*, **175**:955–961.

MARZULLO, G., and J. W. LASH, 1970. Control of Phenotypic Expression in Cultured Chondrocytes: Investigations on the Mechanism, *Develop. Biol.*, **22**:638–654.

MASTERS, C. J., and R. S. HOLMES, 1972. Isozymes and Ontogeny, *Biol. Rev.*, **47**:309–361.

MINTZ, B., and W. B. BAKER, 1967. Normal Mammalian Muscle Differentiation and Gene Control of Isocitrate Dehydrogenase Synthesis, *Proc. Nat. Acad. Sci. U.S.*, **58**:592–598.

O'NEILL, M. C., and F. E. STOCKDALE, 1972. A Kinetic Analysis of Myogenesis *In Vitro*, *J. Cell Biol.*, **52**:52–65.

PAUL, J., et al., 1973. The Globin Gene: Structure and Expression *Cold Spring Harbor Symp. Quant. Biol.*, **38**:885–890.

PRZYBLYLA, A., and R. C. STROHMAN, 1974. Myosin Heavy Chain Messenger RNA from Myogenic Cell-Cultures, *Proc. Nat. Acad. Sci. U.S.*, **71**:662–666.

ROSS, J. I. IKAWA, and P. LEDER, 1972. Globin Messenger-RNA Induction During Erythroid Differentiation of Cultured Leukemia Cells, *Proc. Nat. Acad. Sci. U.S.*, **69**:3620–3623.

RUTTER, W. J., R. L. PICTET, and P. W. MORRIS, 1973. Toward Molecular Mechanisms of Developmental Processes, *Ann. Rev. Biochem.*, **42**:601–646.

SOLURSH, M., and G. C. KARP, 1975. An Effect of Accumulated Matrix on Sulfation Among Cells in a Cartilage Colony: An Autoradiographic Study, *J. Exp. Zool.*, **191**:73–84.

URSPRUNG, H. (ed.), 1968. "Stability of the Differentiated State," Springer-Verlag.

WESSELS, N. K., and W. J. RUTTER, 1969. Phases in Cell Differentiation, *Sci. Amer.*, March.

WHITTAKER, J. R., 1974. Aspects of Differentiation and Determination in Pigment Cells, in J. Lash and J. R. Whittaker (eds.), "Concepts in Development," Sinauer.

WILT, F. W., 1974. The Beginnings of Erythropoiesis in the Yolk Sac of the Chick Embryo, *Ann. N.Y. Acad. Sci.*, **241**:99–112.

YAFFE, D., and H. DYM, 1972. Synthesis and Assembly of Myofibrils in Embryonic Muscle, *Curr. Topics in Develop. Biol.*, **5**:235–280.

CHAPTER 18

Development of the Immune System

At the present time research on the development, nature, and function of the immune system is producing a tremendous body of fact and theory. In this chapter we will focus on the developmental questions that have arisen and on the background of antibody structure and formation necessary to understand them.

The immune system is considered primarily a system of defense at the molecular level. The targets are molecules recognized as foreign to the individual; the weapons are proteins called *antibodies* (or *immunoglobulins*). The cells responsible for antibody production are those of the lymphoid tissue. In mammals this includes the thymus, bone marrow, lymph nodes, spleen, certain tissues of the gut (Peyer's patches), and the fetal liver.

ANTIBODY STRUCTURE AND FUNCTION

As discussed in Chapter 2, protein molecules are composed of chains of polypeptides that are folded and interconnected in a complex, three-dimensional organization. If one were able to view the surfaces of proteins (or nucleic acids or polysaccharides as well), there would be valleys, protrusions, and a myriad of different spatial and electronic configurations. Each species of protein would have a predictable, detailed profile; changes in amino acid sequence of such a protein that arose during evolution would cause this profile to vary from animal to animal. The longer the time since the divergence of two animal species, the greater the difference one would expect in their macromolecules. Amino acid sequence analysis has indicated the nature of the changes that occurred in a variety of proteins over evolutionary time.

If proteins extracted from one animal, such as a mouse, are injected into another species of animal, such as a rabbit, the latter will recognize these proteins as foreign, i.e., distinct from its own proteins. It will respond to them by the production of antibodies. Any substance that evokes the production of antibodies is termed an *antigen*. Substances that are antigenic to one person or to one species of animal might not be antigenic to another; i.e., they may not be recognized as being foreign. Antigens can include polysaccharides and nucleic acids as well as proteins.

Once produced, the antibody is capable of reacting with the antigen responsible for its production, and the antigen is inactivated and destroyed. The most remarkable feature of the immune system is its specificity. If a particular antigen, such as measles virus, is injected into an animal, the antibodies formed in response to that injection are highly specific; they will combine only with measles virus protein and not with protein obtained from another source. The injection of polio virus protein or a foreign hemoglobin will result in an entirely different group of antibody molecules. Several very important questions are raised by these observations. How can certain antibody molecules combine with one antigen and not with another? That is, what is the basis of antibody specificity? This question can be answered by considering antibody structure and variability, discussed below. Another question concerns how a given antigen can invoke the production of an antibody that can specifically combine with it. This question will be considered in the next section.

How can an antibody specifically combine with the antigen responsible for its synthesis? Antibodies are globular proteins or immunoglobulins. Like other proteins, they have predictable spatial and electronic surface configurations. In the following discussion only one type of immunoglobulin (IgG) will be described, though there are several classes (IgG, IgA, IgM, IgD, IgE), which are composed of different types of polypeptide chains. A more thorough discussion of antibody structure can be found in Putnam (1969) and Hood and Prahl (1971).

Immunoglobulin molecules are composed of two pairs of identical polypeptide chains, held together primarily by disulfide bonds. The polypeptides of one pair each contain approximately 110 amino acids (light chains), while the other pair is much greater in its length (heavy chains). The amino acid sequence of proteins can be determined by the stepwise removal and identification of one amino acid at a time along the polypeptide chain. The first step in amino acid sequence analysis is to obtain a preparation of purified protein, because contaminating proteins with a different amino acid sequence will greatly confuse the analysis. Under normal conditions it is impossible to obtain a purified preparation of a given antibody since each individual produces many different antibody molecules, all of which are similar enough in structure to be very difficult to separate. Even after the injection of one antigen, antibodies with many different combining sites (and therefore amino acid sequence) are produced, all capable of combining with some part of the antigen.

Amino acid sequence data has been obtained from immunoglobulins of patients with multiple myelomas, tumors of lymphoid cells. In patients with these tumors, large amounts of single antibodies are produced and secreted. The particular species of immunoglobulin produced presumably depends upon the particular cell that became malignant. Different patients produce different species of antibody. When the amino acid sequences of several light and heavy chains of immunoglobulins from different patients were compared, an important pattern was revealed. In the group of light chains that were studied, it was found that one-half of each chain was constant in amino acid sequence while the other half was variable. The conclusion was that if all the light chains of the immunoglobulin molecules of one person were compared, one-half of each chain would be constant and the other half variable.

Analysis of heavy chains of IgG indicates that approximately one-quarter (the amino end) of each has a variable sequence; the remaining three-quarters is constant among all IgG heavy chains examined. The specificity of antibodies derives from the different amino acid sequence of the variable parts of both their light and heavy polypeptide chains. It is not known how many different light or heavy chains a person can synthesize; figures from 1,000 to 10,000 of

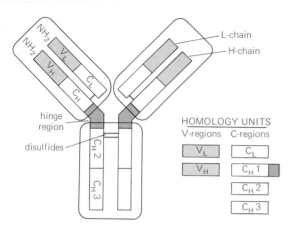

HOMOLOGY UNITS

V-regions   C-regions

V_L		C_L
V_H		C_H 1
		C_H 2
		C_H 3

Figure 18.1 A model of an immunoglobulin (IgG) molecule. V, variable portion of a polypeptide chain; C, constant portion of a polypeptide chain; subscript H represents heavy chain; subscript L represents light chain. [*After Smith, Hood, and Fitch, Ann. Rev. Biochem.,* **40** *1971.*]

each have been proposed. Presumably, antibodies with all possible combinations of light and heavy chains are possible; if there were 10,000 of each, there would be 10^8 (10,000 × 10,000) different immunoglobulin molecules possible. Whatever the actual number might be, it is clear that the ability of the immune system to produce a tremendous variety of different antibodies is one of the most remarkable biochemical feats of living systems, and many important questions about mechanisms arise.

The structure of an IgG molecule is shown in Fig. 18.1. Each half of the molecule has one heavy and one light chain. Each half has its own combining site, though one half of the molecule is identical with the other. IgG molecules are divalent (two combining sites). This property allows large complexes of interconnected antigen and antibody to build up, much the same way that large precipitates of sperm can be formed from the interaction of multivalent fertilizin- and antifertilizin-bearing sperm. It is at the combining site of each antibody that the variable portions of both the light and heavy chains are located. Analyses of these sites have revealed much of their structure (see Singer and Doolittle, 1966).

GENETIC BASIS OF ANTIBODY VARIABILITY

In the previous discussion, combining-site specificity was attributed to the variable portions of the polypeptide chains that make up each site, while the constant portions contribute to that part of the immunoglobulin molecule that is the same among antibodies (Fig. 18.1). If the capacity to produce thousands of different immunoglobulins exists within each individual as a result of the thousands of different variable portions of each chain, an equivalent number of genes that code for these polypeptides must also be present. One question of basic importance is whether the thousands of different genes required are present at the beginning of development in the DNA of the sperm and the egg, or whether this great diversity arises during the development of each animal. In the latter theory it is suggested that as a result of duplication, mutation, and recombination, the large numbers of variable sequences are generated from what was originally a very few genes. Arguments advanced in behalf of the

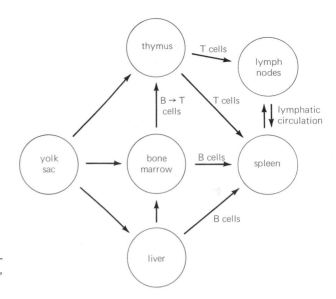

Figure 18.2 Cell migration pattern during the development of the immune system. [*After Auerbach, "Concepts in Development," Sinauer, 1974.*]

former theory (*a germ-line theory*) are by Hood, in Haber (1972), and for the latter theory (*a somatic-recombination theory*), in Gally and Edelman (1970). If the germ-line theory is correct, the variable gene diversity has arisen during evolution. In the somatic-recombination theory, the diversity arises by some special process in the immune cell line during development and differentiation. The final determination of this question awaits the analysis of germ-line DNA for its content of immunoglobulin genes. The presence of both a variable and a constant portion of each polypeptide chain presents several basic problems. Does one gene code for those constant regions, which are of identical amino acid sequence? If so, these polypeptide chains are coded for by two different genes, and some joining mechanism must exist at some point in the sequence of steps leading to protein synthesis. The most likely place is at the DNA level; some mechanism would be required to move the constant gene beside the appropriate variable gene so that an RNA containing the information from both genes in tandem could be transcribed. Several theories have been proposed to account for the production of a constant and a variable gene in tandem.

The evolution of a mechanism whereby one piece of DNA can be inserted in some manner into a variety of locations in the genome would have general significance for differentiation. In the course of lymphocyte differentiation, each cell becomes determined so that it synthesizes only one particular species of antibody. In other words, if a suspension of cells of a lymph node were prepared, each cell would be capable of producing only one particular antibody molecule (discussed below). If one constant gene is utilized in different polypeptide chains among different lymphocytes, the process whereby that gene becomes fixed in each cell may be the step where the future synthetic activities of that cell line are specified. The process of determination in general is one of the most poorly understood in developmental biology. If biochemical specification occurs by this mechanism in the immune system, it may occur in some similar manner during determination in other cell types. If a switching mechanism for this process does exist, it seems to operate only within one chromosome rather than between chromosomes, since the variable and constant portions of all immunoglobulins are genetically linked, i.e., in the same chromosome. In addition, all the immunoglobulins produced by a single antibody-producing cell are derived from one of the pair of homologous chromosomes, while the allele of this protein on the other member of the pair remains silent. This observation comes from the study of immunoglobulins made by cells known to be heterozygous, in which only one allele is expressed. This contrasts with other cases, such as hemoglobin, where both alleles are known to be expressed. It appears, therefore, that a special mechanism exists in the specification of lymphocyte differentiation where alleles on one homologous chromosome are excluded.

The alternative basis for the two-gene–one-polypeptide concept is that there are many constant genes and each variable gene is associated with a constant gene. In this case the specification of lymphocytes to produce an antibody would occur by some other mechanism. There are very difficult problems to overcome in the maintenance of a number of genes in an identical state over periods of evolutionary time. The evidence suggests the number of constant genes is very limited. The problem of maintaining identical copies of genes is not confined to the immune system; it is present in the genes for ribosomal RNA, transfer RNAs, and histones. In each case there appear to be a number of copies (from a few in the case of tRNAs to hundreds in the other two) of identical genes present in the germ line from generation to generation. How do these genes avoid becoming altered by mutation to form genes with diverging nucleotide sequence? A proposal has been made that one gene is used as a "master" and the copies are corrected at certain times against the master copy. Whatever the mechanism might be, it is clear there are many basic problems in genetic function that are not yet understood. Analysis of information storage and utilization in the immune system may be the most challenging of all.

CLONAL SELECTION THEORY

Regardless of the means by which cells of the immune tissues acquire a great number of different genes that code for immunoglobulins, some mechanism must exist whereby appropriate antibodies are produced in response to specific antigens. The theory presented in detail by Burnet (1959) to explain the general basis of antibody production, the *clonal selection theory,* has gained virtually complete acceptance. The theory is based on several premises. One major premise is that as the cells of the immune tissues differentiate, they become capable of producing only one species of antibody molecule. The theory assumes that the entire spectrum of possible antibody-producing cells is present within the lymphoid tissues *prior to stimulation by antigen* and, therefore, independent of the presence of foreign materials. The theory is a selective one. The antigen is somehow capable of selecting the appropriate antibody-producing cell, which responds by proliferation to produce a clone of cells capable of producing antibody that will combine with the antigen and inactivate it. All aspects of the theory have been corroborated.

Inherent in clonal selection is some mechanism whereby antigen can "select" the appropriate antibody-producing cells from among all the lymphocytes in the tissues. Recent studies have clearly indicated that the basis for the selection process is localized at the surface of the antibody-producing cells; receptors capable of combining with antigen are embedded within the membrane itself.

DIFFERENTIATION OF LYMPHOID
TISSUES IN MAMMALS

403
Development
of the
Immune
System

The development of the immune system begins with the appearance of a group of large hemopoietic (blood-forming) stem cells in the yolk sac. As in the case of the primordial germ cells, which also originate in the yolk sac, the stem cells of the lymphoid system migrate from their place of origin to the appropriate embryonic sites. The original concept of stem-cell migration via the blood-stream came from the analysis of twin cattle in which blood cells from both individuals populated the tissues of each twin. The stem cells of the yolk sac are capable of differentiating into a wide variety of different types of cells of both the myeloid (red blood cells, polymorphonuclear leukocytes, monocytes, mega-karyocytes) and the lymphoid (lymphocytes) line. The direction of differentia-tion that each of these cells eventually takes appears to result from the influences it receives after it reaches its specific differentiation. Those that migrate into lymphoid tissues become lymphocytes. Cells destined to produce lympho-cytes are first detected in the embryonic thymus, which forms from the third and fourth branchial pouches and plays a critical role in the development of the entire mammalian immune system. In the mouse, if the thymus rudiment is removed at the tenth day of gestation and is cultured in vitro, no evidence is found of lymphoid cells in the culture. If, however, the rudiment is explanted at day 12, lymphocytes are present in large numbers, suggesting that the thymus has been "seeded" by migrating stem cells between the tenth and twelfth days of development. Once these lymphoid stem cells are present, the rudiment is capable of self-differentiation in vitro.

Once in the thymus, the large lymphoid stem cells proliferate in the cortex of the thymus to produce a population of smaller lymphocytes (present by day 16 in mice) called *thymocytes,* which now bear distinctive markers on their surface. Two of the surface markers are called *theta* and *TL (thymus leu-kemia) antigens.* The term antigen is used because they are detected by in-jecting these cells into another animal, which then produces antibodies against these particular surface components. The final steps in the development of thymus cells involve the acquisition of the ability to interact specifically with antigen. This process gives them the ability to participate in a variety of im-mune functions. Cells from the thymus that have become mature and are now specified to produce only one type of antibody molecule are said to be *im-munocompetent* and are called *T cells.*

The main role of the thymus is to receive and send out lymphocytes. The greatest flow of cells through the thymus is during the period of development of the immune system, but the flow continues at a diminishing rate into adult life. In the initial stages of thymus development, the cells are derived from the yolk sac. Then they are derived from the liver, and after birth, cells from the bone marrow are found to enter the thymus. Presumably all these cells can be con-verted into mature T cells having characteristic surface structures and func-tions. From their maturation in the thymus, T cells migrate through the lym-phatic and blood vessels into a variety of lymphoid tissues, including the spleen and the lymph nodes. These two sites are said to be "thymus-dependent"; they must be "seeded" by T cells arriving from the thymus. If the thymus of a new-born mouse is removed (a thymectomy), T cells, as detected by their surface an-tigens, are absent in the circulation, and the thymus-dependent tissues have a severely depleted lymphocyte population. In the mouse the first week after birth is a time of active "seeding" of thymus-dependent tissues by T cells. Removal of the thymus in the newborn mouse precedes the appearance of a significant number of circulating lymphocytes. In man congenital defects in the thymus are found on occasion, and the symptoms are similar to those of thymectomy in the mouse.

Under normal conditions it is difficult to determine the extent to which cells enter and leave a particular organ, such as the thymus. To measure thymus cell turnover, the thymus can be removed and in its place can be grafted a thymus whose cells have been labeled with ^{3}H-thymidine. Under these conditions there is a rapid loss of labeled cells from the thymus and an appearance of radioactivity in lymph node and spleen tissue. In a matter of days there is essentially a completely new population of host cells in the thymus, and the old population has been replaced. In addition to the seeding of lymphocytes, the thymus is responsible for the secretion of a hormone, thymosin, which appears to act in some manner upon the differentiation of the thymus-dependent lymphoid tissues. If, for example, a thymus graft into a thymectomized mouse is kept within a container that allows macromolecules out but not cells, there is considerably greater development of the peripheral lymphoid tissues, even though none of the implanted cells can leave the graft. Secretion of thymosin into the circulation seems to have a compensating effect for lack of cell immigration.

Thymus-derived cells (T cells) are only one of two main types of lymphocytes; the others are thymus-independent and are called *B cells*. The precise origins of B cells in mammals are not known with certainty. They probably have migrated from the yolk sac to the liver and the bone marrow, though the steps in their differentiation into immunocompetent cells are not well known. As in the case of T cells, the differentiation of B cells occurs in the absence of antigen and is correlated with surface changes that allow the cell to interact in a specific manner with the appropriate antigen.

The receptors on the surface of B cells are known to be immunoglobulins with the same specificity as the immunoglobulins that the B cell will eventually produce in great amount. Antigen-specific receptors are also present on the surface of T cells, but their nature—whether immunoglobulin or not—remains unclear.

The mechanism responsible for clonal selection appears to have been described with the unraveling of the relationship between surface receptors and cell function. The interaction of the receptor and the antigen triggers the proliferation of antibody-producing cells and the secretion of antibody with the same specificity (and thus guaranteed combining ability) as the interacting receptor. This is described in detail below.

ROLE OF T AND B CELLS

Before the effects of thymectomy and the subsequent deficiency in T cells can be understood, a brief examination of the types of immune response is necessary. There are two broad categories of immunity, cell-bound and humoral. In cell-bound immunity, the antigen-combining sites are carried at the surface of a lymphocyte and the destruction of the antigen involves the direct participation of the lymphocyte. Humoral immunity refers to the secretion of immunoglobulin molecules into the blood as soluble antibody. These two types of immune response can be dissociated to a large extent. In humans, for instance, there is a disease (congenital agammaglobulinemia) in which humoral antibody is deficient and cell-bound immunity is normal. In contrast, congenital thymus deficiencies have greatly impaired cell-bound immunity with relatively high serum antibody levels.

CELL-BOUND IMMUNITY

Cell-bound immunity is completely within the province of T cells and is implicated in several functions. The best-studied immune response utilizing T cells is graft rejection. Many of the proteins and glycoproteins located on all cell surfaces are highly specific markers to which the immune system can respond. One group of macromolecules, the histocompatability antigens, is particularly important in the recognition of foreign cells. Histocompatability antigens are coded for by a number of different genes (approximately 15 in mice) for which many different alleles of each are present in the population. The probability that two individuals will have the same alleles for all the histocompatability genes is very unlikely, even among nonidentical siblings. Graft rejection is therefore a virtual certainty after tissue transplantation in all but identical twins and highly inbred strains of laboratory animals. Differences between individuals at certain of the histocompatability loci result in very rapid rejection, while others are considered weak antigens and rejection is a more prolonged process.

The basis of graft rejection is an attack by T cells that have proliferated in response to the presence of foreign tissue containing antigenic determinants. In mice that have been deprived of thymus tissue from birth, graft rejection does not occur and such grafts will remain in place. One special case of tissue rejection by immunocompetent T cells is the graft-versus-host reaction, which has been widely studied. If spleen cells are injected into an animal that has been irradiated or thymectomized and is thus unable to reject foreign cells from another individual, a gradual process of host rejection by the descendants of the injected cells will occur. The spleen cells will seed the lymphoid tissues of the host; being immunocompetent themselves, they will be stimulated by the presence of the host tissue, which is recognized as foreign. The tissues of the host will gradually be destroyed. The graft-versus-host reaction has been observed in humans under certain clinical conditions. In one report, an infant was born with a severe thymus deficiency that had prevented the development of his immune system. In an attempt to provide him with a population of functioning lymphocytes, spleen cells from a very young sister were injected into him. These would be expected to seed his lymph nodes, spleen, and other tissues and to provide him with a basis to attack foreign molecules. In this case, however, the injected cells had already been specified, and they contained cells capable of reacting against their new host. In the ensuing months, host tissues were destroyed by cell-bound lymphocytes that found the tissues foreign. The infant died from what is termed "wasting disease."

The ability of T cells to destroy cells containing foreign surface molecules is believed to play an important role in the detection and destruction of potential tumor-forming cells. As discussed in detail in Chapter 19, the conversion of a normal cell to the malignant state is accompanied by changes in the nature of the cell surface, changes that should make that cell vulnerable to attack by immunocompetent T cells. In this capacity T cells carry out a process termed *immunological surveillance,* whereby the surfaces of cells are continually examined for the appearance of antigenic molecules. Inherent in this theory is the concept that tumor cells are being formed and destroyed throughout life and only those malignant cells that escape immune destruction can lead to the formation of tumors. It is the concept of immunological surveillance that provides investigators with the reason for the existence of such a complex, cell-mediated immune function.

The evidence for immunological surveillance is indirect at the present time. One line of evidence has been obtained from studies of cells in which induced or naturally occurring immune deficiency exists. The theory predicts that if immune function, and therefore surveillance, is greatly diminished, an increased incidence of malignancy should result. There are two types of conditions in humans where the effect of immune deficiency can be studied: the organ transplant patient who has been given immunosuppressive drugs to interfere with his ability for graft rejection and patients, particularly children with genetic defects, whose immune system has suffered destruction or congenital absence. In both cases there is a striking increase in tumor formation, manyfold greater than in the general population.

Another prediction that can be made from the theory of immunological surveillance is that tumor cells from an animal should be antigenic to that animal, at least under certain conditions. The ability of an animal to produce antibodies against its own tumor cells has been reported many times. In fact, humoral antibodies produced in response to tumor cell surface antigens may be responsible for coating tumor cells, thereby preventing sensitized T cells from reaching the tumor cell and destroying it. In this latter case tumor growth can be enhanced. Under other conditions, tumors can be induced, removed from the animal, irradiated to destroy their ability to proliferate, and injected back into the animal, where they will induce an immune response that can destroy the tumor cells. It is clear, therefore, that immune destruction of tumor cells can occur.

The mechanism whereby T cells are able to destroy foreign cells is not yet known. Presumably it relates to their ability to produce a variety of highly active substances, one of which has a cytotoxic action on other cells and could lead to their destruction. These substances, termed *lymphokines,* inhibit cell migration, chemotactically attract other cells, cause other cells to divide, and have cytotoxic action. Many of the important steps in lymphocyte activity remain to be worked out.

HUMORAL IMMUNITY

The ability of an individual to secrete specific antibodies into the bloodstream is one of the bases of our defense against invading pathogenic organisms, whether as a response to an infection itself or after immunization. The cells responsible for the production of circulating immunoglobulins are the plasma cells that are located in the lymphoid tissues and are descendants of the B cells. The plasma cells are the end products of the B cell line, which have differentiated to produce large quantities of proteins that can be released to the outside.

Though the appearance of immunocompetent B cells occurs independently of the thymus, it was found that thymectomy greatly reduced the ability of an animal to produce circulating antibodies against a variety of antigens. Similarly, if B cells alone are injected into a mouse whose immune system had been destroyed by radiation, the injected B cells are not capable of reacting strongly to antigen. If, however, T cells are injected along with B cells, a full response by the B cells can result. Even though it is the B cell that is responsible for antibody production, the T cell is required in some "helper" role. In addition a third type of cell, the macrophage (a nonimmunocompetent cell), appears to play a critical role in this complex. The macrophage probably makes the first contact with antigen, but the subsequent steps remain unclear. The precise nature of the interaction between these cells, whereby the B cell is stimulated, has not been completely worked out. Both types of lymphocytes are capable of combining with antigen, the B cell via its immunoglobulin and the T cell by some undefined receptor. The evidence suggests that the T cell binds to a large part of the antigen so that the appropriate B cell can react with one small part of it (an antigenic determinant) and become activated. Another possible function of the T cell in this interaction is to produce a division-stimulating substance to cause the B cell to proliferate and form a clone of cells (called *blast cells*), all specified to make the same antibody. Some of these blast cells will then differentiate into plasma cells and begin to secrete antibody. It is believed that others will remain in the lymphoid tissues as "memory" cells to respond rapidly at some later date if that antigen becomes reintroduced. It is the memory aspect of immune response to which booster immunizations are geared; the reintroduction of antigen can cause a much more rapid production of antibody than occurred after the initial injection.

The ability of a specific antigen to stimulate the humoral response is an interesting developmental phenomenon. The binding of a specific antigen to the surface receptors of immunocompetent cells triggers a complex sequence of events beginning with proliferation and progressing to the differentiation of a highly specialized, antibody-secreting plasma cell. An interesting sidelight to the story of immune differentiation is the effect of a variety of compounds extracted from plants. These materials, called *lectins*, are generally glycoproteins that are capable of binding to certain macromolecules on the surfaces of animal cells. Certain lectins are capable of inducing small, nondividing lymphocytes to proliferate and differentiate into plasma cells and produce significant quantities of immunoglobulins. These results indicate that lymphocyte differentiation can be stimulated by nonspecific molecules (lectins) as well as specifically by antigen.

TOLERANCE

One of the most important questions to be considered in the development of the immune system is the basis for discriminating foreign substances from those of the body itself. How does an animal learn "self" from "non-self"? Since the specification of a given immunocyte to produce a given antibody is believed to be a random process, presumably cells are formed that have the capability to produce antibodies that could combine with the body's own materials. Antibodies of this type are called *autoantibodies*. Under normal conditions autoantibodies cannot be demonstrated. There is some mechanism whereby the cells that become specified to produce autoantibodies are either eliminated or blocked in some highly effective manner. The thymus is believed to be responsible for screening cells for their capacity to produce autoantibodies.

The term *tolerance* is used to denote a state where a particular antibody cannot be produced. Tolerance is a condition that occurs normally toward an animal's own tissues, but tolerance to foreign antigens can be artificially induced. During normal development there is a period where the immune system learns about "self." If foreign tissues are introduced during this period, they can be considered along with the animal's own proteins and will be considered as part of "self" from then on. Foreign cells that are capable of inducing tolerance, i.e., are *tolerogenic*, are ones that can become part of the host they are injected into and remain there to proliferate and develop a permanent population. Cells of the lymphoid system are highly effective in establishing tolerance. If spleen cells from one newborn mouse (mouse A) are injected into a genetically different newborn (mouse B), they take up residence in the host's lymphoid tissues and are not rejected. Mouse B comes to recognize them as if they had been there from the beginning of development. If, at a later time, a piece of skin were to be grafted from mouse A to mouse B, the graft would remain in place. If, however, a graft was made from a third, unrelated mouse (mouse C), the skin would be rapidly rejected. The immunological paralysis is highly specific; only cells capable of producing antibodies against A and B are inactivated. For a substance to be recognized as "self," the immune system must come into direct contact with this molecule during some early stage. In some cases there are macromolecules that are never present in the general circulation and remain antigenic throughout life. Spermatozoa, found only within the lumens of the seminiferous tubules, contain such materials. Injection into a hamster, for example, of an extract of its own spermatozoa results in the formation of autoantibodies and the complete destruction of the sperm content within the animal's own gonads.

In certain disease states (autoimmune conditions), the production of autoantibodies becomes activated and extensive tissue destruction can ensue. Autoimmune diseases can result from a variety of problems. In Hashimoto's disease, fluid normally kept within thyroid follicles and out of reach of the immune system leaks into the general circulation and is recognized as foreign by the lymphoid tissues, which had never been exposed to these substances during normal development. Autoantibodies are produced in response and attack the thyroid. Rheumatoid arthritis and rheumatic fever are both considered autoimmune conditions. Analysis of serum indicates a rise in autoantibodies with age in humans, and autoimmunity has been implicated as a basic factor in the process of aging.

DIFFERENTIATION OF ANTIBODY-PRODUCING CELLS

The ability to respond to a specific antigen reflects the presence within the lymphoid tissues of an antibody-producing cell that can be stimulated to divide and differentiate. In studies of the fetal lamb there is evidence that the ability to respond to a specific antigen is in some way a genetically programmed event. In these studies the pregnant ewe is operated on to expose the fetal lamb. It can be challenged with a given antigen and its ability to respond by antibody production can be monitored. Results indicate that materials become antigenic in a predictable sequence at predictable times. For example, the fetal lamb can respond to injections of the virus ϕx at approximately 41 days (gestation is 150 days), ferritin at approximately 56 days, skin grafts at approximately 75 days, ovalbumin at approximately 120 days, etc. In each case a response is not found prior to its predicted time of appearance. The explanation for this program is not presently available, though there are sufficient differences in the relative time of lymphoid tissue differentiation in the lamb, as compared with a mouse or a human, that different mechanisms may be present among mammals. There is no evidence in the mouse for such a genetically programmed development of immunocompetence.

FETAL ANTIGENICITY

409
Development
of the
Immune
System

With the evolution of the placental mammal, a new challenge to the immune system had to be overcome. As a result of the genetic contribution of the father, the mammalian fetus bears histocompatability antigens on its cell surfaces that should cause the fetus to be recognized as foreign by the maternal immune system. Considering the intimate vascular relationship between mother and fetus, a basic question in reproductive physiology is the mechanism by which the fetus is maintained rather than being rejected. There is good evidence that the developing fetus does provide antigenic stimulation to the maternal system. Yet the immune response remains ineffective, except in rare cases such as that associated with a difference at the Rh locus, which leads to the condition of erythroblastosis fetalis. Generally, however, even after the mother is previously immunized by injection of cells of the father, the developing fetus is not attacked. Protection of the embryo is not a property conferred by the uterus. Even if implantation has occurred in a completely abnormal site such as the fallopian tubes or the peritoneum, immune destruction does not occur.

As described by Beer and Billingham (1974), there appear to be two factors in operation to protect the fetus. Graft rejection is mediated by sensitized T lymphocytes (cell-bound immunity). Under certain conditions the destructive ability of these cells can be blocked, primarily by the presence of circulating humoral antibody. The exact mechanism in which the blocking occurs is not known, but the effect in malignancy can be to enhance the growth of the tumor and in the fetus to protect it from destruction. The other protective factor appears to be mediated, in some unknown way, by the trophoblast. For some reason trophoblast cells, even when separated from the developing fetus, are highly resistant to immunological destruction, though there is no doubt that they carry histocompatability antigens and are recognized as foreign.

The analysis of the nature of the immune system in the past decade has been a particular success story. To understand immune function, from either a physiological or a developmental perspective, we must understand its incredible specificity. How does an organism develop the ability to respond in a highly specific manner to the presence of a foreign substance, and what is the mechanism of this response? In this chapter we have described the structure of the reacting molecules, the immunoglobulins; the underlying genetic basis for immunoglobulin structure; the clonal selection theory, including the basis for clonal selection by antigen at the surfaces of the immunocompetent cells and speculations as to the means by which each potential clone becomes specified; the histological aspects of the differentiation of the lymphoid tissues; the division of immune function into cell-bound and humoral antibody and the developmental basis for each; and a variety of related topics of developmental interest. Information on the nature and complexity of the immune system continues to accumulate at a great pace. The possible role of the immune system in two of the greatest challenges we face, cancer and aging, has further stimulated immunological research.

READINGS

AMOS, B. (ed.), 1971. "Progress in Immunology," Academic.
AUERBACH, R., 1974. Development of Immunity, in J. Lash and J. R. Whittaker (eds.), "Concepts in Development," Sinauer.
——, 1972. Studies on the Development of Immunity: The Response to Sheep Red Blood Cells, *Curr. Topics in Develop. Biol.,* 7:257–280.
BEER, A. E., and R. E. BILLINGHAM, 1974. The Embryo as a Transplant, *Sci. Amer.,* April.

BENACERAF, B., and H. O. McDEVITT, 1972. Histocompatibility-linked Immune Response Genes, *Science*, **175**:273–279.

BILLINGHAM, R. E., 1974. Immunological Tolerance and Its Possible Role in Development, in J. Lash and J. R. Whittaker (eds.), "Concepts in Development," Sinauer.

BURNET, F. M., 1970. "Immunological Surveillance," Pergamon.

——, 1969. "Cellular Immunology," Cambridge University Press.

——, 1959. "The Clonal Selection Theory of Acquired Immunity," Cambridge University Press.

EDELMAN, G. M., 1973. Antibody Structure and Immunology, *Science*, **180**:830–840.

FRIEDMAN, H. (ed.), 1975. Thymus Factors in Immunity, *Ann. N.Y. Acad. Sci.*, **249**.

GALLY, J. A., and G. M. EDELMAN, 1970. Somatic Translocation of Antibody Genes, *Nature*, **227**:341–348.

HABER, E. (ed.), "Two Genes, One Polypeptide Chain," *Fed Proc. Amer. Soc. Exp. Biol.*, **31**:176–209.

HOOD, L. E., and J. PRAHL, 1971. The Immune System: a Model for Differentiation in Higher Organisms, *Advan. Immunol.*, **14**:291–351.

KABAT, E. A., and M. M. MAYER, 1961. "Experimental Immunochemistry," 2d ed., Charles C. Thomas.

KATZ, D. H., and B. BENACERRAF, 1972. The Regulatory Influence of Activated T Cells on B Cell Responses to Antigen, *Advan. Immunol.*, **15**:1–94.

METCALF, D., and M. A. S. MOORE, 1971. Haemopoietic Cells: Their Origin, Migration, and Differentiation, "Frontiers of Biology," vol. 24, North-Holland Publishing Company, Amsterdam.

MILLER, J. F. A. P., 1972. Lymphocyte Interactions in Antibody Responses, *Int. Rev. Cytol.*, **33**:77–130.

MOLLER, G. (ed.), 1972. "Lymphocyte Activation by Mitogens, *Transp. Revs.* vol. 11.

OWEN, R. D., 1945. Immunogenetic Consequences of Vascular Anastomoses Between Bovine Twins, *Science* **102**:400–401.

PORTER, R., and J. KNIGHT (eds.), 1972. "Ontogeny of Acquired Immunity," CIBA Foundation Symposium, Elsevier.

PUTNAM, F. W., 1969. Immunoglobulin Structure: Variability and Homology, *Science*, **163**:633–644.

RAFF, M. C., 1973. T and B Lymphocytes and Immune Responses, *Nature*, **242**:19–23.

SINGER, S. J., and R. E. DOOLITTLE, 1966. Antibody Active Sites and Immunoglobulin Molecules, *Science*, **153**:13–25.

SMITH, R. T., R. A. GOOD, and P. A. MIESCHER, 1967. "Ontogeny of Immunity," University of Florida Press.

STERZL, J., and I. RIHA (eds.), 1970. "Developmental Aspects of Antibody Formation and Structure," Academic.

—— and A. M. SILVERSTEIN, 1967. Developmental Aspects of Immunity, *Advan. Immunol.*, **6**:337–459.

WEISSMAN, I. L., 1967. Thymus Cell Migration, *J.Exp. Med.*, **126**:291–304.

Malignancy

Cancer can be defined as a disease involving heritable defects in cellular control mechanisms, resulting in the formation of malignant and usually invasive tumors. The development of a multicellular organism consists of cell multiplication, growth, cytodifferentiation, and morphogenesis proceeding together to an organized end. To some extent each of these component processes is independent of the others and has been studied as such so far as possible. In this connection malignant tumors represent an exceptional opportunity to study some component processes in the absence of others. A malignant tumor is the result of unrestricted cell growth and cell multiplication, comparable with tissue culture in vitro but taking place within the body, without response to the normal growth-controlling agencies. Typically such a tumor consists of a single prevailing type of cell which may or may not retain obvious characteristics of the tissue from which it arose. In teratomas, a special class of malignant tumors, various cell types are evident, and compared with the process of development as a whole and apart from the quality of malignancy, only the phenomenon of morphogenesis appears to be lacking. Consequently, malignant growth may be seen as the inverse of organized development, and the study of one may throw light upon the other.

CARCINOGENS

Any tissue in the body that is capable of cell division may become cancerous, with varying degrees of malignancy. The problems involved seem endless, although inquiry falls into a few main categories: the nature of the instigating agents, the changes produced within the cells, and the changed behavior of the cells with regard to normal tissues. The clinical picture does not concern us here. The general inquiry into the nature of the cancerous transformation, however, has much in common with the search for the "organizer" of the vertebrate embryo. In both cases the initial efforts concerned the nature of the causative agents and their common property. In both cases the effective agents were found to be numerous and, in the main, to have no recognizably significant physical or chemical properties in common. In both cases, therefore, interest turns from the nature of the agents to the nature of the response and to whatever aspect of the cell machinery may be responsible for the response. The action of the inducing agents, however, remains vitally important. In spite of their diversity, each in some way interferes with the precise controls of cell growth and multiplication. Yet it does not follow that the control system is affected in the same way by all, except insofar as all the agents may be disruptive.

At one end of a chain of events are the various carcinogenic agents. They include ionizing radiations that penetrate a cell, namely, ultraviolet radiation, x-rays, and the various radiations emitted from radioactive elements. They include a host of chemical compounds, particularly the polycyclic hydrocarbons such as, dibenzanthracene, benzopyrene, and methylcholanthrene, which belong to the same general class as the sex hormones and cholesterol. And they include the viruses that invade and replicate within animal and plant cells and in many specific cases induce tumorous growth.

The remainder of the chain is the cell itself. Is the carcinogenic effect, whatever the agent, exerted at the DNA level, at the cell membrane, or on enzymatic processes between? The answer may vary according to the agent and the type and developmental age of the cell.

TYPES OF MALIGNANT TISSUES

Two main categories of tumors are recognized: (1) *Carcinomas* derive from epithelial tissues and generally retain at least some vestige of their epithelial character. They are known as *adenocarcinomas* when the epithelial character is fully retained. (2) *Sarcomas* are of connective-tissue origin, such as those derived from fibroblasts and chondroblasts, yielding *fibrosarcomas* and *chondrosarcomas,* and a host of others.

There are some tumors that do not fall into the above two categories, such as *lymphomas,* as in leukemia, characterized by an increased production of leukocytes; *melanomas,* derived from pigment cells and usually scattered; *gliomas,* derived from glial cells in the central nervous system; and *teratomas,* which exhibit manifold cell differentiations otherwise associated with embryonic development.

THE MALIGNANT TRANSFORMATION

Cell Division

The *capacity* for growth, division, and movement is much the same for normal and for malignant cells, at least in many cases. In tissue culture, normal cells, when fully released from inhibitory factors, grow and divide at much the same rate as malignant cells, as long as certain conditions are met. The difference is that in the body, cells grow at a maximal rate only in unusual

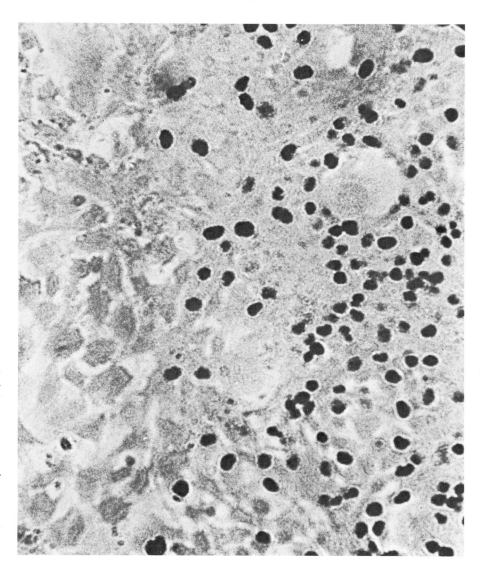

Figure 19.1 Autoradiograph of the edge of a ^{3}H-thymidine-labeled Rous sarcoma focus. The region with the black (labeled) nuclei contains infected and transformed cells. The unlabeled region contains normal cells. This is a graphic illustration of the capacity of virus-transformed cells to continue growing while their sister uninfected cells are inhibited from growing. [*Courtesy of H. Rubin.*]

circumstances and stop when normal tissue structure is restored. Malignant cells grow indefinitely (Fig 19.1), as though the body were only a culture medium serving as a nutritive support. In fact, most kinds of tumors in the body give off small clusters of cells from their periphery, as *metastases,* which circulate until they lodge in some other region, where secondary growths become established. In any case, the maximum rate of growth and cell division attainable by a tumor is no greater and is generally less than that attainable by normal cells cultured under optimal conditions.

With regard to cell proliferation, if, for example, the greater part of a rat's liver is cut off, the liver regenerates rapidly, growing at the rate of about a billion cells a day during the first 4 days. This rate is faster than that of any malignant growth recorded. Growth and cell proliferation then slow down until by the seventh day most of the amputated liver has been regenerated and the growth is less than one-tenth of the peak. In hepatomas, i.e., primary liver cell tumors, growth is slower but continues indefinitely.

The Cell Membrane

The concept of the cell membrane has changed in recent years from one of a relatively static, structural organelle to one of tremendous dynamism and importance in the regulation of cellular activities. The cell surface, apparently more than any other site, becomes modified as the consequence of the cell's becoming malignant. It may be that the large number of intracellular changes accompanying transformation can be considered secondary consequences of some as yet uncertain primary surface event.

One factor should be considered in the following discussion. Nearly all the observations are made upon cells transformed by oncogenic viruses, and there are questions of how general the properties of virally transformed cells are in comparison with other sources of tumor formation. Viruses are used for the ease with which they transform a wide variety of cells growing in culture, for the predictable nature of the events that follow addition of the virus at well-defined times, and for the temperature-sensitive viral mutants, which transform cells at a lower permissible temperature but are ineffective if the temperature is raised. By the use of temperature-sensitive mutants, transformation and reversion can be studied by simple temperature shifts in one direction or the other. In addition, transformation by viruses occurs in response to the integration of a small, well-studied genetic element. Resulting modifications in the cell's behavior can ultimately be explained in terms of this new genetic information. Scattered evidence from spontaneous or chemically transformed cells has corroborated results obtained with viruses.

Most cell membrane studies are performed on cultured cells that show a characteristic response to surface contact by another cell. The membrane of a normal cell, when contacted by another cell, ceases its activity, and movement in the original direction is halted. The cells may move apart in opposite directions, or stable intercellular junctions may form. When normal cells become surrounded on all sides by other cells, their motility ceases; they are not capable of moving over one another. This characteristic is termed *contact inhibition of movement*. The direct result of contact inhibition, as seen in the behavior of cells in culture, is the formation of a layer of cells on the surface of the culture dish that remains one cell deep, i.e., a monolayer (Fig. 19.2). A monolayer is maintained by the cessation of division of the cells on the dish. Once cells reach a continuous sheet, the mitotic index drops to a very low level. The term contact inhibition, therefore, refers to an aspect of normal cell behavior other than its membrane activity, namely, the inhibition of DNA synthesis and cell division. The inhibitory effect on DNA synthesis by cell crowding is completely reversible. If the cells are transferred to a new dish at lower density, they rapidly divide until they again become confluent—i.e., form a continuous sheet—and they cease proliferation. Contact inhibition of cell division illustrates the ability of information received at the cell surface—in this case with respect to proximity of neighboring cells—to be transferred to the intracellular compartment to regulate metabolic activity.

One of the first-described and best-studied properties of malignant cells in culture is their general lack of contact inhibition of both cell movement and cell division. The movement of a malignant cell is not obstructed or diverted when it is confronted by either a malignant cell or a normal cell, nor is its division potential reduced. As a result, cultures of malignant cells form clumps rather than monolayers and are capable of proliferating to many times the cell density of normal cell cultures (Fig. 19.3).

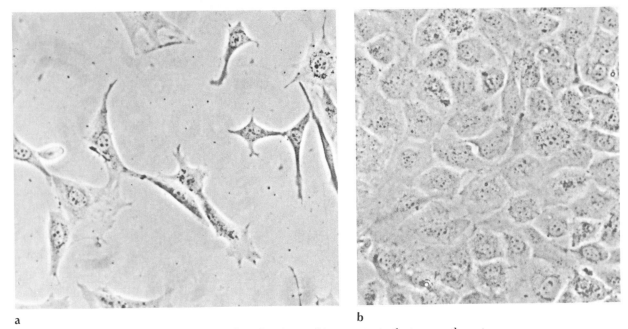

a

b

Figure 19.2 Normal cells growing (*a*) at low density making contacts that cause them to adhere to one another and (*b*) at high density where they have formed a mosaiclike arrangement in a monolayer and are contact-inhibited. [*Courtesy of R. Dulbecco.*]

Figure 19.3 Cells transformed by viruses generally overlap one another (*a*) and form multilayered clumps and irregular patterns (*b*).

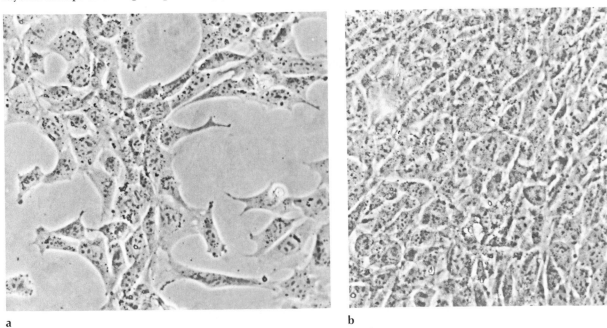

a

b

415

In addition to differences in contact inhibition between a normal cell and its corresponding transformed condition, many other distinguishing surface features have been reported. The transformed state is one of general loss in adhesivity, both between malignant cells and between these cells and their substrate. Cancer cells form relatively weak interactions with one another and with the coated glass or plastic surface upon which they are grown. This decreased intercellular adhesion is reflected in the wandering of cancer cells over one another in contrast with normal cells, whose contacts lead to closely applied membrane surfaces.

Another difference related to those described above is the tendency for normal cells to become coupled to one another under conditions in which their transformed counterparts remain isolated. When grown in culture, normal cells form low-resistance junctions so that low-molecular-weight substances can pass between cell compartments in passageways across the extracellular space. Fluorescent dyes or small ions are rapidly passed from cell to cell by these channels. Malignant cells, however, are generally unable to transfer small molecules, as illustrated in the following experiments. Cells growing in culture can be manipulated so that a line can be constructed in which each cell makes contact with the ones on each side. Fluorescein injected into one cell will readily diffuse into all the cells in the line via the communicating cell junctions. If, however, a malignant cell is placed into the line as one of the links of the cell chain, dye does not pass through the tumor cell (Fig. 19.4). When the cancer cell is reached, transfer stops.

Another change in cells after transformation by oncogenic viruses is the ease with which they can be agglutinated by plant lectins. Lectins are proteins or glycoproteins, extracted from plants, that can bind to specific molecules at the surfaces of animal cells. Examples of these lectins are concanavalin A, wheat-germ agglutinin, pokeweed mitogen, and numerous others. Each lectin

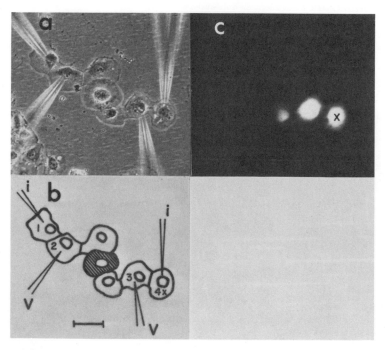

Figure 19.4 Lack of coupling between a cancer cell and the adjoining normal cells. The middle cancer cell was manipulated into the gap in the line of normal cells. *a* The seven cells in a line; the middle cell is malignant. Microelectrodes for measuring electrical coupling are seen penetrating the cells. *b* Tracing of the cells; the cancer cell is black. *c* Dark-field photograph after injection of a fluorescent dye into the last of the normal cells in the line. The fluorescence rapidly penetrates the two adjoining normal cells but does not move into the cancer cell because of lack of coupling. If a normal cell had been manipulated into this line of cells, the dye would have passed through it. [*Courtesy of R. Azarnia and W. Loewenstein.*]

is capable of binding to one particular chemical group projecting from the cell membrane or cell coat. The typical reactive group is a sugar residue occupying part of a small polysaccharide chain, an oligosaccharide of varying length, which is in turn attached to a protein in the membrane or cell coat. Lectins are multivalent; i.e., they have more than one combining site and are therefore capable of bridging the gap between two cells and holding them together. The result of this interaction is the formation of clumps of cells, hence the term *agglutination.*

It is generally found that transformed cells are more readily agglutinated than the corresponding normal cells. In some cases, at least, the change to the malignant state may be accompanied by a change in the position or distribution of lectin-combining sites within the membrane. Redistribution of membrane lectin receptors suggests increased membrane fluidity, which may be one of the basic consequences of the transformed condition. Increased agglutinability can also be obtained by brief treatment of *normal* cells with proteases, indicating that removal of surface peptides can mimic the transformed state. Not only does protease treatment of normal cells increase agglutination by lectins; it can also cause cells that had been previously contact-inhibited to undergo another round of DNA synthesis and cell division. This is another feature that mimics the transformed state. Though the normal cells are poorly agglutinable, lectin binding rises markedly during the time the cell is in mitosis. It appears, at least in agglutination by lectins, that transformed cells, protease-treated cells, and mitotic cells have surface features in common.

THE ROLE OF CYCLIC AMP

How are events at the cell's edge able to dictate policies of growth and division that must be regulated within the cell itself? Intracellular communication is an aspect of cell biology that has been difficult to study and is therefore poorly understood. The contact-inhibited state is believed to result from the formation of a "messenger" molecule, cyclic AMP, at the cell membrane, which then acts by some unknown mechanism to inhibit the cell's division machinery.

The evidence for the involvement of cyclic AMP in the transformation process is largely indirect, but a large body of correlative data supports this concept. In the previous section, high lectin-mediated agglutinability was correlated with transformation, protease treatment, and mitosis. Cells in all these states are also characterized by decreased levels of cyclic AMP. Not only do cyclic AMP levels rise and fall in relation to the activities of the cell, but the addition of this compound or related ones can actually cause the cell to change its observed phenotype. For example, treatment of transformed cells with cyclic AMP causes them to temporarily become more adhesive to one another and their substrate, to become less motile, to lose their agglutinability, to regain their normal morphological appearance, and in some cases to regain their contact inhibition of cell division. Similarly, the ability of protease treatment to stimulate a round of cell division in contact-inhibited normal cells is blocked by the addition of cyclic AMP. The dramatic effect of cyclic AMP on cell behavior is shown in Fig. 19.5. Under certain conditions, normal Chinese hamster ovary cells do not exhibit contact inhibition and they grow in multilayered clumps. Cells in these clumps are randomly oriented (Fig. 19.5a). The addition of cyclic AMP to these cells converts them to elongated, fibroblastlike cells, which are contact-inhibited and grow as a monolayer (Fig. 19.5b).

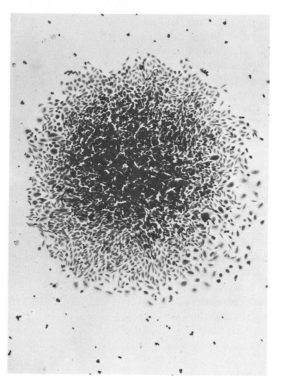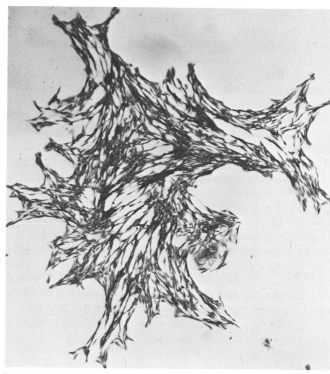

a   b

Figure 19.5 Effect of cyclic AMP on the morphology of a colony of Chinese hamster ovary cells. *a* Cells grown on standard medium where contact inhibition does not occur. *b* Cells grown in the presence of dibutyryl cyclic AMP are now contact-inhibited. [*Courtesy of A. Hsie and T. Puck.*]

The lowered cyclic AMP levels following transformation and the reversal of the malignant phenotype by the addition of cyclic AMP strongly suggest that altered cyclic AMP levels may be a basic causative event in transformation. Cyclic AMP levels are controlled by two factors: the rate at which the compound is synthesized and the rate at which it is destroyed. Synthesis is catalyzed by the enzyme adenyl cyclase, a component of the cell membrane. Degradation is brought about by the enzyme phosphodiesterase, which is within the cell. Comparison of enzyme levels between dividing and nondividing cells and transformed and nontransformed cells indicates that the level of adenyl cyclase drops as cells increase their growth rate. This alteration would be expected to decrease the levels of cyclic AMP in rapidly dividing cells.

Cells can be infected with temperature-sensitive mutants of oncogenic viruses. As long as the cells are grown at the higher, nonpermissive temperatures, no evidence of transformation is seen. If, however, these previously infected cells are dropped to the lower, permissive temperature, decreased cyclase activity can be found within 10 minutes, a very rapid event during transformation. Not only is the cyclase activity lowered; it has been reported that its kinetic properties are altered as well. In contrast with changes in cyclase activity, the increased agglutinability characteristic of the transformed state occurs only after one round of DNA synthesis following the shift to permissive temperatures. If DNA synthesis is blocked in these cells, no increase in agglutinability is seen.

The general theory has emerged from these studies that genetic changes associated with the transformation to the malignant state are accompanied by rapid changes at the cell surface. Analysis of the proteins, glycoproteins, and glycolipids of the cell membrane in the normal and transformed states indicates a variety of alterations. It is proposed that these membrane alterations mediate their effect on cellular activities via the decrease in cyclic AMP content, presumably resulting from a drop in the activity of the membrane-bound adenyl cyclase. Once the cyclic AMP levels are lowered, many or all of the properties of the malignant cell result. In a sense, the malignant cell is frozen in a condition typical of rapidly dividing, mitotic cells and is released from the normal growth controls.

One important feature of this theory is that the malignant state results from what is basically a quantitative change in the cell's activities rather than a qualitative one. In other words, the properties of the malignant state are believed to result from a decrease in a substance (cyclic AMP) found in normal tissues rather than from an entirely new control mechanism.

However, the presence of totally new macromolecules at the surface of the tumor cell is well-documented. A wide variety of new antigens have been reported at the surface of malignant cells, although their role in the cell's phenotype has not been determined. It may be that these surface antigens have no effect upon the internal activities of the malignant cell, but rather are involved in some extracellular event by which the malignant cell must interact with its environment. It should be kept in mind that these hypotheses have been worked out in virally transformed cells, which may not be typical of the malignant state; numerous exceptions have been reported, and current research should soon either bear out or refute this theory.

CHROMOSOMES

Early in this century Boveri (1902), from studies of the effects of multipolar mitoses on developing sea urchin eggs, related developmental abnormalities to the resulting abnormal distribution and combination of chromosomes. This led him to the concept of the individuality of the chromosomes. He also suggested that the multipolar mitoses, already known at that time to be common in many tumors, were responsible for the abnormal character of tumor growth. The modern concept that tumors originate as the result of somatic chromosomal mutation, from whatever causes, is a direct descendant of Boveri's hypothesis.

Chromosomal abnormality, usually associated with abnormal mitoses, is a common feature of many tumors. Tripolar and tetrapolar mitoses are frequent in many kinds of tumors, with inevitable irregular distribution of the two sets of chromosomes among the three or four progeny. As a rule, divisions of this sort are associated with the deeper parts of a tumor and may be regarded as a product of an unhealthy internal environment. All such cells are probably capable of few further divisions at the most and are on the path to death. Vigorously growing, peripheral cancer cells typically divide by regular bipolar mitosis. Yet they are still often characterized by an abnormal chromosome number and numerous unusual chromosomes formed by a variety of abnormal events. For example, in the highly malignant mouse line A9HT it is estimated that only 40 percent of the chromosomes remain even grossly normal. The important question is whether chromosomal abnormalities are the basis of the malignant transformation or a result of it.

If chromosomal changes indicate the underlying variation in genic material on the molecular level, different carcinogenic agents produce different patterns. Numerous inductions in hamsters by means of a virus and a chemical carcinogen, 7,12-dimethylbenz(a)anthracene, yielded fibrosarcoma tumors histologically indistinguishable. Yet most of the virus-induced tumors had one or more additional chromosomes of chromosome pairs, 5, 6, or 10; most of the chemically-induced tumors had additional chromosomes of pair 11. Similar experiments on the rat produced comparable results.

ONCOGENIC VIRUSES

One of the primary difficulties in the attack on cancer has been the inability to generalize all cases. This inability extends to every aspect of the subject and is reflected in the spectrum of cells that can become malignant, the nature of the agents that facilitate the conversion to the malignant state, the susceptibility of different tumors to different treatments, and the properties of the different malignant cells. The difficulty is clearly shown in the variety of opinions that accompany the topic of viral oncogenesis, i.e., the transformation of normal cells to the malignant state by a virus. Some investigators feel that every tumor will ultimately be shown to have a viral basis, while others believe that only a small percentage of human tumors are virally derived. All intermediate opinions can be found, and at the present time the literature on this subject is very complex and is becoming increasingly confusing.

Studies of viral disease date back to Jenner and Pasteur in the last century, and the concept has been firmly established that a virus is an external agent. It could enter a cell and replicate within it, killing the cell and releasing mature virus particles that could reinfect additional cells (*horizontal transmission*). Studies with bacterial viruses (*bacteriophages*) have shown, however, that a virus infection need not progress in that way. In certain cases there were viruses that could infect a susceptible bacterium, integrate its DNA into the bacterial DNA, and be carried along with the host genome from generation to generation without producing mature virus particles and without any apparent damage to the cell. In other words, there appeared to be two states in which a viral genome could exist: one as a part of a cytopathogenic (cell-killing) infection and the other as a part of a "temperate" infection, where the virus remains hidden in the host DNA. The capability of the temperate virus to emerge as a cytopathogenic agent remains, as shown by the reaction to ultraviolet radiation of a bacterium harboring such a virus. Within a short period after radiation exposure, the viral genome is replicated in a typical infective manner. Many mature viral particles emerge simultaneously with the death of the cell.

The transformation of a cell by an oncogenic virus is analogous in many ways to the temperate infections of bacteria by bacteriophage. The viral genome becomes hidden within the host-cell DNA, and the genomes undergo replication together as the virus is passed from each cell to its progeny at cell division. Unlike the typical temperate bacteriophage infection, the oncogenic virus does not remain transcriptionally inactive. Rather, it produces RNAs which become translated into proteins that profoundly disturb the host cell's metabolic machinery. The presence of the oncogenic virus is manifested as the transformation of a normal cell to the malignant state.

Viruses were first reported in tumors as early as 1908, when extracts were found to transmit leukemia through successive passages from fowl to fowl. In 1910 Rous began his pioneering work on the propagation of virus-induced sarcomas. The virus causing chicken sarcoma (Rous sarcoma virus or RSV) has been maintained for over 60 years and is still busily investigated in many countries. Evidence for the involvement of viruses as causative agents in human cancer has been very difficult to obtain; only recently has definitive evidence accumulated.

Oncogenic viruses are broadly divided into two categories based on the nature of the nucleic acid of their genetic material, i.e., the nucleic acid in the mature virus particle released from one cell and capable of infecting another cell. The DNA tumor viruses are in one group; the RNA tumor viruses are in the other. Both groups are clearly implicated in human tumorigenesis (tumor formation).

DNA Tumor Viruses

Most of the DNA tumor viruses that have been studied contain very small genomes and are not believed to be a natural factor in tumor formation. These viruses are highly infectious; cells growing in culture as well as cells growing within the body are susceptible to transformation by the addition of the virus particles. Remarkably enough, the genomes of these viruses—including polyoma virus and simian virus 40 (SV40)—contain genetic information to code for fewer than 10 genes. Presumably, interference with a very limited number of normal cell functions can remove that cell from its normal restraints and convert it into an invasive tumor cell with all the modifications in its morphology, biochemistry, and behavior discussed above. Evidence from temperature-sensitive mutants of polyoma virus indicates that only two gene functions may be responsible for transformation. Because of the limited number of genes they use in transformation, these viruses are well-suited for study of the basis of malignancy.

Two types of host cell are studied in tissue culture in connection with each virus: (1) the "productive" host cell, in which the virus multiplies unchecked within the cell until the cell is killed; and (2) the "transformable" host cell, in which the virus causes little or no productive infection but induces changes similar to those of cancer cells. For transformation studies, cell clones derived from a single cell and therefore uniform in composition are employed. Thus the effect of the virus can be studied without interference from other forms of cellular variation, and transformed cells can readily be compared with normal cells of the same clone.

When suitable clone cells are exposed to viruses of this sort, many viral particles are taken up intact by the cells and accumulate around the nucleus. Most of the particles remain inert, but some lose their protein coat, and their naked DNA core enters the nucleus. Various experimental results show that the transforming process is caused by the incorporation of viral DNA into the host genome and that it is not caused by the viral protein coat.

Integration into the host DNA occurs via the formation of covalent bonds and numerous viral genomes can be incorporated into a variety of host chromosomes. Mutation in the viral genetic material can abolish the ability of the virus to transform the host cell. For example, in a temperature-sensitive mutant line of polyoma virus, the virus can cause either transformation or production, depending on the kind of cell it infects, at a temperature of 31°C; but at 39°C, the effect of the mutation shows up, the virus becomes inactive, and the host cells remain unchanged.

A striking effect of infection with polyoma virus, in cells that normally have a very low rate of DNA synthesis, is an induction of cellular DNA synthesis. A very active incorporation of labeled precursors into DNA begins a few hours

Figure 19.6 Tumor growing from small graft of virus-induced renal adenocarcinoma of an adult frog into the tail of a tadpole. [*Courtesy of R. W. Briggs.*]

after infection and leads to synthesis of DNA that is about two-thirds cellular and one-third viral. When the DNA synthesis begins, three enzymes involved in DNA synthesis also become active. One of these enzymes is thymidine kinase, which appears to be altered by the attachment of a viral protein. In normal, uninfected, crowded cultures, the activity of these enzymes is slight; the activity is much greater in less crowded, uninfected cultures where cell growth and division are relatively rapid. In the infected cultures, even when crowded, activity of these enzymes is high. In other words, virus infection induces a set of activities that are high in growing cells, such as regenerating liver, and center around DNA synthesis. According to Dulbecco, the important point is that the DNA growth complex is induced because the virus removes the growth inhibition caused by crowdedness, and therefore neutralizes the regulatory mechanism that inhibits the growth of the cells in crowded cultures.

Transformation is mediated via transcription of a restricted section of the viral DNA. These several expressed functions allow transformation to occur without formation of viral capsule proteins, which would lead to formation of infectious virus particles that would kill the host cell. An example of a tumor initiated by a DNA-containing virus in amphibians is shown in Fig. 19.6.

SV40 and polyoma viruses (along with a larger type, the adenoviruses) have been used most extensively in the study of the transformed state. Another class of DNA viruses, the herpesviruses, has been implicated in a number of human tumors. The first clear indication that a herpes-type virus was involved in cancer came in 1964. Tumor cells from patients with Burkitt's lymphoma, a rare lymphoma endemic to Africa, were found to contain a virus, since called the Epstein-Barr virus (EBV) after its discoverers. As with other herpesviruses, a large percentage of the population harbors them, evidenced in this case by the presence of serum antibodies against this virus in most healthy individuals. For unknown reasons, in some individuals the virus leads to transformation of certain types of cells to a malignant condition.

Other types of herpesviruses are associated with one condition in a large number of persons and with cancer in a small subpopulation. Herpes simplex I virus typically causes eruptions in the mouth region, such as cold sores. Herpes simplex II is responsible for certain venereally derived genital infections. Both of these viruses have been implicated in a growing number of malignancies. The reason that only a small percentage of persons harboring these viruses develop tumors is not known, but those with tumors possess certain antiviral antibodies not found in healthy persons. These antibodies include ones against a class of antigens believed to be responsible for transformation.

RNA Tumor Viruses

RNA viruses known to be oncogenic in mammalian cells are classified in two groups: type-C viruses, the most diverse, are primarily associated with leukemias and sarcomas; type-B viruses are associated primarily with mammary gland carcinomas. Research on the relationship of these viruses to the mammalian genome and on their involvement in cancer is becoming more and more complex.

The RNA tumor viruses are unusual among viruses because they contain a covering of cell membrane obtained as they are released from the host cell by budding. This process (Fig. 19.7) does not kill the cell. The mature, infectious virus (*nucleocapsid*) consists of an inner core, in which the viral RNA resides, together with several proteins. The RNA occurs as one molecule that sediments at approximately 70S (molecular weight of approximately 12×10^6 daltons). The core protein that has received the most intensive study is the RNA-dependent

Figure 19.7 Budding of a murine Friend leukemia virus from the surface of a cultured leukemic cell. [*Courtesy of E. de Harven.*]

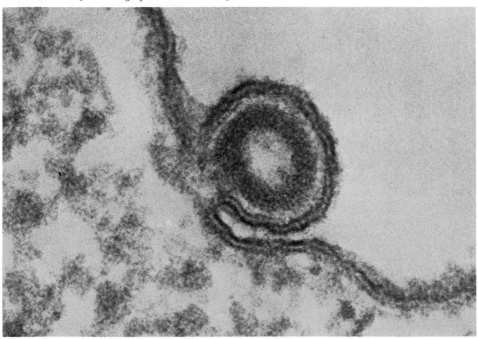

DNA polymerase, commonly known as *reverse transcriptase*. After the infectious particle has entered a host cell, this enzyme functions to make a complementary copy of the RNA genome in the form of DNA, which is then inserted into the DNA of the host cell. Insertion is believed to be accomplished by other core enzymes: a nuclease that makes a break in the host DNA and a ligase that repairs it after the viral DNA copy is inserted. The core is surrounded by an inner membrane; this is in turn surrounded by the outer lipid envelope in which type-specific viral antigens are found. These antigens are believed to be a factor in determining which types of cells can be infected.

When cell-free extracts of infected tumor cells are injected into hosts of the same species, not only is malignancy transmitted but so is the tumor-tissue type. For example, in the chick an extract of fowl chondrosarcoma gives rise to chondrosarcoma when injected into another fowl; fowl endothelioma extract acts upon endothelial cells. Rous sarcoma extracts, injected into the chick, induce sarcomas and lymphosarcomas, particularly of the liver and spleen. The same extract injected into ducklings evokes no response. Only if massive injections are made into the ducklings, within a day or two of hatching, are tumors induced. In this case widespread tumors of the skin, digestive tract, etc., appear in the duckling. That is, epithelial carcinomas are produced rather than mesodermal sarcomas; the agent has undergone change in the transfer and in fact can no longer readily induce tumors in the chick. In those cases where a particular RNA tumor virus can infect a variety of species or tissues, the tumor-specific antigens that appear as a result of the viral presence are always the same. They are characteristic of that particular virus.

RNA viruses were clearly implicated in human cancer when type-B virus particles were identified in certain samples of human milk. It was soon established that human breast tumor cells contained RNA in their polyribosomes that was complementary to labeled DNA probes prepared from the mouse mammary tumor virus. Since normal cells did not contain any evidence of viral RNA, it was strongly suggested that the presence of a human virus very similar to that causing tumors in mice was responsible for human breast cancer. In mice this condition is passed from generation to generation via virus particles in their milk, and the potential for such transfer in affected human mothers has been considered.

The earlier work with oncogenic viruses such as polyoma virus, SV40, adenovirus, and Rous sarcoma virus (RSV) had demonstrated the infectivity of these particles. It was believed that if cancer was generally attributable to viral agents, they presumably had entered from the outside as all other viruses were known to have acted. The provirus theory of Temin (1969), for example, suggested that the intervention of an external viral genome was responsible for virally induced cancer. A cell infected by an RNA virus incorporates the genetic information of the virus into its own DNA via the reverse transcriptase; it thereby acquires the capacity to produce more virus to infect neighboring cells and/or to behave as a malignant cell to initiate tumor formation. If cancer could be explained, even in only a few types, as the result of an infectious agent, it is difficult to understand why there is virtually no evidence of its being passed from person to person as are other communicable viral diseases.

It has been known for many years that certain tumors of mice were transmitted vertically, i.e., through the fertilized egg from mother to offspring, the adults of each generation developing the tumor. These studies provided evidence that the viral genome can be inherited through the gametes and subsequently transmitted from cell to cell via the normal mitotic process without giving any indication of its tumorigenic properties. At some point in the life of each affected mouse, conditions within that animal are reached that provoke the expression of the virus, and the ensuing malignancy is revealed.

The possibility that all tumors are a manifestation of viruses already present in the organism at the time of fertilization is most clearly stated in the *oncogene theory* proposed in 1969 by Huebner and Todaro. The oncogene theory attempts to explain why certain cells of certain members of a population become malignant while all the other trillions of cells in the body that also contain virus do not. The theory suggests that even though the entire viral genome is present, certain genes may be expressed and not others. It is proposed that the *oncogene* represents that fraction of the entire viral genome (the *virogene*) needed to transform the cell, and its expression or lack of it is controlled independently of the remaining viral genes. The maintenance of the normal state in the oncogene theory depends on the repression of the oncogene. The malignant transformation results from the disruption of this repression.

The oncogene theory is based on the premise that all cells harbor hidden virus genomes, which presumably represent infections that occurred at some past evolutionary time. The strongest evidence for the theory is the demonstration that all cells growing in culture can be shown to harbor endogenous viruses. Even cells taken from strains with low tumor susceptibility or from members of wild populations can be induced by a variety of chemicals or radiations to produce type C viral particles. Generally the particles released by these cells are not infectious to the cells of the strain from which they were derived but can be used to infect unrelated cells. The production of viral particles is proof of the presence of the viral genome, but it is not proof that these viruses are involved in the conversion to the malignant state. In fact, it has been proposed that the presence of endogenous virus has an antitumor role.

The phenotype of cells harboring certain of these viral genomes can be highly variable. In some cells there is no evidence of the viral presence; in other cells the presence of viral antigens can be demonstrated, while in other cases mature viral particles are also found. All of these conditions, including the production of a complete virus, can occur in a "normal" cell, one that is neither malignant nor in the process of being destroyed by a virus. In some cases embryonic cells are characterized by the production of type-C virus particles, but this production stops without any sign of malignancy. Virus production may then reappear when the animal is older. Cases have been reported in which cells harbored several endogenous viruses. The relation between the presence of a viral genome and the induction of cancer remains unclear.

DNA-RNA hybridization studies have been used both in support of and against theories that depend on endogenous virus as the cause of cancer. It is generally accepted that tumor viruses share some DNA sequences with normal host-cell DNA, but the work of Spiegelman and his coworkers suggests that tumor cells contain additional DNA sequences not found in the genome of the normal cell. In other words, even though some genes of the virus (or very similar ones) may be present, some sequences are missing and thus an entire tumor-causing virus is not present. If this view is correct, it suggests that the endogenous type-C viruses demonstrated are not responsible for tumors that develop in those cells. The evidence presented in numerous articles by Spiegelman's group on a variety of malignancies is based upon the use of labeled cDNA probes. They are made by the reverse transcriptase from RNAs isolated from virus particles taken from the tumor cells in question. For example, in one study virus particles were isolated from leukemic cells. A labeled cDNA was synthesized and fragmented into appropriate-size sequences. This probe was then hybridized exhaustively with normal cell DNA until all labeled sequences also present in normal DNA (shared by both) were removed. Any remaining labeled DNA should represent viral DNA sequences absent in normal DNA. The existence of these remaining sequences would be strong evidence against the oncogene theory. It was found in the experiments that DNA sequences were left over and that these sequences would hybridize to cells taken from all 10 cases of leukemia, but would not hybridize to any normal DNA tissue. In two cases DNA from identical twins was tested; one had leukemia and the other did not. Only the leukemic twin possessed sequences that would hybridize with the residual labeled DNA, which strongly suggests the tumor-causing DNA sequences were picked up at some time after fertilization. Because these experiments are sufficiently sensitive to detect one viral copy in 50 cells, Spiegelman concludes that vertical transmission of tumor-causing viral information does not occur.

In an extension of the provirus hypothesis, Temin (1971) proposed the *protovirus theory*. It is concerned with RNA-directed DNA synthesis as a mechanism of information transfer in normal cell processes, such as differentiation, and is not exclusively concerned with oncogenesis. The protovirus hypothesis suggests that cancer viruses arise from protoviruses that are segments of genetic information randomly brought together through a variety of genetic events, rather than depression of an oncogene. Moreover, the hypothesis considers that cells do not come into being with a fully formed viral genome, but only with the potential for assembling that information. In this view, the egg cell contains in its descendants the potential (as a result of mutation, recombination, translocation, or some other process) for the genetic development of somatic cells that may lead to the *de novo* synthesis of the information for the malignant state. One prediction of the protovirus theory is the presence of reverse transcriptase in normal cells, since it would be involved in normal activities requiring DNA synthesis from RNA templates. Evidence has been presented for the widespread presence of the enzyme, though the subject remains controversial.

CHEMICAL CARCINOGENESIS

The briefness of this section reflects the lack of understanding of how the malignant transformation can occur in response to carcinogenic chemicals. Chemicals, probably more than other factors, are responsible for a large percentage of the malignancies that are a consequence of our chemically complex environment. The tremendous diversity in molecular structure of the chemicals known to be carcinogenic has led to a search for some unifying principle. Many investigators in this field believe that to be carcinogenic, a chemical must react with the macromolecules of the cell; specifically it must have a region of electropositive charge making it an electrophilic reactant. The cell contains a variety of enzymes that are capable of oxidizing a wide spectrum of organic molecules and in the process can convert them to electrophilic carcinogens. The most important group of enzymes with this capacity are the oxygenases. Ironically, they provide the cell with a means of detoxifying a wide variety of chemical compounds. Because the nature of the carcinogenic chemicals is not clear, after various cellular enzymes have modified them in what may be a complex series of reactions, it is difficult to determine with certainty their precise molecular target within the cell. It is believed that the carcinogenic influence is mediated either directly or indirectly through mutagenic alterations in the structure of the DNA. It is difficult to consider any other target that would allow the effect of a chemical exposure to cause a cancer to appear many years later (a well-documented occurrence). The malignant phenotype could not be retained through each successive cell cycle unless it was a stable genetic change. A persistent point in studies of chemical carcinogenesis is the possibility that transformation involves the activation of an endogenous oncogenic virus. Transformation by chemical carcinogens can occur with very high efficiency in cells growing in culture, and in at least some cases there is no evidence of the involvement of a tumor virus. This point is very important because it poses the question: Is there more than one basic way to transform a cell or can all malignancies be explained as a consequence of viral activity? Further study is necessary to answer this question.

GENETIC BASIS OF SUSCEPTIBILITY

A question of great importance in the development of preventative measures is why certain individuals develop tumors and others do not. Is the basis for tumor initiation and progression in a given individual simply a chance phenomenon or is there a genetic potential? The evidence suggests there is a significant genetic factor that must be considered. Two possible bases for susceptibility can be envisioned; both are probably factors to one degree or another. The susceptibility may be a property of some tissue with a systemic influence, whose malfunction causes an increased susceptibility in the cells of the body at large, or it may be a property of the cells that become transformed.

The prime candidate for systemic influence on tumor formation is the immune system. Tumor immunologists have established a very close relationship between tumor formation and failure in one way or another of the immune system. The theory of immunological surveillance was presented in Chapter 18. Briefly, it states that one of the prime functions of the immune system is to destroy tumor cells recognized as foreign by T lymphocytes. Transformation can generally be shown to be accompanied by the appearance of tumor-specific surface antigens, to which the immune system can respond. It is believed that tumor formation results from the immune system's failure, for some unknown reason, to destroy the initial tumor cells. Successful tumor formation is often accompanied either by a marked general decrease in immune function or by the presence of serum factors that blocked T-cell destruction of the tumor cells. Similarly the much greater incidence of malignancy in persons whose immune system is deficient provides additional evidence for the role of immunocytes in the control of human cancer formation. Many investigators feel that manipulation of the body's own natural defense system holds the greatest promise for human cancer prevention and therapy. Information about tumor immunology is accumulating very rapidly; we have touched on only a few of the many important observations.

Although cancer does not seem to be generally inheritable, an inherited susceptibility of specific tissues has been demonstrated. For example, some mouse strains are highly susceptible to mammary cancer; others have low susceptibility. It has been established that these differences arise from genetic differences in the cells of the mammary tissue rather than from other genetically induced circumstances in the body or gland.

Allophenic mice have been used to probe the importance of a cell's genetic construction as opposed to its environment, with respect to the likelihood of that cell becoming malignant. Embryos from strains of high-tumor susceptibility have been fused with strains of low-tumor susceptibility, and the nature of the tumors formed in these mosaic animals has been analyzed. In one study of liver tumors (hepatomas) in allophenic mice, it was found that 9 of 11 tumors contained only cells of the highly susceptible strain. In other words, the developing tumor containing one type of cell did not cause transformation of the other type of cell. In two cases, however, the hepatomas were found to contain cells of both genotypes, suggesting that the cells of the low-susceptibility strain were influenced in these two animals. In addition, these latter two cases suggest that tumors need not arise from the clonal proliferation of one transformed cell. Similar studies on mammary-gland tumors in allophenic mice from high- and low susceptibility strains produced no mixed tumors; all malignant cells were of the high-susceptibility genotype.

A polygenic basis for neoplasia has been demonstrated in some tumors of inbred strains of mice. These tumors are based on the presence of several genes in specific allelic form. Individually, these genes are harmless, as demonstrated by outcrossing the susceptible strains to unrelated mice. But the collective effect of the several genes shifts the metabolic balance toward the malignant phenotype.

Another means of demonstrating differences in genetic susceptibility of cells to malignancy is to test their ability to be transformed in tissue culture. If SV40, for example, is added to cultures of cells derived from different individuals, a marked difference is found in the number of cells that become transformed; some cells are more susceptible than others. Certain genetic conditions, such as Down's syndrome and Fanconi's anemia, are associated with a much higher incidence of malignancy than is found in the general population. This same difference is also seen in tissue culture; cells from a child with either of these conditions can be 50 times or more susceptible to transformation by added virus. Since these experiments are carried out under conditions completely removed from the body's influence, it must be concluded that susceptibility can be a property of the genetic makeup of the individual cells being examined.

ANALYSIS OF MALIGNANCY BY CELL FUSION

A persistent question concerning the malignant state is whether transformation results from the presence of information or from the absence of a mechanism that inhibits growth or cell division. The fusion of a malignant cell with a normal cell might be expected to provide information with regard to this problem. In two recent studies in different laboratories, those of Lowenstein and of Harris, such a fusion has produced hybrids that were either normal or much less malignant. In one case an epithelial liver tumor cell was fused with three different types of normal cells. The tumor cell prior to fusion had the following properties: it was electrically uncoupled, would grow without contact inhibition, and was highly tumorigenic if injected into a suitable host. The normal cells had just the opposite properties, as did the hybrid in every case.

In the other study a highly malignant line, A9HT, was used in fusion with normal fibroblasts, lymphocytes, or macrophages. All the resulting hybrids were much less tumorigenic except one—the only one associated with chromosome loss. In those hybrid cells that produced tumors, the malignant cells were also associated with a reduced chromosome number. In other words, tumor growth did not result from proliferation of all hybrid cells but from selective outgrowth of those that had lost chromosomes as they divided. These authors

conclude that malignancy and its suppression are chromosomally determined.
Malignancy is believed to be a consequence of the loss of genetic functions,
which are then restored by the introduction of the normal chromosome set.
Whether the loss involves a cellular function, some viral repressor gene, or
some other activity is not known. The interpretation of cell-fusion experiments
as they relate to the analysis of malignancy remains a controversial topic.

Most species of bony fish have elaborate patterns of pigment cells in the
epidermis. The cells are of neural-crest origin and each pattern has a genetic
basis. Hybridizing related species yields unusual combinations of genes. Hybrids between platyfish and swordtails, two species of *Xiphophorus,* almost
always develop melanomas derived from large pigment cells, or macromelanocytes. Other types of pigment cells and all other kinds of cells in these hybrids
remain essentially normal. No other cell type becomes malignant, even though
all have the same genetic constitution. The interaction of several genes, in the
particular circumstance of differentiation of macromelanocytes, appears to be
the decisive requirement for malignant transformation in these cells. That is,
abnormal programming of normal gene function, rather than unique cancer-
producing genes, seems to be responsible in cases such as this.

TERATOMATOUS DEVELOPMENT

The capacity of cells other than eggs to proliferate and undergo diverse differentiation, even with some semblance of embryonic organization and form, is seen
in those malignant tumors known as *teratomas.*

Teratomas are tumors, mostly of germ-cell origin, composed initially of
undifferentiated embryonal-type cells. Some of these cells may differentiate,
giving rise to malignant teratocarcinomas consisting of both embryonal and
mature tissues. Teratomas may be simple in composition, or they may contain
almost all the different kinds of tissues of the body. In some cases so-called
embryoid bodies (Fig. 19.8) are produced, which resemble embryonic stages of
the parental species. Teratomas occur in all classes of vertebrates, with the possible exception of cyclostomes, although the incidence varies greatly from
species to species even within a single class. Occasionally they arise from the
pineal or the adrenal gland and elsewhere; these are rare compared with those
associated with the testes and ovaries. Most studies have been made on teratomas of the testes, either experimentally induced in fowl and mice or spontaneously arising in strain 129 mice at about 12 days of gestation. The degree of
malignancy is extremely variable and depends mainly on which cell type becomes fully malignant. They can be transmitted experimentally.

The common germinal origin of teratomas is demonstrated by the experimental means of induction. They are readily induced in mice and occasionally
in birds by the injection of copper or zinc salts, with or without gonadotropic
hormones, at times when the diploid spermatogonia are actively dividing. If the
genital ridges of the male fetus of susceptible mouse strains are transplanted to
the testis of adults, about 75 percent develop into testes with multiple teratomal
centers. However, teratomas can also be induced in mature testes.

There is strong evidence that all teratomas such as these arise from pluripotent undifferentiated cells. In fetal mice the tumors consist at first of undifferentiated cells of a generally embryonic character; they become histologically
more complex as the animals age. Direct evidence that adult-type tissues in
mouse teratomas are derived by differentiation of pluripotent embryonal stem
cells comes from an elegant in vivo cloning technique designed by Kleinsmith

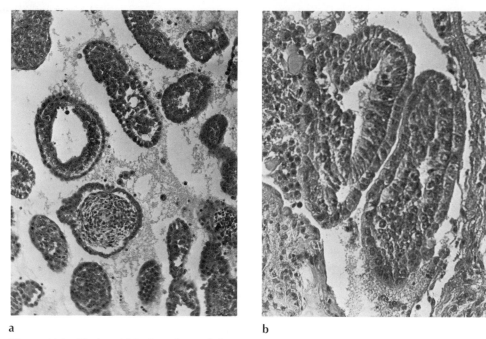

a   b

Figure 19.8 Embryoid bodies derived from a transplanted testicular teratoma of mouse (see text for discussion). [*Courtesy of L. C. Stevens.*]

and Pierce (1964). They dissociated cells of small embryoid bodies, taken from a transplanted teratoma of strain 129, and transplanted them directly into mice. Forty-three tumors grew from single stem cells, composed of as many as fourteen well-differentiated tissues in addition to the original embryonal carcinoma type of cell. In fact single embryonal carcinoma cells are clearly multipotent and capable of producing most of the somatic tissues of the body, although different cells vary in the assortment of cell types they produce.

In one set of experiments, a clonal-tissue strain of multipotent cells was isolated from a transplantable teratoma of a particular inbred strain of mice; it produced teratomas containing at least 10 types of tissue when reinoculated into mice. When subclones were isolated, however, two types of growth became distinguishable in vitro. One became densely piled, tumor-forming, and multipotent like the parental teratoma cell strain. The other was slow-growing, spreading, and somewhat epithelial, but usually not tumor-forming and not multipotent histologically. We may, therefore, make the following conclusions:

1   Spermatogonia are multipotent undifferentiated cells.

2   They are normally destined to proliferate and differentiate as spermatocytes and finally as spermatozoa.

3   They are able, when proliferating as teratoma cells, to differentiate to form most of the specialized somatic-cell types characteristic of the species.

As a rule the embryonal carcinomas first formed are composed of cells that are not only multipotent but also highly malignant, although most of the differentiated tissues they give rise to are generally benign. What we see, in fact, is an initial malignant change in the spermatogonial cell, which transforms it from a well-behaved constituent cell of the germinal epithelium into an unrestrainedly multiplying and invasive cancer. But this very process in effect sets the sperm mother cell free from its original directives under circumstances that enable it, as a multipotent cell of unlimited proliferative capacity, to express its full histogenetic potential. It is a natural experiment and a remarkable performance.

Teratoma Differentiation

What can such a cell do apart from perpetuating the original undifferentiated but malignant type of cell? This depends on circumstances we know little about, for the composition of teratomas is extremely variable. Some teratomas may be mostly embryonal, either entirely undifferentiated or with neural tissue. Most of them contain notochord, together with respiratory, alimentary, and glandular epithelia, and cartilage, bone, and marrow. Many teratomas have hair and sebaceous glands. Various degrees of tissue organization may be seen in them. Some transplantable, i.e., malignant, teratomas may consist entirely of myoblastic cells, although at first they consist of a variety of tissues; others may become entirely neural. Microenvironmental influences seem to be responsible for their development. These influences may be no more than local variations in electrolyte concentrations within each population of cells. The undifferentiated, multipotent cells need little directing in order for them to give rise to the multiplicity of cell types characteristic of the body. But to form an embryo as distinct from an assortment of tissues, supracellular organization of another order is required.

Origin of Teratomas

Two theories concerning the origin of teratomas have been favored. According to one, teratomas originate from germ cells. The other is that they originate from embryonic totipotent cells that have escaped the influence of embryonic organizers. The former interpretation has been adopted in the foregoing account. Supporting evidence comes from the discovery that mice that are sterile because of a genetically determined absence of primordial germ cells do not develop teratomas; their normal litter mates do. This means that the tumors *are* derived from primordial germ cells.

On the other hand, Stevens, who has made intensive studies of spontaneous teratomas, has also found supporting evidence for the alternative theory (Stevens, 1970). In preliminary experiments two-cell (1-day) eggs of mouse strain 129 were implanted in adult testes. Development was normal for about a week, after which the embryos became disorganized mixtures of embryonic, immature, and adult tissues, for as long as 60 days. The delay in onset of differentiation of some cells was attributed to disruption of normal intercellular relationships. When 3- and 6-day mouse embryos were similarly implanted, a comparable mixture of undifferentiated, immature, and adult tissues arose. Several of the embryos, however, gave rise to serially transplantable tumors, indistinguishable from transplantable teratomas derived from spontaneous teratomas of the same strain of mouse. They were apparently derived from undifferentiated stem cells. As in spontaneous mouse teratomas, embryoid bodies are produced when tumor cells are grafted intraperitoneally. Typical teratomas accordingly can arise either from primordial germ cells or from disorganized population of undifferentiated embryonic cells. The distinction between these two kinds of stem cells therefore appears to be purely semantic.

Embryoid bodies have been investigated, and the literature on them has been reviewed by Stevens, and by many others. The debated question is whether they are truly comparable to mammalian embryos of any stage. They arise not directly from the spermatogonia but from undifferentiated embryonal carcinoma stem cells of the tumor. They lack typical organization, but then so do normally fertilized rat and mouse eggs when grafted to many extrauterine sites. On the other hand, grafts from transplanted embryoid bodies derived from a transplanted testicular teratoma of a strain 129 mouse develop formations remarkably like early mouse embryos that have undergone morphogenesis. According to Stevens they form neural folds, amnion, coelomic epithelium, somite material, and yolk sac, all in proper spatial relationships to one another. When some sublines to transplantable teratomas are grafted into the peritoneal cavity, thousands of free-floating embryoid bodies similar to mouse embryos 5 and 6 days of age appear in the peritoneal fluid. He states that mouse embryoid bodies not only look like normal mouse embryos but have similar embryonic potency. He concludes that they are homologous to embryos.

BLASTOCYST IMPLANTATION

The process of tumor invasion has some similarities with, and some differences from, blastocyst invasion during implantation. In rodents, during trophoblast attachment there is an adherence phase at the implantation site—dependent on an increase in estrogen—when the maternal plasma membranes of the uterine epithelial cells become completely flattened and are intimately related to the overlying trophoblast. This state appears to be a prerequisite for epithelial destruction and invasion of the maternal tissues by the trophoblast. Invasion occurs as a result of penetration between, and phagocytosis of, epithelial cells. The trophoblast of the blastocyst exhibits growth-anaerobic-energy production, invasion, and even metastasis, comparable to the properties of a carcinoma. When melanoma cells, which act more as discrete individuals, are transferred to an implantation site, they migrate between the uterine epithelial cells. Tumor passage is complete within a few hours, if estrogen has prepared the epithelium for blastocyst attachment. In the absence of estrogen, neither blastocyst attachment nor melanoma invasion occurs. The similarities among cultured, cancer, and embryonic cells suggest that a significant part of the program of cancer is intrinsic to every cell in the body by virtue of the genetic endowment providing for procreation.

In summary: We have tried in this chapter to describe briefly recent information that has accumulated about the nonclinical, cellular aspects of the malignant state. Why is a cell released from the normal control mechanisms for growth and division to produce mitotic descendants that will destroy the individual? The most pressing problem is to find a means to prevent the malignant transformation or to render it innocuous. Inasmuch as we have not been able to accomplish this in a state of ignorance—in the way, for example, Jenner was able to prevent smallpox by vaccination—it is currently believed that we must discover the underlying cause of the transformation process and the characteristics of the transformed cell. Toward this end a tremendous research effort, particularly in the past decade, has accumulated a mountain of data. Whether this effort will turn up the key to a completely effective clinical program remains to be seen. But analysis of the truly significant findings of recent years makes us more optimistic than ever before.

AARONSON, S. A., and J. R. STEPHENSON, 1973. Independent Segregation of Loci for Activation of Biologically Distinguishable RNA C-type Viruses in Mouse Cells, *Proc. Nat. Acad. Sci. U.S.,* **70**:2055–2058.

ANDERSON, W. B., T. R. RUSSEL, R. A. CARCHMAN, and I. PASTAN, 1973. Interrelationship Between Adenylate Cyclase Activity, Adenosine 3',5' Cyclic Monophosphate Phosphodiesterase Activity, Adenosine 3',5' Cyclic Monophosphate Levels, and Growth of Cells in Culture, *Proc. Nat. Acad. Sci. U.S.,* **70**:3802–3805.

AZARNIA, R., and W. R. LOEWENSTEIN, 1971. Intercellular Communication and Tissue Growth. V. A Cancer Cell Strain that Fails to Make Permeable Membrane Junctions with Normal Cells, *J. Memb. Biol.,* **6**:368–385.

BURGER, M. M., 1973. Cell Surface Alterations in Transformed and Mitotic Normal Cells Monitored with Plant Agglutinins, *Neoplasma,* **20**:579–581.

CONDAMINE, H., R. P. CUSTER, and B. MINTZ, 1971. Pure-Strain and Genetically Mosaic Liver Tumors Histochemically Identified with the Beta-Glucuronidase Marker in Allophenic Mice, *Proc. Nat. Acad. Sci. U.S.,* **68**:2032–2036.

DULBECCO, R., 1969. Cell Transformation by Viruses, *Science,* **166**:962–968.

HOUCK, J. C., and H. HENNINGS, 1973. Chalones: Specific Endogenous Mitotic Inhibitors, *FEBS Letters,* **32**:1–8.

HSIE, A. W., and T. T. PUCK, 1971. Morphological Transformation of Chinese Hamster Cells by Dibutyryl Adenosine 3',5' Monophosphate and Testosterone, *Proc. Nat. Acad. Sci. U.S.* **68**:358–361.

National Academy of Sciences Symposium on Cancer in *Proc. Nat. Acad. Sci. U.S.,* **69**:1009–1064.

NICOLSON, G. L., 1973. Neuraminidase "Unmasking" and Failure of Trypsin to "Unmask" B-D-Galactose-Like Sites on Erythrocytes, Lymphoma, and Normal and Virus-Transformed Fibroblast Cell Membranes, *J. Nat. Cancer Inst.,* **50**:1443–1451.

NOONAN, K. D., and M. M. BURGER, 1973. The Relationship of Concanavalin A Binding to Lectin-Initiated Cell Agglutination, *J. Cell Biol.,* **59**:134–142.

Research News Series in Science: *Science,* **183**:940, 1066, 1181, 1279; **184**:552.

SHOPE, R. E., 1966. Evolutionary Episodes in the Concept of Viral Oncogenesis, *Perspectives in Biol. and Med.,* **9**:258–274.

STEVENS, L. C., 1975. Spontaneous Parthenogenesis and Teratocarcinogenesis in Mice, 33rd Symposium, The Society of Developmental Biology, Academic.

———, 1973. Developmental Approach to the Study of Teratocarcinogenesis, *Bioscience,* **23**:169–172.

SWEET, R. W., N. C. GOODMAN, J. R. CHO, R. M. RUPRECHT, R. R. REDFIELD, and S. SPIEGELMAN, 1974. Presence of Unique DNA Sequences After Viral Induction of Leukemia in Mice, *Proc. Nat. Acad. Sci. U.S.,* **71**:1705–1709.

WIENER, F., G. KLEIN, and H. HARRIS, 1974. Analysis of Malignancy by Cell Fusion, *J. Cell Sci.,* **15**:177–183.

CHAPTER 20

Assembly of Cells and Tissues

Self-assembly phenomena are evident at all levels of biological organization. Cells assemble to form tissues. Tissues react and assemble to form organ components. Partial organs may reconstitute whole organs. Fragmented whole organisms may reassemble to form new wholes (Chapter 24). These activities are based on cell movements, cell differentiation, intercellular matrices, cell communication, and changing interactions as the assembly processes continue.

A developing organism, like any complex machinery, may be seen as a functioning whole or as an assembly of parts. Investigation of the inductive effects of one tissue upon another within the developing system, considered in Chapter 12, represents analysis working from the highest level of organization to lower levels. The complementary approach is to study the capacity of completely dissociated cells of tissues, organs, and organisms to reassemble and differentiate. We are particularly concerned with the means by which normally stationary cells move about when in culture, with the cause of their immobilization when they come together, with the nature of mutual cell adhesion in general, and with the phenomena of self-assembly of cells and their means of communication with one another. These are all properties of great importance in the development and maintenance of multicellular organisms and notably in the construction of form and pattern in tissues and organs.

TISSUE SORTING AND ASSEMBLY

In experiments performed by H. V. Wilson (1907) with red and yellow sponges, mixed cell suspensions from the two genera at first formed randomly mixed aggregates but later sorted out as separate aggregates, each consisting of cells of but one genus or the other. Embryonic tissues from different species can be dissociated and be caused to reaggregate as mixed assemblies forming one tissue. In fact, if presumptive chondroblasts (stellate mesenchyme cells destined to become cartilage-forming cells) from the limb buds of chick and mouse embryos are cultured together for several days, both kinds contribute to the formation of typical cartilage. The cartilaginous matrix of the mouse cells merges with that of the chick cells. Embryonic mouse and chick cells derived from homologous tissues at comparable stages of development are able to form interspecific mosaics and to participate jointly in the histogenesis of such chimeric structures. Regardless of the taxonomic distance, intermingled cells become assorted and matched selectively in accordance with their functional similarity. Kidney cells from both species join to form chimeric tubules; neural retina cells form chimeric rosettes; chondroblasts form chimeric cartilage, and so on. Tissue type dominates over genetic constitution.

More recently a new technical and conceptual approach to sponge reaggregation has been employed by Humphreys. He used cold calcium- and magnesium-free seawater, i.e., seawater devoid of divalent cations, to dissociate sponge tissue into its constituent cells, and a rotatory agitating apparatus to accelerate reaggregation. By means of these techniques, a specific requirement for the divalent calcium and magnesium cations was established for sponge-cell adhesion. However, low temperature was found to inhibit adhesion of such chemically dissociated cells even when the divalent cations were added back to the cells; mechanically dissociated cells aggregated rapidly under the same conditions. This difference is shown to be due to a factor released into the supernatant fluid during chemical dissolution of sponge tissue. When this factor is added back to the chemically dissociated cells along with divalent cations, the cells adhere rapidly even at low temperatures. Moreover, the factor is species-specific, causing adhesion only of cells from the same species.

These results have been interpreted as indicating that sponge cell adhesion is composed of three components: cell surface (as represented by whole cells), divalent cations, and an intercellular material. Cellular aggregation appears to depend on intercellular protein integrity and on the presence of charged linkage groups, for which calcium is necessary. The several components, separated during chemical dissociation of cells, are capable of spontaneously and species-specifically reassembling themselves into an apparently normal cell adhesion. Thus sponge cells appear to be held together by an intercellular material bound to each cell surface by specific bonds involving divalent cations. The active constituents of the species-specific factor have been termed *cell ligands* by Moscona, to indicate that they participate structurally in the linking of cells into multicellular systems.

Disaggregation and reaggregation experiments with amphibian embryos show that the sorting-out process and mutual rearrangement of tissues depend on differences already established in the gastrula and neurula stages. According to the classical work of Townes and Holtfreter (1955), the different cell types in a composite aggregate derived from the gastrula become sorted into distinct homogeneous layers whose stratification corresponds to the normal germ-layer arrangement. (Cells were dissociated by brief treatment with a high-pH medium.) Amphibian material has been notably suited to this investigation, as it has for experimental embryology generally. Amphibian cells are relatively large, and different kinds vary greatly in degree of pigmentation. Consequently cell movements can be followed with comparative ease. Thus in an aggregate of ectoderm, endoderm, and mesoderm cells, Holtfreter was able to see the

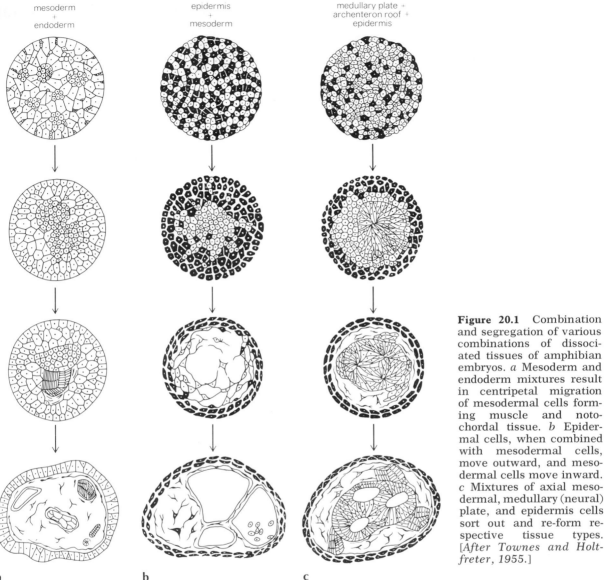

mesoderm + endoderm

epidermis + mesoderm

medullary plate + archenteron roof + epidermis

Figure 20.1 Combination and segregation of various combinations of dissociated tissues of amphibian embryos. *a* Mesoderm and endoderm mixtures result in centripetal migration of mesodermal cells forming muscle and notochordal tissue. *b* Epidermal cells, when combined with mesodermal cells, move outward, and mesodermal cells move inward. *c* Mixtures of axial mesodermal, medullary (neural) plate, and epidermis cells sort out and re-form respective tissue types. [*After Townes and Holtfreter, 1955.*]

a

b

c

lightly pigmented mesoderm cells vanish before his eyes as they moved into the depths of the tissue mass; nearly pigment-free endoderm cells and darkly pigmented ectoderm cells moved to the periphery to replace them.

In mixed aggregates of ectoderm and mesoderm, the ectoderm cells at first mingle with the mesoderm but are later expelled to the surface, where they form a separate epidermal layer; i.e., an initial affinity is later lost. Prospective neural-plate cells and prospective epidermal cells separate to form neural tube and epidermis, respectively. Neural and epidermal tissue can be kept from separating, however, if some mesodermal cells are present to form an intermediate layer adhesive to both (Fig. 20.1).

The directed movements appear to be of two kinds: (1) inward movements, as manifested by the cells of the neural plate, or of the mesoderm, which have been combined with either epidermal or endodermal cells, and (2) outward movements and peripheral spreading, as manifested by epidermal cells. Tissue segregation becomes complete because of the emergence of a selectivity in cell adhesion. When they meet, homologous cells remain permanently united to form functional tissues, whereas a cleft develops between certain nonhomologous tissues (e.g., between neural or endodermal tissues and adjacent epidermis).

Both sorting-out and reassembly processes have been more intensively studied as more sophisticated procedures have been employed, particularly by Moscona, for inducing disaggregation and reaggregation of embryonic cells of chick and mouse. The method primarily employed uses brief trypsin digestion to disrupt intercellular adhesions; this is followed by cell suspension and rotation to bring about forced reaggregations. Such a procedure is readily controlled and standardized with respect to all cellular and environmental parameters. Like mixtures of amphibian cells, mixed cell suspensions of either chick or mouse embryos first form randomly mixed aggregates and then sort out within each aggregate according to histological type. The forces initially binding cells together in aggregates are clearly nonselective and unstable; the selective adhesion to form segregated tissue within an aggregate is acquired later and is stronger. Such a sorting-out is seen when procartilage cells from a 7-day chick embryo are commingled with about 10 times their concentration of retina cells from the same embryo. When coaggregated and allowed to develop, the two types of cells sort out, the retinal cells constructing retinal structures and the procartilage cells forming cartilaginous masses.

TISSUE HIERARCHY

Employing similar procedures and material, Steinberg has shown that a hierarchy exists in the positioning of tissues relative to one another. This is a phenomenon of vital significance concerning the mutual responses of germ layers, as seen in the experiments on amphibian germ layers described above and in the construction and reconstruction of organs. Chick embryo tissues were disaggregated and caused to reaggregate as various paired combinations. Procartilage, heart, and liver cells, among others, were combined in different pairings. A hierarchy of tissue types is apparent. Thus when heart tissue is combined with procartilage, the heart cells become peripheral, the procartilage internal. When heart tissue is reaggregated with liver, the liver cells become peripheral, the heart cells internal. Large heart aggregates, however, tend to surround smaller liver aggregates, indicating that the relative masses of the tissues within a combined aggregate are important in addition to the qualitative differences associated with cell type.

Two hypotheses have been advanced to explain the process of cell sorting in mixed aggregates. In one hypothesis, Moscona proposes that cell adhesion is cell-type-specific. Specificity of adhesion is thought to be conferred on cells by virtue of extracellular surface coatings of specific adhesive macromolecules. According to this hypothesis, dissociation results in removal or inactivation of these surface macromolecules, allowing cells to make initial unspecific adhesions. Cell sorting is thought to occur once cells reestablish normal surface complements of specific adhesive macromolecules, allowing the reestablishment of type-specific cell adhesions. In this hypothesis, the extracellular matrix plays an essential part.

The alternative is Steinberg's differential adhesion hypothesis, which does not involve the extracellular matrix. This hypothesis proposes that in certain circumstances (i.e., where cell sorting leads to a sphere-within-sphere arrangement of tissues, displayed by pigmented retinal epithelium-neural retina combinations) adhesion between dissimilar cells is stronger than adhesion between the cells that constitute the peripheral layer. The differential adhesion hypothesis predicts that neural retinal cells adhere better to pigmented retinal cells than they do to one another. The two hypotheses differ in their assumptions about the nature of adhesion between dissimilar cells. The differential adhesion hypothesis appears to account easily for the whole spectrum of related aspects of behavior now recognized. This includes (1) the rounding-up of irregular tissue fragments; (2) the occurrence of sorting-out; (3) the pathway by which sorting-out takes place; (4) the spreading of a fragment of one kind of tissue around a fragment of another; and (5) the tendency toward a particular equilibrium configuration, which is independent of the cell distribution at the start. The differential adhesion hypothesis also predicts the existence of a sixth phenomenon, a hierarchical ordering of equilibrium configurations.

Control of tissue rearrangements is a central problem of developmental biology. Cell sorting results not only in the establishment of homogeneous tissues but also in the arrangement of these tissues in a fairly accurate reflection of their normal position in the embryo. The formation of normal tissue arrangements in the embryo also employs morphogenetic movement. Thus there is some hope that answers to questions of control of cell movement during cell sorting can be applied to questions of control of cell movement during morphogenesis.

This reestablishment of normal architecture of tissues and organs by cell sorting is a counterpart, at the tissue and organ level, of the phenomenon of molecular self-assembly. Both in molecular self-assembly and in cell sorting, normal structure is regenerated by initially disordered populations of subunits (protein molecules or cells, respectively). When single-cell suspensions prepared from kidney, liver, or skin of 8- to 14-day chick embryos are scrambled, recompacted, and transplanted to the chorioallantoic membrane of 8-day embryos, they are able to give rise to remarkably complete and morphologically well-organized organs of the respective kinds. The various tissue components have their normal mutual relations and functional activity. *The results reemphasize that internal "self-organization" is one of the most basic problems in the study of development, in contradistinction to contemporary preoccupation with external inductions.*

CELL LOCOMOTION AND CONTACT INHIBITION

The studies of individual cells in tissue culture—particularly those by Weiss and his colleagues over many years—have shown that cells in suitable culture medium, separated from their neighbors, usually move continuously and nondirectionally over a glass surface. Contact of this type, i.e., contact with a surface other than that of another cell, does not inhibit movement; movement continues but in a way that preserves contact. Yet the cells do not move by amoeboid movement; they flatten and glide over the substratum without psuedopodial formation. Nor is there any evidence of protoplasmic flow. Such cells move across a glass surface by making intermittent contacts resulting from ruffling, peristaltic movements in the whole plasma membrane. The ruf-

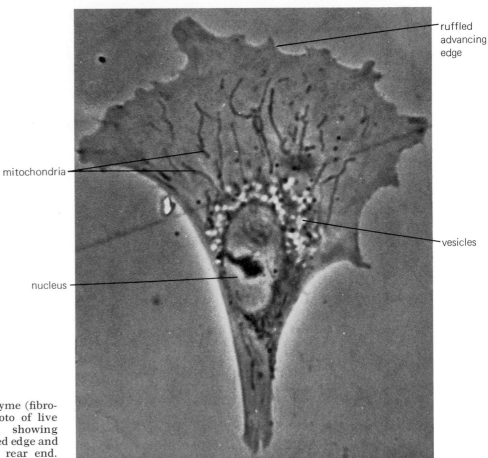

ruffled
advancing
edge

mitochondria

vesicles

nucleus

Figure 20.2 Mesenchyme (fibroblast) cell (phase photo of live cell) in locomotion, showing broad advancing ruffled edge and tapering, contracting rear end. [*Courtesy of N. K. Wessells.*]

fles are waves of large-scale expansions that travel along the cell membrane (Fig. 20.2). Phase and interference microscopy show that the leading edge of a moving fibroblast consists of an exceedingly thin, fanlike membrane, 5 to 10 μm wide and closely applied to the substratum. This membrane undergoes continual folding movements that beat inward, i.e., appear as ruffles. Cultures of isolated embryonic cells of amphibian embryos show wandering cells with the same kind of thin, advancing, fanlike edge. In a migrating cell, the undulating membrane that pulls the cell forward is filled with a network of microfilaments. Cell migration, however, typically requires a substratum over which to move, and cells may vary in shape according to its nature (Fig. 20.3).

There is evidence that glycoproteins of the cell surface turn over rapidly in contact-inhibited cells but not in growing cells. Thus, molecules that turn over in cells that are contact-inhibited may be intimately involved in the maintenance of the cell surface structure necessary for contact inhibition. In other words, *molecules that maintain the normal structure of the cell surface must be replaced continually when cell growth is inhibited.* Contact inhibition commonly involves cessation of cell growth and division, that is, during the state of *confluence,* when cells are in full contact and immobile. (See Fig. 19.2.)

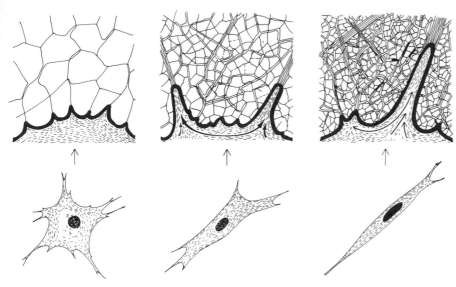

Figure 20.3 Structure of mesenchyme cells in three media of (from left to right) increasing plasma fibrous concentrations. Showing protoplasmic flow directed along main paths of fibrous gel structure. [*After Weiss and Garber*, Proc. Nat. Acad. Sci., **38**:270 (1952).]

CELL SURFACE PROPERTIES

The surface properties of a cell primarily depend on the molecular species at the cell surface. The synthesis and breakdown of these molecules, and in some cases their transport, are largely determined by metabolic processes. The plasma membrane, in fact, is characterized by a definite surface specificity related to genetic type and even to organ type. These specificity factors are often primary determinants in cell associations, and every cell type may well have characteristic surface proteins that determine specificity. This specificity, however involves proteins variously conjugated with polysaccharide. When the cell coat is removed from sponge cells of like type, they will not reaggregate until additional cell coat is formed or cell-coat factor has been added to the media, i.e., glycoprotein plus lipid. In vertebrates the coat material is mainly mucopolysaccharide or glycoprotein assembled in the Golgi apparatus and transported to the cell surface, with incorporation of the transport vesicle membrane into the plasma membrane (Fig. 3.9). In the case of embryonic chick cells (10-day), immunological studies involving immune agglutination and immunofluorescence, by Goldschneider and Moscona, have demonstrated the existence of tissue-specific antigens on the surface of embryonic chick cells. It is clear that tissue-specific cell-surface antigens exist in embryonic cells and represent a phenotypic expression of cell differentiation. These antigens could have a role in histospecific cell recognition and cell association during histogenesis and the organizational maintenance of tissue integrity.

Accordingly, differences in cell-surface antigenicities may be a characteristic, perhaps universal, attribute of cellular differentiation. In addition to cell-type or tissue-specific antigens, shared classes of antigens may typify the surfaces of cells with a common lineage, such as neural retinal and brain cells. Another class of surface antigens may be shared by cells of mesenchymal origin, such as various connective tissues and contractile and skeletal elements. Finally, antigens obviously exist that are common to all cell surfaces in the organism or in a group of organisms. These would include transplantation antigens, blood-group antigens, and various receptor substances that are not cell-type or tissue-type-specific.

There is strong evidence that complex polysaccharides exist on the surface and play an important role in recognition and communication between cell and cell and between cell and environment. Enzymes are also present, especially transferases. Most intracellular and surface transferases are probably bound to membrane components, including the plasma membrane. Roth and Roseman have proposed that recognition and communication may result from interactions between the glycosyltransferase enzymes and cell-surface glycosyl acceptors. (Transferases are named according to the particular nucleotide sugar transferred, i.e., used as a donor.) The probable origin of surface glycosyltransferases is the Golgi apparatus. Surface carbohydrates are derived from the unfolding of Golgi vesicles after they fuse with the plasma membrane. Therefore, any enzymes responsible for prefabricating surface carbohydrates within Golgi vesicles would also be placed at the surface.

According to the model, if two cells possess surface enzymes and appropriate substrates, and if these components are unable to interact with each other on a single cell surface, the enzyme-substrate-binding reaction will then occur between these two cells when they make contact with each other. Such enzyme-substrate complexes are of less specificity and also more general occurrence than antigen-antibody complexes, although both represent "lock-and-key" mechanisms possibly affecting the growth patterns of cells. In such a system, the glycosyltransferase would serve as a "lock." Transglycosylation between two contacting cells in a culture could be among the initial surface events that eventually lead to contact inhibition and decreased growth.

INTERCELLULAR CONTROLS

The characteristics of a tissue depend upon the individual phenotypes of constituent cells and collective action among these cells. Collective action arises especially from direct cell-cell communication (nerves, electric coupling) and indirect (hormonal) connections (Fig. 20.4). Especially appealing in a communication system for collective tissue-specific action is cyclic AMP, which appears to be a component common to both direct and indirect communications.

Figure 20.4 Control mechanisms in cytodifferentiation, between adjacent cells, between cells and remote sources of information, and by way of extracellular matrix. [*After Grobstein, 1966.*]

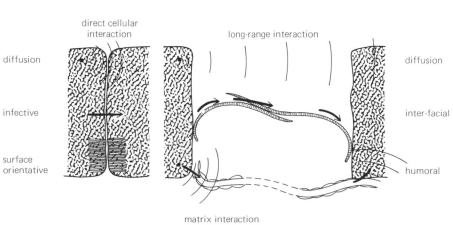

Apart from the simplicity of one common component, cyclic AMP offers to coordinate cells in tissue-specific action by integrating external signals at cell-membrane levels and internal signals within the cytoplasm.

There are several ways in which signals can be transmitted: by junctional transmission, by diffusion through intercellular fluid or matrix, and by way of systemic circuits. Epithelial cells, for example, are electrically coupled and there is a free flow from cell to cell of many substances up to 500 molecular weight. That is, the cells do not behave as isolated units but are truly integrated into a higher-order junctional unit, the tissue. Only at the level of macromolecules—proteins, RNAs, etc.—are coupled cells truly isolated from each other.

Apart from the concept and the evidence for direct junctional communication between electrically coupled cells, intercellular communication in higher animals has generally been considered to take place in one of two ways. One is by direct communication from cell to cell by way of nerves. The other is by indirect communication by way of chemical messengers within the circulatory system or diffusion within intercellular matrix, i.e., as hormones or their equivalent. Important similarities between these two modes have long been obvious; for example, the transmission of signals across synapses in the nervous system is generally by chemical rather than by electrical means. Synaptic transmission, in fact, is a highly specialized function carried out by a few unique, low-molecular-weight neurotransmitters; hormonal control is a complex and diverse set of functions carried out by many different chemical messengers of various size, structure, and chemical complexity.

Hormonal Control

Recent experimental evidence indicates that neural transmission and much of the hormonal system may share a common biochemical mechanism. The point of view is emerging that both neural transmission and hormonal transmission essentially are highly developed forms of cell-to-cell junctional transmission on the one hand and of intercellular diffusion transmission on the other.

The basic elements in this widespread biochemical control mechanism are: calcium ions, cyclic AMP, intracellular microtubules, microfilaments, secretory vesicles, and a class of enzymes known as protein kinases, which phosphorylate specific proteins with ATP as a substrate. Since its discovery, cyclic AMP has been implicated as an intermediate in the action of many peptide hormones and in the release of neurotransmitters at synapses and neuromuscular junctions. The enzyme responsible for synthesis of cyclic AMP is bound to the plasma membrane of almost all animal cells; the enzyme responsible for its degradation (phosphodiesterase) is located in the internal cytoplasm. In this system a first messenger, which is an external stimulus capable of interacting only with selected target cells, those having receptors on their surface. The receptor-messenger complex then activates a membrane-bound enzyme (adenyl cyclase, leading to increased synthesis of cyclic AMP within the cell (Fig. 20.5). This increased concentration of cyclic AMP then acts as a second messenger, activating one or more processes or enzymes. According to Sutherland:

1   The first order of specificity resides at the cell surface, where a highly specific selection of intercellular messengers operates.

2   A second order of specificity is determined by the structural and biochemical uniqueness of each specific cell type.

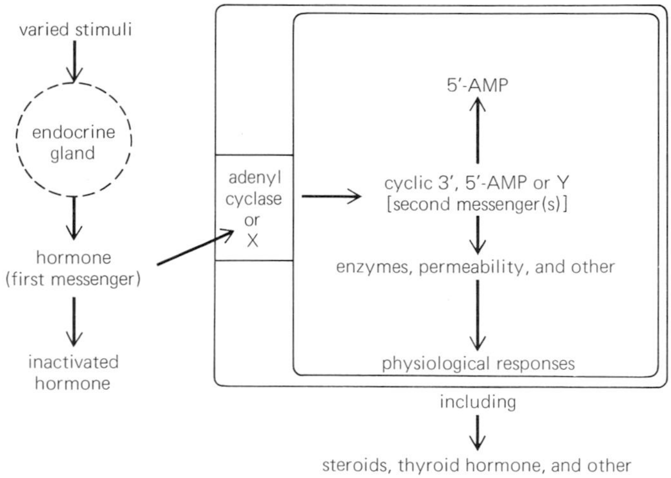

Figure 20.5 The two-messenger hypothesis of hormone action. The hormone is the first messenger; it circulates in the blood, binds to the plasma membrane of the target cell, and activates adenyl cyclase. Cyclic AMP, the second messenger, is generated on the inner surface of the cell membrane, diffuses through the cell, and brings about the appropriate physiological responses. [*After E. W. Sutherland, 1972.*]

3 A third order of specificity has three aspects, whether, where, and what: whether or not the particular cell secretes a product in response to stimulation, where the product is released, and what specific product is released.

With these orders of specificity, the organism has an endless number of possible unique responses while employing a common biochemical device. This particular control system appears to be one of the most universal mechanisms for integrating the intracellular responses of animal cells with specific extracellular stimuli.

For stimuli received by a cell from a distance, the exposed cell membrane represents the primary receptor, particularly its constituent proteins. Cell-surface proteins are *intrinsic proteins*, associated with the membrane in a permanent fashion, and *peripheral proteins*, which have a weaker, more temporary association. Insoluble substances combine with receptor sites to produce intracellular effects. Specific membrane receptors have been identified for a number of polypeptide hormones such as vasopressin, growth hormone, adenocortisone, and insulin. The insulin receptor, recently isolated from adipose tissue, is a protein with specific solubility and binding characteristics. Comparatively few such molecules are present in the membrane of each adipose cell, and the insulin molecule need not penetrate beyond the membrane to exercise its effect. Moreover there is an apparent relation between hormones and calcium with respect to membrane structure and function.

The epithelial cells in the mammary gland of the mature, nonpregnant animal undergo virtually no proliferation. In contrast, the cells in the gland of the pregnant animal undergo extensive proliferation. Mammary gland explants from mice in mid-pregnancy respond rapidly to insulin in terms of increased DNA synthesis. After one to several days in culture, the virgin tissue acquires sensitivity to the hormone comparable to that of pregnancy tissue, independent of the presence of exogenous insulin. That is, tissue isolation or pregnancy can confer insulin sensitivity on the gland. In general, actions of such hormones are to be regarded as telegraphic or triggering messengers rather than transmitters of basic information.

443

On the assumption that the environment dictates gene expression in epidermal cells, Bullough suggests the hypothesis that a concentration gradient of some chemical messenger exists between the basal and the more superficial layers. Such a system might work as a negative feedback to suppress mitosis and to confine it to the basal layer. Working with this concept as a basis, Bullough and his colleagues have extracted an antimitotic chemical messenger from pig epidermis, which they have called the *epidermal chalone*. This extract appears to be of central importance in maintaining the stability of the system and seems to be a glycoprotein of relatively low molecular weight.

This substance is tissue-specific but not species-specific. Both in vivo and in vitro, mitosis in mouse epidermis can be suppressed by epidermal chalone extracted from a variety of mammals, including man, and from the skin of a codfish. Therefore it is not even class-specific. The cell mechanism that emits the message and the one that receives it and acts upon it may accordingly be basically the same throughout the vertebrate kingdom. What is true of epidermis probably holds for every other type of tissue; that is, all are probably tissue-specific but without class distinction. Chalones with comparable properties have also been extracted from liver, kidney, lens, white blood cells, and hair bulbs—each specific for the type of its tissue of origin but able to affect corresponding tissues in other classes of vertebrates.

A chalone extracted from adult *Xenopus* kidney specifically inhibits mitosis in the pronephros, or larval kidney; a chalone extracted from lymphoid organs inhibits the stimulation of lymphocytes by phytochemagglutinin. Both these subjects are tissue-specific but not species-specific.

ROLE OF MESODERM

Much of the pioneering work with tissue culture in relation to tissue pattern and morphogenesis has been that of Paul Weiss and his colleagues, beginning with his discovery that connective-tissue cells in culture tend to move along lines of least resistance in the culture media. Orientated tracts of protein subunits resulting, for example, from stress induced in the medium are followed by the mesenchymatous cells, i.e., through "contact guidance." This is probably a factor in outgrowth of nerve fibers. This phenomenon is clearly of great importance with regard to formative movements of cells and tissues. A general feature of epithelial tissue, for example, is that it requires a substrate over which to spread. Chick embryo epidermis when cultured alone fails to grow and loses its skinlike organization. Yet the normal organization is maintained if a suitable substratum, whether it be live dermis, frozen or killed dermis, or collagen gel, is present.

The skin of vertebrates serves well as a model system of a tissue. It consists of two layers, the epidermis and the mesenchymal dermis, with a basement membrane between. The epidermis consists of a basal layer of columnar cells which are loosely united as an epithelium resting upon the basement membrane, together with a number of layers of progressively keratinized cells externally. All cell division takes place in the basal layer; cells above the basal neither divide nor synthesize the DNA which must precede mitosis. Following division, both daughter cells remain basal cells for an indefinite period; yet every time a basal cell divides, a nearby cell begins to move toward the skin surface. Once free of the basal layer, such cells change from columnar to cuboidal to flat and progressively produce the mixture of proteins that consti-

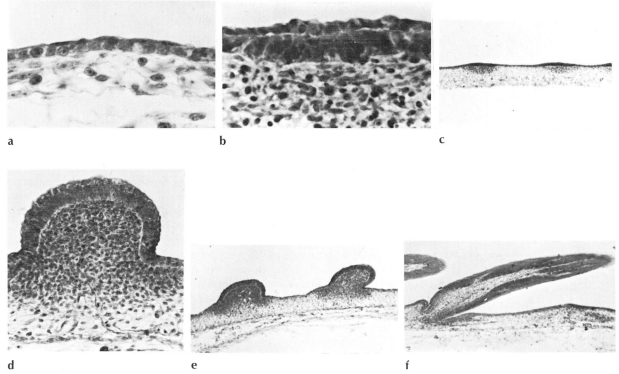

a   b   c

d   e   f

Figure 20.6 Stages of normal embryonic feather development, high-power details showing epidermal differentiation and dermal papilla *(DP)* *a* Preplacodal stage, 6-day skin. Two-layered epithelium, cuboidal cells covered by flat peridermal cells; mesenchyme forms a loose subjacent network; feather papillae are not yet defined. *b, c* Placodal stage, 8-day skin. Epithelium has palisaded into a thickened placode of columnar cells covered by a peridermal layer; dermal condensation beneath the placode forms a discrete dermal papilla. *d, e* Feather bud in hump stage, 10-day skin. Dermal papilla has greatly increased in volume and has elevated the placodal epithelium; blood vessels invade the papilla from the underlying connective tissue. *f* Elongation phase. [*Courtesy of B. Garber.*]

tute keratin. At the same time they form stable connections, desmosomes, with their immediate neighbors. Consequently the epidermal cells external to the basal layer migrate toward the surface bonded together as a continuous sheet.

Differentiation of embryonic skin and the other specialized derivatives of the integument—such as hairs, feathers, and scales—is based on specific interactions between dermal and epidermal components. Separation of the two interacting skin components has provided insights into the relative contributions of the two tissues to the initiation and maintenance of special structures. In normal development of feathers (Fig. 20.6), four stages are generally recognized:

Preplacodal stage In the 5-day embryo the ectoderm is a simple epithelial layer of cuboidal cells overlaid by flat peridermal cells, the underlying mesoderm being a loose mesenchyme network.

Placodal stage In the 7- and 8-day embryo the feather germs (primordia) first appear as localized nodes, or centers of dense cell populations, along the middorsal line of the embryo, the ectodermal cells now becoming columnar and forming placodes while the underlying mesenchymal dermis condenses into dermal papillae. Other rows of feather germs later appear successively on either side of the primary row, i.e., the feather germs originate progressively both posteriorly and bilaterally.

Hump stage In the 8- to 10-day embryo the dermal component grows rapidly and raises the ectodermal component to form the feather bud.

Elongation stage The feather germ elongates, and condensed dermal papilla cells are evident at the feather base.

The capacity of dissociated and subsequently reaggregated embryonic cells to develop into organized structures changes with the age of the cells at the time of their dissociation, i.e., it changes as their differentiation progresses. Thus aggregates of cells dissociated from 5- to 8-day-old embryonic skin (preplacodal and placodal stages) form well-developed, typical feathers enclosed in large, thin-walled keratinized epithelial vesicles in the chorioallantoic membrane. Aggregates of cells dissociated from 10-day embryonic skin (hump stage) form imperfect feathers and skin, normal in cell types but poorly constructed. No feathers of any sort, only dense and extensive sheets of dermis and keratinized epidermis, form from aggregates of 12- and 14-day-old skin cells.

Feathers are exceedingly complicated structures that vary in morphology and function on different parts of a bird's body. Although feathers are made almost entirely by ectodermal cells, the mesoderm controls the type of feather that will form from the ectoderm. Three types of experiments demonstrate this fact: (1) When a block of mesoderm from the thigh of a chicken embryo is inserted beneath the ectoderm covering the proximal portion of an embryonic wing, the wing ectoderm forms leg feathers. Both the feather morphology and the arrangement of feathers on the wing surface are characteristic of leg. (2) A combination of feather-forming mesoderm and ectoderm located in an area that does not form feathers results in feather development. (3) If a piece of ectoderm destined to form feathers is combined with mesoderm from the lower leg, where "scales" normally form, the ectoderm forms scales. It has no intrinsic stability for feather formation. All three of these results are consistent with the conclusion that *mesoderm controls the kind of specialized structure* (scale or type of feather) *that will form from ectoderm.* This conclusion, however, has to be qualified, for a remarkable experiment by J. L. and A. J. Coulombre shows that the corneal epithelium (ectoderm) of a 17-day-old chick embryo, when supplied with dermis (mesoderm) from the flank of a mouse embryo, develops feathers (Fig. 20.7). The *stimulus* to form feathers in place of corneal differentiation is supplied by mouse mesoderm, which in a mouse would have induced hairs. The *capacity* to develop feathers rather than hairs is part of the ectodermal repertoire of chick ectoderm.

TISSUE PATTERN FORMATION

Sheets of skin from the middorsal area of 6-day embryos, maintained in organ culture, show that the first change in the dermis in connection with feather development is the appearance of cells elongated in an anteroposterior direction, while small clusters of cells appear marking the sites of the first row of dermal papillae. At the 8-day stage the entire dorsal feather area (field) is organized into a latticelike system of oriented dermal cells linking the sites of the dermal papillae. Epidermis alone shows a generalized meshwork, but dermis shows an additional fibrous pattern. It first appears as a midline streak and then extends laterally, i.e., corresponding to the order of appearance of the

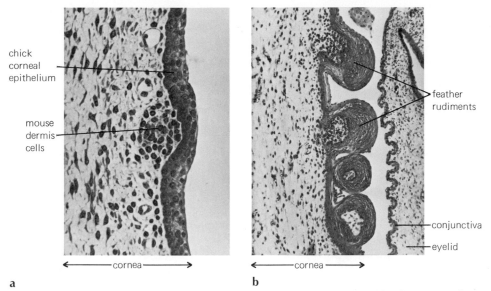

chick
corneal
epithelium

mouse
dermis
cells

feather
rudiments

conjunctiva

eyelid

← cornea →

← cornea →

a

b

Figure 20.7 Induction of feathers in chick cornea by flank dermis cells of mouse embryo. *a* Axial section of the epithelium in the corneal region of a 17-day-old chick embryo. At 5 days of incubation the lens of this eye was replaced by a block of flank dermis from a mouse embryo (0 mm crown-rump length). A group of mouse cells lies just beneath the chick epithelium. *b* Feathers are forming from the corneal epithelium. Mouse cells are present in the feather pulp. [*Courtesy of J. L. and A. J. Coulombre.*]

feather germs. The pattern of the fibrous material and the pattern of feather buds are the same, both spatially and temporally. The fact that the enzyme collagenase, which breaks down collagen, inhibits the development of the fibrous material and of feather germs, as well as other evidence, indicates the collagenous nature of the fibrous lattice and its importance.

A birefringent, fibrous dermal lattice has a strikingly gridlike organization and, as already stated, is collagenous. The development of dermal papillae coincides with a characteristic distribution pattern of dermal cells in relation to this fibrous lattice: elongated cells align along the tracts of the lattice; rounded cells form clusters at the intersections of the lattice, which represent the sites of the future dermal papillae (Fig. 20.8). Cell clusters at the lattice intersections are the precursors of the dermal papillae and arise by aggregation of cells that migrate along the fibrous tracts. Whether the fibrous material is directly involved in cell guidance, or whether this is due to nonfibrous materials associated with the fibers, is an open question. The fibers might conceivably provide a visible indication of some organization at a finer level.

That the fibrous lattice plays a role in skin development is indicated by the following results: (1) Treatment of skin with collagenase, which disrupted the organized structure of the lattice, caused a reversible inhibition of skin development. In skin of the "scaleless" chicken mutant, both the birefringent lattice and the dermal condensations are absent. Although collagen synthesis proceeds normally, an organized dermal lattice does not form. Evidence suggests that the absence of a fibrous lattice is not the result of a reduced synthesis of collagen but is probably the result of failure of synthesized collagen to become organized into a lattice.

Feather-forming skin of the chick thigh tract is capable, in isolation, of autonomous pattern formation. Separated lateral and medial halves of the tract

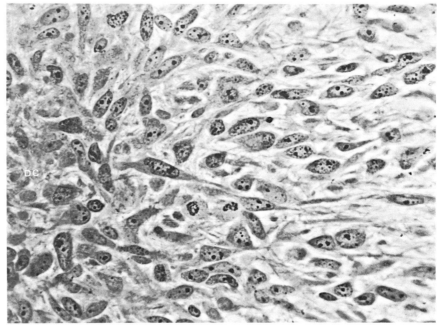

a

Figure 20.8 Pattern of dermal condensations relating to feather germ formation in dorsal skin of chick embryo. *a* A dermal-cell condensation on the left, and oriented cells pointing toward a neighboring condensation. [*From Wessells and Evans, 1968.*] *b* Diagram of a portion of an embryonic feather tract to show the relative positions and sequential appearance of aligned fibrous material and dermal cells during development of papillae. The primary row contains major groups of aligned fibers and cells (B–B) extending anteroposteriorly between successively forming papillae; this midline region contains a full, continuous spectrum of the stages in fiber and cell alignment, as related to papilla formation. In the lateral regions, the major bands of aligned fibers and cells (C–C^1, D–D^1) extend diagonally from the more mature medial papillae toward the prospective lateral papillae; thus, a cross section (A–A^1) through the lateral skin does not coincide with the directions of fiber and cell alignment. [*After Moscona and Garber.*]

A–A^1 hypothetical plane of cross section
B–B^1 primary row of fibers and cells between papillae
C–C^1 }
D–D^1 }   bands of oriented cells and aligned fibers
a–p   anteroposterior axis (midline axis) through the primary
             row of feather germs
stippled circles—developing papilla
open circles—prospective papilla
solid lines—aligned fibers and dermal cells
broken lines—prospective bands of aligned fibers and cells

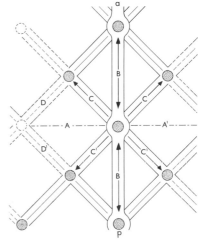

b

can each initiate the development of spatially ordered feather primordia (Fig. 20.8b). Therefore, no one row serves as a specific "initiator row" in whose absence the entire area of skin remains devoid of feathers. Apparently all the skin within the feather tract is capable of forming a first row of equally spaced primordia and of adding secondary rows in the normal pattern.

The mechanism controlling pattern formation must act, accordingly, over a shorter distance rather than over the whole tract, probably a distance not greater than the width of one primordium. Both in vivo and on the chorioallantoic membrane, a misplaced primordium is propagated as a whole new row within the pattern. Thus a single, misplaced primordium can act as a whole new frame of reference within the pattern. This strongly suggests that each individual primordium not only is a component of the pattern but acts directly in the actual extension of the pattern. The simplest explanation of pattern generation, therefore, is that the place where each primordium forms is determined by some influence from the adjacent primordia, once they themselves are established. This would account for the change in the pattern caused by a single, misplaced primordium.

Retinal Pattern

A very different example of lattice pattern is seen in the retina. The retina of fish and birds and possibly other classes of vertebrates exhibits a lattice pattern in the distribution of rods and cones, and particularly in the distribution of a variety of types of cones. The study of this subject extends from the beginning of the century (Shafer, 1900) to the present (Morris, 1973). Shafer mapped the position of double and single cones in the anterior region of the retina of the fish *Micropterus salmonides*. He found a remarkable correlation between the distribution and orientation of single and double cones on the one hand and a system of intercrossing coordinates on the other. Single cones occur in the middle of each lattice space; double cones are midway on each coordinate section between crossovers. Further, the separation line in each double cone is at right angles to the coordinate line.

The system is somewhat more complex in the chick (Fig. 20.9). Rods, double cones (a principal and an accessory cone), and two types of single cones appear in the chick retina, with associated differences in the synaptic structures. The types of receptors are arranged in a hexagonal lattice pattern. The pattern in the mosaic is regarded as the outcome of an evenly spaced distribution of receptor types (Fig. 20.10). The pattern appears to be formed, during the development of the retina, from an array of stem cells. Each stem cell gives rise, by sequential division, to the four receptors in the repeating group of the pattern, according to one hypothesis.

This hypothesis has been tested in a study of the times at which the receptor types complete their final S phase. Tritiated thymidine is injected at a series of incubation times and the embryos are then reared to hatching. Analysis of the results lends support to the contention that the receptor types depend on cell lineage, but not from one stem cell. Each receptor cell in a repeating group is probably formed, in the final cell cycle, from a different precursor cell. The problem of diversified differentiation remains acute, and so does that of the periodic patterning of the several cell types in a complex mosaic.

When dissociated neural retinal cells of 6- to 10-day-old chick embryos are grafted as a pellet (a small compacted mass) onto the chorioallantoic membrane and are allowed to develop, complete retinal structures are reconstructed.

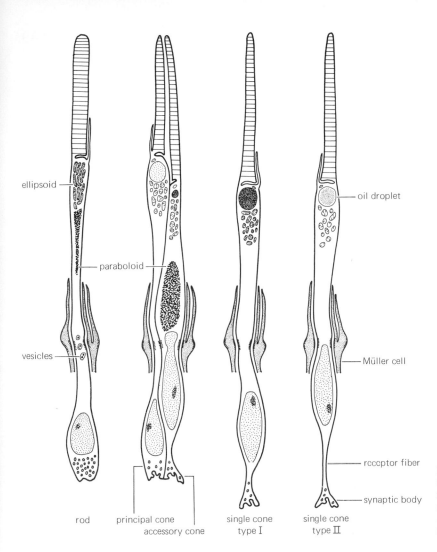

ellipsoid

paraboloid

oil droplet

vesicles

Müller cell

receptor fiber

synaptic body

rod   principal cone   single cone   single cone
             accessory cone   type I   type II

Figure 20.9 Differentiation of five types of visual receptors in the chick retina. From left to right: rod, double cone (two types), single cone type I and type II. [*After V. B. Morris and C. D. Shorey, 1967.*]

Particularly well-oriented retinal structures, possessing three nuclear layers and two plexiform layers, form when the retinal cells of 6-day-old embryos are used. The fundamental steps in this complete reconstruction are: rosette formation, formation of a fibrillar lumen, differentiation of receptor and ganglion cells, fusion of the fibrillar lumen, fusion of the receptor lumen, and finally the formation of a three-layered neural retina. The completed structure of the retina is shown in Fig. 15.14.

ORGAN FORMATION

The development of an organ consists of two fundamental events: (1) the development of form, such as branching, and (2) the specific differentiation of constituent cells. These two features are independent of one another, and are the basic distinction between morphogenesis and cytodifferentiation or his-

450

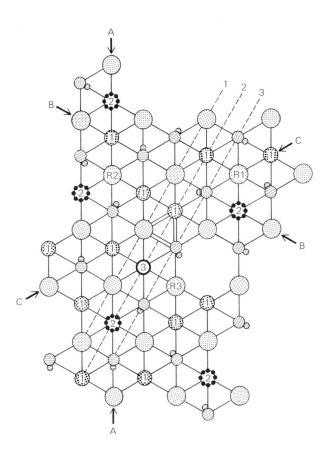

Figure 20.10 Pattern of the receptors in the peripheral retina of the chick. Rows of receptors (AA, BB, and CC) intersect at angles of 60°. Each of these rows is composed of repeating sequences of one rod and two other types of receptors. Another pattern is indicated along the broken lines: broken line 1 is a row of rods, broken line 2 is a row of single cones. A third regular pattern, visible throughout the lattice, is a triangle of receptors consisting of one rod, one single cone, and one double rod. (An example is indicated with double lines.) [*After V. B. Morris, 1970.*]

togenesis. The two processes work together, at least in the sense of proceeding together temporally. Both depend on the same definitive population of cells, but they are concerned with entirely different sets of cell properties. Cytodifferentiation was discussed at length in Chapter 17. Here we are mainly concerned with morphogenesis, or generation of form.

Epithelial-mesenchymal Interaction

Early development of a unit of lung, kidney, or secretory gland is in each case characterized by ingrowth and branching of the epithelial component, while loose mesenchyme condenses around the branches (Fig. 20.11). Dense areas of mesenchymal tissue become visible around each branch. Synchronized development and intimate relations of the two components suggest an interacting mutual control system. Separated components, cultivated in vitro, do not undergo differentiation but do so if they are brought into close association.

Some epithelia require specific homologous mesenchyme (e.g., salivary and bronchial epithelium) for characteristic development. Salivary epithelium exposed to salivary mesenchyme on one side and lung mesenchyme on the other develops branching on the salivary mesenchyme side and remains smooth where it is in contact with lung tissue. Other epithelia (e.g., pancreatic or skin epithelium) will develop normally under the influence of mesenchyme from

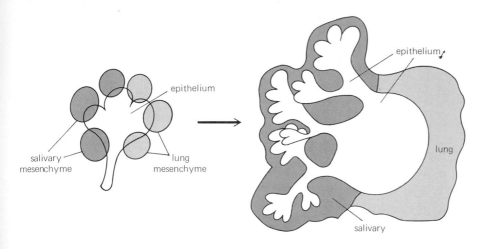

Figure 20.11 Influence of mesenchymal specificity on epithelial morphogenesis. *a* Salivary epithelium freed of all adhering mesenchyme cells and combined with pieces of salivary mesenchyme on the left and lung mesenchyme on the right. *b* After 3 days of culture, only the left half of the epithelium has undergone branching morphogenesis. The right side, in contact with lung mesenchyme, remains smooth and does *not* branch. [*After Wessells, 1973.*]

several sources, or even in the absence of mesenchyme if culture media are supplemented with embryo extracts. Morphogenesis may involve progressive branching (as in salivary, lung, or ureteric bud epithelia), or the cells may assume tissue-specific patterns (e.g., acinar arrangements in the pancreas, basal-cell orientation and proliferation in the skin). In several instances, the characteristic morphogenesis of an epithelium is modified by the mesenchyme with which it is grown, producing an epithelium that reflects the origin of the mesenchyme.

Epithelial morphogenesis can occur under conditions where the epithelium and mesenchyme are separated by a porous filter (Grobstein, 1967). These studies have apparently demonstrated that direct mesenchymal contact is not required for the interaction, particularly with regard to kidney tubule induction. Recent experiments by Nordling, Saxén, and others, however, tend to exclude free diffusion of inductor molecules as the effector factors; they also do not support observations that cytoplasmic processes invade a filter and make contact with tissue on the other side. More and more attention is focusing on the role of extracellular material as a determining agency.

Based mainly on studies of the development of the salivary gland, Bernfield and Wessells have proposed the following explanation: Since morphogenesis proceeds in a precise and highly ordered fashion, the factors involved in this process must be closely integrated. A hypothetical model for the interrelationship of morphogenetically active surface-associated material and of the putatively contractile microfilaments can be formulated. This model accounts for all the available data and makes predictions that are subject to experimental verification. The model is based upon the following premises: (1) The microfilaments in the cells at the basal surface of the epithelium are contractile. (2) Mucopolysaccharide-protein complexes are present near the epithelial surface. (3) Collagen fibers are also present near the epithelial surface and arise by the interaction of collagen (synthesized predominantly by mesenchyme) with the mucopolysaccharide-protein complexes. (4) Regions of accentuated microfilament contractility, which result in cleft formation in an epithelium, are caused by localized areas of surface-associated mucopolysaccharide-protein (Fig. 20.12).

If the mesoderm, or its extracellular secretions, plays a pivotal role in epithelial morphogenesis, it becomes crucial to know whether that effect is a

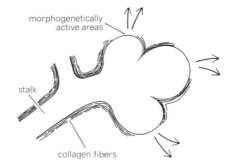

Figure 20.12 Location of collagen fibers around a developing salivary gland unit. Collagen fibers are believed to stabilize the branching by accumulating in the indentations; their removal by collagenase is followed by loss of the branched contour. Collagen is not accumulated in the morphogenetically active areas, i.e., those that will soon indent. But newly synthesized mucopolysaccharide is localized there.

direct one upon the organelle machinery or whether it is indirect via the nucleus or genes of the epithelial cell. It is possible that specific mesoderm regulates microfilament contraction. The demonstration that mucopolysaccharides at the epitheliomesenchymal interface are required for salivary morphogenesis suggests these compounds are involved in this regulation. Until the contractility of the microfilament apparatus is proved, however, and an effective assay for contraction is perfected, such a regulatory role for specific mesoderm will remain an intriguing hypothesis.

Altogether, experimental results raise a number of questions: Is the pattern of deposition of newly synthesized acid mucopolysaccharide controlled by the mesenchyme? Does the mesenchyme control the presence and location of microfilaments and microtubules and the dependent epithelial branching? Above all, what distinguishes one mesodermal subpopulation from another?

EXTRACELLULAR MATRIX

Experiments by Urist (1970) on bone morphogenesis are also illustrative. Demineralized cortical bone matrix was used as a substratum for bone morphogenesis by postfetal mesenchyme cells. The matrix is demineralized and implanted intramuscularly in allogenic rats, where mesenchyme cells abound. Mesenchyme cells invade old vascular channels and begin restriction toward bone-cell differentiation. Once determination is established, a cell population develops osteogenic competence, the not-yet-activated state of readiness to respond to a bone morphogenetic substratum. The quantity of woven bone deposited by *progeny* of osteoprogenitor cells is proportional to the *mass* of preimplanted matrix. All evidence suggests that the total three-dimensional structure of the bone matrix imposes the bone morphogenetic pattern. Preparations of bone matrix, which are lipid-free, low in glycoprotein, and divested of all but traces of intracellular material, retain morphogenetic properties.

The explosive increase in total cell population, the changing character of the differential cell counts, and the percentage of the volume of bone collagen resorbed before bone cells differentiate point to a causal but indirect relationship between the implanted matrix and bone morphogenesis. How the morphogenetic pattern is imprinted on a small cell population and reprinted on all the larger cell populations developing after a few days is a mystery.

A wide variety of extracellular substances may act as morphogenetic substrates and as cues for subsequent differentiation. In this light, the genetic control of collagen synthesis may be an intermediate step, or means, for determining specific patterns, for example, feather patterns or in retinal differentiation. When matrix components are appropriate, cells will react with the matrix carbohydrate component. In so doing they undergo change and also induce change in the matrix, so that a new situation arises and successive changes become possible. In a very real sense, the extracellular matrices represent a continuous supracellular agency, integrating populations of cells into organized and differentiating patterns. At the same time each cell as an individual entity contributes to the pattern. This area of investigation is still in its infancy; at least it offers some promise of placing abstract concepts of morphogenetic fields and the "wholeness" of the organism and organs in a tangible context.

READINGS

ARGYRIS, T. S., 1972. Chalones and the Control of Normal, Regenerative, and Neoplastic Growth of the Skin, *Amer. Zool., 12*:137–149.

ARMSTRONG, P. B., 1971. Light and Electron Microscope Studies of Cell Sorting in Combinations of Chick Embryo Neural Retina and Retinal Pigment Epithelium, Wilhelm Roux's *Archiv, 168*:125–141.

BERLINER, J., 1969. The Effects of the Epidermis on the Collagenous Basement Lamella of Anuran Larval Skin, *Develop. Biol., 22*:213–231.

BERNFIELD, M. R., R. H. COHN, and S. D. BANERJEE, 1973. Glycosaminoglycans and Epithelial Organ Formation, *Amer. Zool., 13*:1067–1083.

———, and N. K. WESSELLS, 1970. Intra- and Extracellular Control of Epithelial Morphogenesis, 29th Symposium, *Develop. Biol.,* suppl. **4**:195–249.

BULLOUGH, W. S., 1962. The Control of Mitotic Activity in Adult Mammalian Tissues, *Biol. Rev., 37*:307–342.

COULOMBRE, J. L., and A. J. COULOMBRE, 1971. Metaplastic Induction of Scales and Feathers in the Corneal Anterior Epithelium of the Chick Embryo, *Develop. Biol., 25*:464–478.

GARBER, B. B., and A. A. MOSCONA, 1972. Reconstruction of Brain Tissue from Cell Suspensions. II. Specific Enhancement of Aggregation of Embryonal Cerebral Cells by Supernatant from Homologous Cell Cultures, *Develop. Biol., 27*:235–243.

GOETINCK, P. F., and M. J. SEKELLICK, 1972. Observations on Collagen Synthesis, Lattice Formation, and Morphology of Scaleless and Normal Embryonic Skin, *Develop. Biol., 28*:636–648.

GOLDSCHNEIDER, I. and A. A. MOSCONA, 1972. Tissue-Specific Cell-Surface Antigens in Embryonic Cells, *J. Cell Biol., 53*:435–449.

GROBSTEIN, C., 1967. Mechanism of Organogenetic Tissue Interaction, *Nat. Cancer Inst. Monogr., 26*:279–299.

HAY, E. D., 1973. Origin and Role of Collagen in the Embryo, *Amer. Zool., 13*:1085–1107.

HUMPHREYS, T., 1963. Chemical Dissolution and *in vitro* Reconstruction of Sponge Cell Adhesions, *Develop. Biol.,* **8**:27–47.

KRATOCHWIL, K., 1969. Organ Specificity in Mesenchymal Induction Demonstrated in the Embryonic Development of the Mammary Gland of the Mouse, *Develop. Biol., 20*:46–71.

LAWRENCE, I. E., 1971. Timed Reciprocal Dermal-Epidermal Interactions between Comb, Mid-dorsal, and Tarsometatarsal Skin Components, *J. Exp. Zool., 178*:195–210.

LINSENMAYER, T., 1972. Control of Integumentary Patterns in the Chick, *Develop. Biol., 27*:244–271.

LUDUENA, M. A., and N. K. WESSELLS, 1973. Cell Locomotion, Nerve Elongation, and Microfilaments, *Develop. Biol., 30*:427–440.

MADERSON, P. F. A., 1975. Embryonic Tissue Interactions as the Basis for Morphological Change in Evolution, *Amer. Zool., 15*:315–328.

MANTZ, E., H. M. PHILIPS, and M. S. STEINBERG, 1974. Contact Inhibition of Overlapping and Differential Cell Adhesion: a Sufficient Model for the Control of Certain Cell Culture Morphologies, *J. Cell Sci., 16*:401–419.

MORRIS, V. B., 1970. Symmetry in a Receptor Mosaic Demonstrated in the Chick from the Frequencies, Spacing and Arrangement of the Types of Retinal Receptor, *J. Comp. Neurol., 140*:359–397.

———, and C. D. SHOREY, 1967. An Electron Microscope Study of the Types of Receptor in the Chick Retina, *J. Comp. Neurol., 129*:313–339.

MOSCONA, A. A., 1962. Studies on Cell Aggregation and Demonstration of Materials with Selective Cell-Binding Activity, *Proc. Nat. Acad. Sci., 49*:742–747.

OTHMER, H. G., and L. E. SCRIVEN, 1971. Instability and Dynamic Pattern in Cellular Networks, *J. Theoret. Biol., 32*:507–537.

RAWLES, M. E., 1963. Tissue Interaction in Scale and Feather Development as Studied in Dermal-Epidermal Recombinations. *J. Embryol. Exp. Morphol.*, **11**:765–789.

ROTH, S., 1973. Molecular Model for Cell Interactions, *Quart. Rev. Biol.*, **48**:541–563.

SAWYER, R. H., 1972. Avian Scale Development. I. Histogenesis and Morphogenesis of the Epidermis and Dermis during Formation of the Scale Ridge, *J. Exp. Zool.*, **181**:365–384.

SAXÉN, L., 1971. Inductive Interactions in Kidney Dvelopment, 25th Symposium of the Society of Developmental Biology, Academic Press.

—— et al., 1968. Differentiation of Kidney Mesenchyme in an Experimental Model System, *Advan. Morphog.*, **7**: 251–293.

SPOONER, B. S., 1974. Organogenesis in Vertebrate Organs, in J. Lash and J. R. Whittaker (eds.), "Concepts of Development," Sinauer.

SPOONER, B. S., and N. K. WESSELLS, 1972. An Analysis of Salivary Gland Morphogenesis: Role of Cytoplasmic Microfilaments and Microtubules, *Develop. Biol.*, **27**:38–54.

STEINBERG, M. S., 1970. Does Differential Adhesion Govern Self-Assembly Processes in Histogenesis, *J. Exp. Zool.*, **173**:395–434.

STUART, E. S., B. GARBER, and A. A. MOSCONA, 1972. An Analysis of Feather Germ Formation in the Embryos and *in vitro*, in Normal Development and in Skin Treated with Hydrocortisone, *J. Exp. Zool.*, **179**:97–118.

SUTHERLAND, E. W., 1972. Studies on the Mechanism of Hormone Action, *Science*, **177**:401–407.

SYMPOSIUM, 1973. Factors Controlling Cell Shape during Development, *Amer. Zool.*, **13**:941–1129.

TOOLE, B. P., 1973. Hyaluronate and Hyaluronidase in Morphogenesis and Differentiation, *Amer. Zool.*, **13**:1061–1065.

TOWNES, P. L., and J. HOLTFRETER, 1955. Directed Movements and Selective Adhesion of Embryonic Amphibian Cells, *J. Exp. Zool.*, **128**:53–120.

UNSWORTH, B., and C. GROBSTEIN, 1970. Induction of Kidney Tubules in Mouse Metanephrogenic Mesenchyme by Various Embryonic Mesenchymal Tissues, *Develop. Biol.*, **21**:547–556.

URIST, M. R., 1970. The Substratum for Bone Morphogenesis, 29th Symposium, *Develop. Biol.*, suppl. **4**:125–163.

URSPRUNG, H., 1966. The Formation of Pattern, *Develop. Biol.*, **25**:251–277.

WANG, H. 1943. The Morphogenetic Functions of the Epidermal and Dermal Components of the Papilla in Feather Regeneration, *Physiol. Zool.*, **16**:325–350.

WEISS, P., 1961. Ruling Principles in Cell Locomotion and Cell Aggregation, *Exp. Cell Res.*, **8**:260–281.

——, and A. C. TAYLOR, 1960. Reconstitution of Complete Organs from Single-cell Suspensions, *Proc. Nat. Acad. Sci.*, **46**:1177–1185.

WESSELLS, N. K., 1970. Mammalian Lung Development: Interactions in Formation and Morphogenesis of Tracheal Buds, *J. Exp. Zool.*, **175**:455–466.

——, and J. EVANS, 1968: The Ultrastructure of Oriented Cells and Extracellular Materials between Developing Feathers, *Develop. Biol.*, **18**:42–61.

WISEMAN, L. L., M. S. STEINBERG, and H. M. PHILLIPS, 1972. Experimental Modulation of Intercellular Cohesiveness: Reversal of Tissue Assembly Patterns, *Develop. Biol.*, **28**:498–517.

CHAPTER 21

Aging

Cellular Aging
Extracellular Aging
Hormones
Aging and Growth

The outward signs of aging are obvious; yet the underlying bases for the deteriorative processes that occur in all animals are very poorly understood. As an animal ages it becomes increasingly sensitive to a wide variety of destructive agents, whether they are internal physiological disturbances or external stress. The effect of age-related physiological changes on life span is reflected in a typical survivorship curve for humans (Fig. 21.1). In humans after the age of maturity there is a progressive increase (approximately twofold every 8 years) in the probability of death with time. Our recent technological accomplishments have had little effect either on the general shape of this curve or upon our life span; they have succeeded primarily by increasing the number of persons who live out the expected human life. It is estimated that the elimination of the major causes of death in humans—i.e., cancer and heart disease—would serve only to increase the *average* life span by 10 or 12 years and would have very little effect upon the maximal span itself. If we are to achieve a significant increase in life expectancy, we must have a basic understanding of why an organism ages. It is this question that will occupy the bulk of this chapter.

Figure 21.1 Survival curve of a human population.

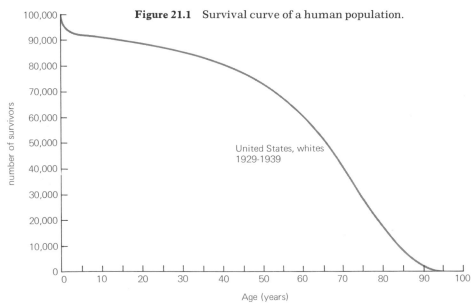

United States, whites
1929-1939

number of survivors

Age (years)

Aging is a complex subject; many basic observations have been made of age-related changes, i.e., those changes correlated with increasing age. One of the most important tasks is to determine which of these changes are primary events that could be directly responsible for the survival curve of Fig. 21.1 and which are either secondary manifestations or independent processes not responsible for causing age-related death. If the primary events of aging can be established, a theory that purports to explain the basis of aging must take these into account.

One of the most important facts that must be incorporated into any theory of aging is that each species has a characteristic life span. In other words, there is an overriding genetic component, passed on from generation to generation, that restricts the life of each animal. Aging cannot, therefore, be explained merely as a consequence of physical-chemical laws, which would be expected to act equally on all animals. Which aspects of the genetic information cause the life of a mouse to span approximately 2½ years while the life of a human is many times that length? At present there is no information available to shed light on this basic question. In the mouse there is an acceleration of the entire spectrum of age-related processes in comparison with the human; a 2½-year-old mouse can be considered in many ways to be physiologically equivalent to a human approximately 30 times that number of years. Any theory of aging, therefore, must be based on primary events that occur much more rapidly in short-lived animals than in long-lived ones. The size of the animal is one factor that has been considered. A mouse is many times smaller than a dog or a human, but what of a horse that outweighs a human but has half the live expectancy? Smaller animals often have higher metabolic rates, and it can be argued that increased metabolic activity produces an accelerated aging process. It is hard to explain, however, how this could account for the thirty- to thirty-five-fold difference in the expected life span of a mouse and a human. If many animals are compared, the correlation between metabolic rate and life expectancy is not that high. A better correlation is between life expectancy and relative brain weight. Those animals with a proportionately larger brain have a greater life span, but the meaning of this correlation is obscure.

Another basic question is why an animal should age at all. Why should all animals be subject to destructive processes that will ultimately claim their lives? Natural selection acts to adapt populations, from generation to generation, to changing environmental conditions. The essence of natural selection is survival, i.e., survival to reproduce. Yet survival is severely limited by the aging process. It appears that there is little selection for longevity, and what selection does exist is relative to the particular species being considered. The reason for this condition stems from the lack of biological advantage in living to a post-reproductive age. In fact, according to some evolutionary theory, there is a selective disadvantage for a population to maintain individuals who will only compete for limited resources with those currently reproductive. As an animal progresses through its reproductive period and into its postreproductive years, there is less and less selective advantage for maintaining physically optimal health. The acceleration of the aging process, reflected in the curve of Fig. 21.1, can be viewed as a reflection of the decreasing selective advantage for mechanisms that act to maintain the state of the animal. Or possibly it reflects an increasing selective advantage for mechanisms to shorten the reproductively unproductive years.

The most readily observed effects of aging are changes in the individual's nature. Physiological measurements of organ function, nerve conduction velocity, muscle power, etc., indicate a decreasing capacity with age. It is generally believed that these more easily observed alterations reflect a basic, progressive deterioration in the elements of which the tissues are composed. In this discussion we will consider two sites, the cellular and the extracellular, in which age-related events occur. There is no doubt that progressive changes take place both within cells and in their surrounding environment. The principle controversy in the field of aging is which of these two sites within the tissues is the primary one from which the aging of the whole animal results. Some of the evidence is contradictory: many of the interpretations are controversial. In the following pages we will simply present some of the basic observations that have been made and a little of the speculation about their significance.

CELLULAR AGING

Theories that attempt to explain the aging process as a result of defective intracellular processes are based upon several assumptions. The underlying assumption is that there is a finite frequency of accidental error in the biochemical operations of every cell. Over long periods, these errors might accumulate to produce a cell with defective function or they might result in the death of that cell. First we will present some of the evidence that indicates cells do age. Then we will examine whether it is feasible that cellular aging can explain the aging of a whole animal or whether it is merely an accompaniment.

Biochemical mistakes or damage can occur at numerous sites and manifest themselves in numerous ways. Any change in the linear base sequence in the DNA will result in the continual production of erroneous RNA, which will result in its altered regulatory or template properties and subsequent effect upon all processes in which that gene is involved. Alteration of the DNA template can result from damage—known to occur after most types of radiation—or from a mistake during replication by insertion of an incorrect nucleotide. Alterations in the genome of cells outside the germ line are called *somatic mutations*. Such mutations would be expected to be random, and each cell would have its information content affected in a different way.

The best evidence that individual cells undergo deterioration has been obtained with cells growing in culture. In 1965 it was reported by Hayflick that when human lung fibroblasts are followed in tissue culture, the number of divisions these cells can undergo is limited. To perform this experiment, a small piece of tissue is removed, the cells are dissociated, and a certain number of these single cells are transferred to a culture dish allowed to attach to the surface and divide. After a number of divisions the cells are removed from the dish and placed into suspension; a small percentage are used to inoculate new culture dishes, just as the first had been done. These cells will continue to divide and cover the new dish, after which the process can be repeated. Each time the cells are removed from the dish and plated on a new dish at a lower concentration, they are said to be *subcultured*. If cells are subcultured numerous times, a point is reached where they stop dividing and the cell strain dies out. This has been found for many types of cells. It is generally reported that the number of divisions the strain goes through determines its life span, rather than the time that has passed during the experiment. This is clearly an example of age-related cellular death.

Tumor cells provide a significant exception to the rule that cells undergo a limited number of doublings in culture. Malignant cells have no such restriction; they continue to divide in essentially an immortal way. Tumor cells are often characterized by an abnormal chromosome number, which may be related to their immortality in vitro. Interestingly, occasional cells derived from a normal donor will continue to divide rather than become senescent, as in most cases. When the chromosomes of these peculiar cells are examined, they are found to be aneuploid, like the malignant cells, and they behave in other respects as if they were tumor cells. Cells that undergo this change are said to be a *cell line* as opposed to a *cell strain,* as in cells that retain the diploid number of chromosomes and have a restricted division potential. The frequency with which cells become a cell line is related to the species from which they were derived. Mouse cells will frequently become altered in this way, human cells only rarely.

If aging and ultimate age-related death of an animal result from intracellular damage, it would be expected that cells from a short-lived species would have less potential for cell division than those from a long-lived animal. Similarly, cells from a young animal should be less capable of extended division than cells of an older individual. In a general way, human fetal lung fibroblasts are capable of approximately 50 divisions before they lose this ability; those from an adult at maturity are capable of approximately 30; and those from more aged individuals are capable of less. These numbers, however, are averages, and in one case an 87-year-old man was reported to have cells capable of an average of 29 further divisions. In other words, there is convincing evidence that cells age, but it is equally clear that we do not run out of *all types of cells* and then die as a result. If we take the value of 50 divisions (believed to be an underestimate) for all cells of the fetus, sufficient cells for many lifetimes could be produced. If the exhaustion of the capacity of cells to divide is responsible for age-related processes, a search must be made for a tissue that is particularly sensitive, which could secondarily affect the other tissues of the body in a destructive way. A candidate would be one or more of the endocrine glands, whose effects on the function of the whole body are well known. Another is the lymphoid system; we will return to this subject below.

Up to this point in the discussion it has been implied that the effect of the accumulation of biochemical errors would simply be the lack of ability to continue to divide. Actually this is only one manifestation of progressively defective cellular function and one likely to require an exceedingly high error level. Presumably, as errors occur during the early divisions, cell function is adversely affected; the additive effect upon the tissue containing these cells might be seen as tissue aging.

Mistakes in chromosomal structure can be minute, as in a change of one nucleotide in one gene, or massive, as in a visibly altered chromosome. In the latter case we speak of a chromosomal aberration, and the incidence of chromosomal aberrations with age has been examined. The cells of the liver have been widely studied. There is a good correlation between the frequency of damage visible in the chromosomes of liver cells and the age and life span of the animal. In other words, a mouse at 2½ years (near the end of its life) has many more aberrations than a dog of that age. Similarly, a dog of age 12 has many more aberrations of its liver cells than a correspondingly aged human. As the chronological age of each of these organisms increases, so does its incidence of chromosomal aberrations.

Why should the cells of a mouse age more rapidly than those of a human? We cannot answer this. Why certain animals have a greater error frequency than others is an open question; yet the observations indicate that such is the case. It has long been found that the overall spontaneous mutation rate for germ cells is roughly—very roughly—inversely proportional to the life span of the species. It may be that natural selection has actually led to an increased intrinsic (inborn) error frequency in animals that would have overpopulation problems if their life were increased. Also, without some inherent level of mistake by mutation, there could be no variation upon which natural selection could operate. In other words, a low but finite level of error production might be selected for under conditions of a changing environment that would require changing adaptions among the members of populations. Aging then could result from a continuation of these errors into the postreproductive period, by which time their cumulative effect would be sufficient to have progressively destructive effects.

Up to this point we have considered the accumulation of simple, randomly occurring mutations. To understand the potential for cellular damage inherent in the occurrence of somatic mutation, we must consider the "error catastrophe" concept proposed by Orgel. In this concept it is pointed out that certain types of errors are likely to produce a great number of subsequent errors. Consider, for example, a mistake occurring in a DNA polymerase gene that results in an enzyme that will make further mistakes during replication. Such a mistake would be considered an error catastrophe, and examples of altered enzymes that cause an increased number of mistakes are known from studies of bacterial viruses. Replicational enzymes are only one place where an error catastrophe could occur. Proteins are needed for transcription and translation, and altered proteins that serve these functions could similarily be expected to rapidly fill the cell with an entire spectrum of defective proteins.

Is there evidence that as cells become older, they have an increasing content of deficient proteins? This is a controversial subject, like most observations in this field, but there is good evidence that such is the case. For example, if the activity of the enzyme liver aldolase is compared between 3-month and 31-month-old mice, it is found that the cells of the older mouse contain increasing quantities of proteins that resemble the enzyme (by immunological criteria) but are no longer enzymatically active. Presumably mistakes have produced an enzyme with an amino acid sequence similar enough to be recognized by antibodies against the enzyme but sufficiently different so that it is inactive.

As cells grow in culture, they become filled with enzymes that are thermolabile, i.e., enzymes that are inactive at elevated temperature. This suggests that temperature-sensitive mutations are occurring as would be expected from altered amino acid sequences. This observation and the ones above suggest there is a correlation between the aging of cells and the appearance of defective proteins. The critical question is whether the relation is a causal one. Evidence that it is the increased level of errors that actually brings on senescence comes from the use of the compound 5-fluorouracil, which becomes incorporated into RNA and produces subsequent errors in translation. In the presence of this compound, cells become prematurely filled with thermolabile enzymes and undergo premature senescence, i.e., early cessation of division.

The aging of cells as they grow in vitro has been described above. By *serial transplantation,* whereby cells from one animal are repeatedly transplanted from one host to another, the longevity of cells in vivo can be estimated. With this technique, the descendants of the cells of the original transplant can be maintained in the bodies of animals of any age rather than be exposed to a continually aging environment. In other words, the technique of serial transplantation allows one to dissociate the cell from its normal environment, yet maintain it within an appropriate physiological container. Several types of tissues, including skin, mammary gland, and spleen cells, have been treated in this way. In all these cases the proliferation of cells is limited, just as the in vitro experiments. However, these transplanted tissues will outlive, to a considerable extent, the animal that they were originally taken from. The results of these experiments, therefore, are inconclusive. They confirm that cells undergo aging in vivo but do not establish if this phenomenon is responsible for the age-related death of the animal.

One of the main lines of evidence cited in support of theories of cellular aging has been obtained by irradiation. It is a well-established fact that irradia-

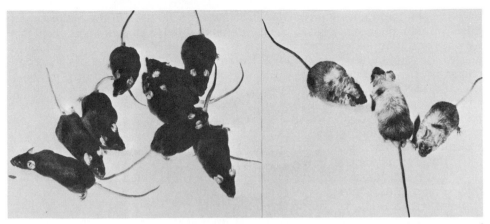

Figure 21.2 Two groups of mice that were originally identical. Mice on the left are control animals; mice on the right received a large but nonlethal dose of radiation. Only three mice of the irradiated group remain alive; these are "old" and senile. [*Courtesy of H. J. Curtis.*]

tion, in proportion to the dose, has life-shortening effects. Remarkably, animals whose life expectancy has been shortened as a result of such exposure undergo the signs of aging prematurely. Figure 21.2 shows two groups of littermates of mice. The group exposed to x-radiation shows the debilitating signs of age at a chronological age well in advance of the normal time for these animals. The means by which the radiation is administered and whether the effects are truly mimicking the natural aging process are controversial and beyond the scope of this book. If we assume that radiation is accelerating the natural aging events, the most likely explanation for its action is via somatic mutation, i.e., changes in the DNA.

Much of the evidence to support a cellular basis of aging comes from the study of mammalian cells in culture. An entirely different type of cell culture, that of protozoa, has also provided evidence in the study of aging. Protozoa are at the same time a single cell and a whole animal. Therefore, the question of whether evidence from studies of single cells can be applied to the whole organism is no longer relevant. Early studies indicated that ciliates that continued to grow and to reproduce asexually (by mitotic fission) reached a point of senescence; they stopped dividing and died. If these cultures were allowed to undergo sexual reproduction (conjugation), many of the cells would rejuvenate; they would continue to divide and the culture could be maintained.

Two important parallels can be drawn from studies on ciliates and aging in cultured cells of mammals. In the first, both types of cells gradually lose the ability to divide after continual mitotic division. As ciliates grow and "age," at first there is little or no evidence of altered proteins; but after a time, defective proteins are abundant.

The second parallel is found in the rejuvenation following sexual reproduction. Ciliates are unusual in having two types of nuclei, very large macronuclei and very small micronuclei. The micronuclei are believed to have a complete set of all the genes, while the macronuclei have many copies of each, i.e., repeated DNA. The macronucleus is responsible for the daily cellular activities; presumably, errors in the macronuclear DNA are responsible for the altered ciliate protein described above. One of the events in sexual reproduction or conjugation, whereby two individuals come together, is the destruction and subsequent re-formation of the macronucleus. The re-formation is under the direction of the micronucleus, which has undergone a meiotic division. Presumably the DNA of the new macronucleus is identical in information content with that of the new micronucleus; any errors that had accumulated in the old macronucleus would have been "erased." The ciliates that leave the conjugal event (the exconjugants) are given a "fresh genetic start": they have a new micronucleus due to meiosis and nuclear fusion between individuals, and the old macronucleus is destroyed. The relative value of each of these events in rejuvenation of the culture is unclear.

In the reproduction of higher organisms it appears that the offspring of a pair of aging individuals are also given a "fresh genetic start." This important fact must be taken into account in any theory of cellular aging. If cells age as a result of the accumulation of mutations, why isn't this state passed on to each offspring, as it is in cells growing in culture?

Even mice whose own life spans have been shortened by irradiation produce offspring that have normal life spans. The effects of the irradiation are not transmitted through the germ-cell line.

There are two sets of DNA to consider, that of the germ cells and that of the rest of the body cells. Only mutations in the germ-cell line have to be considered in terms of mistakes passed on to the next generation. Because mistakes do not seem to accumulate and to be passed on, there must be some differences between these two groups of cells.

The question raised in this discussion is why the germ cells, which had undergone numerous mitotic divisions as gonial cells, do not become genetically defective. Several possibilities could be offered in explanation. It may be that in some way the mistake-producing factors are absent in the germ-cell line. This is most conceivable if natural selection has actually favored a low level of inherent error-producing mechanisms. They could possibly be excluded from the germ-cell line. Another possibility is that DNA repair activity is more effective in the germ-cell line than in other cells. The presence of enzymes that can recognize altered regions of DNA and repair them is well established, though their extent and mechanism of operation in the cells of higher animals are poorly understood. Another possibility is that cells in the germ line with an altered genetic content are somehow recognized and destroyed. The majority of human oogonia originally in the fetal ovary disappear during the life of the individual. It is possible that the eliminated oocytes are somehow recognized as defective and are selectively destroyed.

Evidence that germ cells do age is incontestable. The increased incidence of Down's syndrome in offspring of older mothers reflects the increasing likelihood of abnormal meiotic divisions in the older woman. Yet, even considering this evidence, the genome of the oocyte may be no more defective than that of the younger person. Meiotic difficulties very likely reflect an aging process of the oocyte cytoplasm during its long prophase state and may be unrelated to alterations in the DNA.

Before questions of cellular aging within the mammalian body can be considered, a distinction must be made as to the nature of the cells involved. A certain percentage of the cells of the mature animal, including neurons and muscle cells, are formed during the developmental period of the life cycle and are not replaced during the entire life of the organism. The study of a postmitotic cell for signs of aging allows one to separate aging processes from mistakes made during division. Neurons or muscle cells, once formed might be expected to accumulate errors during their long life. These errors might be expected to reduce the capabilities of each cell and to cause deteriorating changes in the physiological properties of the tissue. Both nervous and muscle tissue undergo age-related physiological change.

Another class of cells produced continually throughout the life of the animal include circulating blood cells, lymphoid and bone marrow cells, skin cells, mucous membrane epithelial cells, etc. These cells are produced with a finite lifetime, from days to months, and are destroyed. Use of radioactively labeled cells indicates that in many cases these cells are not removed on a random basis; rather, as a cell's lifetime in the body increases, its chance of becoming destroyed also increases. This is an important observation, because it indicates there are mechanisms by which aging cells can be marked and mechanisms whereby they can be destroyed. These short-lived cells can be shown to age in very short periods, while longer-lived cells show no such changes in these short time periods. Different cells seem to undergo different rates of age-related deterioration.

Another class of cells can be distinguished that either continue to divide or retain the capacity, to some degree, throughout the life of the organism. Examples are hepatocytes, osteoblasts, chondrocytes. In this group are the many types of stem cells that are partially differentiated, at least to the extent that they can give rise to only one or a limited variety of differentiated cells. Aging to this group of cells would be reflected in their inability to renew the tissues they are responsible for as well as in their decreased ability to function physiologically. Each type of cell must be considered individually: each may have its own error frequency, its own molecular turnover rate, etc., and each may contribute in a different way to the overall aging process of the animal.

However, cell proliferation in regenerating liver is similar in young and old rats. Also, the generation time of intestinal cells of very old mice is only slightly lengthened, and there is no dying out of this population. Serially transplanted mouse skin has been reported to survive at least 6 years, that is, more than twice the normal life span of a mouse. Mice, being short-lived, should have cells with less than the human doubling capacity of 50. However, in one recent study, mouse tongue epithelium showed a minimum of 146 and an average of around 565 doublings over the life span, with no significant difference in cell division between 3-, 13-, and 19-month-old animals. The results of these types of studies remain contradictory and the effect of cellular aging on cell division remains open to discussion.

As stated above, theories of cellular aging must explain the entire age-related spectrum of changes responsible for the curve of Figure 21.1. Can an increased likelihood of malignancy, increased heart disease, etc., be accounted for by underlying cellular damage? One theory has been presented that utilizes the effect of somatic mutation and its consequences on one organ system, the lymphoid system; it then explains the remainder of the aging process by the secondary effects on all tissues that result from a decreasingly efficient or increasingly destructive immune system.

The immunological theory of aging provides the best hypothesis to date to explain a mechanism whereby cellular aging could account for the entire spectrum of age-related changes. The elements of the theory are as follows: The primary organ responsible for aging is the thymus gland. The thymus is unusual among the body's tissues in that it reaches a maximum weight in humans from age 7 to 11 and declines from that age until it has essentially disappeared in late middle age. In other words, the thymus seems to operate under its own program, independent of that of the rest of the body.

Why does the thymus undergo atrophy? Proponents of this theory suggest that the high rate of proliferation of lymphoid cells exhausts the number of divisions a cell strain is capable of and causes a depletion in the cells of the bone marrow or other lymphoid tissues that can enter the thymus. An experiment utilizing the technique of serial transplantation has illustrated that immune cells can undergo their "allotted" number of divisions in vivo and die out. In this experiment donor mice were injected with a single antigen (2,4-dinitrophenol or DNP) to induce the proliferation of clones capable of producing antibodies against it. The spleen, which now will contain a greatly increased, number of the anti-DNP immunocytes, was removed and dissociated to a cell suspension. A fraction of these cells were injected into mice of the same strain that had been irradiated to destroy their immune response. These irradiated mice now produced antibodies to DNP as a result of the proliferation of the cells derived from the original response in the first donor. The spleen from the first host was then removed and the cells were injected into a second irradiated host, into which in turn DNP was injected to induce another proliferation, as monitored by the presence of antibodies in the blood. In this experiment Williams and Askonas found that antibodies against DNP could be produced at high levels through four transplants, at decreasing levels in the fifth through seventh, and could not be produced in the eighth host. These results indicate that cells of the original donor could be stimulated to divide in vivo a limited number of times before senescence and, finally, death. It is estimated that these cells underwent approximately 90 divisions, a value that fits closely with many obtained by in vitro studies. The results suggest that cell division is restricted *within the body* and that the immune system is particularly sensitive because of its high rate of division. The immunological theory of aging suggests that age-related effects in the whole animal are explained on the basis of secondary effects resulting from an increasingly deficient thymus function. According to Burnet, virtually all immune functions, humoral or cell-mediated, diminish sharply in effectiveness with age. There are several ways in which a less effective immune system can be deleterious. Decreasing humoral antibody production results in a reduced ability to mount an antibody response to infectious diseases. Immunological surveillance depends upon cell destruction of recognizable abnormal cells. With decreasing thymus function there would be an expected curtailment of the ability of the immune system to destroy newly formed tumor cells (whose number might be increasing as a result of accumulating mutation). Therefore there would be an increased incidence of malignancy. The thymus is believed to be responsible for the removal of immune cells that can produce autoantibodies, i.e., antibodies against one's own tissues. With diminished thymus function, an increase in the number of "forbidden clones" and an increase in autoantibodies might be expected. The effect of autoimmune reactions is tissue destruction, which could account for all the degenerative changes in all body tissues. The appearance of numerous autoantibodies with age is well documented.

EXTRACELLULAR AGING

A significant percentage of the dry weight of an animal resides outside the cell in the extracellular space. The extent to which a tissue is composed of extracellular material varies greatly, reaching a maximum in the supportive tissues of the body. The primary components of the extracellular space are mucopolysaccharides and fibrous proteins, particularly collagen and elastin, which are secreted out of the connective tissue cells in which they are synthesized. Collagen is estimated to account for up to 40 percent of the body protein, is present in extracellular spaces of virtually all tissues, and has been suggested as the primary site for age-related changes.

Several properties of collagen suggest it is responsible for the aging process. That collagen undergoes molecular modification with age is primary to the theory. (The molecular organization and assembly processes were described previously.) The fibrous protein molecules are polymers of tropocollagen monomers, each composed of three polypeptide chains. In the newly polymerized molecule the tropocollagen monomers are held together by noncovalent bonds. As collagen is maintained under physiological conditions, covalent cross-linking takes place both within the tropocollagen monomer (among the three chains) and between the monomers. These cross-linking reactions have profound effects on both physicochemical and biological properties of collagen. For example, the ease with which collagen can be extracted and dissociated drops markedly with age until it is essentially insoluble by the time of maturity in mammals. From that point through old age, cross-linking continues and its effect can be measured. One study of its changing properties has utilized collagen fibers from rat tail and their resistance to shrinkage. If collagen fibers are heated to 65°C, they shrink in length unless maintained at their original length with attached weights. The amount of weight required to prevent shrinkage is a measure of the extent of cross-linking and, therefore, of aging of the collagen molecules. Verzar has found that 2-month-old rat-tail collagen can be maintained by 1.5 g, 5-month by 3 g, and 30-month by approximately 10 g. Changes in cross-linking of collagen can be correlated with expected life span. The collagen from a 2½-year-old mouse is heavily cross-linked, while that of a 2½-year-old human is not.

Most body components studied reveal a significant replacement or turnover level which ensures that any given molecule will eventually be destroyed. The extracellular mucopolysaccharides, for example, are turned over with half-lives of days to a month. Collagen, in contrast, is essentially nonrenewable. Only the most recently synthesized collagen molecules are generally found to be susceptible to replacement. As a result, collagen molecules produced as early as the embryonic period can remain in the body for life; there they undergo the cross-linking reaction that convert them to an increasingly altered form.

The theory of aging based on collagen is analogous to the theory based on intracellular changes in that the evidence of age-related modification is indisputable. The question is whether or not all the other age-related events are explainable as a consequence. The primary chemical modifications are believed to directly affect a wide variety of physiological activities, as a result of the widespread distribution of collagen. For a cell to maintain a healthy intracellular composition, it must receive oxygen, nutrition, ions, hormones, etc., from its environment and release carbon dioxide and other waste products. The occurrence of collagen in spaces between cells suggests that it could play a critical role in the exchange activities between a cell and its environment. The presence of large amounts of collagen in the lining of all blood vessels would similarly affect movement from the blood into the extracellular space as well as affect the distensibility of the arterial wall. Because collagen is a major component of bone, tendons, ligaments, etc., its aging could have marked effects on the proper functioning of these tissues and thus could interfere in various structural functions.

HORMONES

Since the endocrine and the nervous systems act, often together, to enable an organism to adapt to environmental changes, these systems are also being examined as possible sites of aging pacemakers. The role of hormones in aging may be studied by means of their effects on enzyme induction. A number of stimuli, many of them acting indirectly by stimulating the release of hormones, induce the synthesis of enzymes by animal tissues. As animals age, their ability to respond to the stimuli may be modified in a variety of ways. The response may be slowed and decreased in magnitude; or it may be diminished or enhanced but not altered in rate; or it may be delayed but eventually reach the same magnitude as in young animals.

A number of hormones are ultimately under the control of the nervous system, and it is possible that aging pacemakers are located in the brain. The marked decline in hormonal output by the ovary during menopause, for instance, is not due to intrinsic decline in the capacity of the gland to secrete the hormones. Ovarian activity and estrous cycles (analogous to menstrual cycles in primates) can be reinitiated in aged rats by stimulating an area of the brain known to control reproductive hormone secretion.

AGING AND GROWTH

Some investigators believe that aging, whether caused by intrinsic or extrinsic factors, is a generalized property of all normal cells. Others have proposed that a limited population of cells controls the course of aging throughout the body. Many think that a combination of mechanisms causes the complex phenomenon of senescence. The problem may be relatively difficult to solve in animals such as the higher vertebrates because of the extreme complexity of the body in terms of cells, tissues, and extracellular materials. All aspects or properties of the organism are clearly involved in the general process, and possibly no single one can be assigned responsibility for the overall phenomenon. Aging is a widespread, a nearly universal process in organisms. An intensive and comparative study of aging in lower multicellular forms both of animals and plants may in the end be more profitable and enlightening. The study of aging in creatures that have no hormonal system, if there truly be any, would at least be a salutary counterpart to studies on animals with elaborate hormonal systems.

Above all, perhaps it should be emphasized that aging and growth cannot be divorced from one another. The limits of growth in virtually all organisms are generally predetermined at the onset of development, although the innate potential for growth may become stunted by environmental factors. Growth as such may be analyzed in terms of cell multiplication, cell enlargement, cell replacement, and other features such as accumulation of extracellular substance. Yet the phenomenon itself, including the factors that determine both the rates of growth and the limits of growth, is not understood. Aging is essentially an extension of the growth process into negative values; that is, the process is seen as increase as long as cell multiplication exceeds cell death and as decrease when cell death exceeds cell multiplication. The process is a continuous one throughout life, and the waning of the process actually begins in early development. When the underlying growth-controlling property becomes better understood, so will the phenomenon of aging and death.

READINGS

BURNET, F. M., 1974. Intrinsic Mutagenesis: A Genetic Basis of Aging, *Pathology,* 6:1–11.
COMFORT, A., 1964. "Ageing: The Biology of Senescence," Holt, Rinehart and Winston.
CRISTOFALO, V. J., 1974. Aging, in J. Lash and J. R. Whittaker (eds.), "Concepts in Development," Sinauer.
DANIEL, C. W., 1972. Aging of Cells During Serial Propagation *in vivo, Advan. Gerontol. Res.,* 4:167–199.
HAYFLICK, L., 1965. The Limited *in vitro* Lifetime of Human Diploid Cell Strains, *Exp. Cell Res.,* 37:614–636.
HOLLIDAY, R., and G. M. TARRANT, 1972. Altered Enzymes in Aging Human Fibroblasts, *Nature,* 238:26–30.
KOHN, R. R., 1971. "Principles of Mammalian Aging," Prentice-Hall.
KROHN, P. L. (ed.), 1966. "Topics in the Biology of Aging," Wiley-Interscience.
ORGEL, L. E., 1973. Ageing of Clones of Mammalian Cells, *Nature,* 243:441–445.
STREHLER, B. L., 1961. "Time, Cells, and Aging," Academic.
————, 1960. "The Biology of Aging," Waverly.
TANZER, M. L., 1973. Cross-Linking of Collagen, *Science,* 180:561–566.
VERZAR, F., 1963. The Aging of Collagen, *Sci. Amer.,* April.
WALFORD, R. L., 1969. "The Immunological Theory of Aging," Williams & Wilkins.
WILLIAMSON, A. R., and B. A. ASKONAS, 1972. Senescence of an Antibody-Forming Cell Clone, *Nature,* 238:337–339.

PART V

RECONSTITUTIVE, SELF-ORGANIZING SYSTEMS

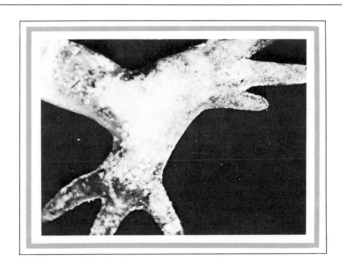

Metamorphosis

Reconstitution and transformation are primarily concerned with the whole organism. Analytic studies therefore pertain to the highest levels of organization. The diversity of forms available for such studies is immense. Relatively few have been investigated intensively. The following chapters present an assortment of topics, including metamorphosis in animals, polymorphic development, and reconstitutive phenomena.

The developmental system, seen as a continuously maintained although progressively elaborating and changing organization, the very molecules of which are in perpetual flux as long as life persists, is a reality whose essence is elusive. Yet any change in the genetic information appears as some sort of change in the developmental outcome, and any subtance to which cells and tissues are sensitive can alter the course in some degree. Hormones, which are themselves the products of development, have such a role and act on cells and tissues in various ways to modify or modulate the timing and direction of events. Yet no more than the so-called inductors, organizers, and organ-forming substances of the embryo can they be considered to be truly developmentally instructive.

The most spectacular shifts in the precise control of growth and form in a rapidly changing developmental system, in both animals and plants, are the metamorphoses seen in the developmental cycle of many marine invertebrates, in the holometabolous insects and anuran amphibians, and in the initiation of flowering in the higher plants. These events are both challenging and potentially enlightening. Attention focuses mainly on the nature of the target tissue on the one hand and on the nature of the triggering, usually hormonal, agents on the other. It should be kept in mind, however, that hormonal activity in a developing system is possible only in organisms already sufficiently developed to produce hormones. Hormones are unlikely to be present in embryonic stages, nor are they likely to be operative at the time of metamorphosis of the small larval organisms of marine invertebrates such as sea urchins and ascidians.

Metamorphosis is a widespread developmental phenomenon. It is usually associated with a dramatic change in habitat and consequent way of life, such as the change from a planktonic to a benthic existence in the sea urchin, from an aquatic to a terrestrial existence in frogs and toads, and from nonflying to a flying existence in insects. Such changes in environment and activities demand equally rapid transformations of the structure and function of the living machinery.

METAMORPHOSIS AND EVOLUTION

The general significance of the more specialized types of marine larvae has long been debated. An early, generally discarded interpretation is that they represent ontogenetic relics of ancient ancestral types. Eggs, being conservative, do retain old ways of doing things. But the generally accepted current belief is that echinoderm larvae, ascidian tadpoles, and nemertean larvae are evolutionary inventions interpolated into an originally more direct developmental cycle. The various special types of insect larvae are similarly regarded. On the other hand, amphibian larvae, both anuran and urodele, are almost certainly retentions of an ancestral type of larva, with some modern improvements. They are retained because of persisting advantages, for amphibians, of continuing to develop and grow in their primitive freshwater environment.

Each group presents a developmental-evolutionary problem. In the first, which includes the marine invertebrates and the insects, the nature of the egg and the genome have been changed from that associated with a relatively more direct development to a more complicated course. The development of the egg is forced into a new path to yield a viable organism strikingly different from the adult; this is accomplished without harming the capacity to develop the adult organization. In the second group, the amphibians, the genome (and the egg as a whole) has evolved so as to produce a terrestrial tetrapod in place of an ancestral lobe-finned fish. It has done so without changing the particular character of the early freshwater vertebrate type of egg, which follows the old developmental path for a considerable developmental distance.

In both groups a dual system of development is very evident. In both groups the egg exhibits a specific early organization that relates to the development of the first of the two organismal stages. In one group this special organization has been added to the primary developmental process leading to the mature adult. In the other group a comparable organization has been retained as an inheritance of an ancient type. In terms of development, the two situations have much in common, although they are different enough to call for separate discussion.

Several fundamental developmental, and evolutionary, problems accordingly confront us. The development of an organism adapted to two very different environments at different times during its life span implies the operation of two sets of environmental selection pressures. Whatever such selection for functional phenotypes may have been, an internal developmental selection of genotypes may well have been the primary factor in determining evolutionary direction. In the examples of metamorphic life cycles just mentioned, at least two effective genotypes, i.e., two virtually independent sets, exist together in the same genome.

METAMORPHIC TRANSFORMATION

Transformation during development is typical of most animals. In many, where no radical change in life style occurs, the course of development may be a gradual, progressive change from one condition to another. Or the change may be sudden but not so superficially remarkable that it goes by the name of metamorphosis. Such is the shift from fetal structures and adaptations to postnatal life in human beings and other mammals. Metamorphic change during the developmental cycle is an acceleration or condensation of essentially the same basic processes characteristic of most forms of development. Primarily it consists of the differential destruction of certain tissues, accompanied by an increase in growth and differentiation of other tissues. This is seen in spectacular form in the development of the starfish (Fig. 22.1). A bilaterally symmetrical larval form, (the bipinnaria larva) designed for living as a plankton organism, is replaced by a radially symmetrical bottom-living type of organism that has developed within the larva.

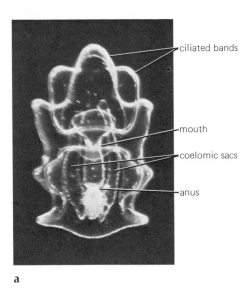

a

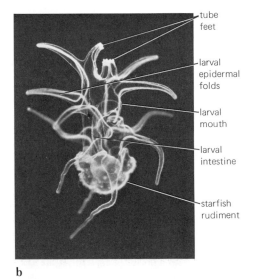

b

Figure 22.1 Metamorphosis during development of the starfish *Asterias. a* Bipinnaria larva with extensive ectodermal ridges bearing locomotory cilia and intestine, all exhibiting a bilateral symmetry. *b* Older bipinnaria larva with rudiment of juvenile starfish forming from portions of internal tissues and exhibiting a radial symmetry; the two organizations coexist for a while as a dual planktonic organism. *c* Fully metamorphosed stage, as a benthic (bottom-living) juvenile starfish with arms yet undeveloped, larval tissues resorbed or sloughed off, and clearly radially symmetrical. [*Courtesy of D. P. Wilson.*]

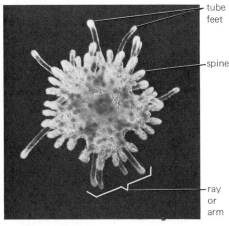

c

471

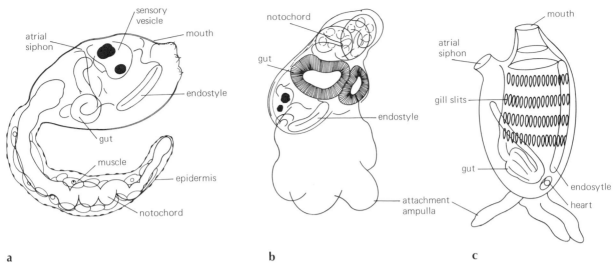

Figure 22.2 Metamorphosis in an ascidian. *a* Metamorphosing tadpole showing resorbing tail. *b* Attached metamorphosing tadpole, with tail nearly completely resorbed. *c* Fully metamorphosed ascidian with functional internal filter system, showing inhalant siphon (mouth) and exhalant siphon.

Among lower chordate animals, metamorphosis occurs in dramatic form in ascidians, particularly with regard to absorption of the tail. At the time of fertilization, the ascidian egg is essentially programmed to develop into a tadpole larva. All the specializations of the egg appear to be related to this production. Yet not all of the egg is directed to this process, for some features of the permanent, or adult-type, organism slowly develop during the rapid formation of the tadpole structure. When the period of larval activity comes to an end, however, and larval tissue is resorbed (Fig. 22.2), the residual takes a great leap forward, so to speak. It is released from the dominating presence of tadpole organization and at the same time receives a new nutrient supply in the form of autolyzed tadpole-tail tissue. The factors that trigger tail resorption of the tadpole, which is the most striking feature of ascidian metamorphosis, are still unknown. The active role of contractile microfilaments in the contraction, or resorption, of epidermis and notochord of the tail has been demonstrated in many species of ascidians by Cloney and by Lash.

INSECT METAMORPHOSIS

Insects, in both egg and adult form, have become fully terrestrial. The most primitive insects lay small but yolky eggs on land, which develop directly to the adult state without passing through special larval stages or through a process of metamorphosis. Special larval forms, especially those of holometabolous insects (those that undergo pupation), are relatively new evolutionary inventions interpolated into the originally direct course of development. This holometabolous transformation is surely as radical an alteration of form as graces the animal kingdom. The extraordinary fact is that a caterpillar hatches from the egg of a butterfly; the subsequent change of the caterpillar into the butterfly is merely the return of the metamorphosed young to the form of its parents. The transformation of the caterpillar is a visible event reenacted with each generation. The legs of a caterpillar, for example, are not primitive structures representing an early step in the development of the adult legs, because the legs of the adult exist within the larva as distinct structures, segregated off as imaginal discs. The larval legs serve as legs but are relatively new structures evolved for the special conditions of larval life and are sacrificed in the return toward the ancestral form.

Developmental Cycle

The eggs of the large *Cecropia* silkworm moth hatch as larvae after 10 days; they subsequently molt four times as they grow some 5,000-fold to mature as fifth-instar larvae, all the while transforming leaves into silkworm. They then enter pupation; the pupa is enclosed in a cocoon (Fig. 22.3).

The completion of the cocoon signals the beginning of a new and even more remarkable sequence of events. On the third day after a cocoon is finished, a great wave of death and destruction sweeps over the internal organs of the caterpillar. The specialized larval tissues break down. But meanwhile, certain more or less discrete clusters of cells, tucked away here and there in the body, begin to grow rapidly, nourishing themselves on the breakdown products of the dead and dying larval tissues. These are the imaginal discs, which throughout larval life have been slowly enlarging within the caterpillar. Their spurt of growth now shapes the organism according to a new plan. New organs arise from the discs. Also, some less specialized larval tissues, such as the epidermal layer of the abdomen, are transformed directly into pupal tissues. Pupation is followed by a developmental standstill, a diapause, lasting 8 months. This device allows the pupa to survive the winter and emerge at an appropriate time the following spring.

Then comes a second period of intense morphogenetic activity. The result is a predictable pattern of death and birth at the cellular level as the specialized tissues of the pupa make way for the equally specialized tissues of the adult moth. Spectacular changes occur throughout all parts of the insect: in the head, the formation of compound eyes and featherlike antennae; in the thorax, the molding of legs, wings, and flight muscles; in the abdomen, the shaping of genitalia and, internally, the exorbitant growth of ovaries and testes. In the newly formed skin we can witness the strangest behavior of all—the extrusion and transformation of tens of thousands of individual cells into the colorful but lifeless scales so typical of moths and butterflies. After 3 weeks of adult development, the process is complete (Fig. 22.4). The full-fledged moth escapes from the cocoon and unfurls its wings.

Extent and Timing of Metamorphosis

The many orders of insects show a great variation in life cycles. Of the winged orders, the exopterygote insects have wings that develop internally, as in stone flies, termites, dragonflies, cockroaches, and locusts. All these insects have a series of larval stages that lack wings and have immature reproductive systems. They exhibit a gradual transition to the winged, sexually mature adult, a process called *incomplete metamorphosis*. Each nymphal stage molts into the next stage, which may have slightly more developed wing buds and reproductive system. The greatest change even in this general type, however, is seen at the last, or nymphal-adult, molt, when a dramatic growth of wings and reproductive systems takes place.

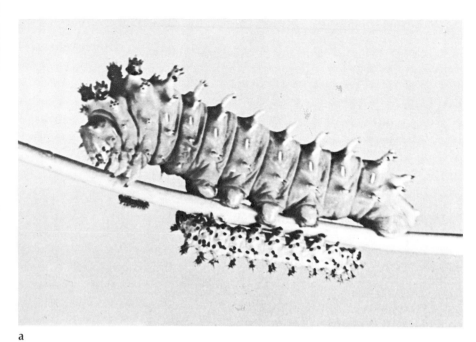

a

Figure 22.3 Life history of the *Cecropia* silkworm. *a* First-, third-, and fifth-instar larvae. *b* Larval-instar larva hatching from egg. *c* Larval-pupal molt within cocoon. *d* Pupa within cocoon. *e* Adult male. [*Courtesy of L. I. Gilbert.*]

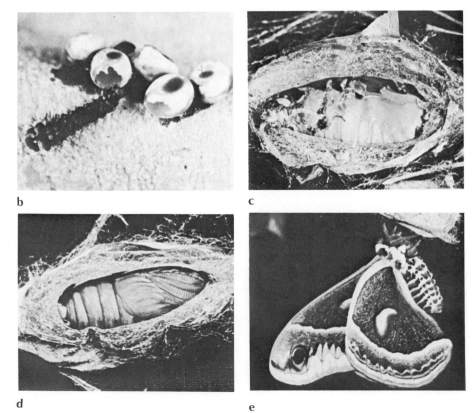

b

c

d

e

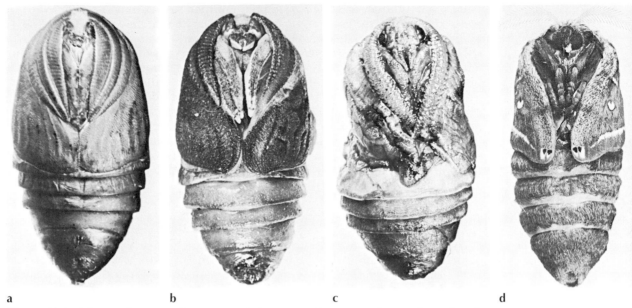

Figure 22.4 Advanced stages of pupation of *Cecropia* silkworm. *a, b* Female and male pupae. *c, d* Later stage of female and male pupae, respectively. [*Courtesy of L. I. Gilbert.*]

The other group of winged insects are the endopterygotes, with wings and other structures developing internally in invaginated imaginal epidermal pockets. They include moths and butterflies, bees and wasps, flies, and others. Metamorphosis is described as complete. Larval stages lack any external evidence of wings and reproductive organs. The transformation into the adult is a two-step process, the fourth or fifth instar, or larval stage, molting into a pupa and the pupa into an adult. In all members of this group of insect orders, not only are reproductive systems, wings, and compound eyes present in the adult and absent in younger, larval stages; but with changes in feeding habits, extensive changes occur in mouth parts and intestine, while muscle requirements may be drastically different in larva and adult. No system, in fact, remains unaffected by the metamorphic changes occurring during the pupal stages.

Preparation for the development of the adult organization is seen, however, in very early development stages, mainly as the segregation of imaginal buds or discs. They represent a consortium of prospective organ structures, awaiting the time of metamorphosis for their potential to be released. In all insects the role of the juvenile hormone is the same, that of blocking the factors responsible for differentiation of tissues into adult forms. The insect hormones appear to be primarily concerned with the timing of events rather than with determination of their character. Whatever the mechanisms involved, they are primarily triggering agents or inhibiting agents of processes that are set to go.

Temporal control of hormones, however, must itself be under control, but under the control of what? It has been known for some time that a momentary exposure of *Drosophila* embryos to light leads to hatching on another day at the same hour as that of the exposure. A biological clock of some sort clearly is involved. Harker (1965) studied timing during pupation in *Drosophila*, particularly with regard to the time taken to complete three developmental stages, namely, eversion of the head to the appearance of yellow eye, from yellow eye to wing pigmentation, and from wing pigmentation to hatching (eclosion). Pupae were kept under different light conditions: 12-hour light—12-hour darkness; 12-hour bright light—12-hour dim light; and continuous darkness. In another experiment, she used 12-hour light—12-hour darkness; 4-hour light—20-hour darkness; and 18-hour light—5-hour darkness. The duration of each stage is affected by the time of day, relative to the light cycle, when the stage is entered. The rate of development of a pupa entering a stage during the light period is related to the time interval since the light "on" period; the preceding dark period has no effect. Since the developmental rates are maintained even in constant darkness, the rate is affected by factors that follow a diurnal rhythm. The form of the rhythm is apparently determined by both "on" and "off" signals, but the *timing* is determined by the two signals acting independently of each other. This is clearly an unfinished story.

Molting and the Molting Hormone

Insects have been studied mainly with regard to their external features and structures, which consist of cuticle laid down by a single layer of epidermal cells. Internal organ systems are as important to the insect as to any other animal but are even less amenable to experimental, developmental, or genetic studies. It seems, therefore, that in the insect the epidermis is the chief agent of morphogenesis, although our ignorance may be bliss and seeing is believing. However this may be, the general characters of the cuticle change in successive stages of growth. Since the cuticle is a mosaic made up of the contributions of each individual epidermal cell, the growth activity of each cell, at each stage of the whole developmental history, is firmly registered in the characters of the little patch of cuticle it lays down. And since the cells constituting the single epidermal sheet not only lay down cuticle, a process incompatible with cell division, but are also responsible for growth and change of form, which requires cell multiplication, these two processes do not occur at the same time. Accordingly the growth of insects takes place in cycles, in which mitosis and cellular growth alternate with the deposition of a new cuticle and the shedding of the old, i.e., in molting cycles. All insects are subject to this pattern of growth and its restraints.

The sequence of events is under precise hormonal control. In brief, certain stimuli associated with the state of nourishment cause the brain to discharge the "brain hormone" from the neurosecretory cells of the pars intercerebralis. This hormone in turn activates the endocrine organ known as the *prothoracic gland,* which then secretes the molting hormone, *ecdysone.*

Ecdysone is a cyclic compound of small molecular size. Just as the same thyroid hormones are produced in all classes of vertebrates, the hormone ecdysone is produced by all insects and other arthropods that have been investigated. Molting cycles are characteristic of all classes of arthropods. Ecdysone extracted from insects causes molting in shrimps, while ecdysone from shrimps causes molting in insects. It is an activator of a nonspecific type. The growth and molting cycles of an insect are more specifically controlled, however, by a third hormone, the juvenile hormone (Fig. 22.5), secreted by the corpora allata. They are endocrine glands located near the brain. A general pattern of hormonal control in insects accordingly emerges, although there are differences among insect groups.

In *Drosophila melanogaster*, during the prepupal period. the imaginal discs are converted in a matter of hours into the basic form of the adult insect. There are extensive gross morphological changes involving the evagination of the

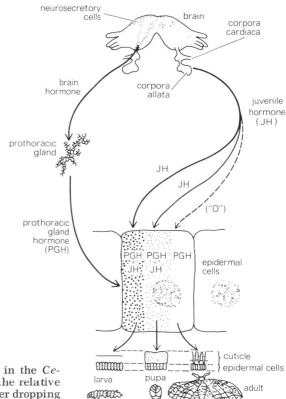

Figure 22.5 The endocrine control of growth and molting in the *Cecropia* silkworm. The nature of the molt is determined by the relative levels of the two hormones, PGH (ecdysone) and JH, the latter dropping steadily through the life cycle. [*After Schneiderman and Gilbert, 1959.*]

appendages, fusion of the discs into a continuous sheet of tissue, and formation of the cuticle. Discs invaginated in pockets during larval life evaginate at the onset of metamorphosis. Evagination and RNA synthesis in the discs can be evoked in vitro by ecdysone.

Differential response must be a property of the target tissues. For example, many of the cells of the epidermis are highly differentiated and are no longer capable of division or of renewal of the cell cycle; other cells lying between the groups of specialized cells remain dormant or undifferentiated.

Under the impact of ecdysone, at each molt the old cuticle is loosened and thrown off, the specialized epidermal cells are resorbed or discarded, and the ordinary epidermal cells that have been stimulated to grow and divide give rise to new cuticle and to new groups of specialized cells. In fact, ecdysone acts directly upon those cells that are in a state of dormancy. Within a few hours the nucleolus is enlarging, RNA begins to accumulate in the cytoplasm, and mitochondria enlarge and multiply by subdivision. By the time the old cuticle is thrown off, the renewed epidermal growth has been virtually completed, with locally expanded regions folded compactly while awaiting release from cuticular confinement. Remarkably, the muscles of the larva, e.g., of *Rhodnius*, dedifferentiate between molts and redifferentiate muscle fibers shortly before the next molt occurs. To a degree the organism is renewed on each occasion and may therefore be said to undergo a degree of metamorphosis. As a general but not absolute rule, molting occurs each time the volume of the growing animal doubles. Such is the cyclic basis of growth, which underlies the more spectacular changes commonly seen in the life history of many insects and crustaceans.

In holometabolous insects, whether fruit flies or giant saturniid silk moths, the life cycle consists of usually four of five larval molts, a larval-pupal molt, and a pupal-adult molt. The larval-pupal-adult transformations constitute an extensive metamorphosis. In the silkworms metamorphosis is usually interrupted soon after pupation by a prolonged pupal diapause, during which development usually ceases. Sexual maturation, which is a part of metamorphosis, occurs during the construction of the adult during pupation. Six stages follow the hatching of the embryo: four (in some, five) larval stages (or instars), the pupation phase, and the mature adult. The intermittent molting, with its discard of the old and replacement with the new, allows control both of phase duration and of remodeling during the span of individual life. In the absence of ecdysone, for instance, the insect lapses into a state of development standstill. When ecdysone is again secreted, this state, the diapause, is terminated and growth is resumed.

The dual nature of the development of the egg is evident and important. On the principle of first come, first served, the embryonic development leads directly to the formation and function of the insect larva—whether it be the so-called nymph of a grasshopper (resembling its parent except dimensionally and in the absence of wings), the dragonfly nymph (remarkably different from the adult in being adapted to aquatic life), or the grub or caterpillar (which must be entirely remodeled as a pupa).

In every case the developing system, having been diverted to some degree during embryonic development, moves toward expression of the adult organization. The adult organization is latent but ready-to-go, so to speak. The hormonal controls operate to determine when the major event occurs, to what extent development can be temporarily arrested, and how long juvenile states may be prolonged. For example, in the presence of the prothoracic gland hormone (PGH), juvenile hormone (JH) promotes larval development or maintains the *status quo* and so prevents metamorphosis. The presence of JH in an immature insect, whether larva or pupa, ensures that when the immature insect molts, it retains its larval or pupal characters and does not differentiate into an adult. When the insect molts in the absence of JH, it differentiates into an adult. In other words, withdrawal of JH initiates metamorphosis. Conversely, implantation of the JH-secreting gland from a second-stage larva to a fourth-stage larva maintains the larval state, in effect inhibiting metamorphosis, so that larval growth continues and a giant larva is produced (Fig. 22.6*d*).

Quantitative differences are as significant as the extremes of presence and absence, as is seen in the response of epidermal cells to JH. When the larval epidermis molts in response to ecdysone (PGH), the response varies as follows:

1   In the presence of a high concentration of JH, the cells secrete larval cuticle.

2   In the presence of a low concentration of JH, the epidermal cells secrete a pupal cuticle.

3   In the absence of JH, the epidermal cells secrete the adult, or imaginal, cuticle directly and omit the pupal molt.

Moreover, if the corpora allata are removed in the last larval stage of the honeybee or the *Cecropia,* for instance, instead of a normal pupa appearing, a

Figure 22.6 Experiments on effect of molting hormone on pupa size. *a, b* Dwarf pupae of moth, resulting from the removal of the corpus allatum (source of the molting hormone) from third- and fourth-instar larvae. *c* A normal pupa. *d* A giant pupa produced by implanting an extra corpus allatum from a young larva into one that had already reached the stage at which it would normally pupate.

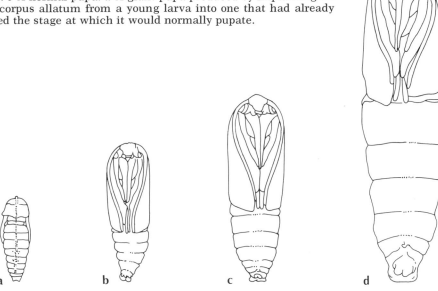

monstrous form intermediate between a pupa and an adult is developed. However, if these glands are surgically removed during one of the earlier stages, the larvae undergo precocious pupation at the very next stage and eventually develop into midget-sized adult insects. The larval form is developed in the presence of a high concentration, the pupa in the presence of a very low concentration, and the adult when the hormone is completely absent.

Pupal Reorganization

Metamorphosis in the insect in its complete form is complex indeed, for there is a relatively great disruption of old tissues and a correspondingly great degree of new development. Moreover, not only is there much variability among different insects, but in every case each tissue in the assembly that constitutes a larva undergoes changes particular to its own character. The cells of some tissues commit suicide. In others, they may multiply, for example, to give rise to a new intestine in place of the old. Or they may have persisted throughout larval life as undifferentiated, though not undetermined, cells of imaginal buds or discs and be permitted at last to fulfill their destiny. Within the confines of the pupal epidermis, the broken-down tissues yield a veritable nutritive soup. This promotes massive proliferation and reconstructive processes by the less specialized cells that survive the cellular massacre or mass suicide, whichever it may be.

Two main types of larval tissue have been recognized with regard to growth and metamorphosis. Many tissues grow by increase in cell size and undergo disintegration at metamorphosis; the corresponding adult tissue is formed from imaginal discs that were not functional parts of the larval tissue. In the second class, tissues grow by cell division and are carried over, with or without modification, into the adult. Some other tissues behave in a manner intermediate between these two methods.

The muscle system is a case in point. In some of the more primitive orders, the majority of larval muscles are carried over into the adult stage. On the other hand, in the thorax of the honeybee, for example, no larval muscles remain unchanged, although most of them are associated with the development of adult muscles. In general, metamorphosis involves the destruction of some larval muscles, the rebuilding of others, and the formation of muscles that were never represented in the larva. In muscles that disappear, the cross-striations are lost, fiber bundles lose their connections and separate, nuclear membranes disappear, and nuclei degenerate. Only when the tissue is disintegrating do phagocytes pick up the pieces. The rebuilding of a muscle from larva to adult involves the replacement of large nuclei (which have multiplied by amitosis) by smaller nuclei, which multiply by mitosis and have been sheltered in the larval muscle. At metamorphosis the large nuclei degenerate. Each of the small nuclei becomes enclosed in a small bag of myoplasm, thus forming the myoblasts, which construct new adult muscles.

A comparable situation is seen in the reconstruction of the intestine, in the mosquito, for example. Larval growth is accomplished solely by increase in cell size. At metamorphosis the adult tissue is formed by the simultaneous division, reduction in size, and increase in number of these same larval cells. The great increase in size of the intestinal cells, associated with larval growth as a whole, is accompanied by replication of chromosomes in the individual cell, with the largest cells having as many as 32 sets of chromosomes. During metamorphosis these cells divide until daughter cells are produced having the normal diploid sets. The new cell population gives rise to the new intestine of adult character.

Other types of tissues have cells which grow large but do not divide during larval growth, although the tissues may be augmented by growth of associated small reserve cells. These tissues also undergo excessive chromatin replication but of a different sort. Such cells do not subdivide at metamorphosis; characteristically they suffer cell death, and they may or may not be replaced, depending on organ function.

Hormones and Gene Activation

Giant interphase chromosomes occur in the highly differentiated giant cells of Dipteran larval and adult tissues. They have been much exploited as material for gene activation studies, particularly by Beerman and subsequent workers. They are enclosed in a typical nucleus and attain a length of at least 10 times, and a cross section of up to 10,000 times that of normal univalent interphase chromosomes. These chromosomes are polytene. That is, they are multivalent in the fashion of a rope consisting of thousands of strands, as a result of repeated chromatid replication (up to 14 times) without mitotic contraction and separation (Fig. 22.7). A peculiar type of local structural change occurs in giant chromosomes, which is called *puffing*. Puffing as such is a function of single bands (or pairs of bands, or bands in conjunction with adjacent interbands). A close correlation exists between puffing of specific chromomeres and the developmental state of the cell.

The giant chromosomes of the salivary glands have opened the door to a visualization of the process of gene activation, particularly in relation to metamorphic events. Just before pupation, the salivary glands show a sharp change in their synthetic activity, secreting a brownish fluid in place of their previously clear secretion. At the same time striking changes occur in the pattern of

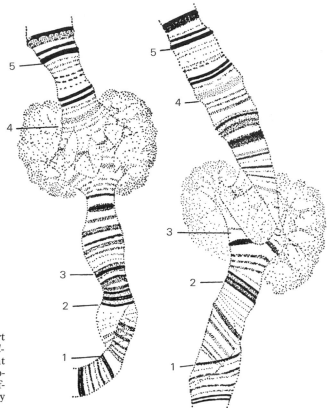

Figure 22.7 Puffing in insect chromosomes. A short section of one of the chromosomes of a fly, *Trichocladius*, from a cell of a salivary gland. Five prominent bands (numbered) can be recognized in each chromosome. The same chromosome region is seen from different lobes of the salivary gland, showing a strikingly different pattern. [*After Beerman, 1966.*]

puffing of the giant chromosomes. Most of the puffs that had been prominent during larval life now collapse, the DNA strands seeming to fold back into the chromosome to re-form compact bands. Meanwhile new puffs form at a series of other specific loci.

Pupation itself is the response to an increasing concentration of ecdysone and a decreasing concentration of juvenile hormone. When ecdysone is injected into an immature larva, therefore, conditions are established that favor premature pupation, which then takes place. In this experiment, 2 hours after the injection of ecdysone, the pattern of puffing in the salivary glands shows a changeover from the larval to the pupal type. Accordingly, the primary effect of ecdysone is to alter the activity of specific genes, and this action is documented in the giant chromosomes. Cells are made to undertake synthetic acts accompanied by derepression and utilization of fresh genetic information.

The correlation between ecdysone level and the puffing of the giant chromosomes indicates some sort of connection but says little concerning its nature. Does ecdysone, or any other hormone, exert its effect partly or wholly by intervening with the pattern of information retrieval from the genome? By what mechanism do the relatively small and simple molecules exert such complicated and fundamental effects? How is the transition from the use of one set of information to another instigated in all cells of an organism? The question is raised whether ecdysone and juvenile hormone exert their effects partly or entirely through intervention with the patterns of information retrieval. What is their mechanism of action? Studies have been made on isolated cells and tissue in culture employing ecdysone at a critical level as the test substance. Little has been done with juvenile hormone. It is postulated that ecdysone causes a cell to accumulate potassium ions, since the primary set of puffs can also be induced without ecdysone by increasing intracellular or intranuclear concentrations of K^+. Accordingly the stimulation of K^+ uptake by cell and by nucleus may be the primary effect of ecdysone (Fig. 22.8). Results are summarized as follows:

1 Within 1 minute after application, the electrical potential difference across the nuclear and cell membranes begins to rise and continues to do so for about 12 minutes, until it reaches a value of about 15 mV (millivolts).

2 Within 15 minutes, isolated nuclei from epidermal cells show a general increase in RNA synthesis.

3 Within 15 to 30 minutes, the "primary set" of puffs appears.

4 Within 60 minutes, the resistance of the nuclear membrane has risen to about twice its original level.

5 Within 65 to 72 hours, the "secondary set" of puffs appears.

6 This is followed by a series of events such as enlargement of nucleoli, swelling of mitochondria, and stimulation of mitosis that precede the actual molt.

Figure 22.8 Probable ecdysone and possible juvenile hormone action. Arrows pointing to transport systems indicate that effectiveness of these systems is modified; this might also be achieved by changes in membrane permeability, leaving the transport systems themselves unaffected. [*After Kroeger, 1968.*]

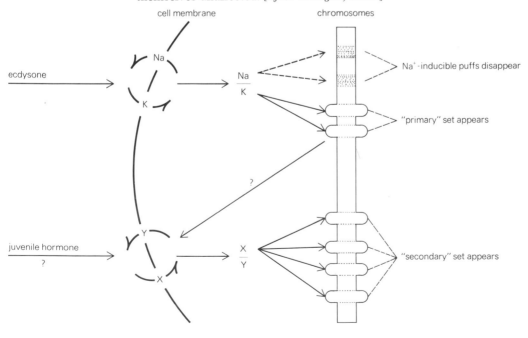

Although the appearance of the primary set of puffs is the first easily demonstrated effect of ecdysone, during normal development this event is preceded by the disappearance of a number of puffs in a specific sequence. These disappearing puffs can be made to reappear by an increase in Na^+ of a salivary-gland cell, suggesting that a lowering of intracellular Na^+ causes these puffs to disappear and that this is another effect of ecdysone in low concentrations. Extreme sensitivity to electrolytic disturbance of the intracellular and intranuclear environment is evident. Clever suggested that mRNA synthesized in the puffs of the primary set directs the synthesis of proteins that alter transport or permeability functions of the cell in such a way that the intracellular solute undergoes further alterations, and that these changes then cause the loci of the secondary set to become puffed. He concluded that molting depends not on the activation of a *pattern* of genes (such as $A + B + C \cdots$) but on activation of a *sequence* of genes ($A \to B \to C \to \cdots$), of which only the first is hormonally activated. However, these are only guidelines. In any case, it is surprising that such a coarse environmental change has such a fine genetic effect. This is a problem not yet understood.

The premise is that most if not all features of a cell are determined by its population of protein molecules. Any fundamental changes in a cell, therefore, might be expected to involve alterations in the composition or activity of its protein pool. In view of the process of DNA→RNA→protein information transfer, the protein complement of a given cell should reflect that set of cistrons in the genome that is being transcribed. Therefore, if only part of the information stored in the genome is used at a given time, the most efficient way of doing this would be to allow some cistrons to form messenger RNA while others are kept inactive. Thus in autoradiographic experiments, one would expect to find RNA synthesized at certain loci, but not at others.

Experiments on the giant chromosomes of cells of salivary gland excretory tubules and on the midgut of dipterans, using tritium-labeled RNA-precursor molecules and autoradiography, show that some regions incorporate more labeled precursors than others, and that the synthesized material is RNA. They also show that for the same *organ* taken from animals at the same developmental stage, *this pattern is constant*. The pattern is tissue- and stage-specific. Accordingly RNA synthesis is discontinuous along the axis of the giant chromosomes. The active regions are seen as puffs, made up of DNA, RNA, and protein, the DNA being much less tightly coiled than elsewhere. The RNA produced in the puffs appears to migrate through the nuclear sap and into the cytoplasm in the form of ribonucleoprotein granules. They are thought to consist of ribosomal precursors and other ribonucleoprotein particles associated with messenger RNA.

It has been shown by Beerman and others that production of secretory granules in the apical cells of salivary glands is correlated with the appearance of a subterminal puff on the third chromosome. This suggests that the puff produces RNA essential for specific synthesis of secretion granules by apical cells. More recent investigations of the proteins released into the lumen of the gland disclose certain apical cell-specific varieties, possibly coded during RNA synthesis under control of the puff.

By comparing puffing patterns from different stages of development and from different tissues, one can determine whether genomic-activity patterns change during development and whether they are tissue-specific. Puffs appear and disappear, ranging from barely discernible to 20 bands. They begin to form at a single band but progressively incorporate neighboring bands, which suggests that during puff development more and more cistrons are stimulated

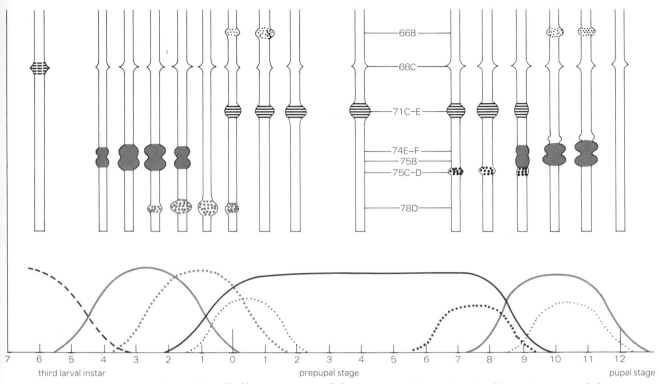

Figure 22.9 Puffs appearing and disappearing during the third larval instar and the pre-pupal stage at the base of chromosome arm 111 L of *Drosophila melanogaster* salivary glands. Numbers indicate hours before or after puparium formation. [*After Becker,* Chromosoma, **10**:*654 (1959), by permission of Springer-Verlag.*]

to deliver their information in a sequential way (Fig. 22.9). About 10 percent of the giant chromosome bands are puffed at any one time. Drastic changes in the pattern of puffing occur shortly before the first signs of molt preparation, while during the last larval instar, preceding pupation, 15 percent of the chromosomal bands are puffed at the same time.

Kroeger concludes that those puffs which are present at all times, change their activity little if at all during metamorphosis, and are shared by many or all tissues, are those involved in cellular functions common to all cells, such as respiration, carbohydrate metabolism, and so forth. They form by far the larger group of puffs. In contrast, the smaller group of puffs that appear and disappear in preparation for a molt may mediate the less common chemical reactions characteristic of a specific step in metamorphosis. It seems, therefore, that the genome exerts permanent control over the chemical and morphological events that occur in the cytoplasm during metamorphosis.

The hormonal message therefore appears to act at two sites. At the *cell membrane* it causes an alteration of the intracellular and intranuclear electrolyte media. At the *chromosomal* level this shift in milieu is translated into a differential pattern of mRNA synthesis. The following questions are crucial:

1 Which part of the cell is dispensable, and which part is necessary for the formation of those coherent patterns that occur during development and may be termed "strategic patterns"?

2 At what site or by what interaction of cell parts is this "strategy" elaborated? Is coordination a purely nuclear process, arising, for example, by an interaction of chromosomal sites, or do cytoplasm and gene cooperate in activating any single site on the chromosome?

Since transplantation of cytoplasm of nerve tissue from the excretory (Malpighian) tube into the cytoplasm of salivary-gland cells does *not* alter the puffing pattern of the host cell but rolls it back to a more juvenile pattern, tissue-specific patterns are *not* elicited by the cytoplasm. That isolated salivary-gland nuclei can also undergo a similar rollback shows that a cell nucleus devoid of all observable cytoplasm can form a more juvenile pattern and implies that strategy is purely nuclear. Moreover, when as many as three-quarters of the chromosomes or chromosome parts are removed from isolated salivary-gland cells, rollback changes still occur, showing that strategy does not involve mutual interaction of chromosomes.

METAMORPHOSIS IN AMPHIBIANS

The amphibian egg and larva are, in their general organization, clearly a retention of an ancient ancestral type, serving only while development proceeds in the original freshwater environment. Amphibian metamorphosis is in essence a release or activation of the genomic set underlying the adult organization, which requires for its expression a mass of tissue that is minimal but greater than that of the egg. Concomitantly the genomic support for the larval organization is withdrawn and specifically larval tissues resorb. Frogs, toads, and, in a less spectacular way, urodeles transform from an aquatic gill-breathing larva to a lung-breathing terrestrial animal. The general course of development through this life cycle is well known (Fig. 22.10). Two transformations take place:

1 Certain adaptive structures formed during embryonic development—namely, the ventral suckers and the external gills of the anuran tadpole and the balancers of the urodele larva—are resorbed during early functional life. These are merely resorptions of precociously formed structures; they are not a part of the general metamorphic event, which occurs much later, and in anurans includes the resorption of the tail. They disappear when they have served their purpose.

2 Almost every organ system of the frog undergoes alterations during metamorphosis. Before the onset of metamorphosis, the tadpole, a vegetarian, is a fully aquatic creature with well-developed gills, a long flattened tail, lidless eyes, horny rasping teeth, and a long coiled intestine. After the completion of metamorphosis the froglet, no heavier and usually somewhat lighter than the tadpole that gave rise to it, is a lung-breathing creature with no tail, with well-developed limbs, with eyelids, and with teeth, gut, and other structures associated with its carnivorous habits. Even structures that persist into the adult undergo changes. For instance, the skin thickens, becomes more glandular, attains an outer keratinized layer, and acquires a characteristic pattern of pigmentation. The brain becomes more highly differentiated. At the cellular level, cell modifications are evident in eyelids, limbs, lungs, tongue, eardrum, operculum, skin, liver, pancreas, and intestine. Horny teeth are lost, and the tail and the larval cloaca atrophy. Probably no cell or tissue or organ remains entirely unaffected.

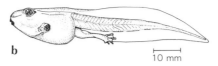

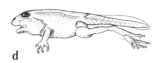
1 mm

10 mm

Figure 22.10 Typical anuran metamorphosis (*Rana pipiens*). *a* Premetamorphic tadpole. *b* Prometamorphic tadpole (growth of hindlimbs). *c* Onset of the metamorphic climax (eruption of forelimbs, retraction of tail fin). *d, e* Climax stages, showing gradual appearance of the froglike organization.

Biochemical Changes.

At the same time many physiological and biochemical changes take place. According to Frieden, the biochemical alterations may be considered to have direct adaptive value or to serve as a basis for morphological, chemical, or other changes that have adaptive value relating to the change from freshwater to land. For example, among the most important adaptive changes are the shift from ammonotelism to ureotelism (i.e., from the excretion of ammonia to the excretion of urea), the increase in serum albumin and other serum proteins, and the alteration in the properties and biosynthesis of hemoglobins. The development of certain digestive enzymes and the augmentation of respiration also contribute to the success of the differentiation process. During metamorphosis, there are many additional important chemical developments, which may be secondary to the primary morphological or cytological transformations that aid in the adjustment to land. These include alterations in carbohydrate, lipid, nucleic acid, and nitrogen metabolism. Major modifications in water balance, visual pigments (vitamin A), pigmentation, and tail metabolism are also observed. Finally, there is a partial mobilization of the enzyme machinery to promote the metamorphic process and the colonization of the land.

It is not yet certain whether the frog and the tadpole enzymes differ in their basic subunits or whether they are made up of the same subunits but in different proportions. The synthesis of what seems to be a new enzyme during metamorphosis of the tadpole to the frog, with each enzyme serving in what appears to be the same metabolic role, indicates that biochemical differentiation from the stage of the fertilized ovum to the tadpole stage involves a different, or modified, genetic expression from that in the biochemical differentiation of the tadpole to the adult frog. A similar situation has been reported for the hemoglobins of the tadpole and frog (Cohen, 1970).

Frogs metamorphose after various periods of growth, according to the species. It was recognized early that the attainment of a critical species-specific size, rather than the duration of growth, is crucial. Thus, in nature, bullfrog tadpoles metamorphose at the end of the third summer-growth season in the North, but at the end of the second in the South, after having attained a certain size. The time required depends on the mean environmental conditions. It has also long been known that adding iodine to the water or feeding with thyroid-gland tissue causes metamorphosis to occur earlier, at a smaller size (Fig. 22.11). Elimination of iodine from the diet postpones it. Conversely, elimination of iodine and therefore of thyroxine by thyroidectomy of the tadpole results in failure of metamorphosis to take place. Nevertheless, such a tadpole may continue to grow and become sexually mature although still a tadpole. This phe-

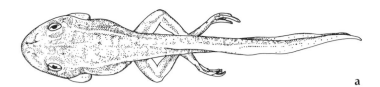
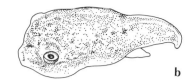
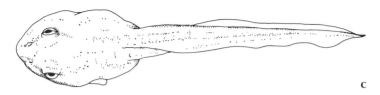

Figure 22.11 Hormones and metamorphosis. *a* Normal metamorphic stage. *b* Premature metamorphosis following exposure of young tadpole to thyroxine. *c* Inhibition of metamorphosis following removal of either the thyroid or the pituitary gland.

nomenon is known as *neoteny*. From the first, therefore, the iodine-containing thyroxine of the thyroid gland has been studied intensively with regard to the timing of metamorphosis and the metabolic effect of the hormone. Any vertebrate hormone, however, is a component in a complex interacting hormonal system, in which pituitary hormones are particularly involved.

In nature, the perennibranchiate or permanently gilled salamanders grow to sexual maturity as permanently aquatic creatures that retain larval features, such as external gills, and do not undergo metamorphosis. Typically they have relatively inactive thyroid glands, and they do not respond to thyroxine or iodine treatment. They are also remarkable in having tissues that consist of comparatively enormous cells, as though the larva had grown to adult size by means of cell enlargement rather than cell proliferation. The phenomenon calls for further analysis.

Hormonal Control

So far, hormone activity in development has been approached in several ways and with regard as much to the development and differentiation of the vertebrate reproductive and other systems as to the questions of metamorphosis.

1 The initial concern is to show that particular hormones influence and participate in the control of differentiation of various target structures, by administration of excess hormone or removal of its source. In the case of thyroxine in relation to amphibian metamorphic events, the task of proving this relationship has been mostly accomplished.

2 A more analytical concern is to identify the specific developmental processes that are subject to hormonal interference during critical periods of development.

3 It is necessary to interpret the hormone action in terms of cellular mechanisms.

4 Finally, and prospectively, efforts are being made to fit the effects of hormones on target tissues with the central doctrine that differentiation reflects the emergence of selective protein synthesis preceded by differential repression or derepression of the coding genes.

487

The hormonal system has been investigated during many years by Etkin, who long ago emphasized that the schedule of metamorphic events depends on the concentration of thyroid hormone, while the *sequence* of the events is inherent in the tissues. Most tissues respond when a critical threshold is reached, but some respond earlier and some later. Thyroid hormone concentration in the blood and tissues of the tadpole gradually increases during the last two-thirds of larval life up to the phase of metamorphic climax, and then undergoes a sudden drop. At a critical point in the development of the tadpole, some factor, presumably controlled by a genetic mechanism, renders the hypothalamus sensitive to the low level of thyroid hormone already circulating in the blood. The hypothalamus is the midventral part of the brain, derived from the infundibulum, which mediates the neural control of the pituitary gland.

The neurosecretory apparatus of the hypothalamus responds by secreting a thyrotropin-releasing factor (TRF), which stimulates the anterior pituitary to secrete a thyroid-stimulating hormone (TSH), which turns on the orderly increase of thyroid secretion. This increase in thyroid hormone then trips the orderly sequence of tissue changes that transform the tadpole into a frog. If the part of the hypothalamus attached to the pituitary is removed, metamorphosis proceeds through the early stages but stops abruptly at the climax. The presence of the hypothalamus seems to be necessary for the completion of metamorphosis. Isolation from the pituitary inhibits the hypothalamus from attaining a high level of TSH activity. Nevertheless, animals thus inhibited continue to grow and may achieve gigantic size.

Etkin and coworkers have shown that another pituitary hormone, prolactin, is also involved (as an inhibitor) in the overall control of metamorphosis (Fig. 22.12).

At the level of endocrine action we again see the developmental control is effected by a balance between inhibition and activation rather than by simple stimulation. The pituitary-thyroid axis is kept at a low level of activity in the growth phase of the tadpole's development by negative feedback, and at metamorphosis its activation is brought about by hypothalamic action. The complexity of this push-pull type of interaction in governing metamorphosis is further emphasized by the discovery of the role of prolactin as a thyroid antagonist in amphibian development. Whether this substance acts at the peripheral level or as a goitrogen or in both ways, its role again emphasizes that development is controlled by a dynamic balance of plus and minus factors. Etkin calls attention to a fascinating aspect of this particular interaction, which is the manner in which it appears to have been exploited as the mechanism for the evolution of a "second metamorphosis" in the common newt.

This urodele, after a typical first metamorphosis that produces the land form, and after a period of growth on land, then undergoes a second metamorphosis for the return to water in order to breed. This second metamorphosis has been shown to be under the influence of prolactin, presumably resulting from a shift in the balance between the pituitary factors, prolactin, and TSH, rather than from an activation of one of them. In other words, the first metamorphosis is induced by a shift in favor of TSH, the second metamorphosis by a return to the predominance of prolactin.

Metamorphosis involves alteration of larval tissues that normally acquire sensitivity to thyroid hormones long before significant quantities of such hormones are released into the circulation. In general, structures that metamorphose early are more sensitive than those that undergo change later. Whether this variation is related to differences in threshold values or to differences in total thyroxine requirements has been in debate. However, by using greatly lowered hormone concentrations for long periods of time, up to a year, Kollros has shown that different tissues have different thresholds. Successive

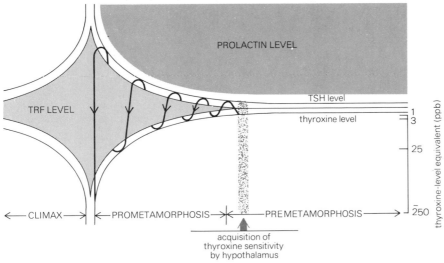

Figure 22.12 The interaction of endocrine factors in determining the time and pattern of anuran metamorphosis. In the early premetamorphic period the thyroxine level is very low; it remains so until just before prometamorphosis begins. At this time, the mechanism of the hypothalamic thyrotropin-releasing factor (TRF) becomes sensitive to positive thyroxine feedback, thereby initiating prometamorphosis. The increase in TRF provoked by the action of the initial thyroxine level on the hypothalamus stimulates increased release of TSH (thyroid-stimulating hormone), which acts in turn to raise the thyroxine level. This leads to a spiraling action which raises the thyroxine level and thereby induces prometamorphosis, with its characteristic sequence of changes. The positive feedback cycle leads to maximal activation of the pituitary-thyroid axis, thereby bringing on metamorphic climax. During early premetamorphosis, prolactin is produced at a high rate (dark shading). With the activation of the hypothalamus, the production of prolactin drops, under the inhibitory influence of hypothalamic activity. As the level of TSH rises during prometamorphosis, that of prolactin decreases. The growth rate of the animal therefore falls, and the metamorphosis-restraining activity of prolactin diminishes. Thus the premetamorphic period, in which growth is active and metamorphosis is inhibited, is characterized by the predominance of prolactin over TSH. The reverse situation exists during metamorphosis. The time of shift in hormone balance is determined by the initiation of positive thyroid feedback to the hypothalamus. This varies greatly among species. The pattern of change during metamorphosis is regulated by the pattern of the feedback buildup and is much the same in most anurans. [*After Etkin, 1968.*]

metamorphic events have different and somewhat higher thresholds from preceding ones.

Thus limb development, inhibited during most of the growth period of the tadpole, apparently needs a progressive booster at a certain stage (Fig. 22.13). This may be associated with the enormous growth that anuran hind limbs finally undergo during metamorphosis, compared with urodele limbs, which remain relatively small and require only developmental release. In the frog, however, as hormone concentrations increase, tissue responses become progressively more rapid, until maximum rates of change are attained. In effect, at high concentrations, all metamorphic events become crowded together, and the time sequence is disturbed; the tail begins to resorb before limbs become well developed, so that without providing means of locomotion and other essential factors, the transformation leads to death.

Difference in tissue sensitivity is seen in a striking form in an early experiment in which an eye cup was transplanted to a tadpole tail, where it differentiated. During metamorphosis the eye moved forward as the tail resorbed and finally came to rest in the sacral region when metamorphosis was complete (Fig. 22.14). Transplanted limbs and transplanted kidney tumor are likewise unaffected by the degenerative processes in the surrounding tail tissue.

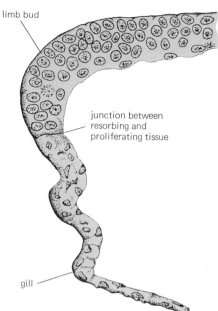

limb bud

junction between
resorbing and
proliferating tissue

gill

Figure 22.13 Differential response of limb-bud
and gill tissue to thyroxine; the line separating
the two districts, one growing, the other degenerating, is very sharp.

Perhaps the most striking single feature of the hormonal control of amphibian metamorphosis is that a single hormone, the low-molecular-weight compound thyroxine, evokes multiple responses from diversified tissues. Responses
are specific although the inducer varies only quantitatively. Moreover, they are
both constructive and destructive, depending on the target tissue. Thus, in
response to triiodothyronine, a companion hormone of thyroxine, biosynthesis of
nucleic acid is decreased in the tail but increased in the liver. Similarly,
thyroxine induces rapid aging and destruction of the red blood cells of the metamorphosing tadpole, which carry tadpole-type hemoglobin; simultaneously (or
later) it stimulates the development of cells that synthesize the adult frog type
of hemoglobin exclusively. The agent is the same, but the response is cell death
and cell proliferation, respectively, in the two erythrocytic cell populations.

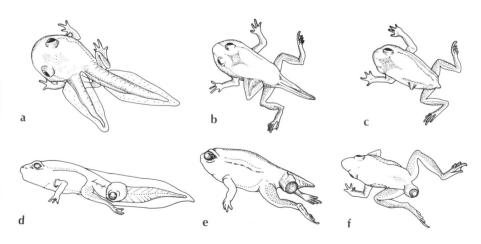

Figure 22.14 Organ specificity of metamorphic
responses in tadpoles. *a–c*
Tail tip transplanted to
the trunk region undergoes
atrophy simultaneously
with the host's tail. [*After
Geigy*, Rev. Suisse Zool.
48:483 (1941).] *d–f* Eye
cup transplanted to the tail
remains unaffected by the
regressing tail tissue.
[*After Schwind, 1933.*]

a   b   c

d   e   f

The problem, therefore, is: What general property of thyroid hormone is responsible for these effects? The association with level of basal metabolism in higher vertebrates suggests that an increase in oxidative metabolism may be the discriminating factor. However, there is no increase in oxygen uptake during spontaneous metamorphosis. On the other hand, a flood of metabolites, resulting from tissue destruction, is immediately available for rapid protein and nucleic acid synthesis.

Tail Resorption

Changes in the fine structure of the tail muscle, involving myofibrils, mitochondria, and sarcoplasm, occur before any appreciable shortening of the tail takes place. Although absence of lysosomes in these cells suggests that such changes do not depend upon contained lysosomal enzymes, lysosomal (phagocytic) digestion accomplishes most of the visible tail resorption (Fig. 22.15). Experimental evidence indicates that thyroid hormone acts directly upon peripheral tissues to accelerate metamorphic changes at both a morphological and a biochemical level.

Tail isolation culture has been used as a model to study the direct metamorphosing action of thyroid hormone at the biochemical level. The process of tail resorption has been investigated in isolated tails or pieces thereof, of *Xenopus* in particular. Isolated tails respond to thyroxine. Involution always begins at

Figure 22.15 Regression of tadpole tail, in metamorphosis of *Xenopus laevis*, is accomplished by lysosomal digestion of cells. As metamorphosis proceeds, the enzyme concentration increases (the absolute amount of enzyme remaining constant). Eventually the stub contains almost nothing but lysosomal enzymes, and it falls off. [*Partly after Etkin, and Weber.*]

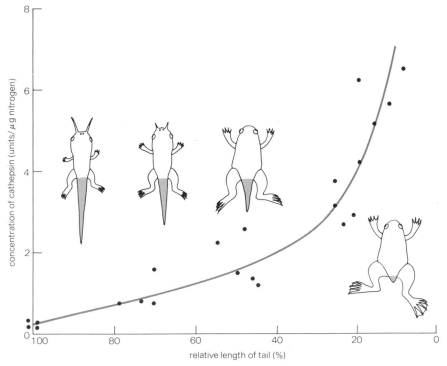

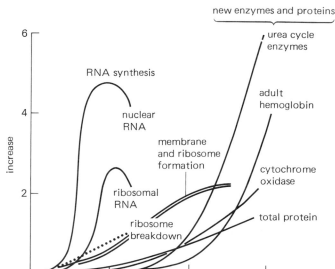

Figure 22.16 Sequential stimulation of rates of RNA and phospholipid synthesis in relation to the increases in enzymes or protein synthesized upon the precocious induction of metamorphosis in *Rana catesbeiana* tadpoles with triiodothyronine. Curves show the rate of rapidly labeled nuclear RNA synthesis; specific activity of RNA in cytoplasmic ribosomes labeled before induction; rate of microsomal phospholipid synthesis; urea cycle enzymes (carbamyl phosphate synthetase); cytochrome oxidase per milligram of mitochondrial protein; appearance of adult hemoglobin in the blood; total liver protein per milligram of wet weight. The values are expressed as percentage increases over those in the noninduced control tadpoles. The decreasing values in curves of RNA synthesis reflect the dilution of specific radioactivity in precursor molecules due to the onset of regression of tissues such as the tail and intestine. [*From J. R. Tata, in "Biochemical Actions of Hormones" (G. Litwack, ed.) vol. 1, pp. 89–133, Academic Press, New York, 1970.*]

the very tip, and the typical pattern of metamorphosis follows: thickening of the epidermis, migration of pigment cells, and involution of notochord, neural tube, and muscle cells.

Inhibition of RNA synthesis with actomycin D or of protein synthesis with puromycin or cycloheximide completely abolished regression that had been induced in tail-organ cultures by triiodothyronine. This indicates that additional RNA and protein synthesis are essential for the process at the onset of regression in cultured tails. A basic question remains: Does the general patterned process of tissue regression and cell death trigger the release of the new phenotypic development, or is the differential destruction of the "juvenile" structure a response to the activation of the new phenotype?

According to Tata (1971), what is perhaps of utmost importance in the study of the sequential events between the initial burst of RNA synthesis, following triiodothyronine adminstration, and the appearance of newly synthesized proteins is the turnover and distribution of ribosomes in the cytoplasm (Fig. 22.16). During this period there is a complex process of breakdown of "old" RNA together with alterations in polysome profiles of the endoplasmic reticulum consisting of (1) a response to growth stimulus contained in newly formed ribosomes and (2) a topographical segregation on the endoplasmic reticulum of differently precoded polyribosomes carrying out the synthesis of different groups of proteins.

PERSPECTIVE ON METAMORPHOSIS

Amphibian metamorphosis accordingly is an important postembryonic developmental process in which nonreproductive structures of the larval form of the amphibian change drastically to an adult form during a brief discrete period.

The change is accompanied by dramatic adaptive changes in numerous biochemical systems, many of which appear to be highly temperature-sensitive and involve genetic control of protein and RNA biosynthesis and their repressors. Two different types of experimental approaches—administration of varying concentrations of thyroxine to tadpoles and analysis of thyroid gland activity during various phases of normal metamorphosis—demonstrate the important controlling role that hormone concentration plays in amphibian metamorphosis. The normal metamorphic pattern is the result of direct specific responses of individual target organs to various concentrations of thyroid hormone. The timing of these responses is due to variations of certain qualities inherent in the tissues. These variations include time of onset of sensitivity as well as threshold and rate of response. The unfolding of metamorphic events as one of the important aspects of cellular differentiation, on the one hand, and as a profound change in the general organization of tissues and organs, on the other, remain fundamental problems for all developmental biologists.

READINGS

BARRINGTON, E. J. W., 1968. Metamorphosis in the Lower Chordates, in W. Etkin and L. Gilbert (eds.), "Metamorphosis," Appleton-Century-Crofts.

——, 1961. Metamorphic Processes in Fish and Lampreys, *Amer. Zool*, **1**:97–106.

BERGER, C. A., 1938. Multiplication and Reduction of Somatic Chromosome Groups as a Regular Developmental Process in the Mosquito, *Culex pipiens, Carnegie Inst. Washington Pub.*, **496**:209–232.

BERRILL, N. J., 1955. "The Origin of Vertebrates," Oxford University Press.

CLEVER, U., 1965. Chromosomal Changes Associated with Differentiation, in "Genetic Control of Differentiation," Brookhaven National Laboratory, Symposium in Biology, no. 18.

CLONEY, R. A., 1961. Observations on the Mechanism of Tail Resorption in Ascidians, *Amer. Zool.*, **1**:67–88.

COHEN, P. P., 1970. Biochemical Differentiation during Amphibian Metamorphosis, *Science*, **168**:533–543.

ETKIN, W., 1968. Hormonal Control of Amphibian Metamorphosis, in W. Etkin and L. Gilbert (eds.), "Metamorphosis," Appleton-Century-Crofts.

——, 1966. How a Tadpole Becomes a Frog, *Sci. Amer.*, May.

FRIEDEN, E., 1961. Biochemical Adaptation and Anuran Metamorphosis, *Amer. Zool.*, **1**:115–150.

GILBERT, L. I., and H. A. SCHNEIDERMAN, 1961. Some Biochemical Aspects of Insect Metamorphosis, *Amer. Zool.*, **1**:11–52.

HARKER, J. E., 1965. The Effect of Photoperiod on the Developmental Rate of *Drosophila* Pupae, *J. Exp. Biol.*, **43**:411–423.

HENSEN, H., 1946. The Theoretical Aspect of Insect Metamorphosis, *Biol. Rev.*, **21**:1–14.

KALTENBACH, J. C., 1968. Nature of Hormone Action in Amphibian Metamorphosis, in W. Etkin and L. Gilbert (eds.), "Metamorphosis," Appleton-Century-Crofts.

KEMP, N. E., 1963. Metamorphic Changes of Dermis in Skin of Frog Larvae Exposed to Thyroxin, *Develop. Biol.*, **7**:244–254.

KOLLROS, J. J., 1961. Mechanisms of Amphibian Metamorphosis, *Amer. Zool.*, **1**:107–114.

KROEGER, H., 1968. Gene Activities during Insect Metamorphosis and Their Control by Hormones, in W. Etkin and L. Gilbert (eds.), "Metamorphosis," Appleton-Century-Crofts.

LAMBERT, C. C., 1971. Genetic Transcription during the Development of the Tunicate *Ascida callosa*, *Exp. Cell Res.*, **66**:401–409.

LASH, J. R., A. CLONEY, and R. R. MINOR, 1973. The Effect of Cytochalasin B upon Tail Resorption and Metamorphosis in Ten Species of Ascidians, *Biol. Bull.*, **145**:360–372.

LISK, R. D., 1971. The Physiology of Hormone Receptors *Amer. Zool.*, **11**:755–768.

LYNN, W. G., 1961. Types of Amphibian Metamorphosis, *Amer. Zool.*, **1**:151–162.

SCHNEIDERMAN, H. A., 1967. Insect Surgery, in F. W. Wilt and N. K. Wessells (eds.), "Methods in Developmental Biology," Crowell.

SCHWIND, J. L., 1933. Tissue Specificity at the Time of Metamorphosis in Frog Larvae, *J. Exp. Zool.*, **66**:1–14.

TATA, J. R., 1971. Hormonal Regulation of Metamorphosis, *Symposium, Soc. Exper. Biol.*, **25**:163–181.

WEBER, R., 1967. Biochemistry of Amphibian Metamorphosis, in R. Weber (ed.), "Biochemistry of Animal Development," vol. II, Academic.

WHITTEN, J., 1968. Metamorphic Changes in Insects, in W. Etkin and L. Gilbert (eds.), "Metamorphosis," Appleton-Century-Crofts.

WHYTE, L. L., 1960. Developmental Selections and Mutations, *Science,* **132**:954, 1694.

WIGGLESWORTH, V. B., 1966. Hormonal Regulation of Differentiation in Insects, in W. Beermann (ed.), "Cell Differentiation and Morphogenesis," North-Holland Publishing Company, Amsterdam.

———, 1959. Metamorphosis and Differentiation, *Sci. Amer.,* February.

WILLIAMS, C. M., 1963. Differentiation and Morphogenesis in Insects, in J. Allen (ed.), "Nature of Biological Diversity," McGraw-Hill.

Regeneration

Virtually all the phenomena and problems associated with development generally, especially those associated with the vertebrate embryo, are inherent in the regeneration of a limb. The development of limb buds, as we have seen, more or less parallels the early development of the embryo as a whole. It begins with an initial and relatively undetermined stage, i.e., the spherical egg or the circular limb disc, with little more than primary polarity, and develops mainly as the result of interactions between epithelial (epidermal) and mesenchymal (mesodermal) tissues, leading to tissue differentiation and pattern elaboration. A comparable event is seen in the reconstitution or regeneration of a part from the whole at later stages of growth and development, even in fully grown and mature organisms. The process of reconstitution of the vertebrate limb accordingly offers further opportunity to analyze the morphogenetic and histogenetic events responsible for the creation of such a structure. The situation differs from embryonic limb development inasmuch as the stump from which a new limb, following amputation, is produced already consists of differentiated cells and tissues. The following account, therefore, extends the analysis of limb development already given and also serves as an introduction to the general phenomenon of regeneration widely encountered among lower animals.

LIMB REGENERATION IN VERTEBRATES

Limb regeneration has been studied mostly in amphibians, particularly in salamanders of various ages. In these forms the limbs are readily regenerated throughout life, although more rapidly when the amphibian is young and small. In fact no other vertebrates exhibit such a wide capacity for regeneration of missing parts, including tail and snout and even the eye to some extent. In the case of the limb, some of the more outstanding earlier experiments are summarized graphically in Fig. 23.6 (see caption).

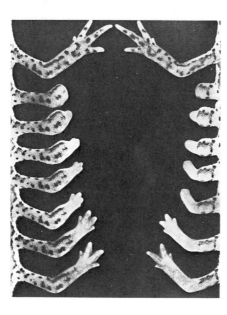

Figure 23.1 Regeneration of forelimb of salamander. (*Left*) Amputation below elbow. (*Right*) Amputation through upper arm. [*Courtesy of R. J. Goss.*]

The Blastema: I

When a limb is amputated, a process of restoration begins immediately, in which three phases are recognized: a period of wound healing, a period of blastema formation, and a period of differentiation (Fig. 23.1). The present discussion of the blastema is limited to that of the limb. It is described in broader context toward the end of this chapter.

The similarity between the morphogenesis and differentiation of the blastema in a regenerating adult or larval amphibian limb and limb embryogenesis has been noted many times. The regeneration blastema, like the embryonic limb bud, is composed of a mound of mesodermally-derived cells in close contact with an epidermal covering that is thickened apically into a ridge. The ridge has been shown to direct the accumulation of blastema cells into a mound at the tip of the amputated stump. Many questions arise, however. What is the source of blastemal cells and what are the steps in tissue differentiation? To what extent are blastemal cells formed through processes of dedifferentiation and redifferentiation, and to what extent do they form from undifferentiated stem cells? Both sources are possible, and the question raises the matter of stability of the differentiated state. Cell-to-cell interactions, cell affinities, and self-assembly processes are involved. So are extraneous influences, such as radiation (Fig. 23.2) and drugs, and perhaps above all is the genetic control of cytodifferentiation. All of these are contained in one fascinating phenomenon, which has the potential to illuminate much of differentiation and morphogenesis.

Three phases are evident in the regeneration process as a whole:

Wound healing This process consists essentially of epidermal cells migrating from the basal layer of the adjacent epidermis toward the center of the wound. Active migration of this epithelial layer of cells continues until the wound is closed.

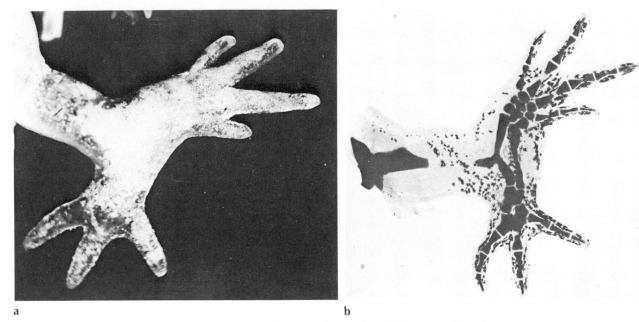

a   b

Figure 23.2 *a* Photo of live supernumerary three-digit hand extending below normal hand, resulting from ultraviolet irradiation of a developing right forelimb of *Ambystoma* larva, and *b* stained section of same, showing skeleton. [*Courtesy of E. G. Butler.*]

Blastema formation Cells accumulate beneath this newly formed epithelial covering, and the combined cap of epithelial and subjacent cell mass is known as the *blastema*. As such, it has the general properties associated with a limb bud or an egg insofar as it has the potentiality of growing and differentiating into a highly organized unit structure. The production of the blastema continues for some time before developmental events become discernible through cell division and cell migration. Epidermal cells continue to accumulate at the apical region, possibly through further migration but certainly in part through mitotic division of cells initially forming the cap. Mesenchymatous cells progressively accumulate beneath the cap, so that an epithelium-mesenchyme reacting system is established, resembling that of a limb bud or a feather bud but on a much larger scale.

Differentiation The limb blastema passes through several definable stages during the course of regeneration. Morphologically, in the adult newt at 20°C, 15 days after amputation, the blastema is filled with undifferentiated cells; by 20 days the blastema has become a *cone,* the *palette* stage (a flattened cone) is reached at 25 days, the *notch* stage, representing the first sign of digits, is reached at 30 to 35 days. From then on digital pattern becomes progressively in evidence, the precartilaginous skeleton condenses, and a complete limb is present by 75 days (Fig. 23.3).

The general questions that arise are already familiar. What is the role of the newly formed ectoderm, and what is the role of the mesodermal elements in the subsequent processes of differentiation and organization? What is the developmental sequence? And so on. The new questions relate to the fact that the blastema cells derive from mature epidermis and from internal tissue that contained fully differentiated muscle, nerve, and cartilage, together with connective-tissue cells (fibroblasts or mesenchyme).

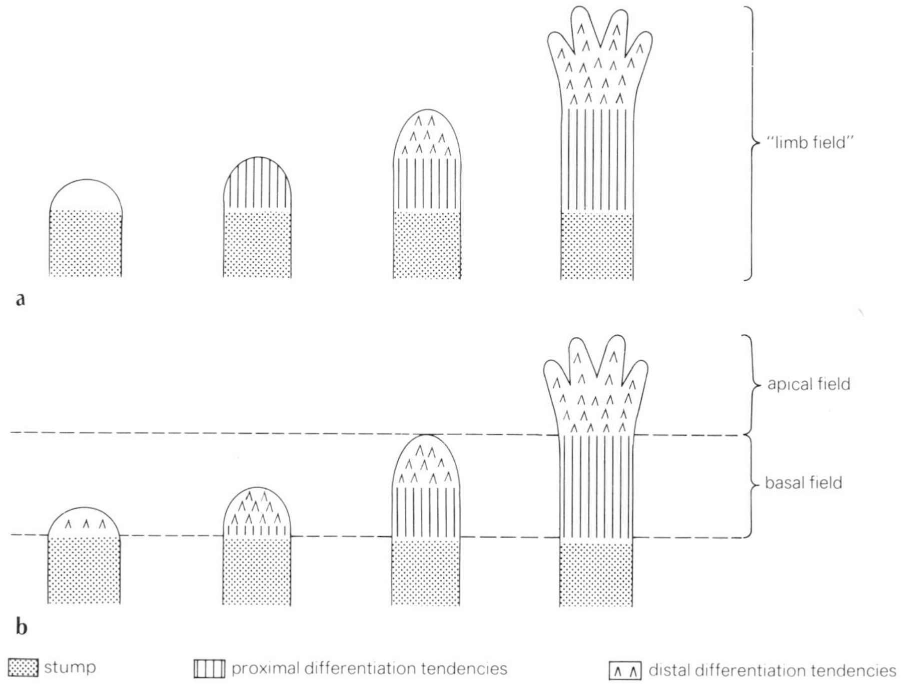

"limb field"
a
apical field
basal field
b
stump
proximal differentiation tendencies
distal differentiation tendencies

Figure 23.3 Two concepts of regional organization in the limb regenerate. Four successive stages of regeneration are shown, from left to right. *a* The youngest blastema is depicted as being morphogenetically neutral. Limb pattern arises as a result of determinative events proceeding from stump distalwards. *b* The youngest blastema has distal differentiation tendencies. Proximal differentiation tendencies appear later than distal ones. [*After Faber, 1965.*]

Dedifferentiation

The source of the mass of mesenchymatous cells constituting the bulk of the blastema has been a problem plaguing analysis of limb regeneration for many years. Following amputation, the residual differentiated tissue of the stump, mostly cartilage and muscle, undergoes extreme disintegration and apparent dedifferentiation e.g., cartilage cells lose their matrix, muscle cells their myofilaments. At the same time the mesenchyme cells beneath the epidermal cap increase in number enormously (Fig. 23.4). The problem has been to ascertain the connection between these two events. Opposing interpretations, not entirely exclusive of one another, have been variously adopted. The points at issue have been questions not of plausibility but of fact. Possible interpretations are:

1 Is the apparent dedifferentiation of mature muscle and cartilage cells a true return to an undifferentiated state? If so, they can obviously give rise to a mass of undifferentiated blastema cells. It has been extraordinarily difficult, however, to establish whether or not true dedifferentiation and subsequent redifferentiation may actually take place.

2 Are the disassociating and otherwise changing cartilage and muscle cells degenerating and in fact dying, allowing their products to stimulate and support rapid multiplication of any unspecialized mesenchyme cells present? A dependent population replacement of this sort would be effective and is known to occur in regenerative processes in some other forms (e.g., ascidians). In this event no transformation of cells is called for, only differential multiplication.

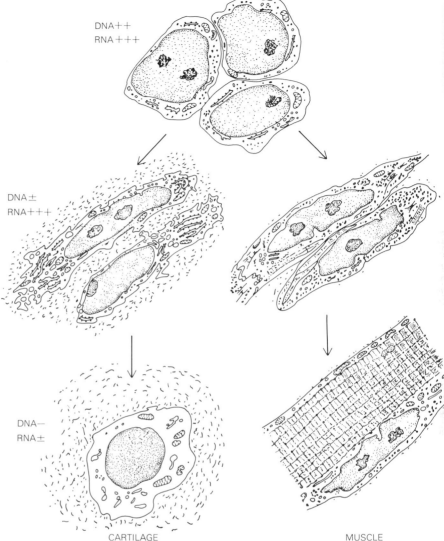

Figure 23.4 Changes in fine structure of mesenchymal cells as they aggregate within the limb blastema (*top*) and differentiate into cartilage (*left*) and muscle (*right*). In cartilage, the newly formed differentiated products are destined for the extracellular compartment. They are synthesized and secreted by the granular endoplasmic reticulum and Golgi complex. In muscle, the differentiated proteins (myofibrils) are intracellular in location. They seem to be synthesized by free ribosomes in the cytoplasm without the intervention of the granular endoplasmic reticulum. The muscle cell contains only a few profiles of granular reticulum and has a smaller Golgi apparatus than the cartilage cell. It later acquires a special kind of smooth-surfaced reticulum. Also depicted in the diagram are the relative amounts of DNA and RNA synthesized by the cells in the developmental stages illustrated. [*After Hay, 1965.*]

DNA++
RNA+++

DNA±
RNA+++

DNA—
RNA±

CARTILAGE

MUSCLE

3 Do the cartilage and muscle cells merely appear to dedifferentiate? That is, do they lose their distinctive histological character, but in actuality retain their fundamental character and as such contribute to the blastema? This phenomenon of pseudodedifferentiation is commonly seen in tissue culture—as, for instance, collagen dependence of muscle differentiation—and has been termed *modulation* by Weiss. If this is the case, however, in a blastema, then we are faced with another problem, because the implication is that modulated cartilage, muscle, and other cells, having been mixed together, subsequently sort out according to their kind, i.e., like to like, and also become reassembled in the new configurations of the developing limb structures.

The long-standing difficulty has been the failure in following the history of individual cells during the crucial period, that is, in tracing individual cartilage or muscle cells from the original stump tissues to whatever their destiny may be, or in determining the source of the mesenchyme cells with any precision. Electron-microscopic studies support the contention that the differentiated cells of the stump do become morphologically undifferentiated cells in the blastema. What is less clear is whether they redifferentiate into new cell types.

Redifferentiation

When the stumps of amputated limbs are treated with tritiated thymidine and the tissues are fixed at later intervals and radioautographed, the pattern of incorporation of the thymidine indicates that DNA synthesis begins 4 to 5 days after amputation in all differentiating tissues within 1 mm of the wound. In animals into which thymidine has been injected before amputation, only the epidermis of the limb shows incorporation of the tracer. When this is followed by amputation, the labeled epidermis migrates over the wound surface and forms a labeled apical cap, which remains labeled throughout blastema formation. None of the labeled epidermal cells contribute to the internal blastema.

Other evidence shows that cells from the body proper do not contribute to the mesenchymal blastema. Blood cells, for instance, that appear at an early stage in the limb do not derive from the blood-forming organs of the body. The dedifferentiating tissues of the stump, more or less by default, give rise to the unspecialized blastema cells. Evidence that cartilage cells can dedifferentiate and subsequently redifferentiate into muscle cells, or vice versa, is supplied by labeling experiments of a different kind. The question is a general one of vital significance: can the daughter cells of a highly differentiated vertebrate cell, following mitosis, exhibit a variety of differentiations, or must they perpetuate the parental type? Can they truly dedifferentiate and redifferentiate, or only modulate?

The crucial experiment consisted of grafting triploid salamander cells of a known differentiated type into the limbs of diploid hosts, amputating the limb, allowing limb regeneration to occur, and then examining the regenerate to see whether the triploid cells had given rise to cell types other than that of the original graft cells. The grafts consisted of pure cartilage, pure muscle, cartilage plus perichondrium, and epidermis, i.e., the various types typically present in the stump of an amputated limb, but introduced separately into the hosts. Host limbs were previously exposed to x-irradiation to discourage host cells from participating in the regeneration process when the host limb was amputated. Triploid cells are recognizable as having three nucleoli in the interphase nucleus instead of two.

When the graft tissue consists of pure cartilage or of cartilage plus perichondrium, the marker appears subsequently in the regenerated limb in the following cell types: cartilage, perichondrium, the connective tissue of joints, and in fibroblasts, but not in muscle. When pure muscle is grafted, the marker appears in all the above cell types and in muscle cells as well; no regeneration occurs when pure epidermis is grafted. Similar experiments made independently but employing both tritiated thymidine and triploidy (used either independently to mark graft and host cells differentially, or simultaneously to label the same cell) have provided cross-checks on any uncertainties in either method alone. Again, clean cartilage grafts give rise to morphologically dedifferentiated blastema cells, which redifferentiate almost exclusively into chondrocytes that retain their specific character through at least five divisions; and, again, muscle tissue contributes to both muscle and cartilage, *though it is highly significant* that muscle tissue consists of connective-tissue cells as well as contractile elements. The question whether real dedifferentiation takes place, with subsequent redifferentiation along another line, still receives a somewhat dusty answer.

Blastema as a Self-organizing System

The cone stage is of particular interest morphogenetically because not only do the various tissues and structures differentiate within the regeneration outgrowth, but they form in continuity with the stump tissues to produce an anatomically and functionally complete limb. Only those structures distal to the plane of amputation are formed. A long-standing explanation has been that the differentiated tissues of the limp stump induce the undifferentiated blastema to redifferentiate the lost parts in conformity with the stump organization. The failure of young blastemas to continue their differentiation when transplanted to foreign sites and the ability of older blastemas to do so have supported this interpretation.

The validity of this has been tested by Stocum by removing cone-, palette-, and notch-stage blastemas and grafting them to the body (the dorsal fin) of the larval salamander, with or without a stump. Whether the stump is included or not, whole blastemas are able to self-organize into all the skeletal and muscular components of the lost limb distal to the level of amputation. Distal parts of blastemas grafted in the same way develop hand structure; proximal parts develop the more proximal parts. In other words, the limb blastema as early as the cone stage is not continuously influenced by the surviving stump tissue but is a self-organizing system already imbued with a pattern representing the prospective regional structure. This concept was formulated earlier by Coe with regard to regeneration in nemertean worms.

Blastemas of all three stages are able to differentiate precartilage and striated muscle in vitro in complete absence of the stump. Inclusion of stump in an explant does not enhance the frequency of differentiation of precartilage and muscle in the blastema, and it actually appears to be detrimental to development of the regenerate. It has been concluded that by the time the blastema has reached the cone stage, it is not dependent upon inductive messages from the stump for differentiation but is a self-differentiating system. The process as a whole is summarized graphically in Fig. 23.5.

Nevertheless a blastema has received an imprint of regional character by the time amputation of the blastema becomes possible, so that in some way it already represents that portion of the limb that has been amputated, neither more nor less. If a forelimb of a salamander larva is transplanted to the region of the hindlimb, or vice versa, and the transplant, after healing, is partly reamputated, what develops depends on the original character of the stump rather than the site to which it is transplanted (Fig. 23.6a). If a thin transverse slice of forelimb, for example, is healed onto the stump of a hindlimb, a new forelimb regenerates.

Epidermis derived from stump epidermis, moreover, is not essential. If the epidermis from the stump is removed following amputation and the stump is then surrounded by lung tissue, the limb that regenerates is well provided with normal epidermis (Fig. 23.6b). There is, however, one striking limitation to the regenerative capacity of a mutilated limb. If a limb is amputated longitudinally, rather than transversely, the injured surface heals but does not regenerate as a whole. If such a split limb is then cut transversely, a distal regenerate forms, which is normal in cross section and structure (Fig. 23.6c).

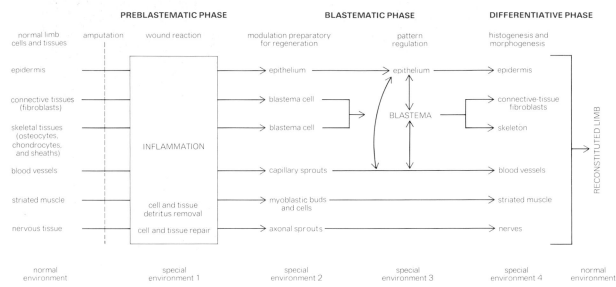

Figure 23.5 A concept of the regeneration process in amphibian amputated appendages. With the exception of the final reconstitution of the amputated appendage, this diagram could also serve as a summary of repair processes in all vertebrates. [*After Schmidt, 1968.*]

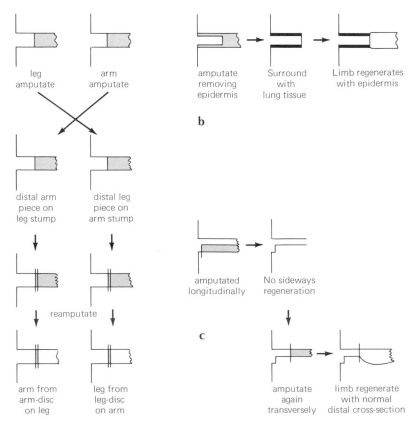

Figure 23.6 Regeneration of salamander limb in different circumstances. *a* Leg and arm amputated and regrafted on to arm and leg stump respectively, then cut off again leaving disc of arm or leg on stump of other kind; result is regeneration according to type of disc. *b* Regeneration of limb from stump devoid of epidermis; result is complete regeneration including new epidermis. *c* Amputation of limb longitudinally, resulting in no regeneration, followed by transverse amputation; result is complete regeneration, followed by transverse regeneration of whole distal portion from reduced base. [*After Needham, 1942.*]

A somewhat comparable relationship exists between amphibian limb regeneration and the presence of anterior pituitary hormones. Limb regeneration does not occur in hypophysectomized urodeles. If, however, limbs are allowed to regenerate for varying lengths of time prior to hypophysectomy, there is a gradual emancipation from the influence of the anterior pituitary gland, and regeneration takes place. Therefore, anterior pituitary hormones act early in regeneration to initiate steps that do not require further presence of the hormone. Larval urodeles can regenerate a limb in the absence of anterior pituitary hormones, but this ability is lost following metamorphosis. In hypophysectomized adult urodeles, the ability to regenerate limbs is restored by anterior pituitary extract or by autografting or organ-cultured anterior pituitary gland.

Neural Trophic Factor

Regeneration of the limb blastema of vertebrates, particularly amphibians, and of regeneration blastemas of many invertebrates is normally dependent upon a critical supply of nerves at a very early stage. Many nerve endings in fact enter the epidermal cells. However, if a limb is first denervated and then amputated, or if nerves are by any means blocked from penetrating the epidermis, no regenerative outgrowth occurs. The stump tissues merely undergo degenerative changes. Yet once the process of dedifferentiation and blastema formation has taken place, interference with the nerve supply no longer has any effect. The influence of nerves is something other than nerve function as such and is not due to acetylcholine (Fig. 23.7). The agent is known as the *neural trophic factor*. What it is and how it works are still unsettled, although the establishment of neural-epidermal junctions seems to be an essential condition in such nerve-dependent regenerations.

Dependence of regeneration upon neural factor, however, is not universal. Embryonic limb buds, for instance, comparable to though smaller than regeneration blastemas, develop without initial neural stimulation. Similarly, salamander limbs that have been denervated and maintained nerveless for a month or

Figure 23.7 Comparison of acetylcholine content and acetylcholinesterase activity during the course of regeneration of forelimbs of adult newts. Acetylcholine (ACH) levels are high during the phases of formation, accumulation, and rapid growth of the regenerate and drop during the period of morphogenesis and cytodifferentiation. Acetylcholine levels can be correlated with the levels of the enzyme that destroys it, cholinesterase (CHE). Even though the timing of high ACH levels would fit with it having a trophic role, such does not appear to be the case. [*After Singer, David, and Arkowitz*, J. Embryol. Exp. Morphol., **8**:98 (*1960*).]

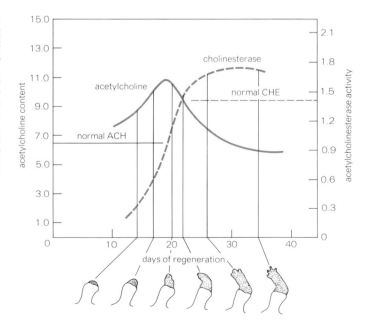

more, by repeated denervation at 5-day intervals, acquire the capacity to regenerate amputated limbs. In other words the dependency is not absolute.

Mammals do not significantly regenerate lost parts. The inaccessibility of mammalian embryos makes it impossible to be sure of this point in fetal mammals. An exception is the marsupial. It is born at a relatively very early stage, after which it migrates to the maternal pouch and attaches to the nipples. The newborn North American opossum has proved to be uniquely suited for studies of replacement of the mammalian limb. Since this marsupial is born without lymphocytes, xenoplastic as well as homoplastic transplants are tolerated. Supplementary nerve tissue was transplanted to newborn hindlimbs and the limbs were amputated immediately above the ankle. The implant remained in place, and distal limb regeneration resulted. Control experiments indicate that neither the trauma of simple amputation and of implantation nor the implantation of other tissues can evoke the response that results after nerve tissue is implanted. These studies demonstrate that young opossum limbs are capable of regenerating when additional nervous tissue is supplied.

REGENERATION AND ELECTRICAL FIELDS

Efforts to stimulate limb regeneration in placental mammals have followed investigation of electric fields in normal and regenerating amphibians (Fig. 23.8). Adult frogs are ordinarily unable to regenerate limbs, but limb regeneration can be stimulated by the implantation of small electrogenic bimetallic couplings in the amputation stump. Regeneration occurs only if the orientation of the coupling enhances the distal negativity and is lacking or much decreased with all other orientations. The initial or primary stimulus for this process may be a relatively simple electric field requiring only a minimal current level acting upon a population of susceptible cells.

It is now known that the direct current potentials measurable on the intact surfaces of all living animals demonstrate a complex field pattern that is spatially related to the anatomical arrangements of the nervous system (Fig. 23.9). The surface potentials appear to be directly associated with some element of the

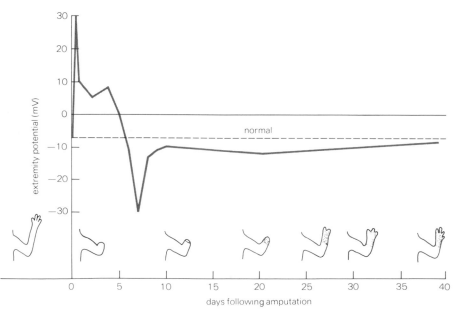

Figure 23.8 Voltage changes in adult-newt forelimb during regeneration. Zero point on horizontal scale immediately precedes amputation. Very high peak in positive voltage curve is concurrent with limb amputation. Secondary positive peak is observed on the fifth day. Negative maximum is reached on the eighth day. Negative bias is maintained until limb regeneration is complete. Normal limb voltage is about −10 mV (interrupted line) at point of amputation. Lower figures show schematically the stages of regeneration. [*After Becker, 1961.*]

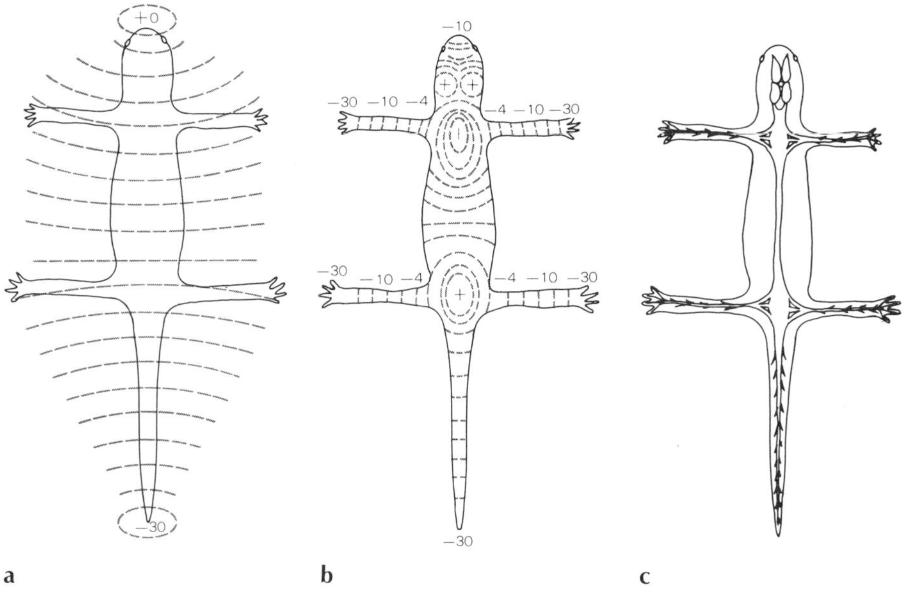

Figure 23.9 Bioelectric field of adult newt. *a* Total body potential, with tip-of-nose reference electrode and tip-of-tail recording electrode; animals are immersed in fluid. *b* Field plot found using two-electrode equipotential line-plotting technique on an animal kept moist but not immersed in fluid. *c* Gross arrangements of the central nervous system in the adult newt. [*After Becker, 1961.*]

nervous system. They can be measured directly on peripheral nerves, where they demonstrate polarity differences depending upon whether the nerve is primarily motor or sensory in function. The existence of standing electric potentials in a conducting medium implies the existence of a steady current flow. Experiments have demonstrated that such a current exists, longitudinally, in the neural elements.

Three general possibilities are that (1) bulk ionic currents and fields may directly modify the surface charge pattern on the membrane of sensitive multipotent cells and thus transmit information to the cell machinery, (2) cells can be directly influenced by changes in the electrochemical environment at or near an electrode interface, and (3) cells can be indirectly influenced by changes in enzyme concentrations or configurations produced by electrochemical reactions at the electrodes.

Small direct currents and electric fields stimulate tissue regeneration and healing of fractures. In the bone system, Becker has shown that stress-generated potentials are probably used by the organism in the normal processes of growth and repair. Externally applied electricity designed to stimulate bone growth consists of direct currents ranging between 10^{-6} and 10^{-3} A with applied potentials between 0.1 and 10 V. Electrical stimulation of this sort results in partial regeneration in the forelegs of laboratory rats. Bone, cartilage, bone marrow, muscle, nerves, and blood vessels all grow as far as the first joint, although what prevents completion of regeneration beyond that level is not known.

The continuity of the tissue that transmits the dc potentials during regenerative healing, however, is restored in a shorter time than is possible by nerve restoration. Schwann cells appear to be involved in this process. Schwann cells originate from the neural crest and are totally absent if the neural crest is removed. During development they migrate proximodistally along growing nerve fibers, as was seen by Harrison (1904) in living nerve fibers in the skin of the frog tadpole tail. They attach only to unmyelinated portions of the nerve but form myelin sheaths only around axons exceeding 0.6 μm in diameter. Glia cells in the brain appear to have a comparable relation to central neurones and

505

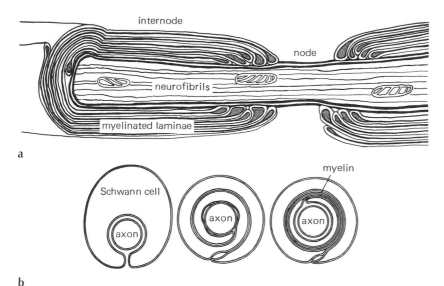

Figure 23.10 Diagram illustrating myelination of axons in peripheral nerves by Schwann cells. *a* Axon enclosed by the Schwann cell, with the development of myelin. *b* Cytoplasmic process of the Schwann cells wrapped around the axon and the formation of lamellae of compact myelin. [*After J. D. Robertson*, J. Biophys. Biochem. Cytol., **4**:349 (1958).]

are also derivatives of the embryonic neurectoderm. Although myelination is not essential for the development and functioning of axons, they greatly increase the conduction velocity of the nervous impulse.

Following section of a nerve, Schwann cells (Fig. 23.10) migrate outward after a delay of several days, although they do so immediately if an already degenerating nerve is cut again. Migration either is inhibited by a healthy nerve fiber or is accelerated by products of nerve degeneration. Mammalian Schwann cells migrate at about 0.3 mm per day and eventually bridge gaps, thereby providing mechanical support and guidance for axons growing out of the proximal nerve stump.

The Schwann and glia cell system invests the whole vertebrate nervous system and appears to be primarily responsible for maintaining the characteristic high-level dc electric potential system. Becker has proposed that the basic system, consisting of the glia and Schwann cell continuum, is an analog-type transmission system using varying levels of direct current as its signal. An analog computer processes continuous quantities such as voltage, resistance, etc.; a digital computer processes discrete numbers as in a binary system, with one digit (0 or 1) representing the "on" and "off" state as in an electronic device or nerve cell discharge. This analog system is conceived as being involved in the receipt of damage or injury stimuli, which we perceive as pain, and in the various growth processes of repair and regeneration. It interlocks with the nervous system and is regarded as a more primitive property of cells and tissues. There are two electrochemical links of great significance in the operation of the system. One is between the dc system and the nervous system, which it invests. The other is between the dc system and all body cells whose basic functions it is said to control.

Investigation and understanding of the electrochemical properties of organisms are still in their infancy although long recognized and utilized in physiological and clinical study of the heart and brain. It is notable that Becker's report on the significance of bioelectric potentials is published in volume one (1974) of a new journal, "Bioelectrochemistry and Bioenergetics." Both electrical conduction and regenerative processes are fundamental properties of organisms independent of and antedating the presence of sophisticated nervous systems. Jellyfish, for instance, even though they do possess a well-developed network-type nervous system, exhibit reflexes that work without involving the nervous system at all. These reflexes depend on the mechanism and behavior of certain epithelia absolutely devoid of any nerve or muscle. The epithelia receive external stimuli, convert them into electrical signals, and conduct them in all directions by a rapid all-or-none type of conduction, at a velocity and with a refractory period comparable to unmyelinated nerve fibers of vertebrates, finally reaching effector muscles. The electric field must be regarded as a universal property of tissues and its possible role in developmental control systems recognized.

The existence of electric fields has long been recognized in hydroids. Hydroids, including *Hydra,* have been widely used in experimental studies of regeneration from the very start of developmental biology, with particular reference to the nature and effect of polarity. *Hydra,* however, is discussed in the context of asexual development, which is related to regeneration but goes beyond it in scope. This is examined in the next chapter.

Lund (1921) showed that in the hydroid *Obelia,* polarity has an electrical basis, there is an electrical potential difference between the two ends of a regenerating piece of hydroid, and this can be neutralized or reversed by sending an electric current through a stem in the direction opposing its own bioelectric polarity. The imposed electric field has to be only slightly greater than the inherent field. He reasoned that since an applied field of the same order of magnitude as the natural inherent field, but of opposite sign, could change the site and reverse the direction of differentiation, the inherent field must under natural conditions determine the site and direction of differentiation. Tests were made on stems of *Tubularia,* another hydroid to ascertain whether conditions that determine the site and direction of regeneration do so by producing a polarized (bioelectric) field prior to visible regeneration. The tests show that conditions favoring regeneration at the ends of stems do so by first making those ends electronegative. Conditions that retard regeneration locally tend to make that region electropositive. This and other experiments on *Tubularia* by Rose are described at length in his book "Regeneration" (1970).

HEAD REGENERATION IN INVERTEBRATES

The Blastema: II

In most cases of regeneration (other than in hydroids) undifferentiated cells, whatever their source, gather as a group at the wounded area and constitute the blastema. Here regeneration is initiated. In flatworms (planaria), these undifferentiated cells are termed *neoblasts.* They are generally considered to be totipotent, i.e., they are capable of forming any and all of the missing tissues and organs. There is at present some dispute as to their origin. Earlier they were considered to be reserve cells in the body of the planarian. Vital-dye experiments and electron micrograph studies, however, show that neoblasts may arise from dedifferentiation of intestinal and other differentiated cell types. There is also evidence that blastema formation depends initially on the presence of cells already available, inasmuch as (1) a high mitotic activity does not necessarily cause blastema formation, and (2) blastema formation is sometimes possible when mitoses are inhibited. Blastema formation begins with the determination of the distal part, and this occurs as soon as wound healing is over.

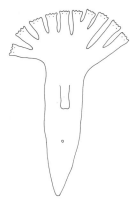

Figure 23.11 Multiple potentiality in head field of planarian. When a decapitated anterior end is partially split by a number of cuts, and when the parts are prevented from re-fusing, each part regenerates its own head although it is still attached to a common body.

Wound healing juxtaposes dorsal and ventral tissues, which exhibit different patterns. Healing institutes new patterns near the level of the wound. Longitudinal incisions (prevented from re-fusion) in the anterior end of a transected flatworm result in the formation of a corresponding number of small but complete heads (Fig. 23.11).

In regeneration the situation is even more complicated than in embryogenesis because of the presence of the old tissue. The remaining tissues may influence regeneration in an inductive, or inhibitory, manner; their influence may be specific upon one tissue or may be general, in the establishment of polarity, for example. Not only do the old tissues influence the formation of new tissue, but the old tissue itself undergoes a reorganization in the course of regeneration. This type of reorganization is termed *morphallactic regeneration.*

Hierarchical Induction

Induction phenomena are well-documented in planarian regeneration. It has been demonstrated that the brain induces eye formation. In a series of experiments in the 1950s, Lender and his group worked with *Polycelis nigra,* which has numerous eyes forming a rim around the anterior region. If the brain and part of the eye rim are removed, subsequent removal of the "brain" blastema every 2 days prevents regeneration of eyes. Eyes regenerate before optic nerve connection occurs. Therefore, Lender concluded that the brain was capable of inducing eyes "at a distance" through chemical substances he called "organisms." If "brainless" planaria were raised in an extract of planarian brains, the eyes also regenerated.

Transplantation of the head into the postpharyngeal region caused a supplementary pharynx to be regenerated. Removal of the induced pharynx caused another one to be regenerated. A prepharyngeal fragment differentiates a pharynx inside the old tissues. A postpharyngeal fragment regenerates a pharynx within the blastema but not before the brain and eyes develop. From experiments such as these, the investigators conclude that the brain induces a prepharyngeal zone, which induces a pharyngeal zone capable of forming a pharynx.

Based on these demonstrations of inductions and inhibitions in planarian regeneration, the Lender-Wolffian school has presented a model to explain regeneration in planaria (Fig. 23.12). The brain induces the formation of eyes and also of a prepharyngeal zone. It also inhibits the formation of supernumerary brains. The prepharyngeal zone induces a pharyngeal zone, followed by the formation of the pharynx. Inhibitory substances from the pharynx prevent additional pharynges from forming. The anterior region also induces the gonads and copulatory apparatus.

Effect of Tissue Extracts

Many experiments have been made on a variety of organisms concerning the existence of inhibitory substances in relation to regeneration of anterior or posterior parts, particularly of *Tubularia,* of the nemertean worm *Lineus,* the annelid *Clymenella,* various flatworms, and in relation to regional suppression of developing parts in vertebrate embryos.

In all such cases an aqueous extract of tissue from an anterior part of an organism, when added to the culture medium in which regenerating is taking place, tends to prevent the formation of the anterior part, while allowing posterior regeneration to proceed. Extracts of posterior tissue blocked posterior regeneration but allowed anterior regeneration. In flatworms, if a brain is

Figure 23.12 *a* Sequence of induction in regenerating flatworm from left to right: brain first differentiates, which induces differentiation of eyes along anterior and anterolateral margin, to constitute head structure; head induces prepharyngeal region and then the pharyngeal region posteriorly, which induces reproductive organs posteriorly. [*After Wolff, 1962.*] *b* Window is cut out of forepart of flatworm, and head regenerates within it, whether or not original head is amputated. [*After Bromstedt, 1955.*]

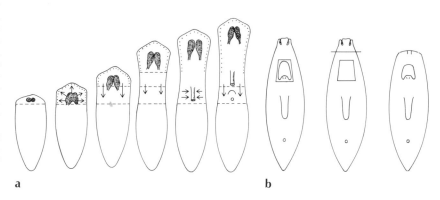

a   b

grafted to a headless piece, the latter regenerates all parts except the brain, while pharyngeal extract inhibits reconstitution of a new pharynx but permits other regeneration to proceed. In chick embryos, extracts of anterior brain suppress the development of that part of the brain; midbrain extracts inhibit development of midbrain and anterior brain, but not of posterior brain or spinal cord; and spinal cord extracts suppress spinal cord and all brain development anterior to it. That is, the whole central nervous system can be suppressed by extracts of the most posterior unit. Accordingly there is good evidence that specific repressors of differentiation exist in tissues, although it should be noted that differentiation is a term applied here to form and structure differentiation rather than to cell-type differentiation.

The concept of a "time-graded regeneration field" to explain interactions occurring in planarian regeneration has been fully presented by Brønstedt in his book "Planarian Regeneration" (1970). This concept is that there is a regenerative "high point" located anteriorly and centrally in the worm where the neoblasts begin to differentiate first. These neoblasts would differentiate into a brain. As these neoblasts differentiate into nerve cells, they prevent other cells from becoming brain. These neoblasts then differentiate according to the next choice open—that of eyes. Therefore, there exists a sort of hierarchy of differentiation possibilities open to a neoblast. What it actually becomes is determined by these gradients of time and space as well as by interactions with its fellow cells.

Nemertean worms are spiralians distantly related to flatworms but more advanced in having a tubular gut rather than a sac-like gut. In these worms the distinction between the regenerated blastema and the body is much clearer. They have been less exploited than the planarians, especially the polyclad members of that group, because they are less accessible and not so readily cultured in the laboratory. If developmental biologists will utilize organisms on the basis of their suitability for specific problems rather than on their proximity to specific laboratories, the spiralians will be the source of much developmental information in the future. Here, then, is a case in point.

Apart from early descriptive accounts of regeneration, most of what is known about the process in nemerteans is from a series of experimental studies by Coe. The worms are long and slender. A worm 100 mm long may be divided into as many as 80 transverse pieces, each capable of regenerating and reorganizing into a whole worm. In fact, by successive divisions of the regenerated minute worms, miniature worms were produced, almost microscopic in size and not more than one two-hundred-thousandths of the volume of the original. That is, they were about the size of an ordinary *Paramecium*.

509

A feature of nemertean morphology of special interest concerning regenerative phenomena is the extension of the anterior end of the body well beyond the mouth. This preoral region contains the brain, the sensory structure, and the anterior portion of an invaginated proboscis and sheath peculiar to this group of animals. It is therefore simple to amputate an anterior piece that lacks the intestine entirely. Another feature is the presence of two widely separated lateral nerve cords, so that pieces of worm can be readily sectioned longitudinally in such a way as to produce quadrants with or without a segment of nerve end. Those that possess nerve cord regenerate from both ends; those that lack nerve cord do not regenerate.

Cuts immediately instigate a coordinated migration of epidermal and connective tissue cells toward both cut surfaces, and the wounds are thereby closed and healed. The cuts also activate the dormant cells situated throughout the body in the parenchyma. These migrate anteriorly and posteriorly to collect in large numbers beneath the new epidermis covering the cut ends. Anterior and posterior blastemas are thus formed. Posterior regeneration thereafter is closely similar to normal growth. Anteriorly the process is as follows:

1   Localizations soon become manifest in the blastema, and the cells congregate in three areas: the two lateral are the primordia of the cerebral ganglia and the median is that of the new proboscis and sheath (Fig. 23.13).

2   These primordia in turn appear to act as induction centers for other head organs, particularly a tube joining the proboscis to the exterior, and the cerebral sense organs. A new mouth invaginates to form the foregut, which joins the anterior end of the old gut remnant.

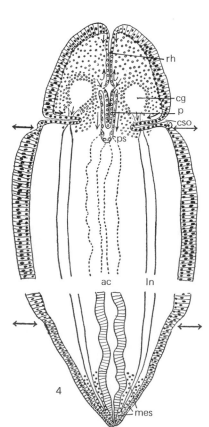

Figure 23.13 *Lineus socialis.* Blastema with differentiated primordia of cerebral ganglia (*cg*) with new lateral nerves growing posteriorly to join nerve cords of original fragment; *cso*, invagination of new epidermis to form cerebral sense organs; *rh*, rhynchodeum; *p*, new proboscis growing posteriorly in the new sheath (*ps*). The posterior end shows the elongation of the original organ systems, with migration and incorporation of mesenchyme cells (*mes*). Fifteenth day of regeneration. Arrows indicate location of cuts. [*After Coe, 1934.*]

3 As soon as the regenerated part has become individualized, when all organs of the new head are restored, it *reorganizes all the tissues of the original fragment into units of smaller size*. An essentially new individual of harmonious proportions results.

When transverse cuts are made so as to remove the anterior portion of the head as well as the entire body posterior to the cerebral sense organs, the missing anterior tissues to be replaced are organized by those remaining. If all trace of the digestive system has been removed at the other end, an entirely new digestive canal is replaced by mesenchyme cells, which migrate posteriorly.

The blastema is considered to be a self-determining system comparable to the early embryo. The constituent cells are evidently multipotent and capable of differentiation into any of the new organs. Once activated, they and their descendants complete the regenerative processes. The primary organization center is evidently associated with part of the nerve cords, which are capable of activating the regenerative cells and of controlling their bipolar migration. Secondary organization centers result as soon as the primordia of the organ systems have become differentiated in the self-determining blastema.

More recent experiments, comparable to those on flatworms, have shown that both anterior and posterior regeneration can be specifically inhibited in pieces of *Lineus* cultured in media containing extracts of tissues from the anterior and posterior regions of the worm itself. The proposed hypothesis states that anterior regeneration is governed by a hierarchy of regions extending from head to tail, *each possessing a different differentiation pattern and each determining the succeeding regions by inhibiting them from attaining levels of differentiation already present in preceding regions*. Likewise, posterior regeneration is governed by a similar hierarchy extending from tail to head, the more posterior regions by inhibiting them from forming patterns already existing behind them. This hypothesis is clearly in keeping with those suggested by Brønstedt and by Lender and Wolff for differentiation control in flatworms. The positional information theory proposed by Wolpert may be compared with the above concept of a double gradient system.

Blastemas and Reorganization

The remaining group of worms, also capable of remarkable regenerative and reorganizational performance, are annelids, or segmented worms, especially the more diverse and even beautiful marine polychaete annelids. Anatomically the annelids are more advanced than flatworms and nemerteans. They are divided into a series of body segments, each of which has much in common with the other segments and at the same time has morphological and physiological features distinctively its own. Therefore the segmented worms offer several advantages to the investigator of regenerative phenomena:

1 An anteroposterior polarity or axis is present, comparable to that of others.

2 A regional differentiation exists along the primary axis.

3 New body segments form from the posterior zone of growth, whether in normal posterior growth or regenerative posterior growth.

4 Blastema formation occurs at the onset of anterior regeneration.

5 Reorganization of old body structure takes place under the influence of new anterior regenerating tissue.

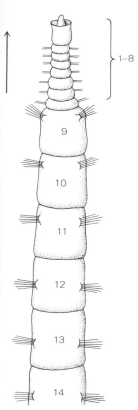

1–8

9

10

11

12

13

14

Figure 23.14 Polarity and reconstitution in the polychaete *Clymenella*, showing polarized (anteroposterior axis) structure and reconstitution, anteriorly or posteriorly, of whatever number of segments are required to restore the original total of 22 segments. In this instance, segments 1–8 are regenerated from the anterior surface of segment 9.

As stated above, these phenomena are recognized in flatworm and nemertean regeneration. In polchaete regeneration they are more clearly defined. Body segmentation makes every region along the axis numerically definable. This is immediately apparent in the anterior and posterior regeneration of pieces of certain polychaetes such as *Clymenella* (Fig. 23.14). A common species of this genus consists of 22 segments. These are formed very early during the juvenile stage; further growth occurs through enlargement of individual segments.

Any segment or group of segments separated from the rest will regenerate the missing anterior and posterior parts and will do so exactly. If the anterior eight segments are amputated, eight are replaced. In a piece consisting of original segments 13 and 14, twelve will be regenerated anteriorly and eight posteriorly, so that the two old segments come to be numbers 13 and 14 in a new worm consisting altogether of 22 segments. The problem is the same as in the specific determination of the number of body segments (including tail) in vertebrate embryos and adults. No satisfactory explanation has yet been given for the basic nature of the posterior rhythmic growth responsible for segment production, or for the precise limitation of such growth among the many creatures that exhibit it.

Many annelids—polychaetes and others—are unable to regenerate more than a few segments anteriorly, no matter how many have been removed. Moreover the capacity in such cases usually diminishes along the anteroposterior axis. In most cases, however, regeneration posteriorly takes place in the expected manner.

A theory of growth limitation proposed by Moment holds that annelids continue to grow by the proliferation of voltage-producing units until, by the summation of these units, whether segments or cells, a critical inhibitory voltage is built up. The formation of these units occurs in distal growing regions, and it is in such terminal zones that the inhibitory voltage finally attains a critical value. Subsequent growth of the segments and of the cells of which they are composed is usually very great, but it is primarily by cell enlargement, not by cell proliferation.

A special case of limitation of anterior regeneration is associated with the most striking example of reorganization (*morphallaxis*) of the remainder of the body. It is seen in the sabellid polychaetes, the so-called fanworms, feather dusters, etc., which inhabit long parchment tubes of their own making. They feed by extruding a flowerlike crown of tentacles from one end. The body of the worm is divisible into a specialized three-segment head, a thoracic region of from seven to twelve or more segments, and an abdomen consisting of a large but indefinite number of segments. The obvious difference between thoracic and abdominal segments is that the pattern of bristles and hooks on each segment is reversed in one compared with the other, as though the worm had been twisted through 180° at the thoracic-abdominal junction (Fig. 23.15*a*). This has functional significance for the life of the worm in its tube, but in the present connection it is of interest in the reorganization process mentioned above.

The capacity for regeneration in a sabellid worm is the same throughout the body, at whatever level from head to tail. Posterior regeneration is not notably different from that of other polychaetes, but anterior regeneration is always restricted to three segments. These develop from the blastema, which forms from any anterior cut surface. As with the head blastema of the nemertean and that formed from the stump of an amputated amphibian limb, the head blastema of a sabellid is clearly a self-contained, self-organizing developmental system. As such it is an exceptionally promising subject for further analysis of the processes leading to the elaborate structure of the combined three anterior segments: prostominal segment with brain, peristomial segment with tentacle

Figure 23.15 Reconstitution in the polychaete *Sabella*. *a* Anterior end of worm showing crown of tentacles, junction between "head" and thorax, and junction between thorax and abdomen. The bristle tuft and row of hooks characteristic of each segment are reversed in position in thoracic segments compared with abdominal segments. *b* Stage in reconstitution of abdominal piece of worm, showing regenerating "head" in front of the junction with the thorax and a gradation in the stage of transformation of abdominal-type segments into thoracic-type segments. *c* Completed reconstitution of an individual from a piece consisting of four originally abdominal segments. A new functional "head" has regenerated anterior to the left arrow, the four originally abdominal segments have transformed into thoracic segments, and 19 new abdominal segments have regenerated posterior to the arrow on the right.

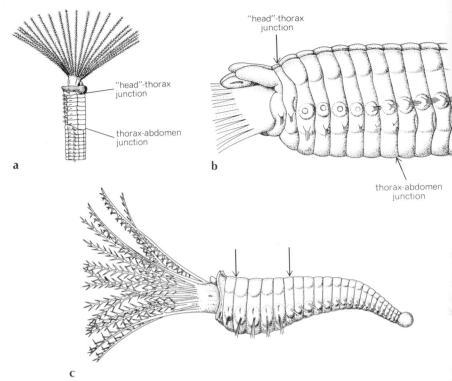

crown, and collar segment associated with tube building. A basic question to be answered is why such a definitive three-segment unit should form, whatever the number of segments removed.

What defines the potentiality of the blastema? In a species such as *Clymenella*, does the blastema determine how many segments are added to the anterior end of the original piece, or does the old tissue determine the extent of the outgrowth? Or is there an interaction at the junction between old and new?

The sabellid situation is not so much enlightening as challenging. If a piece of the abdominal region of a sabellid is isolated, a blastema forms at the anterior end, giving rise to the typical anterior three head segments. No thoracic segments are regenerated, but a number of the most anterior, originally abdominal, segments become transformed into thoracic-type segments (Fig. 23.15*b*). The transformation is seen as a progressive disappearance of the parapodial bristles and hooks, beginning in the most anterior segment, and their replacement with comparable structures in the inverse position. Simultaneously, changes occur in the anterior part of the intestine.

Apparently a "morphogenetic field" of some sort is established by the presence of the blastema, which in effect represents the whole new organization. In the absence of thoracic replacement by distal regeneration of new tissue, reorganization of old tissue is the only alternative if normal structural and physiological relationships are to be restored. As a rule, the number of abdominal segments transformed to the thoracic type is about the same as that in a normal, intact worm. However, in one species at least, *Sabella pavonina*, a beam of intense light at the blue end of the spectrum directed at the developing blastema may cause the transformation process to extend a tenfold distance down the length of a worm. Repeated amputations of the developing head of a single worm may have the same effect. This effect calls for further investigation.

Bipolar Head Regeneration

Anteroposterior polarization may be replaced by a bipolar phenomenon resulting in regeneration of anterior structure from both ends.

Bipolar regeneration has been induced in *Sabella* (Figs. 23.16, 23.17) by means of exposure to colchicine. Colchicine inhibits all regeneration, but when colchicine-treated pieces are returned to normal seawater, a head may regenerate from each end. When such a two-headed piece is bisected, however, the anterior portion regenerates a tail posteriorly, and the posterior portion regenerates a head anteriorly. The original polarity is regained. The interpretation offered is that colchicine reversibly disrupts the normal array of microtubules in the nerve cord; i.e., it causes a temporary depolarization, while the production of neurosecretory granules is not inhibited. It is suggested that in the presence of colchicine, neurohormone concentrations in the most posterior segments increase beyond the threshold level for tail regeneration, thereby abolishing the axial gradient; and in response to the increased levels, the cells of the posterior regenerate engage in morphogenetic events that lead to the formation of head structures.

It has long been known that very short pieces of a stem of the hydroid *Tubularia* and similarly short pieces of a flatworm generally reconstitute "head" structure at both ends. This was explained by Child in terms of his theory of metabolic gradients: When the two cut surfaces are close together, the metabolic rates at the two ends are not sufficiently different to establish an effective polarizing gradient, and both ends accordingly develop as dominant regions. Normal head reconstition (regeneration) and bipolar development are shown in Figs. 23.18 and 23.19.

Figure 23.16 Bipolar head regeneration in *Sabella*. Following exposure to colchicine, a typical three-segment head regenerates from the healed posterior cut surface in place of a tail as in normal regeneration. Reorganization of abdominal segments to thoracic segments takes place under the influence of each head. If bisected, the original anterior portion, however, now regenerates a tail, while the original posterior portion regenerates a head. [*Courtesy of T. P. Fitzharris.*]

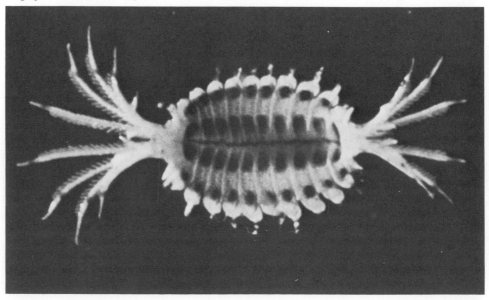

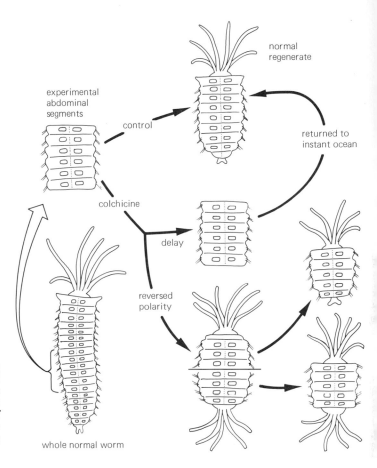

Figure 23.17 Diagram of experiments showing bipolar head regeneration, involving reversal of polarity at posterior end of worm fragment following exposure to colchicine. Note, when bipolar piece subsequently is bisected, each half regenerates according to normal polarity, posteriorly and anteriorly respectively. [*Courtesy of T. P. Fitzharris.*]

Figure 23.18 *a* Reconstitution of a new head (hydranth) from the distal part of a piece of *Tubularia* stem. Four stages, from left to right: pigment-band stage representing future tentacle zones, later stage with tentacle ridges in proximal but not in distal zone, completed hydranth still in original position within cuticle, and functional hydranth extended beyond cuticle. *b* Prospective development of parts isolated from reconstituting *Tubularia* stem. [*After Davidson and Berrill*, J. Exp. Zool., **107**:473 (1948).]

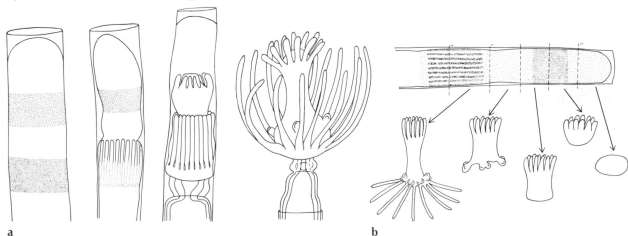

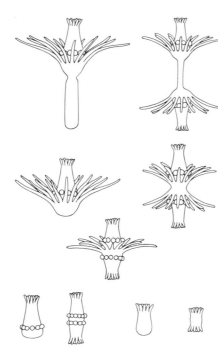

Figure 23.19 Independence of apical region in hydroid *Tubularia*. Partial regeneration occurs in short-stemmed pieces of stalk, which may be uniaxial; it gives rise to as much of the rest of the organism as can be formed from the available material, with apical structure forming at the expense of more proximal structure. Short pieces also commonly produce whole or partial hydroid structure at each end. [*After Child, 1915.*]

Bipolar regeneration also occurs in very short pieces of the abdominal region of the ascidian *Clavelina*. The anatomy of this ascidian is not important here, except that a nerve cord is not present. In this ascidian, Brien demonstrated that the timing of cuts is as important as the distance between them. If short pieces are isolated by cuts made almost simultaneously, anterior (thoracic) structure forms from both surfaces. If the posterior cut is made an hour, more or less, *after* the first cut, typical anterior and posterior regeneration occurs at the two surfaces respectively; i.e., the original polarity of the tissue persists. The *orientation*, presumably of macromolecular components, may be more significant than concentration gradients of either ions or molecules in determining and maintaining tissue polarity. The dc electric current of injury may well be responsible for establishing the initial direction of polarization. That is, in short pieces resulting from simultaneous cuts, the polarizing current produces its effect in opposite directions from the two ends.

For nearly a century, investigations of reconstitutive development, both regenerative and reorganizational, have been conducted on a wide assortment of organisms, mostly invertebrates. The literature is vast and has been reviewed at considerable length in another publication (Berrill, 1961). In the present context, space permits only a brief sampling of the rich diversity of material and experiments; although it is perhaps sufficient to serve as a general indication of the scope of this field of enterprise and to give minimal leads to the literature. This is continued in the following chapter on Asexual Development, which inevitably overlaps the more specific aspects of regenerative development just described.

BECKER, R. D., 1974. The Significance of Bioelectric Potentials, *Bioelectrochemistry and Bioenergetics*, **1**:187–199.

BERRILL, N. J., 1961. "Growth, Development and Pattern," (Chaps. 11, 12), Freeman.

BRØNSTEDT, H. V., 1970. "Planarian Regeneration," Pergamon; also *Biol. Rev.*, **30**:65–126 (1955).

COE, W. R., 1934. Analysis of the Regenerative Processes in Nemerteans, *Biol. Bull.*, **66**:304–315.

FABER, J., 1971. Vertebrate Limb Ontogeny and Limb Regeneration: Morphogenetic Parallels, *Advan. Morphog.*, **9**:127–149.

FITZHARRIS, T. P., 1973. Control Mechansims in Regeneration and Expression of Polarity, *Amer. Sci.*, **61**:456–462.

GOSS, R. J., 1968. "Principles of Regeneration," Academic.

HAY, E., 1966. "Regeneration," Holt, Rinehart and Winston.

KIORTSIS, K., and H. A. L. TRAMPUSCH (eds.), 1965. "Regeneration in Animals and Related Problems," North-Holland Publishing Company, Amsterdam.

LIVERSAGE, R. A., and K. R. S. FISHER, 1974. Regeneration of the Forelimb in Adult Hypophysectomized *Notophthalmus* (*Diemictylus*) *viridescens* Given Embryonic or Adult Chicken Anterior Pituitary Extract, *J. Exper. Zool.*, **190**:133–141.

LUND, E. J., 1921. Experimental Control of Organic Polarity by the Electrical Current, *J. Exp. Zool.*, **54**:471–491.

MIZELL, M., and J. J. ISAACS, 1970. Induced Regeneration of Hindlimbs in the Newborn Opossum, *Amer. Zool.*, **10**:141–155.

NEEDHAM, J., 1950. "Biochemistry and Morphogenesis," Cambridge University Press.

ROSE, S. M., 1970. "Regeneration," Appleton-Century-Crofts.

———, 1970. Differentiation during Regeneration Caused by Repressors in Bioelectric Fields., *Amer. Zool.*, **10**:91–100.

SCHMIDT, A. J., 1968. "Cellular Biology of Vertebrate Regeneration and Repair," The University of Chicago Press.

SINGER, M., 1973. "Limb Regeneration in Vertebrates," Addison-Wesley.

SMITH, S. D., 1963. Specific Inhibition of Regeneration in *Clymenella torquata*, *Biol. Bull.*, **125**:542–555.

STOCUM, D. L., 1968. The Urodele Limb Regeneration Blastema: A Self-organizing System, *Develop. Biol.*, **18**:441–456, 457–480.

THORTON, C. S., 1970. Amphibian Limb Regeneration and Its Relation to Nerves, *Amer. Zool.*, **10**:113–118.

TUCKER, M., 1959. Inhibitory Control of Regeneration in Nemertean Worms, *J. Morphol.*, **105**:569–600.

WALLACE, H., 1972. The Components of Regrowing Nerves which Support the Regeneration of Irradiated Salamander Limb, *J. Embryol. Exp. Morphol.*, **28**:419–435.

CHAPTER 24

Asexual Development

Asexual Reproduction in Coelenterates

> Structure of *Hydra*
> Individuality
> Maintenance of form and growth
> Reconstitution of form
> Positional information theory
> Development of reaggregated tissue cells
> Polymorphic development

Asexual Reproduction in Tunicates

> Budding in ascidians
> Bud development
> Budding in thaliaceans

Meristems
Questions and Answers

Asexual reproduction in animals appears to be an exploitation of a general capacity for regenerative growth that is common in some degree to most living organisms. As a rule the process consists of setting apart a small fragment of tissue, physically or physiologically separate from the parental body and capable of developing into a new whole. Asexual reproduction may be concerned with the formation of colonial systems consisting of many individuals associated in various degrees of organic or physical intimacy. In some cases they form a true superorganism in which the life and function of the individual are subordinated to the life and function of the whole. In other cases, such reproduction may result in the production and liberation of large numbers of free individuals, building up enormous populations while circumstances are favorable, although with minimal genetic variation.

Whatever purpose it may serve, the process of asexual development varies greatly according to the cell and tissue constitution of the segregated fragment. In the polychaete *Dodecaria,* for example, the individual worm breaks up (*autotomy*) under certain natural conditions into single segments, and each segment then heals and regenerates anteriorly and posteriorly to become a new complete individual. The phenomenon and the problems are those of regeneration described in the preceding chapter. In other cases—e.g., the buds of ascidians such as *Botryllus*—the segregated tissue may consist of so few cells that the term regeneration becomes a misnomer, for we see a developmental phenomenon as complete as that displayed by any egg.

Two aspects of asexual reproduction should be distinguished. One is the means of segregation and constitution of the reproductive unit; the other is the manner of development of such a unit. The former is generally recognized as the process of budding, and the latter as the development of the bud. The association of these terms with plant reproduction, apart from seeds, is fully recognized, for asexual reproduction in animals has much in common with that in plants. Among animals the process is exploited mainly in aquatic groups that are either sessile (attached to a solid surface) or are drifting or floating forms with little or no directive locomotion. These are the tunicates (particularly the orders ascidians and thaliaceans), the coelenterates (or cnidarians), certain polychaete and planarian worms, and the sponges and bryozoans. In plants it is seen in the production and development of spores and bulbs and in the development of every shoot. Among protists (single-cell organisms of either plant or animal character) it is the predominant form of reproduction. Altogether this is an enormous field of inquiry and no more than a brief introduction is possible in this chapter. An extensive survey of the phenomena and literature is contained in the book "Growth, Development and Pattern" by Berrill. The present account therefore highlights certain of the more interesting examples.

ASEXUAL REPRODUCTION IN COELENTERATES

The best-known and most-studied organism that reproduces by budding and also by egg and sperm production is *Hydra*. Buds and eggs develop directly into small hydras, differing little except that buds develop as hollow outgrowths of the body wall whereas eggs cleave to form an elongate, ciliated embryo. Called the *planula*, it develops a mouth and ring of tentacles at one end, as in the development of a bud. As long as environmental conditions of food, space, temperature, etc. remain optimal, budding hydras are virtually immortal; so are their budding progeny. Following sexual maturity and reproduction, however, a process usually incompatible with budding, the individuals commonly regress and may or may not recover. The onset of sexual maturation is generally a seasonal response to changing environmental circumstances, and fertilized eggs may alone survive adverse conditions the adults cannot tolerate. The development of the hydra bud cannot be separated from the succeeding growth and maintenance of the juvenile and adult stages, for it is all one continuous process. Even the process of budding itself must be seen as an integral part of the cellular activities that constitute a hydra.

Structure of Hydra

It is no accident that, among animals, *Hydra* has been so intensively studied over the years. Simple in gross structure, it is essentially a tube with a mouth (an oral cone, or hypostome) and a ring of hypostomial tentacles at one end, and an adhesive foot, or basal disc, at the other. It is simple in tissue structure, consisting of two epithelial layers, the epidermis and gastrodermis, separated by a thin layer of collagenous noncellular mesoglea. It is small, about 10 mm long and 1 mm wide when extended; yet it is large enough to be readily observed and amenable to operation. It is composed of about 100,000 cells, a seemingly large number, yet relatively small. There are only 17 distinguishable kinds of cells, representing a much smaller number of basic types. Yet despite its comparative simplicity of structure, the organism presents most of the familiar problems concerning the maintenance of form and the diversification of tissues and cells encountered in the study of multicellular organisms generally.

Hydra has been a classic subject for analysis ever since its discovery more than two centuries ago. The Abbé Trembley in Holland observed and experimented on hydras, employing very simple means. He saw the process of reproduction by budding. He succeeded in cutting the small animal in two and observed the regeneration of the amputated part; he managed to insert a hair through the mouth of a hydra and pull the creature inside out, subsequently observing the process of recovery to the normal state. Such was the beginning.

Individuality

A hydra is a strongly polarized multicellular organism that is maintained by an uninterrupted production and flow of cellular elements, combined with a certain rate of differentiation and aging of the cells. The system has to be recognized as the direct consequence of a series of interacting and balanced processes constituting a steady state rather than a fixed, structural pattern. Not only form but also size is a property of the specific state characteristic of this organism. When, for example, the heads and bases of hydras are amputated and the trunks are grafted together in series, the giant tube thus formed, although regenerating a new head with tentacles, does not remain a single giant individual. Each portion asserts its individuality, regenerates head and stalk, and separates. It is significant that individual separation occurs sequentially, beginning with the unit farthest from the regenerated head (Fig. 24.1).

Maintenance of Form and Growth

The pioneering work of Brien and Reniers-Decoen more than 20 years ago laid the foundation for the present analysis of the subtle processes of growth and maintenance in hydras. They grafted various portions, such as hypostome and the upper part of the body column, of individuals which had been stained with a vital dye—neutral red, methylene blue, or Nile blue sulfate-into various levels of the body column of unstained individuals. Such stained material migrates toward the basal disc, where it eventually disappears. When grafted immediately beneath the tentacle ring, stained tissue migrates toward the tentacle tips. The interpretation was made that hydras possess a growth region, or special growth zone, just below the level of the tentacles, where relatively rapid cell division is supposed to occur in both epidermis and gastrodermis. Only the hypostome, i.e., the conical and expansible tissue between mouth and tentacles, appears to be stable.

According to this interpretation, supported by Burnett, a region of maximal growth appears to exist as a subhypostomal growth zone beneath the ring of tentacles. As cells multiply, new tissue forms most rapidly in this region. It continuously moves not only toward the base of the organism but also distally into the tentacles, displacing older tissue until the aging tissue reaches the extremities, where it is sloughed off.

Recent analyses by Shostak show that in the gastrodermis, at least, there are four separate self-generating cell populations. A population at each end of the body column supports the tentacles and the basal disc, respectively. Two populations meet at the lower edge of the budding region and support the development of buds, although they can also expand and produce lengthening of the body. Altogether this is a different picture of tissue maintenance from that of a subtentacular growth zone. Yet there is no doubt of a general movement of the epidermal (epitheliomuscular) and gastrodermal (digestive) cells down the length of the body column. Since the pattern and rates of cell division do not

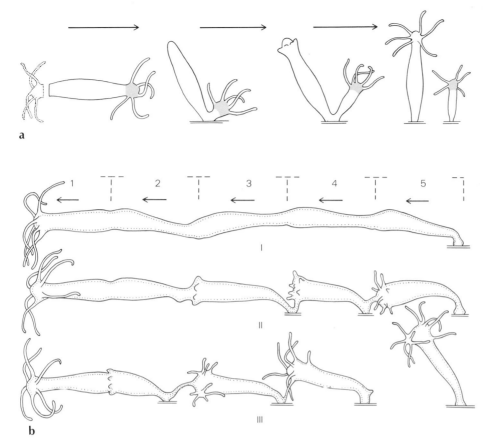

Figure 24.1 Polarity and individuality in *Hydra*. *a* Head of hydra (shaded) grafted to foot of decapitated hydra: decapitated hydra regenerates new head from its anterior cut surface, grafted head grows new column of its own, and the two individual hydras eventually separate. *b* A series of five decapitated hydras are grafted tandem to form a single long column. The original anterior region of each decapitated hydra reconstitutes a new head (hypostome and tentacles), commencing with the most posterior original individual, the process proceeding anteriorly according to their original polarity. [*After Tardent*, Arch. Entwickl.-mech., **146**:640 (1954).]

satisfactorily explain it, what does? Does the mesoglea play a role? This has been suggested. It is probably significant that mesogleal strands, bands of interstitial cells, and the succession of bud initiations all move in a spiral course in the column.

There is still agreement that a band of column material which appears stationary exists just below the tentacles. From this region tissues move distally along the hypostome, outward along the tentacles, and proximally down the column to the buds or onto the stalk. Yet studies by Campbell of the distribution and frequency of cells in division along a hydra column, together with related studies of the incorporation by cell nuclei of tritiated thymidine, suggest that cell growth and division are much more widespread through the column than has been supposed (Fig. 24.2). The existence of a restricted and exclusive growth zone is in doubt. *The body column of a hydra may be viewed as an expanding cylinder whose elongation is balanced by tissue loss at the two ends.* Since tissues at the two ends of the column are moving in opposite directions,

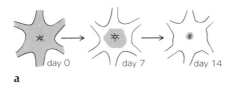

a

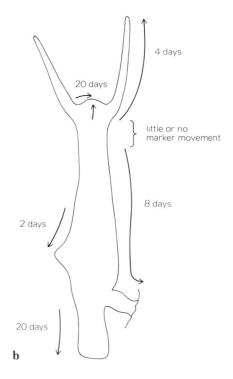

4 days

20 days

} little or no
marker movement

8 days

2 days

20 days

b

Figure 24.2 Tissue-movement pattern, based on movement of tissue markers. Numbers indicate the approximate time (days) for a marker to move along the path shown by the arrow. *a* Movement along the hypostome. *b* Movement distally and proximally from the stationary zone below the tentacles. [*After Campbell, 1967.*]

there has to be one intermediate column level where tissue does not move with respect to the animal's structure. *Therefore a stationary region must be present regardless of how the growth is distributed along the column.*

The two epithelial sheets of tissue described above are the primary cellular structure (Fig. 24.3). The epidermis consists of large epitheliomuscular cells, unspecialized interstitial cells, various nerve cells, and sting cells (cnidocytes) containing a nematocyst. The gastrodermis consists of large gastric epitheliomuscular cells, together with more specialized gland cells and mucous cells. *Hydra* in fact may be regarded as essentially a single cell layer, or epithelium, adhering to each side of a cylindrical collagenous endoskeleton. Cells move proximally over this endoskeleton, the two layers tending to move at different rates. The completely isolated mesoglea retains the shape of the animal and remains elastic. New epidermis slipped over denuded mesoglea adheres and migrates.

The problem of form in a fully grown and well-fed hydra necessarily includes the initiation and growth of buds from a level about two-thirds down the body column, since the buds are an integral part of the individual until the time of their separation (Fig. 24.4). Furthermore, the growth and development of the hydra form begins with the formation of the bud rudiment. In fact, the rate of lengthening of a hydra is 10 times greater during its development as a bud than it is following detachment from the parent. Buds begin to form on a new individual only after the parental rate of growth is already decreasing. During the process of bud formation both parental epidermal and gastrodermal tissue extends outward as the tubular body column of a bud, so that much of the growth of the parental body column as a whole becomes channeled into the growth of buds. Well-fed hydras bud continually; underfed hydras may not bud at all.

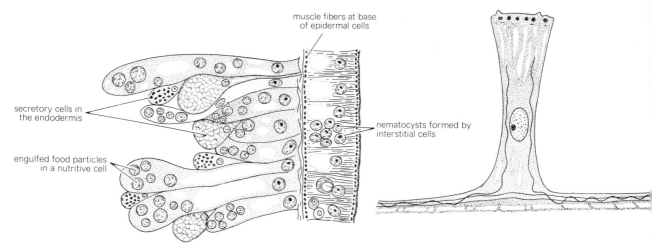

muscle fibers at base of epidermal cells

secretory cells in the endodermis

engulfed food particles in a nutritive cell

nematocysts formed by interstitial cells

Figure 24.3 Histology of *Hydra*. *a* Section through the gastric region of the body wall. *b* An epitheliomuscular cell. [*After Hyman, 1940.*]

Figure 24.4 Hydra with tentacles expanded and with a number of buds forming on the body column. Successively forming buds arise in helical arrangement, seemingly according to available space on the narrow column in the budding region. [*After Brien and Decoen, 1949.*]

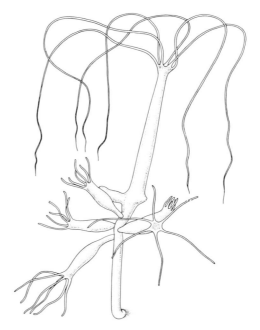

Reconstitution of Form

The problem of form in *Hydra* relates not only to the growth and maintenance processes seen in the normal cycle. A hydra can regenerate a hypostome and tentacles rapidly and repeatedly after all interstitial cells have been destroyed by exposure of the hydra to nitrogen mustard. Normal proportions can be retained or reconstituted apparently even without any cell division at all. For example, a starved hydra keeps its shape while slowly diminishing in size; a minced hydra rapidly reorganizes into a complete animal or animals, mainly through reassembly of the constituent cells. A decapitated column regenerates

523

a new hypostome and tentacle ring, though the time necessary for initial hypostome determination is less when the cut is made distally and becomes progressively greater as the cut is made more proximally. Amputation at the basal disc is followed by regeneration of a new basal disc. A hypostome grafted into the side of the body induces the outgrowth of a new column and tentacles. Hydras partially divided lengthwise and fused together longitudinally, thereby forming individuals with an excess of tentacles, subsequently reduce the tentacle number to normal, and so on. In most cases the key event seems to be the initiation or formation of a new hypostome, from which all else follows. This was well demonstrated by Chalkley (1945), who found that in masses of minced body sections new organization centers first appear as hypostomal outgrowths, and also that the number of such centers varies directly with the volume of tissue in the mass.

The crucial question is: How is a distinction made between the hypostome and the rest of the form? Burnett suggests that the differentiation and maintenance of a polarized cellular form in hydras is at least in part controlled chemically by a diffusible factor concentrated in, and probably produced by, nerves of the hypostome.

From crude extracts of *Hydra*, a substance of molecular weight of about 900, and probably a peptide, has been isolated and enriched. It activates head and bud formation. The head-activating substance, mainly produced by or at least stored by nerve cells, occurs as a gradient decreasing from the hypostomal to the basal region. From the nerve cells the substance is released steadily or, dependent upon certain stimuli, in minute concentrations. Since the granules containing head-activating activity are present as a concentration gradient decreasing from the hypostomal to the basal region, this release would suffice to build up and maintain a gradient of freely diffusible head-activating substance.

Two simple mechanisms are available for generating stable gradients of a substance:

1 A simple diffusion mechanism involving continuous production of a substance by a source and continuous removal by a sink. Either the sink or the source must be located at one end of the axis.
2 A mechanism involving polarized, or unidirectional, transport of a substance coupled with back diffusion.

Neither of these appears to be fully satisfactory; in each case, while many results are explainable, others are not. Experiments involving tandem grafting (Fig. 24.1*b*) represent a promising approach to the gradient-control question.

Positional Information Theory

The concept of positional information, already discussed, has been developed by Wolpert and associates with particular regard to the problems of organization presented by *Hydra*. The older concepts of the relation of gradients to regulation of form, as in hydras when pieces are removed or added, have remained vague and unsatisfactory. Positional information was recognized by Driesch at the beginning of this century as the cell or tissue property that causes them to undergo specific differentiation according to their position in the system. The present concept represents an attempt to introduce a more rigorous and quantitative conceptual framework for considering pattern formation and regulation.

The basis of the proposed mechanism is that cells first have their position specified with respect to certain boundary regions, as in a coordinate system. This positional information is then interpreted by the cells according to their genome and developmental history. Once the idea of position specification is accepted, our attention is drawn at once to the specification of the boundary regions and the properties of the system that enable position to be specified. According to Wolpert, a hydra may be regarded, along its main axis, as a bipolar field. He defines a field as that set of cells which have their position specified with respect to the same coordinate system or boundary regions. The hydra field is bipolar, since the two boundary reference regions appear to be the head and foot ends. The variation in positional value along the hydra may be represented by a gradient in some cellular property, which decreases steadily from the head to the foot end. For this gradient to provide positional information, a fixed value must be assigned to the head and foot ends, and the values reestablished when a head or foot is removed. A sophisticated discussion of this concept as it relates to *Hydra* is included in "The Developmental Biology of the Cnidaria" (1974) together with reports of many recent investigations, a symposium.

Development of Reaggregated Tissue Cells

Separated cells of hydra reaggregate and develop into normal animals in essentially the same way as dissociated tissues of sponges. Suspensions of hydra cells produced by mechanical disruption of hydra tissues in a suitable culture medium reaggregate spontaneously in dense cell suspensions, but especially when the cells are centrifuged together. Suspensions and aggregates contain cells in approximately normal proportions of interstitial cells, cnidoblasts, nerve cells, gland cells, and epitheliomuscular cells of ectoderm and endoderm. Reaggregates develop or regenerate tentacles, hypostomes, and basal discs in 3 to 5 days, but only when the reaggregates consist of at least 15 percent epithelial cells and a total minimum of about 50,000 cells. Histological analyses show that more than half the nerve cells of the aggregate have differentiated from incorporated interstitial cells.

According to Gierer and colleagues (1972), development of reaggregates begins at once and takes the following course:

1   Within a few hours the aggregate acquires a smooth surface and a clear outer layer surrounding an orange core, representing the two primary layers.

2   A hollow sphere is formed by the end of the first day.

3   Tentacle buds appear and usually spread irregularly over the whole surface before the end of the second day.

4   Hypostomes appear and the tentacles begin to collect around the hypostomes, or are resorbed, after 2½ to 3 days.

5   After 5 days the regenerate is able to feed on brine shrimp (*Artemia*) larvae.

6   The hypostomes eventually divide up the tissue, and several normal individuals develop, capable of budding later on.

Clearly, the capacity to form or re-form the organized shape and the cell and tissue activities we recognize as a hydra is a property of any assemblage of hydra cells that consists of a minimum number and diversity. Within such an aggregate local centers self-assemble as hypostomes of specific, innate dimensions, each of which organizes adjacent tissue in competition with other centers.

Polymorphic Development

Hydra is a solitary hydroid of the coelenterate class Hydrozoa. Most of the members of this class exist in two forms: the hydranth or polyp, which resembles a hydra, and the medusa or jellyfish. Where the medusa is present as part of the life cycle, it is the sexual stage, although in some species even the medusa may reproduce by budding in addition to sexual reproduction. The presence of two such different types of organisms in the typical hydroid life cycle raises the same questions concerning genomic control as the metamorphoses in sea urchin, frog, and insect. A difference is that in hydroids and also in the other medusa-forming coelenterates, the Scyphozoa, both hydranth and medusa may be produced from the parental somatic tissue and not necessarily from an egg. These phenomena present challenging problems, such as the initial determinative event that directs a particular small area of somatic tissue into one developmental path (hydranth formation) or the other (medusa formation), and the developmental process (morphogenesis) whereby one product is formed rather than the other.

A hydroid colony commonly produces new individuals from various sites along its system of stems and connecting basal stolons. New growths arise as outgrowths from stem or stolon, resembling an early stage of bud outgrowth in hydras. The terminal part of such an outgrowth typically develops into a feeding polyp, or hydranth, which consists essentially of rings of tentacles surrounding a gastric column. Alternatively, an outgrowth may develop into a medusa of different form and size from a hydranth and complete with internal canals and marginal sense organs. Eventually the medusa is set free to grow to sexual maturity (Fig. 24.5). The same parental tissues are involved in the production of both types of individual.

What determines which course of development will be taken is far from being understood, although temperature and light are among external factors, and nutrition and cell relationships are among internal factors. However this may be, the important fact is that one of two or more very different paths of development, leading to the formation of very different kinds of individuals, may be taken by groups of cells with the same genetic constitution and from adjacent regions of the same parental structure.

Transformative Development The egg of the common jellyfish *Aurelia*, like that of virtually all hydrozoan and scyphozoan coelenterates, hydra included, develops into a small elongate, cilia-covered planula larva. In *Aurelia* and other scyphozoans, the planula attaches by one end and develops a mouth and ring of tentacles at the other; i.e., it becomes a hydralike polyp, or scyphistoma (Fig. 24.6). The polyp grows and produces buds laterally from the body wall in essentially the same way as hydras do, the buds separating and becoming attached alongside the parent polyps which they replicate. Extensive polyp colonies are thus produced, as in hydras, that persist throughout most of the year. Each polyp grows to a certain maximum size, with individual growth otherwise being siphoned off, so to speak, through the process of budding.

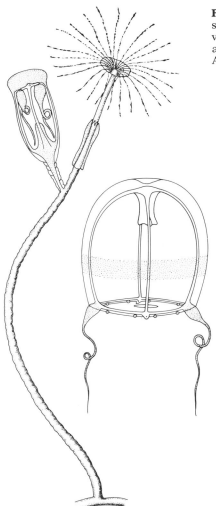

Figure 24.5 Polymorphic development in hydroid, showing fully formed hydranth with a fully developed medusa growing from stalk, and a liberated, expanded medusa. [*After Rees*, J. Mar. Biol. Assoc. U.K., **23**:*1, (1939).*]

Figure 24.6 Strobilating scyphistomas of *Aurelia*, both polydisc and monodisc. [*Photo by Clarence Flaten, courtesy of Dorothy Spangenberg.*]

In nature, during spring months, polyps undergo a segmentation, or strobilation, process. That is, transverse epidermal constrictions mark off a series of segments of the trunk, forming in sequence beginning at the distal end and eventually consuming all but the basal part of the polyp (Fig. 24.7). During the process of constriction each segment develops the basic organization of a medusa, complete with radial symmetry, gastric filaments, statocysts, and pulsating musculature. The young medusa, set free as an ephyra, grows massively to become a sexually mature aurelia. This life cycle is of course well known, but it exemplifies again that diverse forms—polyp and medusa—can be expressed by the same genome under different circumstances, and also that here there is an actual transformation of polyp (hydranth) into multiple medusae. Segmentation initiates the process and is followed in each segment by a true metamorphosis (Fig. 24.8). The residual polyp, following strobilation, regrows and repeats the process year after year.

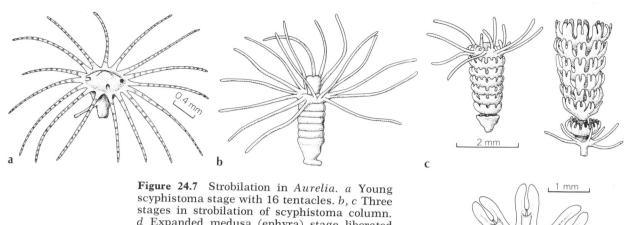

Figure 24.7 Strobilation in *Aurelia*. *a* Young scyphistoma stage with 16 tentacles. *b, c* Three stages in strobilation of scyphistoma column. *d* Expanded medusa (ephyra) stage liberated from top of strobilating column. [*After Uchida and Nagao, 1963.*]

Many attempts have been made to identify the environmental factor or factors responsible for triggering the strobilation process. Several have been implicated, particularly temperature; a preconditioning by exposure to comparatively low temperatures appears to be generally necessary. The only dependable effective agent so far discovered, by Spangenberg, is iodine. It is effective as iodide or as thyroxine when added to artificial seawater used as a culture medium for laboratory-maintained *Aurelia* polyps. Natural seawater normally contains iodine in trace amounts, and since the iodine content undoubtedly fluctuates with the seasonal growth and decay of iodine-binding seaweeds, iodine may well be the trigger in nature as well. In any case, it is striking that

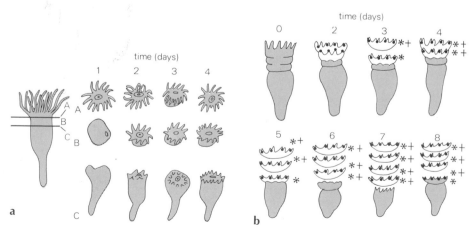

Figure 24.8 Strobilation in *Aurelia*. *a* Regeneration of segments of polyp stage, to reconstitute new polyp. *b* Time sequence of medusa (ephyra) development and liberation. [*After Spangenberg, 1967.*]

* pulsing   + gastric filament   ☐ medusa tissue
• statocysts   filament   ▨ polyp tissue

iodine and thyroxine are capable of initiating a profound metamorphosis in such unrelated organisms as jellyfish and amphibians. What the significant change may be that iodine brings about in the tissue metabolism of the responsive organisms remains a question for the future.

Alternative Differentiation   Depending on circumstances, the same tissue may give rise to either a newly developed individual (asexual reproduction) or to differentiated sexual tissue, male or female. This is evident in hydras. The middle region of the column may be heavily involved in forming bud outgrowths, which successively develop and detach, with both the gastrodermis and epidermis taking part; under certain other conditions, the epidermal cells of the same region differentiate into testes and/or ovaries, when budding usually ceases (Fig. 24.9).

An even more striking case is seen in certain small jellyfish (the medusae of *Rathkea*, a marine hydrozoan). Medusae are formed and set free from the small hydralike polyp. But instead of growing directly to a sexually mature state, they proceed to form exclusively epidermal buds on the manubrium, which develop directly into new medusae. These are set free successively, to grow and produce similar medusae in turn, until enormous populations are established. The procedure continues as long as the ocean temperatures remain below about 7°C. When the temperature rises above this level, the budding process stops and all medusae differentiate testes or ovaries from the tissue that

Figure 24.9   Mature sexual form of *Hydra* (male), showing development of translucent testis in the epidermis of the trunk, and suppression of budding.

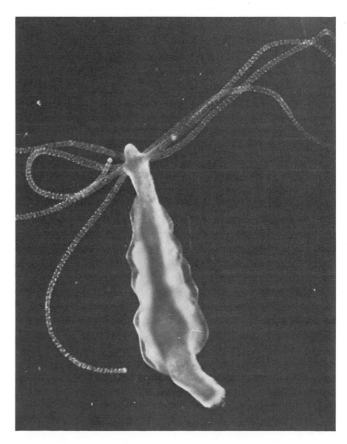

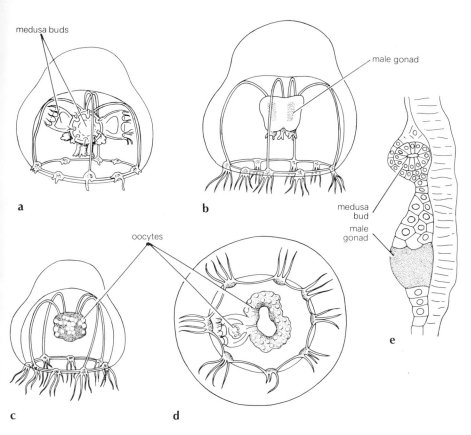

medusa buds

a

male gonad

b

oocytes

c

d

medusa
bud
male
gonad

e

Figure 24.10 Conversion from medusa-bud production to sexual reproduction in the medusa of *Rathkea octopunctata*. *a* At low temperatures medusa buds form successively from the ectoderm of the manubrium. *b, c* At higher temperatures medusa-bud production ceases and the same ectodermal tissue differentiates into either male or female gonad, according to the genetic sex of the parental individual. *d* Sexually differentiating medusa produces sexually differentiating medusa bud. *e* Section of manubrium wall shows simultaneous origination of medusa bud and a male gonad from the ectoderm.

had previously been involved in budding (Fig. 24.10). In this case only the epidermis is involved in the process of bud production. It is the same epidermal tissue which becomes sexually differentiated. The two processes may well be competitive. Yet there is clearly a temperature-operated switch, at least with regard to the initiation of sexual differentiation.

Thus somatic tissue in coelenterates and at least some other kinds of animals, often initially consisting of a very few cells indeed, can readily develop asexually into complete new organisms capable of becoming sexually mature individuals; or they can produce sex cells. Furthermore, somatic development may take different paths, leading to different individual forms, depending on circumstances, even though the constituent cells have the same genetic constitution.

ASEXUAL REPRODUCTION IN TUNICATES

Tunicates, fully qualified members of the phylum Chordata, exhibit virtually every conceivable form of sexual and asexual reproduction, a versatility matched only by the coelenterates. Both kinds of reproduction appear to have been fully exploited in relation to environmental circumstances. The habitats range from the intertidal zone to the oceanic abyss and the open sea, as is also true for coelenterates. In ascidians, a tunicate class, the asexual process is exclusively concerned with the formation of colonial systems consisting of mats or masses of tunic material in which numerous small ascidian individual zooids are embedded. This encrusting form of growth enables species to flourish in habitats otherwise unavailable. Multiplication and dispersal of such colonial ascidians remain functions of fertilized eggs and the larvae they develop into, just as in the case of individually large solitary, or single, ascidians. In both types the organism remains attached following the settling and metamorphosis of the larva.

Budding in Ascidians

In ascidians the budding process takes many forms. Buds produced by different species differ widely in their tissue constitution, depending on what part of the parental organism is included. They vary from substantial segments resulting from constriction, or strobilation, that undergo regular regeneration of the missing parts, to minute discs or spheres consisting of very few cells. The latter are as simply constituted as any gastrula and are very much smaller. Inasmuch as ascidian eggs typically develop into chordate, tadpole larvae, which undergo metamorphosis, a comparison of the development of the most simple and smallest ascidian buds with such development is informative.

The development of the ascidian egg has been described in several places earlier in this book, with regard to the organization of the egg and cleavage pattern, with regard to gastrulation and neurulation, with regard to the tadpole larva and its metamorphosis into a miniature ascidian. The duality of such egg development is evident. On the one hand, the egg develops into a chordate larva, and the organization of the egg, cleavage pattern, and gastrulation appear to serve this end primarily. The swimming, nonfeeding tadpole larva, with its neurosensory-musculature equipment, functions as a special site selector for the permanent settlement of the organism. On the other hand, from the start, but more slowly, the egg develops the permanent organization of the ascidian, which continues to develop through the metamorphic period into the juvenile and later adult condition. This brief outline is a necessary basis for comparison with the development of a bud.

First, it should be mentioned that even in egg development, the tadpole stage is not an essential step in the process of becoming a young ascidian. Ascidians generally occupy the multiple attachment sites available along rocky shores, lagoons, reefs, etc., where site selection is a vital need. Some, however, inhabit the vast mud and sand flats of the continental shelf, where there is little or no need for site selection. In nearly all such species, the egg develops directly to form a miniature ascidian without forming a chordate embryo or tadpole larva. Egg size, developmental rate, gastrulation, time of hatching—all remain unaltered; but the larval enzymes responsible for sensory, tail muscle, and notochord differentiation in tadpole development are absent. The lack of these is apparently sufficient to convert the characteristic indirect course of development into a direct development. Nevertheless much of what is considered to be typical egg development remains.

Bud Development

The development of a bud is in sharp contrast with that of the egg, whether the latter is direct or indirect. The course of development is strikingly simple and direct, as, for example, in *Botryllus* and *Distaplia*. In both of these, as in other ascidians that have minimally constituted buds, such as *Perophora,* the bud primordium consists of two layers of tissue. The outer layer is derived from the parental epidermis; the inner layer is of ectodermal origin in *Botryllus,* of endodermal origin in *Perophora.* The epidermal layer in every case is already a specialized tissue whose cells secrete the external tunicin that forms a supporting extracellular coat or tunic for the organism, and from which the phylum (Tunicata) gets its name. The epidermis of the bud inherits the character of the parental epidermis. It continues to secrete tunicin. As a boundary epithelium it plays a role in shaping the body as a whole, particularly since the body wall consists only of the one-cell-thick epidermis and the extracellular material. The inner layer of bud tissue is therefore responsible for developing the whole internal organization and the cytodifferentiations associated with it. The origin of the internal layer in terms of the three primary germ layers recognized in embryonic development apparently has no significance. In every case the internal layer involved in bud formation has remained a simple limiting membrane, the cells of which presumably have undergone no histological or cytological specialization. Such cells may be regarded as units of no less potency than eggs and with nothing of the egg's elaborate specialization. Some mesenchyme cells may be included between the two basic layers constituting a bud.

In the two chosen examples, the colonial organism contains numerous individual ascidiozooids several millimeters long. In *Botryllus* the zooid is ovoid; in *Distaplia* it is slender and much longer with a very long posterior vascular extension. Body form is a specific character that is very readily perceived. In *Botryllus* the bud primordium is initially a disc of enlarged atrial (ectodermal) epithelial cells associated with a corresponding area of overlying epidermis. It shortly converts into a two-layered vesicle (Fig. 24.11) with unmodified epidermis externally surrounding an inner sphere of enlarged epithelial cells. Such primordia arise from the lateral body wall of the parent. In *Distaplia,* buds arise from the distal end of the long posterior epidermal extension of the body containing a tubular epithelial extension known as the *epicardium.* The buds form by constriction of the epidermal structure and are pinched off as minute, two-layered vesicles resembling those of *Botryllus* formed from the bud discs. Apart from the different sources of the buds in these two genera and the need in *Botryllus* to convert a disc into a vesicle, the starting point for development is virtually identical: a double-layered epithelial sphere with some resemblance to the late gastrula stage of an amphioxus and various invertebrates. The bud

Figure 24.11 Direct development in the buds of two types of ascidians, showing development of double-layered disc of *Botryllus* bud into stage with six primary organization divisions by invaginative and evaginative foldings, and comparable stages of bud of *Distaplia.*

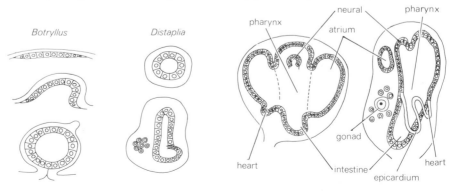

vesicle in both *Botryllus* and *Distaplia,* however, is relatively minute. In *Botryllus* the disc stage is recognizable when only eight somewhat enlarged somatic cells are present.

Starting with the closed sphere stage (Fig. 24.11) and considering mainly the inner formative layer, two folds divide it into a median and two lateral divisions, thereby establishing the right and left atrial cavities and the central pharyngeal sac, i.e., the primary spatial divisions of the organism-to-be. Then evaginations from the central chamber establish the intestinal loop posteriorly, the heart ventrally, and the nerve-tube dorsally. Somewhat later the walls of the central sac become perforated simultaneously by rows of minute stigmata or prospective gill slits. At exactly this stage, neither sooner nor later, the bud primordia of the next generation appear as slightly thickened discs in the outer wall of the right and left atrial cavities. Before this the external form has been more or less completely acquired, although the dimensions are less than one-sixth of the final size.

Further development consists mainly of expansion and histological elaboration. Throughout the whole development the epidermal layer plays a relatively minor role, conforming to or developing the shape of the whole and producing as a structure of its own only the stolonic outgrowth that unites the bud to the colonial system of vessels.

The fact that it is possible to describe the developmental processes so briefly even in outline indicates to some extent the monumental directness of the phenomenon.

Several points merit further emphasis. One is the rigorous correlation of the features characterizing any given stage, so that if the developmental stage of one feature is known, the stage as a whole can be accurately defined. The separation of the heart evagination indicates a definite degree of development of, for example, the digestive loop or neural complex. In the development of pattern there is accordingly an invariable relationship at a given moment, with certain exceptions to be discussed later. There is no shifting in the first appearance of a character to an earlier or later stage. Such constant relationships, while obvious and possibly universal, gain rather than lose significance by virtue of their general occurrence.

Another point is the general relationship of a stage of development to its spatial dimensions.

The sphere stage already mentioned is less than one-tenth of a millimeter in diameter, consisting of the order of 100 cells. It is no more than a tenth of a millimeter long when the atrial divisions and neural, heart, and intestinal evaginations are all discernible, and the characteristic shape of the organism is already emerging. It is hard to conceive how the gross architecture of the organism could be expressed in a smaller entity or by significantly fewer cells.

With minor change, the above description could apply to the development of the *Distaplia* bud. The main difference relates to the markedly different body proportions and structural organization of the *Botryllus* and *Distaplia* zooids. These differences are evident in some degree almost from the beginning of bud development, showing that the property of wholeness as indicated by specific shape is a dynamic feature from first to last.

Budding in Thaliaceans

The thaliaceans, another class of tunicates, are pelagic inhabitants of the ocean without attachment to the sea floor at any time. In them, reproduction takes place by both sexual and asexual means. In one kind represented by *Pyrosoma*, budding results in the formation of a complex multizooid swimming organism. In the other two kinds, represented by *Salpa* and *Doliolum*, budding is primarily a means of producing exceedingly large numbers of separate free-swimming individuals. In all three cases the budding is effected by serial epidermal constriction, or strobilation, of a slender tubular structure called the *stolon*, which grows out from the base of the thorax. New individuals are set free from the end of the stolon, much as the ephyrae are set free from the strobilating scyphistoma of *Aurelia*.

MERISTEMS

Production in hydras and in those medusae that produce medusa buds from the manubrium follows a characteristically sequential course. New buds are continually produced at a critical distance from the distal end of the organism or manubrium, as the case may be. Older buds and their adjoining parental tissue shift proximally accordingly. Bud rudiments appear initially to be of essentially the same size, and the number of buds present at any one time depends on the circumference and extent of the total area involved. In other words, irrespective of the details of the budding process in any particular case, buds are initiated and exist in direct relation to available space. In essence the procedure is meristematic and may be compared to the situation in the vegetative and floral meristems of the higher plants.

The shoot or the flowering apex, as the case may be, shows two phenomena:

1   A series of well-defined territories becomes established in sequence immediately below the tip of the meristem.

2   Each territory is the site of a more or less independent development leading to leaf, shoot, or flower formation, depending on various circumstances.

This is an oversimplification, for the subject is vast and complex, and investigation of the development of meristematic units is still in its infancy.

The active growth centers are characterized by increased metabolism, cell division, and growth, resulting in the outgrowth of a leaf or bud. The fundamental problems are the same as those associated with local asexual development of buds of colonial animals, particularly hydroids, bryozoans, and tunicates. These are essentially threefold:

1   The initiation or establishment of a local territory as an independent growth center within the general organization of the parental organism, which includes the question of positioning within the meristematic system

2   The properties of such a growth center, or the territory involved, which determine what type of developmental path will be followed

3   The course of subsequent development of the unit in terms of morphogenesis, histogenesis, and cytodifferentiation

The term *phyllotaxis* has long been used to denote the regular spacing of successive leaves or other primordia on the surface of a meristem, and accordingly the arrangement of the developed structures on the mature stem. It refers not only to the regularity of the spacing but to the particular character of the spacing. The growth centers which are formed on the flank of the meristem are started near the apex a certain initial distance apart in series and at a certain distance from those already forming the ring of centers already below. As a rule the series thus formed are arranged either in a close spiral or as a number of whorls extending from the meristem apex to its base. Accordingly there are both primary and secondary growth centers. The primary center is the distal meristem itself, from which growth of the shoot apex as a whole proceeds. This region exhibits a rhythmic growth, which is seen as a regular change in shape correlated with the initiation of each secondary center. During this growth the apex passes from a minimum to a maximum volume. Each secondary center initiated successively from the apical region, whatever its manner of formation may be, represents a local region of increased growth rate relative to the rate of growth of its immediate surroundings. A rhythm in the frequency of mitosis is evident in the meristematic zone immediately distal to the zone of initiation of the primordia.

It becomes increasingly evident from the studies of the plant meristem and equally from studies of the development of eggs and other developmental units that the great technical problem arises from the fact that in all cases the most important developmental events occur in the beginning. This of course is far from surprising; yet it means that the primary analysis concerns events taking place either in single cells (though they may be large, as in the case of the apical cell of a meristem and all animal eggs) or in a group of apical meristem cells and the buds of colonial animals. So much must go on in so little space, or in so little mass of living material, that analytical progress has been severely retarded by technological difficulties. The need, with regard to experimental analysis, is to isolate the growing systems so that they can be studied under various conditions in the laboratory. Animal eggs, of course, are ready-made for such a procedure and have therefore been exploited in this way for nearly a century. The asexual developmental units of plants, excluding spores, and of those animals that exhibit such development constitute a different situation, since the developmental units are usually not only initially much smaller than most animal eggs but are typically dependent on tissue continuity with the parent organism if they are to grow and develop.

Figure 24.12 *a* Lateral view of whole-shoot meristem from a dormant vegetative bud of spruce, showing domelike apical meristem at the top, and helical whorls of primordia (secondary fields). [*U.S. Forest Service Photograph No. 520097, by J. A. Romberger, reproduced by permission.*] *b* Extension and subdivision of morphogenetic fields. [*After Nieuwkoop, 1967.*]

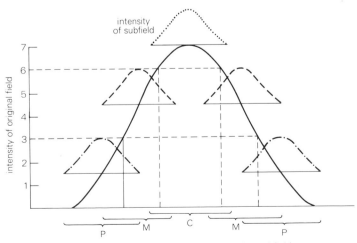

a   b

Recently, however, Romberger and his coworkers (1970) have evolved a technique for maintaining excised shoot meristems of Norway spruce and other plants under laboratory conditions, thus making the meristematic system, normally hidden and almost inaccessible, available for experimental study (Fig. 24.12). A comparable situation has prevailed in the study and experimental approach to the early development of the eggs of mammals, which are minute and are of exceptional interest but normally develop out of sight and out of reach within the mammalian womb. The domelike meristem of the spruce is about 0.3 mm in diameter and somewhat less in height. To culture it one must, while maintaining sterility, expose it to view, cut if off with a microtool, causing as little damage as possible, and transfer it to a suitable nutrient medium. The culture must then be kept sterile and be nurtured under a controlled environment while its growth response to various treatments is periodically observed. The practical problems are legion. For plant scientists the problem is comparable to that of growing test-tube mammalian embryos, though the difficulties are not as great.

QUESTIONS AND ANSWERS

The meristematic process, the strobilating process, and the morphogenetic process as a whole—as seen in the initiation and development of bud primordia—remain challenging subjects for analysis. These phenomena are to be pondered, and they call for an understanding of the nature of morphogenetic fields far beyond anything we now have. The distance from the concept of gene regulation seems almost infinite, and the prospect is wide open.

The great variety of phenomena and organisms available for study, although for the most part difficult to obtain and often hard to cultivate, holds much promise for students of developmental biology for generations to come. It is this ongoing activity that is most meaningful rather than the attainment of dogma. The philospher A. N. Whitehead wrote that "the process itself is the reality," and this phrase applies equally and cogently both to developmental processes and to activity of the developmental biologist.

READINGS

BERRILL, N. J., 1961. "Growth, Development and Pattern," Freeman.
———, 1951. Regeneration and Budding in Tunicates, *Biol. Rev.*, **26**:456–475.
———, 1950. Budding and Development in Salpa, *J. Morphol.*, **87**:553–606.
———, 1941. Spatial and Temporal Growth Patterns in Colonial Organisms, 3rd Symposium, *Growth*, **5**:89–111.
BRIEN, P., 1968. Blastogenesis and Morphogenesis, *Advan. Morphog.*, **7**:151–204.
BURNETT, A. L. (ed.), 1972. "The Biology of Hydra," Academic.
CAMPBELL, R. D., 1967. Tissue Dynamics of Steady State Growth in *Hydra littoralis*, I: Patterns of Cell Division, *Develop. Biol.*, **15**:487–502; II: Patterns of Tissue Movement, *J. Morphol.* **121**:19–28.
GIERER, A. et al., 1973. Regeneration of Hydra from Reaggregated Cells, *Nature New Biol.*, **239**:101–103.
ROMBERGER, J. A., and C. A. TAYLOR, 1970. Culture of Apical Meristems and Embryonic Shoots of *Picat abies*, *Tech. Bull. U.S. Dept. Agriculture*.
ROSE, S. M. 1970. "Regeneration," Appleton-Century-Crofts.
SCHALLER, H., and A. GIERER, 1973. Distribution of the Head-activating Substance in Hydra and Its Localization in Membranous Particles in Nerve Cells, *Develop. Biol.* **29**:39–52.
SHOSTAK, S., 1974. The Complexity of Hydra: Homeostasis, Morphogenesis, Controls, and Integration, *Quart. Rev. Biol.*, **49**:287–310.
SPANGENBERG, D., 1971. Thyroxine-Induced Metamorphosis in *Aurelia, J. Exp. Zool.*, **178**:183–194.
STEEVES, T. A., and I. M. SUSSEX, 1972. "Patterns in Plant Development," Prentice-Hall.
SYMPOSIUM, 1974. R. L. Miller, ed., The Developmental Biology of the Cnidaria, *Amer. Zool.*, **14**:437–866. (32 articles on *Hydra*, Hydroids, and Scyphozoa.)

PART VI

APPENDIX

CHAPTER 25

Methods in Cell Biology

CELL FRACTIONATION

A section of Chapter 2 deals with the nature of the ribosome, a particle so small that it is seen as a mere dot in the electron microscope. One question that must be satisfied is how investigators have learned so much about something so small. The ribosome exists as a part of a cell, and to perform biochemical studies of its nature, the integrity of the cell must first be destroyed. In higher organisms the cell is a fragile unit, whose outer membrane can be broken or dissolved by numerous treatments including pressure, shearing or grinding forces, ultrasonic vibration, detergents, or osmotic shock. Once the cells are broken and have formed an homogenate, some procedure must be used to obtain a preparation containing only the part of the cell under study. The term *cell fractionation* refers to the separation of the contents into purified fractions. The fractionation of the cell's components is desired for many reasons, and many techniques have been designed to meet this need. Typically, cells are fractionated by differential centrifugation, which describes the fact that different parts of the cell will sediment toward the bottom of a centrifuge tube at different rates of centrifugal force. In a eukaryotic organism, if a nuclear preparation is sought the homogenate is centrifuged at low centrifugal force (below $1,000 \times g$), the nuclei are spun to the bottom, and the supernatant is removed. If mitochondria are sought, the nuclei are first removed, the supernatant is then centrifuged at greater speeds (approximately $12,000 \times g$), and the mitochondria are spun out. If ribosomes are sought, as in this example, the nuclei and the mitochondria are first removed, the supernatant is subjected to ultracentrifugation at approximately $100,000 \times g$, and the ribosomes pellet at the bottom of the tube. The postribosomal supernatant now consists of the soluble phase of the cell's protoplasm and those particles too small to be easily removed. In actual practice, many more procedural steps would be required to obtain a purified organelle preparation, but the principle is that outlined above. Technological advances and creative energy in cell biology continue to allow greater sophistication in all methodology, cell fractionation included. For example, techniques of subnuclear purification include procedures for the isolation of nucleoli, nuclear membrane, specific types of chromosomes, and even the nuclear pore complex itself.

SUCROSE DENSITY GRADIENT CENTRIFUGATION

In ribosome assembly it is clear that each of the two subunits of the bacterial ribosome, the 30S and 50S particles, can be isolated from the other. To begin to separate cell components as similar as these two particles, a more sophisticated technique must be employed. One can still use the centrifuge, but an environment within the tube must be constructed that takes advantage of differences in properties of the components. The major difference between the 30S and the 50S subunit is the greater mass of the latter. These two particles are easily separated in a sucrose density gradient. To perform this operation, one must begin with a centrifuge tube filled so that the bottom contains a high cencentration of sucrose, and the concentration decreases linearly or nonlinearly toward the top, producing a gradient of sucrose. A typical gradient to separate ribosomal subunits might have 40 percent sucrose at the bottom and 10 percent sucrose at the top. To begin the separation, a small volume containing the ribosomes is carefully layered on top of the gradient. Since its density is less than 10 percent sucrose, it will form a layer without mixing. The tube is then centrifuged at high speed (generally above $30,000 \times g$), which drives the particles down into the gradient. If centrifugation is done at very low Mg^{2+} levels, the two subunits of each ribosome come apart from each other. The velocity with which a particle sediments depends upon its molecular weight. The greater the molecular weight, the faster it moves; therefore these subunits become separated within the gradient. As a particle sediments through the tube, the increasing gravitational forces it experiences cause the particle to accelerate while the increasing viscosity of the sucrose produces a counteracting effect.

This same technique can be used to fractionate larger-size particles, such as polyribosomes. Each polyribosome consists of a messenger RNA thread and ribosomes, along with the various factors needed for protein synthesis and the nascent polypeptide chain. The bulk of the polyribosome is composed of ribosomes; the number of ribosomes attached to a given mRNA will determine how rapidly that polyribosome will sediment in a sucrose gradient. Generally, larger mRNAs will have a greater number of ribosomes in their polyribosomes and will be found closer to the bottom of the tube after centrifugation. The procedure generally used is to homogenize the cells, centrifuge the homogenate to pellet the nuclei and the mitochondria, layer the supernatant (containing the polyribosomes) over the sucrose gradient, and then centrifuge the contents. If membrane-bound polyribosomes are to be examined, they must first be dissociated from their membrane attachments, a feat generally accomplished with detergents, such as sodium deoxycholate. An example of a polyribosome gradient is shown in Fig. 9.4. As in the separation of the ribosomal subunits, density gradient centrifugation allows onc to spread the various elements of a mixture into their component parts, in this case the various-size polyribosomes. The use of labeled amino acids or uridine prior to homogenization allows one to analyze which polyribosomes are most actively synthesizing protein and which polyribosomes contain newly synthesized RNA.

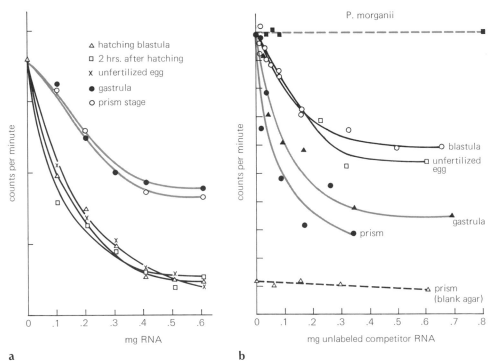

Figure 25.1 Comparison of populations of RNA present at different stages of development, using competition by unlabeled RNA of the binding of labeled RNA to DNA. In both experiments labeled RNA is incubated with DNA adsorbed to a filter in the presence of increasing concentrations of unlabeled RNAs from various stages of development. The greater the percentage of RNA species in common between the labeled and unlabeled populations, the greater will be the drop in the radioactivity (counts per minute) bound to the filter at the end of the incubation. *a* In this experiment the labeled RNA is made by blastula-stage embryos. The unlabeled RNAs from the gastrula and prism, both later stages than the blastula, are less effective competitors than RNA from earlier stages, indicating that many of the species of RNA being made by the blastula are no longer present after gastrulation. [*After Glisin et al., 1966.*] *b* In this experiment the labeled RNA was made by the prism (a postgastrulated embryo); the competition curves indicate that RNA present in the unfertilized egg and blastula contains a significant percentage of the species of RNA being made by the prism, but a significant percentage are absent. The top curve (labeled *P. morganii*) shows the effect of unlabeled RNA from a starfish; there is no competition against the labeled sea urchin RNA. [*After Whiteley et al., 1966.*]

Density gradient centrifugation can be used to separate macromolecules as well as particles. For example, if the ribosomal pellet was first extracted for its RNA, a mixture of 18S and 28S RNA would be present together. If this mixture were layered over a sucrose gradient (in this case 5 to 20 percent), these two rRNAs could be separated as easily as the 30S and 50S subunits in the previous sucrose gradient. The S values of a particle or molecule refer to its sedimentation velocity.

We have arrived at the place where the components of the original mixture have been separated, but they remain in the tube and somehow must be analyzed. The problem is to displace the contents from the tube for analysis without disturbing the separation. This is generally accomplished by carefully puncturing the bottom of the tube and collecting the drops into different tubes. The first drops to emerge are at the bottom of the tube, and soon drops will fall that contain the 50S subunit (or 28S rRNA in the last example). Eventually drops will emerge that contain the small subunit (or the 18S rRNA). Collection of sample from the top of the tube can also be made. The amounts in each collection tube, or fraction, can be determined with the spectrophotometer or radiation counter.

SEDIMENTATION EQUILIBRIUM CENTRIFUGATION

In the previous section we discussed the use of a sucrose density gradient to facilitate the separation of a mixture of two particles or macromolecules. In that example, the longer the tubes were centrifuged, the farther into the gradient the materials would move. If left long enough they would pellet at the bottom. We will consider another type of gradient centrifugation, this time using DNA extracted from germinal vesicles of *Xenopus* oocytes. We begin with a centrifuge tube containing a solution of cesium chloride. To this solution we mix in the sample of DNA, place the tube in the proper holder, and centrifuge it at high speeds for a few days in the ultracentrifuge. During the centrifugation, the cesium ions are so heavy that they can be influenced by the centrifugal force, and a gradient of cesium chloride is formed. To shorten centrifugation, one can begin with a preformed gradient as for sucrose. This gradient of cesium chloride is also a gradient of density, due to the different concentration of cesium along the length of the tube. As a result the DNA, in this case, sediments to a position in the gradient having a CsCl density equal to its own. If DNAs of different buoyant density (different guanine plus cytosine content) are present, they become separated. If proteins are present, they are less dense and will go to the top of this particular gradient. If RNA is present, it is more dense and will go to the bottom. Single-stranded DNA is more dense than double-stranded DNA. In these latter examples the CsCl gradient can be used to purify as well as to separate these molecules. The contents of the tube can be removed and the amounts determined, as in the sucrose gradient.

Sedimentation equilibrium centrifugation has been an important technique in determining that the synthesis of rRNA during amphibian oogenesis takes place upon selectively amplified rDNA (p. 96). If DNA is extracted from somatic cells of *Xenopus*, such as liver cells, and is centrifuged on a cesium chloride gradient to equilibrium, only one DNA peak, with a density of 1.699 g/cm^3, is found. If, however, DNA is extracted from germinal vesicles collected from *Xenopus* oocytes and is then centrifuged in a similar manner, two distinct peaks are found. One of these peaks has a density of 1.699 cm^3; the other peak has a higher density of 1.729 g/cm^3. Since the bulk chromosomal DNA of *Xenopus* has a guanine plus cytosine content of 40 percent while the ribosomal DNA has 63 percent, it would be expected that the high-density peak contained the DNA that codes for rRNA and was present within the many nucleoli of the germinal vesicle. In the somatic-cell DNA, no high-density peak is seen, since in these cells having only two nucleoli, the rDNA should account for only about 0.1 percent of the genome (450 copies of ribosomal RNA genes per haploid set of chromosomes). This is too low a value to detect in these gradients. In the gradients of oocyte DNA, however, the rDNA accounts for a minimum of nearly 50 percent of the chromosomal DNA and represents a striking selective gene amplification.

QUANTITATION

Many techniques have been developed whereby the quantity of a particular macromolecule can be measured. Some of these are highly specific for one type, e.g., for DNA, RNA, protein, polysaccharide, or lipid. Some methods utilize enzymes, others the measurement of specific chemical reactions, and others the ability of these molecules to absorb light. This last technique is widely used; it is rapid and can be adapted to measure most macromolecules. The instrument that measures the absorbance of light by molecules in solution is the spectrophotometer. It has the capacity to produce light of a single wavelength, which passes as a beam through a slit and then through a quartz cell (cuvette) in which the macromolecule to be measured is kept. If purified DNA is to be measured, the wavelength used is generally 260 nm in the ultraviolet spectrum. The beam of light passes through the DNA solution, and what is not absorbed is measured by a photocell on the other side of the cuvette. The amount of light that is absorbed by the DNA (or other molecule) is proportional to the concentration of DNA; the greater the DNA concentration, the less light will be picked up by the photocell. In this way the concentration of DNA is determined.

If the material to be measured is radioactive, an alternate means of determination can be used that requires very little material. Radiation monitors take advantage of the fact that radioisotopes emit particles of specific energy (and therefore specific distance of travel). The most commonly used instrument is the liquid scintillation counter, for which the radioactive material is placed in a vial to which a liquid sensitive to radiation is added. Particles emitted by the radioisotope strike molecules in the added solution, which react to bombardment by emitting flashes of light. These tiny flashes within the vial are detected and amplified by the instrument, and the amount of radioactivity can thus be measured.

AUTORADIOGRAPHY

Autoradiography takes advantage of the ability of a particle emitted from a radioactive atom to activate a photographic emulsion, much like light or x-rays activate the emulsion that coats a piece of film. If such a photographic emulsion is brought into close contact with a radioactive source, the particles emitted by the source leave tiny, black-silver grains in the emulsion after processing. Autoradiography is used to analyze radioisotopes within cells and tissues, or sections of tissues, that have been immobilized on a slide or electron microscope grid. The emulsion can be purchased in two forms. In the liquid form, the slide containing the tissue is dipped into the fluid and withdrawn, leaving a thin film over the tissue. In the other type, the emulsion is already in the form of a thin film, which is floated on water to a position on top of the slide. In either case these operations are performed in the darkroom and the slides are then put aside in a lightproof container to allow the film to be exposed by the emissions. The longer the slide is left, the greater will have been the number of emissions, and therefore the greater will be the number of silver grains. After the desired exposure time, the slides are developed in the darkroom, in the same manner a piece of film is developed, and examined under the microscope. Wherever radio-isotope was present in the tissue, as in a section of a fly ovary (p. 101), silver grains will be found in the layer of emulsion directly over those sites.

Autoradiography, therefore, allows one to see where in a cell or tissue the radioactive molecules that were administered have become localized. In addition, since the number of silver grains can be estimated or even counted, the quantity of radioactive molecules can be determined.

INHIBITORS

The use of inhibitors to probe function is widespread. There are specific inhibitors for the disruption of a multitude of biological processes. Some inhibitors are analogs, which are effective because they resemble a biological molecule and the cell cannot distinguish between the inhibitor and the proper molecule. Once the analog is used in place of the proper molecule, either the further synthesis of the product is halted or the product is nonfunctional. For example, cordycepin is an analog of adenosine and blocks poly A metabolism as a result. Puromycin resembles an amino acyl-tRNA molecule and is added to the growing polypeptide chain; the entire nascent chain then falls off the ribosome without elongation. Many inhibitors work to block specific enzymes. For example, there is a potent RNA polymerase inhibitor isolated from mushrooms, alpha-amanitin, which blocks RNA synthesis by binding to the enzyme. Actinomycin D blocks RNA synthesis in an indirect manner by attaching to the DNA and stopping the movement of the polymerase at that point. Other inhibitors have particular effects on biological molecules, such as the ability of colchicine to cause the depolymerization of microtubules and therefore the dissolution of the spindle apparatus.

The general method for the use of an inhibitor is to add the compound at one specific time and watch for a disruptive effect at a later time. In the example of meiosis (p. 86), an inhibitor of DNA synthesis is added at the stages of meiosis and abnormalities are recorded. If the inhibitor is added during zygotene, the ability of the chromosomes to properly synapse and form the synaptonemal complex is blocked. The conclusion is that the synthesis of DNA at zygotene is somehow needed for this morphological process to occur; in other words, a causal relationship is implied.

Interpretation of inhibitor studies must be made with caution. First it is important to show that the inhibitor is working, by measuring the effect on the specific synthetic process. Inhibitors are often large molecules that may or may not penetrate a given cell. If no effect is seen, the reason may be the lack of penetration and subsequent inhibition rather than that the synthesis is unnecessary. Comparison of the effect of actinomycin D in different systems illustrates the permeability problem. Mammalian cells growing in tissue culture are inhibited at less than 1 μg/ml while a comparable inhibition in sea urchin embryos requires over 20 μg/ml. The difference, presumably, reflects the different penetration rates rather than differences in the sensitivity of RNA synthesis to this inhibitor.

Another difficulty that is harder to evaluate is the possibility that the observed effect is not due to the specific inhibition but to a side effect. For example, actinomycin D is known to have an effect on respiration; it is therefore difficult to assign its blocking of a certain process, such as cleavage in mammalian eggs, to its inhibition of transcription rather than to its inhibition of respiration or some other event.

Clearly the most important tool for the analysis of cell structure is the electron microscope. The theoretical limit of resolution of a given type of microscope is restricted by the wavelength of the illuminating source. In the light microscope, using light of the shortest wavelength, the theoretical limit of resolution is approximately 0.2 μm. In other words, if two structures being examined are not separated by at least that distance, one could not see them as distinct entities in the light microscope. Instead they would be so close together that they would appear as one structure. In the electron microscope, illumination is by means of electrons, whose wavelength is vastly shorter than that of visible light; the limit of resolution is therefore vastly greater. As a direct result of the electron microscope, the tremendous body of knowledge of the complexity and structure at the subcellular level has been gained. We are all accustomed to the sight of the elongate mitochondria with its numerous membranous elements, the ribosome-studded membranes of the rough endoplasmic reticulum, or the many other features in common to many cell types or characteristic of only one or a few types of cells. In the world of the cytologist of only a few decades ago, the structures within a cell were either unknown or recognized at a poorly defined level.

Two types of electron microscopes have been developed and both have been used to study a multitude of processes that occur in developing systems. The most familiar type is the *transmission electron microscope,* which is used to analyze the structure of very thin sections of tissue. Before sections can be prepared, the tissue must be subjected to a prescribed series of treatments. The first step in tissue preparation is fixation. The tissue is immersed in a fixative that has the following properties: It causes the cessation of all the cell's activities and its rapid death, and it maintains the structure of the cell as close as possible to that of the living state. It is of obvious importance, when one examines cell structure at the termination of the procedure, to have confidence that what is being observed is a reflection of the true structure of the cell rather than an artifact produced after the cell was fixed. The most common fixatives in use for electron microscopy are formaldehyde, glutaraldehyde, and osmium tetroxide. These may be used singly, in sequence, or in combination.

After fixation, the tissue is dehydrated by transfer through a series of alcohols of increasing concentration. It is finally placed in a solution of liquid plastic, which is allowed to penetrate into the spaces of the cells by replacement of the previous solvent. This tissue is then placed in the oven, which causes the molten plastic to harden as a supporting medium of the tissue. Blocks of tissue are then prepared and very thin sections of plastic-embedded tissues are cut. Sections for the electron microscope are typically about 500 Å in thickness (1 cm equals 10^8 Å). These sections float on water as they come off the knife and are then picked up on small grids, which act as a support in a manner analogous to the slide for a light microscope section. The sections on the grids are then stained by floating the grids on drops of solutions of heavy metals, typically uranium and lead, which become complexed with the tissue. Because these heavy metals interfere with the passage of electrons through the tissue, those parts of the cell that have bound more of the stain will appear relatively darker on the viewing screen.

One point should be kept in mind when examining a series of electron micrographs. Each micrograph represents the state of the cell at only one point in time, and any suggestions concerning the dynamic processes of that cell must be based on conclusions that compare many different micrographs at different stages in the process.

The freeze-fracture technique uses the transmission electron microscope in an entirely different way. The first step is to place the tissue on a small metal disc and freeze it by dropping it into liquid freon or a similar freezing fluid. This disc is then placed in a special freeze-fracturing apparatus, which maintains its frozen state and cracks the tissue in half. The fracture planes characteristically run along surfaces and within membranes, and these parts of cells have been studied best by this technique. Following the fracture, the open surfaces of the tissue are still held in place by the apparatus, and heavy metals are used to coat these surfaces with a very thin layer. Once the coating has been made, the tissue that served as the template is discarded and the metallic cast, or replica, is then examined in the electron microscope. Since the molecular metallic layer was able to fit itself to the contours of the fractured surface, we are provided with an elegant replica of that contour. That the technique works is demonstrated by the micrographs of Figs. 4.7 and 4.14. This technique, in contrast with that used in the scanning electron micrograph described below, allows one to retain the high resolution of the transmission electron microscope.

The other type of electron microscope is the *scanning electron microscope,* which is used to observe the nature of the cell surface. In this procedure tissue is fixed but not sectioned. Instead, the specimen is dried under special conditions and covered with a very fine layer of heavy metal, which again acts to block the penetration by electrons. The resulting image in the scanning EM reveals the intricate three-dimensional nature of the outer boundary layer. This tool has recently been used to explore processes where surface events play a significant role in the activity. These include the changes in egg surface at fertilization, the surface of migratory embryonic cells, and the surfaces of cells during cleavage.

PURIFICATION AND FRACTIONATION

The need to purify a particular protein or other macromolecule is not the only reason one would use fractionation procedures. Information on the variety of proteins, RNAs, or polysaccharides can be of great importance in understanding cellular activity. For example, one can ask how many different proteins make up a microtubule or a chromosome, or how many RNAs are present in the ribosomes, or how great a variety of sulfated polysaccharides exist at the cell surface. Answers to these questions require a means of separating the molecules so that their variety can be displayed. A related question to the ones above concerns the synthesis of a given species. For example, one may inquire whether the proteins of microtubules are being synthesized by the embryo and also about their variety. Questions of synthesis are best answered with isotopes. The embryo can be provided with radioactively labeled amino acids for incorporation into proteins made prior to homogenization. After incubation, the microtubules are purified and fractionated to determine which of the proteins under study are labeled. The question has been answered.

Each type of macromolecule—RNA, DNA, protein, polysaccharide, or fat—has properties that enable it to be prepared free of contaminating impurities. The preliminary steps in most isolation and purification procedures involve the differential solubility of these different macromolecules. Cells are generally homogenized, and the homogenate or cell fraction treated with solutions that selectively dissolve or precipitate the desired material. For example, if one were extracting DNA, the homogenate might first be shaken with phenol, possibly in the presence of a detergent and high salt; these are conditions that remove the protein from the DNA and precipitate it while the DNA goes into solution in the aqueous phase. The addition of ethanol to the aqueous DNA solution causes the DNA to come out of solution (along with any RNA), and the fibrous DNA can be wound on a glass rod (leaving the finely precipitated RNA behind). The next step in a purification procedure is often the treatment of the material with enzymes that will digest any remaining contaminant (RNA, protein, or polysaccharide in this case). By this time we should have a relatively pure preparation of that macromolecule, but we might want a particular species and must continue the purification. We might be purifying one RNA species (e.g., 18S rRNA), one protein species (e.g., collagen), or one polysaccharide (e.g., chondroitin sulfate). To reach this goal, more sophisticated procedures must be employed to separate a mixture of molecules into its spectrum of individual components.

Certainly one of the greatest gifts to the developmental biologist from the biochemist has been the tremendous number of materials made available, which allow the fractionation of these macromolecules. Two species of macromolecules with a different linear sequence of components will inevitably have different physical properties. The dramatic effect of a single amino acid substitution in one polypeptide chain of the hemoglobin molecule of a sickle-cell anemia victim is a clear illustration of this fact. The most common differences between species are molecular weight, ionic charge, solubility, shape, and density. A given fractionation procedure generally depends on more than one of these properties. In the technique of electrophoresis, for example, the population of macromolecules is placed in an electric field, with the positive electrode on one side and the negative electrode on the other. Under these conditions a macromolecule with an overall negative charge—i.e., it has more negatively charged groups than positively charged ones—will migrate toward the positive electrode. The greater the negative charge, the faster will be the migration; therefore this mixture of species will begin to separate out into its components on the basis of charge. Although they all began at one spot, those species carrying the greatest negative charge will move farthest toward the positive electrode. The mobility of these molecules in an electric field, however, is affected by other properties as well. Larger molecules, as might be expected, move more slowly. Similarly, certain shapes are more conducive to rapid migration than others. The distance a given species will migrate in a period of time is a complex matter and two different molecules are not likely to be the same.

Different techniques utilize different physical properties; therefore, fractionation procedures often involve more than one method to ensure maximum separation. In the example above, consider that the maximum separation by electrophoresis has been obtained and the protein being isolated is migrating closely with a contaminating species. This pair of proteins can be removed and subjected to a different technique that depends on a different basis of separation—for example, one that depends most heavily on molecular weight, such as gel filtration with Sephadex. Sephadex consists of tiny beads perforated by holes of very specific diameters. Different Sephadex grades have different-size holes for use with various molecular-weight ranges. These beads allow molecules up to a certain molecular weight inside and exclude molecules with a larger molecular weight. Consider that the protein being isolated has a molecular weight of 100,000 and the contaminant, 50,000. In this case a column of Sephadex G-75 beads can be made within a tube. This grade of Sephadex allows molecules of 50,000 to penetrate the beads, but those of 100,000 remain outside. When a solution containing these two proteins is poured through the column, the solution that first drips out the bottom contains the protein being studied. All of the contaminant remains held up in the beads. Other major fractionation procedures take advantage of differences in solubility or sedimentation. Studies in immunology have provided some of the most powerful fractionation techniques, based on the specific interactions of antibodies and their antigens, but these are beyond the scope of this book.

NUCLEIC ACID HYBRIDIZATION

Results obtained by nucleic acid hybridization (either DNA to DNA or DNA to RNA) are discussed in several places in this book. The technique is complex, and so many variations can be used that a discussion of these methods rapidly moves far beyond the limits of an introductory textbook. On the other hand, the technique is the only available method to analyze nucleic acids from the standpoint of their nucleotide sequence, from which their entire informational content is derived. Without some understanding of the potential that the technique offers in the study of nucleic acid metabolism, the student cannot appreciate our current knowledge of molecular information processes during development or any other event.

The underlying principle of all hybridization experiments is that single-stranded nucleic acids of complementary sequence will reanneal (hybridize) with one another to form a double-stranded molecule held together by the formation of hydrogen bonds. Reannealing can occur between two single-stranded DNA molecules or between a single-stranded DNA molecule and an RNA molecule (see also pp. 22–23).

Certain preparatory steps are required in all hybridization experiments. The nucleic acids to be used must first be purified. DNA must be converted to a usable form, which requires converting the double-stranded helix to single-stranded molecules and in some cases breaking up the fragments of DNA into smaller pieces. In all experiments the nucleic acids to be hybridized must be mixed together at sufficient concentration and given sufficient time of incubation for the complements to find one another. The temperature and the ionic composition of the media are of critical importance in determining how closely two molecules must be complementary to one another before they will reanneal. The higher the temperature and the lower the salt, the closer the two strands must complement one another before they will remain attached; i.e., the percentage of possible hydrogen bonds formed between the two strands must be greater. In all experiments the hybridized nucleic acids—whether they are DNA-DNA hybrids or DNA-RNA hybrids—must be separated from the nonhybridized fraction. In some cases this is carried out by hydroxyapatite chromatography, and in other cases nonhybridized DNA or RNA can be washed away or selectively destroyed (see below).

The reannealing curve on p. 23 shows the basic hybridization procedure. Double-stranded DNA is converted to single-stranded molecules by heat, and the solution is cooled to a temperature (60°C) at which reannealing can proceed. The longer the period of time, the greater is the percentage of DNA in a double-stranded state. Those sequences present at the greatest concentration reanneal more rapidly. In order to plot a reannealing curve, some method must be used to determine the percentage of the original DNA that has reannealed at the various times of incubation. Reannealed, double-stranded DNA has different properties from nonreannealed, single-stranded DNA and this difference is used for their separation. When the mineralized material of bone—a particular type of calcium phosphate called hydroxyapatite—is ground up into fine particles, it is capable of binding DNA. The hydroxyapatite crystals are packed into a column through which solutions of DNA can be passed. At low phosphate concentrations (e.g., 0.03 M), both single- and double-stranded DNA binds to the hydroxyapatite. At intermediate phosphate concentrations (e.g., 0.12 M), only double-stranded DNA binds while single-stranded DNA passes through and can be collected. At high phosphate concentration (0.5 M), neither DNA will bind. To determine the percentage of the DNA that has reannealed after a given period of time, the solution is passed through the column in 0.12 M phosphate. The double-stranded molecules are bound while the single stranded DNA comes through and can be measured. After the single-stranded molecules have come through, the phosphate concentration can be raised to 0.5 M and the double-stranded molecules previously bound are removed, collected, and measured. The reannealing curve of Fig. 2.3 is obtained in this manner. It reflects the fact that the more copies of a particular base sequence there are in the genome, the greater will be their concentration. Thus, these complements will reanneal more rapidly and their contribution to the total curve will be represented closer to the y axis of the graph. The distribution of hybrids in the curve of Fig. 2.3 separates the DNA sequences into two groups, the repeated and the nonrepeated, and the methods of working with each are generally quite different.

Question 1: Are mRNAs coded from repeated or nonrepeated genes? Before one can begin to ask what type of DNA sequence is responsible for a specific protein, a method must be available to obtain large quantities of the nucleic acid that carries the code for that protein. In the search for a suitable protein with which to approach this question, we must find a cell whose synthetic activities are dominated by the production of one single protein molecule, so that the corresponding mRNA (or mRNAs if more than one polypeptide chain is involved) can be purified and separated from all other mRNAs. One such cell that fits this bill is the hemoglobin-producing erythroblast. From the polysomes of this cell, a small quantity of hemoglobin mRNA can be isolated. To convert this small quantity of unlabeled RNA into a larger quantity of highly radioactive DNA with the code for hemoglobin, we take advantage of a special enzyme that can be prepared from certain cancer-causing viruses. These viruses contain an enzyme, reverse transcriptase, which uses RNA as a template and synthesizes a complementary copy of DNA from it. This is the reverse of the normal transcriptive process; hence the name. With the aid of this enzyme, one can take any preparation of RNA and produce from it, in the test tube, a copy of radioactively labeled DNA by using labeled DNA precursors.

Once the specific labeled DNA is available, a small amount of it is mixed with a large excess of total, unlabeled DNA; the mixture is heated to separate the strands of the double helix and is then allowed to reanneal. Reannealing of a preparation of total DNA forms a curve just like the one in Fig. 2.3. In this case, however, one sequence, of all possible sequences, is represented by a few radioactive molecules. If this sequence is identical with a sequence in the repeated DNA, it should be found in the rapidly reannealing fraction (left part of curve). If it is identical with a sequence in the nonrepeated fraction, it should take as long to find a partner as all the other nonrepeated sequences; radioactivity should appear in the hybrid fraction only after very long times of incubation (right-hand part of curve). The analysis of several mRNAs, including that for the polypeptide chains of hemoglobin, suggests they are transcribed from the nonrepeated fraction of DNA; i.e., these sequences reanneal together with nonrepeated DNA. Messenger RNAs for the histones, however, hybridize with DNA sequences that are repeated a few hundred times and thus are assumed to be transcribed from moderately repeated genes.

Question 2: How great a variety of RNAs are stored in the unfertilized egg? Because experiments with repeated and nonrepeated DNA are handled separately, the question becomes: How great is the variety in each DNA fraction? Only RNAs complementary to nonrepeated DNA will be considered at this time. Students who wish to examine the more complex methodology for utilization of repeated DNA may refer to Hough and Davidson (*J. Mol. Biol.,* **70**:491, 1972).

Before one can hybridize RNA to nonrepeated DNA, this type of DNA must be isolated in a pure state uncontaminated by the presence of repeated sequences. This is accomplished by allowing the total DNA to reanneal long enough for all the repeated sequences to hybridize to one another, but with most of the nonrepeated ones still present as single strands. When the reaction has proceeded to this point, the reaction mixture is passed through a column of hydroxyapatite. The double-stranded (reannealed, repeated) DNA sequences bind to the column, while a nearly pure fraction of nonrepeated sequences are collected as they drip through.

To complete the experiment, the single-stranded, nonrepeated DNA is combined with a great excess of the RNA to be tested; the two nucleic acids are allowed to hybridize. To give the investigator a simple means of following the DNA sequences, radioactively labeled DNA is used. In a sense the labeled DNA sequences can be divided into two groups: those to which the RNAs can bind and those to which they cannot. Presumably those DNA sequences that become hybridized were active during oogenesis as templates for the synthesis of the complementary RNA molecules that become stored in the egg. Even though there is only one copy of each DNA sequence per haploid amount of DNA, the RNA is in such great excess that there are sufficient collisions and the reaction is driven to completion, whereby all DNA sequences that have RNA complements will hybridize. At the end of the incubation, the reaction mixture is passed through the hydroxyapatite column to which the labeled DNA-RNA hybrids are bound, and the unhybridized labeled DNA fragments pass through. The hybrids can be simply washed off the column (by raising the salt concentration or raising the temperature to break the strands apart) and the percentage of the original DNA sequences can be determined—i.e., the percentage of the radioactivity that became stuck to the column as a hybrid. In the present example, using RNA extracted from the oocyte, it is found that 0.6 percent of the labeled, nonrepeated DNA sequences form hybrids. Because only one of the two strands of the genes is being transcribed (the sense strand), the value can be doubled to give 1.2 percent of the nonrepeated genes active during oogenesis in *Xenopus,* producing RNAs for storage in the egg (p. 203).

Question 3: To what extent are the RNAs made during early sea urchin development the same species present in the unfertilized egg? This question, unlike the previous ones, asks for a comparison between two populations of RNA: one present at the time of fertilization and the other synthesized during development. Before this question can be answered, those RNAs synthesized at a particular stage must be distinguished from those that are simply there in the cells and had been synthesized at an earlier stage. This distinction is determined by the use of a radioactively labeled RNA precursor, such as ³H-uridine. If embryos of the desired stage are incubated in this label, we can expect it to be taken up by the embryos and incorporated into newly synthesized RNA. Those RNAs present at that stage but synthesized at an earlier time cannot be labeled.

The experiments to be described (Fig. 25.1) are termed *competition experiments* and involve only the repeated DNA sequences. These experiments provide no information concerning transcription from nonrepeated genes. The results of two sets of competition experiments are described on page 205. Each analyzes a separate question and the results complement one another. The curves in Fig. 25.1 (p. 541) are *competition curves*. They reflect the binding of labeled RNA synthesized at one stage to DNA in the presence of unlabeled RNA from a variety of stages. In Fig. 25.1a the labeled RNA is made by incubating a culture of sea urchin blastulas in ³H-uridine for a brief period and then extracting the RNA. Those molecules of RNA containing ³H were being made at that stage.

The procedure for hybridization of RNA to repeated DNA is quite different from that previously described. The first step is to prepare a solution of purified, total DNA and to denature it into single strands by heat. This DNA solution is then allowed to drip through a nitrocellulose filter to which the DNA strands become adsorbed The solution continues to leave single-stranded DNA adsorbed to the membrane until a point of saturation is reached and no more DNA can be bound. The DNA on this filter is now immobilized. That is, it cannot move around and therefore it cannot bind to itself; it remains single-stranded. These DNA-bearing filters are now placed in a solution containing the RNAs and are kept in an appropriate salt concentration (e.g., 0.3 M NaCl-.03 M NaCitrate, pH 7.2) at an appropriate temperature (63°C); the RNA will bind to the DNA. If the filters are incubated in a solution where the only RNA present is labeled (such as labeled blastula RNA of Fig. 25.1a), a certain percentage of the radioactivity that was originally added will be bound to the filters at the end of a suitable incubation time. The radioactivity that remains associated with the filter represents ³H-RNA that is bound in a complementary way to the immobilized DNA. In Fig. 25.1a, the far left end of the curves converge. This value reflects the amount of ³H-blastula RNA bound in the absence of any unlabeled RNA. The curves in this figure fall into two groups. We will follow the curve obtained from the binding of ³H-RNA from the blastula in the presence of unlabeled blastula RNA (triangles). It drops steeply and in the tube containing the greatest amount of unlabeled RNA (.6 mg), very little ³H-RNA is bound. The reason for the shape of this curve is that as more unlabeled RNA is added, it becomes more and more difficult for a given ³H-RNA molecule to bind because there are more and more of these same molecules that are unlabeled. The basic assumption in competition experiments is that two different species of RNA (different base sequence) will not compete with one another. In other words, if there are any species of ³H-RNA that are not represented in the unlabeled competing population, the binding of that species of ³H-RNA should not be affected by all the other unlabeled molecules. When one is testing unlabeled RNA from the same stage as the labeled RNA (in this case unlabeled blastula versus labeled blastula), there cannot be any labeled species not present in the unlabeled population, since they are from the same stage. Therefore, the unlabeled RNA would be expected to completely wipe out the binding of the ³H-RNA, which is what is found.

However, there are two other curves (those of the unfertilized egg and the hatched blastula) that are indistinguishable. The conclusion is reached that these other two stages also contain all the RNAs that are being made by the blastula stage. In other words, the population of RNA made at the blastula appears to be the same population present in the unfertilized egg at the end of oogenesis. If the competition curves of RNA from the gastrula and the prism larvae are examined, they do not compete as well. These curves level off at half the counts per minute. The reason they level off is that these stages do not contain all the species of RNA being synthesized by the blastula. They do contain a significant percentage, since the curve drops to a considerably lower point. But the fact that it levels off indicates all the ^{3}H-RNAs that can be competed against have done so. The remaining counts that are bound reflect species of RNA made by the blastula stage that are no longer present in the later gastrula or prism embryos.

In the curves of Fig. 25.1b, the labeled RNA is being synthesized by the prism stage and the unlabeled RNAs are from either the same or an earlier stage. The results indicate that the unfertilized egg and the blastula contain about 60 percent of those RNAs being made at the prism, and the other 40 percent represent new species not present before gastrulation. It must be kept in mind that all the results presented on the sea urchin reflect RNA that is complementary to the repeated fraction of the genome. The nonrepeated DNA sequences are on the filter, but they are at too low a concentration to participate to any significant extent in the binding.

Additional questions concerning the origin of tumor-causing viruses and the appearance of tissue-specific mRNA have involved hybridization techniques and are considered in Chapters 17 and 19.

CELL-FREE PROTEIN SYNTHESIS

One property of a population of RNA that can be measured is its ability to direct amino acid incorporation into protein, i.e., its template activity. To measure this property, a technique has been developed that uses the protein-synthesizing machinery of one type of cell and the mRNA of the cells under study. For example, a preparation can be made from bacteria that contain all the necessary ingredients for protein synthesis (the ribosomes; initiation, elongation, and termination factors; the tRNAs and their activating enzymes; an energy-generating system, etc.) except that they lack mRNA. When mRNA, from whatever source, is added, this added RNA can be used by the protein-synthesizing system to translate into protein. The system is termed *cell-free* because the cells that donate the ribosomes and other ingredients have been homogenized and no intact cells are used. Since rRNA and tRNA are not capable of serving as templates for protein synthesis because of the changes in their nucleotide bases (such as methylation), the amount of amino acid incorporation is proportional to the added template-active RNA. To arrive at the percentage of the total RNA that can be used as a template (4 to 5 percent on p. 204), the RNA being studied is compared with that of an RNA known to be pure mRNA, such as viral RNA. In the present case the viral RNA causes 20 to 25 times greater amino acid incorporation per milligram of RNA; therefore only one-twentieth to one-twenty-fifth of the total egg RNA is template-active.

In this section a general approach to measure the amount of RNA synthesized per unit of time is described. The same general procedure would apply to the determination of any product using a radioactive precursor with appropriate modifications. The availability of a precursor relatively specific to the macromolecule to be measured greatly simplifies the determination procedure. For the measurement of RNA synthesis, the most widely used precursors are ^{3}H-uridine or ^{3}H-guanosine. Before being incorporated these molecules must be converted to the triphosphate form (UTP or GTP), which is utilized by the RNA polymerase in RNA synthesis. The triphosphates are soluble under many conditions where RNA is not, such as in 70 percent ethanol or cold 5 percent trichloroacetic acid or 0.6 M perchloric acid. To measure the amount of labeled precursor incorporated into RNA, the cells are homogenized; the homogenate is treated with a solution that renders the unincorporated precursor soluble and the RNA (containing the *incorporated label*) insoluble and therefore precipitated. The radioactivity in the precipitate is a measure of the added uridine or guanosine that was incorporated during the period of incubation. To be certain that all the label was actually incorporated into RNA and not, for example, into DNA after conversion into a DNA precursor, the susceptibility of the labeled product to RNase can be measured. If all the radioactivity becomes soluble after enzyme treatment, it had all been incorporated into RNA.

Up to this point the only consideration has been the value of incorporation of precursor. This is not necessarily a measure of synthesis. When a labeled precursor is used, the rate of synthesis is reflected by three values: incorporation, uptake, and pool size. Assume that between two stages, A and B, there is no actual change in the synthesis of RNA. Assume also that between these stages there is a twofold increase, for some reason, in the permeability of precursor into the embryo. In other words, if the same number of embryos is placed in the same concentration of ^{3}H-guanosine, the embryos of stage B will *take up* twice as much isotope. This means that twice as many GTP molecules in the cell will be radioactive; and when the incorporation value is measured, it will be twice as high for B as for A, though no actual change had occurred in the synthetic rate. A changing precursor uptake pattern is a common observation during development, and therefore uptake must be measured to establish synthetic rate. Uptake can be measured as the amount of radioactivity present as precursor.

The other value necessary to measure the actual synthetic rate is pool size. The term *pool* refers to the amount of precursor actually available for synthesis at a given time. In the previous example, no change in synthesis occurred between stage A and B. Now assume there is no change in uptake or actual synthesis, but there is a change in the amount of uridine or guanosine that the embryo is making. If in stage B the embryo has made enough guanosine so that its pool has doubled (there are twice the guanosine molecules available for synthesis), then the percentage of labeled GTP molecules in the cells relative to the total number will be one-half, and this will result in half the value of incorporation. To measure the size of the pool, the actual quantity of precursor in the embryo must be measured. If both uptake and pool size are known, then incorporation values can be converted into true synthetic rates. The determination of these values can be very complex.

Index